A Queer World

A Queer World

The Center for Lesbian and Gay Studies Reader

EDITED BY

Martin Duberman

NEW YORK UNIVERSITY PRESS
New York and London

NEW YORK UNIVERSITY PRESS
NEW YORK AND LONDON

Library of Congress Cataloging-in-Publication Data
A queer world : the Center for Lesbian and Gay Studies reader / edited
by Martin Duberman.
p.   cm.
Includes bibliographical references and index.
ISBN 0-8147-1874-4 (clothbound : alk. paper). — ISBN
0-8147-1875-2 (paperbound : alk. paper)
1. Homosexuality.   I. Duberman, Martin B.
HQ76.Q44   1997
306.76'6—dc21   96-53390
                    CIP

New York University Press books are printed on acid-free paper,
and their binding materials are chosen for strength and durability.

Manufactured in the United States of America

10 9 8 7 6 5 4 3 2 1

To those who did so much to make the Center for Lesbian and Gay Studies (CLAGS) a reality—its board members, staff, and volunteers.

Contents

A Queer World

Introduction

Martin Duberman

The Center for Lesbian and Gay Studies (CLAGS) came into formal existence at the City University of New York Graduate School in April 1991. But its beginnings go back to the spring of 1985, when I first invited a few scholars to meet in my living room and talk over possibilities for establishing a research institute that would encourage and disseminate reliable scholarship on gender and sexual nonconformity. CLAGS went through a protracted struggle to come into existence and a difficult journey of survival and growth. Its many public successes were matched by periodic internal strife over how best to implement the feminist and multicultural values on which it had been founded. But that history must be left for some future telling.

The purpose of this anthology is not to recount or analyze the story of an organization, but to make available some of the more substantial fruits of its work to date. As early as 1987 and while still in its infancy, CLAGS staged its first public event—"New York City Lesbian and Gay History and Culture"—and soon after began the monthly colloquia at which scholars presented their work-in-progress. In the intervening years, there have been dozens of such occasions, frequently playing to packed auditoriums and often marked by passionate debate. Literally hundreds of scholars, activists, and cultural workers (a single individual often embodying all three) have taken part in informal panel discussions, given formal papers, or presented slide shows, videos, and films.

Some events have drawn scholars from abroad; and people from widely scattered points around the United States have made the trek to New York to attend a given conference. But overall, participation has been mostly confined to those living on the East Coast corridor. The many who have been kept away by logistics from CLAGS events have often lamented to us "how much we wish we could have been there."

Through *A Queer World* (and a second anthology, *Queer Representations*, which is soon to follow), they now, in some sense, can be. Our goal at CLAGS has always been to disseminate to as broad an audience as possible the often original, controversial, illuminating findings that cutting-edge scholars and activists have presented at our events. The opportunity to gather much of that scholarship into two anthologies has made that goal a reality.

But it has not been easy to decide which of the many presentations given at CLAGS over the years should be included—and in what form. Initially CLAGS did not tape its events, and then for several more years did so only sporadically. By the early nineties we were routinely recording all our conferences and colloquia—but that has produced a different problem: how to sort through and select from what has grown now to be a very large archive.

As editor of these anthologies, I've had to deal with the additional fact that any number of speakers—and among them some of the most eloquent and challenging—used no notes at all or spoke from bare outlines. How many of them would prove willing to reconstruct and elaborate on their off-the-cuff remarks, or to invest the effort needed to re-address a subject they had taken on years before and might feel quite done with—especially since that might entail rethinking prior views and incorporating the sometimes massive amount of scholarship that had accumulated in the years since?

Happily, many did prove willing, and they and I have worked together— sometimes through many months and drafts—to produce substantial new essays that bear only a tangential relationship to the material as first presented at a CLAGS event. In a few instances pieces do appear here in very nearly the form in which they were originally given—for example, much of the section "Genes, Hormones, and the Brain." But in most cases a tape transcription has merely been the starting point for the creation of a much revised article.

This has inescapably meant that the "truth" of the historic moment has been sacrificed: What you read here, in most instances, is not what you would have heard had you attended the CLAGS event in question. But this has seemed to me and to the contributors a necessary sacrifice. In our minds, it would have been a foolish disservice to the advancing state of lesbian, gay, bisexual and transgender studies not to allow—indeed encourage—individual authors to rethink and restate their earlier presentations.

That decision made, the shape of the anthologies hardly became a given. A mountain of material had to be reduced, choices made between essays, and coherent frameworks created for grouping those selected. More than a hundred voices are heard in these two anthologies, but some hundred others who have presented work at assorted CLAGS events are not.

Circumstances dictated many of the final choices. To give but one example: fourteen people presented papers at CLAGS's 1994 conference "Homo-Economics," but only half of them are in this volume. Why? For the same varied reasons that other CLAGS presenters are missing: they had no prepared text, or no tape of what they said existed, or what did exist proved too sketchy and outdated to warrant an overhaul. In other instances, some CLAGS presenters had already published their expanded remarks elsewhere, and in a form that (to them or to me) seemed too distant from their starting points to justify inclusion here. On the other hand, I have made room for a few reprints when the original venue was one of limited circulation and the essay seemed of special importance.

The pieces once chosen and revised, I then had to grapple with how to group them. Anthologies whose aim is to *transform* standard categorizations of knowledge (and within each category, to question received notions of truth) nonetheless require some coherent arrangement, or at least the appearance of coherence. Because many of the individual essays in this collection cross disciplines and resist traditional labels, I have tried to keep the section titles general and inclusive. But the fact remains that an essay such as Vivien Ng's "Looking for Lesbians in Chinese History" could as readily have been included under "Ancient Genealogies" in the second (forthcoming) anthology, *Queer Representations*, as under "The Terrains of History" in which I have placed it in *A Queer World*. Moreover, even those sections that seem "obvious" in their organization—like "Laws and Markets"—contain individual pieces with information or insight of obvious relevance to issues of gender, identity, and politics.

Yet porous as the anthologies' divisions are, they do (hopefully) represent certain logical clusters of data, perspective, or analysis—as they most certainly represent the apparently persistent human need to name and group elusive, disparate phenomena. The (perhaps frightening) nominalist alternative is to emphasize instead the irreducible particularity of all experience and the (perhaps comforting) inauthenticity of all efforts to generalize from it.

Similarly, the reader should not expect this—or, in a burgeoning field, *any*—anthology to be comprehensive. My choice of essays for these two volumes has necessarily been confined to presentations made over the years at CLAGS-sponsored events. Needless to say, brilliant work in lesbian and gay studies has been done in many other venues, and under a variety of sponsorships.

But I *would* make the claim that these anthologies (like CLAGS itself) are distinctive in the amount of attention they pay to the social sciences and to public policy issues. While neither ignoring nor disparaging the significant theoretical work that has been done in cultural, literary, or media studies, these volumes aspire to broaden both the informational base and the agenda of lesbian, gay, bisexual, and transgender studies. Which inescapably means that they aspire as well to express the remarkable range of distinctive voices that are perhaps the most characteristic and dramatic strength of this rapidly emerging field of inquiry.

Martin Duberman
November, 1996

One

Mapping Identities:
Gender and Sexuality

A. Whose Identity?

1

The Girl I Never Want to Be: Identity, Identification, and Narrative

Judith Roof

If difficulty in writing this essay is any indication, I apparently have a deep resistance to issues of identity. This probably comes from having horrifying early identifications with Cubbie, Moochie, Beaver Cleaver, Imogene Coca, and Eve Arden. I've never thought of myself as having a discernable Identity (with capital *I*) and have religiously avoided—nay eschewed—anything associated with those automatic appurtenances of my so-called whiter-than-white, hyper-WASP, Midwestern, middle-class birthright, in my case, affiliations with the Presbyterian Church, Job's Daughters, people from Upper Arlington, Republicans, capitalists, and the red, white, and blue. I even wanted to change my name. Probably my ability to buck Identity as a category has been a part of my white bourgeois privilege, an example of the identity paradoxes of individualism. As I got older I found myself identifying against and excepting myself from institutionalized identity categories, i.e., against the French department when I studied French, the English department when I studied English, law when I was in law school, a group called (improbably) Gay Women Sapphoncified when I came out, women's studies when I began to do feminist work, and any university I've ever worked at. It looked as if I was somehow running from group identities or strongly reasserting them in some intensely oppositional manner. But as I review my identity history, a pattern emerges, superficially a pattern of resistance, perhaps a pattern of opposition, but more likely a pattern defined by its repeating structure. In every instance, what seemed to function as something like an identity was more dependent on a posture of outsideness, of other-than-ness, of self-differentiation where position in relation to was more important than any group identity category.

Now of course, this is a fiction, an identity narrative that works layered over the net of group identities presumably rejected, but in abeyance and to which I can still lay claim. The apparent contradiction and interaction between my outsider position and group identities are organized by some set of dynamic structures that underlie identities. Individual identity, linked to ego, is the illusion of a completed process, filling in for a loss that occurs at the mythical primal moment when the first recognition of Other simultaneously produces loss and makes structure and eventually coherent identity necessary. Identity, produced, as Lacan suggests, through discourse, is more specifically a set of positions within relational structures linked to mechanisms of identification and vice versa; that is, the kinds of identifications made by anyone who is no longer an infant are driven by positions already taken within structure. This identity/identification circle operates, at least after ego is formed, in a reciprocal relation with narrative, and by narrative, I mean ideologies of ordering evident in our culturally-determined understanding of storiness—of the possible shapes relations can take. Narrative may be an effect of cultural ideologies and material organizations such as the nuclear family, or the product of more abstract object relations, or some phantasm of unconscious processes and language, or it may produce all of these, or all of the above. Narratives are enabled by identifications and identifications are produced by narratives; together they provide the specific ideologically informed and historically mutable discursive process that defines not only the positions (and identities) possible, but also codifies the mechanisms—the plots—that link identity and position. Thus, to return to identity, identity is a position within largely hidden narratives that drive identifications. What I am going to undertake in this essay is an exploration of the relation between identification and narrative, the link between identification and identities, and finally, how a recognition of the role of narrative might relieve and enlarge strategies of identity politics in the fiction we call the gay and lesbian community.

Here is a true story of an ethically difficult and unresolved instance of identity overreaction from the files of my perpetual struggle with identity, which I think might demonstrate how understanding the contrary narrative mechanisms underlying identifications might relieve the anxieties of identity politics. It is with great reluctance that I use my own example; I noticed as I was struggling with this essay that this section stubbornly remained gloppy and fairly incomprehensible. I don't think anyone is ever reliable about themselves as text, and I am still very suspicious of this reading and the ways it probably serves to rehide the very dynamic I'm trying to bring to light. I could have made all of this up, and I probably won't give you enough information for you to know the difference.

Last spring, I taught a graduate seminar in feminist theory. The class had the usual assortment of representatives from prominent group identity categories: liberated males, gay, straight, and bisexual, reluctant females, excited females, a female excited by crystal power, an African American female, a Korean female, a French female, two lipstick lesbians, and one conspiratorial dyke. Of all the students in the class, I had the most identificatory angst with the dyke. While I liked, even admired and desired, the lipstick lesbians, I hated the dyke. I disliked her smug presumption that we had a "special relation"—even had anything in common because we were both gay. I thought her assumption that she knew everything about lesbians and feminism because she was a lesbian and her insistence on lesbian power, on the lesbian's natural superiority, insight, post-modernity, and radicality blind, self-serving, uncritical, and stupid. It wasn't long before I found myself asking friends, "Am I like her?"

So what's the story here? Is this just a superficial account of taste based on physical appearance, style, and good vibrations? It might be, except my more or less violent overreaction to this student, my protesting too much, signals that something else is going on. Feeling guilty and vulnerable and like a really bad teacher, I tried at the time to account for my reactions by borrowing secondary screen narratives about identifications—essentially pop psychology explanations, versions of which you all know.

Version 1: the plot of internalized homophobia, or the bad doppelgänger story. Judging from certain gross physical similarities, is she me? Can I be taken for her? In which case am I not who I thought I was? Or will I disappear into her who will be me? Or I saw something of myself in this student, and not liking what I saw, I resisted the identification. Or I saw something I feared about myself in her and projecting and displacing my fear of this, I hated her instead. All these accounts equate identity and identification, assuming that identification is a mirrored narcissism stimulated by some evident similarity that results in a struggle for self-differentiation against some self-evident identity. These are the tragic stories of one girl's inability to face the truth, of a fear of really being the other, of an identity sadly mistaken about itself—it is Oedipus.

Version 2: the plot of sibling rivalry. The student's possessive display of lesbian identity created a competition over what lesbian identity means: if she is a lesbian, can I also be, and be different from her, or am I automatically like her, and what if I don't like what she is? The account here equates group identity categories with personal identities, and again relying on a mechanism of mirroring narcissism, poses identification as an automatic effect of identity. This story's crisis, however, focuses on the assumption of difference initially premised as same through the overlay of group identity. It is the comic story of unmasking, of finding to one's relief that the other one isn't oneself, of finding one's identity through the unmasking of the other—it's a Bacchic case of mistaken identity.

These two stories and their variations occult the identificatory processes they illustrate. In offering identity as both narrative resolution and answer to the question of who am I and why I hate her, the stories shield the fact that I can't know who I am and I probably don't hate her; in effect, the narratives that are about identifications subordinate identificatory process to their illusory identity results. I suspect that two mechanisms combine to make identification and its constructing narratives disappear: One is the decoying emphasis on identity—on the self, on the completed subject—which works to draw attention away from other processes; and the second is that identifications are the products of multiple, conflicting narratives that present an impenetrable confusion at identificatory points; this confusion is hidden by an overlay of screen narratives about and accounting for identifications. The narratives constructing identifications hidden beneath the masking totality of identity may be multiple and conflicting, but they are myriad in a particularly ordered and discernable way.

But then how do I find out what the real stories are (if there are any)? If I pretend these stories are symptomatic narratives through which an unconscious reveals itself in a typically Freudian kind of way, I read for repetitions and glitches that offer deductive threads to other unseen narratives lying within. What strikes me if I do that is the number of times the motif of mistaken or usurped identity appears. But already conclusory in these stories, identity, both the student's and my own, is in all cases my projection of identities within the limits of the scenario generated according to some other sense of relation between myself and others—in other words, according to my positional relation within the underlying narrative structure I am trying to locate. What then can the repeated notion of mistake tell me? I am mistaken about myself, she is mistaken about me, I am mistaken about her, and someone had better be mistaken or I am her, or maybe I am her and anything else is a mistake.

It seems to me that this mistake motif is, like identity, yet another screen, but a screen that symptomatically reproduces my initial denial of the fear that I am like her. I'm going in a circle. Given the circular reciprocal relations among the terms "identity," "identification," and "narrative," any place I begin to analyze is not necessarily either the first term or the first cause. My initial impulse is to look to psychoanalysis, which sees identifications as a way of accounting for incipient infantile positionings that create gender and sexual identities. Though there is some confusion in Freud's work about which kinds of identifications occur when, he generally considers two broad types: narcissistic identifications linked to someone one wishes to be and anaclitic identifications linked to someone one would like to have. Both secondary in the sense that they occur after the subject has already positioned itself, these identifications occur not through some mechanism of superficial mirrored gender similarity—not through the introjection of images that characterizes primary identifications, but rather are sustained and defined by underlying narratives of desire. The narcissistic narrative goes something like this: You are what I wish to be. I wish to be you because I wish to be such that I would want to be me. In other words, I want to be in the place occupied by the subject of my own desire. The anaclitic narrative goes like this: I want to be you because I want to have you. Wanting to be what I want to have means being in the place of the object of my own desire. These two types of identification merge into one narrative, one story of the interdependence of subject and object, of being and having, a narrative sustaining desire where being is having and having is impossible.

And I suspect that this interdependence creates a circle that can regress infinitely, identification framing identification, reiterating the same sandwiched dynamic, while the genetic first cause of identification—loss—remains perpetually deferred. The stories generated to account for identifications merely reiterate the circular interrelation of being and having as mutually causative, a relation that echoes a circuit between identification and narrative itself, and screens the workings of both from our view. Accounts of identification prevent us from seeing identification's primal scene, referring us instead to identification's effects or to another identification. It is as if obscuring processes of identification will hide the loss identifications and their contribution to identity conceal. But it is only by seeing this underside that we can understand why identity itself is so tortured and why identity politics is so difficult.

This series of interlocked desire narratives defines the terms and positions of the subject's identifications; since few trouble to uncover it, identificatory choices often seem illogical, unaccountable, or politically incorrect. The example comes to mind of my stalwart identification with James Bond, which goes beyond the visual pleasures of narrative cinema. It's not simply an identification with the masculine, or with patriarchy, or with the narratively and ideologically poised protagonist, but is rather an identification grounded in a complex set of narratives about power, a desire for power, and the power of the desirer that produce an identification with the place of the powerful, rule-breaking, unorthodox dude with great toys.

I also apparently identify with the Witty Butcher's Wife's position in Freud's narrative about her, since I keep using her story as an example. If you recall, the Butcher's Wife identified both with her husband's desire for the woman who could not satisfy him and with the woman he desired. Her identifications were with the position of the desirer in relation to an unfulfillable desire and with the position of object of desire in relation to another's desiring. The nifty thing about the Butcher's Wife is that her interwoven desire narratives permit her to be in both places at once: both desirer and desired, and perhaps this is her ultimate desire. In identifying with the Witty Butcher's Wife, I reiterate her desire narratives and add one of my own: the desire to be in the place perceived as desiring an unfulfilled desire and of being in both places at once, which is, in effect, to be in the place of the desire I desire.

But the structuralism of psychoanalysis, which seems highly appropriate to an examination of identity as a narratively determined position within structure, is also somewhat tautological; its narratives of identification with position are also dependent on an underlying notion of identification as a kind of inevitable lurch toward a sameness somehow already recognized. The Witty Butcher's Wife identifies with her desiring spouse because she already desires an unfulfillable desire registered in her dream as the caviar she wants but tells her husband not to get for her. The infant in Freud's account of infantile sexuality identifies with her father's desire because she already wants mother.

So if I continue my self-analysis of my identificatory angst with these repetitions of primal imagistic identifications, where do I end up? Am I like my student? Do I look like her? Not really. Do I act like her? No. Is it the worst thing in the world to be her? Yes, because in her association to me, she is in the place where I imagine I once was in relation to my own lesbian teacher of feminist theory, and it is around that position that the identificatory story lies.

The story—or the worst-case scenario—that I project on this student is that, of course, I was madly in love with my own teacher and acted toward her in many of the ways this student seemed to be acting toward me. But this projected similarity is not simply a repetition of historical circumstances— another mirroring; but rather, if I perceive of my identifications with her as positions in narratives of desire, the way I rewrite the scenario reveals the structure of my identifications. For one thing, I have repositioned myself in relation to what I have projected as an uncanny specter from my past. I am not what I was; I am now what my teacher was: I have situated myself in the place of the object I once wanted to both be and have. In this sense, my projections onto the student seem to be a rejection of an old position and the reaffirmation of a new one; they are the elements in a narrative of fulfilled desire. The narrative is about becoming what I wanted to have.

But that's too easy and it certainly doesn't account for my animosity, unless hostility is a necessary posture of rejection. In my scenario two different narratives coexist: a narrative of unfulfilled desire—of wanting to want some-one I could never have—and the narrative of fulfilled desire I have projected on the student—of being in the place of the object of another's desire by which I have redefined my own position. Both of these, however, are my narratives; and though they conflict, they necessarily work together. What then is my identificatory position in the collision of these narratives? What are the narra-tives that draw these narratives together?

This is the last step of this narrative desirathon, even though it's probably not the end, since there is probably a perpetual circle here wherein identifica-tory position determines narrative and narrative constructs identificatory posi-tion. If my concept of identity is, like the student and the Witty Butcher's Wife, in the position of the desirer of an unfulfilled desire, and if I have made the student represent a narrative of unfulfillable desire in which I am the object, what the collision of the two narratives implies is that underneath my position of desirer is a position of wishing to be the object of an unfulfillable desire. Those two positions do not necessarily clash as long as I don't actually occupy the place of the object of someone else's desire, but in this case, where it appears that I have succeeded in actually having my desire fulfilled by being in that place, my identificatory positions in narrative crash, the identity that covers over this process is brought into question, and I place the blame on the other where I have already projected the disturbing story. This is not to suggest that all of this happened with the advent of the student, but that I have maybe always been beset by conflicting narrative identifications whose unity and cooperation I have sustained by placing myself in the position of the outsider—the one who cannot be in the place of the other's desire. What I've always thought was my identity—the position outside—is in fact a cover for a discordant desire to be the object of another's desire. The outsider narrative constitutes a compromise narrative that allows two conflicting desire narratives to coexist.

If conflicting positions within narrative define identifications and if identities are screening totalities of compromise formations that hide the nefarious activities of identification, identity and identifications are in some conflict with one another. This creates a real problem in group identity politics where notions of identity tend to be equated with identifications and where individual and group identity are assumed to belong to the same categories. There are several difficulties here, and I'm going to use lesbian groups as an example of what those difficulties might be. That is of course assuming the fictions already represented by the term "identity."

1. The narrative multiplicity underlying identifications suggests that any identity politics premised on an assumption of mirroring, of group association cemented by a common bond or identity, may be looking at the wrong or an overly simplistic idea of identity except insofar as the categories of group identity coalesce with and inform narratives of position within structures of desire. Even if we take desire as a group premise, as in the case of lesbians, individual lesbians still position themselves differently within desire narratives.

2. Lesbian identity is not what it seems to be, and there is a difference between the identities of individual lesbians constituted through the interface of very different identificatory narratives and a lesbian group identity. There is a tendency to believe that individual lesbian identities are derived from group identity, as in, for example, Lillian Faderman's understanding of lesbians as those who define themselves as such. But while the existence of a visible group probably plays a part in the desire narratives of individuals, that part will be different for different women. This means that there is not an automatic or essential group identification either.

3. Individual lesbians will identify differently within groups; in other words, they will position themselves differently in relation to identity groups in a way that fits into their own positioning in identity narratives. Thus, there is no reliable single way of understanding the relation between individual and group.

4. The lack of alignment between individual lesbians and a lesbian group identity means that group identity, like individual identity, is a fiction that must be maintained through a compromise formation analogous to that sustaining individual identity.

5. The means of maintaining compromise formations sustaining lesbian identity is narrative. Rather than more or less unconsciously struggling to

patch the inevitable rends in those identities and the differences within them through oppressive calls to conformity and definition, might not a consciousness of the processes that underlie identifications and their difference from identities work to shift the teetering fictional bases for lesbian group identity?

Understanding the difference between group and individual identity and understanding identity as a fabrication of unities might forestall expectations of uniformity, coherence, and compliance that make identity communities oppressive, splintered, and politically inefficacious. Seeing the basis for joint action not as a shared identity, but rather as sets of shared purposes gets rid of the confusion between homogeneity and motivation that plagues group identities and prevents the coexistence of what are, for the purposes of joint action, individual identity differences, differences in individual position, multiple group identifications, and incomplete identifications with groups. In this sense the personal is not the political. Though positions in desire narratives that constitute individual identity myths take from cultural ideologies linked to histories of oppression and group position, to equate individual identity with a notion of the interpellated subject is to ignore the very source of the dynamic that makes micro-political politics fail—the failure to comprehend that the levels of difference extend beyond the social and the material.

What this means is not that identity is indeterminate or so widely individualistic as to be useless, but rather that identity should not be the sole basis for group action. As in the working of narrative ideology in the structuring of individual identities, the stake in obscuring identificatory narrative processes always works to hide the loss that motivates the production of such unities in the first place. Consciousness of those processes at least brings the terms of identity production into view, replacing an illusion with the marked differences it conceals. In a way, this is akin to the project of announcing and owning one's differences as a way of reforming communitarian politics, but it differs in terms of the kinds of differences and processes it makes visible. The problem with positional confessions is that they always take place within the boundaries of group identity politics, meaning that owning differences is tantamount to claiming membership in multiple other group identities—I am white, bourgeois, Protestant, Euro-American, and so on. In other words, such a process merely reiterates the identity problem on a slightly more specific level. Understanding identity itself as a fictional result of a process that is itself ideological might help us understand the production of the categories of differences as well as the positions within that production that articulate social categories differently within individuals.

So does this mean that tracing the narrative genesis of my unsisterly distaste for my student cures my dislike and makes us work happily together as participants in a conscious compromise toward a greater good that will benefit us both? Maybe. Does it mean that I can stay in the same room with her without wincing? Probably not.

2

The Event of Becoming

Jewelle L. Gomez

When I was about eleven years old I was visiting the small city in Rhode Island where my mother lived with my stepfather. Pawtucket was a failing mill town, predominantly white, of various ethnicities. Its working-class homes were spiraling downward in the late 1950s, before the phenomenon of gentrification. It was a cheap and manageable town for my fair-skinned, straight-haired mother, who resembles the Wampanoag side of the family more than I do. It had seemed like a comfortable place for her and her white husband.

One day, while sitting on the steps outside my mother's home I was approached by a boy a bit younger than I. He eyed me warily and asked what nationality I was. I replied that I was an American. He looked puzzled, then said, "No, I mean what nationality are you?"

I was adamant. "American."

"No," he said, "you know what I mean."

The beginning of anger stretched my words tightly in the air.

"You said what nationality, that means nation. I'm from America, so I'm American. What are you?"

He looked at me in fear and then disgust and said, "You don't know what you're talking about," then ran down the street to his own stoop.

He went back, I'm sure, to his white parents who'd sent him. He had the air of a child on a mission he did not quite understand, but he knew I had not responded satisfactorily. I was sure that he'd expected me to say I was a "nigger," just as his father and mother had probably identified me. The look of expectation in his eyes was a betrayal. In siding with his parents' ignorance he betrayed our natural alliance as children. I felt crushed.

But I had a major advantage over that child. I knew what he was doing and he did not. As a black person in the United States—even as a child—I recognized a trap being set by a white person. I saw, at eleven years old, what black meant to white America, and I knew that by stating my blackness I might set in motion a series of events that had historically never meant anything good for me. So, precocious little wench that I was even then, I whipped out another identity I knew would stump him and his parents, whose devious hand I sensed guided his bumbling inquiries.

And lest my behavior be dismissed today as fanciful paranoia, the fact is that within months of that encounter my mother and her family were beseiged with hate phone calls; garbage was dumped and burned on her tiny lawn. Her neighbors threatened her home and her life when they realized that by American I also meant black.

So the question of identity and its complexities is not just an academic one for me. I never had the privilege of relaxedly theorizing who I was in this world, even as a child. Each hypothesis I might create was met with a specifically defined reality and the question of survival. Interestingly enough, this reality and the experiences it offered me did not seduce me into an insistence on a rigidly guarded identity. I recognized the wondrous spectrum of elements that begin the construction of my identity—lesbian, African American, Wampanoag, Ioway, Bostonian—to just begin. Coming of age during the political movements of the 1960s helped me learn an early appreciation of the power and the value of identification. But the complexity of identity didn't escape me. After all, my mother was an acceptable neighbor on one day and a target of violence the next, simply because of others' interpretation of her identity. This life lesson also helped me develop a critical stance toward any element that was viewed as fixed, unmitigated, or eternal.

Now that I've been given the opportunity to do some theorizing, I'd like to share some linked but not necessarily linearly related thoughts and feelings on my two responses to the question of identity—appreciation and caution.

First, I suggest that the question of identity as posed in this country is one that would be almost unrecognizable in other countries. Most nations begin from a more articulate definition of who its citizens are, rightly or wrongly, and then develop attitudes and institutions which allow for assorted variations, as well as for colonialism. In the eighteenth and nineteenth centuries the concept of a "British subject" became so expansive that it could, at one time, have taken in just about every existing ethnic group. I'm not suggesting that the British have been especially liberal in their acceptance of immigrant African or Caribbean "subjects" any more than the citizens of Germany today absorb Asian and African immigrant workers. But those nations start from a unified whole—whether real or imagined—and the United States does not.

The idea of "American" (and I, of course, use that word imprecisely when I use it to speak only of U.S. citizens) embodies resilient refugees from many other shores. Consequently the struggle for identity is more focused, more strident for citizens of the United States. We are continually, as a nation, seeking a way to pull together the unifying threads that make us a nation. And when we speak of Americans we think of an amazing array of mostly European immigrants who escaped their countries, explicitly choosing the United States because of its mythology. Most often the United States has been extolled as a place where one could escape the oppressions of the past (religious, economic, social, judicial) and create a new life, that is, a new identity.

It is this tabula rasa ideal that sets much of the tone for the development of the American national persona. After being bathed in the fire and water of a transatlantic journey and surviving to step on to the frightening and alien shores of America, the new arrivals must surely have deemed it only fair that life be allowed to begin anew. And that idea of newness, that disconnection from all that went before, alongside the sense of a vast expanse of wilderness (supposedly unclaimed) shaped the embryonic American identity.

That American identity most often comes into greatest relief when we speak of the deeds of explorers/exploiters such as the Pilgrims, cowboys, and settlers of the western migration or those who survive victimization—European immigrants who endured antagonism to become successful. Both mythologies were shaped to emphasize a simplistic heroism—good against bad. Personal fortitude and ingenuity winning out over mindless evil or ignorance. John Wayne versus the wild Indians; Horatio Alger versus poverty. In this country politicians play most successfully to people's belief in this mythology. The good citizens are asked to defeat the forces of evil: antifamily homosexuals, pornographers, the lazy poor, the violent people of color, all those too "weak" to overcome their circumstance. The polyethnic nature of our beginnings makes such fractional-izations an easy strategy.

There has been much discussion in literary circles in the past few years of the deconstruction of words and ideas, stripping them down to allow them to stand independent of meaning, stark against a page; that old tabula rasa, if you will. We learn much when we are able to look at roots and at the flotsam and jetsam that have little meaning in and of themselves, but that linger in the wake of words and ideas. We strip away the attendant realities until we look at the empty space that lies there, waiting to form itself into motion, object, concept.

But people are not artichokes. It is very helpful in a therapeutic situation to peel each leaf and get to the heart of what has formed a personality. But in human social interaction it is by exploring the full construction and interaction of the layers of character that we find the heart. To twist an old geometry principle—the whole equals more than the sum of its parts.

Any writer or literary critic would acknowledge that it is those layers both personal and social that make our fictional characters memorable. When most effective our stories reflect the plurality of who we are both individually and as a nation. Because of who I am when I wrote my novel *The Gilda Stories*, the questions of real (fictional) life and those of national identity had to be considered. I made the choice not to discard but to utilize those questions in developing the plot, themes, and characters. If a youthful-looking, dark-skinned woman is walking down a lonely country road at night and encounters two men dressed like beds, that is, wearing sheets and hoods, with what dilemma are they presented? Well, two conflicting desires begin: both are rooted in fear and need for a sense of power. So there is murder and there is rape. The conflict: whether to rape her or kill her. Of course the resolution is that they can do both, first rape, then lynch. They assume that they can accomplish both deeds successfully, anonymously, because history has shown them it's possible.

But shortly into the encounter they realize they have misidentified their prey. Like the little boy on my mother's stoop, they see only what they've been told to see. On that road she is not simply a lone dark woman; she is that and more. She is someone with powers—physical or mystical, or maybe just a gun. She is a lone dark woman who is also more than simply that description, and the inability of those men to absorb a constructive concept of who she is will cost them their lives. For them identity is reached through a reductionist theory. It says that black women are one particular set of things: powerless, sexual prey, not intelligent. These men are unable to see her identity in a constructive way, that is, a circle of elements forming a whole. But whether this encounter takes place in the eighteenth century or the twentieth century, whether it is on a dark country road or in a U.S. Senate judiciary hearing room, the definition of the identity of that lone dark woman will not (for the white males who've intercepted her) be broad enough to include other things she might be—a crack shot, a black belt in karate, a reputable lawyer who'll no longer be silent about harassment, a vampire.

Many of us who've been categorized and oppressed fear that to identify oneself as a specific thing—black, lesbian, Jewish, Italian, American—is to reduce yourself to a single element that excludes all other possible elements. The concept of identity as a reductionist rather than constructive expression is continually reinforced in this culture, where ethnic or social identity is rarely used as part of a normative stance. Sociological surveys pinpoint specific identities in order to categorize and assess and market information. The Kinseys, the Nielsens, the Bureau of the Census introduce the slots into which we must all fit. And once we are slotted, wheels will turn and things will happen. Homosexuals will be known as lonely white men, television shows with all-black casts and no laugh track will not be produced, and candidates for office will decide on which neighborhood to focus their campaign. We have come to accept negative social consequences from such identification.

Why is that, when evidence also shows that creating specifics doesn't have to be limiting or exclusionary? The success of the film and television business depends on precisely that principle—anyone in the world should be able to identify with Shirley Temple, Sylvester Stallone, or a purple dinosaur. The concept of "world literature" also presumes such identification. People rarely think, What an ethnic oddity Leopold Bloom is, let's drop Joyce from the canon;

or, the working poor of Victorian England are irrelevant, so don't bother reading Dickens. We can accept the perspectives of Joyce or Dickens as extremely specific and at the same time broad and relevant. We now must insist on giving the same credence and value to other perspectives, including our own.

Marilyn Frye speaks of "the event of becoming a lesbian (as) a reorientation of attention in a kind of ontological conversion." When we use this constructive approach, identification becomes a shift in perspective rather than a closing of one's eyes. To identify ourselves can open a way into discussion. Rather than reducing us to familiar elements, it can offer an introduction into the many layers that construct who we are. To say that I am a lesbian is not the same as saying that I am *only* a lesbian. Identifying myself as a lesbian shifts the emphasis, suggesting a place to begin, not a place to end.

I first read James Baldwin's *Giovanni's Room* around 1961 and was not surprised to find that it was about gay men. In one section one of the characters, seated in a bar, coyly observes the patrons and says, "All these men, all these men and so few women. Doesn't that seem strange to you?" "Ah," said Giovanni, "no doubt the women are waiting at home."

Because I knew myself to be a lesbian I identified with the men in that bar, eyeing each other in a way that was forbidden. I experienced the thrill of recognition of my place with these people. I saw the hot mix of limbs and sweat that was the reason for being there and found joy in it. At the same time I transmuted the experience and was able to understand that I was also at home with the women—the women who I knew were not merely waiting. Our imagination allows each of us this possibility of being party to both experiences.

Perhaps it would be easier for us to acknowledge the many places where we reside if we could learn to accept the basic, natural permutation that is our lives. We are perpetually defining and redefining ourselves. The baby, the youth, the teenager. I am now learning my identity as middle-aged in preparation for my identity as an elder. These are precise identities that we take on, reshape, fill up as we need to over the course of our alloted time on this planet. As we move into the next definition, what we have been does not evaporate to make way for the next phase. It is embedded in who we are. That infamous inner child! We can hold on to all those other things we've been and make what we are more whole. My identity as a lesbian is tied up with James Baldwin's literary representation of gay men; with Mercedes McCambridge, a particularly dykey actress of the 1940s; with Gwen, my high femme best friend from high school; as well as with Stephen, the heroine of *The Well of Loneliness*. My early experience of lesbians as women in flannel shirts and Frye boots gives more resonance to my experience today of lesbians in three-piece suits or in transparent body stockings. When I can reconcile those experiences, those identifications, I have created a larger whole, not a smaller self.

In order to really appreciate the opportunity that the advent of lesbian and gay studies presents, I must also explore the history that made the idea possible in our lifetimes. The labor movement, the civil rights movement, and the antiwar and women's liberation movements each created new realities to be layered onto the idea of what it meant to be an American. In examining that process of development I see the areas where we need to continue to expand our idea of what our identity as lesbians or gays can mean. And in doing so, I hope we avoid making the same mistakes made in the past.

The emergence of black studies and Africana studies departments, the result of student activism of the 1960s, provided a strong base for the redefinition of black identity in this country. But what it also did was help to isolate blackness from the other layers that made up the totality. I think this occurred not because there is inherently anything wrong with black studies, but rather because black identity was not being looked at within a full political context. Blackness was being taught in reaction to racism. The effort was to affirm the goodness and value of being black, to retell the history of being black in a positive light. Offering a fuller political context rather than being simply reactive would have accomplished the goal and would have allowed for a linking of the struggle for black liberation with other liberation struggles in general. This is not what happened: consequently women and lesbians and gays were (and still are) relegated to lesser roles in the development of that area of study. And students of the various ethnic studies programs see each other primarily as competitors for limited funds and greater victim status. Again, this is not because there is anything wrong with black studies; rather, the programs have eschewed any active political position other than the one immediately connected to that one element of identity—blackness. The idea of what black means is reduced to the most obvious.

The advent of women's studies in the 1970s created another whole set of political dilemmas, but it did offer the possibility for fuller development because it was not just trying to reshape the idea of who women are but was also advocating a specific political philosophy—feminism. Modern feminism grew naturally out of a reassessment of the political movements in this country's history. It postulates the inclusion of all elements when assessing a political situation. It calls for a constructive perspective rather than a reductive one. Raising the questions of race, ethnicity, physical difference, and class broadens our analysis to include not just vindication of those who are oppressed at the moment but also an examination of how oppression occurs systemically. The implication is that not just one element of society needs to be changed; all the power dynamics of society are due for realignment. The questions about the focus and effectiveness of women's studies (or any of the attempts to address the inadequacies of traditional educational institutions) as an academic discipline remain, but the value of feminism as a political perspective should not be overlooked.

The insult often hurled at "minorities" by conservatives is that we're practicing identity politics. Well, all politics is identity politics, whether it is built around an affiliation with African Americans, Chicano farmworkers, the Family

Values Coalition, the Teamsters, the National Rifle Association, or the Republican Party. There is nothing innately wrong with making a case for the improvement of one's group position. The problem comes when we ignore the full picture and rely on only one element of our identity to direct our thinking and action. We usually end up with the belief that our position is the only one to be taken into consideration, that there is one perspective that must predominate. In politics, as in our personal lives, we must learn how to integrate the many identities we hold and understand that those identities are sometimes fluid, not static. It is much easier to grab onto a picture of ourselves and continually reinforce it than leave the picture frame open like a shoebox, into which will fall the new information we gather. I enjoy being called a lesbian, a writer, a Virgo, a Bostonian, a woman, an African American, or any of the other identities for which I qualify. And I will gleefully correct you if you seem to indicate that one of those must preclude the others. The little boy questioning me in Pawtucket didn't understand what he saw or heard when I called myself an American, which is sort of the equivalent of saying "all of the above."

In her writing Audre Lorde repeatedly insisted on her right to be seen as all the elements of her identity: black, poet, mother, lesbian, warrior. She said, "There's no such thing as a single issue movement, we do not live single issue lives." Moving through and yet carrying each of the issues and identities that form us create this event of becoming ourselves. It is an ongoing work whose shifting perspective I consider a burden sometimes, but more often a gift.

3

Whose History? The Case of Oklahoma

Michael Moon

I used to say that I had enjoyed wasting my youth in New York but had truly wasted my childhood in Oklahoma, but I have recently come to distrust the too ready association of places like Oklahoma with waste and worthlessness. Attempting to look afresh at my own memories of Oklahoma and beyond them to the stories of other people(s) who have inhabited the place, I start with Michelle Wallace's remark in her collection *Invisibility Blues*:

> I've become fascinated by the unwillingness of "American history" to include Oklahoma in its big picture. It's like one of those nuclear dump sites, some place nobody wants to know anything about.
>
> Perhaps it remains this frightening unknown quantity because its population didn't whiten until the 1920s. Years after all the unwanted Native Americans in the Southeast were rounded up and herded to the "Indian Territory," most notably in the Trail of Tears—ex-slaves began to rally there as well because of the rumors that black men were prosperous in the territory—the possibility of Oklahoma entering the Union as an Indian or black state was seriously considered.[1]

African Americans first came to the then newly created Indian Territory (roughly the eastern half of what became in 1907 the state of Oklahoma) in the 1830s, along with the so-called Five Civilized Tribes (Cherokee, Creek, Choctaw, Chickasaw, and Seminole peoples), who, like their white neighbors in the South from which they had been forcibly removed, were slaveholders (in fact, part of the reason they had been given the accolade "civilized" by their white neighbors is that they held slaves; they also farmed, tended to live in settlements or towns, and had been relatively amenable to Christian missionary efforts—all of these characteristics setting them off for white settlers from the Native peoples of the Plains). Many African Americans who had been slaves in the Territory stayed there after they were emancipated, and many more immigrated from the South in the decades after the Civil War. Blacks established towns, newspapers, and universities in the Territory in substantial numbers in the last decades of the nineteenth century, and some of these towns (Langston, Boley, Clearview) still survive as African American communities.

Ralph Ellison, born in Oklahoma City, has written vividly of the rich cultural scene that black musicians created there in the 1920s, including such legendary figures as Jimmy Rushing, Walter Page, Eddie Durham, Lester Young, and Count Basie, all of whom were collectively and individually developing their art in and around the city during jazz's formative years. In his memoirs of his childhood in Jazz Age Oklahoma City gathered in *Shadow and Act*, Ellison makes clear that the day-to-day production of a powerfully innovative and improvisatory African American blues-and-jazz culture, far from being a monoracial phenomenon, involved frequent projection and identification across racial identities that had generally been stigmatized by whites. In the drugstore where he worked as a teenager, Ellison writes, the regulars regaled each other with "stories of Jesse James, of Negro outlaws and black United States marshals, of slaves who became chiefs of Indian tribes and of the exploits of Negro cowboys."[2] According to Ellison and other students of nonwhite Oklahoma histories, these uncanny, stereotype-shattering characters were of a piece with the actual social communities that produced and circulated these narratives of crossing.

It is of course no accident that the composite characters in the tales young Ellison acquired in the drugstore—these people who in their lifetimes had been both slave *and* Indian chief, or cowboy *and* Indian—have largely disappeared from the historical record; by their very existences as members of mixed and/ or multiple social groups they have defied the white-racist sanction against miscegenation of all kinds, at the same time that they have contradicted ideals of "full-" or "pure-bloodedness" on all sides. These crossings of identities in Ellison's and other writers' stories about the mixed fixity and fluidity of race and social roles in the histories of the West intrigue me because they remind me in somewhat disorienting ways of the recent resistance among queers to being confined to one ready-made, supposedly transparent identity, such as "gay man" or "lesbian." Looking back at some of the underexplored histories of cross-racial identification and self-identification in the history of the West with the aid of our recent thinking about the difficulties and possibilities of identifying and building alliances and coalitions across gender, sexuality, and "perversion" may help us recover or discover some of the connections between race, political resistance, and queernesses that have existed in the past—and that exist in the present, however precariously or provisionally.[3]

It certainly struck me as possibly both grotesque and ridiculous when it first occurred to me to take the history and geography of Oklahoma as a subject for queer theory, for critical "race" theory, and for critical regional studies. Oklahoma is, after all, a notoriously homophobic state; the Oklahoma legislature's response to the widespread drive for gay rights in the late 1970s was to vote to honor its favorite daughter, Anita Bryant, a former "Miss Oklahoma," at the height of her Florida fagbaiting days, and it was to Tulsa that Bryant returned when her "Save the Children" campaign collapsed. The state has also been a notoriously racist one, its history of mistreating its successive African American populations, which dwindled significantly for a long time after the Tulsa Race Riot of 1921, unfortunately paralleled by its destructive attitudes toward its large Native populations. Both groups have survived, but they have done so in the face of decades of malign neglect from the government and racist terrorism from white hate groups.

One of the reasons I have wanted to think about and study Oklahoma is that I wanted to stop feeling like a frightened fugitive from the place—more than twenty-five years after leaving it. I grew up in Kay County, at the north-central border of the state, and as an effeminate boy who liked "all the wrong things"—piano, opera, theater, and fashion—and wilfully ignored "all the right things"—football, basketball, baseball, and track—I experienced the place as simply toxic, as a place that would like to kill me and other people like me.

When I saw the 1983 film *Silkwood*, the lesbian character played by Cher seemed emblematic to me of the queer kid who stays in places like Oklahoma, drifting in and out of potentially fatal environments and situations as if that were "no big deal." Karen Silkwood (played in the film by Meryl Streep) and her roommate (Cher's character) worked at a plutonium plant in the north-central part of the state, where basic standards for handling radioactive materials were being routinely violated. Since seeing the film several years ago, I have learned that Karen Silkwood is only one of the more recent of the state's many fatalities that have fallen prey to corporate and federal connivance and thuggery. As her story suggests, accurate information about industrial and atomic hazards and disease and mortality rates can eventually be gotten, though sometimes at hazard to the life of the activist who starts collecting it. Yet the (to me) haunting presence of the lesbian roommate in the story suggests further that there are as yet no environmental studies for Oklahoma of the no less lethal toxins racism and homophobia, and of their no less damaging and often fatal effects on the present and future of young queer and nonwhite lives.

In doing this project I am trying to resist any notion of "recovering my roots"—idealizing or sentimentalizing where and how I grew up and the people I grew up among—but I'm also trying to resist the cheap if long-established practice of patronizing places like Oklahoma. To continue to condescend to "Bible Belt rednecks" or whatever dismissive label one may have for such places and their inhabitants is to contribute, however redundantly, to the privileging of the coasts of the United States and the coastal metropolises—which, as we have been repeatedly and painfully reminded in recent years, shelter their own brands of intense racist violence and queerhating. There is a strong tendency among academics in the humanities to make places like Oklahoma invisible to students. Oklahoma does not arise as a subject in American literature; it barely figures even in the relatively low prestige subfield of "literature of the American West." (The exception to this rule, as I shall discuss later, is in twentieth-century Native American writing, in which Oklahoma is a major trope.) Many academics come from places like Oklahoma, but from the beginning of our training most of us find ourselves at least implicitly pressured to amnese "insignificant facts" like that, to re-root ourselves imaginarily in a canonical cultural capital such as (for literary studies) Elizabethan England or Puritan New England or Victorian London or modernist Paris. While I have no problem with people reimagining who they are and where they really come from and belong—mass migration and diaspora, real and imaginary, between country and metropolis have, after all, been primary means of communal self-forgings for both African American and queer populations for the past century and more—I do think it is important to try to resist following certain well-worn WASP-academic grooves as we explore the countries of our imaginations.

Surely at least part of the fierce PC-bashing against academics who have been promoting multicultural scholarship and pedagogy in recent years has proceeded from the fury of some white culturati at seeing other white academics declining to perpetuate the racist assumptions that have tended to underwrite most officially supported academic and artistic high culture in this country. White people like myself from working-class families from the sticks have traditionally, through a weird but often effective combination of fosterage and shaming, been considered to make the most faithful defenders of white high culture—because we are supposed to be inexhaustibly grateful for admission to the clerkly classes while remaining susceptible to intimidation on the basis of our allegedly lowly social origins.

To consider for a moment the reverse of the picture I have been composing, I feel it behooves me to say that while Oklahoma has been and remains the site of toxic threats of a number of kinds, I have realized in thinking back about my experience growing up there that at least for some of us in some places it was multicultural and multiracial to what seems in retrospect a remarkable degree, given the backward and whites-only image the state has for many outsiders as well as for some of its residents. Despite such signs of strict segregation in my hometown as the "sundown laws" that were in effect against blacks until civil rights legislation overturned them in the mid-1960s, I went to school with, played with, visited in the homes of, lived across the street from kids and adults who were Chicano, Filipino, and Native American, as well as several shades of "white." Indeed, large pockets of my supposedly hopelessly redneck hometown were in fact in some important ways considerably more racially diverse and interactive than the separatist gay-male social and political scene into which I came out in Manhattan in the late 1970s, when most gay-male activist circles were overwhelmingly white, urban, and middle-class. Even I, given my working-class upbringing and residual working-class identification, often felt out of place and at times more than a little unwelcome in the high-Bloomingdale's-Studio 54-Fire Island Pines ethos in which a lot of queer men my age first tried to figure out what it meant to be gay in the Big City in the years between Stonewall and AIDS.

Yet despite the high incidence of generally positive interaction across race in some parts of my hometown, the Oklahoma history we were all required to study in grade nine was very much a white people's version, with everyone else reduced to the role of "extras," necessary but somehow not central to the plot; Native Americans, Chicanos, and African Americans were made to oscillate between serving as villains and providing local color in these narratives. The state's character as a crucible in which prodigal and desperate political and cultural struggles between and across several races had been waged was not part of the story we heard. The version of Oklahoma history we got reeked of formaldehyde, like the biology lab down the hall on worm-dissection day. We memorized the names of the governors of the state and also the names of the state's seventy-seven counties, which we had to enter correctly on a blank map (critical thinking not being high on the goals list in my junior high). We were given a version of the history of the state in which almost everything of value or interest was left out. For example, I never knew until I started reading Oklahoma history again recently that looking out across the plains from the windows of the second-floor classroom where I was supposedly taught "Oklahoma history," one could almost see the western borders of what had once been the territory of the proud and mighty Osage nation, which extended in our direction to just the other side of Ponca City, barely twenty miles away. White America's bad conscience about our devastating and long-term betrayal of Native peoples has created a particularly charged silence in those parts of the country where some of the worst betrayals have been most recently acted out, whether on the battlefield or in state or national legislatures. No one I knew, in or out of the classroom, ever suggested that the histories of neighboring Osage County and the Native people to whom it had once been promised in perpetuity—"as long as the grass shall grow and the waters run," in the words of the treaties—were very much worth teaching and learning. The kinds of questions children ask—"what happened to them?" "where did they go?" "where are they now, and are they okay?"—seem to have been the very questions our teachers felt they couldn't afford to ask, much less try to answer.[4]

The version of Oklahoma history we got was one long triumphalist white-people fantasy, usually entitled something like "Oklahoma: From Teepees to Office Towers," and often featuring photos of acres of oil wells, including those working away on the front lawn of the state capitol building, and prosperous corporate headquarters like the Phillips Petroleum Tower in Bartlesville, designed by Frank Lloyd Wright. This violently abridged version of the state's history began not with the moundbuilders who lived in the area a millennium ago, or even with the epochal Trail of Tears, but with the spectacular land rushes that began in 1889. The dramatic high point of Ron Howard's recent film *Far and Away*, starring Tom Cruise and Nicole Kidman, is the film's restaging of the Land Rush. This scene—thousands of thundering horses, screaming white men, rickety covered wagons, all careening forward through great clouds of red dust—has been restaged numerous times by Hollywood since it was first filmed in silent days; the last major re-performance of the scene before Howard's took place in Anthony Mann's 1960 film of Edna Ferber's best-seller *Cimarron*. In *Far and Away*, one of the major effects of this colossal and brutal scene of white territorial expropriation is that it simultaneously finally provides a place on which the Irish peasant lad played by Tom Cruise can claim a piece of land on which to ground, after much struggle, his claim to the hand of the fugitive young woman of owning-class family played by Nicole Kidman. The other major effect of the land rush is represented as being the rekindling of erotic sparks between the parents (Daniel and Nora Christie) of Nicole Kidman's character, Shannon, who get turned on to each other again for the first time in years after watching the scene. In the souvenir book of the film, actress Barbara Babcock, who plays Nora Christie, is quoted as saying,

> Seeing the wagons come over that hill was like suddenly being thrown back and knowing what it must have felt like to those people who were trying to stake their claim on a little plot of land. And what happened was this incredible exhilaration. That's the first time he kisses me. Where before we had been alienated from each other, suddenly it's as if we're starting over. It's lovely to think that after all these years, and all this pain and anger, Daniel and Nora Christie have been given a second chance, and can start again with their relationship.[5]

As the film has it, Daniel and Nora Christie, joining thousands of their fellow whites grabbing land, grab each other for the first time in a long while. Rather than taking Hollywood's depiction of a federally organized land grab as a novel kind of marital aid to be some kind of anomalous absurdity particular to Ron Howard's film, we should probably notice with what nauseating clarity such a moment crystallizes what an exciting turn-on this scene has been—and remains, given its popularity with three generations of white filmmakers and audiences. What get ritually trampled underfoot every time the scene is replayed are the hopes of large numbers of people of color to establish something in that territory besides yet another zone of entrenched white racism.

The aggressive and compulsory heterosexuality of this moment as it's represented in *Far and Away* is especially significant, given that the Land Rush is one of only two moments in which Oklahoma has entered the national and nationalistic imaginary, as confirmed by Hollywood. The other occurred in the early to mid-1930s, and it's in one sense a strange revision of the land rush scene: this other scene is the pathetic one of the exodus of thousands of destitute "Okies" out of the Dust Bowl.[6] The Dust Bowl has been unforgettably represented, first by the extraordinary documentary photography of the Depression, by Dorothea Lange, Russell Lee, Arthur Rothstein, and others, and then by John Steinbeck and John Ford in their respective versions of *Grapes of Wrath*.

Grapes of Wrath may help us find some alternatives to the relentlessly heterosexist plot of *Far and Away*. There is certainly a way of reading *Grapes of Wrath* as a queer text and its hero Tom Joad as a queer character, and I'm surely not the first reader or filmgoer to think so. To cite one example, Woody Guthrie's career as a radical performer and activist seems to have been determinately affected by his cathexis of young Tom Joad as portrayed by Henry Fonda in Ford's film version of the text. It's a good example of a characteristic kind of irony in the history of politics and mass culture that Guthrie was commissioned to make his first commercial recording, his great double album of *Dust Bowl Ballads*, by the RCA Victor Record corporation in an attempt on their part to capitalize on the market created for "authentic Okie Dust-Bowl folk music" by the notoriety of the Steinbeck novel and the success of the Ford film. It was in fact the RCA executives who commissioned him particularly to write a "Ballad of Tom Joad." The excited and clearly smitten young Guthrie is said to have dashed off seventeen verses on his new ego ideal to the tune of his then current favorite record, the Carter Family's rendition of the outlaw ballad "John Hardy."[7] It is also a good example of another characteristic kind of irony, this one in the history of radical populist movements and the queer energies on which these movements have thrived, but which have almost always been disavowed, occluded, "sacrificed" to compulsory heterosexuality. Woody Guthrie was queer for Tom Joad, and that changed not only the young Guthrie's life but through him a lot of other people's—but what one always reads and hears about instead are Guthrie's allegedly rampant heterosexuality and his out-of-control womanizing. Thus are the queer impulses that have energized so many radical movements obliviated.

It should not surprise us that there is an important if largely invisible queer element in young Woody Guthrie's refashioning of himself as a successful political rebel and potential revolutionary outlaw on the model of Tom Joad, *and* a highly marketable "authentic" "folk" commodity for RCA records (although Guthrie subsequently recorded largely for the anticorporate, solidly left Folkways label). Tom Joad is a young ex-con at the beginning of *Grapes of Wrath* and a dedicated and militant labor organizer at the end of it; in neither role is he of any use or value to the mass-culture industries. It is interesting that, in contrast, Woody Guthrie had to pass through a kind of moment of re-formation in relation to one of the corporate "media giants" in the process of passing from being one of many "hillbilly" singers performing on local radio stations around southern California in the 1930s to being a star, albeit a star who remained a radical activist. The population of Oklahoma, which, as Michelle Wallace says, had whitened only in the 1920s, was ripe for exploitation by the national media as a focus for pathos that could be used to "authenticate" not only the Okies themselves but all the other Americans who pitied them (while leaving them to the tender mercies of the labor camp bosses). This process of reprocessing and repackaging the state and its people as an imaginarily all-white theme park (not a theme park actually to be visited) culminated in the 1955 film of Rodgers and Hammerstein's 1943 Broadway hit *Oklahoma*, which aggressively omits people of color from the early history of the state—this despite its being closely based on the 1930s folk play *Green Grow the Lilacs*, written by a gay man of Cherokee descent from Oklahoma named Lynn Riggs.

Grapes of Wrath shows Tom Joad turning from one kind of outlaw into another, from an apolitical, small-time crook to a criminal acting out of a coherent political agenda. The novel and film both begin with his release from the McAlester Penitentiary after serving four years for homicide, and they end with his leaving his family once again, this time to organize other migrant workers. At the end of the novel Joad has killed another man, in a deadly encounter between organizers and company goons. In his leave-taking conversation with his mother, she expresses her fear to her son that "they'll drive you an' cut you down like they done to young [Pretty Boy] Floyd."[8] Pretty Boy, the hero of another of Guthrie's Dust Bowl ballads, was a hometown boy to the Joads; Steinbeck has them hail from Sallisaw, Okla., where Floyd was from. He (along with Bonnie and Clyde) was the last of the many outlaw folk heroes for whom Indian Territory—later eastern Oklahoma—had been famous since the heyday of Jesse James and his gang in the 1870s.[9]

I began by citing Ralph Ellison's memories of complex webs of miscegenation and cross-racial affiliation and identification in the Oklahoma of his childhood, and among our younger African American contemporaries I would mention the work of Art Burton, who has vividly demonstrated in his recent book *Black, Red and Deadly*, the persistence of interest in the kind of outlaw tales of Oklahoma Territory that trouble white-racist assumptions about racial purity and separateness in the history of the western United States. Burton grew up in the 1950s and 1960s starved for the very kind of complex cross-narratives Ellison first heard working behind an Oklahoma City soda counter in the 1920s. Burton discusses how, as a child formed like other children of his and my generation by television and Saturday matinees, he longed for there to have been black cowboys and outlaws and sheriffs and rodeo stars, but did not believe there ever had been. When his Uncle Henry back in Oklahoma tried to tell him that blacks *had* done all these things, Burton as a boy refused to believe him because he had never seen such figures in movies or on television.

With E. J. Hobsbawm's work on the political significance of outlaw legends and outlaw activity among rebel populations in mind, we can perceive how the devotion to outlaw heroes of poor whites like Woody Guthrie and Pretty Boy Floyd himself and Steinbeck's Joads, as well as of older and younger African Americans like Ralph Ellison and Art Burton, has functioned as a form of class protest across racialized boundaries against the powers of the white owning classes of the United States in the twentieth century. In Guthrie's "Ballad of Pretty Boy Floyd," Floyd is a Robin Hood who saves destitute farm families from the depredations of the banks. The text begs the question that has intrigued me ever since I first heard it as a child, "Why is Pretty Boy Floyd 'pretty'?" (As a kid, I didn't hear so many songs about "pretty boys," a population I was violently aware of, that this one shouldn't have struck me.) Photographs of Floyd, which I doggedly pursued, struck me as those of a "Babyface," perhaps (like gangster Babyface Nelson), but (I thought) disappointed as pictures of a "Pretty Boy." Troy Donahue he wasn't. Looking back now, I suspect that what gets articulated in Floyd's nickname is the erotic and homoerotic cathexis that was widely made on outlaw heroes by the people who loved and admired them, and both desired them and desired to be more like them, even as these admirers were also disturbed and frightened by them. It is Indian Territory, remember, that Huck Finn is heading out for at the end of *Huckleberry Finn,* when he decides to escape the intolerable civilities of small-town Missouri domesticity before the Civil War. Leslie Fiedler's reading of Twain's most celebrated novel as a homoerotic romance between a black slave and a white-trash boy (Fiedler's essay "Come Back to the Raft Agin, Huck Honey" was first published in the 1950s) is a provocation that has not yet really been either refuted (although there have been many derisive snorts in its direction from the Twain industry) or advanced. Several attempts like John Seelye's have been made to tell the rest of Huck Finn's story after the end of the novel. Andrew J. Hoffman, an outsider to the small world of Twain scholarship, turned a recent conference of Twainians on its ear by carefully tracing the young Twain's extensive professional and social involvements with other writers who are now known to have been queer or queerish during his early years in the West.[10] I like to think that Huck may have partially supported himself after he got to the Territory by exchanging sex for food, drink, and shelter. Such practices may have been common on the frontier, although for obvious (homophobic and sex-phobic) reasons, we are never reminded by official American culture to remember the pioneering male prostitutes of the Old West. (Tom Spanbauer's recent novel *The Man Who Fell in Love with the Moon* imagines the fortunes of a Native American who grows up as the available male in a frontier whorehouse in the Wild West.) Work like Jonathan Ned Katz's, documenting male-male sexual subcultures among ranchers and ranch hands and tramp and hobo populations, attests to the presence of extensive male-homoerotic possibility on the frontier. Reading work like Joan Nestle's historical essay on what she calls the "shared territories" of lesbians and female prostitutes, or Anne Butler's history of female prostitution in the post–Civil War West, we are reminded that wherever there have been outlaws and female prostitutes in modern societies, including frontier societies, there have been male prostitutes and male and female queers, too. Butler quotes an 1887 *Annual Report of the Commissioner of Indian Affairs to the Secretary of the Interior* to the effect that Indian Territory, even by that early date, had already allegedly become infested with large numbers of what the commissioner calls "tramps, vagrants, whiskey peddlers, prostitutes, and lunatics."[11] In many places like Oklahoma the histories of these groups have been imbricated with the sometimes intersecting, sometimes colliding histories of African Americans, Native Americans, Chicanos, whites, and other peoples. One of the biggest lies the Religious Right and their allies keep trying to foist on themselves and the rest of us is that television's ghost-white Walton Family is an accurate representation of rural American life as well as an ideal to which most Americans aspired in the past and to which all "normal" (Newt Gingrich's term) Americans still aspire. The truth of the matter is that large pockets of places like Oklahoma, which since the onset of the Cold War have been taken to be sites of ultra-"normalcy" and white-middle-Americanness, have been and to varying degrees remain downright funky, politically radical in a multitude of ways, "racially" complex, and significantly and continuously queer. No amount of reactionary rhetoric can make that otherwise.

Notes

1. Michelle Wallace, *Invisibility Blues: From Pop to Theory* (New York: Verso, 1990), 99.

2. Ralph Ellison, *Shadow and Act* (New York: Random House, 1964), 157.

3. My thinking in this essay and in the larger project of which it is a part has been informed by a diverse array of recent theoretical work remarking the histories of crossing between racialized and gendered identities. In addition to Wallace's *Invisibility Blues*, I am indebted to Eve Kosofsky Sedgwick's work on cross-identification, beginning with her essay on Willa Cather (reprinted in *Displacing Homophobia*, ed. Ronald Butters et al. [Durham, NC: Duke University Press, 1989]) and including her introduction to *Tendencies* (Durham, NC: Duke University Press, 1993). I and my project are also indebted to bell hooks's essay "Revolutionary Renegades: Native Americans, African Americans, and Black Indians," in *Black Looks: Race and Representation* (Boston: South End Press, 1992), 179–84; Cherríe Moraga's *Loving in the War Years* (Boston: South End Press, 1983); Gloria Anzaldúa's *Borderlands/La Frontera: The New Mestiza* (San Francisco: Spinsters/Aunt Lute, 1987); the work of Mab Segrest and other white scholars doing antiracist work as "race traitors," for example, Segrest's *Memoir of a Race Traitor* (Boston: South End Press, 1994), as well as the journal *Race Traitor*; and other recent work on hybridity and hybrid identities in postcolonial cultures.

4. For an introduction to the history of the Osage people, see Terry P. Wilson, *The Osage* (New York: Chelsea House, 1988). Osage leader John Joseph Matthews (c. 1894–1979) published two extraordinary histories of the Osages: *Wah' Kon-Tah* (1932) and *The Osages: Children of the Middle Water* (1961).

5. *Far and Away* souvenir book, 119.

6. See Roxanne Dunbar Ortiz, "Two or Three Things I Know about Us Okies," *Radical History Review* (1994), for a rich and provocative account of the political transformation of formerly Progressivist and Socialist Okie families in southern California, through the trial of the cops who beat Rodney King (Simi Valley is heavy Okie and Okie-cop territory).

7. Joe Klein, *Woody Guthrie: A Life* (New York: Random House, 1980), 163.

8. John Steinbeck, *Grapes of Wrath* (New York: Viking, 1939), 537.

9. See Ron Hansen's novel *Desperadoes* (New York: Knopf, 1979), about the exploits

of the Dalton gang, for a gritty depiction of the outlaw subculture of the northeastern Oklahoma area at the turn of the century.

10. See Andrew J. Hoffman, "Mark Twain and Homosexuality," *American Literature* 67, no. 1 (March 1995): 23–49.

11. Anne Butler, *Daughters of Joy, Sisters of Misery: Prostitutes in the American West, 1865–1890* (Urbana: University of Illinois Press, 1985), 11.

4

Latina Lesbians

Mariana Romo-Carmona

I am going to speak from personal experience and from political involvement, and also from many years of not fitting into any kind of accepted or expected mode, so my breaking of a category is extremely personal.

I am a compliance specialist for the City of New York. I review city contracts for compliance with requirements for equal employment opportunity. There is a law on the books called Executive Order 50, which requires among other things that all contractors with New York City grant protection on the basis of nine protected categories, the last of which is sexual orientation. My work puts me in a position in which I constantly have to discuss the issue of gay civil rights with people from Fortune 500 companies, from small companies, from all the very diverse contracting populations that do business in New York City. The reason? They must include sexual orientation in their EEO statement. I won't go into that in detail, but I will say that there is a lot to be gained from being in a position where you try to make people change their mind not against their will, but because their wallet is telling them they have to do it and they have no other recourse.

What I want to talk about is a book called *Compañeras: Latina Lesbians*, which came into print as a self-publishing effort in October 1987 by the Latina Lesbian History Project. The reason we formed the Latina Lesbian History Project—besides the fact that we really needed to do that—was to publish this book. We could not get it published by any other publisher, unless we changed its tone, its voice, and we weren't willing to do that. The two people that right now continue to carry on the work are Juanita Ramos—a black Puerto Rican lesbian—and myself. I want to talk about the process of publishing *Compañeras*.

Latina lesbians have been involved in political struggles at every stage of our independent history, and by that I mean our Latin American and Caribbean history. However, we have been very much hidden and very reluctant to make any kind of political statement that will identify us. This is not new. It happens with every other group. But as part of our decision to finally establish our identity and document ourselves, we wanted to explore the reasons we feel that this constraint is all the more oppressive with us.

We see the Latina Lesbian History Project as an archive for a history of ourselves that is ever expanding. We are reclaiming that history. And we exist as a link in the very recent connection between Latina lesbians in the United States, Latin America, and the Caribbean.[1]

As I said before, as Latina lesbians we have been very silently involved—even those who have been active participants and leaders of progressive movements in Latin America and outside, which do not recognize our existence or our contribution to the struggle. Nor do they see our issues as valid, or as needing to be part of the agenda of the struggle. Basically what this means is that, in order to be "good Latina lesbians," we must be faceless (that is, in the closet) when working with Latino and Third World groups; and we must also be faceless when we are working within white gay groups; that is, we can be colored enough to be used as a minority component (in that way, you know, we are very much welcome), but we can't be too colored. If we were, we would pose a threat because we would begin to join the issues of other people of color, and we would begin to question and confront the racism not only within our own Latino communities, but the racism that we face as Latino gays and lesbians within the largely white gay movement.

As a result of this, it has been very difficult to defend not only our identity, but also the need even to have an identity. The members of the Latina Lesbian History Project will start to do that by focusing on ourselves and starting from there, as *Latina* lesbians in this country.

You may be familiar with the concept of straddling a fence that was written and talked about by a Latina lesbian poet and writer, Gloria Anzaldúa. We straddle this fence as we attempt to exist within our culture as Latinas without a sexual orientation, and as political lesbians without a culture, being pushed to the other side, *al otro lado*. To claim an identity while one is in this position is suicidal. Yet it must be done. Otherwise, we again die. In this balancing spot, what we are attempting to do is to carve a place, or to carve a self, without yet having achieved a new self. In other words, we want to destroy old assumptions about ourselves while we are still over here constructing new assumptions and a new identity that we are not really sure will be viable, respected, or supported; we are not sure whether it can even survive, in any case. I think this construction of a new identity is most dramatic when we have to do it with our family. We are here destroying the notion of ourselves as Latina women within our family, within our culture, with no guarantee that the door will be open once we present our families and our culture with this new identity that we are having the temerity to present to them. Later I will discuss what happens when we attempt the same process while working within the white lesbian-gay community or movement or political entity.

The work of building, or creating, the book *Compañeras* started in 1980, when Juanita Ramos, after working for a long time in all kinds of different compartmentalized movements—the lesbian and gay movement, the Latino left movement, the lesbian and gay Latino (very small) part of a larger lesbian and gay movement—finally came to understand that what was needed was something that focused on Latina lesbians, nothing else.

She started to make contact with different groups to solicit submissions to this anthology. The whole process took seven years; it had to be abandoned many times. At the beginning, when she first started to get submissions for the book, most people who found out about *Compañeras* and really wanted to participate didn't feel they could write. And these were precisely the women she wanted to have in this book. These were the women's lives that needed to be in that book. So at that point she decided to include, perhaps, one or two interviews. She went with a tape recorder and just said, "Well, let's talk about you. Let's talk about your life. How did you begin?"—basically, "What is your story?" Even though she intended to do only one or two, perhaps three, of these interviews that could later be converted into different essays within the book, she ended up with fifteen oral histories. The important part about that process was that something was happening each time a woman began to speak about her life. This was evident later on during the editing of the book. Each time a woman began to speak about herself as a Latina lesbian, she began to analyze her life within the context of everything she knew but had never questioned. She did this without any kind of academic guidance,[2] without talking to people who were used to studying and coming out with conclusions, without having any kind of a tradition that said, "It's okay for you to talk about simply being a Latina lesbian." It revolutionized how we were looking at our community. Were we looking simply at Latina lesbians who were academics, who had been well educated, who had been trained to make statements about what it meant to be a Latina lesbian in the United States, or were we looking at the whole of our community?

What we found was that there were certain common threads, of course, and one of the greatest ones was our connection to our family, how we are lesbians within the context of the family and the community, and how important it was for each woman who was telling her own story to remember, in the context of her relationship to the women in her family, the first time she realized she was a lesbian. Here what we found was a response to racism that was so ingrained in our experience as Latina lesbians in the United States that we weren't aware that within the white political movement there was no room for this kind of understanding. We compared our experience to the experience of other lesbians and gay men of color. For example, how can Black gay men continue to be Black and gay men and still be part of their community, and not have to leave that behind once they enter the white gay male world? How can Asian lesbians continue to be Asian and lesbians and not have to respond to being exoticized, to being taken for being passive and inscrutable, and somehow representing this exciting "otherness," and still continue to retain a part of their culture that makes them Asian? This is what we were looking at. How can Latinas abandon our supposed voluptuousness and love for food and loud music and accented language and still bear to carve out an identity that is very much lesbian? How can we continue to have children, to be parents, to be part of all of our families, part of the struggle of different political groups, for the liberation of our people as a whole, and still be lesbian and still be gay? Very often we found that those of us who had been involved in different political movements were expected to drop the issues of our people and trade them for only a gay liberation strategy. This is precisely what we needed to find; to read about it, to share it with each other was a kind of confirmation for us as we put this book together.

The last thing I wanted to touch on is that as people who have taken the route of publishing the written word (but in a way that does not bind us to the structured publishing of political effort or literary effort, and that somehow seeks to mesh the two and to give freedom to ourselves as both political beings and creative beings), we recognize a responsibility to continue to change and to open up the categories that we have been brought up under, so that we make room for the generation that is developing now. In other words, this is something we want to bring to everybody: the responsibility that each one of us has to break open these categories that we ourselves have contributed to, and to make room. That is our responsibility.

Notes

1. International Latin American and Caribbean lesbian feminist encuentros, or conferences, have taken place in Mexico (1987), Costa Rica (1990), and Puerto Rico (1992), and have established an international Latin American and Caribbean Lesbian Network (La Red). The first edition of *Compañeras*, published by LLHP, was distributed free at the three *encuentros*. A new edition of *Compañeras: Latina Lesbians, An Anthology*, compiled and edited by Juanita Ramos, was released by Routledge (New York/London, 1994).

2. As we find our society stagnating in a bottleneck of censorship and repression, it is extremely important that we work to preserve those places where there is an active link between grassroots movements and the relative safety of academia. We are witnessing "normalizing" trends such as the academization of queer theory, in which formerly vibrant and cutting-edge efforts at self-documentation, analysis, and history are validated only when they are connected to institutions. The result is a scholarly queer anthropology without resonance in queer reality. In this way we effectively cut off access to parts of ourselves.

5

inciting sites of political interventions: queer 'n asian

Yukiko Hanawa

> It has always been an unstable identity, psychically, culturally, and politically. It, too, is a narrative, a story, a history. Something constructed, told, spoken, not simply found. People now speak of the society I come from in totally unrecognizable ways.
> —Stuart Hall, "Cultural Identity and Diaspora"

> After all, what would be the value of the passion for knowledge if it resulted only in a certain amount of knowledgeableness and not, in one way or another and to the extent possible, in the knower's straying afield of himself? There are times in life when the question of knowing if one can think differently than one thinks, and perceive differently than one sees, is absolutely necessary if one is to go on looking and reflecting at all.
> —Michel Foucault, *Technologies of the Self*

queer 'n asian

> GAPA is for men of all Asian Pacific backgrounds. Whether we are Chinese, Japanese, Filipino, Vietnamese, Korean, Malaysian, Indonesian, Laotian, Hawaiian, Pacific Islander, East Indian, or mixed heritage Asians, and whether we are immigrant or American-born, as gay Asians we all share a common sexual identity, a common racial and cultural bond.
> —Ban Nguyen, "GAPA: Coming Out Together"

Who or what is an Asian American queer?[1] In Boston, San Francisco, New York, and other large cities across the United States today, a number of groups identify themselves as lesbian/gay/bisexual Asian/Asian American/Pacific Islander organizations. These organizations are informed by multiple purposes—political, social, and cultural—and function for some as the precious location from which to craft an Asian/Asian American queer identity. The existence of these organizations is a testimony to the work required, for such an identity requires a mobilization of discourses that acknowledge multiple hegemonies, or "scattered hegemonies," to borrow Inderpal Grewal and Caren Kaplan's term.[2] It invokes, immediately, the need to negotiate the uncertain terrain on which both "race" and "sex" are naturalized *and* denaturalized in North American practices.

In the racial/ethnic sexual discourse of the United States, the very queerness of Asian/Asian American queer subjects is often rendered invisible. It seems as though this polyglot, pantheistic, and polycentric "group" called Asian Americans, often identified (by others as well as by themselves) as a monolithic model minority, could not possibly include individuals with polymorphic sexualities among its members. Membership in such an ethnic group has its privileges, to be sure. Yet the potential benefits are regularly outweighed by the detriments of such membership as the practice of the members is necessarily regulated within a racialist regime. Within *certain* racial practices, the requirement of identification with a group is codified within the logic of structures of *otherness.* This has meant, too often, that the possibility of such identification is dependent on the articulation of not only "difference" from the dominant but also difference from other otherness.[3] If we do not confirm or conform to a useful political/cultural construct of "what we are" or "who we are," we are rendered invisible. That is, without the acknowledgment of our very existence. The specific needs of gay/lesbian Asian/Asian Americans goes unaddressed. This is one condition under which many have come to organize and belong to Asian American queer groups.

Indeed, the statements of intent put out by these groups as they constitute themselves in organizations often explicitly note the fact of both being "Asian American" and thus belonging to an identificatory site within U.S. racial discourse as well as *being* different from simply being Asian American. In 1980, for example, BAGMAL (Boston Asian Gay Men and Lesbians)[4] distributed pamphlets that stated that the members, both "overseas" and "American born" Asians with varied degrees of participation in Asian community life, were both *"Asian* and *gay"* and did "not believe that we have to choose between our race and our sexuality."[5] That is, for those who are *not* identified as lesbian/gay, it implies the inclusion of the other "otherness."

More explicitly, Asian Women, a San Francisco Asian lesbian group identified the uniqueness of *being* Asian lesbians as they identified who they are as follows:

We feel that as Asian lesbians, we have unique and special needs and concerns that no existent group has been able to meet. We'd like to develop some kind of network among women who recognize that we face specific challenges quite different from other Asian women and from other non-Asian lesbians.[6]

And it seems that the 1984 formation of Asian Lesbians of the East Coast (ALOEC) was also specifically tied to the exigency of representing themselves. The group reported in its newsletter that the goals of the organization were to both build visibility in society and to reach out to other, possibly more closeted, Asian lesbians.[7]

That one of the concerns addressed by these groups is the invisibility of Asian gay men and lesbians both in the various ethnic communities and in the dominant gay/lesbian organizations is clear enough. On the one hand, these groups say to the Asian community, we are Asian, even if we are gays and lesbians. On the other hand, to the dominant gay/lesbian organizations they say, we are gays and lesbians even if we are Asian. I want to address in this essay, albeit somewhat speculatively, what the conditions of such invisibility— and activism to counter it—have meant in terms of self-conscious political strategy and positioning by and of Asian Americans. What happens when the terms of political praxis are defined by inclusion/exclusion, invisibility/ visibility?

Let me try to make myself clear that my desire to consider the ways in which political praxis are made possible and limited through the logic of visibility is not to undermine in any way the reality for many of the condition of invisibility, that is to say a condition with material consequences. I am well aware of the ways this "condition of invisibility" has, for instance, directed resources to reconfirm the hetero-normative expectations of the Asian American "community" in ways that immeasurably affect the health and well-being of those who identify as Asian Americans but do not conform to the "visible" representatives. Thus I am not here trying to distinguish between real and unreal consequences—material and non-material—but rather to point out that the focus of this essay will necessarily be on the ways our political language and vision are confined by impulse to correct the "conditions of invisibility."

The problematic of representation I want to propose foregrounds the sites in which "gay," "lesbian," and "Asian" are stabilized—sites that are already present and accounted for in such configurations. I want to take up this stabilizing process and consider how the practice of representation is positioned in this process and in the logic of "Asian American queer." And I am particularly concerned with the ways history and historical representation is deployed as the storehouse of evidence on which the foundation of identity rests. In what follows, I want to posit in a somewhat roundabout way how we might think about the problem of historical representations and its relationship to our present and the future. I am not much interested in establishing protocols for a more effective "identity politics," but neither am I interested in establishing a protocol that allows for the dismantling of "identity." The desire, indeed the need, to question these sites, which due to the exigencies of the moment have coherence, reflects an effort to engage with what I consider to be part of our work, that is, to consider the range of possible political practices that might allow us to continually think and to act. The fixedness of categories prematurely closes that range of possibilities, particularly if it is spoken as an unmediated organic site.[8]

This brings me back to the sameness and difference that are foregrounded in both the GAPA and the Asian Women quotes I referred to earlier. The sameness/difference, that which binds them and separates them from other Asian/Asian Americans and gay/lesbians, are discursive operators that are operationally dependent on a certain sense of framework or borders within which the sameness and difference are contained and self-evident.[9] I want to explore, using what I can of my own engagement with historical practices and what I have learned from working with others, "a passage beyond the fragmentations of identity politics and the various essentialisms at work in it,"[10] a passage that might allow for a common effort. In the terms of Elspeth Probyn:

> This is, then, to go beyond discrete positions of difference and to refuse the crisis mode of representation. It is to make the sound of our identities count as we work to construct communities of caring, to technologize and transform ourselves in the care of others.[11]

asia as the originating site

Asian America includes today peoples who identify or are identified as Asian/Asian American/Pacific Islander. It seems quite simple that in order to claim an Asian American identity, one needs to trace some relationship to a national/cultural group that is or was part of the geopolitical area largely defined as Asia or the Pacific Islands. But this deceptively straightforward identifier immediately raises questions in my mind about the difficulties of that "national/cultural" legacy. After all, "Asia" is a discursive field that has emerged in a historical and political context of centuries of violent conflicts.[12] For a Korean American woman who immigrated to the United States early in the century when Korea was a colonial territory of Japan, surely Asia is a very different place than for a postwar Japanese—referred to in Japan as "children who know no war" (*senso o shiranai kodomotachi*). Though of course many postwar Japanese are hardly children, such a descriptive identifier may say something not only about what one imagines an adult to be in Japan, but also about both how historical knowledge is structured and how *experience* is positioned within such knowledge, as well as the elision of contemporary forms of occupations through multinational capital.

Asia as a site of one's identification is dependent on the ability of this signifier to be recognized as "embodiments," that is, the individual bodies who are in possession of the requisite certification of racial, ethnic, and national citizenship. That is to say, its currency is contingent on "location and history in specific sites."[13] Thus, the singularity of practice within historical sites that are abstracted into modes of being—Asian, in this case—are referenced each time Asia is identified as the site from which the identifier Asia egresses. Yet, the self-evident nature of this explanation, in fact, betrays the logic of such enunciation; it is to refract the very contingent nature of the site being invoked.

While Asian and Asian Americans do not work too well in the current American racial terrain in which Asians live, I do think that these terms have political currency that reflect the historicity of the lexical genealogy. In her 1993 preface to Jessica Hagedorn's *Charlie Chan is Dead*, Elaine Kim has made this point; in writing her book *Asian American Literature: An Introduction to the Writings and Their Social Context*, she "wanted to delineate and draw boundaries around whatever I thought of as Asian American identity and literature." However, she argues that "The lines between Asian and Asian American, so crucial to identity formation in the past, are increasingly blurred: transportation to and communication with Asia is no longer daunting, resulting in new crossovers and intersections and different kinds of material and cultural distances today." Thus, she argues that "Asian American identities are fluid and migratory."[14]

While I have no intention of defending the cultural nationalist attempt to separate Asian and Asian American (and I will make this point quite clear in this essay), I do want to point out that in fact, as the biographical material on the authors included in the Kim book makes clear, one has to have some connection to having lived in the United States to be included as an Asian American author (the exception is Joyce Kogawa, an Asian Canadian). This may seem an obvious point, and one thus not worth making; yet to say that the boundaries between Asian and Asian American are blurred does not necessarily eliminate, it seems, in practice or in our understanding, a necessary relationship of some kind to the United States of America. More flexible, more contested, and more indeterminate, perhaps, but the referential marks are still there.

And as such, if one were to ask (and I am not sure how one would ask such a question without seeming rude), "What are you?" a reply such as "I am Chinese," "I am Vietnamese," or "I am Pakistani" is probably a more common one than "I am Asian American" or even something like "I am Chinese American," "I am Vietnamese American," or "I am Pakistani American." The responses matter because while the question may seem to have remained constant, the identificatory practice may signal the changes in *who* is asked this question, as such practice has its own historicity; and in the rapidly changing post–1960s demographic configuration of Asian America the practice of naming is specifically tied to immigration patterns.

Asian American as an identificatory category is most frequently associated with the Asian American Movement of the 1960s. It seems quite common today to hear people say that Asian American is a category that they do not identify with personally and that they use it in much more limited circumstances than, say, Chinese or Chinese American. While this may lead to a suggestion that perhaps the question of Asia in "queer in asia" is, then, superfluous, there are both strategic and ideological concerns in claiming *Asian* identity in this instance. One is that the political imperative of operating within the circuits of signifiers of normative sexual and racial discourse dictates the ability to *show* that the *invisible* are in fact numerous. More important, perhaps, is that racial "otherness" has played a significant part in the American imagination, particularly since the 1850s, so that even while a specific ethnic group may have been the target of exclusive legislations—the Exclusion Act of 1882, which specified the Chinese, or the Tydings-McDuffie Act of 1934, which named people from the Philippines—these laws were deployed to include larger groups of people who because of their *race* were ineligible for citizenship.[15]

It seems clear that "our" identities are grounded in our relationships to particular national/cultural groups. It would appear that the stakes of identification are quite high, if we judge from the vociferousness of the ongoing battles within the Asian American community. This is not to suggest that the degree of animated positioning is the testimony necessary to convince us of the importance of claiming a *place* to locate representational authority.[16] That is, my point is not to restate the site of contestation but rather to consider the practice of the invocation of history as evidence for representational ownership and authority. It is not easy to simplify what is now an often refereed contestatory locus of "our" political practice, since each gesture toward containment of the problem through the delineation of the *problem* seems only to permute the *problem*, opening up possibilities; but it also draws our attention to the ways in which the very politics of the referential site (Asia) is not outside the racial discourse of the Other, even as (or particularly because) the articulation of *Asia* is supposed to deliver us from the ideology of race through *self-representation* of our racial otherness.[17]

Given that, one of the exemplary texts of this impulse to intervene in the circuitry (or the economy) of representation is the introduction to *The Big AIIIEEEEE!* The editors, Jeffrey Paul Chan, Frank Chin, Lawson Fusao Inada, and Shawn Wong, write,

> Every Chinese American book ever published in the United States of America by a major publisher has been a Christian autobiography or autobiographical novel.[18]

And here they list, among many others, the works of Maxine Hong Kingston— *The Woman Warrior* (1976), *China Men* (1980), and *Tripmaster Monkey* (1989). Christianity and auto-referential writing are cited as the two areas of problems in the cultural politics of representation. It immediately points to the contradictions within the logic of self-representation. On the one hand Christianity is cited here to mark that which is alien, and autobiographical representation as a practice outside that which is *asian*. Yet one could argue that the two are already at tension with each other. That is to say, if Christianity is "spirit possession" and robbing one of the possibility of true representation, then how do we contend with the problematizing of *auto*biography within the logic of *self*-representation? Perhaps the question to ask of the text is, *what* truth does it distort?

> If the woman warrior Fa Mulan; the Monkey of the childhood classic Journey to the West; China's language, culture, and history; the heroes, ducks, and swans of the Chinese fairy tale are all fake, as depicted in the Christian works then what is real? (To prove that) the Christian works to be either fake or white racists. . . . we have to turn to the history of the Asian Chinese and Japanese in white Christianity and in Western historiography, philosophy, social science, and literature.

In a turn to *history* as *evidence* of the duplicity of Christianity—and the categories of Western knowledge—*Asian* Chinese and Japanese history is naturalized as that which is something other than "a narrative, a story, a history." But it may also, quite inadvertently, gesture toward the narrativity of Chinese *American* or Japanese *American* history.[19]

> For the truth of the Chinese culture and history that has been carried and developed into Chinese American institutions by the first Chinese Americans, we have to confront the real Fa Mulan, the real Monkey, the real Chinese first-person pronoun, the real Chinese words for "woman" and "slave" as they exist in the culture and texts of Chinese childhood literature, the ethics that the fairy tales and heroic traditions teach, and the sensibility that they express.

That is to say, one can *simply* (though it is never simple) *find* the *real* Fa Mulan, the *real* Monkey, the *real* first-person pronoun, the *real* words for "woman" and "slave"; these are outside of any specific historicity. This becomes clearer when we understand that the instruction to *find* the real is in the service of the "culture and history" that was embodied into Chinese American institutions. The real that is never changing and stable, then, is the truth that is distorted by the other discourse, the discourse of the West.

While the example of this introduction seems at best extreme and raises many problematics of its own—in its repeated invocations of "truth" for instance—the overdetermined relationship between what is "China" and "Chinese American" cannot be ignored. Namely, it directs our attention to the dyadic logic of the impossibility of a referential site in America for an authentic Asian American identification and *history* as the storehouse where the accoutrements of identificatory practices may be found. This is, of course, the referential system in which cultural nationalism, a site where "collective cultural identities" were forged, that was culturally autonomous of the racialist regime of cultural domination.[20]

In part, the problem is that one is locked into the practice of evidence that assumes either that categories such as race and sex are self-evidential in nature or that the historical production of these categories is outside the production of narrative of spatial representation of *asia*. Furthermore, these examples illustrate that while "Asian American" may have its political origins in the construction of a racial category, "Chinese," "Vietnamese," "Asian Indian," or "Korean American" are ethnic national identities that reflect the modern national conflicts in *Asia* over the past century.

What has historically distinguished the experience of Asians in the United States—thus differentiating them from other immigrants with regard to language difficulties, discriminatory hiring practices, ghettoization, and the like—has been the explicit legislation and praxis that informed and enforced the institutionalization of them as racialized subjects.[21] The contemporary situation has mandated a move toward the blurring of the litmus test. However, it is still operative, necessarily in the impulse to intervene in the racial discourse. When one claims an ethnic identity—and thereby skirts the issues of national identity, and thus questions of immigrant status and citizenship, and race—one places the focus on cultural archives/praxes and knowledge as the reference for identification, still operating within the racialized frameworks of representation.

Thus when asked, "What is an Asian American?" or "What makes one Asian American?" a respondent neatly divide up "America" into citizenship or residency status—documented and undocumented—and "Asia" into *cultural* heritage. "Well, my parents are citizens but they would not think of themselves as Americans. They have *xyz* values." The *xyz*, obviously, can be filled with any Asian national group that one may think of. This understanding of a *cultural* heritage is often bereft of historicity of such praxes that are claimed as heritage and is assumed to be self-evident *as* heritage.

This may, then, be the context in which to consider the criticism of Hwang's *M. Butterfly* and of his "homosexual" subject. Chan and his coeditors conclude that:

> No wonder David Henry Hwang's derivative *M. Butterfly* won the Tony for best new play of 1988. The good Chinese man, at his best, is the fulfillment of white male homosexual fantasy, literally kissing white ass. Now Hwang and the stereotype are inexticably one.[22]

While there are many criticisms—one of which is the questioning of whether the play recirculates the images of an always feminine Oriental Other (even if Hwang had intended it to be ironic)—the question of the viability of a "homosexual" subject outside the Western homosexual *fantasy* seems particularly apropos. Hwang has answered by not answering and noting instead that in fact the play blurs the boundary between gay and straight:

> I think this would apply today to people in Chinese, Italian, Spanish, and some of the other Latin cultures; People in these cultures believe that if you have sex with a man and you do the screwing, you are not gay, but if you're screwed, you're gay. I mean that sort of distinction has existed since time immemorial . . . So what does gay mean at that point?[23]

But does it? If we are still dependent on behavior as a category that can be found in cultural practices from time immemorial then the categories by which we come to recognize these boundaries are not really blurred as such but repositioned outside the discursivity of classification. This relationship between the "Asian" cultural practice and its relevance to practices in the United States, resonates in Alice Hom's discussions of "Asian American parents and their views on homosexuality."

> The knowledge of lesbians and gay men in their native countries and in their communities in the United States serves as an important factor in dismantling the oft-used phrase that a son or daughter is gay or lesbian because of assimilation and acculturation in a western context.[24]

Moreover, there has been some effort within the Asian American lesbian/gay community to find lesbian/gay subjects in the history of Asian societies. For instance, "Her Story," a narrated slide history produced by a member of ALOEC, traces "representation" of "Asian" lesbians from the Kama Sutra to contemporary Asian American lesbian experiences.[25] There is also an emerging field within Asian Studies of works on "traditional Chinese" or "traditional Japanese" homosexualities.

While we may know that when we speak of and write about Chinese Americans or any other Asian American group, we are not in fact necessarily speaking about a group that embodies a national/ethnic cultural essence, still we do seem to be caught in a dilemma. Even forgetting momentarily the strategy of the authentic, continuous link to a national culture, how could we define and identify ourselves *in America?* If self-representation is possible only against a representation of Asia, where does one look for evidence? What archive do we search for evidence to establish the foundation of a historically (as opposed to culturally) validated *identity?* How might it be possible for one to think about the historical relations that would allow us to engage in *creating* positions of politicality? My intention here is to consider, though quite provisionally perhaps, grounds of political relationality rather than evidences for identity politics. It is in this sense that I want to think of the possibility of community: a community that is at once both skeptical of the categories of analysis that assure us a site of belonging (and the possibility of a *history* of such categories) and insistent on the necessity of collectivity for political praxis.

It is this task of thinking about ways to *practice* that is at stake when the terms of racial-sexual identifications are positioned so as to be dependent on what "exists" or "doesn't exist" in an archive defined as "culture." The impulse to organize, which various Asian Pacific lesbian/gay groups cite—to address the invisibility—need not be inherently grounded in such historical archive praxis. It is with this in mind that I want to now turn to what might be learned about our relationship to such histories of discursivities of classifications or historical representations. And in order to do so, I want to look at several same-sex narratives. I call them *same-sex* to gesture away from the overdetermined narrative of sexual subject discourses and gesture toward the specificity of social linguistic practices. My purpose in retelling these stories—some better known than others — is to locate means for creating potential political praxis within an economy of representation that creates the very exigencies of an Asian American political category.

In "Her Story," the slide narrative of "lesbians past and present in Asian culture and history," the national/cultural sites represented are organized similarly to the ways in which one might imagine "East Asian Civilization." That is, the visual representations are organized by India, China, Japan, and North America in that order. As such, almost all of the "modern" representations are images chosen from Japanese examples. The North American images are of contemporary Asian/Asian American/Asian Canadian activists. In considering, below, several same-sex narratives from the 1930s and some contemporary negotiations around the emergence of rezubian subjects in Japan, I want to try to think of ways in which I can trouble historical representations as evidence. The question that I want to return to at the end will be, "evidence of what?"

the case of Masuda Fumiko

Masuda Fumiko, a young woman from a well-known Osaka banking family, and Saijō Erika, an actress from the Kyōdō Film Studio, were apprehended by the police at Nagoya station in the winter of 1934 in a celebrated case of attempted double suicide.[26] Before there had been enough time for the public and journalists to react to their story, the two escaped from family surveillance and disappeared. Two days later they were found again, this time in a hotel. Although in some reports it seems that they had both consumed Adalin (sleeping tablets), it was Masuda who was found unconscious.[27]

The case of Masuda Fumiko and Saijō Erika caught the imagination of the public. It had all the right ingredients: a young woman from a respectable, old family; her partner in crime, a public figure. Fumiko, who used the name Yasumara — at best a gender ambivalent name — sported Eton-style cropped hair, golfing trousers, and tweed jackets. Erika, with softly waved permed hair that touched her shoulders, was accustomed to wearing beaded gowns and stage makeup. Fumiko had taken some family stock certificates to finance a trip that took them from Tokyo to Kyoto, Osaka, Kobe, down to Kyushu, and back to Kyoto.

As Fumiko recovered from the "double suicide" attempt, a series of articles reported their elopement. For several months, reports, follow-ups, exposés, confessionals, and even an essay contest appeared in newspapers and magazines. For instance, Osaka jiji (Osaka daily) carried an eleven-part series on the incident, and most major newspapers, both dailies and weeklies, covered the incident in varying degree. Fujin kōron (Women's central review), perhaps one of the most important women's magazines, began its coverage in March 1935 with the article "Daughter's Romantic Love, Same Sex Love and Mothers," followed by an article by a reporter who had interviewed Saijō Erika right after the suicide attempt. That issue also included two additional articles on the incident, one by Saijo titled "Until Masuda Fumiko, the Masculinely Dressed Beauty, Choose Death," and a short piece by a former classmate of Masuda encouraging her to choose life. The April issue of *Fujin kōron* continued its coverage with a confessional by Masuda titled "The Day I Return to Being a Woman." This was followed by "critique and guidance" from Kawasaki Natsu, an activist social critic known for her involvement in maternal welfare and the conditions of working women. Kawasaki's advice? Masuda should find employment and then get married. The problem is seen as that of a young bourgeois woman of privilege.

It was in response to the confessional by Masuda that an essay contest was organized and the three winning entries published in the magazine's May issue. All together, these reflected the lexicon of the discourses on "same-sex love," "autonomy," "self," and "development." In addition, the magazine of the anti-prostitution organization, *Purity,* published a submission to the contest that had not been chosen for publication in *Fujin kōron.* Entitled "The Facts Are Old but the Problem Is New: Make Masuda Fumiko the Masculinely Dressed Beauty into a Nursery School Worker," this essay positions "woman" as a site in opposition to self that suggests autonomy, selfishness, immaturity, and so forth. The constellation of characteristics of the bourgeois *modan* women were invoked in the interpretations of Fumiko and Erika's liaison. In Fumiko's acceptance of this configuration (and by implication, Fumiko by writing the "confessional" had supposedly acquiesced to this oppositional strategy) that other Fumiko was eradicated and relegated to that which could be narrated in the past tense. Thus perhaps this was a case of "suicide" rather than an "attempted suicide."

What seems peculiar in the narrative that emerges from all these essays is the complete absence of the *body* as the site of either Fumiko's or Erika's story. There are two reasons that I think this is of some significance. One is that the articles that appeared in *Fujin koron* were accompanied by photographs of Fumiko and Erika that were instrumental in the shaping of the narrative—the cross-dressed woman and the non–cross-dressed woman.[28] The other reason, of course, is that the body was very much the site of Fumiko's self-transformation. After all, if she "returned" to being a woman, what had she been in the meantime? I want to come back to this issue of the body, but in order to illustrate my point better, I want to talk about a very different body.

the story of Miyata Sato

In July 1934, an article appeared in a regional newspaper in the northeastern part of Japan titled "Handsome Husband with Long Hair? An Attractive Masculine Woman in her Forties living with a Wife of Another Man Turns into a Man with a Wife."[29] The article was about Miyata Sato, who was thirty-five when her husband died. She supported herself by working as a day laborer and as a farmer after the death of her husband. After a while, however, her voice became lower and she started to grow a beard. Not too long after, she became involved in a relationship with Yokoyama Mitsu, a married woman. The woman's husband protested, and there was some discussion of whether or not Mitsu could be charged with adultery. But since the two involved were both "women" it was decided that no formal charges could be brought. A while later, Miyata Sato became involved with another woman, Setsuko, who was then thirty-four. Like Yokoyama Mitsu, Setsuko was married, but unlike her, she left her husband for Miyata. Her husband tried to convince her to come back to him, but she claimed that she could not leave Miyata. The article reports that "there was much talk about what the two did at night."

The Japanese press seemed quite confused about how to write about these affairs. While the newspaper used the term "same-sex love," it did not describe Miyata as masculine, and certainly she was no "beauty dressed masculinely" like Masuda Fumiko. Instead, as the headline stated, she had *become a man*.[30] The fact that the article claims she had become another sex at the same time it labels this a same-sex story points, perhaps, to the ambivalence of the social linguistic practice that is being reflected. It may also point to a useful departure point for a reading strategy that takes into account the spatial distribution of the modern subject.

The bodies of Miyata Sato, Masuda Fumiko, and Saijō Erika need to be read within a discourse constructed in a rural/urban binary that took as its reference point two well-known figures: the urban *modan gaaru* and the rural girls who were workers. It is not possible here to go into the details of the urban typology except to note that the *modan gaaru* in these urban-rural narratives personified a culture of consumption that defined a new social order based on new personal relationships.[31] In contrast, throughout the 1920s and 1930s, images of the rural woman depended on the inscription of texts with beginnings and ends on her body, where the darkness of her skin from exposure to the sun, the thickness of her calloused hands told stories of labor that exhausted these women, enabling them to feel "nothing, and to think nothing." (This was, wrote a young man, the desirable outcome of farm women's work.)

Compared to narratives of the rural bodies, narratives of the *modan gaaru* were much more spectral. If rural women's bodies were marked by a tale that was biologized, the bodies of *modan gaaru* were almost apparitional. Indeed, the spectral nature of their appearance as harbingers of modernity is etched deeply in our minds along with the tension of our knowledge that the 1930s brought an altogether different urban vision, with growing militarization and expansionism on the Asian continent. In those years before they disappeared, it was the nameless women identified by the requisite signs of self-transformation who came to define that which was *modan*, whether in the body of Masuda Fumiko or the well-known writer Yoshiya Nobuko—sometimes reputed to have been one of the very first women to "bob" her hair—or in nameless representations. In the work of photographer Nojima Yasuzo, for example, the images had titles like "Miss F" or were left untitled, in contrast to his earlier portrait subjects, who had been identified by name or social identity. Rather than depicting individuals, these photographs were of the bodies of urban women that powerfully laced together the "brilliance of the modern metropolis, a stormy eroticism," and the unrootedness of these subjects.[32] The swiftly transforming urban landscape was often haunted by these apparitional figures who disappeared in the mid to late 1930s, only a decade or so after they had first appeared.

A reading of the two narratives that signals the different bodies of urban and rural women and the images that are produced through them within the urban/rural tensions is productive in illuminating a complex discourse network operating in the 1930s. By reading another narrative, that of Yoshiya Nobuko, we may further trouble the ways in which we might negotiate historical representations of same-sex narratives. Yoshiya Nobuko, not insignificantly, is one of the images incorporated in the "Her Story" slide narratives. Of the several twentieth-century Japanese women included—Yosano Akiko, Hiratsuka Raichō, Miyamoto Yuriko—she is, perhaps, the "exemplary" model to consider, in part, because of her lifelong partnership with one woman.

the story of Yoshiya Nobuko

Yoshiya Nobuko was one of the most prolific of woman writers; she almost single-handedly popularized the genre of girl romance and wrote widely, particularly throughout the 1920s and 1930s. The narrative of the girl romance, often situated in a single-sex boarding school, centered around the strong attachments—romantic, and thus idealized—between schoolgirls. With a wide popular base among young readers, she moved on to write novels for an "adult audience" that were serialized in the major dailies such as the *Osaka mainichi* and *Tokyo asahi*. Nobuko lived with Monma Chiyo for over fifty-two years in a well-publicized arrangement in which she adopted Chiyo as her daughter *(yōjo)*. This living arrangement led her to be described as *Monma fujin no danna-san* (the husband of Mrs. Monma) in an amusing article comparing her with the author Hayashi Fumiko.[33] The measure of Yoshiya's popularity may be best understood from the frequency with which she appeared in journals—not only as a writer—in interviews, dialogues, and also as the subject of essays. She shared forums with the likes of Tsuruni Yūsuke and Kikuchi Kan. And, perhaps, as importantly, these articles were not limited to either literary or "women's" journals but appeared in *Gendai, Chuō kōron, Shinchō,* and *Nihon hyōron.*

However, it is in the choice of Yoshiya as *the* woman writer recruited by the navy to tour the troops in Shanghai and elsewhere led by Kikuchi Kan in 1938 that one must consider how her position is constituted.[34] It is also here that the question of choosing evidence from the archives becomes most suggestive and troubling. We learn *about* her tour of China and her response in a *zadankai* she participated in which was published in *Hanashi*. Her claim that "as a Japanese woman, I have advanced to the extreme frontline" in response to the moderator's question, "How far has Japanese women advanced," leaves little room for the reader to question how she positions both her sex and nationality. That is, asked in the context of this roundtable—in the midst of the recitation of the advancing frontline of the Japanese military—her participation *as* Japanese woman and a representative of Japanese women renders it necessary for one to always consider the singularity of practice informing subjectivity, sexual as well as gender subjectivity.[35]

Yoshiya's story is suggestive of the embeddedness of the narratives in the discursive communities operating at any given moment. That is to say, Yoshiya's ability to represent "Japanese" literati is deeply imbricated in the discourse of race and nationality as well as the discourses on sexed bodies, gender, and desire in Japan. Surely, then, this exigency can not be lost on the desire to construct a "ethico-political community", that is "queer 'n asian."[36]

Rereading the cases of Masuda and Saijo and Miyata against the urban-rural terrain, Yoshiya Nobuko and Monma Chiyo's story against the nationalist-imperialist discourse, requires us to consider carefully the meanings of these stories. The discourse on modernity, the rural-urban binary, and national identity are central to the interrogation of all these narratives. And while the same-sex narratives may seem familiar in some ways, the historical and linguistic conditions need to be reconsidered. What exactly is going on in these stories? Are they, for example, part of a history of "sexuality"? And if so, what is "sexuality"—the subject of historical investigations—and what does it mean for us to study "sexuality"?

Finally, let me take you to present-day Tokyo and introduce you to sites of contemporary discursive praxis and productions. The opportunities to negotiate the problem of identity and the movements of identity between and among historical discursivities in different locales are quite clear. While the contemporary situations also require the negotiations of differentially imagined "cultural" spaces in Japan where rural/urban tensions are still manifest, though the discursive operators are homogenized (most significantly through television and other media), it is the ways in which the United States is positioned in the production of "rezubian feminists" that I want to signal. It is also the site rich in its illustrative potentials in that it forces a consideration of the very singularity of the practices that can not be easily connected in a history of sexuality or same-sex genealogy.

the case of Mizuno Makiyo

Mizuno Makiyo was a "master" of the *onabe* bar Kikōshi. *Onabe* bars, which were quite popular in the 1960s and into the 1970s, are bars that cater to a wide range of customers—including middle-aged, "straight" businessmen. These establishments are run by cross-dressing women like Mizuno, who take pride in their absolutely impeccable appearance. Mizuno embodied the Japanese dandy par excellence—well-cut dark suits, cuff links, neatly trimmed crew cut, well-polished shoes, and elegant manners. Many *onabe* bars were located in the fashionable neighborhood of Roppongi in Tokyo, and they charged hefty cover fees. Claiming that it was more "comfortable" to play at these *onabe* bars than in the "high club" atmosphere of Ginza, many of the men brought their favorite hostesses from Ginza clubs to the *onabe* establishments. The bars became part of the "lesbian scene" in Tokyo because of the presence of women like Mizuno.

But Mizuno herself does not define her relationship with women as same-sex relationships, but rather as cross-sexed relationships. And she does not call herself a lesbian, though the nomenclature of sexual subjects is common enough in the Tokyo of the 1980s, when her story was published.[37] That her relationships are neither same-sexed nor "lesbian" is suggestive to those of us interested in considering the multiplicities of hegemonic sites. The possibility of locating Mizuno in current practices of historical representation becomes particularly clear when we consider the recent move toward the appropriation and institutionalization of lesbian identity in Japan.

friday night at Mars Bar

Mars Bar in Shinjuku, Tokyo, is the only "women's bar" in business in Tokyo. M. M., the owner/bartender, opened Mars Bar in late 1985, six months after the opening of Ribonnu, also a "women's bar" in the 2-chōme, or "gay bar," area of Shinjuku. Unlike Kikōshi, where Mizuno worked, Mars Bar self-consciously positioned itself from the start by catering only to women. When M. M. opened Mars Bar, after befriending some lesbians among the women she met at lesbian-feminist gatherings, she forecast the changes that were to come about in the "lesbian scene" during the next few years.

The mid-1980s heralded a clear transition of the Tokyo institutions that accommodated women with same-sex desires. (I use the term "same-sex desire" with trepidation, knowing that it may render invisible individuals like Mizuno.) These were changes not only in styles—the *onabe* to the more androgynous look of M. M.—but more importantly in the construction of a lesbian *identity*.

From 1971 to 1986 Wakakusa-no-kai was the only continuing organization providing social space for women to meet other women. The demise of Waka-kusa-no-kai came when new members who joined in the early 1980s, informed by feminist politics, challenged the autocratic and idiosyncratic nature of leadership—Suzuki Michiko, who started the group, held monthly gatherings at her house and personally interviewed every one of the over five hundred women who joined the group. (She estimates having met over two thousand potential members over the years, on whom she kept files, in which she indicated "masculine quality," "feminine quality," and other characteristics.) What is perhaps significant here is that when Suzuki was challenged by newer members, few came to her defense and there was no overt effort by the rest of the members to continue Wakakusa-no-kai gatherings. It seems that members' lack of a coherent sense of "who they were" contributed to the closing. For instance, a large number of the women who attended the monthly meetings were else-where partnered with men. Even among those women who attended gatherings led by Suzuki over the years, many never revealed their names or gave out information about where they could be contacted. Few of the women thought of themselves as *being* lesbians or women who desired women. What they had in common was not a "lesbian identity," but the fact that they met Suzuki's qualifications for joining the group to meet other women.[38]

In contrast, within a year of Wakakusa-no-kai's closing, several new groups staffed by women, mostly in their twenties appeared in Tokyo at this time. Sappho, Sophia, and Re-gumi Tokyo provided introduction services (Sappho and Sophia), activities (all three), and a newsletter (Re-gumi) that made it possible for some young women to come together for the purpose of meeting other women and pursuing same-sex desires. In the most articulated case, that of Re-gumi (a combination of "re," from "resubian," and "gumi," meaning group), the political impetus behind the organizing came from two women who felt the need to provide a "women-only" space that went beyond facilitating same-sex desires.[39]

By actively seeking out and providing the language necessary to create a community based on shared meanings through newsletters, discussions, and the establishment of a "lesbian library," Re-gumi contributed toward building what historians of sexuality would call a "lesbian discourse," or a unified way of thinking about, talking about, and acting on same-sex desire among women. In this process, women of Wakakusa are stored in the archive of a history of sexual subjects, and someone like Mizuno is relegated to the unrepresentable subjects classification.

Today, Mars Bar and Re-gumi are still protecting that vision of a "women-only" space. When I called Mars Bar from Boston one night, I half expected it to be closed. Yet, speaking to M. M., I was not surprised that of the two places that had opened exclusively as women's bars in 1985, it was Mars that survived. From the start, M. M. was able to attract both Japanese lesbian-feminists and "foreign" lesbians—those belonging to North Atlantic cultures—to her place. This is not an insignificant point. What many of the women who patronize Mars Bar have in common is an identity as lesbians/lesbian-feminists. These women are part of a growing number of women who position themselves consciously among the named subject.[40]

Coda

I want to return to the implications of discursive practices and the building of political community. How do Asian American lesbians make sense out of all these "histories" and "legacies" as we try to locate ourselves in America?[41] What does it mean for one to syncretically claim a cultural/ethnic/racial/ national legacy from someplace called Japan or Asia as one locates one's sexual identity? What will our histories tell us? Which women do we claim as fore-mothers, who will give us a legitimacy for our "lesbian identity"? Aside from the patrons of Mars Bar, none of the women described here has claimed such an identity.[42] While the word "lesbian" (resubian) has had some currency in Japan since the 1920s, it exists only as a transliteration in the Japanese language and for the most part in terms of a discursive locus of social problems, not a site of identity. It seems that if our identities as Asian Americans are grounded in our relationship to a national/ethnic culture, it is crucial that we understand the construction of sexual identity in a social-cultural context such as the Japanese, where the very idea of *identity* itself raises so many vexing questions. Anthro-pologists, linguists, and historians have pointed out that the Japanese "self" always implies a multiplicity of selves in relation to gender, class, geographic region, power, and the like (and not as a result of the postmodernist destabil-ization of the unitary self). These often conflicting and shifting selves are represented by an individual contextually in relation to the particular situa-tion at hand. Furthermore, one of the recurring questions in Japanese discourse in the twentieth century has been the question of what informs one's under-standing of self. How, that is, does one become? Is it through action? Is it through knowledge? Or, is it through object choice? These are questions that are raised in the somewhat ambiguous readings of the cases of those women from the 1930s. But these formulations do not adequately address the question of *identity*, a term that is also used most often in a transliterated form, if used at all.

That the women I spoke of do not claim a *lesbian* identity, it seems to me, is something we cannot simply explain away by stating that they are, for what-ever reason, not choosing an identity. Identification is in itself the problem here. The question is complicated further by the fact that in the Japanese language, as in the Chinese language, there is no word for sexuality.[43] Sexual identity, then, as a concept is doubly controvertible.

There are today Japanese women, like the patrons of Mars Bar, who do self-identify as lesbians, many having been introduced to the category as a self-identifier through feminism. They allow us to understand the ways transna-tional cultural meanings operate and produce new interpretations for transna-tional cultural practices.[44] At the same time they raise questions about the limits of such transnational discursive practices.[45] What does it mean for one to identify as a lesbian? Determining what technologies of self-construction are necessary—both in the act of marking and naming and in the ways of becoming and being—to make it possible to identify as lesbian may actually betray the inherent privileging not only of both sexuality and identity, but of a notion of a coherent subject, as categories of analysis.

This brings us back to the problem of *what* is being acknowledged. To speak of Asian America is necessarily to acknowledge the always already present category of "identity" in our understanding of ourselves. As impossible as it may seem to those of us who live at least our ethnic and sexual identities in English, it may not always be possible to make a coherent connection with those historical subjects that we recognize as "like us."

While I speak here in terms of problems and dilemmas, I like to think that "we" (i.e., Asian American lesbians and gay men) are well positioned to change the discursive contours of "lesbian/gay" theorizing by centering these problems that have been raised by the dominance of metropolitan European languages. It seems that for the time being, we must employ multiple strategies in our attempts to position ourselves not only in relation to each other but also in relation to "Asia." We need to be willing to face the fact that we may not be able to find lost lesbian foremothers in our particular national/cultural histories. That is to say, it is to raise questions about the foundationalist impulse and consolidating urge that are reflected in the legitimization process by a positivist act of pointing to historical evidence. And further, we also need to be able to claim that this genealogy is not particularly necessary for our understanding of who we are and what we are—and what we might be in the future.

One by-product of the attempt to "discover" the genealogy of Asian lesbians and gays is to both naturalize and neutralize the racialized subject that Asians in America are. To claim that we have more of a natural affinity to those men and women who have been in same-sex liaisons in Asia than we have with the "history" of gays and lesbians in America is to ally ourselves with the notion that it is sexual acts that define us rather than the meanings that have been created about these acts. It is to assume that even if the narratives of Masuda Fumiko, Saijō Erika, and Yoshiya Nobuko reflect a discursive trajectory that is historically and linguistically specific, the fact that we are "Asians" naturally provides grounds for identification. In such an assumption, race is naturalized. Even more ironic, however, is that in such an identification, the very process by which an Asian subject position has been created over the past two centuries in the American discourse on national identity and race becomes obscured. Women like Masuda Fumiko and Saijo Erika, though not outside globalized racial discourse, occupied significantly different subject positions than, for instance, those Japanese who lived in the United States in the 1930s or Asians living in the United States today. The case of Yoshiya Nohuko begs our attention to the not so simple notion that even an alternative positionality in relation to the hetero normative familial system is not in itself a means to constitute a critical positionality that the politics of lesbian/gay and queer discourse would demand.

To illustrate this, consider a possible reading of the Masuda case in the Japanese American community in the 1930s. Such a reading would need to take several things into account. First, what would make thinking about this specific case possible would be that copies of *Fujin koron* were available in some of the stores in the larger urban Japanese American communities. Yet the story had different implications for the overseas Japanese. In Japan, the Masuda case came in the wake of a more diffused discourse on schoolgirl crushes—very often located in the culture of single-sex educational institutions as popularized by both media stories and the fiction of Yoshiya Nobuko—and discourses on urban modernity. That discursive terrain was one that would have been foreign to first-generation Japanese living in the United States. And a second-generation daughter, who may have had limited knowledge of Japanese and who was educated in public schools in the United States (and thus exposed to the gender discourses of the 1930s America) would surely have read the photograph of Masuda in a different way than her mother.

For a third- or fourth-generation Japanese American in the United States, such readings on the prewar immigrant community are surely part of a discursive genealogy. What this means, I think, is that the trajectory of the "history of sexuality" in the United States, for example, is quite squarely implicated in such consideration.[46] The relationship of contemporary Asian Americans to this single case multiplies in dizzying possibilities. What, for example, would be the relationship to it of a recent immigrant from India or Pakistan? Or of a second-generation Korean American? In other words, to identify without paying attention to the singularity of the construction of racial/sexual systems and the technologies and mechanisms that inform such systems in the United States, and how they position us differently from those who practice and pursue same-sex desires in areas of Asia, neutralizes one of the impulses behind the organizing of Asian queers, namely, to correct the invisibility of our particular racial, sexual, and gendered subject positions.

So then are history and the legitimacy that we experience in being able to point to others who came before us similarly unimportant? It is with much ambivalence that I have come to examine this process of using historical evidence for contemporary identity formation. I do not mean to argue that Asian American queers should be satisfied with remaining invisible in contemporary political struggles. I certainly do not mean to argue that history does not provide us with ways of understanding our present condition. What I am uncomfortable with is creating a lineage that does not examine the categories by which we identify our evidence. What I want, rather, to do with history is to produce moments of productive contradictions that allows us to imagine how we might *become*.

Such examination is especially important given how the global economy determines demographic shifts, given the increase in queer travel and tourism, and given how the particularities of AIDS are fashioned into international tales of mortality and morality. Finally, it seems to me that we are well positioned to change the shape of queer theorizing by linking geopolitics and the practices of international relations to our understanding of whence queerness comes. For ultimately, to be an Asian/Asian American/Pacific Islander queer is a queerly American experience.

Notes

I am grateful to those who gave me the opportunities to present versions of this essay at Harvard University, Northeastern University, and at CLAGS of the City University of New York Graduate School. The questions and comments of the audience have focused my intentions. Kandice Chuh, Elyssa Faison, Inderpal Grewal, Regina Kunzel, Rosalind Morris, John Treat and the anonymous reader for *positions* have read and commented on different versions of this essay. Tani Barlow, Monica Dorenkamp, and Susan L. Johnson in particular gave me extensive editorial suggestions and comments that sustained the writing. Most of all, I am indebted to Susan L. Johnson for our many conversations over many, many years. She may not recognize herself in this essay, but her insistence and encouragements for clarity prompted me in the negotiation of multiple discourses. And, even as I am keenly aware of my limitations, I have felt guided by her generosity.

1. The term "queer" is used here with the understanding that there are those who oppose such usage. I am using it in this essay as a way to think about contemporary racial and sexual politics as signified in the iconography of "queer and asian." I also read this claiming of this category as "queer" as a gesture toward its engagement with currents of present politics. For a useful discussion of the use of "queer"—as in "queer theory"—see Teresa de Lauretis, "Queer Theory: Lesbian and Gay Sexualities: An Introduction," *differences* 3, no. 2 (summer 1991): iii–xvii. I have also found the more recent commentaries by both Judith Butler and Michael Warner on the usage of *queer* useful in thinking about the ways the term is used in *identity politics:* Judith Butler, *Bodies That Matter: On the Discursive Limits of "Sex"* (Routledge, 1993), 226–30; Michael Warner, introduction to *Fear of a Queer Planet: Queer Politics and Social Theory,* ed. Michael Warner (University of Minnesota Press, 1993), xxvi–xxvii.

2. I have benefited much from Inderpal Grewal and Caren Kaplan, "Introduction: Transnational Feminist Practices and Questions of Postmodernity," in *Scattered Hegemonies: Postmodernity and Transnational Feminist Practices* (University of Minnesota Press, 1994), 1–33.

3. While the reference to "certain" racial practice may seem unnecessarily vague, I do so with the intention of suggesting that it may be possible to consider practices that do not inevitably resort to such articulation. To say that it is inevitable is to claim, it seems to me, to deny any possibility of strategic practices in the time that we live, namely, a time when we are already in possession of "knowledge" of race. The argument in regard to the articulation of differences in relation to both the dominant as well as the other "Other" has been addressed by many. For contemporary political practices, see, for example, Michael Omi and Howard Winart, *Racial Formations in the United States: From the 1960s to the 1980s* (Routledge, 1990).

4. The organization renamed itself later as AMALGM: Alliance of Massachusetts Asian Lesbians and Gay Men, and more recently has gone through a further change in its name as Queer Asian Pacific Alliance.

5. Here I wish to interject that this is not to reinscribe the already held notion that "Asians" are culturally and politically conformist and do not inherently accept *individuality*. I rather think that the social practice of cultural naming is reflective of the specificities of the historicities of its constructions.

6. The pamphlet was printed in English on one side and Chinese on the other. Reprinted in *Alliance of Massachusetts Asian Lesbians and Gay Men Special Newsletter Issue* (summer 1990): 4. AMALGM has recently renamed itself Queer Asian Pacific Alliance, which is a "social, political, and cultural" group for "bisexuals, gays, lesbians

and questioning" people of Asian and Pacific descent. (This new name change is reflected in their Message Board, a telephone information service.)

7. "Who We Are," distributed to members, 1984. *Asian Lesbian Newsletter* 1 (May 1984). Because of the way "Asians" and "Asian Americans" are used in these newsletters, while I refer explicitly to the Asian American/Pacific Islanders community at times, I will also use the term "Asian" to mean this group. When I am referring to Asians in Asia, I will make this clear in the text.

8. In *Sexing the Self*, Elspeth Probyn addresses the very conjunctural reasons which must be taken into consideration in the formulation of the "selves." Here I am taking a bit of liberty in transposing her ideas into the questions of sexual identities and subjectivies as articulated in Asian American politics. Elspeth Probyn, *Sexing the Self* (Routledge, 1993), 167. In thinking about this I have benefited greatly by reading William Haver, "Junshu-shugi no wana: Sogo no ronri no hihan ni mukete," *Shiso no kagaku*, February 1990, 81–90.

9. I am indebted to the discussion by Elspeth Probyn and her citation of Jean Michel Berthelo on this question of discursive operators which works to contain, and "act [to] chiasmatically create discursive relations other than those they seemingly represent." Elspeth Probyn, *Outside Belongings* (Routledge, forthcoming), 22.

10. Christopher Fynsk, "Statement of Interest" presented at the workshop on "Japan Studies" at Cornell University, 17 June 1994.

11. Elspeth Probyn, "Technologizing the Self: A Future Anterior for Cultural Studies" in *Cultural Studies*, Lawrence Grossberg, Cary Nelson, and Paul Treichler, ed. (Routledge, 1992), 54.

12. This is *not* to suggest, as some might charge, that real people do not live in a place that is referenced by "Asia." Rather, it is to suggest, as others have done, that the term "Asia" does not allow for the acknowledgment of the specifically violent ways in which one came to be subsumed under this term.

13. Inderpal Grewal helped me to understand this point more clearly. While it may be possible to signify the historicity of such inclusionary processes, the customary practice of invoking Asia does exactly the opposite. To invoke Asia is to assume a "natural" spatial coherence—even as specific linguistic, political, and ideological praxes are sited—of the geopolitical areas extending from East Asia (the former "Far East") to West Asia (the former "West Asia").

14. Here again, Inderpal Grewal has pointed out the exigency of calling into question *how* such fluidity and migratory identities are, in fact, imagined within frameworks that are much more specific than that which Kim suggests.

15. See Bill Ong Hing, *Making and Remaking Asian America through Immigration Policy, 1850–1990* (Stanford University Press, 1993) for the particular legislative acts and court challenges to such laws. William Wei, *The Asian American Movement* (Temple University Press, 1993) is a useful guide to the post–1960s movement. For a short but very useful discussion of the political construction of Asian American subjectivity, see Sau-ling Cynthia Wong, *Reading Asian American Literature: From Necessity to Extravagance* (Princeton University Press, 1993), 5–7. For a general historical treatment of Asians in America, see Ronald Takaki, *Strangers from a Different Shore* (Little Brown, 1989).

16. It is also noteworthy that not only are there numerous footprints left by those who have tried to steer the direction of this contest, but there are fresh footprints supplementing older ones—now almost unrecognizable.

17. It hardly needs a reminder, perhaps, but this embeddedness of the language and conceptualization of the *problem* is hardly unique to the politics of Asian America. Rather, what I want to consider is the particular way the impulse to self-represent—

within the symbolic logic of the dominant—is mandated by the logic of the ideology that such articulation of the identificatory site is contesting.

18. Jeffrey Paul Chan, Frank Chin, Lawson Fusao Inada, and Shawn Wong, eds., *The Big AIIIEEEEE! An Anthology of Chinese American and Japanese American Literature* (Penguin, 1991), xi–xvi. For specific argument, see the essay by Frank Chin, "Come All Ye Asian American Writers of the Real and the Fake," 1–92.

19. For a very useful discussion of "cultural nationalism" as well as "internal colonialism" and other analytical strategies and their relative positions, see Omi and Winart, 40–45.

20. See Hing, *Making and Remaking Asian America* for an exposition of the capricious history of "racial" definition through legislation.

21. For a discussion of the implication of locating Asian American through ethnicity rather than race, see F. San Juan, Jr., "The Cult of Ethnicity and the Fetish of Pluralism: A Counterhegemonic Critique," *Cultural Critique*, spring 1991, 215–29.

22. Chan et. al 192.

23. John Louis DiGaetani, "M. Butterfly: An Interview with Herry David Hwang" *TDR* 333 (fall 1989):145.

24. Alice Hom "Stories from the Homefront: Perspectives of Asian American Parents with Lesbian Daughters and Gay Sons" *Amerasia Journal* 20:1 (1994): 21.

25. "Her Story" has been shown at Yale University, MIT, the Berkshire Conference on The History of Women, and elsewhere since the mid 1980s.

26. The narrative is pieced together from articles in *Osaka jiji, Fujin kōron, Kaizō, Chūō kōron, Fujo shinbun,* and *Kakusei.*

27. While my reading of this incident is somewhat different and for a different purpose, Jennifer Robertson has also discussed this incident in the context of the etymology of *danson no reijin.* The corpus of her work on Takarazuka is the most sustained scholarship at the present time on female same-sex discourse in Japan in the period from 1910 to the 1940s. See Jennifer Robertson, "Politics of Androgyny in Japan: Sexuality and Subversion in the Theater and Beyond," *American Ethnologist* 19, no. 3 (August 1992): 419–41.

28. See Robertson, "Politics of Androgyny" for the emerging "tradition" of cross-dressing among certain women. In this context, I want to also consider the prevalence of cross-dressing that required the crossing of several borders. In a period when most Japanese women still wore kimono quite regularly, the clothing of choice was often "Western." I will argue that the implication of this "double"—gender as well as racial—crossing is central to the various sexed bodies that are witnessed in the discourse of this period. For a slightly different but nonetheless important discussion of racial/gender cross-dressing, see Miriam Silverberg, "Remembering Pearl Harbor, Forgetting Charlie Chaplin, and the Case of the Disappearing Western Woman: A Picture Story," *positions: east asia cultural critique* 1, no. 1 (spring 1993): 24–76.

29. *Yamagata shinbun,* 14 July 1934.

30. There is a contemporary account, also published in a newspaper, of two sisters in a farming village who both "turned into men," cited in Tomioka Masakata, "Dansei josō to josei dansō," *Kaizō,* October 1938, 105.

31. For discussion of modern urban women, though there are a number of works in the Japanese language as well, the essays by Miriam Silverberg not only have been the most accessible for English readers but also have conceptualized the questions in some of the most creative ways in which gender is refigured in current Japanese historical practices. See, for example, Miriam Silverberg, "The Modern Girls as Militant," in *Recreating Japanese Women, 1600–1945,* ed. Gail Berstein (University of California Press, 1991), 239–66; and idem, "Constructing the Japanese Ethnography of Modernity," *JAS* 51, no. 1 (February 1992): 30–54. Barbara Hamil Sato also proposes a reading

strategy of these urban women in "Kaisetsu, sōsetsu," in *Kindai shomin seikatsu-shi*, ed. Minami Hiroshi (Sanichi Shobō, 1986), 532–38.

32. Kohmoto Shinji and Yuri Mitsuda, eds., *Yasuo Nojima and Contemporaries: One Aspect of Modern Japanese Photography and Paintings* (National Museum of Art, Kyoto and Shoto Museum of Art, Tokyo, 1991).

33. "Yoshiya Nobuko to Hayashi Fumiko," *Nihon hyōron*, February 1939, 238–45. In this same article, however, she is described as forty-four years old and still single and cohabiting with Monma Chiyo. In this context of same-sex love, the article goes on to say that she is the husband and Monma is the wife.

34. See "Kikuchi Kan, Yoshikawa Eiji, Yoshiya Nobuko ni sensō no hanashi o kiku kai," *Hanashi*, December 1938, 58–78 for a "post-tour" report by Yoshiya. It seems particularly appropriate to remind the readers that of the three same-sex narratives that I am presenting here, it is Yoshiya who has been incorporated into, the "Her Story" project cited above.

35. "Kikuchi Kan, Yoshikawa Eiji, Yoshiya Nobuko ni sensō no hanashi o kiku kai" *Hanashi* (December 1938):58–78. Komashaku Kimi provides a very different reading of the positioning of this roundtable and Yoshiya's participation in "Yoshiya Nobuko: onnatachi e no manazashi" *Shisō no kagaku* 9 (1975):55–64. There isn't sufficient space here to discuss in detail the *problem* of how to write a history positioning Yoshiya; however, I want to point out the ways in which we may trouble ourselves here. Taking to task the short-sightedness of Yoshiya's critics, and the assumption that the inclusion of Yoshiya, in this special issue on "women who supported the *system*," is based on such negative assessment, Komashaku points to the ways in which Yoshiya's fiction created a means for women to identify with other women, rather than in competition over men. However, here, "women" is simultaneously the universalized organic subject "women" and the singularity of the those occupying subject positions produced within and through the discourse of *being* Japanese.

36. The term "ethico-political community" is borrowed from Christopher Fynsk.

37. Nawa Kaori "Resubian baā no yoru to yoru" *Bessatsu takarajima* 64 (1987):101–10. See also, for instance, the index category on "lesbian" in the multivolume index of the Ōya Sōichi Bunko for a glimpse of the pervasiveness of "lesbian" as a category in popular writings.

38. For a brief history of *Wakaku-no-kai* see: Hirosawa Yumi "Nihon hatsu no rezubian sakuru: 'Wakakusa-no-kai' sono jyugonen no rekishi to genzai" *Bessatsu Takarajima* 64 (1987):111–19.

39. Hisada Megumi "Genki jirushi no rezubian 'Re-Gumi no gomame' no tōjō" *Bessatsu Takarajima* 64 (1987):120–29. The significance of North American influence, for instance, in these forms of lesbian practice is underscored by the citational practice of juxtaposing a photograph of the lesbian feminist softball team, reprinted from *Our Right to Love* on the same page as the "national" lisiting of information about lesbian groups. *Bessatsu Takarajima* 64 (1987):130–31.

40. Perhaps one of the exemplary texts testifying to the named subject is Kakefuda Hiroko, *"Resubian" de aru, to iukoto* (Kawade Shobō, 1992). Many publications in the past five years implicitly assume the category of sexuality and sexual objects as objects of knowledge. See, for instance, special issues of *Takarajima, Imago, New Feminist Review,* and *Asahi One Theme Magazine: Gender Collection.*

41. My usage of "histories" and "legacies" should be clear to mean not histories or legacies in the sense of a narrative continuity.

42. It seems only appropriate to consider this question when much of the work on the nomenclature of sexual objects in Western scholarship has called into question the usage of those terms not yet used in the specific historical place and time. This is not because we should follow or fall into frameworks already established but rather to call

attention, once again, to the notion of sexual subjects as always already in existence. That is, as I have tried to do in this essay, call into question the concept of sex, as I have tried to call into question the concepts of race and ethnic identities.

43. "Sexuality" is today most often used in its transliterated form. Here, however, what I want to emphasize is the difficulty of grasping whether or not when used in Japan "sexuality" reflects its historicity or genealogy as it almost always does in the United States.

44. Underscoring the discursively connected ways in which knowledge is produced, though often quite troubling, is the large production in Japan today of popular articles, reprinted historical archives, and interpretive essays on "history" and "sex/sexuality." See for instance, the thematic issues of *Imago* 2, no. 9 (1991) and *Asahi One Theme Magazine* 36 (1994); the roundtable on "Japanese Culture and Gender" in *Hihyō kūkan* 2, no. 3 (1994); the reprints of *modern* texts in *Nihon kindai shisō taikei 23: Fūzoku— sei* Ogi Shinzō, Kumakura Isao, and Ueno Chizuko eds., (Iwanami shoten: 1990); and Ueno Chizuko *Seiairon* (Kawade shobō: 1991).

45. Here again, it may be instructive to think about how "thinking from a category" such as *dōseiai* (or same-sex romantic love) renders invisible Yoshiya's national positionality. In another project that I am working on, I will discuss more fully the implications of contemporary historical practice in Japan.

46. This focus has become one of the most productive sites within American history. The number of articles and books published annually testifies to the tremendous force it has become. Most, however, fall in line with a certain chronological framework set out—to confirm or to interpolate—by John D'Emilio and Estelle Freedman in *Intimate Matters: A Social History of Sexuality in America* (Harper & Row, 1988). See also Lisa Duggan for the multiple discourse analysis she applies, particularly instructive in thinking about, for instance, the Masuda Fumiko case: *"The Trials of Alice Mitchell: Sensationalism, Sexology, and the Lesbian Subject in Turn-of-the-Century America" Signs* 18, no. 4 (summer 1993):791–814.

B. What "Gender"?

6

Gender Diversity in Native North America: Notes Toward a Unified Analysis

Will Roscoe

Typically described, in the words of Matilda Stevenson, as men who "adopt woman's dress and do woman's work," male berdaches—or "two-spirits," which is the preferred pan-tribal term among contemporary Natives—have been documented in nearly 150 North American societies.[1] In nearly half of these groups, a social status also has been noted for females who undertook a man's lifestyle, who were sometimes referred to in the Native language with the same term applied to male berdaches and sometimes with a distinct term. Although the existence of berdaches has long been known to specialists in North American anthropology, the subject has been consigned to footnotes and marginal references. In the past twenty years, however, berdaches have become a subject of growing interest. An expanding base of empirical data concerning the social, cultural, and historical dimensions of berdache status has become available.

As a result, a consensus on several points has begun to develop. The key features of male and female berdache roles were, in order of importance, *productive specialization* (crafts and domestic work for male berdaches, warfare, hunting, and leadership roles in the case of female berdaches); *supernatural sanction* (in the form of an authorization and/or bestowal of powers); and *gender variation*. In the case of the latter, cross-dressing was the most common and visible marker, but it has proven a more variable and less reliable indicator of berdache status than previously assumed. In some tribes male berdaches dressed distinctly from both men and women. In other cases, berdaches did not cross-dress at all, or only partly. In the case of female berdaches, cross-dressing was even more variable. Often, female berdaches wore men's clothes only when hunting or participating in warfare.[2]

The sexual behavior of male and female berdaches was also variable. Where data exists, it indicates that their partners were usually non-berdache members of their own sex—that is, berdaches were homosexual, if we define that term narrowly in terms of behavior and anatomy.[3] Some berdaches, however, appear to have been bisexual and heterosexual. This was most often the case when adult men entered berdache status primarily on the basis of visions or dreams. Berdaches participated in both casual sexual relations and long-term partnerships.

A second point of agreement is that berdaches were accepted and integrated members of their communities, as indeed, their economic and religious reputations suggest. In many cases, they enjoyed special respect and honors. In a few cases they were feared because of the supernatural power they were believed to possess. Related to this conclusion has been the abandonment of deterministic hypotheses concerning the "cause" of berdache behavior. This view has a long history, beginning with early contact accounts. As Coreal wrote in the early eighteenth century, describing berdache practices among Natives of Florida, "the boys that *abandon themselves* thus *are excluded* from the society of men. . . . *They employ them* in all the diverse handiworks of women."[4] Such discursive practices predetermine and overdetermine berdaches as the objects of action, never the subjects. The anthropological version of these tropes takes the form of theories that account for berdaches in terms of external forces alone— for example, the suggestion that the berdache role was a social status imposed on men too weak or cowardly to measure up to stringent tribal standards of masculinity. This has been convincingly disproved by evidence of males uninterested or unsuccessful in warfare who nonetheless do not become berdaches and by the actual participation of berdaches in warfare.[5] Consequently, most recent work on berdaches acknowledges the role of individual motivations and talents in determining who became a berdache. Berdaches are finally being recognized as historical subjects—individuals who actually desired to be berdaches because of the rewards that lifestyle offered.

A third area of emerging consensus addresses the problem of translation. Whereas berdaches have been traditionally conceptualized as crossing or exchanging genders, as the terms "transvestite" or "transsexual" imply (or exchanging object choice as "homosexual" suggests), several investigators have begun to argue that berdaches in fact occupied a third gender role, or, in the case of tribes with both male and female berdaches, and distinct terms for each, third and fourth genders.[6]

Both positive and negative evidence supports the argument that berdache status constituted a culturally acknowledged gender category. On the one hand, it easily can be shown that a dual gender model fails to account for many of the behaviors and attributes reported for berdaches—for example, berdaches who did not cross-dress or attempt to mimic the behavior of the "opposite" and those who engaged in a combination of female, male, and berdache-specific pursuits.[7] On the other hand, the consistent use of distinct terms to refer to berdaches, a practice that prevented their conceptual assimilation to an "opposite" sex, is positive evidence that berdache status was viewed as a separate category.[8] These native terms have a variety of translations, from the obvious "man-woman" (e.g., Shoshoni *tainna'-wa'ippe*) to "old woman-old man" (e.g., Tewa *kwidó*) to terms that bear no relation to the words for "man" or "woman," or simply cannot be etymologized (e.g., Zuni *lhamana*).[9]

Although the points made so far apply equally to male and female berdaches, it is clear that female roles were not simply mirror opposites of male berdache roles. Unfortunately, the study of female berdaches lags behind that of male roles, and several features of this status await clarification. Beatrice Medicine concluded that "warrior women," like male berdaches, occupied "socially sanctioned role alternatives." These were "normative statuses which permitted individuals to strive for self-actualization, excellence, and social recognition in areas outside their customary sex role assignments."[10] Some researchers, however, have concluded that female berdache roles were less viable and female berdaches less tolerated than their male counterparts, and others have argued that the term "berdache" should not be applied to women at all. Whitehead concluded that "when women did the equivalent of what men did to become berdaches, nothing happened."[11]

On the other hand, Blackwood has argued that the female berdache role was socially and ontologically on par with male berdache status in the sense of being a distinct alternative identity.[12] At Zuni, I found that the female berdache role was less visibly marked than the male role (i.e., there are no reports of cross-dressing by women), and may have been more variable from individual to individual, but linguistic and religious practices still countenanced a distinct status for women who combined male and female pursuits, as evidenced by the use of the same term, *lhamana*, to refer to both male and female berdaches.[13] It may be more helpful to conceptualize female role alternatives in North American societies as a continuum, with the boundary between temporary and ongoing role variation less clearly marked than in the case of male roles. In this view, female berdaches—women who filled such male roles as hunter, warrior, and chief on an ongoing basis—represent the more elaborated expression of role variations that many women engaged in to a more limited extent at various points in their lives.[14]

The Theoretical Challenge

Derived from the Latin *genus*, or simply "kind, sort, class," "gender" has come to be used by researchers in several fields to distinguish socially constructed roles and cultural representations from biological sex.[15] Indeed, throughout

Western history, popular belief and official discourse alike have acknowledged the role of social learning in sex-specific behavior, but biological sex has always been considered both the origin point and natural limit of sex roles. What we call gender, in this view, *should* conform to sex, a belief that is rationalized alternately on moral and naturalistic grounds. The study of non-Western cultures, however, reveals not only variability in the sociocultural features of sex roles, but, as I will argue below, wide variation in beliefs concerning the body and what constitutes sex.

If gender can be multiple, and potentially autonomous from sex, it becomes crucial to clarify exactly what it denotes. (In fact, definitions of "gender" are rare in the literature of "gender studies.") For the purposes of cross-cultural analysis, I define "gender" as a multidimensional category of personhood encompassing a distinct pattern of social and cultural differences. Gender categories often draw on perceptions of anatomical and physiological differences between bodies, but these perceptions are always mediated by cultural categories and meanings. Nor can we assume the relative importance of these perceptions in the overall definition of personhood in a given social context, or that these differences will be interpreted as dichotomous and fixed, or that they will be viewed as behavioral or social determinants (as opposed to, for example, a belief that behavior might determine anatomy).

Gender categories are not only "models of" difference (to borrow Geertz's terminology) but also "models for" difference. They convey gender-specific social expectations for behavior and temperament, sexuality, kinship and interpersonal roles, occupation, religious roles, and other social patterns. Gender categories are "total social phenomena," in Marcel Mauss's terms; a wide range of institutions and beliefs find simultaneous expression through them, a characteristic that distinguishes gender from other social statuses.[16] In the terms of this definition, the presence of multiple genders does not require belief in the existence of three or more physical sexes but, minimally, a view of physical differences as unfixed, or insufficient on their own to establish gender, or simply less important than individual and social factors, such as occupational preference, behavior and temperament, religious experiences, and so forth.

Since the work of Ruth Benedict and Margaret Mead, anthropological studies of sex roles have focused on the relationship between sex and gender—a relationship that has been described as both motivated and arbitrary. A multiple gender paradigm, however, leads us to analyze the relationship between the body and sex, as well. Although we may allow that morphological differences in infants motivate a marking process, in a multiple gender paradigm the markers of sex are viewed as no less arbitrary than the sociocultural elaborations of sex in the form of gender identities and roles. North American data, for example, make it clear that not all cultures recognize the same anatomical markers, and not all recognize anatomical markers as "natural" and, therefore, counterposed to a distinct domain of the "cultural."

In traditional Zuni belief, for example, a series of interventions were considered necessary to ensure that a child has a "sex" at all. This began before birth, when the parents made offerings at various shrines to influence the sex of the developing fetus. In fact, the infant's sex was still not fixed at the time of birth. If a woman took a nap during labor, the Zunis believed the sex of her child might change. Following birth, interventions intended to influence physical sex continued. The midwife massaged and manipulated the infant's face, nose, eyes, and genitals. If the baby was male, she poured cold water over its penis to prevent overdevelopment. If the baby was female, the midwife split a new gourd in half and rubbed it over the vulva to enlarge it.[17] In this context, knowing the kind of genitals an individual possesses is less important than knowing how bodies are culturally constructed, and what particular features and processes (physiological and/or social) are believed to endow them with sex.

The assumption that the social roles of all societies can be understood in terms of the sex/gender and male/female binaries has been criticized in recent years on both empirical and theoretical grounds. It may, indeed, be arguable that all societies have *at least* two genders, and as suggested above, that these two genders are linked to perceptions of physiological differences. What constitutes anatomical sex, however, which organs (or fluids or physiological processes) are considered the signs of maleness and femaleness, has been shown by scholars in several fields to be as much a social construction as what has been termed "gender."[18]

In sum, if berdaches are to be understood as simply exchanging one gender for another, then they can indeed be interpreted as upholding a heterosexist gender system, as some feminist anthropologists have argued.[19] If they are to be understood as entering a distinct gender status, however, neither male nor female, then something more complex is going on. A multiple gender paradigm makes it possible to see berdache status not as a compromise between nature and culture or a niche to accommodate "natural" variation, but as an integral and predictable element of certain sociocultural systems.

Toward a Unified Analysis

Elsewhere, I have argued for the employment of multidimensional models in analyzing social and cultural differences in sexuality and gender.[20] I suggested that definitions based on single traits such as "gender identity" or "sexual object choice" be replaced with a multidimensional inventory of all the differences to be found in a given cultural context associated with a status such as "berdache" or "homosexual," whether in terms of social role, gender variation, economic specialization, religious roles, sexuality, or subjectivity.[21] A counterpart to multidimensional description and cultural translation is now needed at the level of cultural analysis. Jane Collier and Sylvia Yanagisako offer such an approach in their program for a "unified analysis" of gender and kinship. They point to a growing recognition that the social phenomena of gender and kinship are manifestations of the same sociocultural processes. What is required at this point, they argue, is a methodology capable of analyzing these larger processes without relying on such analytical dichotomies as sex/gender, nature/culture, or domestic/public. They propose a three-part analytical program for this purpose.

The first phase entails the *cultural analysis of meaning*. Here the objective is to explicate the cultural meanings people realize through their practice of social relationships. At this stage of analysis, the investigator needs to ask, "What are the socially meaningful categories people employ in specific contexts, and what symbols and meanings underlie them?" In terms of gender diversity, we would want to know what kind of beliefs are associated with and necessary for the formulation of berdache gender categories. Are gender and sexuality viewed as natural, constructed, inborn, or acquired traits? Is the berdache, therefore, an anomaly, a monster, or a prodigy? How are berdaches conceptualized in terms of the categories and meanings associated with kinship, economics, politics, religion, and other social systems?

The second phase of a unified analysis involves the construction of *systemic models of inequality*. This is accomplished by analyzing the structures that people create through their actions and tracing the "complex relationships between aspects of what—using conventional analytical categories—we might call gender, kinship, economy, polity, and religion."[22] Such "ideal typic models" of how power and social difference are organized in various societies are particularly valuable for comparative purposes. In the case of berdache roles we would want to know the following: What is the position of the berdache as a producer and a consumer within the larger system for creating and circulating power? What avenues of economic specialization are available to the role? What is the position of berdaches in relation to the organization of other genders and the division of labor between them (with special attention to the economic roles of women)?

Being synchronic in nature, systemic models have a built-in bias toward the persistence and continuity of social orders. For this reason Collier and Yanagisako include *historical analysis* as the third element of their program, pointing out that ideas and practices that seem to reinforce and reproduce each other from a systemic perspective can be seen to undermine and destabilize each other from a historical perspective. Historical analysis also leads to the consideration of individual factors in social developments—the motivations, desires, and self-generated meanings of the individuals who participate in "events" and occupy social "roles"—and to an analysis of the construction of subject positions.

A unified analysis can help clarify some of the outstanding issues in berdache studies. For example, what was the relative importance of economic and spiritual dimensions in determining whether an individual became berdache? Here a comparison of berdache roles from two very different culture areas—the Plains and the Pueblos—is helpful. A unified analysis also makes it possible to distinguish individual differences from culturally patterned behavior, and to recognize historical change as a factor affecting both. To illustrate this point, I will review the ethnographic evidence concerning Mohave berdaches.

Plains and Pueblo Berdaches

Perhaps the clearest evidence of the degree to which beliefs functioned independently of economic factors can be found in those cases of vision-induced entry into berdache status by adult men who had not previously manifested berdache traits. This occurred in "vision complex" cultures, especially among Plains tribes, where following supernatural instructions was considered mandatory. Indeed, even successful warriors, if visited with dreams or visions considered berdache-specific, assumed berdache identity.[23] In other words, even though the economic dimension of berdache roles was their most common feature, Native beliefs concerning supernatural experience were sufficient to sanction entry into the status on their own. Future research should focus on the possibility that multiple gender statuses might exist in societies without any economic correlate or where such a correlate had lapsed.

This leads us to ask whether a "vision complex" is the only kind of belief system in which berdache roles could occur. The Pueblo Indians, for example, in contrast to many Plains tribes, lack any manifestation of a vision complex, as Ruth Benedict pointed out in her classic study, *Patterns of Culture*. The cooperative values of Pueblo communities, arising from the collective nature of agricultural production and communal living, de-emphasized all forms of individualism. Direct contact with the supernatural was not sought and not welcomed. Despite the absence of a vision complex, berdaches have been documented in a majority of Pueblo communities.[24] The economic basis of their status was similar to that of Plains berdaches. Pueblo women produced and distributed both food and durable goods, and these products were coded as being female. Specialization in these areas by males entailed no loss in social standing. Nonetheless, Pueblo and Plains Indian belief systems were distinct in how they legitimated multiple genders. Among the Zunis, the berdache role was sanctioned not by individual contact with the supernatural, but through tribal myths that relate the creation of berdache status as an autonomous cultural category, much as gender distinctions, kinship categories, and other social statuses are explained.[25]

The examples of Plains and Pueblo societies provide evidence that berdache status can exist in conjunction with varying subsistence patterns and belief systems. At the same time, despite these differences, neither Plains nor Pueblo economies produced significant inequalities of wealth, and both afforded a basis for berdache status in terms of economic specialization. Similarly, while Plains and Pueblo societies rationalized berdache roles in different ways, both groups shared a basically constructivist view of gender in that neither viewed it as determined by sex, or, for that matter, made a distinction between sex and gender.[26]

Mohave Berdaches

As long as berdaches are culturally recognized *as* berdaches (that is, consistently referred to with a distinct term) and individuals and communities do not engage in a social fiction concerning their anatomy (by suppressing or "forgetting" the individual's actual anatomy or pretending that it had somehow been changed), then cross-dressing alone is not necessarily indicative of a gender-crossing pattern. The sartorial practices of both male and female berdaches have been shown to be far more variable than previously assumed. Clothing and ornament in North American societies constituted a semiotic system for signaling not merely gender but social standing, kinship status, religious status, personal accomplishments, age, and so forth. Cross-dressing itself often occurred in ritual and mythological contexts with little or no reference to berdache status. However, if male berdaches not only wore women's clothing but imitated women's reproductive processes, and female berdaches the reverse, then a sex/gender belief system would appear to be operative, with "berdaches" behaving according to the logic of dual and dichotomous sexes. Such an example appears to be provided by the Mohave Indians of the Colorado River area.

This case is worth examining because it seems to provide the strongest evidence *against* a multiple gender paradigm of berdache roles, and because the Mohave example is frequently cited in the secondary literature as illustrating North American berdaches in general. This is due largely to the detailed ethnographic account of Mohave male berdaches, or *alyha*, and female berdaches, or *hwame*, provided by the psychoanalytic anthropologist George Devereux in the 1930s.[27]

According to Devereux, Mohave berdaches consistently, indeed rigorously, behaved according to the precepts of a cross-gender model—as individuals of one anatomical sex striving to become the "opposite sex." *Alyha* insisted on being referred to by female names and with female gender-references. They only practiced receptive anal and oral intercourse, and whereas they appeared to have achieved orgasm, they discouraged personal contact with and even reference to their male genitals. They used the Mohave word for clitoris to refer to their penises, the term for labia majora to describe their testes, and the word for vagina to the refer to their anuses. A special ceremony served to confirm male berdache status, during which clothes of the "opposite" sex were made and presented to them. Both *alyha* and *hwame* might enjoy casual or long-term relationships with non-berdache men and women. If in a partnership, according to Devereux, they were consistently referred to as a "wife" or "husband," respectively.

What has earned the *alyha* a permanent place in the ethnographic literature, however, is Devereux's account of their elaborate mock pregnancies. These were carried out in excruciating detail, including the simulation of pregnancy through self-induced constipation followed by the "birth" of a stillborn fecal fetus. The whole production culminated with the burial of the "fetus" and the observance of the appropriate mourning rites, in which the *alyha* required her husband to participate. *Alyha* were also reported to simulate menstruation by scratching themselves until they bled.

Devereux's data on female berdaches are less consistent. *Hwame* are not said to have employed male physiological terminology to refer to their genitals, and one informant told Devereux that *hwame* did not necessarily take male names. Some women became *hwame* after having children. They ignored their own menses but followed the taboos required of husbands when their wives menstruated or were pregnant. They did not necessarily cross-dress. Sex between a *hwame* and a woman was performed in a variety of positions, without active/passive distinctions. Like male berdaches, *hwame* were often shamans.

Although Devereux's report provides convincing evidence of cross-gender beliefs and practices on the part of Mohave male berdaches, it poses some difficulties when used to make generalizations. The extreme gynemimetic behavior that Devereux attributes to the *alyha* is unique for North America. Nothing remotely similar to the fake pregnancies of the *alyha* has been reported elsewhere, not even among linguistically related neighboring tribes.[28] In accounting for this apparent discrepancy in North American patterns, a unified analysis provides an effective approach, involving the consideration, in turn, of cultural meanings, socioeconomic structures, and historical factors.

The first test of whether Mohave berdaches represent a case of culturally patterned gender-crossing would be to determine whether the Mohaves believed gender to be dichotomous and fixed, and whether, therefore, a third position was conceptually impossible. In fact, a close examination of evidence reported by Devereux and Kroeber reveals that the social labeling and conceptual patterns of the Mohaves are more compatible with a multiple gender paradigm than a cross-gender model. The use of distinct terms for male and female berdaches, for example, is not consistent with the maintenance of a social fiction of gender-crossing and transformation. In fact, although Devereux states that Mohaves consistently used "he" and "she" in referring to *hwame* and *alyha*, respectively, he later presents extensive quoted material from an informant who repeatedly uses "he" in referring to *alyha*.[29] (Similarly, contemporary Mohaves refer to the nineteenth-century *hwame* Masahay Matkwisa: as "she.")[30] Perhaps the Mohaves' cross-gender references to berdaches were less literal than Devereux understood them. They may have been meant in the same sense conveyed when the pronouns "he" and "she" are placed in quotation marks in written texts.

In fact, a variety of comments recorded by Devereux suggest that, in the minds of most Mohaves, *alyha* and *hwame* retained qualities of their "original" gender and combined them with those of the "opposite" gender, and for this reason were always thought of as distinct from both men and women. "You can tease a hwame," one Mohave told Devereux, "because she is just a woman, but if you tease an alyha, who has the strength of a man, he will run after you and beat you up."[31] *Alyha* were not courted like ordinary girls, nor were they viewed as equivalent to female wives. "He must be awfully hard up to marry a womanly man," was a typical comment concerning a man who chose to marry an *alyha*. According to Devereux, many Mohaves wondered whether the husbands of *alyha* "really thought they were having intercourse with a woman" — in other words, *they* knew that the *alyha* was "really" a man; surely the husband of the *alyha* knew, as well![32]

In explaining the development of berdache orientation, Mohaves credited a combination of predestination, occupational preferences, social influences, and, above all, dreams. As a contemporary Mohave explains, "Dreaming was the very core of Mohave life. It was the source of each individual's special skill, of his prowess as a warrior, and of his success in all his undertakings. A Great Dream might foretell the birth of a male child to his father. Later the dream would return to the child as he grew to manhood and listened to others tell of their dreams. Then he dreamed his own and became a man."[33] In other words, dreaming was key to acquiring gender identity, whether male, female, or berdache. Although all dreams were believed to have originally occurred in the mother's womb, the dreams of *alyha* and *hwame* were not apparent until, as children, they began to express preferences for particular work activities. Devereux was told, "When there is a desire in a child's heart to become a transvestite [*sic*] that child will act different. It will let people become aware of that desire. They may insist on giving the child the toys and garments of its true sex, but the child will throw them away."[34] Although berdache identity is presented as predetermined and nonvoluntary, this passage clearly points to a psychic and not a physiological origin point. At the same time, the role also enjoyed the sanction of an origin myth, which relates the birth of the first *alyha* and the institution of berdache initiation rites by the creator god Mastamho.[35]

In sum, Mohave beliefs combined the two modes of rationalizing berdache status described earlier: supernatural sanction similar to the Plains Indian pattern *and* mythological precedence, as in the case of the Zunis and Navajos. Both rationales are more consistent with a multiple gender paradigm than with a binary, gender-crossing model.

If Mohave work activities were not gender-coded, then the markers of berdache status might be expected to shift to other areas, such as anatomy, but there is no evidence that this was the case. We find the same correlates of berdache status, in terms of social, economic, and religious specialization, in Mohave culture as in other North American groups. In sum, neither the belief system of the Mohaves nor their socioeconomic patterns provide an explanation for the cross-gender behavior attributed to Mohave berdaches. The expectations and beliefs are those of a multiple gender paradigm. Although some berdaches may have insisted on a fiction of gender-crossing, the community as a whole did not go so far. This leaves the consideration of historical factors—or, more broadly stated, the possibility of nonstructural and nonpatterned sources for this behavior.

Gilbert Herdt has pointed out the extent to which Devereux's account of Mohave berdaches conformed to the Freudian theory of homosexuality as a phenomenon of sexual inversion.[36] This lumped together individuals now distinguished by such terms as "gay," "lesbian," "transvestite," and "transsexual." In fact, it would be tempting to define Mohave berdaches as an instance of transsexualism, but this would be misleading. The goal of modern transsexuals has been to appear so convincing as members of their chosen sex that others never suspect they had ever been anything but that sex.[37] As we have seen, the practice of holding public ceremonies to confirm *alyha* status made any such fiction impossible among the Mohaves.[38] Further, the *alyha* Devereux describes appear to have aspired specifically to the acquisition of female *reproductive* functions. Western male-to-female transsexuals, on the other hand, tend to be preoccupied with the inappropriateness of their male genitalia in relation to their gender identification. They aspire more to female morphology than reproductive functions, and the acquisition of breasts takes priority over a vagina. If *alyha* were identically motivated we might expect not elaborate fake pregnancies and simulated menstruation, but attempts to castrate themselves and/or enlarge their breasts (both of which are possible with methods available in a preindustrial society).

Although there is no reason to doubt the accuracy of his reporting, Devereux himself made no direct observations of berdaches, relying instead on the memories of informants recalling events of the late nineteenth century and often relying on secondhand information. Although referring to the existence of other informants, Devereux cites only three specific sources for his data on berdaches—Ñahwera, reputedly the last Mohave who knew the *alyha* initiation songs (but not a berdache himself); an eighty-year-old woman who had heard about (but not seen) the *alyha* ceremony when in her youth; and Hivsu Tupoma, a male shaman who had known Kuwal, a Mohave who, in the late nineteenth century, had had more than one *alyha* wife. It appears that most of Devereux's information concerning berdache pregnancies was provided by Hivsu Tupoma, based on stories he heard from Kuwal. Of course, it must be kept in mind that in a small community the behavior of two or three berdaches might constitute "tradition" for a given generation.

It seems possible, therefore, that the behavior Devereux described had its origins in individual factors more than in cultural expectations and may have been specific to the individuals known to (or heard of by) Devereux's informants, in particular, Kuwal's wives and the dynamics of Kuwal's relationships with them. This leads us to ask what motives besides the desire to cross genders might underlie the imitation of pregnancy by Mohave berdaches. A comment Devereux recorded provides one clue: "Some men who had enough of it [marriage to an *alyha*] tried to get rid of them politely, alleging barrenness of the alyha. But no alyha would admit such a thing. They would begin to fake pregnancy."[39] In other words, faking pregnancy may have been the somewhat desperate stratagem of an individual threatened with the loss of a lover, not unlike cases of hysterical pregnancy in females. Getting the husband to participate in mourning rites for the stillborn "infant" (and burial rites were serious business among the Mohaves) amounted to his capitulation to the fantasy and, therefore, a victory for the *alyha*.

Yet another line of investigation is suggested by a brief passage in Devereux's original article. Reporting on the contemporary (i.e., 1930s) status of homosexuality among the Mohaves, Devereux describes three men "accused of" "active and passive homosexuality," none of whom cross-dressed or had undergone the *alyha* initiation. All three men lived together; two were half-brothers. According to Devereux, "They are usually referred to as each other's wives and are said to indulge in rectal intercourse."[40] What is striking here is the indefiniteness of the role attributions. Devereux invokes the distinction between active and passive homosexuality, but he fails to indicate *who* is active and *who* is passive. In the rest of his article, these distinctions are crucial. One of these men would have to be a husband and another a "wife," and the "wife" would be expected to vehemently insist on the distinction.

Certainly traditional practices were lapsing by the 1930s, which would account for these nonberdache forms of homosexuality, but another possibility worth considering is that not only casual but committed homosexual relationships such as these were a viable option in traditional Mohave culture—alongside the option of being a berdache or a partner of a berdache. Since such a possibility does not fit his preconceived theory of "homosexuality" as sexual inversion, Devereux does not explore it (although he does report that casual homosexual relations were "frequent" in traditional times). This would indeed distinguish the Mohaves from other tribes, where the best evidence at present suggests that committed, sexual partnerships and cohabitation between members of the same gender were rare. If this were an option in Mohave culture, however, then the only motivation for entering the berdache role would be to express a strong sense of gender difference.

As this analysis suggests, Mohave beliefs and practices are more complex than a gender-crossing model would predict. A review of Devereux's original report reveals how Western assumptions concerning gender and sexuality can powerfully shape ethnographic observations and even lead the ethnographer to overlook the presence of social patterns—in this case, the possibility of nonberdache homosexuality. The Mohave case also underscores the importance of allowing for the divergence of individual meanings and motivations from normative beliefs. In small-scale societies, idiosyncratic behavior can too easily be mistaken for a "traditional" cultural practice.

Berdache status was not a niche for occasional (and presumably "natural") variation in sexuality and gender, nor was it an accidental by-product of unresolved social contradictions. In the native view, berdaches occupied a distinct and autonomous social status on par with the status of men and women. Like male and female genders, the berdache gender entailed a pattern of differences encompassing behavior, temperament, social and economic roles, and religious beliefs and practices—all the dimensions of a gender category, as I defined that term earlier, with the exception of the attribution of physical differences. But physical differences were constructed variously in Native American perception, and they were not accorded the same weight that they are in Western belief. Social learning and personal experiences (including ritual and supernatural experiences) were considered just as important as anatomy in defining individual social identity. Viewing female and male berdache roles as third and fourth genders, therefore, offers the best translation of native categories and the best fit with the range of behaviors and social traits reported for berdaches. Conversely, characterizations of berdaches as crossing genders or mixing genders, as men or women who "assume the role of the 'opposite' sex," are reductionist and inaccurate.

Given the presence of multiple genders, what are their social and cultural correlates? The three cases discussed here suggest that most of the variations in the berdache role among different North American societies were related to cultural systems of meaning and historical factors more than differences in prestige systems. Despite a wide variety of subsistence patterns, North American modes of production and division of labor did not in most cases produce significant or fixed differences in wealth and status. At the same time, they also afforded an economic dimension to berdache status in terms of productive specialization. Even so, economic potential alone does not predict the presence of multiple genders. Whereas sedentary horticultural communities may have provided more opportunities for specialization, it was among the Navajos, for historical reasons, that the berdache achieved highest status. Similarly, in terms of belief systems, although a vision complex can serve to rationalize alternative gender statuses and foster entry into the status by individuals who do not manifest the typical traits of berdaches, berdache roles can flourish within cultural systems lacking a vision complex altogether. Finally, we saw in the Mohave case how, even with economic opportunities and beliefs similar to other North American groups, individual motivations, psychological and situational, could powerfully shape the construction of what otherwise appear to be "traditional" features of social roles and the meanings surrounding them.

There are no definitive variables for predicting the presence of multiple genders, but I believe we can specify a set of minimal conditions for the possibility of such statuses. First is a division of labor and a prestige system organized in terms of gender categories, so that the potential exists for women to specialize in production and distribution of food and exchange goods. Second is a belief system in which gender is not viewed as determined by anatomical sex or anatomical sex is believed to be unstable, fluid, and non-dichotomous, and, therefore, an autonomous third category is viable. Third is the occurrence of historical events and individuals motivated to take advantage of these social conditions to construct gender identities. If these conditions are present, then multiple gender roles can develop. Conversely, I would hypothesize that for a given society in which multiple genders were present, it would take not only the elimination of the economic dimension of such statuses, but a lapse in the belief systems rationalizing them and the introduction of a dual-sex ideology to effect a full collapse of such roles.

The next step in berdache studies will be the recognition that gender diversity is not an isolated feature of North American societies but a worldwide phenomenon, represented in most culture areas as well as certain historical periods of Western societies. Gender diversity will become one more part of the story of human culture and history that is anthropology's job to tell.

Notes

1. Matilda C. Stevenson, "The Zuñi Indians: Their Mythology, Esoteric Fraternities, and Ceremonies," in *Twenty-third Annual Report of the Bureau of American Ethnology, 1901–1902* (Washington, DC: Government Printing Office, 1904), 374. For a listing of tribes with berdache roles, see Will Roscoe, "Bibliography of Berdache and Alternative Gender Roles among North American Indians," *Journal of Homosexuality* 14 (3–4) (1987): 81–171.

2. See the examples summarized in Roscoe, "Bibliography," 167.

3. See Charles Callender and Lee M. Kochems, "The North American Berdache," *Current Anthropology* 24 (4) (1983): 443–70, esp. 499; Walter L. Williams, *The Spirit and the Flesh: Sexual Diversity in American Indian Culture* (Boston: Beacon, 1986), 87–109; Roscoe, "Bibliography," 158–59.

4. François Coreal, *Voyages de François Coreal aux Index Occidentales*, vol. 1 (Amsterdam: J. Frederic Bernard, 1722), 33–34 (my trans., emphasis added).

5. See Roscoe, "Bibliography," 162–63; Callender and Kochems, "North American Berdache," 448–49; David F. Greenberg, *The Construction of Homosexuality* (Chicago: University of Chicago Press, 1988), 44–45.

6. Evelyn Blackwood, review of *The Spirit and the Flesh: Sexual Diversity in American Indian Culture*, by Walter L. Williams, *Journal of Homosexuality* 15 (3–4) (1988): 170–71; Will Roscoe, *The Zuni Man-Woman* (Albuquerque: University of New Mexico Press, 1991), 144–46. For the canonical statement on berdaches as gender-crossers, see Henry Angelino and Charles Shedd, "A Note on Berdache," *American Anthropologist* 57 (1) (1955): 121–26.

7. Examples of all these are provided in my studies of Zuni, Navajo, and Crow berdaches. See Will Roscoe, "We'wha and Klah: The American Indian Berdache as Artist and Priest," *American Indian Quarterly* 12 (2) (1988): 127–50; idem, "That Is My Road: The Life and Times of a Crow Berdache," *Montana: The Magazine of Western History* 40 (1) (winter 1990): 46–55; and idem, *Zuni Man-Woman*.

8. For a listing of Native language terms by linguistic family, see the glossary in Roscoe, "Bibliography," 138–53.

9. Of course, many groups have no single term for "man" or "woman" as classes of persons but a set of terms for males and females at different points in life and in different relations to others. Similarly, the Cheyenne recognized not one but two categories of berdaches. The *heeman* (often written *hemaneh*) was a berdache "having more of the male element," whereas the *hetaneman* had "more of the female element." Rodolphe C. Petter, *English-Cheyenne Dictionary* (Kettle Falls, WA: n.p., 1915).

10. Beatrice Medicine, " 'Warrior Women'—Sex Role Alternatives for Plains Indian Women," in *The Hidden Half*, ed. Patricia Albers and Beatrice Medicine (Lanham, MD: University Press of America, 1983), 269.

11. Harriet Whitehead, "The Bow and the Burden Strap: A New Look at Institutionalized Homosexuality in Native North America," in *Sexual Meanings: The Cultural Construction of Gender and Sexuality*, ed. Sherry B. Ortner and Harriet Whitehead. (New York: Cambridge University Press, 1981), 90–93; Williams, *Spirit and the Flesh*, 11, 233–34.

12. Evelyn Blackwood, "Sexuality and Gender in Certain American Indian Tribes: The Case of Cross-Gender Females," *Signs: The Journal of Women in Culture and Society* 10 (1) (1984): 27–42, esp. 29.

13. Roscoe, *Zuni Man-Woman*, 27–28, 232.

14. This is certainly the case in Plains tribes, where references to women joining warfare-related activities are far more numerous than documented cases of female berdaches (see Medicine, "Warrior Women"). In other cases, female berdache status was one of a set of female role alternatives. The Mohave origin myth that accounts for the institution of the male berdache role opens with the creator god Mastamho assigning functions to four distinct categories of women: a mother, a midwife, a female shaman, who is not to marry (the female berdache or *hwame* was usually categorized as a shaman), and a "loose" or promiscuous woman (called *kamaluiy*, a type still recognized today). Alfred L. Kroeber, *More Mohave Myths*, Anthropological Records, no. 27 (Berkeley: University of California Press, 1972), 17–20. The latter is reminiscent of the deviant female status occupied among the Lakota by women who had dreams of the goddess Anuk Ite (Double Face or Double Woman, who also had the power to make men become berdaches). William K. Powers, *Oglala Religion* (Lincoln: University of Nebraska Press, 1977), 197. Seward identified a set of female role alternatives among the Northern Blackfeet similar to those of the Mohave: in the direction of variation by virtue were the roles of the *ninaki*, or favorite wife, and the Sun Dance woman, who is awarded the honor of hosting a Sun Dance in recognition of her uprightness; in the opposite direction were the roles of the *matsaps*, or crazy woman, and the *ninawaki*, or manly-hearted woman, who defied conventions for female decorum by competing and succeeding in male enterprises (without, however, becoming female berdaches, since they remained heterosexually married and never cross-dressed). Georgene H. Seward, *Sex and the Social Order* (New York: McGraw-Hill, 1946) 120–21.

15. The use of the term "gender" to specifically oppose the social to the natural dimensions of sex roles, and thereby question the relationship between them, is fairly recent. Haraway traces the current American usage of the term to the "gender identity" research of the psychoanalyst Robert Stoller beginning in the late 1950s. See Stoller, *Simians, Cyborgs, and Women: The Reinvention of Nature* (New York: Routledge, 1991), 133. See also Suzanne Kessler and Wendy McKenna, *Gender: An Ethnomethodological Approach* (Chicago: University of Chicago Press, 1985), 7.

16. See Judith Shapiro, "Transsexualism: Reflections on the Persistence of Gender and the Mutability of Sex," in *Body Guards: The Cultural Politics of Gender Ambiguity*, ed. Julia Epstein and Kristina Straub (New York: Routledge, 1991), 248–79.

17. Roscoe, *Zuni Man-Woman*, 132.

18. There is a burgeoning literature on all these subjects. For a cogent theoretical critique of the sex/gender binary, see Judith Butler, *Gender Trouble: Feminism and the Subversion of Identity* (New York: Routledge, 1990). For a survey of shifting definitions of sex in Western history, see Thomas Laqueur, *Making Sex: Body and Gender from the Greeks to Freud* (Cambridge: Harvard University Press, 1990).

19. See, for example, Whitehead, "The Bow and the Burden Strap."

20. Will Roscoe, "Making History: The Challenge of Lesbian and Gay Studies," *Journal of Homosexuality* 15 (3–4) (1988): 1–40.

21. I also proposed the concept of "sociosexual specialization" as a culturally neutral term defining a field of study concerned with homosexuality in the broadest sense—that is, encompassing its associations with gender variation as well as sexuality. This synthetic term helps avoid the pitfalls of deploying such ethnocentric categories as "the sexual" or "the erotic," which may not be universally relevant. Since writing this essay, James Clifford pointed out to me the relevance of Rodney Needham's work on polythetic classification, *Against the* Tranquility *of Axioms* (Berkeley: University of California Press, 1983).

22. Sylvia J. Yanagisako and Jane F. Collier, "Toward a Unified Analysis of Gender and Kinship," in *Gender and Kinship: Essays toward a Unified Analysis,* ed. Jane F. Collier and Sylvia J. Yanagisako (Stanford: Stanford University Press, 1987), p 44.

23. See, for example, J. Owen Dorsey, "A Study of Siouan Cults," in *Eleventh Annual Report of the Bureau of American Ethnology, 1889–1990* (Washington, DC: GPO, 1890), 379; Alice C. Fletcher and Francis La Flesche, "The Omaha Tribe," in *Twenty-seventh Annual Report of the Bureau of American Ethnology, 1905–1906* (Washington, DC: GPO, 1911), 133; John Treat Irving, Jr., *Indian Sketches Taken during an Expedition to the Pawnee Tribes, 1833,* ed. John F. McDermott (Norman: University of Oklahoma Press, 1955), 93–95; Victor Tixier, *Tixier's Travels on the Osage Prairies,* ed. John F. McDermott (Norman: University of Oklahoma Press, 1940), 234. Although Callender and Kochems present a table listing tribes in which childhood inclination determined berdache status and those in which visions were considered the precipitating factor, they acknowledge that these modes of entry were not necessarily exclusive. In fact, a close examination of case histories shows that berdache-specific dreams and visions typically served to confirm childhood preferences. Even when dreams were the primary precipitating factor, adoption of berdache occupations typically followed.

24. For sources, see Roscoe, "Bibliography"; idem, *Zuni Man-Woman,* 5.

25. See the analysis of this myth and notes on related data from Acoma, Laguna, and Hopi in Roscoe, *Zuni Man-Woman,* chap. 6 and pp. 251–52.

26. In the Lakota origin myth, for example, gender is weakly marked at the outset, and only over the course of a series of episodes does it emerge as a fully articulated principle of organization in the natural and social worlds. It is portrayed, in other words, as a historical construction (see Powers, *Oglala Religion*).

27. George Devereux, "Institutionalized Homosexuality of the Mohave Indians," *Human Biology* 9 (1937): 498–527.

28. For example, A. B. Holder, "The Bote: Description of a Peculiar Sexual Perversion found among North American Indians," *New York Medical Journal* (50) (23) (1889): 623–25, esp. 624.

29. Devereux, "Institutionalized Homosexuality," 522.

30. However, her name, literally "beautiful girl," is a male name—the kind a Mohave man might have who was lucky in attracting women, which was, in fact, the reason the *hwame* adopted it. Devereux's case study of this woman (in "Institutionalized Homosexuality"), like his other writings on Mohave culture and people, was strongly colored by his psychoanalytic orientation. See Gilbert Herdt, "Representations of Homosexuality: An Essay on Cultural Ontology and Historical Comparison," *Journal of the History of Sexuality* 1 (3): 481–504. Devereux portrays Masahay Matkwisa: (he usually refers to her as Sahaykwisa), who died sometime in the 1890s, as a maladjusted, self-destructive, violence-prone lesbian. Although Devereux's interpreter and key informant during his research in the 1930s, Agnes Sevilla, lived adjacent to Masahay Matkwisa:'s relatives, Devereux apparently never attempted to interview them concerning their *hwame* ancestor. In fact, Masahay Matkwisa: is remembered by contemporary Mohaves primarily as a powerful shaman who specialized in love magic, and not for her status as a *hwame*. Her demise was the result of an overextension, as it were, of her

shamanic practice—she had made too many enemies, human and supernatural, through her constant recourse to magical means of attracting lovers. Similarly, her involvement in prostitution is better understood in terms of the context of the times, when many Mohave women were engaging in sporadic "survival sex" to obtain desperately needed cash or goods. Michael Tsosie, personal communication.

31. Devereux, "Institutionalized Homosexuality," 510.

32. Ibid., 519.

33. Herman Grey, *Tales from the Mohaves* (Norman: University of Oklahoma Press, 1970), 10.

34. Devereux, "Institutionalized Homosexuality," 503.

35. Kroeber, *More Mohave Myths*, 17–20.

36. Herdt, "Representations of Homosexuality," 494.

37. See, for example, Anne Bolin, *In Search of Eve: Transsexual Rites of Passage* (South Hadley: Bergin and Garvey, 1988). This appears to be changing, however. Some transsexuals, for political and personal reasons, are choosing not to assimilate to the "opposite sex," freely acknowledging their previous lives in another gender and rejecting traditional images of femininity. See Sandy Stone, "The *Empire* Strikes Back: A Posttranssexual Manifesto," in *Body Guards*, ed. Epstein and Straub, 280–304.

38. Mohave men and women painted their faces with gender-specific designs. According to Devereux, *alyha* painted their faces with female patterns. However, in the origin myth instituting the *alyha* initiation rite recorded by Kroeber, the face of the initiate is painted with a design that consists of "a vertical stripe down from each eye and another down the nose to the mouth." Elsewhere, Kroeber illustrates this design and labels it a *male* style. Kroeber, *More Mohave Myths*, 20; *Handbook of the Indians of California* (New York: Dover, 1976), 730, fig. 60a; Edith S. Taylor and William J. Wallace, "Mohave Tattooing and Face-Painting," *Masterkey* 21 (6) (1947), fig. 6a. Similarly, although male berdaches assumed female personal names, they did not assume the clan name borne by all the women within a lineage.

39. Devereux, "Institutionalized Homosexuality," 514.

40. Ibid., 498–99. Devereux describes the case of a Mohave man who engaged in both active and receptive anal intercourse while in prison but was not considered a berdache. See also the interview with a gay Mohave man who specialized in crafts and was teased but accepted by other Mohaves. Bob Waltrip, "Elmer Gage: American Indian," *ONE Magazine* 13 (3) (1965): 6–10.

7

The Hijras of India

Serena Nanda

The Hijras of India are a religious community of men who dress and act like women and whose culture centers on the worship of Bahuchara Mata, one of the many versions of the mother goddess worshipped throughout India. In connection with this worship, Hijras undergo a ritual surgery in which their genitals are removed.

This operation—and that is the word they use, the English word—defines them as Hijras, neither man nor woman, or alternately, as sacred female men. Through their identification with the mother goddess and the female creative power she embodies, Hijras have a special place in Indian culture and society. As neither men nor women, themselves unable to create life, they function as an institutionalized alternative gender role of ritual performers, and this is the basis of their traditional occupation. They perform after the birth of a child, traditionally a male child—these days, sometimes, a female child—and also at weddings, both occasions that have an obvious connection to fertility.

Hijras are identified with other ascetics and are regarded with the same ambivalence. They are persons who, while auspicious, are also feared for their powers to curse; like other ascetics, they are also regarded with skepticism regarding their authenticity. Unlike many other ascetics, however, Hijras lead their daily lives within their own highly structured social communities, and their position in Indian society shares features of both a caste within society and renounced ones outside it.

The connection of Hijras with transvestism and the associated flamboyant sexuality may be a source of the stigmatization; in spite of the widespread belief in the Hijras' supernatural powers as sacred men, they do elicit some open ridicule and contempt. This stigmatization works in their favor in an economic sense, however. Being at the bottom of the social ladder, Hijras have nothing to lose in terms of respectability and prestige, and their outrageous behavior, most notably lifting their skirts and exposing their mutilated genitals, along with their perfected verbal abuse when insulted, serves as an effective means by which to extort money from their audiences.

I have only begun to study the relationship between the Hijras as a third gender and male homosexuality. In Hindu culture, male and female are seen as natural categories in complementary opposition. The model of this opposition is biological and essential, but it includes criteria that in the West we would ascribe to gender. Males and females are born with different sexual characteristics and reproductive organs, they have different sexual natures, and they take different and complementary roles in marriage, sex, and reproduction. This essential (in Indian terms) male/female dichotomy is expressed in medical and ritual texts, where bodily fluids and sexual organs are presented as both the major sources of sex and gender dichotomy and its major symbols. However, although each sex is conceptualized as having an essential, innate nature, consisting of physical and moral qualities, these are also alterable, and, indeed, the interchange of male and female qualities, transformations of sex and gender, and alternative sex and gender roles among deities and humans are positive and meaningful themes in Hindu mythology, ritual, and art.

This theme gives meaning to various kinds of sex and gender behavior of actual living individuals in India. The major cultural conceptualization of Hijras as neither man nor woman has nothing to do with male homosexuality. Rather, it is based on the model of the hermaphrodite, a biologically intersexed person. The word "Hijra" is a masculine noun, most widely translated into English as either "eunuch" or "hermaphrodite," suggesting that Hijras are primarily thought of as men who become like women, though females who do not menstruate can also become Hijras. The glosses "eunuch" and "hermaphrodite" both emphasize sexual impotence, which is understood in India to mean a physical defect, impairing the male sexual function both in intercourse (in the inserter role) and in reproductive ability.

Sometimes the word "Hijra," however, is used as a term of stigmatization that implies, though it is not equivalent to, *zenanna*, which literally means "woman," but which connotes a man who has sex with other men in the receptor role. The term "Hijra" is never used in connection with men who have sexual relations with other men or with Hijras in the inserter role, a behavior that is not linguistically distinguished in India. It is thus sexual impotence with women (that is, a defective male organ and the lack of sexual desire for women), not sexual relations with men, that defines the Hijra. As Hijras say, "Never has a Hijra looked upon a woman with a bad eye. We are like bullocks, castrated cattle."

Hijras may be man minus man, or female sacred men, as they transform a negative quality of impotence into a positive female creative power through emasculation, but Hijra identity is never conceptualized as a particular kind of sexual activity or emotional attachment between two men. Indeed, the emasculation ritual is a form of denial of any sexual desire and activity, and Hijras' powers, like those of other ascetics, derive from this total renunciation of sexuality. Where a homoerotic attachment is declared on the part of an individual Hijra, they derive it from a complete gender transformation, that is from man to woman, more similar to a Western construction of transsexualism, than what has been called "male homosexuality."

Homoeroticism, thus, is not part of—is indeed contrary to—the cultural identification of the Hijra. And yet in real life—on the ground, so to speak— there are, I think, some interesting relationships between being a Hijra and male homosexuality. In examining the question of the relationship between the Hijra as a third gender and male homosexuality, one finds a contradiction. If Hijras are men who become something else, then their sexual relationships with men are not really homosexual. I understand that, but I do not have the vocabulary yet to say it any other way. Recruitment to the Hijra community, to the feminine role behavior involved in being a Hijra, and to prostitution is in part related to sexual and erotic attachments of Hijras to men.

There is a widespread belief in India that Hijras recruit their membership by making successful claims on intersexed infants who they come across in their ritual performances for the birth of a boy child. As part of those performances they hold the infant in their arms and rock it and sing certain songs, but in the meantime they also examine its genitals. In fact, some people say that this is the whole purpose of the Hijra performance, to wit, to locate boys born with anomalous genitals and take them away to grow up as Hijras. Newspapers frequently play on this belief by headlining articles about Hijras' "kidnappings" of infants and children.

None of the Hijra personal narratives I have recorded substantiate this claim. Rather, individuals indicate that they join the community in their youth, in preadolescence or early adolescence, either out of a desire to more fully express their feminine gender identity (including the pleasure gained in the receptor role in sexual relations with men), under the pressure of poverty, because of ill-treatment by their parents and peers for feminine behavior, after a period of prostitution, or a combination of all these reasons. All the Hijras I met who were or had been prostitutes said that they had engaged in sexual relations with men in the receptor role during their adolescence, and that this "spoiled" them for heterosexual relationships when they got older.

The term "spoiled" has a physical and social meaning. It is widely believed in India that frequent participation in the sexually receptive role with a male partner will cause "the nerve in the male organ to break, so that it is no longer good for sex with a woman." This physical defect, then, denies them the chance to live their lives as full men—that is, in Indian terms, marrying and fathering children—so that becoming a Hijra is in some ways an attractive alternative lifestyle. It seems to me, in view of the fact that some Hijras *have* married and fathered children, that this reference to having been "spoiled" is not necessarily the way it was, but an explanation informed by hindsight, an adult's interpretation of something that may have been experienced quite differently in adolescence.

In any case, the pleasure that an individual gets from being in the receptive role in a male/male relationship may be an important step for some in becoming Hijra. But by no means do all "passive homosexuals" in India become Hijras.

So I am not in any way viewing this as *the* cause or even a main cause in Hijra recruitment. The process of becoming a Hijra is, in any case, a gradual one, and sexual attachment to men is only one of the—again, in their terms— "feminine-related" activities it draws upon. Hijras are required, when they become Hijras, to exhibit various kinds of feminine behavior. They must wear their hair long like women, wear female clothing and accessories, behave modestly, like women (except in their performances, which real women would never do), do women's work, and dance in approximation of women. Many Hijras I spoke to discussed these aspects of the feminine role, as well as—and in their mind it is connected—enjoyment of the role of the "passive partners" for men in sex (something that is a source of positive pleasure to them, congenial to their desires), reporting an attachment to these behaviors in their early childhood.

For these Hijras, the emasculation operation is a way for them to become physically as much like women as possible, so that they could "have sex from the front"—which they really do not, but say they do—like other women. Their becoming Hijras was very much tied to their wish to have long-term sexual, emotional, and familial relationships with men. In fact, partly because Hijras are outside the structure of social obligation and arranged marriage, which is the norm in India, some of these Hijras express more feelings of romantic love than is generally true of Indian wives. There is variation on a continuum here. Some Hijras who take on many aspects of the feminine role, including a positive feeling about having sex with men, do not undergo emasculation, and many of them seem drawn to the respectability and status of being a wife rather than to the erotic possibilities (which is, of course, true for many heterosexual women as well—another complication).

In spite of the centrality of the renunciation of sexual desire and sexual activity to the definition of Hijras and other ascetics, prostitution is, in fact, a very important way that many Hijras earn their living, acting as sexual receptors for men. I might say that the Hijras do not conceive of their male partners as in any way homosexual. This is not even distinguished linguistically, and when they talk about their value to men as sexual partners, they talk in terms of themselves as women, not as Hijras or males.

So, what to call them? Language becomes, again, problematic here. When one considers the situation of so many desperately destitute children in India, one can see that prostitution, within the context of the protected Hijra culture, can in some way be considered an economic step up, and of course prostitution is not about love and attachment, necessarily, but sex and money. I think this really has not been given enough consideration, at least with regard to the Hijras. However, beyond economics, some Hijras do, in fact, see their commercial relationships with men as at least not contrary to their erotic preferences, and through these commercialized relationships, they do hope to meet a man with whom they can develop a more emotionally satisfying, long-term relationship.

In fact, one of the problems of the "madams" in Hijra houses of prostitution is that whenever the "girls" get a chance to meet a man who would like to have this kind of relationship, they tend to want to run away. Some Hijras are quite frank about the sexually satisfying aspect of their work, and in fact are cynically dismissive of any other reason for becoming a Hijra. Hijras find various ways to cope with their ambivalence about the contradiction between the religious requirements of their role and the actuality that many Hijra lives involve sexual relations with men. On the "propaganda" level, for example, Hijras speaking publicly for the community always disavow the connection between being a Hijra and prostitution, or at most justify it in terms of the increasing constraints on their traditional ways of making a living in the modern world, where nobody appreciates their supernatural powers.

It seems, then, that the relationship between homosexuality and the Hijras as a third gender is complicated. At the level of cultural conceptualization, the two are not related—indeed, the power of the third gender is negated by any sexual behavior. But if we examine how individuals become Hijras, how they relate to their own gender identities as Hijras in the present or in the past, and the economic importance of prostitution, we see a relationship that does, I think, need to be acknowledged and discussed. This is part of the ambivalence toward Hijras on the part of their audiences, and the source of much of the overt public ridicule and contempt, which is displayed mainly by young men, people they call "rowdies."

No respectable Indian would ever dare confront a Hijra, because of the embarrassment over what the Hijras might do in response to insult or skepticism about their authenticity. In India today, there is a more open discussion of male homosexuality, and it will be interesting to see what, if any, influence the dissemination of the gay culture from the West will have on the Hijra identity in India.

Note

In allowing the presentation I gave on the hijras at the 1993 CLAGS conference "At The Frontier: Homosexuality and the Social Sciences" to be included in this volume, I wish to emphasize that this is basically the transcription of a talk rather than a fully articulated paper. A far more detailed account can be found in Serena Nanda, *Neither Man Nor Woman: The Hijras of India* (Belmont: Wadsworth, 1990). My work on the hijras is ongoing; from my continuing interviews with hijras, I see that with the increasing interest in India in gay culture in the West, an increasing identification of hijras with modern gay culture is appearing in the popular press. The impact on traditional hijra culture cannot yet be determined.

8

Are Modern Western Lesbian Women and Gay Men a Third Gender?

Randolph Trumbach

Are modern Western lesbian women and gay men members of a third gender? Do they in their society play the role that the berdache did among the Native North Americans and that the Hijra still plays in certain parts of contemporary Indian culture? In this question there lurk several further and quite difficult questions. For example, is there such a thing as sexual orientation, and can it be found in all times and places? Is this the biological orthodoxy of human bodies: true in all times, in all places, and among all peoples? The historian's answer is a resounding no. There is in nature no such thing as sexual orientation. It is instead the way modern Western culture has described its own third-gender role. But one of the difficulties in studying third-gender roles in different times and cultures is that the wide distribution of the phenomenon across time and place can clumsily be taken for evidence precisely that in all times and places there has been a minority of adult effeminate males (and to a lesser degree, of adult masculinized women) who were passive in sexual intercourse with other males. These then become the proof that nature or biology makes homosexuals and that this will someday be demonstrated if only we look (according to the generation of the scientist) at the right hormone, the right chromosome, or the right structure in the brain.[1]

The first step out of these difficulties is to notice that while some societies have had individuals who constituted a minority third gender of effeminate men or masculinized women, in other societies, sexual desire between biological males (and to a lesser degree between biological females) has been organized around differences in age, and all members of society—not just a minority—participated.[2] Age-structured homosexual behavior is perhaps best known from the cultures of the ancient Mediterranean world. But in both Greece and Rome, in the midst of a system of sexual relations between males one of whom was adult and active and the other adolescent and passive, there were some adult effeminate males. Some scholars take these individuals and declare them the true homosexual biological minority, present at all times and places. But what never seems to be explained in biological terms is the sexual attraction between the majority of the adult men and the boys. Are we to presume that there is a chromosome or a structure of the brain that predisposes all adult men to desire adolescent youths? If the answer is no, then this behavior must be explained in cultural terms. That being so, the behavior of the minority of adult effeminate males in a sexual system in which most adult males have relations with adolescents must also be explained in cultural terms.

The easiest explanation is proposed by Eva Cantarella, who maintains that the minority of adult effeminate males in ancient Greece and Rome were men who had failed to make the transition from the passive to the active role in their early twenties. This was probably always a difficult transition to make in age-structured systems, and these cultural anxieties in ancient Greece can be seen in Theognis's advice to Kurnos to get on with the transition and find a wife. In a quite different time and place, the same anxieties were expressed in the age-structured relations of Renaissance England when Shakespeare in his sonnets also advised his young man to get on with the business of finding a wife. Boys who failed to make this transition became the adult effeminate men of age-structured systems of homosexual behavior.[3]

These men, however, should be sharply distinguished from the adult effeminate men in systems of homosexual behavior structured around the existence of a third-gender role. In third-gender systems the majority of males never undergo a period of sexual passivity, whereas in age-structured societies all males undergo such a period. Instead, in third-gender systems adolescent males and adult males take the active sexual role with the minority of adult effeminate males. Members of this effeminate minority have been deliberately socialized since childhood to grow up to play the role of the passive adult male. Their adult identity is therefore not the result of a failure on their part to make a transition to their appropriate adult role; in contrast, the effeminacy of adult males in age-structured systems is most assuredly the result of a failed transition from a passive adolescence to an active manhood.[4]

With these distinctions in mind we can now turn to the original question of whether modern Western lesbian women and gay men are members of a third gender. The answer can be found in the history of the modern Western homosexual role as it looks when it is placed, first, in the context of the worldwide variations of age-structured and gender-structured homosexual behavior, and, second, in the context of the history of modern Western gender relations. The modern homosexual role for men first appeared in the early eighteenth century. Mary McIntosh was the first to propose this in her famous article of 1968. Unfortunately she did not try to say what form of homosexual behavior had preceded the role before 1700. With even greater misfortune for historical clarity, a single undocumented paragraph by Michel Foucault in the 1976 introduction to his history of sexuality has led his followers to plunge like lemmings into a sea of error. According to Foucault, before the late nineteenth-century discourse on homosexuality, there was only sodomy, a thoroughly confused category that included many forms of behavior and did not stigmatize anyone with a specific homosexual role.[5]

The amazing thing about this statement is, of course, that Foucault argued very strongly in the rest of his book that what seemed to him the repressive structures of modern Western sexuality first appeared in the early eighteenth century. But he did not tie homosexual behavior to this early eighteenth-century transformation; instead he discussed the rise of the literature against masturbation. In doing this he probably reflected the experience of Catholic adolescents in the post-Tridentine world, who were likely to be vigorously questioned about masturbation in the confessional but not about homosexuality, on the prudential grounds that one ought not to suggest possibilities to the innocent and that if one stopped masturbation, one stopped all other sexual transgressions. Some such personal reason is certainly necessary to explain why it never occurred to Foucault to place the modern structures of homosexual behavior in the early eighteenth century where Mary McIntosh had located them eight years before. But McIntosh's vagueness about the nature of homosexual behavior before 1700 also promoted the idea of an unstructured sexual world before 1700 that could be approximated to the more explicit golden age of sexuality that Foucault saw before 1700. She certainly misled me into arguing, in my 1977 article on the two patterns of age-structured and gender-structured homosexuality, that there was a third Western model that was neither of these, and as a consequence I misread what was then the slight amount of work on Western homosexual behavior before 1700. But two years before his death Foucault seems to have changed his mind, and in an interview that many of his followers have yet to deal with, said that homosexuality became a problem in the early eighteenth century.[6]

Two points now follow from this. First, the modern homosexual role newly appeared in the generation after 1700. This has been extensively documented for the Netherlands by Dirk Jaap Noordam and Theo van der Meer, for France by the late Michel Rey, and for England by myself. To this literature I will return, since it makes clear that modern Western homosexual males were members of a third gender. The second point is, however, that this change after 1700 cannot be understood unless one has a very clear view of what the structures of Western homosexual behavior were before 1700. Once these structures before 1700 are firmly described, Foucault's idea of a vague confused sodomitical category before 1700 will finally be destroyed in the minds of scholars.[7]

The clearest description of Western homosexual behavior before 1700 has been given by Michael Rocke in his work on Florence in the fourteenth and fifteenth centuries. Rocke found that in the late fifteenth century, one in every four Florentine males was arrested for sodomy at least once between the ages of fifteen and thirty and that some males were arrested many times. These figures give us reasonable grounds for saying that homosexual behavior was universal among Florentine males. Rocke's figures also show, however, that this behavior was very strictly structured by age. Boys between fifteen and nineteen were always arrested for being sexually passive. Young men between twenty-three and thirty were always arrested for being sexually active. In the transitional age group between nineteen and twenty-three, the same youth could be either active or passive, but when he was active it was always with a younger boy, and when he was passive it was always with an older man. There was no evidence of adult effeminate men who were sexually passive. No other European society has evidence quite of this quality before 1700. But what there is in the rest of Europe by and large supports the idea that the Florentine pattern was the usual European pattern of homosexual behavior before 1700.[8]

In France, Spain, and Portugal (which have the best records outside of Italy), sexual relations were in most cases between active men and passive adolescents. But there were a few adult effeminate men, who ought not, however, to be interpreted as the "true" homosexuals of their societies, but rather as men who had failed to make the transition from passive boy to active man.[9] I do not know why such effeminate adult men do not appear in the Florentine material. The evidence for England and the Netherlands is sparse for the period before 1700, but what there is in the way of trial records, literary texts, and biographical material supports the pattern of relations between active men and passive boys. It is interesting to observe that scholars who work on the literary evidence from England, whether Bruce Smith, Alan Bray, Jonathan Goldberg, or Gregory Bredbeck, do their level best to ignore the age-structured, or as they would tend to say, the pederastical nature of the behavior in their sources. They quote lines about sex between men and boys and then immediately, or within a line or two, transform this into evidence for sexual relations between two adult men. Steve Brown is a sole distinguished exception to this practice. Pederasty is intensely embarrassing to twentieth-century gay men who wish to find people rather like themselves in the high canonical texts of our literature. But the effeminacy of modern homosexual men when they enact their third-gender role seems to be equally embarrassing to an amateur historian like Rictor Norton when he tries to describe eighteenth-century London, or to Gert Hekma in his work on the nineteenth-century Dutch. There is, however, even greater resistance to any attempt to show the continued importance of effeminacy in Western gay communities after 1950, when presumably we all became egalitarian and masculine. Indeed, no paper of mine has ever received so pained a reaction as the one in which I have tried to show that at the heart of gay S/M is a ritual process in which one man transforms another into a woman. These political reactions against pederasty and effeminacy make the work of scholarly analysis much harder, though not perhaps as hard as does the presumption of a biological cause.[10]

The evidence for Europe before 1700 allows one to say quite firmly that homosexual behavior was not in that earlier period organized around a third-gender role played out by adult effeminate men. Instead it was organized around differences in age. The arrest records for England, the Netherlands, and France plainly show, on the other hand, that almost all the men arrested after 1700 for homosexual behavior could reasonably be described as members of a third gender. The evidence for women is more problematical since they were seldom arrested.[11] But to establish the presence of a third-gender role attached to homosexual behavior one needs to be able to describe four things: first, how were individuals socialized into such a role; second, what was the nature of their effeminacy or their masculinized behavior; third, who were the sexual companions of these individuals; and finally, what was the public reception given to the role. Establishing these things makes it possible to say more firmly that after 1700 Europe moved from a system of age-structured homosexual behavior to one organized around the presence of a third-gender role.

Socialization into a third-gender role is the hardest of these four to show historically. There are no accounts like those from Native North American in which parents prepared their children for their future roles. For eighteenth-century England there are texts that say that effeminate boys who played with dolls and boys who were beautiful and delicate, and therefore treated like girls, grew up to be adult effeminate sodomites. But there are other texts that tried to explain the effeminacy and sodomitical desires of men with large, powerful bodies. These are issues, however, that are not easily resolved even by the much better evidence produced by the observation of individuals in the twentieth century. The best eighteenth-century evidence for socialization is negative and indirect. It comes from the legal cases in which adolescents accused adult men of making sexual overtures or forcing sex on them. Some boys fled on being touched, some could tolerate a single sexual encounter but then became profoundly revolted, and a few boys (presumably those who became sodomites) seemed more or less willing until a third party forced the issue. Adolescents were clearly no longer socialized to go through a period of sexual passivity with older men as they must have been in Renaissance Italy. And among adolescents themselves, the new literature against masturbation (of which Foucault made so much, but without tying it to homosexuality) shows that they were strongly discouraged from any experimentation with each other. Sodomy and self-abuse were the Scylla and Charybdis between which eighteenth-century men were to navigate until they came into the safe sea of women's bodies.[12]

The effeminacy of the adult male sodomite is much more easily established than the nature of his socialization. A few men like the Princess Seraphina spent long periods of time in women's clothes and were usually referred to as she and her. But even the Princess sometimes dressed as a man. Many men must have shown no signs of effeminacy until they entered the safe environment of the molly-house, where they could camp and use their female names. Their neighbors were often surprised therefore to learn of their sodomitical identity. The third-gender role in modern Western societies is therefore unlike that in more traditional societies in that it is often not publicly displayed by those who have been socialized into it. On the other hand, some men could be recognized in the street by their effeminacy and blackmailed. It clearly would have made life easier to conceal their identity, but they presumably were unable to do so. This raises a difficult but interesting question that must once again be related to variations in socialization among third-gender men.

The third-gender role in Western societies is, however, entirely dominated by this variation between private and public spheres. Practically all men and many women knew that effeminate sodomites existed. But sodomites could safely enact their role only within the subculture of covert meeting places. Some of these places like the molly-house where sodomites met each other were much safer than those like the public park or the public latrine. But the attraction of the park and the latrine was that they allowed sodomites to have sexual encounters with men who were not sodomites. Western third-gender men, therefore, had sex both with each other and with men from outside their group, whereas the Hijra and the berdache found their partners entirely from outside their groups.

The patterns of third-gender behavior that have been established for a minority of Western males in the eighteenth century has continued down into the twentieth century. It is unfortunately difficult to show this for the nineteenth century since scholars like Jeffrey Weeks and Gert Hekma have tended to study the late nineteenth-century discussions of homosexual behavior and to ignore the patterns of actual behavior in the subculture. Weeks has produced some material for England, and Michael Sibalis and William Peniston have very recently published studies of France that establish that the patterns of behavior that Michel Rey described for eighteenth-century Paris were present in the nineteenth century both in Paris and in provincial towns. But the recent work on the twentieth century by Weeks, Hekma, George Chauncey, and Elizabeth Kennedy and Madeline Davis establish with certainty the continuity over three centuries of a third-gender role for both women and men in Western Europe and North America.[13]

Weeks's book is composed of fifteen interviews with older homosexual men selected from twenty-five he conducted in 1978–79 with the purpose of exploring the development of homosexual subcultures and identities. The interviews mainly document life in London, since most of the men were either born in London or came there to escape life in the provinces. London for homosexual men played its usual dominating role in British culture. But there are occasional glimpses of homosexual life in places like Liverpool, Aberdeen, and Wales, which show that the London patterns existed elsewhere and document a third-gender role that cannot be tied to either urban conditions or metropolitan life. The memories start just before World War I and continue through the beginnings of gay liberation in the 1970s but tell mainly of the period between the two world wars. Six of the men were working-class, four lower-middle-class, and five upper-middle-class. The men who were most informative about life in the subculture were working-class. Some men objected to the term "gay" as American and misleading and preferred "queer" or the expression being "so." But it is also apparent that relatively few Englishmen between the two world wars conceived of themselves in terms of the homosexual identity that the high culture had begun to produce in the late nineteenth century.[14]

This independence of life in the subculture from the norms of the high culture meant that the subculture was déclassé. One very class-conscious man explained that his acceptance of his homosexuality was long delayed by his concern that homosexual sex was something one did with inferior people. Men who acted out the homosexual role most fully in public by effeminate movement, the use of women's names, and transvestism were working-class prostitutes, some of whose customers were probably heterosexual men—a pattern that went back to the eighteenth century. On the other hand, young middle-class men who had not yet become conscious of their identity sometimes acted with an unconscious effeminacy in public that allowed them to be confidently seduced by older men who were already active in the subculture. This suggests that their internalization of their role had occurred during the years that they lived with their families and long before their entrance into the subculture. There was a rigid categorization of homosexual men before World War II into either active or passive (butch or bitch) roles in the sexual act. This categorization was carried furthest by homosexual men who had as sexual partners only men who were married then or eventually to women. They classified these partners as not being homosexual and always took with them what they thought to be the feminine role. But some homosexual men married women, before they realized their exclusive interest in men, or as a means to cure such an interest, sometimes under "therapeutic" intervention. Some men insisted that they had been "born" with their desires, which can be carelessly interpreted as evidence for a biological cause, or more discriminatingly used to argue for a deep unconscious socialization.

Middle-class men were more likely to move in private networks than in the more open world of pubs and private clubs, cinemas and theater galleries; no one mentioned the parks. But some isolated middle-class men never found anyone to introduce them into a network and all their lives used only the more dangerous world of "cottaging" or sex in public toilets, where they were subject to arrest and were unlikely to find a long-time partner, but where presumably they could hope to encounter the occasional heterosexual man. Men of all classes formed partnerships that lasted from seven to thirty years. They were either exclusive or open relationships, and either largely secret or fully endorsed by their families and their heterosexual friends. Some men never entered into such relationships; others preceded or followed them with periods of living alone. There were sometimes gay marriages with one man dressed as the bride (a custom going back to early eighteenth-century Paris and London), but these seem really to have been more send-ups than genuine. Two of the men in 1978 did call for the legalization of gay marriages, and one man insisted that he had always sought love, not sex.

From this it is evident that the male homosexual role was as much influenced by the ideology of romantic marriage and separate male and female spheres as any other part of the modern Western gender system. After 1970 the gay liberation movement attempted to gain public legitimacy for this despised role. It succeeded to the extent that some London schools began to teach children that homosexual couples could legitimately form families. But the mass of the English public and the parliamentary elite rejected this challenge to the modern gender system. Earlier in the post–World War II period the elite had accepted the decriminalization of private homosexual behavior, which they apparently found compatible with the maintenance of the gender system, though the general public did not.[15]

The patterns found in Western Europe since the eighteenth century have so far not been clearly established in the United States for the eighteenth and nineteenth centuries. But George Chauncey's book on early twentieth-century New York City establishes the presence in the United States of a Western male third-gender role that by then must have been two centuries old and shows that there was a common culture on both sides of the North Atlantic world. The first and most original part of the book analyzes the sexual interaction before 1940 of "normal" men with "queers" and "fairies." He is especially interested in the Italian and Irish men who had sex with effeminate male prostitutes, only some of whom were transvestites. Jewish men were much less likely to engage in such relations. This discussion is very valuable, since usually in the anthropological and historical studies of third-gender males like the American berdache or the Indian Hijra, their sexual partners from the majority are never discussed. Chauncey's working-class Italians and Irishmen engaged in homosexual relations without having a homosexual identity. Middle-class Anglo-American men, on the other hand, did not. Chauncey sees the difference as one of class. But it is possible that the Italian men came from a Mediterranean culture in which sexual relations between men and boys were still licit, and that this made their sexual interaction with "queers" easier. The case of an Italian boy who had sex with a man is understood by Chauncey and his American source in terms of the effeminate role, but the dynamic was probably one of differences in age. The Irish are a harder case, since we know nothing of homosexual relations in Ireland, especially before the Famine. Chauncey does not discuss the interaction of poor "normal" Anglo-Americans with "fairies" who were prostitutes.[16]

There were two other kinds of sexual interaction between "normal" men and gay ones. The tough young male prostitute whose customer was a "queer" reverses the dynamic that occurred between the "fairy" prostitute and the "normal" man, but he unfortunately is not discussed in the first part of Chauncey's book and makes only a brief later appearance, even though both types of male prostitution can be found from the eighteenth century onwards.

Chauncey also mentions but does not analyze the many cases in which gay men were prosecuted for sexual relations with "normal" boys who were not prostitutes. The effeminate male prostitute was, however, the average man's idea of a "queer." This was difficult for gay middle-class men to accept, but it is unlikely as Chauncey suggests that this was anything new, since prosperous men had faced this difficulty for two centuries. But the "fairy" prostitute did eventually become marginalized in gay culture after 1940. And in the last generation such individuals sometimes have identified themselves with the newly created medical category of the transsexual who is not supposed to be a gay man at all.

In the second part of his book Chauncey describes in dazzling detail the social world gay men made for themselves in the rooming houses, YMCAs, and apartment buildings where they lived and the cafeterias where they ate. He contrasts their relatively dangerous sexual encounters in parks, streets, and public toilets, where violence from "normal" men and arrest by the police were always a possibility, with a fascinating chapter on the development of gay bathhouses, which the police did not raid and where all sexual encounters were necessarily with other gay men.

The third-gender role among American women in twentieth-century Buffalo, New York, is vividly described by Elizabeth Kennedy and Madeline Davis. They argue for the appearance in the 1950s of a new kind of butch, who dressed in working-class male clothes most of the time, went to the bar every day, and fought back when provoked by straights or lesbians. This limited her economic opportunities. Such a woman worked in a factory, drove a cab, tended bar, or pimped. She was likely to be arrested because of her public violence. Kennedy and Davis insist that it was from such experience that there grew a sense that lesbians were a distinct people who deserved better treatment; they claim that the gay liberation movement had its roots in such a culture, and that the defiant spirit of the liberation movement was therefore not simply copied from the student and the Black Power movements. It is possible that they are right, but they do not really show that individuals from this bar culture became active in the liberation movement.[17]

The butch women of the 1950s were masculine, but not like men, and not at all like passing women, who could not be distinguished from men and who were known to the lesbian community but not part of it. Butches wore pants. They cut their hair short. Those who had large breasts camouflaged them. Some wore men's underclothes but others did not. But the butch was as much identified by her mannerisms as by her clothes—the way she walked, sat, held a drink, her tone of voice, her unfamiliarity with traditional female manners. When one butch was handed a purse during a police raid to help her against a charge of public transvestism, she carried it like a football. A butch took the active role in sex, but Kennedy and Davis insist that her aim was to give pleasure to a femme and that in this she differed from the heterosexual male's pursuit of his own pleasure. The butch ideal was to be untouchable herself, to give pleasure but not to receive it, to keep her clothes on in bed, to experience spontaneous orgasm, to be a "stone butch." In practice many butches were otherwise, and one wonders how new the ideal was in the light of Anne Lister's description of her sexual preferences in the early nineteenth century. The adoption of these clothes and manners was not simply a consequence of living in the lesbian world. A girl in a reform school was able to enact most of this behavior on her own. The behavior was therefore very probably the consequence of a gender role into which women had been socialized in childhood.[18]

It is striking that Kennedy and Davis do not give a systematic description of the role of the femme. It makes their book really a history of the butch role. This is of some consequence since lesbians came in butch/femme dyads. The omission is no doubt partly the result of having interviewed too few femmes. But the dominance of the butch is also the result of the relationship between the homosexual minority and the heterosexual majority that is the subject of the last and most interesting chapter of the book. In that chapter Kennedy and Davis argue by drawing on a distinction of George Chauncey's that homosexual identity among lesbians in Buffalo, and generally in Western culture, changed in the 1940s and 1950s from one based on gender identity to one based on object choice. By this they mean that in the older paradigm the butch was unmistakably homosexual or "queer" but the femme was not, and that in the newer paradigm femmes as well as butches considered themselves gay or lesbian. Kennedy and Davis claim that increasing sexual awareness in the general culture of all women allowed lesbian women to develop an identity based on sexual feelings; it was no longer necessary to use masculine behavior to mark sexual identity.[19]

Femmes were not separated from most women by their femininity; only contact with the lesbian community or involvement in a lesbian relationship made them different. While butches were likely to feel that they had been born gay, femmes had to acquire their identity. Women were likely to come out as femmes and then turn butch—"today's love affair is tomorrow's competition"—a neat inversion of the gay male situation in which the active man became a queen—"today's trade is tomorrow's competition." The difficulty with this argument is that Kennedy and Davis say repeatedly that butch/femme roles became more rigid at precisely the moment that the switch from a homosexuality of gender inversion to one of object choice occurred. They suggest that adherence to the two roles was a response to the decreasing importance of gender in lesbian identity, but this seems odd since surely butch/femme roles are forms of gender behavior, and if they are not, Kennedy and Davis do not adequately explain what they are instead.

The solution to this conundrum probably lies in a different conceptualization of the transition that ties it to changing relations with the heterosexual majority. Until 1950 lesbians were butches—members of a third gender who combined elements of male and female behavior—and like third genders in other societies, they could feel that they sought their sexual partners from among the general population of ordinary feminine women. After 1950, however, all women who had sexual relations with other women were likely to view themselves as part of a subculture, and a lesbian's preferred partner was no longer a straight woman but another lesbian who could be identified by her membership in the subculture. The lesbian world had begun to separate itself from its previous integration with the straight world, and in the context of that separation, the rigid adherence to butch/femme roles became the means of stabilizing the community. It is also likely, however, that femmes came to share to some degree the sense of gender difference that the butch had always had, and it would be important to look for evidence of this.

The likelihood of such a transition in the lesbian world is reinforced by a parallel change in the male gay world. Gert Hekma has argued that until the 1950s in the Netherlands, the preferred partner of an effeminate man or queen was a "real" man or a straight man. Queens went to gay bars to socialize with each other and then left for the toilets to pick up straight men, though in practice they must often have settled for another gay man. Beginning in the 1950s, however, gay men went to bars to pick up other gay men for sex. Hekma, like Kennedy and Davis, would also argue that in this context, gender became less important. In the male world (where there was no dyadic structure parallel to butch/femme) this would have meant that the effeminacy of gay men became less marked.[20]

But I am skeptical about the decline in effeminacy. Some forms of public effeminacy probably did disappear, but all men in the subculture continued to be concerned, no matter whether they were tops or bottoms (the current New York jargon—does it show a revival of role playing or is it evidence that it never disappeared?), about the possibility that they might display effeminate behavior. One could therefore argue that when the gay male world separated itself from the straight world after 1950, because their preferred sexual partner was no longer a straight man, all homosexual men became queens. The importance of effeminacy was therefore heightened, not lessened, and this would exactly parallel the reinforcement of butch/femme roles in the lesbian community of the 1950s. One can even argue that the growth of a leather and S/M community among men—which is often cited as evidence for the decline of effeminacy—demonstrated the continued importance of male/female roles since at the heart of S/M there was a ritual process in which one gay man transformed another into a woman.[21]

But whatever the role of gender in the new homosexual community that emerged in the 1950s, it is very likely that it was that community's sense of its separateness from the straight world that prepared the way for gay liberation as a mass popular movement after 1969. Third-gender people in the Western world had entered a new phase in their history in which they had sex almost exclusively with each other, and in this way became quite different from the berdache or the Hijra. Within a generation of this change, gay men and lesbian women therefore sought to enter into legal marriages with each other and to become as couples the legal parents of children, a situation similar to that of the berdache who took a husband from among the warriors of his tribe—and yet profoundly different.

Notes

1. For third-gender roles, see Gilbert Herdt, ed., *Third Sex, Third Gender* (New York, 1994).

2. Randolph Trumbach, "London's Sodomites: Homosexual Behavior and Western Culture in the Eighteenth Century," *Journal of Social History* 11 (1977): 1–33; David F. Greenberg, *The Construction of Homosexuality* (Chicago, 1988).

3. Eva Cantarella, *Bisexuality in the Ancient World* (New Haven, 1992).

4. Randolph Trumbach, "Gender and the Homosexual Role in Modern Western Culture," in Dennis Altman et al., *Which Homosexuality?* (London, 1989).

5. Mary McIntosh, "The Homosexual Role," *Social Problems* 16 (1968): 182–92; Michel Foucault, *The History of Sexuality*, vol. 1: *An Introduction* (New York, 1978).

6. Didier Eribon, *Michel Foucault* (Cambridge, MA, 1991), 316.

7. Dirk Jaap Noordam, "Sodomy in the Dutch Republic, 1600–1725," in *The Pursuit of Sodomy*, ed. Kent Gerard and Gert Hekma (New York, 1989); Theo van der Meer, "The Persecution of Sodomites in Eighteenth-Century Amsterdam," in *The Pursuit of Sodomy*, eds. Gerard and Hekma; idem, "Sodomy and the Pursuit of a Third Sex in the Early Modern Period," in *Third Sex, Third Gender*, ed. Herdt; Michel Rey, "Parisian Homosexuals Create a Lifestyle, 1700–1750," in *'Tis Nature's Fault*, ed. R. P. Maccubbin (New York, 1987); Randolph Trumbach, "The Birth of the Queen: Sodomy and the Emergence of Gender Equality in Modern Culture, 1660–1750," in *Hidden from History*, eds. Martin Duberman, Martha Vicinus, and George Chauncey (New York, 1989); idem, "Sex, Gender and Sexual Identity in Modern Culture," in *Forbidden History*, ed. John C. Fout (Chicago, 1992).

8. Michael Rocke, *Forbidden Friendships* (New York, 1996).

9. See the literature cited in Randolph Trumbach, "Erotic Fantasy and Male Libertinism in Enlightenment England," in *The Invention of Pornography*, ed. Lynn Hunt (New York, 1993), 388–89.

10. Bruce R. Smith, *Homosexual Desire in Shakespeare's England* (Chicago, 1991); Alan Bray, *Homosexuality in Renaissance England* (London, 1982); Jonathan Goldberg, *Sodometries* (Stanford, CA, 1992); Gregory W. Bredbeck, *Sodomy and Interpretation* (Ithaca, NY, 1991); Steve Brown, "The Boyhood of Shakespeare's Heroines," *SEL: Studies in English Literature* 30 (1990): 243–63; Rictor Norton, *Mother Clap's Molly House* (London, 1992); Gert Hekma, "Homosexual Behavior in the Nineteenth-Century Dutch Army," in *Forbidden History*, ed. John Fout; Randolph Trumbach, "Ritualizing Sexual Behavior: From Eighteenth-Century Libertinism to Modern S/M" (public lecture, University of Amsterdam, June 8, 1993).

11. Randolph Trumbach, "London's Sapphists: From Three Sexes to Four Genders in the Making of Modern Culture," in *Third Sex, Third Gender*, ed. Gilbert Herdt.

12. Randolph Trumbach, "Sodomitical Assaults, Gender Role, and Sexual Development in Eighteenth-Century London," in *The Pursuit of Sodomy*, eds. Gerard and Hekma.

13. Jeffrey Weeks, *Coming Out* (London, 1977); idem, *Sex, Politics and Society* (New York, 1981), chap. 6; idem, "Inverts, Perverts, and Mary-Annes," in *Against Nature* (London, 1991); Gert Hekma, *Homoseksualiteit, een Medische Reputatie* (Amsterdam, 1987); Michael Sibalis, "The Regulation of Male Homosexuality in Revolu-

tionary and Napoleonic France, 1789–1815," in *Homosexuality in Modern France*, eds. Jeffrey Merrick and Bryant T. Ragan (New York, 1996); William Peniston, "Love and Death in Gay Paris: Homosexuality and Criminality in the 1870s," in *Homosexuality in Modern France*, eds. Merrick and Ragan.

14. Kevin Porter and Jeffrey Weeks, eds., *Between the Acts* (New York, 1991).

15. Stephen Jeffery-Poulter, *Peers, Queers, and Commons* (New York, 1991).

16. George Chauncey, *Gay New York* (New York, 1994).

17. Elizabeth Kennedy and Madeline Davis, *Boots of Leather, Slippers of Gold* (New York, 1993).

18. Helena Whitbread, ed., *I Know My Own Heart: The Diaries of Ann Lister, 1791–1840* (New York, 1992); idem, ed., *No Priest but Love: Excepts from the Diaries of Ann Lister, 1824–1826* (New York, 1992), on which see Randolph Trumbach, "The Origin and Development of the Modern Lesbian Role in the Western Gender System," *Historical Reflections/Réflexions Historiques* 20 (1994): 287–320.

19. George Chauncey, "From Sexual Inversion to Homosexuality," *Salmagundi*, nos. 58–59 (1982–83): 114–56.

20. Gert Hekma, "The Amsterdam Bar Culture and Changing Gay/Lesbian Identities," in *Sexual Cultures in Europe* (conference paper, Amsterdam, 1992).

21. Trumbach, "Ritualizing Sexual Behavior."

9

Third Genders, Third Sexes

Gilbert Herdt

The title of this essay questions the existence of third genders and counterposes them in relation to homosexuality. It is best to tip my hand at the beginning. Yes, third genders exist, but I would also suggest that these always occur apart from another analytical category, namely, the third sex. We might distinguish these, definitionally, on the basis of learned cultural characteristics, especially social roles, in the case of third genders; for third sexes, however, virtually all the criteria involve more material traits, such as a small penis or a large clitoris.

The eighteenth-century Mollie and the North American Indian berdache are third genders. The Indian Hijra is a third sex. Historical study has emphasized gender and the sociocultural meaning of folk biologies, suggesting that in fact we are more concerned with our discursive ideologies of relatedness than with their literal essences in the objectified time and space world of the sexologist (among other creatures who participate in the Foucaultian production of technologies of sexuality in the last century and gender in this one). In short, it is the tradition, it is the cultural genitals that we might find of interest, those icons of tradition that reproduce and bring pleasure on the levels of nature and culture.

Emphasis on a third sex and a third gender is an implicit challenge to the long-reigning paradigm of sexual dimorphism predominant in Western discourse. Many postmodern theorists have examined the pitfalls of continuing to objectify the sex/gender dichotomy of the past, which is probably culture-bound and scientifically misleading. In some times and places, persons are grouped into divergent categories of ontology, identities, tasks, and institutions that have resulted in more than two kinds of persons, which Westerners would typically class as male and female, masculine and feminine. Studies of sexual deviance and third genders have typically conflated the two.

Generally, sexual conduct has been ignored as a constitutive criterion leading to the formation of a divergent sex/gender category, or inclusion within one. But having now split apart third sex from third gender, as I have also done in a recent book on this topic, I face another problem. This is the categorical homosexual, an idealized historical construct that labors under the signs of sin, disease, and deviance, a creature I would not like to encounter, even in my worst Sunday afternoon daydreams, for fear I might not recognize it, so vast, so ambiguous, so shadowy and convoluted are its dimensions. Indeed, in a recent book, *Children of Horizons*, a study of the rise of gay and lesbian culture and adolescent identity in Chicago, I went to great lengths to distinguish the identity categories "homosexual" from "gay and lesbian," on the grounds of our historical and cultural analysis.

These are distinctions to which I will return. Before I compare divergent sexualities and gender, let me mention how I first met the categorical third sex myself. I was in New Guinea in the mid-1970s, doing fieldwork among the Sambia. Their culture recognizes the existence of what they call the *kwolu-aatmwol*, that is, "a person of transformation," a female thing changing into a male thing; what we would call "hermaphrodites," or what medical practitioners would refer to as "five alpha reductase hermaphrodism."

One of these persons, a shaman named Sakulambei, I have studied for some years, a person who I think I would be fair in describing as neither male nor female, who is not homosexual, and who is certainly not gay. He began to challenge me, by talking with me inside my own thoughts, to wonder whether Sambia observed a three-sex system in their attributions of nature and culture. For Sambia, the *kwolu-aatmwol* begins at birth with the sex assignment of the infant into a third category, and fans out in development to embrace origin myths and social practices. People such as the New Guinea *kwolu-aatmwol* certainly confirm the existence of persons across time and space who in the West European tradition had been marginalized and stigmatized.

Although much has been written about gender variations and deviations of late, especially within the historical study of homosexuality, we must surely wonder (as has Randy Trumbach) how Foucault could have so ignored the historically earlier sodomite. I believe the reason is that Foucault never seriously questioned his epistemology of dimorphism, whether two sexes or genders are in the nature of things, be they defined as biological or social, whether in our species or others. Medical sexologists still continue to reflect the naturalism of this kind of dimorphism.

Their sense of faith and a commonsense view must make us wonder, with historians such as Trumbach and Thomas Laqueur, about the transformations and the perception of two-gendered bodies. Just how did things ever get to be this way in the nineteenth century? From a larger spectrum of possibilities around the world, we in Western culture arrived in the nineteenth century with a two-sex system. A funny thing, this, because if we turn to the German sociologist Georg Simmel, at the turn of the century, we find him already complaining that there are too many categories and two few sexes to explain the immense varieties of human experience.

Anthropology's own encounter with traditional societies has repeatedly demonstrated divergent sexualities and classifications, and how often these have been misunderstood. Over the past century, for example, the North American Indian berdache has been prominent in the cultural imagination, in our thinking about exotic societies, even if the more radical implications of the phenomenon have been ignored, as Will Roscoe has pointed out. These cross-cultural variations in anthropology were always played down when it came to discussions of normal reproductive sexuality and kinship, that is, discussions of whether there are but two sexes and genders in human nature. This, too, was largely due to the intellectual, social, and morally defined strictures of sexual dimorphism as we inherited them in late Victorian anthropology.

Aside from this general prejudice of Western epistemology, our difficulties in dealing with divergent categories stem primarily, I believe, from the long neglect of sexuality, not only in anthropology, but in social studies at large. Until recently, we remained preoccupied with gender, but had scarcely begun to conceptualize sexual desire; and while social reproduction continues to charm much of social theory, our understanding of pleasure and the erotic aspects of social relations remains dull. Recent studies have anticipated a new approach to the question of a third sex; among these, one thinks immediately of Foucault's own addition of *Herculine Barbin*, an account of an early nineteenth-century French hermaphrodite.

The book reveals the effects of the modern period's ideology of dimorphism, the existential awareness of being insufficiently male and female. As Foucault puts it, Herculine was "a boy/girl, a never/eternal masculine/feminine who committed suicide after being forced to change from one sex to the other because he and she was incapable of adapting himself to a new identity." Take note that Foucault's appeal to identity is unusual for him, suggesting an unresolved problem in the epistemology of desire: how to express a desire in the absence of a corresponding social category. A century later, the inability to fit the normative categories of sex and gender would plague American transsexuals—eventuating in the transgender movement.

The ethnomethodologist Harold Garfinkel has cynically chided the essentialism of Western ideas of dimorphism: "This composition is rigorously dichotomized into the natural, moral entities of male and female," and provides for persons who are "naturally," "in the first place," "in the beginning," "all along," and "forever one or the other." Many scholars have thus predicated their work on the assumption of dimorphism so prevalent in the literature since before Darwin. Thus, when late Victorian anthropologists encountered persons classified as berdache in the cultures of American Indians, such persons were often misinterpreted as biologically abnormal hermaphrodites.

Later, they were classified as homosexuals, using that pathological nosology of Freud's Vienna. Such interpretations violated, of course, the cultural phenomenology of these third-gender roles in Native North America. But likewise, anthropologist Niko Besnier from Yale has shown a similar problem in the Pacific, from the time of Captain Cook on to the present; that is, the misinterpretation and mislabeling of third gendered roles such as the Mahu among the Tahitians. It is in this light that Will Roscoe's account of the third gender helps inject a much-needed cultural analysis into the understanding of transformed systems of personhood and precolonial economy, insisting on understanding, as Walter Williams did before, the common denominators of berdachehood in such societies, common denominators that suggest that the berdache was typical of this culture area throughout North America.

Thus, it seems to me that we should think of the berdache as being a characteristic core feature of the area of the world, whereas in fact, the phenomenon has seldom been treated in this way. Where I would find fault with Roscoe is in the general absence of attention to the erotic, to the formation of sexual conduct and erotic relations among such persons. As George Devereux pointed out in the 1930s about the Mohaves, the male berdache experience involves sexual interaction with another person defined as a masculine male partner in the tribe, a person who penetrates him anally and gives him an orgasm that is said to be rapturous—and yet, while rapturous, the berdache does not permit his partner to touch or handle his own penis.

This fact was never explained, and neither was the sexual excitement. Such a sexual ontology is remarkable because it posits a clear form of preferred sexual excitement that is a probable basis of the appeal of the role. No anthropologist has ever explained why such forms of sexual desire created the perfect fit between individual and culture among the berdache, nor, indeed, why this form of sexual excitement would be aesthetically attractive. That the berdache was characteristic of a major region of Native North America and the Pacific Rim and that it was based on the construction of gendered roles is pretty clear, but let us also uncover the erotic, whenever this embodies the native ontology in the being and the bodies of persons making a seamless fit between the inner world and the social surround.

In short, we would not lay these classification systems at the door of the structure of the mind, but rather that of culture; while theorists might agree with Nietzsche's dictum that all categorization involves treating unequal things as similar, they have not refigured their classification of sex or gendered things in this light. According to the views of Darwin and late Victorian social theorists, including Freud, there were but two categories of normal human nature, male and female, whose essences and anatomies placed them in opposition. Nineteenth-century sexologists and sexual reformers were preoccupied with the problem, having created classificatory schemas that included the Uranian, the homosexual, the intermediate sex, the psychic hermaphrodite, and other quaint notions to identify persons whose minds or bodies or actions seemed to defy dimorphism. The same was true of their successors in the earlier twentieth century, beginning with sexological work and continuing with the zoologist Kinsey, that great quantifier of American orgasms.

Kinsey well understood the difficulties involved in classification when he remarked that it is the human mind that categorizes, while nature does not. The moral ideology of dimorphic reproduction and its dualism of heterosexual/homosexual has changed greatly over historical time, as Trumbach has so well argued, changing the thinking of many of us who study sexuality. Nearly three centuries ago, the desire for the same sex was punished by death in many Western nations—in Holland, for example, after the late seventeenth century, many people were put to death. The evidence suggests that some of the sodomites, according to their diaries and love letters, desired the same sex before a category name existed to describe or explain this desire. The early executions were secret, because sodomy was loathsome, a crime against God and nature that should not be discussed in public. This privacy and secrecy thwarted the emerging category.

As the sodomite network of the early modern period comes into existence, the age-structured system begins to decline, and as age-structured relations decline, so too does there emerge a new category, what Theo Van der Meer has called the "he-whore," in the Netherlands, a third gendered role, first in Holland, perhaps, then in England and other areas of Western culture.

It drew on the imagery of a sexualized woman, unknown before, and also one who was beyond the confines of normal culture. This, it seems to me, is quite essential in our rethinking of the emergence of heterosexuality in the later modern period. None of these evolving ideas were able to successfully challenge the social insistence on lumping together things regarded as equal, or splitting others apart, marginalizing what is unclassifiable to residual categories, such as the hermaphrodite.

Male and female had become the fundamental duality of human nature in the time of Freud and Kinsey. Only now, in the late twentieth century, are we able to look afresh at the historical and anthropological evidence to ask once again the question asked in the nineteenth century: How is it possible, perhaps even inevitable, for alternate genders and sexual categories to emerge in certain times and places, transcending dimorphism?

However, we should not believe that in all times and places this has occurred. Some scholars have taken this fact to the logical conclusion of believing in some eternal law of dimorphic human nature, including currently, the brain scientist Simon LeVay, who believes in a kind of tantric dimorphism that would have made even Freud blush.

We are dealing with multiple cultural and historical worlds, in which persons of divergent sexual and gendered nature exist on the margins of society. They may pass as normal to remain hidden from the official ideology and everyday commerce of social life. For this reason, they may, upon discovery, become icons in history and popular culture, sanctioning normal male/female dimorphism, a kind of betrayed matter out of place, which symbolizes boundary blurring, the anomalous, the unclean, the tainted, the morally inept or corrupt, the monsters of the cultural imagination of the Renaissance, and the vampires of Anne Rice novels.

The third sex and gender, we might say, to paraphrase Lévi-Strauss's famous idea on totemism, are ready-made for objectifying first and second sexes, laying ready the subjectification of third sex desires in those who have such desire. Classification systems of sexual and gender things thus need to be taken apart, put back together again, in the exercise of defining what is sexual nature and what is gendered culture. Here, an enormous burden is placed on the representation of the other, unloading our prejudices about what is natural and normal in order to create or think about the homosexual or the transsexual or the hermaphrodite. There is much of good value in this line of postmodern work, though one has the sense that too often it is based on weak or insubstantial observations, the burden borne almost exclusively by the study of representations.

But other observations derive from longer-term study. Serena Nanda's wonderful work, based on longitudinal field study on the Hijra of India, raises profound questions about the historicity and the culturality of the third sex in the Indian tradition. Her rich ethnography questions both the interpretation of Hindu ontology (and Western epistemology by comparison) in understanding Otherness, especially in her effort to compare the Hijra to the Mollie, the Hijra to the berdache, the homosexual to the berdache, and of course, the Hijra to that Western, two-spirited caste known as the transsexual. It does matter, I think, what the third sex and gender looks like and acts like, whether among the Hijras, the sodomites of the eighteenth century in Holland or England, or women who dressed in men's clothes in historical Europe. What were they like? How did they speak? What was their behavior? Hijras, for instance, shatter stereotypes of male and female. Their appeal to the Mother Goddess and their ritual blessings demonstrate the power not just of the sexual, but of the sacred, as this is deployed in the legitimation of the category.

Now some may question the focus on three entities. Why not four or five or myriad other categories of sex and gender? The presence of only two categories, a dyad, creates an inherent relationship of duality of spirit and flesh, an inevitable oppositionality, an instability. When, however, a third category or class is introduced, a new dynamic develops between the dyadic agents. As the sociologist Simmel's classic essay on the triad points out, "The dyad represents both the first synthesis and unification, and the first separation and antithesis. The appearance of the third party indicates transition, conciliation, and the abandonment of absolute contrast."

Thus, the code of thirdness should not be taken literally to mean that in all times and places, there are only three categories possible for human life. We would want to entertain the possibility of multiple categories in human lives. However, many of the examples from history and culture pivot around the question of a third nature, which impinges on characteristics of a deeper structure of ontology and epistemology and the way we humans characterize things into twos and threes. Thus, it is no wonder that as a gay and lesbian cultural system has emerged in contradistinction to heterosexuality since the nineteenth century, the identity of the closet homosexual has receded, and simultaneously, in this recent period of what we might call "sexual communism" and "sexual democracy," the queer and bisexual have emerged as new constructions, resulting in the attempt to create an alternate symbolic reality in competition with a hegemonic order of an aging social tradition.

In short, sex and gender systems may be thriving in diversity, but have not left behind the third other. Many scholars in the social sciences have treated the berdache and Hijras and kindred cultural systems apart from male and female, seeing them as alternatives to the universalizing tendencies of our narrow-minded Western dualism. The great question remains: How did these people get to be this way? How did Hijra and berdache persons find their way into such cultural roles and strata systems? It was not, surely, purely accidental. How were the cultural forms of such traditions socialized and instantiated, not just in the social rules of conduct, which are relatively simple, but in the whispers of their private lives, or the preoccupations of their sexual ones?

The standard social science notion of recruitment to roles and the learning of norms sits awkwardly on this tired paradigm, because taboos bar public passage into the margins beyond culture. These were emergent systems created as much by antithesis and incitement to rebellion as by opposition to norms, in the sense of those typical cauldrons of social pressure that convert raw people into overly socialized and cooked actors. I am sympathetic to the effort to locate, historically and socially, these constructions in the marketplace of culture.

However, by saying this, I believe we should resist the reduction of the full human person to merely a social, gendered, or sexual role. And we should resist the reduction of the third sex to sexual orientation, for these are not the same phenomena. We might deepen our interest in other issues concerning desire or pleasure, in erotic partnerships that are transformed in social and historical places, looking to those symbolic spaces in society for, as John Gagnon once wrote, "the ineluctable opportunities for being and expressing new desires in emerging social places, far from the crowd, close up to one's chosen partner, of whatever social and sexual orientation, who would recreate society in the most intimate of encounters."

Here, it seem to me, we still have much to learn—not just about the body, but also about the role of concepts, of spirit, of mind, and of political subversion—as we build on the revolution that has occurred in social history and anthropology during the past generation. The missing key to much study of third sex and gender is an understanding of the desires and attractions of the person. Especially in those instances of recruitment or advancement to a new position, let us consider the man who becomes a Mollie, the Mojave child or Zuni child who becomes a berdache, or a young male of India electing to have himself castrated. In these quarters, we are pretty much ignorant of the reasons desires are transformed into these third sex and gender categorical positions.

How much of this is the product of ontology, of a sense of being different that identifies with the category? How much comes from social and sexual pressures that produce normative dimorphic hierarchies? We must find this out by focusing on the concept of desire, by facing the challenge of linking those cross-cultural forms to the transition to modernism in our own Western tradition since the time of the Renaissance. If my intuition is correct, this match between emergent desires and cultural classification is the missing key to understanding the emergence of third sex and genders across time and space.

10

Gender Identity Disorder in Boys: The Search for a Constitutional Factor

Susan Coates

Gender identity disorder (GID) of childhood is a very rare syndrome, first classified in the *Diagnostic and Statistical Manual of Mental Disorders* (third edition), characterized by a persistent and determined wish to be the opposite gender coupled with an intense dislike of one's own gender. Boys with the syndrome are referred for clinical evaluation far more frequently than girls by a ratio of approximately five to one (Zucker and Green 1992). The onset of the disorder almost invariably occurs between the ages of two and four, and once established, it is surprisingly stable and usually proves refractory to all but the most intensive psychodynamic and family interventions. Several features of the syndrome as it occurs in boys have been repeatedly noted since the very inception of the diagnosis. It typically emerges during a limited time frame in development in families with chronic problems in affect regulation (Bradley 1985; Marantz and Coates 1991; Wolfe 1990). It typically occurs in sensitive boys (Stoller 1968; Coates 1992) who are avoidant of rough-and-tumble play (Bates, Bentler, and Thompson 1979; Green et al. 1983) and who are described by their mothers as beautiful (Stoller 1968; Green 1974; Zucker et al. 1992). The symptoms of the disorder, so dramatic and disturbing to the outside observer, are invariably tolerated and/or encouraged by the parents. And finally, all observers agree that there appears to be a constitutional diathesis for the development of the disorder, though it has proved difficult to conceptualize what that diathesis might be.

The primary purpose of this essay is to provide clarification as to the role of constitutional factors in the etiology of childhood gender identity disorder. Secondarily, I will briefly consider what light, if any, such a clarification sheds on the normal development of gender identity. Phenomenologically, the manifestations of gender identity disorder are quite striking and include both intrapsychic and behavioral manifestations. Gender disordered boys display the following characteristics: they express the wish to be a girl; some claim that they will be a girl when they grow up; and they prefer stereotypically feminine activities, such as playing with Barbie dolls. They enjoy playacting the roles of girls; they like to dress up in girls' clothes; they show an intense interest in cosmetics, jewelry, and high-heeled shoes; and they prefer girls as playmates. Many, but not all, of these boys also display anatomical dysphoria, in the form of an intense dislike of their penis and/or a wish to be rid of it.

Detailed individual case reports have been repeatedly described in the literature. Research and extended clinical experience over the past ten years have gradually yielded a complex etiological model for the development of the disorder in which psychodynamic and familial variables interact during a sensitive period in the child's development to produce a fantasy of fusion of self with mother. Once established, the cross-gender identification becomes entrenched in part because it helps the child in various ways to restore a more satisfactory relation to the mother in reality, but also in part because it enables the child to function more autonomously. Such is the contribution the cross-gender identification makes to the child's management of anxiety that the child experiences it as a "solution." As development proceeds, however, the child's creativity and spontaneity become increasingly consumed in the repetitive, stereotyped, and joyless enactments of the cross-gender identification while his social adjustment becomes increasingly precarious in the face of continued peer rejection.

It is important to bear in mind that the collateral clinical features associated with the syndrome are not required for the diagnosis, which instead concerns only the focal area of the disturbance of gender. What defines the essence of the syndrome, and what makes it so disturbingly provocative at first glance, is that these children give every indication that they feel they would be better off if they were girls. The syndrome thus seems analogous to the adult condition of transsexualism, wherein a person protests that he is a man trapped in a woman's body, or vice versa. In fact, research into childhood gender identity disorder was initially spurred by the search for childhood analogs to the adult condition, since adult transsexuals typically report severe anatomical and gender dysphoria for as long as they can remember. The possibility that a little boy can insist that he really feels like a girl and maintain that identification despite adverse social and psychological consequences raises important questions as to how gender identity gets established in both normal and abnormal development. The possibility that a constitutional diathesis may be required for the disorder, in turn, raises tantalizing questions about the psychobiological roots of femininity and masculinity. In fact, as I shall argue, an understanding of the constitutional diathesis for the development of gender identity disorder does indeed shed light on the ordinary processes whereby small children come to feel that they are boys and girls. But, as the reader shall see, the light shed on the issue of the psychobiological roots of masculinity and femininity is indirect at best. To anticipate our conclusion, the study of constitution leads paradoxically to a greater appreciation of both the role of environmental and experiential factors and the complexity of the nature-nurture interaction—even in an area so seemingly biological as sex and gender.

Terminological Background

The implications of a putative constitutional factor in the development of gender identity disorder can be more precisely stated; though this requires a terminological excursus. In the world of contemporary research, an essential distinction is made between sex and gender. Sex refers to the chromosomal status at birth (46XX for girls, 46XY for boys). Except in certain rare physical disorders, this status will be further reflected in the neonate's external genitalia, which for both parents and physicians are the hallmark of sex. Gender, by contrast, is a social-psychological construct; it designates how persons are categorized by others and how they categorize themselves. Within the category of gender, three further distinctions are typically made. *Gender role* describes the outwardly observable activities, proclivities, and attitudes that are associated with cultural expectations of masculinity and femininity. *Gender identity* is the complementary intrapsychic sense of oneself as being either male or female. A quite masculine man, for example, may nonetheless find that he prefers to perform many of the nurturant and supportive tasks vis à vis his children that are traditionally associated with the maternal role, or that he rather prefers activities like making floral arrangements. In either case, one may speak of a degree of gender nonconformity. Some men are comfortable with gender nonconforming interests; others are not. Thus it may happen that a man may be disturbed by his interest in a stereotypically "feminine" activity and may come to entertain doubts as to how completely "masculine" he is. Or else, if he resentfully elects to suppress his proclivities, he might come to entertain seemingly inexplicable thoughts about how nice it might be to be a woman. In either case, one can also speak of (mild) gender dysphoria. Clearly, however, such fluctuations can occur within a normal range and bode nothing whatsoever vis à vis the overall mental health of the individual.

Disturbances in core gender identity are another matter. *Core gender identity*, a term first proposed by Stoller, refers to the affectively laden sense that one is the "right" sex. If you ask even small children whether they are a boy or a girl, they will respond with something like indignation. "Of course I am a boy," the child will respond, "what a silly question!" Moreover, even though boys and girls at different times feel disadvantaged in terms of the range of activities permitted them, children of both sexes can readily come up with reasons why it is "better" to be the sex that they are. This affectively colored sense of one's gender becomes consolidated in almost all children by the age of three and a half and remains stable thereafter. In terms of the child's developing affectivity, core gender identity appears to reflect the confluence of both hedonic pleasure in being a particular gender and the child's rudimentary sense of propriety (Kohlberg 1966; Emde et al. 1991), that is, the child's sense of how things *should* be. In a child's vocabulary, it is "good" to be the "right" sex— indeed, what else could one be?

On the basis of his clinical experience and the available research literature, Stoller supposed that among the factors contributing to core gender identity was a basic biological contribution. Equally, he proposed that in extreme boy-hood femininity (which at that time he equated with childhood transsexualism) this biological contribution was at least partially skewed in the direction of greater "femininity" in boys. He was the first to note that these boys were *experienced* by their mothers as more beautiful than other boys (Stoller 1968, 1975), an observation that has since been replicated in empirical studies (Green 1974). Zucker et al. (1992) have recently found that this finding holds up when attractiveness is rated by others, extending the observation beyond just the reports of the mothers' experience. Relying on the reports of the mothers, Stoller further theorized that gender identity disorder resulted from a pro-longed "blissful symbiosis" between a constitutionally predisposed child and a basically bisexual mother, lasting several years. The consequence of this pro-longed symbiosis, in Stoller's view, was that the developing child did not make the switch to a masculine identification. (He hypothesized that all children begin life with an innately feminine orientation and along with Greenson [1968] believed that boys have to dis-identify with their mothers in order to develop a masculine identification.) Something akin to "imprinting" was at stake in Stoller's theory, such that the inborn constitutional factor became fixed through prolonged contact with the mother. In his view, the resulting feminine identification, though problematic socially, was otherwise nonconflictual for the child.

Many of Stoller's original observations of "extremely feminine boys," such as their sensory sensitivities, their unusual artistic capacities, and their unusual beauty, as well as his observations of maternal depression and paternal inaccessibility as collateral features of the syndrome, have withstood the test of further observation and research. Moreover, his belief that the disorder could come about only when a confluence of many factors came together in a single time frame is shared by nearly all of those who have been long-term systematic observers of the disorder. To be sure, the deficiencies of the "blissful symbiosis" aspect of his etiological hypothesis are now well known, in large part thanks to research efforts spurred by his important conceptualization of the idea of core gender identity and by his challenging psychodynamic formulations. Even still, if we put "blissful symbiosis" to one side, the question remains as to how the constitutional elements noted by Stoller (unusual beauty, unusual sensitivities, etc.) could contribute under any set of circumstances to a profound disturbance in core gender identity. It is easy to think of the traits enumerated by Stoller as somehow "feminine," but is that characterization reflective of a truly innate biological difference or only a by-product of our particular culture with its particular stereotypes?

The Search for Meaningful Sex Differences

The issue of determining the biological roots of gender presupposes that one is able to take gender as a focal object of research and intellectual curiosity generally. However, just this has proved very difficult to do over the millennia. It is really only in the modern age that people have become curious about gender. At the same time, indeed as part of the same processes, interest in gender has become burdened by a great deal of social, cultural, and political concern. Accordingly, before we proceed further, it might be useful to take in the great historical novelty of contemporary research into gender and its social significance. Clarification on both counts is needed before one can appreciate where contemporary research into gender actually stands.

At first glance, for both the naive observer and the member of a coherent, traditional culture, the fact of gender seems to be the most natural thing in the world. Rare anomalies of nature aside, human beings come in only two biologically given sexes at birth, male and female, and they routinely grow up to be only two genders, men and women. Such is the seeming obviousness of one's given biological sex that its cultural patterning as gender has in almost all human societies proceeded as though according to a natural law, even though this often resulted in vast disparities in the status and privileges of one or the other gender. For most of historical time in most human societies, one did not question gender since it seemed the inevitable expression of an innate biological given. This was true even for societies with intermediate classifications such as the Native American category of berdache. That the innate biological given was shaped by cultural standards and enforced by cultural sanctions was a fact that could not be appreciated as such. As a fish would be the last creature to ask about the ocean, men and women for millennia grew up in cultures whose predications of gender seemed "natural" and God-given and thus intellectually invisible. To put it another way, for most of human history, human beings reacted to the issue of gender much as small children continue to do. One's gender, with all its social specifications, was always the "right" gender—what else could it be?

It is only in the modern, post-enlightenment era that social concern, coupled with anthropological research, has focused intellectual attention on the great variability, and sometimes great injustices, attending gender definitions in different societies. Contemporary social scientific interest in understanding gender as a potentially variable social category has been further fueled by the extraordinary rate of change in gender roles in industrial societies during the course of this century. This rate of change, in turn, has been accompanied by political, social, and cultural ferment to the point where gender definitions have become a matter of practical concern for a great many people and an arena for often passionate and fractionated public debate.

Contemporary social concern over gender roles has been accompanied by the spawning of important research efforts in an attempt to disentangle, if possible, what is indeed the biologically given contribution of sex to gender versus what to the contrary is the result of cultural patterning. Though no sophisticated researcher supposes nowadays that a pure nature versus nurture dichotomy applies, and though all researchers now agree that progress can be made only through the study of the interaction of the two (in biological terms, the study of the necessary role of experience and environment in shaping the phenotypal expression of the genotype), the search for identifiable "sex differences" is so important culturally that even weak or uncertain statistical findings that seem to bear on this topic command great public and scientific interest. Underneath this burgeoning research effort, I would suggest, one can often detect either a yearning to find somewhere a true biological anchorage upon which to moor drifting gender definitions or else a contrasting wish to find that all gender is a social construction. The latter urge is consistent with our democratic and egalitarian values, manifested in the belief that all people are created equal, and perhaps also in the no less idealized belief that you can make anything of yourself that you want to (including your gender and sometimes even your sex).

If we look at the outcome of years of psychological research on sex differences, however, we come to a truly remarkable fact. Despite all the contemporary research into "sex differences," that is, inborn, psychobiological differences that can be understood to be conceptually independent of child-rearing practices, the fact is that very little in the way of positive results has been obtained (see Byne and Parsons, in press). Boys are born slightly heavier and taller than girls, but more susceptible to illness, and they will continue to be slightly taller and heavier throughout the life cycle. As toddlers, boys are somewhat bolder and more aggressive, and they are more active explorers of their environment; in particular they will show a preference for rough-and-tumble play (DiPietro 1981). Also, their visual-spatial skills will develop somewhat more rapidly than they do in girls, while their verbal skills will develop somewhat less rapidly. Puberty, including growth spurts, will begin earlier in girls. There may be increased lateral differentiation of the two brain hemispheres in adolescent and adult males as compared to females, but this issue is not yet settled, nor is its significance. And that is about it.

The relative paucity of findings and the fact that all findings show differences of an entirely relative sort, that is, differences that appear only in a sufficiently large statistical sample, rather violate our initial expectations. Boys and girls, and men and women, are different, we tell ourselves, perhaps adding in puzzlement, "Aren't they?" Yet, what research findings that currently exist suggest is that these differences are only a matter of degree, and that the difference in degree is not all that striking. That there are only two genders would lead us to suppose that sooner or later, on some measure yet to be devised, we would see two essentially distinct populations. But what has been observed is not this. What has been observed is two largely overlapping populations, with so much shared variance between them that even a composite score on all the known relevant variables would not allow one to predict the gender of any given subject with any great confidence whatsoever. The question thus arises whether the distinction between the two genders, so clear in our mind, is essentially the result of cultural patterning, or whether, to put the matter crudely, it has essentially been "made up." The innate differences between boys and girls, so far as is currently known, are simply not sufficient to account for the observed cultural disparity in gender.

The History of Clinical Research into Gender

It is in this context that recent clinical and developmental research into the formation of gender has proved to be surprisingly illuminating. Let us begin with the clinical research. The first clear, concise descriptions of gender identity disorder in childhood were elicited by the pioneer sexual researcher Richard Von Krafft-Ebing (1902), at the end of the last century. But Krafft-Ebing's descriptions were uniformly retrospective accounts elicited from adult homosexuals gathered on the basis of a complex etiological scheme that cannot be described further here. Some clinicians even today continue to conflate GID and homosexuality, arguing that cross-gender behavior in childhood is the first manifestation of homosexuality (Zuger 1988). To be sure, there is some statistical support for this as a prospective correlation; current research has produced estimates that 66 percent to 75 percent of gender disordered children grow up to be homosexual (Zucker and Green 1992). However, as a retrospective correlation, the conflation of the two conditions does not hold up. In retrospective studies of clinically unreferred adult homosexuals, about three-fourths have described themselves as gender nonconforming in childhood. Yet this self-characterization includes, in the majority, nothing more than a preference for solitary activities and/or artistic activities as well as the avoidance of rough-and-tumble play (Saghir and Robins 1973; Bell, Weinberg, and Hammersmith 1981; Friedman 1988). Only a minority of adult homosexuals recall cross-gender interests and cross-gender identifications of an intensity that would meet the criteria for a GID of childhood. The upper-level estimate based on current research of adult homosexuals who may have had a GID of childhood is about 15 percent and the true percentage is probably much lower than that. In my view, the supposition that boyhood gender identity disorder and adult homosexuality are manifestations of a *unitary* developmental pattern is both empirically unwarranted and conceptually unsound, nor does such a supposition contribute to our understanding of the specific nature of the childhood disorder.

To be noted is that as long ago as 1907, Albert Moll, as part of a methodological criticism of Krafft-Ebing's (1902) use of retrospective data to infer childhood patterns, presented a clear case of gender identity disorder in which the child did not grow up to be homosexual.

The preliminary descriptions of childhood gender identity during the first era of sexual research by men such as Krafft-Ebing and Moll at the turn of the last century did not lead to a conceptualization of gender as a distinct developmental line, nor did they spawn further research. In part this was due to a functional conceptualization of sexual development, and of sexual behavior generally, as leading to and being consummated in procreation and the further perpetuation of the species. In such a unified functional conception, it was difficult to distinguish gender, an aspect of the self, as independent of sexual orientation, which concerns the gender of one's preferred sexual object. Curiously, though it was the essence of the psychoanalytic redefinition of sexuality that libido was said to be composed of multiple, and functionally independent, component drives, each of which might have its own developmental history and each of which might be conjoined with the others in adult sexual behavior only very poorly or not at all, the lacuna with regard to gender persisted. Psychoanalysis substituted the vicissitudes of desire and defense for the functional conception of its predecessors as the basis for understanding psychosexuality; it did not create a place for gender as pertaining to one's own status independent of desire.

The modern era of research into gender began with the work of John Money and his associates at Johns Hopkins University in the 1950s on hermaphroditic children. These children typically have ambiguous genitalia at birth, with both male and female organs present in various combinations. Money and his colleagues (1955) discovered that such children nonetheless grew up thinking of themselves as unambiguously boys and girls, provided they were assigned to one or another gender at birth and raised that way thereafter. To put the matter into contemporary terminology, core gender identity could be established and maintained even though biological sex was ambiguous. This remarkable and unanticipated finding paved the way for the conceptualization of gender identity as an issue distinct from biological sex and also, perhaps not so obviously, from sexual orientation (Money and Ehrhardt 1972).

Money was the first to define the term "gender role" (Money, Hampson, and Hampson 1955) and the first to differentiate it from gender identity (Money 1973). His researches led not only to Stoller's psychoanalytic investigations, but also to empirical studies of a host of disorders less extreme than true hermaphroditism. Among the latter, one condition in particular deserves mention: congenital adrenal hyperplasia (Ehrhardt and Baker 1974). This rare autosomal inherited disorder involves a genetic defect in cortisone production, and thus in adrenal steroidogenesis. The consequence in a genetic female is that there will be excessive levels of adrenal androgens prenatally, with the result that at birth there will be ambiguous or else fully masculinized external genitals despite normal female internal reproductive organs. Though at one point in time such children might have been raised as males, in recent decades all are raised as female (which is what their chromosomal inheritance dictates) and are given surgical correction and cortisone replacement therapy as needed. The importance of this syndrome theoretically is that owing to the genetic defect, itself not sex-linked, such girls are exposed to excessive levels of the male hormone androgen both prenatally and in early childhood prior to the institution of cortisone replacement therapy. Thus, in addition to the masculinized genitals at birth, these girls are also potentially exposed to androgen-related changes in the structure of their brains. We will return to this syndrome shortly.

The work of Money and Ehrhardt (1972) had a second important consequence, echoed in Stoller's "imprinting" thesis, namely, that it became possible to conceptualize a "critical" or "sensitive" developmental period in the development of gender identity. A "critical" period is a window of time, often quite short in animal species, during which a genotypal capacity either will or will not find its typical phenotypic expression, depending on environmental stimuli. The classic demonstration of a "critical" period is Konrad Lorenz's discovery of "imprinting" in baby ducks. At birth, the ducklings will follow the first large moving object they see—and they will continue to follow that particular object until they reach adulthood. In nature, this mechanism, entirely inborn, more or less efficiently guarantees that baby ducks will follow their mother, a situation of obvious survival value. In the Lorenz home in the countryside, however, the same mechanism led to one duckling trailing along behind the great naturalist wherever he went.

Critical periods occur most strikingly before birth. For the most part prenatally, hormones organize the gender dimorphic structures of the brain. Postnatally, hormones typically serve an activation role (Phoenix, Goy, and Gerall et al. 1959). In some animal species these prenatal critical periods can be quite brief and yet lead to striking alterations in behavior. For example, it is known that female rats, when stressed during pregnancy for even very brief times, have neurophysiological reactions that block the "androgen bath" to the male brain (Ward 1984) that is responsible for prenatal structuralization of the male brain. This observation has led to a series of increasingly more precise experiments with pregnant rats to discover the effects of "depleted" levels of androgen on their offspring. Startlingly, and somewhat misleadingly in terms of its implications, it has been discovered that very high levels of stress in the pregnant rat lead to decreased stereotypical male reproductive behavior and that male rats so affected produce the female lordosis response, allowing themselves to be mounted by unaffected male rats. Moreover, this effect, so enduring during the course of the animal's life, can be achieved by stress on the mother during a time frame of only a few hours' duration during the prenatal period. In short, there is a critical period during the differentiation of the rat's brain prenatally such that the absence of androgen leads to a sexually specific structuralization, resulting in sexually atypical behavior in the male rat after birth (for a discussion of implications for our understanding of the human brain, see Friedman and Downey and Byne and Parsons, both in press).

Such exceedingly brief critical periods (involving a few hours) are increasingly difficult to find, even prenatally, as one moves up the evolutionary ladder and in humans are entirely unknown. This has led to the postulation of a less restrictive concept, that of a "sensitive" period in development, a duration of some length during which the genotypal potential flexibly takes its typical phenotypal shape. If there is a sensitive period for the development of a given trait or capacity, then the expectation is that once the sensitive period passes the trait or capacity in question will either fail to develop or else will develop in an atypical form. In this context, the question raised by Money's research was whether there was a sensitive period postnatally for the development of gender identity.

Indeed there was. Money and Ehrhardt (1972) found that the crucial period was between eighteen and thirty-six months, which they believed was linked to the acquisition of language. When sex-assignment had to be changed for medical reasons after this age, psychological difficulties invariably ensued. Money argued that during this period gender identity was still flexible. After this time, gender identity was fixed.

The suggestion that the establishment of gender identity might be correlated with the achievement of language in the developing child has received independent confirmation from an entirely different line of research. Beginning with Kohlberg (1966), cognitive-developmental researchers have been able to describe a regular developmental sequence in the development of the ability to classify self and others by gender. At age two and a half, approximately one half of all children have achieved this capacity; by age three and a half, almost all children have achieved it. Indeed, it appears that the binomial distinction between boy and girl, and between man and woman, may be the second such categorization achieved by the child (Kohlberg 1966), preceded only by the distinction big-small (see below). Moreover, as Fast (1984) has described and elaborated on in considerable detail, no sooner is this capacity achieved than it also becomes affectively significant for the child. That is to say, once the child can categorize by gender, he or she begins to show a preference for same-gender activities and the company of same-gender peers (Fagot, Leinbach, and Hagan 1986). Though this has only recently been subject to systematic study, it appears that this developing capacity in the child, and its corollary expression in his or her shift toward same-gender activities and peers, ordinarily meets with reinforcement from parents and caretakers. Fathers, in particular, appear to be important in reinforcing gender behavior in both boys and girls, with their sons in particular they negatively reinforce cross-gender behavior. Interestingly, however, children at this early age (two and a half to three and a half) usually have not achieved the further cognitive abilities to understand that gender does not change over the course of life (gender stability) and that it likewise does not change even if one adopts the clothes and/or activities of the opposite gender (gender constancy). In short, from a cognitive-developmental standpoint, this is a vulnerable period, and it should not surprise us that the onset of gender identity disorder typically occurs during it. From a purely cognitive standpoint, gender identity disorder of childhood entails an ability to classify by gender that is defensively employed in cross-gender fantasy in a way that seems to exploit the cognitive immaturity of not having achieved gender constancy and gender stability. The failure of parents of children with GID to discourage cross-gender behavior, first noted by Green (1974) and since repeatedly confirmed by other observers, means that the child's cross-gender enactments go unchecked and, in fact, become subtly embedded in the ongoing parent-child interaction.

The discovery of a sensitive period clinically and of a vulnerable period cognitively in the development of gender identity still leaves open the question of how innate biological factors relating to biological sex may be impacting on self-categorization. One could imagine, for example, that some combination of hormones serving both activating and organizational functions might cause the ability to classify by gender to misfire, as it were, once that cognitive ability comes on line. Let us begin our consideration of this issue by saying that there exists no known mechanism whereby male and female hormones directly cause a "switch" to be thrown with regard to the experience of one's own gender. Nor does the pattern of findings from a whole host of studies on the relation of hormonal functioning to gender lead one to suppose that any such hormone-activated "switch" could exist. This is not to deny that hormones play a role in gender role behavior, but only to assert that they are not *directly* causal in producing a full-blown gender identity disorder.

Here let us return to the topic of congenital adrenal hyperplasia. Girls with CAH have elevated levels of androgen and masculinized genitals at birth. These girls are born, as it were, with two strikes against them. If hormones played a crucial role in gender identity disorder, we should expect that a high proportion of girls would develop the syndrome. Research into these girls instead suggests that they are more masculine and/or less feminine than controls in their *gender role* behavior; that is, they are more active and involved in rough-and-tumble activities (Ehrhardt and Baker 1974; Ehrhardt and Meyer-Bahlburg 1981). They also exhibit somewhat higher levels of gender dysphoria than would be expected in the normal population. Their core sense of being female is largely unaffected, however, and very, very few of them show signs of formal gender identity disorder, both in early childhood and in adolescence.

But there do appear to be intermediate routes whereby the relative status of male and female hormones can indirectly influence one's core experience of gender in the interaction with significant others. Recall that one of the few sex differences found to date is the relative preference of boys for active exploration and rough-and-tumble play as compared to girls. Interestingly, it has also been found that such proclivities can indeed be influenced by prenatal male hormones. Girls with CAH, for example, show a positive preference for rough-

and-tumble play. Similarly, animal experiments have repeatedly shown that a decrease in prenatal male hormones leads to a diminishment in those active behaviors whose analogues in children tend to lead to roughhousing and play fighting with peers. The same biopsychological relation between prenatal hormones and rough-and-tumble play appears to operate in children, though the specific mechanisms governing it are unknown. These findings have led to repeated attempts to document genetic and/or hormonal differences in male children with GID—all without success.

It thus appears that while hormones affect temperament, this impact must be socially mediated in specific ways before it can lead, even indirectly, to the development of GID. Clinical experience bears this out. For example, the father of an otherwise ordinary boy who is passive, fearful, and averse to rough-and-tumble play will often worry about this side of his child and wonder what he can do to help socialize his son sufficiently in masculine pursuits so that he will not be ostracized by his peers. The fathers of some boys with GID, by contrast, will venture to their sons' therapist statements like, "I don't know how I could have sired such a 'wimp'," and at home will withdraw from their boys. Almost always the temperamental fearfulness and motoric inhibition touch some aspect of the father's own unresolved conflicts and insecurity. The same cue leads to different interpretations in the two different kinds of interactions.

Temperament can also indirectly influence the boy's experience of the nascent capacity to classify by gender, particularly when these concepts are first developing. Two aspects of cognition that appear to be "hardwired" from the beginning are relevant. Children appear to be programmed from the start to categorize in binary chunks, for example, big/little, male/female, bad/good, pretty/ugly, and so on. As I mentioned earlier, Kohlberg (1966) even suggests that the first concept that children learn is big/little and the second is male/female. Children create concepts by abstracting from multiple instances of perceptually salient characteristics. For example, when you ask a two-year-old how they can tell the difference between boys and girls, they typically say variations of the following: girls wear dresses or have long hair and boys fight (Kuhn, Nash, and Brucken 1978). For young children, outward appearance (haircut and clothes) and aggression (fighting) are the subcategories subsumed under the boy/girl categorical distinction. Consequently at these early stages of categorization, concepts are grossly overgeneralized and stereotypic, because the child does not have the cognitive capacity to understand subcategories or exceptions to the rule.

For a boy with a shy, inhibited temperament, a nonfighting boy, it must be more difficult at this early age to feel that he really belongs to the category even if he knows how to place himself in the correct conceptual category of boy. My impression is that many boys compare themselves to the other boys and feel that they do not quite fit in, particularly if their peers are very rough-and-tumble and if they do not have other male peers with a temperament similar to their own. From this they move to the feeling that they are more like a girl and, in the context of other, more massively pressing psychodynamics, may come to wish that they were a girl.

Contributing even at an early age, though far more marginally, to this is the fact that boys with GID prefer to play with girls and as a result spend more time in female company. Affiliation patterns of preschoolers are strongly influenced by preferences for children with similar temperaments. This has been particularly demonstrated around differences in aggression, social competence, and social sensitivity (Moller, Culko, and Serbin 1988–89). I would suggest that the boy with GID prefers to be with girls who are less aggressive and more interpersonally sensitive, more like him than rough-and-tumble boys, and this peer affiliation will in turn make him feel less like a boy. The complication for treatment is that this peer preference, though sincerely felt by the child, has already been put in service of a structure designed to deny and mitigate massive trauma.

The point here is that the relationship to peers makes an independent contribution. Boys in our clinic most often identify not liking to fight as a separate and specific reason for not wanting to be a boy. And even when they can make a connection to another shy boy, in their peer group, their temperament remains a complicating factor. Thus, for example, it is not uncommon for such a boy to become upset when his buddy is placed on the opposing team in an intramural sports game; here the heightened capacity for empathic connection (see below) interferes with the normal socialization of competitiveness. The child's insecurity vis à vis his peers, his sense of being not quite like the other boys often predates the development of a GID, which in its turn will lead to frank scapegoating. Being called a "faggot," humiliating in any case, is compounded in these children by the inner sense that there is something different about them to begin with.

Constitution in Boys with GID

A different route to understanding the constitutional diathesis for GID is through the application of concepts derived from other clinical syndromes. Thus, Bradley (1985) has made the important suggestion that these boys may share some of the genetic predisposition for affective disorder. Certainly, there is a great deal of supportive evidence for such a proposition. The high rate of anxiety and depression found in the mothers of these boys (Wolfe 1990; Marantz and Coates 1991; Zucker, personal communication), the collateral finding of borderline pathology in the mothers (Marantz and Coates 1991), the presence of anxiety disorders, depression, and alcohol abuse in a significant percentage of the fathers (Wolfe 1990)—all this points to a strong familial loading for an affective diathesis. The extremely high rate of separation anxiety disorder (55 percent to 60 percent) in these children as well as evidence of depressive symptoms lends support to Bradley's thesis. To be noted here is that if one assumes such a constitutional diathesis to be at work in these children, then one's attention is drawn to the issues of separation and loss as potentially potent traumas that may have a considerable role in instigating the disorder—and this is exactly what one observes clinically in a great many cases.

A different way of conceptualizing the constitutional diathesis required for developing the disorder derives from research into temperament in early development. Boys with GID are typically described as avoidant of rough-and-tumble play, more anxious, fearful in new situations, and more prone to separation anxiety. In this regard they strongly resemble Kagan's (1989) "inhibited" type of child. In Kagan's paradigm, inhibition refers to the degree of fearfulness and uncertainty that a child will manifest in a challenge situation, which consists of the presentation of unfamiliar stimuli in the absence of a primary caretaker. Even at very young ages, children can be reliably ranged on a continuum ranging from extremely inhibited (and thus fearful and timid in the challenge situation) to extremely uninhibited or bold. Here, as with other variables such as curiosity and activity level, one would expect that during the course of development, the child's degree of inhibition would shift and change according to environmental variation and, even more importantly, according to the quality and stability of the interaction with primary caregivers, with the result that initial scores would not by themselves be predictive of later ones. And indeed this is so for the great midrange of children ranging from moderately inhibited to moderately uninhibited.

What Kagan has discovered, however, is that the extremes of the continuum, the 15 percent of children who are extremely inhibited and the other 15 percent of children who are extremely uninhibited, prove to be remarkably stable over the course of the early years of development. Kagan thus proposes that a qualitative distinction applies to these children, or in other words that we are here dealing with constitutional types. Kagan notes in particular that the inhibited type shows a heightened degree of initial arousal in the challenge situation; he believes this is the result of lower thresholds for arousal in the limbic-hypothalamic system.

The phenomenon of behavioral inhibition can be seen as a strategy for coping with a more highly reactive central nervous system. Put in commonsense terms, it takes far less to send an inhibited child's pulse racing; accordingly, such a child is far less adventurous in terms of what he will spontaneously expose himself to in situations of uncertainty. The observed degree of inhibition is the outward behavioral compensation for the inward condition of being readily and highly aroused.

Kagan also notes that among his "inhibited" type there is, among Caucasians, an unusually high percentage of blue-eyed, blond-haired children—approximately 60 percent. Moreover, Kagan (1989) has found that blue-eyed, blonde-haired, shy adults that have high levels of physiological arousal in new situations also have lower olfactory thresholds than brown-eyed males who describe themselves as very sociable. Millidot (cited in Kagan 1989) had previously reported lower tactile thresholds in a comparable comparison of blue-eyed and brown-eyed adults. The biological mediating mechanisms underlying these associations are not yet known. What they suggest, however, is that the presence of blond hair and blue eyes in an inhibited Caucasian child will be further associated with lower olfactory and tactile thresholds. In other words, the high level of internal arousal is reflected in greater sensitivity to these kinds of sensory stimulation.

In addition, shy, inhibited adults (Bell et al. 1990), shy children during their infancy (Kagan et al. 1991), and the first- and second-degree relatives of shy children in comparison to bolds (Kagan et al. 1991) have a greater incidence of allergies, especially hay fever. As well, Teiramaa (1978a, 1978b, 1979) has reported an association between childhood shyness and both greater severity and poorer outcome of asthma.

Children who are shy and inhibited are at risk of developing anxiety disorders and depression (Kagan, Reznick, and Snidman 1988; Rosenbaum et al. 1988). Moreover, parents who have panic disorders, agoraphobia, or major depression have children who have the highest rates of shy, inhibited behavior (Rosenbaum et al. 1988).

The portrait of the boy who is susceptible to developing a gender identity disorder shares some notable similarities with Kagan's inhibited type. Our clinical impression is that boys with GID are often markedly fearful in strange situations (a trait that can be observed well before the onset of the disorder proper) and are very slow to make a transition to new situations. Compared to other children, boys with GID typically need the safe base of their parents for longer periods of time when making these transitions; in clinic situations they will hang at the door, holding mother's hand, and wait for a time before going in on their own. Moreover, these boys typically tend to rely on significant others for clues about novel situations. By the same token, they very often are unusually adept at reading such clues and are able to make correct judgments on the basis of subtle signals. This, too, becomes part of the child's adaptive repertoire. They have an intense gaze and they often search the interviewer's face, trying to read affective and interpersonal clues.

Stoller (1968) first described boys with GID as having unusual sensory sensitivities, involving sight, sound, touch, and olfaction. These same sensory sensitivities as well as a sensitivity to taste have also been striking in the boys that we have evaluated at the St. Luke's/Roosevelt Hospital Childhood Gender Identity Center. These sensitivities are reflected in both an increased capacity to derive pleasure from a particular sensory modality, such as pleasure in colors, music, textures, taste, and olfaction, and in a heightened vulnerability to the dysphoric aspects of sensory experience. For example, a mother may report that her child will spontaneously remark on good smells, such as cookies baking in the oven, but that he will gag when a garbage truck passes. Another child will be described as enjoying music and will demonstrate musical talent but also will cry at unexpected loud sounds such as the doorbell ringing, a vacuum cleaner being turned on, or raised voices. Many boys with GID refuse to wear a new shirt unless the tag is cut out, but by the same token they will derive obvious enjoyment from the feeling of soft textures next to their skin. Similarly, these boys are frequently drawn to bright, vivid colors but will sometimes have strong aversions to dark colors, to the point where, for example, they will refuse to wear black.

Allergies are also notable in boys with GID. In two separate samples of boys, ongoing treatment for asthma occurred in 20 percent (Coates and Person 1985) and 23 percent (Coates and Wolfe, unpublished data) of the two samples, respectively. Allergies such as hay fever and hives are frequently reported as well. Interestingly, like Kagan, we have also found that in a consecutive sample of twenty-five Caucasian children, 60 percent had blond hair and blue eyes.

An obvious question is whether there is a direct relationship between an inhibited temperament and the development of GID. Kagan and Moss (1962) in the Fels Longitudinal Study found that the only characteristic that was stable from the first three years of life into adulthood was what they called passivity at that time, but now call "inhibition." However, boys who were extremely passive at age three grew up to be relatively passive and dependent as adults, and interested in relatively "non-masculine interests" (Kagan and Moss 1962, 276). No studies have yet been done demonstrating a direct relationship between an inhibited temperament and gender identity disorder, but it is currently being investigated in our center. The link, nevertheless, between inhibited temperament and the development of GID is very striking. I would in fact postulate that boys with GID are a subset of Kagan's inhibited type. One can think of temperament as the nonspecific predisposer to the development of GID, one that is compatible with Bradley's (1985) proposal of the genetic diathesis being familial affective disorder. But other environmental and experiential factors must come into play for a GID to come about.

The last point needs emphasis. Even at the level of temperament, Kagan (1989) raises the important question of whether temperament is determined by biology alone or in interaction with the child's early environment. On this point he commented,

> We suggest, albeit speculatively, that most of the children we call inhibited belong to a qualitatively distinct category of infants who were born with a lower threshold for limbic-hypothalamic arousal to unexpected changes in the environment or novel events that cannot be assimilated easily. . . .
>
> However, we believe that the actualization of shy, quiet, timid behavior at two years of age requires some form of chronic environmental stress acting upon the original temperamental disposition present at birth. Some possible stressors include prolonged hospitalization, death of a parent, marital quarreling, or mental illness in a family member. (1989, 161–62)

Although we agree with Kagan that a reactive temperament can be made more reactive by stress, we also share the view of Sroufe (1985) that temperament is codetermined by constitution and the attachment experience from the beginning of life. That is to say, once one moves beyond the neurological and behavioral status of the neonate as observed immediately after birth, one is necessarily viewing something that has evolved in the context of the continuing mother-child interaction.

One should also note that trauma can have a permanent effect on temperament, either exaggerating it or shifting it in a new direction. A growing body of neurobiological literature suggests that significant stress can literally alter the "hardwiring" of the brain, both in terms of neurochemical processes and in terms of the microanatomical structures. Kandel (1983) has been able to demonstrate this process of change even in an animal as primitive as a snail: the changes induced by stress become encoded at the synaptic level. Moreover, recent research (Post 1992) provides evidence that the first episode in a person's life of a primary affective disorder (whether mania or depression) may permanently alter gene expression and thus give rise to a series of changes in the production of neurotransmitters, in receptor site sensitivity, and in the formation of neuropeptides. Thus, while it may take a significant trauma, such as a severe loss, to trigger the first such episode, subsequent episodes become progressively easier to trigger owing to the neurological change. Similarly, though in less dramatic fashion, accumulated stress and trauma in the developing child's life can lead to an exacerbation of his or her original temperament. Not uncommonly in the histories of children who develop GID, one can identify such changes prior to the onset of the disorder. In the case of Colin, reported elsewhere (Coates, Friedman, and Wolfe 1991), for example, the temporary loss of his father and grandmother at age two seemed to effect a shift in his disposition such that he went from being a very sensitive child to being a very oversensitive and anxious child.

Constitution and Attachment

Findings from primate research on the role of temperament and early experience of separation and attachment on the development of depression can help us to illuminate ways that temperament, stress, and attachment relationships interact. The relevance of primate models to the psychobiology of human depression, first proposed by Bowlby (1969), is now no longer in doubt. The infants of many primate species show a distinct pattern of protest followed by resignation when they are separated from their mothers. When the separation persists, the infant monkeys typically develop both neurochemical and behavioral sequelae. These sequelae in turn predispose the individual monkey to develop reactions in later adulthood that appear analogous to human depression, or at the very least to those aspects of human depression that are anaclitic in nature.

What is often not appreciated by psychodynamic clinicians is that there is a considerable intraspecies variation in the degree to which individual monkeys are prone to develop separation reactions in early life and depressive equivalents later on. Indeed, it is possible through selective breeding to develop strains within a given monkey species in which both tendencies are unusually high. Here I would like to report on the remarkable experiments of Suomi (1991a, 1991b) with the Bonnet monkey. Bonnets make a good species to study because in the wild periodic separations between mother and child are the rule, a fact that allows easy comparison with artificially induced separations in the laboratory. What Suomi (1991a) did was to breed one strain of Bonnets in which vulnerability to early separation and subsequent "depression" was quite high and a second group of low physiologically reactive monkeys in which vulnerability to separation was low. The former monkeys he identified as high reactives and the latter as low reactives. Like Kagan, he conceptualized these differences as reflecting differences in neurophysiological reactivity, and he too found that at the extremes of the continuum, approximately the highest and lowest 20 percent temperamental styles were stable over long developmental periods. That is, the high reactives were sensitive to separations and tended to remain so over their life course.

Suomi (1991b) then conducted a remarkable additional experiment on the interaction of temperament and early attachment experience. He divided the high and low reactives into two groups that were raised by two different kinds of mothers. The first were ordinary, competent mothers and the second were mothers who were particularly nurturant. Being an unusually nurturant mother was defined by a willingness to wean the monkey baby slowly rather than abruptly batting the infant off her breast, as is typical of the species; moreover, nurturant mothers remained accessible to their babies as they began to experiment with separating from her and exploring the environment on their own. Half of each group of high and low reactives were raised by each of these styles of mothering.

As they grew older the monkeys were placed in a larger single group, wherein adolescent Bonnets normally form dominance hierarchies. Status in the dominance hierarchy is determined by complex social skills and is a critical measure of adaptive competence in primates. In the group was also placed a pair of "foster grandparents," older monkeys whose presence was designed to keep control over levels of aggression. To Suomi's considerable surprise, the shy, high reactive monkeys raised by the nurturant mothers were the only monkeys to touch base with the "foster grandparents" (particularly the female), and it was these same monkeys who subsequently ended up and remained at the top of the hierarchy. The shy ones raised by the ordinary mothers did not make use of the older parents and ended up at the bottom. The low reactive or bold monkeys all ended up in the middle of the hierarchy, their status appearing to be relatively unaffected by parenting style.

These findings are in keeping with the contemporary psychoanalytic developmental researches (Stern 1985; Emde 1988a, 1988b; Lachman and Beebe 1992; Slade and Aber 1992; Zeanah et al. 1989) that have found that continuities in development grow out of the child-caretaker interaction unit and not out of separate continuities within either the child or the parent. That is to say that in order to make even moderately successful predictions of later childhood on the basis of observations at earlier ages, we must look at the mother-child interaction unit. The significance of Suomi's work in this context is that he has demonstrated that a given temperamental trait (in this case high reactivity) can take variable phenotypal expression depending on the quality of the infant's early attachment relationship. Monkeys bred to be sensitive to separation and later depression, but given the advantage of unusually nurturant mothers and later the availability of "foster grandparents," proved to be unusually robust as adolescents, outstripping not only similarly endowed monkeys in terms of temperament, but also monkeys bred to be bolder and less sensitive to separation.

Constitution and Attachment in the Onset of GID

The foregoing considerations allow us, I contend, to look at the typical etiological constellation leading to the development of GID in a new light. Assuming that children prone to GID are comparable to Kagan's inhibited type, then one would expect them to form unusually close attachments to caregivers and, by the same token, to be unusually responsive to disruptions in the attachment bond. This, in fact, is what is reported and observed with children who develop GID. Often the mothers will report that the early period of attachment was quite close and loving, and that there only began to be significant difficulties at a later age. Moreover, when one begins to chart the impact of trauma, both to the child and to the mother, on the development of the disorder, one invariably finds that in the wake of the trauma, the attachment system between mother and child became derailed. The GID, in turn, arose in the context of this derailment.

If we take matters from the child's point of view, the loss of maternal availability will be a catastrophe. These children depend on their primary caretakers to help modulate their levels of arousal (since they are highly reactive and sensitive to change, transition, and sensory input) and to provide clues as to how one should deal with new situations. Consistent, attuned, and attentive mothering will help modulate a boy's reactivity, will help him create a stimulus barrier and reduce his anxiety in strange situations, and will help him in developing autonomy. However, a boy so predisposed will be far more reactive to inconsistent parenting and disruption of the attachment relationship, and it will be far more destabilizing to him than to a boy of lower reactivity. Put in other terms, these children depend for their very survival affectively on the intersubjective world between self and other; when they lose intersubjective connectedness, as for example with a mother who has abandoned herself to a depression, these children lose more than their objects. In an important way they lose themselves—or at least that is the threat. The restoration of the object in the fantasy fusion of self with mother becomes an important mode for restabilizing the self.

Moreover, some of the same sensory sensitivities that characterize the highly reactive child come to be employed in the reparative cross-gender identification. The child's love of texture, for example, can be redirected in his interest in female attire, his love of colors in an interest in makeup, and so forth. The characteristic stereotyped behaviors that define the disorder thus help bind the very sensitivities whose existence helped bring it into being. Likewise, the ability to imitate feminine behavior, so striking to the observer, involves the redirection through imitation of the child's previous close scrutiny of his significant caretaker. These children were watching Mommy very closely; when they decided that their survival depended on becoming Mommy, they had a whole repertoire of observations to build their mimicry on.

What is essential to understand here is that for the cross-gender fantasy to become locked in, it must revitalize the depressed mother and therefore repair the derailed attachment relationship. For it to succeed in revitalizing the mother it must be fueled by forces within her. Boyhood GID comes about when there is a dance between forces in the child and the mother. The child's own attempt to repair the mother/child bond and thereby mitigate his anxiety, within the parameters set by his temperament, must interlock with powerful maternal psychodynamics in a way that makes the cross-gender identification an improvement on the previous state of traumatic disruption in attachment. It is this interlocking of the boy's and the mother's solution that sets the disorder in motion and contributes to its perpetuation.

One could extend our discussion of temperament still further and note how various collateral features of the disorder also come to have additional meaning when viewed through the lens of the child's constitutional endowment. For example, the absence of a relationship with the father seen in so many cases will compound the child's separation anxiety, already at traumatic levels. Similarly, the schismatic relationship between the parents will mean that the father will fail to intervene in the relationship between mother and son; the son will be left to read the cues that his mother gives out on his own. If, in this context, his otherwise depressed mother becomes enlivened by a display of cross-gender identification, and the father subsequently does nothing to set limits on and redirect the behavior, the child will have discovered an impressively effective coping device for restoring relatedness with his primary caretaker.

Three other aspects of the disorder might also be mentioned here in connection with constitution: poor peer relations, difficulties managing aggression, and response to treatment interventions. In terms of peer relations, it is important to remember that the inhibited boy will be naturally aversive to the very sort of rough-and-tumble play that other boys prefer. On the basis of temperament alone, one might expect these children to more often seek out the company of girls and to be drawn to less aggressive pursuits. When a disturbance in gender identity is added to this, resulting in behaviors that are destined to provoke severe ostracism from other boys, the child's predicament is almost untenable. The clinician, in conjunction with parents and perhaps also teachers, must help the child explore the available interpersonal world in search of male peers whose temperament and interests more closely match his own, or else who are tolerant of having a shy friend.

In terms of the handling of aggression, these children often exhibit dissociative defenses. A trauma will make a bold child more aggressive, even hyperaggressive, but it will make an inhibited child even more inhibited, while his own aggressive drives become projected into the environment. The clinician should be sensitive to the intrapsychic sources underlying this increase in fearfulness and help the child gradually to integrate his own aggressive feelings. As well, in initial assessments the clinician should be aware that these children, though they often present as docile and compliant, are capable of extreme outbursts of aggression once their threshold has been reached. These outbursts, moreover, have typically been met with inadequate limit setting and redirecting from the parents. Work on appropriate limit setting needs to be done both in the office and in the home. This is particularly important, since as treatment proceeds and the cross-gender defenses weaken, hitherto bound aggression in the child will become liberated often in unmodulated ways. It is critical that the father be actively engaged in his son's treatment since fathers have a major role to play in the socialization of their sons' aggression (Herzog 1982) as well as their gender identity.

In terms of treatment responsivity, the existence of a basic constitutional temperament loaded for behavioral inhibition makes these children unusually "resistant" to strategies that emphasize rapid behavioral change and hence, however inadvertently, introduce novelty. In our work with these children, as in our work with their parents, a psycho-educational approach is extremely useful vis à vis the specific issue of temperament. Fathers in particular may need help in learning how to approach and engage their sons. For example, a well-meaning father may attempt to engage his son in a game of catch and only succeed in terrorizing the boy: all primates are afraid of fast-moving objects, and these little boys in particular need to spend much longer periods of time with soft tosses (e.g., with a nerf ball) before they graduate to playing with a harder ball. Moreover, just as a father must learn to engage his extremely shy and timid boy, the boy himself can profit from learning about his disposition and his coping strategies in a way he can understand. Thus, for example, one boy who refused to go to a party was reminded of how he had handled a similar occasion the previous week—he hung at the door for a half hour, and then had a splendid time—and was encouraged to try the same strategy again. Obviously, the same sensitivity to the child's temperament also ought to be manifest in how one frames dynamic interpretations during the course of treatment.

Gender identity disorder of childhood is brought about by complex and multiple factors, biological, interpersonal, and intrapsychic, that interact at multiple levels of development. In any given individual the relative weight of one of these factors over another may vary; the clinician and the researcher must allow for multiple pathways leading to the development of the disorder.

Constitution, in particular, serves as a predisposing factor by lowering the threshold for derailment of the attachment system. In addition, it increases the child's sensitivity to parental wishes. These are filtered through the child's mind, that is, both limited by his cognitive developmental level and distorted by his own conflicts about separation and aggression.

The chronic pathology of the parents leaves the sensitive, reactive child with an insecure, anxious attachment. When trauma or severe marital stress are added, causing maternal depression and severe anxiety, a traumatic derailment of the mother-child attachment bond occurs. This results in a cascade effect that in turn traumatizes the child. When the child's attempts to repair the derailed attachment involve gender content and he succeeds in revitalizing the mother, all the factors necessary for the onset and development of a GID are in place. Many factors come to play a role in perpetuating the symptoms; these involve ongoing internal mechanisms, ongoing interpersonal mechanisms in the attachment relationship, and the child's ongoing experiences with his peers.

What is essential to understand about the specific contribution of constitution is that it does not specifically involve gender other than temperamental differences at the outset. The reparative solution that the child creates involves gender content that becomes overburdened with meaning. On the maternal side, for cross-gender behavior to succeed in revitalizing the derailed attachment relationship, powerful psychodynamics have to be involved. We can understand the disorder only by taking into consideration both the child's and the maternal/paternal psychodynamic contribution simultaneously during a sensitive period of development.

In this essay we have been principally concerned with two subsidiary questions arising out of research into this multiply determined, pervasive disorder of childhood. The first is the role of constitutional factors in predisposing for the disorder. Bradley's suggestion that these children may have an inherited predisposition for affective disorder, clinically manifest in early childhood in a proneness to anxiety states, is valuable and entirely consonant with this author's clinical experience. Further, I have been arguing that these children can also be seen as a subset of Kagan's inhibited type, and on the basis of Kagan's observations, ethological research, and clinical experience, I have been emphasizing in particular the constitutional need for a protective attachment relationship and the vulnerability to disruptions in the mother/child bond. How best to integrate these two overlapping conceptualizations, Bradley's and my own, remains a topic for further investigation. Nonetheless, it is already clear that there is a specific constitutional predisposition for the disorder and that an understanding of this disposition clarifies in important ways the impact of such psychodynamic, parental, and familial risk factors as have otherwise empirically and clinically been identified. Rather than constitute an alternative mode of explanation, understanding the role of constitution deepens our understanding of the psychodynamic etiology of this disorder. To repeat what I have emphasized in this essay one last time, the study of the phenotypal expression of any set of genotypal factors necessarily must take the environment and the individual's experience of that environment through development into account. In gender identity disorder, as well as other stable configurations in childhood, one must look at the interaction pattern between the child and significant caretakers.

The second subsidiary question we have been concerned with has been whether an understanding of the constitutional predisposition to this disorder sheds any light on the psychobiological roots of masculinity and femininity. What we have found is that there is indeed an area of overlap. Boys who are prone to develop gender identity disorder are less "masculine" and more "feminine" in the very restricted sense that they show an aversion to rough-and-tumble play. However—and this point is crucial—in this respect they resemble other inhibited boys who do not develop the disorder. Accordingly, if there is a lesson to be drawn from this research with regard to the general topic of gender, it would be that masculinity and femininity, probably over the course of the life cycle but most certainly in early childhood, reflect the impact of and are embedded in the experience with significant others. In short, becoming a boy or a girl is not biologically preprogrammed in any simple sense. One learns to be a boy or a girl, and to take pleasure in that aspect of the self, only insofar as the environment rewards, supports, and enjoys that aspect in the context of a more general recognition of one's right to be, including one's right to be different.

Note

I would like to express my enormous appreciation to John Kerr, whose probing questions in many dialogues led me to both sharpen my thinking and rethink some of my formulations. Also William Byne offered some helpful suggestions on an earlier version of this essay.

References

Bates, J. E., P. M. Bentler, and S. K. Thompson. 1979. Gender-deviant boys compared with normal and clinical control boys. *Journal of Abnormal Child Psychology* 7: 243–59.

Bell, A. P., M. S. Weinberg, and S. K. Hammersmith. 1981. *Sexual Preference: Its Development in Men and Women.* Bloomington: Indiana University Press.

Bell, I. R., M. L. Jasnoski, J. Kagan, and D. King. 1990. Allergic Rhinitis more frequent in young adults with extreme shyness? A preliminary survey. *Psychosomatic Medicine* 52: 511–16.

Bowlby, J. 1969. *Attachment and Loss, Volume 1: Attachment.* New York: Basic Books.

Bradley, S. J. 1985. Gender disorders in childhood: A formulation. In *Gender Dysphoria: Development, Research, Management,* ed. B. W. Steiner, 175–88. New York: Plenum.

Bradley, S. J., R. W. Doering, K. J. Zucker, J. K. Finegan, and G. M. Gonda. 1980. Assessment of the gender/disturbed child: A comparison to sibling and psychiatric controls. In *Childhood and Sexuality,* ed. J. Samson, 554–68. Montreal: Editions Etudes Vivantes.

Byne, W., and B. Parsons. In press. Human sexual orientation: The biological theories reappraised. *Archives of General Psychiatry.*

Coates, S. 1992. The etiology of boyhood gender identity disorder: An integrative model. In *Interface of Psychoanalysis and Psychology,* ed. J. W. Barron, M. N. Eagle, and D. L. Wolitzky, 245–65. Washington, DC: American Psychological Association.

Coates, S., R. C. Friedman, and S. Wolfe. 1991. The etiology of boyhood gender identity disorder: A model for integrating psychodynamics, temperament and development. *Psychoanalytic Dialogues: A Journal of Relational Perspectives* 1:341–83.

Coates, S., and E. S. Person. 1985. Extreme boyhood femininity: Isolated finding or pervasive disorder? *Journal of the American Academy of Child Psychiatry* 24: 702–9.

Coates, S., and S. Wolfe. In preparation. History, politics and ethics of treating boys with gender identity disorder.

DiPietro, J. A. 1981. Rough and tumble play: A function of gender. *Developmental Psychology* 4: 429–33.

Ehrhardt, A. A., and S. W. Baker. 1974. Fetal androgens, human central nervous system differentiation, and behavior sex differences. In *Sex Differences in Behavior,* ed. R. C. Friedman, R. M. Ricart, and R. L. Van de Wiele, 33–51. New York: Wiley.

Ehrhardt, A. A., and H.F.L. Meyer-Bahlburg 1981. Effects of prenatal sex hormones on gender-related behavior. *Science* 211: 1312–18.

Emde, R. N. 1988a. Development terminable and interminable II. *International Journal of Psycho-analysis* 69:23–42.

———. 1988b. Development terminable and interminable II. *International Journal of Psycho-analysis* 69: 283–96.

Emde, R. N., Z. Biringen, R. B. Clyman, and D. Oppenheim. 1991. The moral self of infancy: Affective core and procedural knowledge. *Developmental Review* 11: 251–70.

Fagot, B. I., and M. D. Leinbach, and R. Hagan. 1986. Gender labeling and the adoption of sex-typed behaviors. *Developmental Psychology* 22: 440–43.

Fast, I. 1984. *Gender Identity: A Differentiation Model.* Hillsdale, NJ: Analytic Press.

Friedman, R. C. 1988. *Male Homosexuality: A Contemporary Psychoanalytic Perspective.* New Haven: Yale University Press.

Friedman, R. C., and J. Downey. In press. Neurobiology and sexual orientation: Current relationships. *Journal of Neuropsychiatry and Clinical Neurosciences.*

Green, R. 1974. *Sexual Identity Conflicts in Children and Adults.* Baltimore: Penguin Books.

———. 1987. *The "Sissy Boy Syndrome" and the Development of Homosexuality.* New Haven: Yale University Press.

Green, R., and J. Money. 1960. Incongruous gender role: Non-genital manifestations in prepubertal boys. *Journal of Nervous and Mental Disorders* 131: 160–68.

Green, R., D. S. Neuberg, and S. J. Finch. 1983. Sex-typed motor behaviors of "feminine" boys, conventionally masculine boys, and conventionally feminine girls. *Sex Roles* 9: 571–79.

Greenson, R. 1968. Dis-identifying from mother. *International Journal of Psycho-analysis* 49: 370–74.

Herzog, J. M. 1982. On affect hunger: The father's role in the modulation of aggressive drive and fantasy. In *Father and Child: Developmental and Clinical Perspectives,* ed. S. H. Cath, A. K. Gurwitt, and J. M. Ross, 163–74. Boston: Little, Brown.

Kagan, J. 1989. *Unstable Ideas: Temperament, Cognition and Self.* Cambridge: Harvard University Press.

Kagan, J., and H. Moss. 1962. *From Birth to Maturity: A Study of Psychological Development.* New York: John Wiley and Sons.

Kagan, J., J. S. Reznick, and N. Snidman. 1987. The physiology and psychology of behavioral inhibition in children. *Child Development* 58: 1459–73.

———. 1988. Biological bases of shyness. *Science* 240: 167–71.

Kagan, J., N. Snidman, M. Julia-Sellers, and M. O. Johnson. 1991. Temperament and allergic symptoms. *Psychosomatic Medicine* 53: 332–40.

Kandel, E. R. 1983. From metapsychology to molecular biology: Explorations into the nature of anxiety. *American Journal of Psychiatry* 140: 1277–93.

Kohlberg, L. A. 1966. A cognitive-developmental analysis of children's sex-role concepts and attitudes. In *The Development of Sex Differences*, ed. E. E. Maccoby. Stanford: Stanford University Press.

Krafft-Ebing, R. von. [1902] 1965. *Psychopathia Sexualis: A Medico-Forensic Study*. Trans. H. Wedeck. New York: G. P. Putnam's Sons.

Kuhn, D., S. Nash, and L. Brucken. 1978. Sex role concepts of two- and three-year olds. *Child Development* 49: 445–51.

Lachman, F. M., and B. Beebe. 1992. Reformulations of early development and transference: Implications for psychic structure formation. In *Interface of Psychoanalysis and Psychology*, ed. J. W. Barron, M. N. Eagle, and D. L. Wolitzky, 133–53. Washington, DC; American Psychological Association.

Lowry, C. B., and K. J. Zucker. 1991. Is there an association between separation anxiety disorder and gender identity disorder in boys? Paper presented at the meeting of the Society for Research in Child and Adolescent Psychopathology, Zandvoort, Netherlands.

Marantz, S., and S. Coates. 1991. Mothers of boys with gender identity disorder: A comparison to normal controls. *Journal of the American Academy of Child and Adolescent Psychiatry* 30: 136–43.

Moll, A. [1907] 1912. *The Sexual Life of the Child*. New York: Macmillan.

Moller, L. C., J. Culko, and L. A. Serbin. 1988–89. Same-sex affiliation in preschoolers: Influence of behavioral compatibility. *Centre for Research in Human Development Research Bulletins* (Concordia University) 7(5).

Money, J. 1973. Gender role, gender identity, core gender identity: Usage and definition of terms. *Journal of the American Academy of Psychoanalysis* 1: 397–403.

Money, J., and A. A. Ehrhardt. 1972. *Man and Woman, Boy and Girl: The Differentiation and Dimorphism of Gender Identity from Conception to Maturity*. Baltimore: Johns Hopkins University Press.

Money, J., J. G. Hampson, and J. I. Hampson. 1955. An examination of basic sexual concepts: The evidence of human hermaphroditism. *Bulletin of the Johns Hopkins Hospital* 97: 301–19.

Phoenix, C. H., C. W. Goy, and A. A. Gerall. et al. 1959. Organizing action of prenatally administered testosterone proprionate on the tissues mediating mating behavior in the female guinea pig. *Endocrinology* 65: 369–82.

Post, R. M. 1992. Transduction of psychosocial stress into the neurobiology of recurrent affective disorder. *American Journal of Psychiatry* 149(8): 999–1010.

Reznick, J. S., J. Kagan, N. Snidman, M. Gersten, K. Baak, and A. Rosenberg. 1986. Inhibited and uninhibited children: A follow-up study. *Child Development* 57: 660–80.

Rosenbaum, J. F., J. Biederman, M. Gersten, D. R. Hirshfeld, S. R. Menninger, J. B. Herman, J. Kagan, J. S. Reznick, and N. Snidman. 1988. *Archives of General Psychiatry* 45: 463–70.

Saghir, M. T., and E. Robins, 1973. *Male and Female Homosexuality: A Comprehensive Investigation*. Baltimore: Williams and Wilkins.

Slade, A., and J. L. Aber. 1992. Attachments, drives, and development: Conflicts and convergences in theory. In *Interface of Psychoanalysis and Psychology*, ed. J. W.

Barron, M. N. Eagle, and D. L. Wolitzky, 154–85. Washington, DC: American Psychological Association.

Sroufe, L. S. 1985. Attachment classification from the perspective of infant-caregiver relationships and infant temperament. *Child Development* 56: 1–14.

Stern, D. 1985. *The Interpersonal World of the Infant*. New York: Basic Books.

Stoller, R. J. 1968. *Sex and Gender. Vol. 1: The Development of Masculinity and Femininity*. New York: Science House.

———. 1975. *Sex and Gender. Vol. 2: The Transsexual Experiment*. New York: Science House.

Suomi, S. J. 1991a. Primate separation models of affective disorders. In *Neurobiology of Learning, Emotion and Affect*, ed. John Madden IV. New York: Raven Press.

———. 1991b. Early stress and adult emotional reactivity in rhesus monkeys. In *The Childhood Environment and Adult Disease*, 171–88. Wiley, Chichester, Ciba Foundation Symposium 156.

Teiramaa, E. 1978a. Psychic disturbances and severity of asthma. *Journal of Psychosomatic Research* 22: 401–8.

———. 1978b. Psychosocial and psychic factors in the course of asthma. *Journal of Psychosomatic Research* 22: 121–25.

———. 1979. Psychosocial and psychic factors and age at onset of asthma. *Journal of Psychosomatic Research* 23: 27–37.

Ward, I. L. 1984. The prenatal stress syndrome: Current status. *Psychoneuroendocrinology* 9: 3–13.

Wolfe, S. 1990. Psychopathology and psychodynamics of parents of boys with a gender identity disorder. Ph.D. diss., City University of New York.

Zeanah, C. H., T. F. Anders, R. Seifer, and D. Stern. 1989. Implications of research on infant development for psychodynamic theory and practice. *American Academy of Child and Adolescent Psychiatry* 28(5): 657–68.

Zucker, K. J. 1985. Cross-gender-identified children. In *Gender Dysphoria: Development, Research, Management*, ed. B. W. Steiner, 75–174. New York: Plenum.

Zucker, K. J., R. W. Doering, S. J. Bradley, and J. K. Finegan. 1982. Sex-typed play in gender disturbed children: A comparison to sibling and psychiatric controls. *Archives of Sexual Behavior* 11: 309–21.

Zucker, K. J., and R. Green, 1992. Psychosexual disorders in children and adolescents. *Journal of Child Psychology and Psychiatry* 33(1): 107–51.

Zucker, K. J., J. Wild, S. J. Bradley, and C. B. Lowry, 1992. Physical attractiveness of boys with gender identity disorder. *Archives of Sexual Behavior*.

Zuger, B. 1988. Is early effeminate behavior in boys early homosexuality? *Comprehensive Psychiatry* 29: 509–19.

11

Bodies in Motion: Lesbian and Transsexual Histories

Nan Alamilla Boyd

Here on the gender borders at the close of the twentieth century, with the faltering of phallocratic hegemony and the bumptious appearance of heteroglossic origin accounts, we find the epistemologies of white male medical practice, the rage of radical feminist theories and the chaos of lived gendered experience meeting on the battle field of the transsexual body: a hotly contested site of cultural inscription, a meaning machine for the production of ideal type.
— Sandy Stone, "The Empire Strikes Back:
A Posttranssexual Manifesto"

My point of departure is that nationality ... nation-ness, as well as nationalism, are cultural artifacts of a particular kind. To understand them properly we need to consider carefully how they have come into historical being, in what ways their meanings have changed over time, and why, today, they command such profound emotional legitimacy.
— Benedict Anderson, *Imagined Communities*

This essay concerns the relationship between bodies and nations, and more specifically, transsexual bodies and lesbian nations.[1] It explores how visible, intelligible, and legible bodies come to reflect, define, and regulate the nation as a boundaried political geography.[2] I suggest that the naturalized body is not simply a duped or docile subject; nor is it free to determine its own form.[3] Rather, the body remains a highly politicized, unstable, and symbolic structure, intimately connected to the state, and as a result, it reflects both nationalism and resistant social movements.

In many ways, the connection between nationalism's history and the body's relationship to the state remains obscure.[4] However, as Michel Foucault explains, while divinely ordained monarchies crumbled in the face of late nineteenth-century West European republicanism and the concomitant rise of state nationalism, state-sanctioned punishments (law) helped transform the body into a political anatomy.[5] Not only did the materiality of the body gain meaning as it became *subject to* new laws and regulations, but paradoxically the body became the *subject of* the state as a (perhaps interchangeable) physical representation of republican ideology.[6] In other words, the body begins to imagine itself meaningfully autonomous and individual only in relation to the collective: the republican state. Thus, the body's subjectivity—its social and political agency— remains linked to its physicality, to the social meaning of human corporeality. In this way, through the nineteenth century, as *individuals* began to participate more dynamically in the body politic, the body through its social and political gestures, indeed its social and political embodiments, began to participate more efficiently in its own regulation and prohibitions.

While the body becomes self-regulating as respectable or heteronormal, for example, in order to affirm an empowered relationship to the state, the body's intelligibility incorporates it within the nation. The nation, as Benedict Anderson argues, functions as "an imagined political community," a community that will never completely know itself—it will never know all its constituents—but it learns to recognize its members (even sight unseen) as part of a limited, boundaried, and sovereign entity, "a deep, horizontal comradeship."[7] The nation functions differently than the state in that the state emerged as the political invention of the Age of Revolution and Enlightenment, as a political geography sovereign through its own efforts and imaginings rather than its God-ordained nobility or territorial sweep. The nation, however, emerged as the state's cultural artifact and constant companion. The nation and nationalism, if Anderson's arguments are correct, claim cultural legitimacy for the state insofar as nationalism replaced religious and dynastic symbols with a secular semiotics of political representation.[8] However, as this essay will demonstrate, while nationalisms reflect, reinforce, and reinvigorate the state, contemporary social and political movements also invoke the language of nationalism in order to resist and restructure the state. In other words, while late eighteenth-century revolutionary movements engineered the hegemony of the modern nation/state in order to resist monarchial and/or colonial tyranny, contemporary resistant movements (anticolonial, socialist, antiracist, queer) often imagine themselves within a cultural system—nationalism—that reinscribes the foundations of state capitalism.

These notes help us understand the body's relationship to both the nation (nationalism) and the state (law), particularly since some bodies matter more than others. Bodies that inhabit or enact naturalized states of being remain culturally intelligible, socially valuable, and as a result, gain and retain the privilege of citizenship and its associated rights and protections. Bodies that matter, as Judith Butler argues, are worth protecting, saving, grieving.[9] Some bodies, however, are less intelligible or unintelligible and are not instrumental or valuable to the state; in fact, these bodies undermine in many different ways the recognition or comradeship central to nationalism's purpose. It makes no difference if these bodies die or if no one grieves them because, as Butler explains, abject bodies—bodies transgressive of borders and boundaries—do not matter. They do not function intelligibly as matter, and they do not have value. How then does the materiality or morphology of the body influence its social value, its political purchase? Do abject or queer bodies retain inchoate or inherently resistant positions vis-à-vis the state? Is it necessary to transition (or pass) from abject to intelligible in order to function within the state (or in order to resist a state-sanctioned, rights-based economy of value)? How do bodies that do not matter become bodies that matter?

Despite twentieth-century antihumanist and anti-essentialist gestures away from the body, the material body continues to influence contemporary social and political movements. For instance, as queers begin to visibly take up public space and imagine themselves part of a larger political community, they often do so around a system of meanings that transforms bodies into specific, cohesive, and authentic identities. Gay men, lesbians, bisexuals, and transsexuals, as increasingly viable subjects in relation to the state, police their own borders, regulating the social territories they inhabit, including their bodies, in an effort to secure and protect limited political entitlements. For example, in June 1994 the Human Rights Campaign Fund (HRCF), a U.S. gay and lesbian lobbying organization, brought antidiscrimination legislation to Congress through several key representatives. If adopted, this legislative package, known as ENDA (the Employment Non-Discrimination Act), would protect lesbians, bisexuals, and gay men in the United States from "job discrimination or special treatment on the basis of sexual orientation."[10] In an effort to speedily secure the bill, however, HRCF refused to use language that would also protect the transgendered from job discrimination.[11] When confronted by transgender activists who argued that ENDA failed to protect the "visibly queer," HRCF countered that trans-inclusive language would set back the legislative process and could cost ENDA twenty to thirty potential congressional votes.[12] In other words, in order to forge a relationship with the state, particularly around legal protections, the lesbian and gay nation regulates its borders and disciplines its body to project an intelligible picture of itself, one with clear boundaries around not just the sexual identity of its constituents but the unambiguous gender (and genital status) of those who might be protected by this legislation. With this move, the queer body becomes coherent and self-regulating in relation to the state, not queer at all, in fact.[13] It becomes, instead, disciplined and intelligible within a state-sanctioned language about appropriately gendered "lesbian," "gay," and perhaps "bisexual" bodies. While the struggle over queer antidiscrimination legislation continues, other theaters of struggle showcase the ambivalent relationship between subject and state, body and nation.[14]

The Theater of Historical Recuperation

History, as this story unfolds, is a battleground, an intellectual territory that serves political purposes, and lesbian, feminist, and transgender communities share a common but sometimes hostile relationship to overlapping historical geographies. In contemporary lesbian history, butch drag or female-to-male cross-dressing has signaled the presence of lesbians. Indeed, in a working-class context, butch iconography was lesbian iconography, and masculine gender codes when worn on an anatomically female body stood in for or advertised lesbian desire and sexuality.[15] However, because of the historical relationship between butchness and lesbian sexuality, lesbian histories often conflate "cross-dressing" (anatomical females sporting masculine appearance for the purpose of advertising lesbian sexuality) with "passing" (anatomical females donning masculine appearance for the purpose of being perceived as men).[16] Lesbian history, for example, particularly in its earlier phase, often documented the history of passing women as a method for bringing lesbians into history because these individuals (when "discovered" to be women) were the most visible and publicly accessible historical subjects.[17] However, transsexuals and transgender community historians and activists take a different approach to the historical recuperation of female-to-male cross-dressers. They argue that anatomical females who passed as men in public might just as easily be recuperated as transgendered men than passing women or cross-dressing lesbians in that their perceived gender identity was male rather than female. In this way, lesbian and transgender communities construct a usable past around the recuperation of many of the same historical figures.[18]

The slide show *She Even Chewed Tobacco*, for example, discusses cross-dressing and passing women in U.S. Western history. Created in 1979, it introduces the character Babe Bean, a "passing woman" who lived in Stockton, California, from 1897–98, and places Bean within a narrative about women's history that suggests that passing women functioned as a cultural precursor to contemporary butch lesbians.[19] The slide show's introductory segment states that in the nineteenth century, "a small but significant group of American women rejected the limitations of the female sphere and claimed the privileges enjoyed by men. They worked for men's wages, courted and married the women they loved and even voted. They did so by adopting men's clothing, hiding their female identities from most of the world and passing as men." *She Even Chewed Tobacco* uses passing women as liminal characters to highlight the gulf between male privilege and female oppression. It positions them within a late-1970s feminist discourse that stresses labor equity, suffrage rights, and lesbian love. Moreover, it tells a Horatio Alger-esque story, embedding a nationalist trope of success within feminist discourse: successful cross-dressing produced women who, as citizens, could vote. In this way *She Even Chewed Tobacco* gives nineteenth-century female-to-male cross-dressers a history as women within the rubric of contemporary lesbian and feminist concerns. No mention is made of cross-gender identity, and the only conclusion one might make about the lives of passing women is that if they lived at a time when they could enjoy economic freedom, political rights, or sexual love for women as a woman, they would not choose to masquerade as men. Indeed, it is this concept of masquerade that underscores the argument that nineteenth- and twentieth-century female-to-male cross-dressers were really women and, in fact, probably lesbians.

Babe Bean is a complicated historical figure, however, because for a short period of time Bean straddled the boundary between man and woman. In August 1897, Bean was arrested in Stockton, California, for cross-dressing. After the arrest s/he stayed in Stockton for approximately a year and became something of a local celebrity. Bean continued to dress entirely in men's clothing, lived alone on a houseboat, and attended meetings at the local Bachelor's Club. However, Bean communicated only through writing and refused to speak aloud, which shrouded the truth of her/his sex. In other words, even though Bean admitted to having a female body, her/his self-presentation was so consistently masculine that some of the citizens of Stockton remained unconvinced of Bean's sex. "The mystery is still unsolved as to whether 'Babe' Bean is a boy or girl, a man or a woman," one news article reported, dubbing Bean "the mysterious girl-boy, man-woman."[20]

In 1898, Bean left Stockton for San Francisco and joined the U.S. military, serving in the Philippines during the Spanish-American War. Bean returned to San Francisco after the war, his arms covered with elaborate tattoos, and he adopted the name Jack Garland. At this time in San Francisco, 1903, cross-dressing was made illegal by city ordinance. And although Garland spent the rest of his life in San Francisco, working as a male nurse and a free-lance social worker, he was not arrested again. However, when Jack Garland died in 1936, after almost forty years of living as a man, his "true sex" was revealed to be female. Jack Garland was born in 1869, daughter of José Marcos Mugarrieta, San Francisco's first Mexican consul, and Eliza Alice Garland.

The late Lou Sullivan, a female-to-male (FTM) transsexual and also an active member of San Francisco's Gay and Lesbian Historical Society (GLHS), published a biography of Jack Garland in 1990 entitled *From Female to Male: The Life of Jack Bee Garland,* which retextualizes Babe Bean's life as the life of Jack Garland. Sullivan states in his introduction that "Jack Garland demonstrated, through his lifelong adherence to his male identity, that his reasons for living as a man were more complex than just his dissatisfaction with the way society expected women to dress. [Jack Garland] was a female-to-male transsexual."[21] Furthermore, while many histories of female-to-male cross-dressers tell the story of how passing women were able to pursue the women they loved under the protective cover of male dress and, perhaps, male identity, this was not the case for Jack Garland. Garland preferred the company of men. Sullivan notes that "he dressed and lived as a man in order to be a man among men," which further unhinges any direct connection between cross-gender behavior and sexuality. In the memoirs he left behind, Jack Garland states that "Many have thought it strange that I do not care to mingle with women of my own age, and seem partial to men's company. Well, is it not natural that I should prefer the companionship of men? I am never happy nor contented unless with a few of 'the boys.' "[22]

While Sullivan rewrites lesbian history to produce a history of visible transsexuals, one cannot overlook Garland's racial, class, and national passings. The turn of the century was a period of intense racial, ethnic, and national consolidation which marked the rise of Anglo-Saxonism, the production of a nationalist discourse of U.S. exceptionalism, and intensified U.S. colonization. Garland's gender certainly did not exist independent of these circumstances. For instance, Garland chose Anglo names for himself, which signals a movement toward white-ethnic or Anglo-American identifications. Moreover, while his silence in Stockton masked, most obviously, the feminine tenor of his voice, it also hid any Spanish language affects that would have destabilized his ethnic and national crossings. Also, for the last decades of his life, Garland wandered the streets of San Francisco and lived in poverty. Here, gender remains inseparable from class—while Garland's maleness allowed for late-night street wandering and urban rescue work, the very public and class-specific nature of his activities reinforced his gender. Finally, Garland's participation in the Spanish-American War and his service to the U.S. military wrapped a cloak of nationalist allegiance around his political subjectivity, highlighting both his masculinity and American-ness. Clearly, the story of Babe Bean/Jack Garland exceeds a singularly recuperative narrative.

Billy Tipton, the jazz pianist and saxophonist whose so called true sex was revealed when he died in Spokane in 1989, provides another example of a historical subject claimed by both lesbian/feminist and transgendered communities. Like Jack Garland, Billy Tipton lived his adult life as a man, over fifty years. Born in Kansas City, Missouri, in 1914, at the age of eighteen he applied for a social security card under his brother's name, Billy, and hit the road as a musician. He formed the Billy Tipton Trio in 1954, recorded two albums, and toured the West until he settled in Spokane in the 1960s. Through these years, Tipton married several times but, according to his lovers, never revealed his female anatomy. Betty Cox, Tipton's lover from 1946–53, claims that Tipton must have used "sexual devices" when making love: "I know it sounds incredible, but I'm a normal healthy woman who enjoys her man . . . [a]nd if that little Billy was alive today, well, I'd still enjoy him."[23] On the other hand, Kitty Oakes, Tipton's third wife, claims that they didn't have sex during their eighteen-year marriage. She notes that Tipton had been injured in an auto accident, explaining "—there was an attraction between us, but it wasn't sexual."[24] Over the course of their relationship, Tipton and Oakes adopted and parented three sons.

Tipton did not have surgery or openly identify as a transsexual; instead, he represented himself, even to his closest friends and family, as a man. Clearly,

Billy Tipton's gender identity was male. Still, critics and enthusiasts have recuperated Tipton as an example of the kind of extreme measures women must undergo to pursue equitable economic opportunities. "[Tipton] apparently began appearing as a man to improve her chances of success as a musician," one reporter noted.[25] Jason Cromwell, a sociologist specializing in female-to-male transsexual identities, refutes this idea. "You don't die from a treatable medical condition if you are simply a woman living as a man so you can take advantage of male privileges."[26] (Tipton died of an untreated bleeding ulcer.) A print graphic published in several transgender community newsletters and magazines takes this idea one step further. It positions a simple "trivial pursuit" question in the center of the page with statements swirling around it; the question reads: "Billy Tipton was a (choose one): a. woman, b. lesbian, c. crossdresser, d. man." A check is placed next to answer d, indicating that the correct answer is that Tipton was a man. Statements protectively encircling the ad read:

> Billy Tipton was a jazz musician. When he died, in 1989, television and newspaper sources proclaimed him to have been a woman who had lived as a man in order to be a jazz musician. "He gave up everything," they said. They were wrong. He didn't give up anything, for he wasn't a woman. The gay community was quick to proclaim Billy as a lesbian. They were wrong, too. Billy wasn't a lesbian, either. Billy was married, with three adopted sons. His family did not know of his female anatomy, but they knew something the newspaper and television and gay press didn't—that Billy Tipton was a man.

In smaller print, in the bottom right corner, a more provocative statement reads, "Billy Tipton was transsexual. . . . His life was not an imposture, and the notion that he was anything less than a man is a denial of everything that he was. Hands off! He's one of ours!"[27] Like Jack Garland, the recuperation of Billy Tipton's life exceeds a simple narrative about women's economic opportunities or lesbian sexual identity. Instead, without denying labor inequity or lesbian history, Tipton's life evidences the uneasy fit between unintelligible bodies and contemporary (recuperative) historical practice.

More recently, Brandon Teena, a twenty-one-year-old who, despite his female body, lived as a man and dated women, was murdered on December 31, 1993, in Humboldt, Nebraska. Three months earlier he had moved from his hometown, Lincoln, to Falls City, where, it was noted, he was "popular with the girls." After a misdemeanor arrest, however, police revealed his anatomical sex to the local press, who published it. This information angered two men, who disrobed Brandon Teena at a Christmas Eve party ostensibly to prove to his girlfriend that he was "actually a female." Early the next morning, on December 25, 1993, Brandon Teena was abducted, beaten, and raped by the same two men; they "threatened to silence her permanently" if he went to the police. A week later, after Brandon Teena filed charges, the same two men murdered him and two of his friends.[28]

The murders attracted a great deal of national attention, particularly after

Brandon Teena's family asserted that the murders would not have occurred had the rape and battery been prosecuted by the local police.[29] Meanwhile, in the gay press, coverage of Brandon Teena's death evolved into a discussion about lesbian and gay civil rights. Pat Phelen of Citizens for Equal Protection, Nebraska's gay and lesbian rights organization, stated that "this incident underscores the need for the state to pass laws protecting the rights of Gays and those perceived as Gay."[30] The National Gay and Lesbian Task Force (NGLTF), San Francisco's Citizens United against Violence (CUAV), and New York City's Anti-Violence Project (AVP) similarly asserted that Brandon Teena's death exemplified the worst kind of violence against women and lesbians:

> Brandon Teena was raped and then murdered for being a woman who broke the rules: she presented herself as a man, dated the prettiest girl in town, and was not sexually involved with men. . . . For all these transgressions, as a woman and as a lesbian, she was murdered.[31]

Because gay press coverage of the events leading to Brandon Teena's death pointedly represented him as lesbian or female, these articles obscure his transgendered identity, erasing its specificity.

For example, Donna Minkowitz's *Village Voice* coverage of Brandon Teena's murder evades a direct analysis of transgender experience in order to buttress lesbian visibility and political subjectivity. While Minkowitz notes repeatedly that Brandon did not identify as a lesbian and that he talked frequently to his lovers and friends about being transsexual, Minkowitz nevertheless identifies Brandon Teena as a confused but sexy cross-dressing butch lesbian:

> From photos of the wonder-boychic playing pool, kissing babes, and lifting a straight male neighbor high up in the air to impress party goers . . . Brandon looks to be the handsomest butch item in history—not just good looking, but arrogant, audacious, cocky—everything they, and I, look for in lovers.[32]

Minkowitz's article ultimately functions as a cautionary tale about violence against lesbians, but it doubles back on itself in a gesture of "blame the victim." Minkowitz's article explains that if Brandon had only found someone to talk to about "her" latent homosexuality, to counsel "her" through "her" intense self-hatred as a lesbian, "she" would not have gotten so embroiled in the pattern of deceit that sealed "her" fate. As the final lines of Minkowitz's article explain, "The frustration she had felt for so long had finally frustrated others, and the fury she could not express was ultimately expressed on her. By men."[33]

Minkowitz's narrative places the facts of Brandon Teena's life, indeed his own statements about himself, within a lesbian and gay paradigm that stresses visibility, pride, and coming out of the closet. Minkowitz understands Brandon Teena's insistence that he was not a lesbian to be the words of an unrealized, homophobic young woman who, had she greater access to social services, might have adjusted to lesbian life.[34] In this light, as Jordy Jones argues in an article for *FTM*, a newsletter produced by and for female-to-male transsexuals, "Brandon Teena was not killed because *she* was a Lesbian, *he* was transgendered. This is neither more or less horrific than if he had been killed for lesbianism, but it is different." Jones continues that "If the queer community makes of Brandon a martyr to a cause, so be it. But if he is to be canonized in any way, it should be done in such a way that respects his right to self-definition."[35] Self-definition is often difficult to pin down where no written sources point to a transsexual or transgendered identity per se, but through his survivors, Brandon Teena speaks clearly. Brandon Teena's mother notes that he never identified as a lesbian but instead wanted to be a man. And his girlfriends, who identified as heterosexual, understood him, if they had knowledge about his genital status, as a preoperative transsexual. Lana Tisdel remembered, "He said he was born female, is a female, but wants to be a male," and another girlfriend recalled that Brandon Teena, "was a woman outside but felt like a man, and . . . was going to have an operation."[36]

Self-definition is central to the recuperation and, perhaps, appropriation of historical figures for presentist means. But gender cannot continue to function as a slippery subset of sexuality, as evidence for a history of sexual outlaws that obliterates the possibility of gender outlaws and erases transgender history and experience. As Jason Cromwell notes in an article on Billy Tipton,

> I know that as an FTM many within our community would like to claim Billy as one of our own. We have so few role models, even though history is filled with females who lived and passed as men. Billy did not have surgery to alter his sex, and he certainly lived during a time when it was available. However, this is true for many FTMs, because the results are not very good and quite costly. Billy left no written explanation for the actions of his life. He left us instead with a life lived for over 50 years as a man. Does his life as a man have no meaning?[37]

What is the meaning, then, of cross-gender behavior and identity? What are the facts of gender when, upon the death of an anatomical female who lived his entire adult life as a man, his so called true identity is revealed to be female and his sexuality is recuperated as lesbian? What is the material substance that determines the truth of one's gendered or sexual identity: written articulation, daily practice, or, finally, genitalia?[38] Clearly, in the last instance—in these cases, hospital beds and autopsies—genitals remain the material fact of gender for many historians, and when gender (which often doubles back as biological sex) determines sexual identity, historical recuperation becomes a tricky political contest indeed. Yet these touchy and not so new questions about the materiality of gender are rarely addressed except by transsexuals and, not surprisingly, in lesbian S/M literature, where a discourse about the body remains central to community life. It is here that a relationship between lesbian and transsexual communities is more articulately fleshed out.

The Theater of Social Space

In the first issue of *Venus Infers*, a magazine for lesbian sadomasochists, Pat Califia poses the question, "Who is my sister?" and outlines some controversies that were raised at the 1992 Powersurge Conference, a conference for leather-dykes that had as its goal the creation of "lesbian only space." The Powersurge Conference was located in Seattle, hosted by the Outer Limits, a Seattle-based women's leather and S/M group. Its program advised that a "lesbian is a WOMAN who considers herself to be a lesbian." Furthermore, it cautioned that the conference organizers would not "be the gender police," so participants should respect this policy, noting that "Because gender lines are bending and fading in these changing times we also have a further clarification for attendance . . . : If you can not slam your dick in a drawer and walk away, then the Amazon Feast and the Dungeon parties are not available to you." However, despite the graphic imagery, two floating signifiers ("lesbian" and "WOMAN") refused to contain themselves during the conference, and the admission policy generated for Powersurge 2 in 1993 changed its tone, specifying that the conference "is open to and welcomes women born women leatherdykes (chromosomal [XX] females only)."[39]

Like the admission policies generated by the Michigan Womyn's Music Festival and the 1991 National Lesbian Conference in Atlanta, which banned "non-genetic women," the 1993 Powersurge Conference policy was generated in response to the participation of transsexuals. However, as Califia observes, this policy excluded lesbian-identified male-to-female transsexuals while it continued to include ex-lesbian female-to-male transsexuals, despite their male appearance and identity, because they remain "chromosomally correct" according to the 1993 admission policy. This raises some peculiar questions about the relationship between bodies and nations—questions that have indeed generated some creative responses (like chromosomal admission tests).[40]

Califia's article stresses the pressing need to address the conflicted relationship between ex-lesbian FTMs, lesbian-identified MTFs, and leatherdykes. Califia articulates her discomfort with continued FTM participation at lesbian (leather) events, particularly while lesbian-identified MTF transsexuals have been excluded. While maintaining the right to self-determination (including the right to identify as a male-to-female transsexual lesbian *or* a female-to-male transsexual lesbian), Califia nevertheless encourages FTMs to take responsibility for their chosen gender. She states that "If someone is taking male hormones, letting their facial hair grow, has taken a male name, changed their legal documents to say they are male, and expects to be addressed by a male name and male pronouns, I can't really visualize that person as being a lesbian."[41] She notes her discomfort as she watches a roomful of lesbians listen respectfully to FTM "leatherdykes" describe how they want to "cut off their tits," while MTF leatherdykes who "love their tits" are not allowed to participate in Powersurge. Thus, on the one hand, while Califia argues that the material that informs gender springs from a number of life experiences and choices (legal identity, hormonal therapy, facial hair, etc.), she concludes that the relationship one determines with her or his physical body ultimately underscores the social fact of gender. In other words, Califia argues that a line between genders does exist, and male-identified individuals, despite their chromosomes, socialization, or genital status, cannot be lesbians. FTMs must place themselves on a continuum that realistically and by choice pulls them into the category "man"—and out of "women only" spaces. So, while the precise boundary between genders remains unclear, the regulatory function of gender boundaries remains uncontested.

Controversies surrounding the Michigan Womyn's Music Festival's entrance policies frame these questions from a different angle. This festival, which has been in existence for twenty years, is a weeklong event where thousands of women gather in a Michigan forest to camp, socialize, attend workshops, and enjoy an impressive line-up of mostly lesbian musicians. Until 1991 the festival had no explicit policy with regard to the attendance of transsexuals (or exactly who "womyn" are), but in 1991 Nancy Jean Burkholder was expelled from the festival after one day of attendance because she was suspected of being a transsexual. Burkholder was not the first transsexual woman to enter the festival. In fact, she had attended the year before, but for some reason in August 1991, security tightened, and Burkholder was expelled because even though this policy remained absent from 1991 festival literature, a security guard asserted that "transsexuals were not permitted to attend the festival."[42] Before she left, however, Chris, the security guard and contact person for the producers, asked Burkholder whether she had had a sex change operation. Burkholder said Chris could look at her genitals, but Burkholder maintained that her surgical history was her own business.[43] This information signals the ambiguity of the festival's policy. Burkholder was being ejected, but was it because of her genital status, her surgical history, her consciousness, or her chromosomes? Chris stated that the festival had a "no transsexuals" policy, and while this may be true, her curiosity about Burkholder's surgical history suggests that morphology may, indeed, have something to do with gender, or in this case with "womyn."

As a result of these events, the 1992 Michigan Womyn's Music Festival's literature got clearer about its policies, stating that the festival was open to "womyn-born-womyn" only. Although no transsexuals were expelled from this festival even though there were several in attendance, the 1993 festival saw the expulsion of four MTF transsexual lesbians and the birth of "Camp Trans," a quasi-refugee colony that pitched tent just outside the entrance to the festival. From this venue transsexuals and friends continued to distribute literature about the festival's exclusionary policy in an attempt to gauge whether the producers' policies matched those of the festivalgoers. Through the next year, the protesters pressured the festival producers, Lisa Vogel and Barbara Price, to state explicitly that their "womyn-born-womyn only" policy really meant that the festival was open to non-transsexual women only, which would raise the stakes not only to the level of explicit discrimination but closer to the body where one might measure one's transsexual-ness against surgical or hormonal intervention. However, the festival producers refused to change their "womyn-born-womyn" policy and in August 1994 "Camp Trans, for humyn born humyns" re-seated itself, hosting a wealth of extracurricular activities, again just outside the entrance of the festival.

In 1994, however, the scab fell off the uneasy peace between S/M and non-S/M dykes as Tribe-8, a raucous band of musicians, performed amid controversy about their ostensibly violent lyrics and stage presence. At the same time, the Lesbian Avengers gathered momentum inside the festival in defense of excluded (transsexual) Lesbian Avengers on the outside. On the sixth day of the festival, after a group of protesters walked to the front gate and challenged the festival's entrance policy with a variety of differently sexed and gendered bodies, the producers agreed to allow transsexuals to enter the festival but still under the rubric of "womyn-born-womyn."[44] This constituted a victory for the protesters in that the meaning of gender was placed within the realm of self-definition, but questions of morphology continued to plague the policing of borders as it remained unclear whether non- or pre-operative MTF transsexuals might enter the festival or whether FTMs at any stage remained within the rubric of "womyn-born-womyn." In other words, how much or in what ways did the body constitute consciousness? Could consciousness exist irrelevant to the body's contours? Could individuals with penises be "womyn-born-womyn"? Might individuals with vaginas be men?

At this point, the compromise/victory engineered at the 1994 Michigan Womyn's Music Festival sounds a lot like Califia's fluid boundary whereby in the end, despite your body hair, legal identity, genital status, or surgical history, you place yourself as a result of your consciousness at any particular point in time on a bipolar gender continuum that admits the existence of a boundary between men and women, male and female. You decide for yourself what you are and whether or not you can, in good faith, enter a gender-bound social space. Even with this fluid and self-determining approach to the meaning and function of gender difference, gender remains foundational to the articulation and function of community. Bodies take on social meaning in relation to, for instance, the lesbian nation only if they can fix themselves in time and space as one gender or another. Despite mutating morphology, or the potentially revolutionary transformation of the body in response to oppressive gender constructs, the ability to articulate oneself intelligibly as one gender or another remains central to the function of community, social identity, political formation, and ultimately the forging of a relationship to the state in the name of separatism or civil rights protections.

Discussion

In order to pose an alternative and more provocative perspective, one that does not necessarily reinscribe a boundary between male and female, I return to

Powersurge's "slam your dick in a drawer" policy. This policy provides an example of a community that encourages gender play as an integral part of its practice but simultaneously struggles to maintain some kind of anatomy-based exclusionary policy around which the dyke part of the term "leatherdyke" continues to make sense. In this case the problem is not male-identification, self-definition, or surgical history but the function of the penis itself. In other words, dykes may have any variety of chromosomal configurations, shifting gender identifications, and most certainly ambiguous bodies, but Powersurge leatherdykes by definition cannot have functioning or particularly sensitive penises—or penises large enough to slam in a drawer. This policy, which remained in effect even though Powersurge 1995 dropped its "women-born-women" requirements, seems to be something of an innovative and practical solution to a theoretical conundrum (although it certainly raises a whole different set of problems). In many ways the "slam-your-dick-in-a-drawer" policy leaves a traditional sex/gender system behind in that sexuality (or dykeness) remains independent of gender and birth bodies. Dykeness has nothing to do with gender, is not something you are born with, nor is it a product of socialization or self-definition. Dykeness becomes a brute manifestation of one aspect of the body rather than an expression of genetic female same-gender or even cross-gender sexuality. Certainly, dykeness in this instance resonates loudly as lack, but because it is read from the body's immediate material form, gender's relationship to sexuality is erased and gender is innovatively excused from the picture.

Along a similar line, in a roundtable discussion, a number of FTMs challenge a sex/gender system that leaves no room for lesbians who are men or men who retain a lesbian history. Mike, for example, reveals that "I never really identified as female, but I identified as a lesbian for a while." He continues,

> Being a dyke gave me options. I knew I wasn't straight; I tried it, and it didn't work. I wanted to be with women. But the more I was out in the lesbian community, and the more I was out into S/M, the more I came to realize that, hey, I didn't fit there either, exactly. For me, it's not about being a man or being a woman, cuz there is some fluidity in there. I identify primarily as male, but I still have roots with the women's community that I don't want severed. I'm thankful that I was socialized female.[45]

Sky, another FTM, similarly unsettles an intuitively clear relationship between gender and sexual identity: "My emotional affinities are still very clearly with queer women. I'm forty years old, and I've been involved with dykes for more than half of my life. I'm not going to give that up . . . the dyke community is home."[46] According to these statements, Mike and Sky's lived practice as women (or lesbians) had become a historical anchor and the material fact of gender (or sexuality) despite their male bodies and male gender identities.[47] These statements suggest a paradigm in which sexual identity has social meaning beyond or outside gender, so that men might, at times, be lesbians—and women, gay men.[48]

These reconfigurations do not necessarily provide evidence for a third sex or third gender, nor do they indicate a postmodern proliferation of genders and sexualities. Instead, the tension between transsexual bodies and lesbian nations suggests a site where sex and gender no longer combine to flesh out culturally intelligible bodies. As Max Valerio argues, "Transsexuals are freaks, outsiders and outlaws in this world. We have lived the unthinkable. Are privy to information and experiences that most people have little conception of. This is our power, our damning glory."[49] Valerio's statement calls attention to the specificity of transsexual experience. He, along with sociologist Henry Rubin and literary critic Jay Prosser, argues that it is the materiality (the daily practice) of transsexual embodiment that confounds and displaces bipolar gender and sexual nationalism.[50] These observations resonate in response to gender and queer theory's appropriation of transsexual bodies as potentially revolutionary cultural artifacts.[51] They also resonate in response to a (lesbian) feminist critique and condemnation of transsexuality.

Most famously, Janice Raymond has argued that MTF transsexuals are dangerous to women and by extension lesbians because they not only colonize femaleness through embodiment, but they provide material for a medical-psychiatric empire to resolve a contemporary gender identity crisis by trading one set of gendered sterotypes for another. Raymond argues that through MTF transsexuals, doctors invade women's social spaces (as well as their bodies) and market the future of gender.[52] Bernice Hausman, in a more recent book, makes a similar claim. She argues that the contemporary concept of gender, as distinct from biological sex, is relatively new and emerged as a psychiatric response to medical technologies employed through the mid-twentieth century to "solve" the problem of intersexuality (or hermaphroditism). With the birth of new technologies such as endocrinology and plastic surgery, doctors found that they could reshape the genitals of an intersexed individual, usually a child, into something less ambiguous. The idea of a core gender identity grew out of these practices because some surgically altered individuals continued to express themselves as the "wrong" gender despite hormonal and surgical intervention. Gender, some psychiatrists reasoned, seemed to be fixed within the body rather than the product of socialization or an immediate expression of morphology. More surprisingly, the body's exterior began to seem more plastic than its interior. However, in Hausman's narrative, the agents of these inimical social changes shift from doctors to transsexuals in that through the late 1950s, as a response to the celebrity of Christine Jorgenson, transsexuals began to use the language of core gender identity to demand genital reconstruction. Thus, through the development and gradual acceptance of sex reassignment surgery as the appropriate medical intervention or cure for "gender dysphoria," transsexuals helped stabilize and naturalize the relatively new concept of gender identity. So while Hausman charts new territory in the history of medicine and its impact on feminist theory, she ultimately (like Raymond) blames transsexuals for normalizing, naturalizing, and codifying a bipolar gender system, fixing biological women into a feminine frame.[53]

As this essay illustrates, however, the meaning of gendered bodies, particularly transgendered bodies, remains complicated by and dependent on the territories (nations) bodies inhabit. Transsexuals do not fix gender in time and space, nor do they always already undermine its insipid naturalization. Rather, in the examples cited above, transsexual bodies reconfigure historical narrative and reterritorialize social space. Contrary to Raymond and Hausman's assertions, these actions upset a fixed relationship between sex, gender, and sexuality. In fact, while this essay does not intend to disrupt or deny the value of separatist practice, it illustrates (through the lens of lesbian nationalism) the function of intelligible bodies to the body politic. It argues that the body politic (the nation) exists for intelligible bodies, and despite anti-essentialist gestures to the contrary, contemporary sex/gender politics often document the absolutely desperate reiteration of bipolar gender as a foundation for sexual nationalism. Finally, this essay poses the specter of the outlaw (particularly as it takes the form of unruly, unreadable, inconsistent, but nevertheless material bodies) and suggests that outlaw bodies sharpen a boundary not between men and women, male and female, or even transsexual and non, but between abject and intelligible. This distinction evidences the possibility that while most bodies, even transgendered bodies, fit neatly or fold back into the body politic as readable, comprehensible, and intelligible, some retain or reclaim a fleeting moment of social and cultural unintelligibility, inhabiting a queer space, I would argue, outside, beyond, invisible to, and perhaps, as a result, in confrontation with the state.

Notes

The author thanks CLAGS, the Center for Lesbian and Gay Studies, for the generous Rockefeller Fellowship that made the producion of this essay possible. Thanks also go to Michael Du Plessis, Elizabeth Freeman, Ben Singer, and especially Alex Harris for insight and support through the writing process.

1. While it is important to distinguish between the terms "transsexual" and "transgender," particularly since access to medical technologies and state entitlements (i.e., change of name, alteration of birth certificate) are often dependent on a medical diagnosis of "transsexualism," this essay uses these terms somewhat interchangeably in order to broaden the category transsexual. For instance, if the term "transsexual" is used to signify a body that has entered into a formal relationship with doctors and the state with regard to "sex reassignment" (with the stated goal of eventually completing "the surgery"—a nonsense term with regard to female-to-male transsexuals who experience a series of surgeries, if any), many pre- and nonoperative transsexuals, particularly female-to-males, fall out of the category "transsexual" and can only be understood as "transgendered." For diagnostic categories, see the American Psychiatric Association's *Diagnostic and Statistical Manual of Mental Disorders*, 4th ed. (1994); for a more comprehensive discussion of the term "transgender" and its relationship to transsexuality, see Susan Stryker, "My Words to Victor Frankenstein above the Village of Chamounix," *GLQ* 1:3 (1994) 251–52; for more information about FTM surgeries,

see James Green, "Getting Real about FTM Surgery," *Chrysalis: The Journal of Transgressive Gender Identities* 2:2 (1995) 27–32.

2. As this essay will explore further, the concept of nationalism ("the nation") refers to both the creation and reiteration of world political and economic borders (i.e., the post–World War II consolidation of the nation-state as the legitimate international political form, most obviously visible in the creation of the United Nations) *and* the contemporary emergence and articulation of resistant, deterritorialized, subcultural, and political movements. While Black Nationalism functions as the most resilient form of state-resistant nationalisms in the United States, more recently one can speak of the Lesbian Nation, the Queer Nation, and the Transgender Nation. See Michael Warner's introduction and Lauren Berlant and Elizabeth Freeman, "Queer Nationality," in *Fear of a Queer Planet*, ed. Michael Warner (Minneapolis: Minnesota University Press, 1993); Eve Kosofsky Sedgwick, "Nationalisms and Sexualities in the Age of Wilde," in *Nationalisms and Sexualities*, ed. Andrew Parker, Mary Russo, Doris Sommer, and Patricia Yaeger (New York: Routledge, 1992); David Evans, *Sexual Citizenship* (New York: Routledge, 1994), particularly his chapter "Trans-Citizenship: Transvestism and Transsexualism."

3. For more on the naturalized body, see Michel Foucault, *Discipline and Punish: The Birth of the Prison* (New York: Vintage, 1979), particularly "Docile Bodies," 136–69.

4. See George Mosse, *Nationalism and Sexuality* (New York: Howard Fertig, 1985) for an account of the rise of state nationalism through the construction of sexually respectable bodies.

5. Foucault, *Discipline and Punish.*

6. See Elizabeth Grosz, *Volatile Bodies: Toward a Corporeal Feminism* (Bloomington: Indiana University Press, 1994); Robyn Wiegman, *American Anatomies: Theorizing Race and Gender* (Durham: Duke University Press, 1995); Thomas Laqueur, *Making Sex: Body and Gender from the Greeks to Freud* (Cambridge: Harvard University Press, 1990); Anne Fausto-Sterling, *Myths of Gender: Biological Theories about Women and Men* (New York: Basic Books, 1985); *Representations* 14 (spring 1986), particularly Catherine Gallagher, "The Body Versus the Social Body in the Works of Thomas Malthus and Henry Mayhew," 83–106. See also Jennifer Terry and Jacqueline Urla, eds., *Deviant Bodies* (Bloomington: Indiana University Press, 1995); Judith Halberstam and Ira Livingston, eds., *Posthuman Bodies* (Bloomington: Indiana University Press, 1995).

7. Benedict Anderson, *Imagined Communities* (New York: Verso, 1991), 5–7.

8. Anderson argues that "print culture" and "print capitalism," particularly the publication and distribution of the popular novel and newspaper, weakened and ultimately replaced historically sacred symbols. *Imagined Communities*, 9–46.

9. Judith Butler, *Bodies That Matter: On the Discursive Limits of "Sex"* (New York: Routledge, 1993), 16.

10. Doug Hattaway, "The Employment Non-Discrimination Act," *HRCF Quarterly* (summer 1995): 6–7.

11. "Trans Community Protests Human Rights Campaign Fund," *AEGIS News* (June 1995): 11.

12. "HRCF Kicks Transfolk Out of National Anti-Discrimination Bill!" *TNT: Transsexual News Telegraph* 5 (summer 1995): 8; Susie Day, "ENDA Discrimination," *Lesbian & Gay New York*, Sept. 17, 1995, 9.

13. Here I stress Michael Warner's use of the term "queer" as an identity that functions to both disrupt the minoritizing logic of toleration and assert a critique of heteronormalcy. See introduction to *Fear of a Queer Planet*, ed. Warner, vii–xxxi.

14. As Foucault notes, in the age of Enlightenment "there will be hundreds of tiny theaters of punishment" where specific territories or functional sites, like HRCF's Employment Non-Discrimination Act, aid the production of disciplined bodies. Michel

Foucault, *Discipline and Punish: The Birth of the Prison* (New York: Vintage, 1979), 113.

15. Joan Nestle, *A Restricted Country* (Ithaca, N.Y.: Firebrand, 1987); Joan Nestle, ed., *The Persistent Desire: A Femme-Butch Reader* (Boston: Alyson, 1992); Elizabeth Lapovsky Kennedy and Madeline D. Davis, *Boots of Leather, Slippers of Gold: The History of a Lesbian Community* (New York: Routledge, 1993).

16. Judith Halberstam provides a historical account of lesbian masculinities in "Female Masculinities: Tommies, Tribades and Inverts," and "Lesbian Masculinity or Even Stone Butches Get the Blues" (unpublished manuscripts).

17. Esther Newton problematizes the slippage between masculinity and lesbianism in "The Mythic Mannish Lesbian: Radclyff Hall and the New Woman," *Signs* 9:4 (1984): 557–75. Nestle's and Kennedy and Davis's recent work (cited above) also clarify the distinction between passing women and butch lesbians by articulating in rich detail the function of butch gender codes as a component of lesbian desire and representation.

18. Jason Cromwell, "Default Assumptions, or The Billy Tipton Phenomenon," *FTM* 28 (July 1994): 4–5; Susan Stryker, "Local Transsexual History," *TNT: Transsexual News Telegraph* 5 (summer–autumn 1995): 14–15.

19. Originally produced by the San Francisco Lesbian and Gay History Project (1979), *She Even Chewed Tobacco* is currently distributed in video form by Women Make Movies. See " 'She Even Chewed Tobacco': A Pictorial Narrative of Passing Women in America," in *Hidden from History: Reclaiming the Gay and Lesbian Past*, eds. Martin Duberman, Martha Vicinus, and George Chauncey, Jr. (New York: Penguin, 1989).

20. Louis Sullivan, *From Female to Male: The Life of Jack Bee Garland* (Boston: Alyson Press, 1990), 31.

21. Sullivan, *From Female to Male*, 3.

22. Sullivan, *From Female to Male*, 4.

23. Betty Cox, quoted by Cindy Kirshman in "The Tragic Masquerade of Billy Tipton," *Windy City Times*, March 1, 1990, 17.

24. Doug Clark, "Billy Tiptop: An Improvised Life," *Seattle Spokesman Review*, January 21, 1990. See also Cindy Kirshman, "The Tragic Masquerade"; Ann Japenga, "A Jazz Pianist's Ultimate Improvisation," *Los Angeles Times*, February 13, 1989.

25. Linda Lee, "Women Posing as Men Pursued Better Opportunities," *Seattle Post Intelligence: What's Happening*, September 10, 1989, 11. While the initial flurry of mainstream press coverage echos this analysis (see "Musician's Death at 74 Reveals He Was a Woman," *New York Times*, February 2, 1989; "Autopsy: Musician Was a Woman," *Newsday*, February 2, 1989), follow-up articles argued that Tipton's sexual or gender identity had more to do with his cross-dressing than his desire to succeed as a musician. See Kirshman, "The Tragic Masquerade"; Clark, "Billy Tipton: An Improvised Life"; and Japenga, "A Jazz Pianist's Ultimate Improvisation."

26. Jason Cromwell, "Default Assumptions, or The Billy Tipton Phenomenon," 4–5.

27. "Billy Tipton Was a (Choose One):" *TNT: Transsexual News Telegraph* 1 (summer 1993): 22. A smaller version of this "advertisement" also appeared in *Engender* 2 (July 1993).

28. "2 Men Held in Slaying of 3 at Humboldt," *Omaha World-Herald*, January 2, 1994; "Rape Report Tied to Killings: Family Says Slaying Were Preventable," *Lincoln Journal-Star*, January 4, 1994; "Woman Who Posed as a Man Is Found Slain with 2 Others," *New York Times*, January 4, 1994; "Her Fatal Deception?" *New York Newsday*, January 5, 1994; "Charade Revealed Prior to Killings," *Des Moines Register*, January 9, 1994; "Questions in Triple Homicide," *San Francisco Chronicle*, March 17, 1994.

29. "Rape Report Tied to Killings."

30. Kristina Campbell, "Transsexual, Two Others Murdered in Nebraska," *The*

Washington Blade, January 14, 1994, 19; Mindy Ridgway, "Queers Have No Right to Life—In Nebraska," *San Francisco Bay Times,* January 13, 1994, 7.

31. Terry A, Moroney, letter to Anthony Marro, editor, *New York Newsday,* January 5, 1994. See also AVP press release, "Anti-Violence Project Calls for Bias Classification in Nebraska Lesbian Murder," January 5, 1994.

32. Donna Minkowitz, "Love Hurts," *Village Voice,* April 19, 1994.

33. Minkowitz, "Love Hurts."

34. In fact, Minkowitz is so sure Brandon Teena was a lesbian that she wonders why Brandon Teena moved from Lincoln, a city with a visible gay community, to Falls City, an even more remote Nebraska town, rather than San Francisco or Denver, "the gay mecca of choice for corn belters." Clearly, Minkowitz can not see the events of Brandon Teena's life and death outside a gay lens. Perhaps Brandon Teena wanted to evade *misrecognition* as a lesbian and as a result chose a city with heightened gender codes so to more effectively live as a man.

35. Jordy Jones, "FTM Crossdresser Murdered," *FTM* 26 (Feb. 1994): 3.

36. Campbell, "Transsexual, Two Others Murdered in Nebraska," 19; "Charade Revealed Prior to Killings," 4B; "Her Fatal Deception?" See also Denise Noe, "Why Was Brandon Teena Murdered?" *Chrysalis* 2:2 (1995): 50.

37. Cromwell, "Default Assumptions, or The Billy Tipton Phenomenon," 5.

38. See Grosz, *Volatile Bodies,* for a discussion of the materiality of subjectivity.

39. Pat Califia, "Who Is My Sister: Powersurge and the Limits of Our Community," *Venus Infers* 1:1 (summer 1993): 4–5.

40. Renee Richards, for example, was asked (but refused) to submit to a Barr body test in which cells from the inside of the cheek are examined to reveal chromosomal distributions. See Bernice Hausman, *Changing Sex: Transsexualism, Technology, and the Idea of Gender* (Durham: Duke University Press, 1995), 12.

41. Califia, "Who Is My Sister," 6.

42. Nancy Jean Burkholder, "A Kinder, Gentler Festival?" *TransSisters* 2 (November–December 1993): 4.

43. Burkholder, "Kinder, Gentler Festival?" 4.

44. Davina Anne Gabriel, "Mission to Michigan III: Barbarians at the Gates," *TransSisters* 7 (winter 1995): 14–32; Riki Anne Wilchins, "The Menace in Michigan," *Gendertrash* 3 (winter 1995): 17–19.

45. "FTM/Female-to-Male: An Interview with Mike, Eric, Billy, Sky, and Shadow," in *Dagger: On Butch Women,* ed. Lily Burana, Roxxie, and Linnea Due (Pittsburgh: Cleis Press, 1994), 155.

46. Sky, in "FTM/Female-to-Male," 158.

47. On the other hand, Henry Rubin argues in a study of FTM identity formation that FTMs often consolidate their gender identities around a vehement disidentification from butch lesbians. Henry Samuel Rubin, "Transformations: Emerging Female to Male Transsexual Identities" (Ph.D. diss. Brandeis University, 1996). See also Ben Singer, "Velveteen Realness" (paper delivered at the CLAGS Trans/Forming Knowledge Conference, May 2, 1996.

48. C. Jacob Hale, "Dyke Leatherboys and Their Daddies: How to Have Sex without Men or Women," paper delivered at the Berkshire Conference on the History of Women, June 8, 1996).

49. Max Wolf Valerio, "Legislating Freedom," review of *The Apartheid of Sex* by Martine Rothblatt, *TNT: Transsexual News Telegraph* 5 (summer–autumn 1995): 26.

50. Henry Samule Rubin, "Transformations: Emerging Female to Male Transsexual Identities"; Jay Prosser, "No Place Like Home: The Transgendered Narrative of Leslie Feinberg's *Stone Butch Blues,*" *Modern Fiction Studies* 41 (fall–winter 1995).

51. For an overview of feminist and queer theory's approach to transsexual identi-

ties, see Kathleen Chapman and Michael du Plessis, " 'Don't Call Me *Girl':* Feminist Theory, Lesbian Theory, and Transsexual Identities" in *Cross Purposes: Lesbian Studies, Feminist Studies, and the Limits of Alliance,* Dana Heller, ed. (Bloomington: Indiana University Press, 1997); and Ki Namaste, " 'Tragic Misreadings': Queer Theory's Erasure of Transgender Subjectivity," in *Queer Studies: A Lesbian, Gay, Bisexual, and Transgender Anthology,* Brett Beemyn and Mickey Eliason, eds. (New York: New York University Press, 1996).

52. Janice G. Raymond, *The Transsexual Empire: The Making of the She-Male* (Boston: Beacon, 1979).

53. Hausman, *Changing Sex.*

12

Creating Good-Looking Genitals in the Service of Gender

Suzanne Kessler

In previous research, I have studied the management of intersexed infants. Through interviews with psychiatric endocrinologists, urologists, and surgeons, as well as reading the management literature, I came to some understanding of how physicians normalize the intersexed condition for the parents. For example, physicians imply that it is not the gender of the child that is ambiguous, but rather the genitals. I analyzed the physicians' gender-assignment decisions and drew some conclusions about cultural factors that influenced those decisions. A major criterion for assigning "male" is the length of the infant's penis and the future ability of that penis to fill a vagina. Finally, in that earlier work, I argued that neither physicians nor parents of the intersexed infant emerged from that experience with a greater understanding of the social construction of gender.

After my article was published I received a letter from an intersexed woman who had read it. I had written, in passing, that there is virtually no information about the handling of intersexuality from the viewpoint of the intersexed individual. She had two main things to say to me. First, she agreed with me that the voice of the intersexed is missing from the professional literature. And second, I had taken for granted too much of what the physicians had told me about the success of the surgery. Somehow, by concentrating on the social decision making and the management issues, I had glossed the whole surgical enterprise, and assumed that while cultural aspects were problematic, technical aspects were not. She begged to differ with me. Her letter precipitated a lengthy correspondence, and I have since corresponded and talked with other intersexuals. I have also talked with parents of newly diagnosed infants, and read about a hundred letters from parents of intersexed infants. In addition, I have plowed through the surgical literature, much like an anthropologist in foreign territory, armed with some knowledge of terminology, but not sharing the taken-for-granted convictions that genital surgery is either necessary or successful. I realized that I was dumb to such issues as what genitals are supposed to look like and how genitals are supposed to function. And the professional literature is written in such a way as to capitalize on this ignorance. Yet this dumbness had proven to be an advantage in helping me see what is between the lines, although those on the front lines of genital surgery would just say I was dumb.

What you need to know about gender assignment is that when a baby is born with ambiguous genitals, a chromosomal test is done. If the baby is XX, then the phallic tissue is reduced in size, labia are made, and a vagina is eventually created if there is none. If the baby is XY, a decision is made about whether the phallic tissue is large enough, or will be large enough if given hormonal treatment, to be a "good" penis. If "yes," then surgery is done to "improve" the phallus and testicles. If "no," then surgery is done to create a clitoris and labia. About 10 percent of intersexed infants are assigned to the male gender, the remaining are assigned to be female. I'll be talking primarily about female genitals, especially the clitoris, the vagina, and the labia.

I will begin with the question of how physicians know when they are confronted with ambiguous genitals. In reading the medical literature, I extracted the following kinds of quotations. Ambiguous genitals are described, I would have to say, ambiguously:

> Their external genitals look much more like a clitoris and a labia than a penis or a scrotum.[1]
>
> The tip should be the expected size for the patient's age.[2]
>
> The size of an enlarged clitoris cannot be stated in exact measurements.[3]

Maybe I was asking the wrong question. Maybe I should ask what normal genitals look like and then I will be able to recognize abnormal ones. At birth the normal clitoris is supposed to be up to 1 centimeter long, and the normal penis between 2.5 and 4.5 centimeters. And then we've got these enlarged clitorises with the intersexed conditions that are between 1.5 and 4. I guess you are just not allowed to have a genital that is between 1 centimeter and 2.5. The genital boundaries have to be considerably separated, which is kind of interesting. I am not sure what that means.

The measurements depend on how something is measured: whether you are measuring the relaxed phallus, the stretched one, the erect one. Ambiguity or decisiveness is at least partially determined by factors such as who is looking, why they are looking, and how hard they are looking. There is considerable vagueness, suggesting that when one encounters a "problem" genital one will know it. Although there are a few studies that report precise measurements of genital size, shape, and location, I can't imagine surgeons standing at the table, as someone has just given birth, with a ruler in hand comparing what's there with some kind of chart, looking back and forth. I've taken some examples from the medical literature reflecting the language of genital surgeons about large clitorises: "imperfect," "defective," "malformation," "anatomic derangements," "deformed," "major clitoral overgrowth," "obtrusive," "grossly enlarged," "ungainly masculine enlargement," "offending shaft," "embarrassing," "offensive," "incompatible with satisfactory feminine presentation or adjustment," "disfiguring," "troublesome," "challenging to a feminine cosmetic result."

These descriptors suggest not only that there is a size and malformation problem, but there is an aesthetic one as well, experienced as a moral violation. The language is emotional. Physician-researchers seem personally outraged. The early items on the list suggest that the large clitoris is imperfect and ugly. The later items suggest more of a personal affront. From the perspective of the viewer, the clitoris is portrayed as offending and embarrassing. Who, exactly, is offended and embarrassed, and why? A comment from an intersexed adult woman about her childhood is relevant: "I experienced the behavior of virtually everyone towards me as absolutely dishonest and embarrassing." What's interesting is that she didn't say she experienced the organ as embarrassing, even though she was not operated on until she was eight. Objects in the world, even non-normative objects, are not embarrassing. People's reactions to them are. Perhaps the last item on the list says it best: the clitoris is "challenging."

My favorite quote of all the reading I've done is "The annals of medical history bulge with strange cases of enlarged clitorises."[4]

What about the language used to describe the micro-phallus, the small penis? I've found that it is not emotional. It is not particularly pejorative. Some common descriptors for the small penis are "short," "buried," "anomalous." There is usually some discussion about whether the micro-phallus is normally proportioned or whether it has a feminine stigmata. Descriptions of the micro-penis, however, are tied quite explicitly to gender role. Here are more quotes:

Is the size of the phallus adequate to support a male sex assignment?[5]

A ten-year-old boy with a small penis was given testosterone ointment, "after which"—I don't know whether it was momentarily or it took a while—"after which he reaffirmed his allegiance to things masculine."[6]

After B's 15th birthday, her penis developed erections. She produced ejaculations and she found herself feeling a sexual interest in girls.[7]

Clearly, once the penis is large enough to support masculinity, with or without extra hormones, everyone will be more comfortable. Once that penis starts to work, it will direct the owner, even if she is a girl, toward a sexual interest in girls.

There is considerably less discussion of how the labia ought to look than how the clitoris ought to. Labial variation is permissible. The labia majora don't have to completely cover the minora. Minor fusion of the labia is acceptable. And it is all right if the prepuce adheres to the clitoris. Here is a quotation from a 1930s marriage manual:

> In some women the inner lips protrude somewhat. The inner lips meet at their upper ends, and when separated, are approximately in the form of the wishbone of a hen, approximately two inches at width.[8]

Then there is the "Hottentot apron." "In all the women of the Bushman, in South Africa, and in some of the Hottentot women (according to one early textbook), "the labia minora hang halfway down to the knees."[9] There were women with this condition (or beautification) who went on tour in Europe and were exposed to people. They lay down and people came and looked at them.

I want to relate this very briefly to female genital mutilation today, one rationale for which is that the labia are considered unsightly and unclean, and if they are not excised they will dangle between the legs and may threaten the penis.[10]

Does the average person have any idea what genitals should look like? Would the average person permit more variation than the average surgeon? Imagine a set of criteria pictures by which someone's genitals would be judged: "How much does the clitoris protrude from the labia?" I located one study of what women know about their sex organs.[11] Women were asked to draw both their internal and external sex organs, and the outer and inner lips of the external genitalia were in fact seldom drawn. So women actually didn't draw labia when they were asked to draw the female genitals. It is, perhaps, more interesting that in this group of women only 41 percent drew the clitoris. One of my students is interviewing surgeons who do genital reconstruction for women who have had genital cancers. One physician told her, "There is usually only a labia majora made by the surgeon, because people are not that sophisticated. They don't require a labia minora, and they are much more difficult to construct. You can fool most of the people most of the time."

Perhaps the labia are so poorly conceptualized because their function is obscure. A nineteenth-century medical text clarifies the function of the labia.

> The labia majora protect the deeper parts. They lead the male organ to them and serve as buffers during coitus. The function of the labia minora is to ensure a more perfect adaptation and act as an irritant for the nerves of the male member at the same time that their own nerves are acted on.[12]

So one wonders who the female genitals belong to. Some 1930s marriage manuals show the same blatant heterosexism in their descriptions of the vagina. There was one picture of the female sex organs, separated into what the author called the "working parts" and the "sensation providing parts."[13] The "working parts" were the fallopian tubes, the womb, the ovary, and the vagina. (I guess the work they do is reproductive work), and the "sensation providing parts" were the clitoris and the labia. The vagina is from the Latin word meaning "sheath": the male sex organ fits into it like a sword into a sheath.

In a 1906 text, a diagrammatic section of the median plane of the female genital organs includes the end of the penis.[14] There is no clitoris. The caption describes the drawing as the "internally more important part of the female sexual apparatus."

More modern scientific literature also blends appearance and function, albeit with more subtlety. Here's a representative description of the clitoris:

> The clitoris is not essential for *adequate sexual function* and sexual *gratification*, but its preservation would seem to be desirable if achieved while maintaining *satisfactory appearance* and function. Yet the clitoris clearly has a relation to erotic stimulation and to sexual gratification and its presence is desirable even in patients with intersexed anomalies if that presence does not interfere with *cosmetic, psychological, social and sexual adjustment.*[15]

The emphases are mine. I have some questions. What is meant by "adequate sexual function"? Is that the same thing as "gratification"? If not, what is "gratification"? Are either of them the same as orgasm? Who would this be desirable for? The patient? The doctor? The natural state of things? And what is a "satisfactory appearance"? How are the four different "adjustments" listed at the end ranked? Is that order accidental?

Before I talk about surgeries on intersexed genitals, I want to summarize what I think are the surgeons' beliefs about female genitals (although never stated, they are important because they underlie surgical practices): The most important thing about the clitoris is that it be small. The labia might just as well not exist. And the vagina is basically just an adjunct to the penis. (I'll provide more support for that statement later.) In Western culture there are no female genitals. (All this should be contrasted with the view of the cultures in Africa and the Middle East that are performing clitorectomies, where clearly the female genitals are very striking and powerful and dangerous, and no matter what their size, they need to be gotten rid of.)

Here is a brief description of some clitoral surgeries. Clitorectomy, which was the earliest, is also called clitoridectomy, or amputation. In the argument for doing a complete clitorectomy, which is sometimes still done today, it has been said that it is not good to have any halfway measures because doing it halfway, removing only the exposed portion, would "allow the bulk of the clitoral shaft to remain and such tissue can become turgid and painful."[16] The technique of "clitoral recession," developed in 1961 by John Lattimer at Columbia Presbyterian, was an operation to reduce or cover the enlarged clitoris without removing it. I thought it interesting that it is acceptable to have a large clitoris as long as it is covered.

Then there is clitoral reduction, which is a technique developed in 1970 by Judson Randolph to preserve more of the erectile tissue. He wrote in a letter (1993), "I came to the conclusion that sparing the clitoris would be more physiologic and more appropriate." One intersexed woman says that half a dozen intersex surgeons she spoke with were uniformly ignorant of the Randolph technique, and the Lattimer technique is the most common and is still used at Columbia Presbyterian today. As far I could tell, from my reading of the literature, there is no size criteria or medical criteria by which one would choose one technique over another.

In reading through the medical literature, I have noted something about the language used to discuss the surgery. It is described as "necessary" not because anyone, or any one profession, has deemed it so, but because the genital itself requires the improvement. Here are some quotations:

> Given that the clitoris must be reduced, what is the best way to do it?[17]

> When the female sex is assigned, an operation on the clitoris, together with other necessary procedures to modify the genitalia, becomes necessary for the establishment of proper psychological and social adjustment.[18]

> The size of an enlarged clitoris demanding clitorectomy cannot be stated in exact measurements.[19]

We have this sense that the clitoris is "demanding," maybe with placards or something, to be reduced. Where does the clitoris get its right to demand reduction? Why, from "Nature." And now that we know that the large clitoris is an affront to "Nature," it is understandable why the language used to describe it is so emotional.

I had some questions when I began reading the literature: How good is the surgery that is performed on the intersexed? How much scarring results from the clitoral reductions, recessions, or creations? Does this affect the ability to experience orgasm? Does it cause irritation or pain? How credible is the appearance? How functional is the vagina? Is it long enough? Wide enough? Does it lubricate enough? How credible is its appearance? Does the vagina scar and tend to close, requiring further surgeries? If so, is this because the surgical techniques themselves are imperfect, or because of patient noncompliance?

I reviewed eleven follow-up studies, published between 1961 and 1992, on intersex surgery. Some of the studies were conducted by the surgeons who developed the techniques, Lattimer and Randolph, assessing the effects of their own surgery; other studies were comparisons of different surgical techniques. It is not always easy extracting from the studies exactly what criteria were used to measure success. Sometimes the language is so vague as to be mystifying: "The surgery yielded an acceptable appearance and, in most instances, satisfactory sexual adjustment leading to an improved psychologic base."[20] Acceptable to whom? Satisfactory in what sense? Improved from what? Compared to what?

Some follow-up studies give more specific criteria.[21] I have grouped the criteria according to categories in the order that I believe is important to physicians. Despite all the discussion about enlarged clitorises, most studies consider that the intersexed patient has been successfully treated if her vagina size and functioning are good. "Vaginoplasty" is the term used to refer to surgery to create a vagina that wasn't there, or to correct an "imperfect" vagina. There are a number of different techniques used on intersexed girls, most of which have been developed on transsexuals. This surgery is also done on women with genital cancers. Vaginoplasty on the intersexed used to be done in early childhood, shortly after clitoral surgery, which is usually performed within the first year. Now vaginoplasties are often delayed until puberty, after the body has finished growing and when the child is old enough to do all the things she has to do to keep the vagina from closing up. It is a quite complicated, tedious procedure. Delaying the surgery is presumably also in the service of reducing the amount of dense scarring. One father of an intersexed child told me he wanted vaginoplasty on his baby daughter delayed as long as possible.

The size of the vagina is related to whether it is used successfully in intercourse. It is sometimes unclear who is evaluating "unsuccessful" attempts at vaginal intercourse. Studies that are explicit about evaluating the vagina suggest that the results are far from perfect. In one study fifteen of twenty-three women who had vaginal reconstruction during infancy had functionally inadequate vaginas.[22]

When vaginoplasty for transsexuals is discussed in the literature, sexual intercourse is described as "useful" in keeping the vagina open, thereby contributing to a successful surgical outcome, as though the whole point is a successful surgical outcome. A specific heterosexual sex activity is seen as useful for the purpose of creating and maintaining a particular anatomy—a new take on anatomy as destiny. You're destined to have the anatomy. You don't want a vagina so you can be functionally heterosexual; you function heterosexually so you can have a vagina. In that sense, plastic dilators are as good as penises.

Based on my reading of vagina measurements, I would say that transsexuals are getting bigger vaginas than adult women. An adult female virgin non-transsexual's vagina is three and a half to four and three-fourths inches, and transsexuals are getting vaginas up to seven and an eighth inches. I don't know if anyone wants to protest that. I guess if you are paying that much "ya gotta get a big one."

A surgeon who does genital reconstruction of women with genital cancer said,

If you can give a patient a functioning vagina, you have accomplished what Eve set out to accomplish. Without a vagina a woman is not normal. It's like having a nose. You can breathe fine without a nose, but you look funny without a nose. The women don't feel normal. I don't think it is very important whether it is ever used.

When asked whether there was consensus in the field about this, he said, "I haven't sat down with other plastic surgeons and discussed it. I am not aware of any psychological studies." Does his answer about not needing to use the vagina suggest that he is not being heterosexist? Or does his requirement of the vagina for complete femaleness reflect what a heterosexual man means by "complete woman" in terms of his own self-interest: the vagina should be there if it is ever needed?

The second criterion is the aesthetics of the anatomy, which is rated by the surgeons. I haven't come across any reference to patients being asked how satisfied they were with the way their genitals look. One researcher says, "Gross appearance of the external genitalia was acceptable, although on close examination the lack of the clitoris was obvious."[23] Having no clitoris is described as an "acceptable appearance." Another researcher evaluated anatomy, rating it as "excellent," "satisfactory," or "unsatisfactory," but he didn't give the criteria by which he judged it.[24] Others suggested that appearance is "unsatisfactory" if the glans is positioned too high or if there is persistent prominent size.

The third criterion is discomfort: "No prepubital girl," according to one study, "expressed any discomfort of the clitoris or described troublesome erections."[25] I wonder exactly who would be troubled by these erections, and what was troubling about them. Other researchers mention frequent erections and constant irritation and pain.

Some researchers, who are apparently unwilling to ask their patients direct questions, display their naïveté when they describe why erotic response can't be directly assessed. Thus one study reports, "some patients, of marriageable age, are still single, and any relevant conclusion regarding the erotic response of the glans is hard to determine."[26] I guess unless you're married, there would be no way to test whether your genitals were working or not. From a follow-up study of transsexuals' surgery, the researcher makes reference to male-to-female transsexuals having the "sensation of orgasm."[27] That phrase is in quotes in the original article. Is there a difference between an orgasm and merely the "sensation" of an orgasm? I found that in other articles, too, erotic response is described as having the "sensation of an orgasm." I suspect that isn't quite an orgasm yet.

The fourth criterion is the occurrence of complications, such as "cysts" or "fistulas." This is rated by the surgeons, and there is very little discussion of this. One gets the *sense* that the surgical procedures are pretty good in avoiding such complications. This is in striking contrast to the result of mutilations performed under unsterile conditions in Africa.

The final criteria are marriage and pregnancy. As evidence of the success of the surgical technique, one researcher cites the case of a twenty-one-year-old intersexed woman who was married and was in the final month of her second pregnancy.[28] Another mentions two women from the sample who were married.[29] Although marriage and pregnancy are not referred to in every intersex follow-up study, the emphasis on the vagina suggests that the ultimate test of the vagina is a successful marriage and eventually a pregnancy. In other words, heterosexuality.

The heterosexism of the researchers is evident in the way they interpret some of their data. In one study of eighty adult females, thirty-eight reportedly had no sexual experience.[30] And yet twelve of those thirty-eight, according to the researcher, had been judged as having an "adequate" vagina. Only three of the thirty-eight women admitted to being lesbian. The researchers were mystified: "If the women had good vaginas, why weren't they using them?" Part of the answer to this naive question is reflected in the ambiguity of the language used to describe the results, which might also reflect the ambiguity of their questioning of the subjects. Throughout that article, the following terms were used interchangeably: "heterosexual activity," "sexual intercourse," and "sexual experience." The researchers may have concluded that the women were not sexually active if they implied they did not have penile-vaginal sexual intercourse, as if sexual intercourse were the only sexual activity one could do with a male or female partner. In addition, we have no way of knowing how comfortable the women felt confiding their lesbian activity to the physicians. Some of the adult intersexed women I have been in contact with are lesbians, and one of them claims that many intersexed she has met are.

I believe that, given the medical histories of these women, with large numbers of doctors examining, poking, and photographing their genitals, from birth to adolescence, it is not surprising that they have an aversion to anybody looking at or touching their genitals.

I'll make a few concluding statements about the follow-up study. The sense one is supposed to get is that the surgery is pretty good. The external genitals could pass inspection, medical complications are few, and if women would only comply with the tedious procedure of dilating their vaginas and having whatever additional surgeries are prescribed, they would have "good enough" vaginas for sexual intercourse. Any self-critiques of the medical profession are available only between the lines, as suggested in the following quotation. "We have learned, in some instances bitterly, the absolute essentiality of a structured, regular, comprehensive program from infancy into adult life."[31]

Some patients are not compliant with the physicians' recommendations. For example, they refuse to dilate their vaginas, have additional recommended surgeries, or be available for follow-up studies. This noncompliance is discussed in terms of how it reflects poorly on the patient; it is not seen as reflecting on the procedure itself. Noncompliance is described as "unfortunate" because it interferes with the surgeon's opportunity to "do his job" and "fix it" once and for all, or it interferes with the researcher's ability to get accurate follow-up statistics.

If, instead of evaluating the surgeries from published follow-up studies, we ask the adult intersexed women directly, the medical intervention seems less benign. One intersexed woman I've communicated with said, "If I apply a vibrator to the inside of my vagina, the only result is an irritating, itching sensation. Sex therapists tell me this is typical of scar tissue." She also says both her external and internal genitals are scarred and she has pain and is unable to have an orgasm. After examining her genitals one doctor characterized them as "an area a couple of centimeters in diameter with no feeling, and everything else is fine. You'll get someone to hold you nice and you'll be okay."

She told me of another intersexed woman who said that the result of reduction was so sensitive as to be painful, and she chose to have the clitoral recession in order to eliminate the pain. She asserts that the surgery caused immense damage to her sexual response. Then there is the case of an intersexed male who was born with a small penis. He had ten reconstructive surgeries by the time he was eighteen years old. The results were very bad. Doctors told him that another six operations would have him in "ship shape." Instead, he opted to have the penis removed and is now living as a woman with a female partner. Surgeons working with intersexed children don't talk to their patients about sexual response, and, lord knows, their parents don't want to talk about the sexual response of these infants. How can the surgeons refine their procedures or their skills?

An interesting contrast between transsexuals and intersexed is that, in one particular study, most of the transsexuals interviewed seemed willing to trade sexual gratification for having their bodies look right.[32] From my talks with adult intersexed, I don't think that they would make that trade of function for form. I see the inflated evaluation of the follow-up studies as serving to provide justification for the surgeries. Earlier, I talked about how the language of surgeons portrays medicine as merely taking its cues from Nature. While medicine is obeying Nature's command to reduce large clitorises, it is also attuned to Nature's commitment to evolution. "Given diagnostic progress, a more orderly surgical approach has developed."[33] "The surgical management is receiving increased attention as clinical insight, directing the assignment of sex, gains refinement."[34] "The tragedies of yesteryear rarely occur. Now, gender is assigned with confidence."[35] Surgical interventions are presented as progressive and surgeons are presented as more and more insightful and confident about gender. Given this conception of a forward-moving clinical specialty, we can make more sense of why genital surgery is promoted, in spite of the lukewarm follow-up data.

From the doctor's point of view, infants with indeterminant sex should be considered "a neo-natal, psycho-sexual emergency."[36] "There is certainly legal limbo awaiting the hermaphrodite who refuses surgery and wishes to maintain a sexually ambiguous body."[37] Yet the intersexed I've corresponded with say they would have been happier without the surgery and should have been permitted to develop an intersexed identity. In none of the follow-up studies I read is there any indication that a criterion for success includes the adult reflection on having had the surgery. One intersexual wrote me,

Parents have to decide whether they want an aesthetically acceptable child, or a happy, healthy, intact child. Before allowing them to decide in favor of the former, the child should better be adopted by someone else, who is more tolerant, or even killed.

The following table contrasts the conventional terminology of medical professionals (on the first line) with the unconventional terminology of adult intersexuals (on the second line). It's obvious that meanings differ depending on whose concerns are voiced.

Presurgical genitals	Intervention	Postsurgical genitals
"deformed"	"create"	"corrected"
"intact"	"destroy"	"damaged"

There are advantages to reducing the number of genital surgeries on intersexed infants. This would require educating doctors about extending the range of what is considered normal. It would also involve a different education for parents, and the development of support networks. I mentioned earlier that I had read over a hundred letters from parents of intersexed children. Most of them had never met anyone in their situation. The doctors don't, apparently, link up people. The way things are handled now, I believe that the parents' anxiety about their children's health is resolved through the genital surgery. These parents have a lot to be anxious about beyond the intersexed condition, since many of the children have life-threatening medical conditions. The consequence of resolving the anxiety through surgery is that there is no possibility for the intersexed child to experience her/his undamaged genitals or develop an intersexed identity, whatever that would be.

The political thrust for reducing the number of surgeries could come from children's rights groups who could expand their agenda and fight for the right of children not to be cut. There is an anticircumcision group called No Harm that is fighting on behalf of boy babies.

Is female genital surgery cosmetic surgery? In certain respects it is conceptualized as a design issue. I take as evidence for this claim the way surgeons write about clitoroplasty, which makes it seem akin to dressmaking or creative hairstyling. The word "fashion" comes up over and over. "Fashioning a cosmetic clitoris"[38] that is not expected to have any function. "Fashioning a nipple to simulate a glans clitoris."[39] "Preserving the feminine contour."[40] "Rearranging labial tissue to eliminate feminine folds"[41] (around the penis). The clitoris is referred to, in some places, as "plicated," which is a term from dressmaking having to do with making pleats. I haven't looked carefully at other surgical language, for example, heart-bypass surgery, but I suspect that it is not as fashion-oriented.

In female genital surgery there is a sense that nothing too difficult or too serious is going on. This contrasts with Marjorie Garber's analysis of the language used to describe the surgical construction of the female-to-male transsexual's penis.[42] It is consistently referred to, in the medical literature, as "not easily accomplished," "fraught with rather serious hazards," "still quite primitive and experimental," "likely to produce poor cosmetic results." Garber says that "in sex reassignment surgery, there remains an implicit privileging of the phallus, a sense that a real one can't be made, but only born."

Gender is equated with genitals, and the dimorphism of gender has demanded the dimorphism of genitals. Women's bodies may be underprivileged, but they certainly attract the attention of the cosmetic surgeons. In fact, there is a similarity between the language used to describe clitoroplasty and the language of elective surgery. Diana Dull and Candace West discuss ways that cosmetic surgeons rationalize doing elective surgery, that is, surgery that by its own definition is unnecessary.[43] Cosmetic surgeons describe elective surgery as a "normal, natural pursuit to correct objectively flawed features." Cosmetic surgeries are neither "luxuries" nor "investments," but rather "interventions that are needed." Once women's bodies are seen as essentially in need of repair, then surgery is seen as a moral imperative.

So then I ask, under what conditions could genital surgery be seen as elective? Who would the market be? How could such surgery not be seen as evidence of psychosis? I imagine that the justification would go something like this. "My self-esteem is tied up with my clitoral size, and I'd feel more feminine with a smaller clitoris," or "I'm a lesbian and in my community large clitorises are important. I'd like my clitoris to be 'lifted' and my prepuce designed." Or "I don't feel enough like a woman with my short, or long, or irregular labia." Imagine Madonna getting a labia elongation or clitoral implants.

Imagine some further features of this scenario: genital surgery ambulance chasers, looking for genitals to correct, not content to rely on the short supply of major "errors." Thus far, it is acceptable to have plastic put inside your skin—breasts, vulva molds, and penile implants—but if without benefit of a surgeon, you attach the plastic outside your skin, then it's just falsies or dildoes.

There is some indication that transsexuals already think of genital surgery as cosmetic surgery.

> In one sample (of transsexuals) over one third had undergone second and third genital surgeries for the purpose of cosmetic improvement, indicating a possible interest in beautifying the genitals.[44]

Many surgeons claim to provide cosmetic clitorises for male-to-female transsexuals, skin tabs that do not provide erotic sensation. They tend to disappear within two years. I guess there is a short warranty.

Who has a right to these new surgical parts? I noticed a recent *Los Angeles Times* ad that many of you may have seen: "Men only; penile enlargement; penile lengthening; financing; Dreams do come true." What is striking to me is not that penises are being enlarged and lengthened at the same time that clitorises and labia are being reduced, but that the ad needs to caution, "Men only." I suppose it is meant to deter female-to-male transsexuals, but maybe it is meant for any woman to take heed and squelch her desire for a penis.

Once genital parts become as commonly "correctable" as noses, there may be no limit to who requests them. And maybe there shouldn't be. Since genitals are the primary sign of gender, then for those of us interested in destabilizing gender, the avenue may be through denaturalizing, and thus destabilizing genitals. I think there is a radical potential in treating genitals as bodily ornaments.

The following is a transcription of the discussion (in part) that took place following Suzanne Kessler's presentation of her paper at a CLAGS colloquium.

QUESTION: You spoke at the very beginning about the genetic determination—if it's XX, or if it's XY, then you proceed. But you really didn't give time to that, and I wonder how much you think that that is a factor in families', in parents' decisions to go ahead with this surgery. If I can understand your talk, it's that we should at least try to understand intersexed people better, and try to really examine it in a more neutral way, and then make a determination about how to proceed, really based on the choices of the individuals and the families. But I think that there seems to be a strong push to go along with the sexual dimorphism of the society.

KESSLER: The parents really take their cues from the doctors. They're so distraught by this, and they don't know what to do. It's not like they are given a choice: "Would you like to keep the child this way or that way? Would you like to go with the chromosomes or go with the gonads?" or "How do you want to do it?" So they look to the doctors, who are rather confused for the first couple of days, naturally, because they don't know yet what the condition is. Once they make their decision, "Oh, this is congenital adrenal hypoplasia," or whatever they determine it is, then they come back to the parents and say, "Now we know what gender your child is. Now we know what to do. We just have to do a little snip and tuck here, a little simple operation. Bring her back in nine months. We'll do it." And often, as I mentioned, there are so many other medical emergencies going on around this child, that the gender stuff seems to get pushed to the back burner. It is not something the parents focus on. They're so happy to have that part of it resolved, and they can deal with the other things, like whether the child is salt-losing, that they'll say, "Okay, let's do the surgery. Let's at least get that clarified." So anxiety gets handled that way. And clearly the dimorphism is perpetuated by the doctors, who I guess we can't expect to act alone in this, and somehow be the vanguard of a movement.

QUESTION: How many intersex babies are born in the population?

KESSLER: It is a hard number to get a handle on. It is not like a chromosomal disorder that gets registered. I've heard estimates of "less than 1 percent" to "up to 4 percent." Even 1 percent seems high. If you talk to your average pediatrician, you see a couple in a lifetime, I would say. And the people who are doing the major work, see maybe ten a year. But that is because people come from all over. So I don't think it is extraordinarily common, even when you add all the conditions together.

COMMENT: A couple of comments I'd like to make here because I don't know how many other transsexuals there are in the room, and I may be the only one. If I'm not, please let me know so I can shut up. Some of us don't care about which chromosome mix we have—we know what we are inside. That biomedical determination is irrelevant, because frankly I don't cut it in the world functioning in the other gender role. I do cut it well the other way, as most people get to know me. And unfortunately, in terms of cosmetic surgery, we are involved in, beyond medical issues, psycho-social issues where we do want to, quote-unquote, "look normal." It's really unfortunate because we do. We are all under such pressure to be normal. Even gay folk are under pressure to be normal. And I constantly hear, being an outsider in the neighborhood, in the community, all sorts of peer pressures going on as "who can do what with who?" And these are things that in the next hundred years, hopefully, our society will straighten out.

QUESTION: Did you interview people who did not undergo surgery as infants, and who are being allowed to develop into whomever they developed into?

KESSLER: Not personally, but someone I communicated with had. This was the example of someone whose mother was offered the surgery and the mother was horrified. So I can't vouch for whether the person ended up quite okay. I'm not even arguing that, in fact, the intersexed I've spoken to who said they would have been okay, would, in fact, have been okay. I'm not naive about that. I'm just saying, from where they are sitting now, they say they would rather have not had it. Now, the parents that I've interviewed—one, in particular—there were no questions about whether their daughter should have the surgery. She is going to have the vaginoplasty. The parents—it's interesting—they tell me things like, "Well, you know, these kind of girls have a higher intelligence than other girls, but they don't turn out lesbian."

QUESTION: What about chromosomal ambiguity? There could be various other kinds of, like, extra Xs or extra Ys.

KESSLER: Most of the intersexed conditions I'm talking about, the chromosomes are not abnormal. Most of us in this room, my guess is, have no idea what our chromosomes are.

QUESTION: How often, in your estimation, is it an exaggeration of a condition that really needs correcting?

KESSLER: Can we imagine these things not needing correcting? Can we imagine letting them be? And one way to get to that would be for everybody to start just monkeying around with their genitals.

QUESTION: But considering what actually is . . . can't you just say, "Well, it's a girl," even though . . .

KESSLER: It's a girl with a big clitoris.

QUESTION: Right.

KESSLER: Why not? I mean, what kind of support would that require? What kind of a doctor would be able to say that? What kind of parents would be able to handle it? What kind of world could that kid grow up in? I've read cases of parents who have said they didn't realize anything was unusual about the clitoris until the doctor told them. "I thought that's the way they looked." Does everybody really know what the range is? I think a lot of these parents, if they were told, would answer, "Well it's kind of large. Well, so is her nose, really, you know."

QUESTION: Really what you are indicating here, on some level, is that there is this very wide gap between opening up a kind of discourse on gender and, on the other hand, genitals; that where looking at a less binary conception of gender obviously is not translating into opening up a sort of dialogue about continuums and so forth in relation to genitals. What surrounds an individual's understanding of their genitals? How do you see that opening up? I'll just give you one brief anecdote. I did have a patient who, for many years had some irregularity with her hymen, some very minor irregularity. And it took her about a year to tell me. She had never gone to a gynecologist because she was afraid to have this looked at. She had never had sex because of this, what she perceived of as a deformity. When it was looked at and explored, it was an incredibly minor variation. This was an educated, politically aware person. Right? And it took years.

KESSLER: This is *the* question: the sense of where it's going, what it's basically about. I'm interested in destabilizing gender and thinking about ways to do that. One possibility is, let's get a political movement going and let's just stop some of these surgeries. And I think that is a good direction. But on a more theoretical level of gender and what it is all about, I kind of like the idea of treating genitals as just ornaments, as not primary signifiers, as nothing special. And if you can somehow show that they are not dimorphic, they are just another body feature in some way, and there is a continuum, and people can fool around with it, and not take it quite so seriously, then maybe gender would somehow collapse under that.

COMMENT: But as a culture, we already do that with female genitals. We take them not seriously. We treat them as ornaments. They don't exist. You remove them. The clitoris—you get rid of . . . And male genitals—if you are going to do that, how do you make male genitals less serious? How do you reframe things so that penises are ornaments, are no big deal?

QUESTION: Looking at genitals as ornaments suggests that genitals are not the primary signifier or need not necessarily be a primary signifier of gender. You know, parents want to know, "Is it a girl or a boy?" What replaces genitalia, if you say you could separate genitals from gender? What replaces, or is there something else that will replace, or could replace, genitals as the primary signifier for gender? Is it the chromosomal analysis?

KESSLER: Well, that wouldn't be a step forward, as far as I'm concerned. If we said there was nothing primary, there was nothing essential . . . Okay, there was going to be gender, but it's really a decision, somewhat of a performance, or whatever you want it to be, maybe people would take *that* seriously. Because performances are easy to change, if gender becomes grounded only in performances, then the social construction of gender will ultimately cause gender to be taken less seriously.

COMMENT: And it seems to me that the chromosomal stuff, legitimately or illegitimately, has a kind of weight. When the genitals are confusing, the doctors say, "What are the chromosomes?"

QUESTION: So, suppose you have, which is one possible condition, someone with XY chromosomes with a clitoris and labia and a vagina? They are gender "interesting"?

KESSLER: There are some women with that condition who don't discover it until they are twelve, thirteen years old, or even later, that they are XY, and they are women. So, chromosomes seem like the least likely thing to hang it all on. I think maybe the problem with the other ways of treating female genitals (as trivial) is that it is not the woman who is instituting alterations, it's the culture.

COMMENT: It's the surgeon.

KESSLER: It's the surgeon, or the multilators, or whoever is doing it.

COMMENT: They are size-queens.

KESSLER: Reverse size-queens. There is a certain amount of time it takes to determine what the best medical treatment is, and what the medical condition is, and what is necessarily to be done. But once you look at the baby, and you see, well, it's an XX baby, and no major medical condition, or maybe the child has to take some kind of medicine for the rest of her life, but we don't have to touch the genitals. It's just, "it's a girl." It's a girl, and, yes, her labia are fused a little. I mean, I don't know if I would want to be the parent under that circumstance and have to be the pioneer and do this.

COMMENT: Or you are in a community, or a type of community, with a family and everything, and "I'll raise it as a girl," and then at the age of ten or twelve she wants to be a boy.

KESSLER: Or, if she wants to have a vagina when she is old enough, let her go pay for it herself. My guess is, before this century, or before medicine became so sophisticated, there probably were lots of people walking around with genitals that were different. It's only because we *can* do something about them that we feel that we *must*. You historians probably know those kinds of things.

COMMENT: The civil law in the South before the nineteenth-century was that people could choose and the only thing that they couldn't do was change their minds once they decided which gender they wanted to be.

KESSLER: And in a culture where your land ownership goes along with your genitals, it becomes more important to stick with whatever you've picked.

QUESTION: I guess I am still confused on the point of whether it's okay to have transsexual surgery, because I'm hearing a lot of the notion that "surgery is bad." But I don't really hear that about transsexual surgery.

KESSLER: Well, one of the things I wanted to say is that in some clinics where the surgeries are being done, you have to sign a form, saying that you realize that you may lose your ability to have an orgasm, and that you may have intense scarring. And unless you are willing to sign that consent form, you're not going to get the surgery. My understanding is that there is a willingness to put up with that for the way it looks.

QUESTION: Right. And I'm asking, do you think that that's okay? Is it okay for somebody who walks in and really knows . . . It's not just doctors who are forcing you to have plastic surgery. Believe me, it really follows the laws of the marketplace. And there are a lot of people, and more and more, who are barging in and demanding new noses, new hips, new whatever. You know, I can see where the objection is coming from, but I'm wondering if you are saying that it is really not okay for transsexuals to come in saying, "I want this surgery."

KESSLER: I have real mixed feelings about it, not to say I don't feel that they have a right to pay their money and get whatever kind of body they want. Part of me feels that it is unfortunate that people would have to go through that extreme surgery and spend that amount of money to just be whatever gender they want to be, but given that that is what genitals mean—gender in our culture—I can understand why they want to have the genitals that belong to their gender.

COMMENT: But it's so odd that function doesn't go along . . . I mean, nobody would have a nose job if they couldn't breathe after the nose job.

KESSLER: Well, I think this is the great secret: that the surgeries are not very good.

COMMENT: I want to say one thing. I think it is very important to recognize that transsexuals are adults, you know, and they have a right to make any kind of decision they want to make about their bodies. I don't think we should even talk about operations for transsexuals at the same time that we are talking about infants that are not able to choose anything. I mean, if you mutilate an infant, then that is for life. There is nothing you can do about it. When the child is old enough to make a decision, it is too late. So these are two entirely different things that we are talking about.

QUESTION: Are you saying, Suzanne, that the transsexual operation is not successful, or rarely successful? My understanding was that a lot of people who go through transsexual surgery are, in fact, orgasmic.

KESSLER: Some are not. When you actually read the follow-up studies, it is not as successful, in terms of orgasm and having what is called a "functional" vagina, able to hold a penis. There are a significant number in every study who would not be defined as sexually functional. That usually is not enough to make them regret having done it. But I do think, however bad the results are, my sense of the reading is: they are better than the intersex surgeries. They are better in terms of sexual functioning, and they are better in terms of just discomfort.

QUESTION: I would like to ask a question. You said early on that 90 percent of the surgeries on the babies are to make them girls. Why?

KESSLER: It's easier. That is the pat answer: "it's easier." Now, that means that you can create a female with no problems, a perfectly good-looking, functioning female. I think that there is some question about whether the functioning is that good.

QUESTION: But what about biological reproduction?

KESSLER: Well, there are some intersexed conditions where there is fertility, if you have the internal organs and all the hormones are working well. Most of the intersexed conditions are not fertile.

QUESTION: What happens to these little girls when they grow up?

KESSLER: A lot of them are being followed up. They must have psychologists and sociologists beating down their doors finding out if they are tomboys. But some parents get real scared if there is any sign of, quote, "masculinity" in these girls. There is really good counseling going on in Amsterdam, the effort made to counsel the parents not to get so scared when their daughters start showing signs of tomboyism, because lots of girls show signs of tomboyism and "don't overreact by that." So they give them a lot of counseling ahead of time of what to expect, because some of these parents go overboard in trying to socialize femininity in these girls.

QUESTION: About the point you made about orgasm, it occurs to me that they *were* using a kind of rigorous differentiation between orgasm and the sensation of orgasm. It's recognized by doctors that there is a physiological set of responses that define orgasm, and that orgasm is defined in terms of the stages which involve autonomic, neurological discharges which create effects in the body.

KESSLER: Yes. These were not physiological measures.

QUESTION: So, when you talk about "the sensation," you could talk about having, feeling, the sensation of orgasm without necessarily having the sympathetic discharge, which in the normal physiological female, would cause, usually, lubrication of the vagina.

KESSLER: So, since they weren't using physiological measures, all they could say was "sensation of orgasm." That is interesting.

Postscript

Readers will note that this essay contains more questions than answers. It reflects my preliminary reading of the surgical literature and interview data. Based on feedback from CLAGS seminar participants and SUNY/Purchase College women's studies faculty, I am preparing a more formal analysis of the issues introduced in these musings. I am more concerned than I indicated in this essay with the proliferation of cosmetic genital surgery and can now marshal more arguments against using it to destabilize gender.

Notes

1. Jared Diamond, "Turning A Man," *Discover*, June 1992, 71–77.
2. John K. Lattimer, "Relocation and Recession of the Enlarged Clitoris with Preservation of the Glans: An Alternative to Amputation," *Journal of Urology* 86, 1 (1961): 113–16.
3. Robert E. Gross, Judson Randolph, and John F. Crigler, Jr., "Clitorectomy for Sexual Abnormalities: Indications and Technique," *Surgery*, February 1966, 300–308.
4. L. T. Woodward, *Sophisticated Sex Techniques in Marriage* (New York: Lancer Books, 1968).
5. Kurt Newman, Judson Randolph, and Kathryn Anderson, "The Surgical Management of Infants and Children with Ambiguous Genitalia," *Ann. Surg.* 215, 6 (June 1992): 644–53.
6. Frank Hinman, Jr., "Microphallus: Characteristics and Choice of Treatment from a Study of Twenty Cases," *Journal of Urology* 107 (March 1972): 499–505.
7. Diamond (n. 1 above).
8. M. J. Exner, *The Sexual Side of Marriage* (New York: W. W. Norton, 1932).
9. Henry J. Garrigues, *A Textbook of the Diseases of Women* (Philadelphia: W. B. Saunders, 1894).

10. J. Ruminjo, "Circumcision in Women," *East African Medical Journal,* September 1992, 477–78.

11. Lucille Hollander Blum, "Darkness in an Enlightened Era: Women's Drawings of their Sexual Organs," *Psychological Reports* 42 (1978): 867–73.

12. Garriques (n. 9 above).

13. Helena Wright, *The Sex Factor in Marriage* (New York: Vanguard Press, 1931).

14. August Forel and C. F. Marshall, *The Sexual Question* (Brooklyn: Physicians and Surgeons Book Co., 1906).

15. Judson G. Randolph and Wellington Hung, "Reduction Clitoroplasty in Females with Hypertrophied Clitoris," *Journal of Pediatric Surgery* 5, 2 (April 1970): 224–31.

16. Gross, Randolph, and Crigler (n. 3 above).

17. Lattimer (n. 2 above).

18. H. Kumar, J. H. Kiefer, I. E. Rosenthal, and S. S. Clark, "Clitoroplasty: Experience during a Nineteen-Year Period," *Journal of Urology* 111 (1974): 81–84.

19. Gross, Randolph, and Crigler (n. 3 above).

20. Judson Randolph, Wellington Hung, and Mary Colainni Rathlev, "Clitoroplasty for Females Born with Ambiguous Genitalia: A Long-Term Study of Thirty-seven Patients," *Journal of Pediatric Surgery* 16, 6 (December 1981): 882–87.

21. A. Sotiropoulos, A. Morishima, Y. Homsy, and J. K. Lattimer, "Long-Term Assessment of Genital Reconstruction in Female Pseudohermaphrodites," *Journal of Urology* 115 (May 1976): 599–601; Lawrence E. Allen, B. E. Hardy, and B. M. Churchill, "The Surgical Management of the Enlarged Clitoris," *Journal of Urology* 128 (August 1982): 351–54; F.M.E. Skijper, H. J. van der Kamp, H. Brandenburg, S.M.P.F. de Muinck Keizer-Schrama, S.L.A. Drop, and J. C. Molendaar, "Evaluation of Psychosexual Development of Young Women with Congenital Adrenal Hyperplasia: A Pilot Study," *Journal of Sex Education and Therapy* 18, 3 (1992): 200–207.

22. Allen, Hardy, and Churchill (n. 21 above).

23. Sotiropoulos, et al. (n. 21 above).

24. Randolph, Hung, and Colainni Rathlev (n. 20 above).

25. Randolph, Hung, and Colainni Rathlev (n. 20 above).

26. Kumar et al. (n. 18 above).

27. Sara Perovic, "Male to Female Surgery: A New Contribution to Operative Techniques," *Plastic and Reconstructive Surgery* 91, 4 (April 1993): 708–9.

28. Allen, Hardy, and Churchill (n. 21 above).

29. Rose M. Mulaikai, Claude J. Migeon, and John A. Rock, "Fertility Rates in Female Patients with Congenital Adrenal Hyperplasia Due to 21-Hydroxylase Deficiency," *New England Journal of Medicine* 316, 4 (January 1987): 178–82.

30. Mulaikai, Migeon, and Rock (n. 29 above).

31. Newman, Randolph, and Anderson (n. 5 above).

32. June Martin, "The Incidence, Frequency and Rate of Genital Satisfaction of Sixty-four Post-Operative Male-to-Female Transsexuals Reported to Be Experienced during Various Sexual Behaviors: A Descriptive Study" (unpublished manuscript, 1988).

33. Randolph, Hung, and Colainni Rathlev (n. 20 above).

34. Allen, Hardy, and Churchill (n. 21 above).

35. Newman, Randolph, and Anderson (n. 5 above).

36. Barbara C. McGillivray, "The Newborn with Ambiguous Genitalia," *Seminars in Perinatology* 16, 6 (1992): 365–68.

37. Perovic (n. 27 above).

38. Howard W. Jones and William Wallace Scott, *Hermaphroditism, Genital Anomalies, and Related Endocrine Disorders* (Baltimore: Williams and Wilkins, 1958).

39. Allen, Hardy, and Churchill (n. 21 above).

40. Randolph and Hung (n. 15 above).

41. Newman, Randolph, and Anderson (n. 5 above).

42. Marjorie Garber, "Spare Parts: The Surgical Construction of Gender," *Differences: A Journal of Feminist Cultural Studies* 1.3 (1989): 137–59.

43. Diana Dull and Candace West, "Accounting for Cosmetic Surgery: The Accomplishment of Gender," *Social Problems* 38, 1 (February 1991): 54–70.

44. Martin (n. 32 above).

Two

The Terrains of History: New Stories,
New Methodologies

13

"Homosexual" and "Heterosexual": Questioning the Terms

Jonathan Ned Katz

In the late 1970s and early 1980s, as I researched a second book on homosexual American history, I was astonished to discover that the now common, unquestioned bifurcation of people, their emotions and acts, into "homosexual" and "heterosexual" was a recent manufacture.

The terms "homosexual" and "heterosexual," I learned, were coined by a writer (not a medical doctor), Karl Maria Kertbeny, and are first known to have been used by him in a private letter of May 6, 1868, to Karl Heinrich Ulrichs, another pioneering sex reformer. Kertbeny first publicly used the term "homosexual" in 1869, in a petition against the German law criminalizing "unnatural fornication." The label homosexual was then appropriated by late nineteenth-century medical men as a way of naming, condemning, and asserting their own proprietary rights over a group then parading into sight in the bars, dance halls, and streets of Europe's and America's larger cities.

At the same time, the label heterosexual was also appropriated by doctors as a word for the erotic intercourse of men with women. But since such intercourse was not necessarily reproductive, the word "heterosexual," well into the twentieth century, continued to signify a bad, immoral relation.

The words "homosexual" and "heterosexual," I learned, were first printed in an American publication, a medical journal, in May 1892, raising a new and interesting question: How were the intimacies of the sexes categorized in April, and, of course, earlier? In their debut appearance, I noticed, the terms "heterosexual" and "homosexual" defined two kinds of sexual perversion, judged according to a procreative standard. A list of "Sexual perversions proper" included "Psychical hermaphroditism or heterosexuals." A note explained that "heterosexuals" were persons in whom occur "inclinations to both sexes," as well as inclinations "to abnormal methods of gratification."

Only gradually, I began to realize, did American medical publications agree that the word "heterosexual" referred to a "normal" male-female eroticism. In 1901, a Philadelphia medical dictionary was still defining "heterosexuality" as "Abnormal or perverted appetite toward the opposite sex." In 1910 Havelock Ellis was still protesting that we "have no simple, precise, natural word" for the "normal sexual love" of the sexes. As late as 1923, I discovered, the authoritative Merriam-Webster dictionary was still defining "heterosexual" as a medical term meaning "Morbid sexual passion for one of the opposite sex."

Only in the first quarter of the twentieth century, I finally realized, did heterosexuality's doctor advocates succeed in constructing and distributing it as a signifier of sexuality's Standard Brand. Their regularization of eros paralleled contemporary attempts to standardize masculinity and femininity, intelligence and manufacturing. The doctors' heterosexual category proclaimed a new erotic separatism, a novel sex orthodoxy, that forcefully segregated sex "normals" from sex "perverts," and set "hetero" over "homo" in a hierarchy of superior and inferior eroticisms. But only gradually did the idea that there were such creatures as heterosexuals and homosexuals emerge from the narrow realm of medical discourse to become a popular, commonplace notion.

Upon historical examination we find that "homosexual" and "heterosexual," the terms we moderns take for granted, are fairly recent creations. Though presented to us as words marking an eternal fact of nature, the terms "heterosexual" and "homosexual" constitute a normative sexual ethic, a sexual-political ideology, and one historically specific way of categorizing the relationships of the sexes.

The terms "heterosexual" and "homosexual," I suggest, also arise out of and help maintain a historically specific way of socially ordering gender and eroticism. "Heterosexual" and "homosexual" refer to groups, identities, and even behaviors and experiences that are time-limited, specifically modern phenomena, contingent on a peculiar institutional structuring of masculinity, femininity, and lust.

Many researchers now commonly agree that sexual and gender categories, erotic identities, communities, meanings, and institutions are historical and change over time. But even theorists of the social construction of sex have continued to posit an ahistorical "homosexual behavior." For example, a historian from whom I have learned a great deal refers to the distinction "between homosexual behavior, which is universal, and a homosexual identity, which is historically specific." But only the most mechanistic, biologistic idea of "behavior" permits this distinction between a universal behavior and historical identity.

Even as we labor to historicize sexuality and gender, many historians continue to assume that, whatever a behavior was called in its own time, we now know its real name and character: That behavior was *really homosexual, heterosexual, or bisexual.* Our epistemological hubris and ontological chutzpah prevent us from understanding the varieties of sexuality and gender within their own social structure and time.

If sexual behavior is more than just a conjunction of organs, if it is always shaped by the particular system within which it functions, and if it always includes a mix of socially defined feelings and meanings, behavior is just as historically relative and constructed as identity.

Don't get me wrong. Some sexual acts similar to those performed in New York last night were no doubt performed in New Amsterdam in the early colonial American era. But that early colonial sexual behavior was enmeshed within a different economy. So profound is the historically specific character of sexual behavior that only with the loosest accuracy can we speak of sodomy in the early colonies and "sodomy" in present-day New York as "the same thing." In another example, to speak of "heterosexual behavior" as occurring universally is to apply one term to a great variety of activities produced within a great variety of sexual and gender systems.

Radical social constructionists, myself among them, posit the historical relativity of sexual behaviors, as well as of identities, meanings, categories, groups, and institutions. Such relativity theory is no longer particularly radical when applied to the changing historical emotions and institutions of "the family," for example. But it remains subversive when applied to erotic and gender history, for it challenges our stubborn, ingrained idea of an essential, eternal heterosexuality and homosexuality.

It is particularly unsettling, I think, to speak of heterosexual history, for that history challenges our usual, implicit, deterministic assumption that heterosexuality is fixed, timeless, biological, synonymous with the conjunction of female and male organs and acts. To the contrary, I argue, heterosexuality (like homosexuality) has an unheralded, various past, and an open, undetermined future. To paraphrase Karl Marx, women and men make their own sexual and affectional history. But they do not make this history just as they please. They make it under circumstances given by the past and altered by their political activity and organization, and their vision of a valued future. Erotic and gender relationships are always under construction and reconstruction within specific historical settings.

In the last sentence, let us note, I fall back into a mode of speech suggesting the existence of some essential, universal eroticism and gender always being reconstructed. Such is the power over our minds of essentialist thought that I know no way to avoid it. But the move away from a history of homosexuality and heterosexuality to a history of eroticism and gender does, I think, empower a pragmatic, strategic conceptual advance, allowing us to ask new questions.

When, for example, we stop positing the Eternal Homosexual, we are encouraged to ask how men in early and mid-nineteenth-century New York City structured their erotic relations with men, what thoughts, judgments, and physical acts of theirs we can find evidence of, and what words they used about those relations.

My social constructionist hypothesis does not, by the way, suggest that heterosexual or homosexual feelings are less real, profound, or legitimate because they are socially constructed, simply that they are not omnipresent, not a biological fate.

In order, then, to understand the historical diversity of the sexes' relations, I challenge researchers to suspend temporarily, at least, our usual universalizing heterosexual/homosexual hypothesis. If we stop projecting those categories on societies in which they did not operate, we can open our eyes to the historical varieties of gender, affection, and eroticism past.

14

Telling Tales: Oral History and the Construction of Pre-Stonewall Lesbian History

Elizabeth Lapovsky Kennedy

    Oral history has been central in creating knowledge about lesbian and gay male life before Stonewall. This is particularly true for working-class lesbians, whose oppression as women and as lesbians, combined with race and class oppression, has made it unlikely that they leave many written records. However, even upper-class women, unless they were inclined to the literary world, were not likely to leave documents about their lesbianism.[1] Despite the prominence of oral testimony in lesbian and gay history, there has been surprisingly little discussion of the problems and possibilities of the method.[2] Most theoreticians of oral history have come to see the practice as revealing two different but complementary kinds of "truth." First, oral history adds new social facts to the historical record. Second, being based in memory, it explores subjectivity—and individual's interpretation of the past.[3] In my own work I have been hampered by the fact that the tradition of gay and lesbian oral history has thought much more about the former, what I will call for want of a better term the "empirical," than the latter, and has not fully considered the interconnections between the two.[4]

    The "empirical" concerns of lesbian and gay oral history emerged from the desire to document and legitimize lesbian and gay history at a time when most people thought no such thing existed. The spirit of the early gay and lesbian history projects, such as the Lesbian Herstory Archives in New York City, the Buffalo Women's History Project, and the San Francisco Lesbian and Gay History Project, was to grab a tape recorder and go out and record the memories of our elders before they were lost. The urgency with which lesbians and gays went in search of their history, first in grassroots community projects and later in the academy, to reclaim a history before its bearers died, encouraged a focus on dates, places, names, and events. Furthermore, the fervent desire to legitimize their findings, and therefore gay and lesbian history, encouraged a downplaying of the oral and subjective nature of the life stories that were collected. At that time, "serious" history emphasized objectivity and viewed first-person narratives with suspicion.[5] But this kind of defensiveness is no longer necessary. Most social historians have transcended the polarization between the reliability of social facts derived from written sources—letters, newspaper accounts, court records—and those from oral sources. They have come to understand that many newspaper accounts are based on interviews and recollections, and that letters and diaries are first-person accounts. Furthermore, postmodern thinking has questioned the objectivity of historical accounts, revealing the partiality of all sources. In fact, today in gay and lesbian studies it is "empirical" work that is on the defensive.[6]

In the past fifteen years the most forward-looking oral historians have come to understand the subjectivity and orality of their sources as a strength rather than a weakness.[7] They have explored how oral testimony—the actual storytelling—conveys unique information and how the subjective—what the past means to a particular individual—adds new dimensions to history. They have also emphasized the interactive process between the historian and interviewee in constructing the interpretation, and have considered the political uses of their work. These kinds of exploration are very appropriate for gay and lesbian history. Not being born and raised in a public lesbian and gay culture, each gay and lesbian person had to construct his or her own life in oppressive contexts, a process that oral history is uniquely suited to reveal. Furthermore, the celebration of the twenty-fifth anniversary of Stonewall, which occasioned the writing of this essay, has accelerated the formation of powerful cultural myths about the place of Stonewall in gay life. Self-consciousness about how research methodologies contribute to this process is very timely.

This essay argues that while gay and lesbian historians need to continue with the "empirical" uses of oral history—adding social facts to the historical record and analyzing how social institutions change—we also need to expand our understanding of what can be learned from oral sources. First, I will consider how close examination of storytelling styles can reveal information about cultural and class differences among lesbians. Second, I will explore how we can learn more about the meaning of lesbian identity by embracing the subjective. Third, I will discuss the cultural uses of memory in the interpretation of the gay and lesbian past. And finally, I will examine the constructed nature of oral histories, focusing in particular on how the myths of Stonewall both expand and limit historical research. Together these considerations add new dimensions to the writing of gay and lesbian history and help clarify the meaning of Stonewall.

Letting the Style of Storytelling Be Evidence in Its Own Right

My own experience working with the oral histories for *Boots of Leather, Slippers of Gold* was that black and white working-class lesbians were exquisite storytellers. The life stories we collected for the most part were breathtakingly beautiful documents of survival and resistance in very difficult situations. At first my proletarian bias led me to assume that this was because most of the interviews were with working-class lesbians. As active agents in shaping a public lesbian community and identity, working-class lesbians were conscious about their place in history and therefore highly articulate. But as more and more oral histories of middle- and/or upper-class lesbians have been published, as in *Inventing Ourselves: Lesbian Life Stories* or *Cherry Grove, Fire Island*, I have had to revise this perspective.[8] Despite their commitment to a life of discretion and privacy, many upper-class women also tell compelling stories. It seems that a significant number of lesbians are good storytellers, no matter their class or cultural group.

Audre Lorde's *Zami: A New Spelling of My Name*, which the author describes as a biomythography, provides some clue as to why this should be.[9] Though Lorde is writing about a black working-class experience, her insights seem applicable to many lesbians. Because the majority of lesbians grow up in a heterosexual culture, they have no guidelines and no patterns for creating a homosexual life.[10] They, therefore, are constantly creating their lives, developing a biomythography, so to speak. Lesbians who are completely private are no exceptions. They cannot passively accept the traditional structure of a woman's life; they must create their own guidelines for living, and therefore actively engage the process of storytelling.

Because storytelling plays a prominent role in lesbian life, we can scrutinize the style of lesbian stories for what it tells us about the culture of the narrator. Do styles differ significantly, and can they provide a new window onto class, racial-ethnic, and regional variations in lesbian oppression and resistance? In *Boots of Leather, Slippers of Gold* we marshal all kinds of evidence to make our points, but we never use this sort of analysis of the structure and style of storytelling.[11] I cannot think of any other lesbian and gay oral historians who do so. It seems an appropriate time to open up this new direction of analysis.

Buffalo working-class lesbians who were "out" in the 1940s and 1950s tell the story of their finding, building, and enjoying lesbian community with excitement and humor. The structure of their stories conveys their connection to audience and community. For example, Arlette, a black fem, remembers how she was intrigued by mannish-looking women the first time she saw them on the street:[12]

> The first time I saw really gay women, mannish-looking women was here in Buffalo, New York. And I didn't know what they were. I really thought that they were men. . . . The first gay lady I saw here . . . to me she was fascinating. I kept

looking at her, and I said, "That's a good-looking guy, but it's a funny-looking guy. . . ." I could never tell if she was a man or a woman 'cause I never got close enough to her, but there was one strange thing, she would have on lipstick. I said, "This woman's different." She's got on men's clothes, her hair was very nice, cut short. She treated a lady like a gentleman would with a lady out, but I said, "Is that a man or a woman?" So I made it a point to get close enough to hear her voice, 'cause I knew if I could hear her talking I could tell. Then I found out, this is a woman. And I said, "Golly, got on men's clothes and everything, what kind of women are these?" Then I started seeing more women here dressed in stone men's attire. I said, "Well, golly, these are funny women." Then they kind of fascinated me. What could they possibly do? Everybody wants to know what can you do. I got curious and I said, "I'm going to find out."

This small fragment is like a dance of anticipation and curiosity. It captures many of the significant ingredients of black working-class lesbian life: the drive toward and excitement of finding lesbians, the importance of the appearance of studs for creating lesbian visibility, the daring of fems who sought out studs. Most important for this analysis, the storyteller makes herself an active partici- pant in the process of discovery of community, telling us explicitly what she said and thought. It also conveys a connection to a wider audience, "everybody," and the humor is based on the public's curiosity about lesbians.

These same ingredients of humor, agency, and community appear in the "Robin Hood" tale of Sandy, a white butch, about her return to the Carousel, after having been forbidden entry due to unacceptable behavior. (The Carousel was a popular bar that had a fairly respectable reputation, catering to upwardly mobile lesbians in the front and rough-and-tough lesbians in the back.) Sandy vividly conveys the way butches envisioned themselves as fighters for justice:

Oh yeah, Jamie was working there. I punched her out so that didn't go over good. So I was barred. That really pissed me off. Because when the Canadians and all that would come over they would go to there. It was a little nice, they'd go there and I'd wanted to be in there too. The girls would be there. So I got really mad about that. Who the hell was I with, I think it was Ronni. We were down at the Chesterfield, I'm pissed off. I says, "I'm going up to that Carousel," and I already had a plan. So we go up to the Carousel, I says, "Pull in the driveway." There was a driveway right beside the bar, so she pulled in there and I got out of the car and I went to the back of the Carousel where these windows with screens on them was where the kitchen was. So I ripped the screen off, opened the window and I got in. Now I'm in the kitchen. Course, out of the kitchen is the back room, the bar naturally is to the front. So I went in the kitchen and I'm looking around, the big cooler, so I open up the cooler; I'm looking in there. There was all these cream pies and butter and all this shit. So I go to Ronni, here, we're loading the car up, with this butter and cream pies. So now, she says, "Come on Sandy," she was chicken, she says, "Get out of there, get out of there." I says, "Wait a minute," I seen these big trays of chicken, all cooked. It must have been for some party or something, I don't know. So I said, "I'll be right with you." So I get out one of these trays, there was some towels there, put a towel over my arm, take the tray and I went in the back room from the kitchen. I had a good time then. Now nobody really knows that I'm barred, but they got everything right, "Chicken tonight." I'm going around giving all this out to all the kids in the back room.

About two trays of chicken I handed out. Of course I didn't go to the front or anything. Somebody had to go out to the front, and they were eating chicken. He goes, "Where'd that chicken come from?" "Why Sandy's back there." "What?" They're yelling "That God damn Sandy." I dove out the back window. And I was barred good then. There was no way of ever getting back in there. And Ronni says, "But I got so sick of those God damn cream pies." It was better than starving. Pulled the old waiter bit.

Sandy's story captures her pride in her tough behavior, her ability to stick up for her rights, her resentment that this was not accepted in the better bars, and her refusal to be limited in the bars she could enter. Also, she takes care of her own kind: the other tough lesbians who were in the back room. All these themes reappear throughout her life story and in those of others in her community. Her style is direct: "I said, she said"; and she consistently portrays herself and her friends as active agents in shaping their lives. The story also expresses a sense of community as it interweaves several voices in one tale. Her antics make sense only in the context of others' actions.

As we listened to and worked with these oral narratives, we realized that these stories were not told for the first time to us, the oral historians, but that they had been shared before with friends at parties and in bars. Sometimes we inadvertently repeated questions to a narrator after several years had elapsed, and we would hear remarkably similar stories, embellished with similar details. This made sense to us because working-class lesbians spent a lot of time socializing together in explicitly lesbian space. Their lives were defined by finding and supporting other lesbians in a hostile environment and by developing strategies to live with some dignity and pride. What better way to accomplish this than by sharing stories about these successes and defeats? Essentially we were tapping into an oral tradition that supported lesbians, allowing them to survive in a hostile environment, very much like the oral tradition of African Americans in the South or industrial workers in Italy.

The content and style of these stories are radically different from those of middle-class lesbians of an earlier time, who not only did not announce their lesbianism to the world, but also never talked about being lesbians with each other. They therefore never shared stories about lesbian life and community. This tendency can be seen in the life story of Julia Reinstein, an eighty-eight-year-old woman who lived as a lesbian from 1928 to 1942 in South Dakota and rural western New York. During this time Julia's status as a successful teacher— not her lesbianism—defined her public identity.

Nevertheless, she had an active lesbian sexual life, and once she settled down with a partner, she developed a small, intimate circle of lesbian friends. The recurrent refrain throughout her story is "It just wasn't talked about." Julia reminisces about the time she and Dorothy, her lover, spent with another lesbian couple who owned a hair salon in Deadwood, South Dakota, in 1930.

Well they decided that they would start a sauna of their own, so they established a sauna in connection with their hair salon, and it was quite popular with the ladies, because they didn't have to go up to where the big sauna was, which was obviously for men, built for men, and masculine. And they [the couple] lived in the apartment in one of the two apartments upstairs over it, and they rented out the next apartment. Well, when Dorothy, the first year that I went to teach in Deadwood and I met Dorothy, and fell in love with her and she with me, I was having the girls do my hair. And Dorothy said, well she always had somebody in Rapid City do her hair, [but] she would try them, and so we both of us used to go to the sauna together. And of course that led us immediately to the fact that the other two were lesbians, so there were the four of us. We would very often go late in the afternoon for our sauna and then the four of us would have dinner together. Now we talked about everything but being homosexuals . . . never talked about it. Maybe occasionally, Heidi [who] was the older of the two of them, Heidi would say, well, I left something good down in Denver . . . something like that, but it was never, we never talked about it. And this is what I keep saying to so many, many people, in that period of time it just wasn't talked about. We knew it existed, we accepted it or didn't accept it, but it was there.

The silence about lesbianism did not diminish Julia's ability to construct an interesting and compelling life story, but her stories lack the dramatic flair characteristic of working-class lesbian stories. They have not been fine-tuned over a lifetime or used to engage an interested audience in the comedy and tragedy of being lesbian. Julia's stories were not told at the time the events took place; they have come to be told only recently as the contemporary lesbian community began to seek out the stories of its elders and also as Julia prepared to tell these stories to her daughter. They were not part of bringing lesbianism into the public world, but rather reflect the crafting of a private world where lesbianism could flourish.

The contrast between Julia's storytelling style and that of Arlette and Sandy illuminates the nature of class relations in pre-Stonewall lesbian communities. It provides a different kind of evidence for the argument that working-class lesbians took leadership in developing a public community in ways that middle-class lesbians did not.[13] The humor, agency, and community that are part of the fabric of working-class lesbian stories help confirm the analysis that working-class lesbians were key in laying the groundwork for the Stonewall rebellion and the gay liberation movement. Furthermore, by looking at the style of storytelling, the reader comes to see precisely how working-class lesbians took leadership: not merely "what they did," but how, through the sharing of stories, they created a unique community and culture.[14]

Taking Advantage of First-Person Narratives to Gain New Insights about Lesbian Identity: Being Out or Being Discreet

In her work on Italian fascism, Luisa Passerini argues that oral history adds a critical dimension to the study of fascism.[15] Because of the uniquely subjective nature of life stories, she contends, oral histories provide a way to learn about an individual's struggle with the authority of fascism. What makes some individuals conform to the arbitrary power of the state while others resist it? How do individuals construct strategies of resistance? Passerini views these as some of the most important questions in history. Her questions about fascism strike me as parallel to questions in lesbian and gay history about how individuals cope with and resist heterosexism and homophobia. How do individuals decide to construct and express their identities?

In the mythology of gay and lesbian history, before Stonewall, gays lived furtive, closeted, miserable lives, while after Stonewall gays could be free and open. Stonewall is quintessentially about being out of the closet, about fighting back, about refusing to be mistreated anymore.[16] However, the rich subjectivity expressed in personal narratives of lesbians and gay men expands our understanding of the construction of identity, problematizing the concepts of "hidden" and "out" and making the division between them less rigid.

In Buffalo, black and white working-class lesbians during the 1940s and 1950s—I hesitate to extend this generalization to gay men—took leadership in being out. One of the central tensions in lesbian bar life was between those who were more out, more public, and those who were more discreet. Being out was expressed through butch-fem roles, or by appearing in public as a butch or as part of a butch-fem couple. In *Boots of Leather, Slippers of Gold* we were able to document that between the 1930s and 1950s working-class butches and fems became bolder, took more risks, and actively developed a sense of community and consciousness of kind. Lesbians of the 1940s gathered together on weekends and built a public social life; rough-and-tough lesbians of the 1950s pushed this assertiveness and openness to the point where they wore their men's clothes as much as possible, went out to socialize every day of the week, and fought back when needed. This visibility, however, was not in and of itself liberating because, in the antigay climate of the times, it entailed embracing the terrible stigma of being "queer," of being a "dyke." Before the 1970s, lesbian and gay life was based on an insoluble paradox. For most lesbians and gay men, to be out to the public entailed being engulfed by stigma and, therefore, isolated from sustained and meaningful relationships with other than a small group of similarly stigmatized people.

Life stories of the working-class women who were leaders in creating and defending lesbian community express this contradiction: The freedom that comes from socializing with your own kind and pursuing your romantic attractions is always shaped by the pain of being a complete social outcast. The life story of Sandy, whose leadership was undisputed in the 1950s, is riddled with bitterness as a legacy of her struggle to build a lesbian life. The other side of the fun of being with her lovers and friends and distributing free chicken to her comrades is a feeling that her life has amounted to nothing because of who she is.

You know it pisses you off, because like today, everything is so open and accepted and equal. Women, everyone goes to where they wear slacks, and I could just kick myself in the ass, because all the opportunities I had that I had to let go because of my way. That if I was able to dress the way I wanted and everything like that I, Christ, I'd have it made, really. Makes you sick. As you look at the young people today that are gay and they're financially well-off, they got tremendous jobs, something that we couldn't take advantage of, couldn't have it. It leaves you with a lot of bitterness, too. I don't go around to the gay bars much any more. It's not jealousy, it's bitterness. And I see these young people, doesn't matter which way they go, whatever the mood suits them, got tremendous jobs, and you just look at them, you know, they're happy kids, no problems. You say "God damn it, why couldn't I have that?" And you actually get bitter, you don't even want to know them. I don't anyway. 'Cause I don't want to hear about it, don't tell me about your success. Like we were talking about archives, you know where mine is, scratched on a shit-house wall, that's where it is. And all the dives in Buffalo that are still standing with my name. That's it, that's all I got to show.

The oral histories from working-class lesbians who were much more cautious than Sandy in the 1940s and the 1950s—that is, they did not always wear men's clothes and were not always willing to physically fight men who insulted them—convey less self-hate and bitterness. Also, those women whose families accepted their gayness did not seem to have as much self-hate and bitterness. Sandy's parents had been divorced when she was young, and she had no relationship with her father and a very difficult relationship with her stepfather. Her relationship with her mother was also tense, with little communication and understanding. In contrast, Marty, who came out explicitly to her parents and involved them in her life, seems to have internalized no stigma about being gay. She was unambivalently ebullient about gay life, despite the fact that she had been the subject of many insults and fights due to her appearance and her work as a bartender in a gay bar. Her lovers and friends regularly came to her parents' house for Sunday dinner, and she discussed aspects of her life with her mother, including her relationships. The only time Marty was concerned about discretion was in relation to her family. She avoided activity that would cause her parents unnecessary trouble with their neighbors or their extended families. This evidence suggests that the connection we, the children of Stonewall, make between happiness, freedom, and being out is much too simplistic.

My interviews with Julia Reinstein confirm and complicate this point. From 1928 to 1942 Julia lived happily as a lesbian, completely satisfied with her life. This was true despite the fact that she was not public about her lesbianism. Julia reminisces:

Now Dorothy and I realized we were both teachers, and we couldn't do anything. But at the same time we were together a great deal. But we were very careful about being casual. There was never any exhibition of affection. We were just good friends. We did things together. When we were traveling we kidded everybody about our common pocketbook, and things of that sort . . . we always travelled together by putting the same amount of money into a purse, and one of us handled it and paid all the bills. And then when we got low we added more to the purse. . . .

When I got up here [to Buffalo] . . . I realized that lesbianism was much more public, and I guess I kind of stayed away from it. I didn't feel myself closeted as we talk about it today. It was just kind of personal or natural . . . we'd gone down to Letchworth Park a lot, but so did a lot of other women who were straight. There wasn't that fear, there didn't seem to be. I can't think of any time . . . I can think of in a crowd, and some[one] was, talking about homosexuals or gays. They would talk about the gays, but almost never, when I think back, they didn't talk about lesbians. It was the gays that made the conversation if there was one.

Although Julia considers herself completely private about her lesbianism, this characterization is not entirely accurate. Her father and mother—divorced when she was very young—knew about it. Her father aided and abetted her liaisons in South Dakota, and Julia and her lover actually lived for a period in western New York in her mother's house, sharing a room. In this context, being discreet was not a terrible problem. "Good behavior" was expected of women of her class and particularly of teachers, whether they were lesbians or not. She was used to those strictures and did not find them terribly confining. Julia explains the importance of family in her life.

I was part of the community. Of course in Castile [New York], everybody knew my family. First they were settlers. Second they were the upper echelon. And they all knew me from the time I was a kid. And in Silver Springs [New York] you could count on one hand those people who were considered the top part of the village. Dad was one of them because he had the largest store.[17] And he had political influence, and my uncle had political influence. These things meant something to me. I was proud of them. I didn't want to do anything that would have impaired those importances to my family. I was family oriented, I am going to admit. Lesbianism was very, very private, even after my father died. It didn't begin to come out at all, until after I was doing my graduate work, and I was in New York enough times to see what city lesbianism was. And when I got to Buffalo and thought that I might try to get into it. Again I was outside of the main line of the city, see I was on the edge, and I was only here during the teaching week. If I had lived here it might have been different but see I came to Warsaw every weekend.

For a woman like Julia, being a lesbian was just one of many aspects of her life, albeit a very important one, and she managed to keep her many identities in balance. Coming out publicly would have been more of a burden than a freedom. In most ways, her discretion did not limit her life or make it particularly unpleasant. The only negative result that she hints at is that when her lover of twelve years left her she was relatively isolated: her small circle of friends were all in couples, and she could not easily meet another woman lover. In essence, she married on the rebound. Julia, like Marty, seems to have avoided internalizing the stigma of being lesbian. In her case, acceptance by her family and the privilege of her class gave her full confidence that her attraction to women was a good thing.

These life stories from lesbians in western New York challenge the simple equations of discretion and secrecy with furtiveness, despair, and self-hate, and of openness with liberation and happiness. They suggest that class relations and social position played a very important role in shaping whether discretion was restricting and painful for lesbians in the mid-twentieth century. At least for some upper-class women, being discreet allowed them to live multifaceted lives as teachers and respected citizens and as lesbians.[18] Their families continued to protect their reputations as upstanding members of the community. The severe restrictions on the behavior of all upper-class women made the requirements of discretion unremarkable. In contrast, once working-class women gave up the protection of a marriage, they had little promise of reward—financial stability or community respect—for accepting the social restrictions of discretion. Coming out gave them the excitement of associating with others of their own kind, the ability to find partners when a relationship broke up, and pride in who they were. But the virulently antigay climate of the 1940s, 1950s, and 1960s meant that for many their lives could not be multifaceted, but had to be marked first and foremost by the stigma of being "queer," "butch," or "gay."

These life stories also suggest that the distinction between open and secret needs to be refined to indicate the context in which it occurred—that is, to clarify to whom one was open or hidden—and to specify relationships between parents and children. Although Julia defines herself as completely discreet, her parents were, in fact, fully aware of her relationships with women and were part of a system of discretion that protected her. Although Marty sees herself as completely open and proud of her life during the 1950s, even with her parents, she felt compelled to be discreet in aspects of her life that would affect her family. She was careful not to do things that would embarrass them with their neighbors or other members of the extended family. Although Sandy was completely open in her daily life, never backing down from an occasion to defend herself as a lesbian, she never fully shared her lesbianism with her family, who she felt would not accept it. These life stories suggest the chillingly simple proposition that when daughters were accepted by their families, as in the case of Marty and Julia, their lives were whole and productive, no matter whether they were discreet or open.

In *Cherry Grove, Fire Island*, Esther Newton approaches the dichotomy of "closeted before Stonewall" and "out after Stonewall" from a different, though complementary, angle.[19] She documents the creative lives that gay and lesbian residents crafted in their resort community through the medium of theater and drag and later through sex, despite the fact that most denizens were closeted in the city. She suggests that there are different styles of being gay, one in the camp/theater tradition, the other in the democratic egalitarian tradition, and that being out (identifying as lesbian and gay) means something different in each tradition. I like this approach, particularly because it adds the specificities of gay life and history to discussions of differences that have heretofore been explained primarily in terms of the social relations of class. The life stories of lesbians in western New York bear out Newton's interpretations. Certainly for working-class lesbians, being out during the 1940s and 1950s was expressed through the performance of butch-fem roles, which were at the center of an elaborate and vital culture. Because this form of being out stigmatized them as deviant, difference characterized their politics. In contrast, Julia's lifestyle as a teacher, respected citizen, and discreet lesbian has much more in common with the egalitarian democratic tradition of gayness of the homophile movement, which argues for assimilation to and acceptance by the mainstream. Neither tradition can be simply characterized as discreet or open, happy or discontented. The meaning of these various stances toward the world changes in different social contexts and historical moments.

Understanding Memory as a Cultural Phenomenon

Recent theorists of oral history analyze memory as a part of culture in ways that might be extremely useful for gay and lesbian historians. For example, Alessandro Portelli's analysis of oral histories of workers in Terni, an industrial town in northern Italy, vividly shows that oral histories can contribute much more than new information about dates, places, and events.[20] The workers' stories about the murder of Luigi Trastulli, a twenty-one-year-old steelworker, by police varied as to the date; some dated it in 1949, which in fact is the correct date, while many others dated it 1953, at the same time as a mass strike. This inconsistency could be taken to show the unreliability of oral history and the faultiness of memory. Portelli suggests otherwise. Although the stories in this case do not help in ascertaining dates, which can be obtained from other sources, they do relay information about how workers think about their lives and the value they give to dignity and pride. Portelli argues that many people had moved the date to 1953 because in their minds the mass strikes of that time avenged the death of Trastulli. It was too painful to consider that a fellow worker did not die for a major cause, and that his death had not been avenged. Thus oral histories, if sensitively used, can provide a window into how individuals understand and interpret their lives.

This kind of interpretation is essential for gay and lesbian oral history. In writing *Boots of Leather, Slippers of Gold*, which is based on oral histories with forty-five narrators, we came upon many cases where narrators' memories were internally contradictory or conflicted with one another. An example that was significant for the development of our analysis involved disagreement about the quality of bar life. For some narrators, time in the bar was the best of fun, for some it was depressing, and for others it was both. We came to understand that these contradictory memories conveyed precisely the freedom and joy and the pain and limitation that characterized bar life in the mid-twentieth century.

Lesbian and gay history provides fertile ground for the scrutiny and interpretation of memory. For instance, in his book *Stonewall*, Martin Duberman questions whether a dyke started the Stonewall riots by swinging at the police when they ushered her into the paddy wagon, as reported in the *Village Voice*.[21] Some of Duberman's narrators are sure it was a dyke, while others are adamantly sure it was not. An appeal to the validity of the written source does not have much utility in this case, because gays and lesbians know how frequently the press can be wrong. In trying to reconcile these different views, Duberman says that there were many things going on at once, and it was hard to know what actually started things off. In fact, Duberman records a variety of views as to what started the riot.

Another way to use the information of the disputed nature of the Stonewall story is to consider what this disagreement tells us about the contested relationship between men and women in the gay community. The assignment of agency to women by participants in Stonewall is completely in keeping with women's role in the bar community. Lesbians were always known as "trouble" and respected as good fighters. In the gay imagination, based on the experience of the 1950s and 1960s, it is highly likely that a woman would start swinging. Yet at the same time, the denial of women as leaders in fighting back reverberates with the dominant view of women in heterosexual society as passive with little skill in fighting. It also encapsulates the male-dominated atmosphere in the Stonewall Inn. Women, when there, were made invisible. One Buffalo lesbian who went sporadically to the Stonewall Inn and was in fact there on the night of the riots, but left to meet a blind date shortly before 11 P.M., remembers always being mistaken for a drag queen.[22] The conflicting memories about how the Stonewall riots started concisely capture the cultural process of making lesbians and women invisible in history.

Given that social constructionists have analyzed the formation of both gay and lesbian identities, there is surprisingly little research on the relationships of gay men and lesbians at any point in history.[23] What struck Davis and me in our research was how many women insisted that men and women got along perfectly in the past, unlike today. As our research proceeded, we gathered evidence that suggested that these statements were ideological. Women and men socialized together on some occasions but not on others, and there was always an underlying tension between the men and women in public life, if not in personal relationships. In *Boots of Leather, Slippers of Gold*, we suggest that the narrators emphasized this harmony to highlight how different the situation was in the past, when there was no ideological commitment to difference between gay men and lesbians as there is today. But as I think more about memory and the constructed nature of lesbian and gay identity, I wonder whether the narrators aren't affirming the unity of women and men that they saw as important for survival.

Constructing the Interview and Interpretation: The Biases of the Stonewall Metanarrative

Researching the Stonewall riot, like studying any major historical event, reveals both the possibilities and limitations of oral history. To do so we need oral histories to correct the historical record of life before and at the time of Stonewall; we also need to be fully aware of how the myth of Stonewall, as the central event of twentieth-century gay and lesbian history, constructs the nature of the oral histories we collect and the interpretations we derive from them.

Unquestionably, Stonewall is a key moment for lesbian and gay history. It did transform the lives of many gays and lesbians, and it also became the turning point for the rapid spread of a new kind of gay and lesbian politics and movement. But the history is more complicated than that, and oral history has begun to indicate this.[24] Oral histories show that working-class women, who were rendered invisible by the politics of Stonewall, made an active contribution to developing the sense of solidarity and pride that made Stonewall possible. And although Stonewall is quintessentially about being out, many working-class lesbians and gay men were out before Stonewall.

Such correctives to the historical record are extremely important and are unquestionably the strengths of oral history. But at the same time, oral histories have been shaped by the myths of Stonewall. Many scholars in empirical fields have come to question abstract standards of objectivity and to understand the constructed nature of interviews and their interpretation. The general orientation of contemporary anthropologists, feminists, and oral historians is to encourage reflexivity—that is, the conscious identification of the social position of the interviewer and interviewee—and to recognize that knowledge is the result of a dialogue between the two. In most situations, this involves an awareness of the power differentials, due to class and race privilege associated with most researchers. The implications of such an approach are immense, easily a subject for an entire article or book.[25] Here I will narrow my focus and suggest some of the ways in which the centrality of Stonewall in the iconography of most lesbian and gay researchers shapes or biases oral history research.

By periodizing twentieth-century lesbian and gay life as pre- and post-Stonewall, we are creating a metanarrative, an overarching story, of lesbian and gay history, in which we understand bar communities, resort communities, and homophile organizations as laying the groundwork for the development of gay liberation politics. By definition, seeing Stonewall as a major turning point in gay and lesbian life commits researchers to a certain vision of gay and lesbian history, one that makes central the creation of a fixed, monolithic gay and lesbian identity, most often understood as white and male. A pernicious effect of this metanarrative of Stonewall is that it tends to camouflage women's voices and make racial/ethnic groups and cultures invisible.

To do an adequate job in revealing lesbian participation in pre-Stonewall life, we need to combine homosexual and women's history.[26] Davis and I attempt this in *Boots of Leather, Slippers of Gold,* and although we were successful in placing lesbians at the center of the study, we were not able to escape telling lesbian history from the perspective of the development of a fixed lesbian identity. Rather, we explicitly embraced this bias. We were interested in understanding the ways in which lesbian bar communities were predecessors to gay liberation. The beginning perspective was very useful because it allowed us to reveal the ways working-class lesbians built solidarity, developed a consciousness of kind, and expressed pride in being lesbian in the 1940s and 1950s. From this, we were able to argue that bar communities provided a tradition of being public to gay liberation and were also a fertile ground in which gay liberation could grow. For a lesbian to swing at the police, as was possibly done at Stonewall, was a mode of being in the world that Buffalo lesbians had already perfected. As important as this perspective was and is to our work, it also limited the work, skewing it toward the necessity of building a stable lesbian and gay identity.[27] I am not so much concerned that work like ours is partial, because all research is; rather, I am interested in bringing to the fore the people the Stonewall myth excludes. A perfect example of the repercussions of our perspective was our unwillingness at the beginning of the research process to interview women who were no longer living as lesbians. We felt that people had to be gay "through and through." As a result we missed interviewing many women who had been fems in the community of the 1940s and 1950s. Who else did our perspective exclude? *Boots of Leather, Slippers of Gold* is a history of survivors: those who were bold and brazen and could survive the stigma and the ugliness of oppression. Some women were no longer able to tell their stories, having been wasted by alcohol or sickness. Others never felt comfortable in the bar community due to the prominence of roles and/or working-class culture and wanted to forget it. When we located potential narrators and asked them to share their memories of lesbian community during the 1940s and 1950s, several people turned us down, expressing some variation of "what [lesbian] community?" In their minds, the divisiveness outweighed the solidarity and had not allowed them to thrive.

The writings of lesbians of color in the last fifteen years have made amply clear that lesbians of color do not have one single identity, but rather multiple identities.[28] In the case of African American lesbians in Buffalo, they were part of the larger bar community, but they also maintained their own African American house parties and bars. They cannot be considered, nor did they consider themselves, lesbians first and African Americans or Native Americans second, or vice versa. Therefore a metanarrative that focuses on the formation of a unitary lesbian identity and politics might include African American and Native American women, as *Boots of Leather, Slippers of Gold* did, but by definition communities of color cannot be the central focus. We need therefore to orient the interviews and open our interpretive frameworks to multiple centers of lesbian life and to ask fundamental questions about how these varied points interact rather than assume that they fit together in a linear history of Stonewall.

In arguing, as I have done throughout this essay, that there is a tremendous amount to be learned by fully exploring the subjective and oral nature of oral histories, I have also suggested that the "empirical" and "subjective" should not be falsely polarized. They are fully complementary. I am convinced that gay and lesbian oral history is at a point where, to grow, it needs to fully embrace the subjective and oral nature of its documents. By doing so its "empirical" goals are not compromised but expanded.

Notes

This essay is a revised version of material originally presented at a CLAGS conference and then as a paper at the New York University conference "Gay Lives and Liberation in Greenwich Village and New York City Circa Stonewall," April 29, 1994. I want to thank Chris Staayer for inviting and encouraging me to participate in that conference, even though my research is not on New York City. Thanks also to Jeff Escoffier, who encouraged me to revise the paper for publication and worked with me to speed up the final revisions. The comments of Adina Back and Molly McGarry from the *Radical History Review* editorial board were very helpful and aided the revision process. And thanks to the insightful comments by members of my writing group (Carolyn Korsmeyer, Carol Zemel, Betsy Cromley, and Claire Kahane) on an early version of the paper and to Susan Kahn and Michael Frisch for giving me helpful feedback on the penultimate draft.

1. For instance, in her study of Cherry Grove, Esther Newton uses as her primary source oral narratives or interviews. Esther Newton, *Cherry Grove, Fire Island: Sixty Years in America's First Gay and Lesbian Town* (Boston: Beacon, 1993). The unquestionably upper-class lesbians who helped found the community did not leave substantial written sources—letters, diaries, or newspaper accounts—to construct the history. I am currently interviewing a highly literate eighty-eight-year-old woman who has not left an elaborate written record of her lesbian life. The paucity of material on lesbians other than oral histories is hard to remember in the halls of academe, where written texts predominate. Recently, I gave a presentation on *Boots of Leather, Slippers of Gold* at the University of Chicago, and one of the first questions was why I relied so heavily on oral history. The student immersed in literary texts had never stopped to think that if we are to know much about working-class lesbian life, an important source will be personal memories. Elizabeth Lapovsky Kennedy and Madeline Davis, *Boots of Leather, Slippers of Gold: The History of a Lesbian Community* (New York: Routledge, 1993).

2. A telling example of this lack was the absence of a paper devoted explicitly to the methods and meanings of oral history at the Stonewall History Project Planning Conference, held in September 1992. This conference brought together scholars and activists from around the country to help plan museum exhibits in New York City for the twenty-fifth anniversary of Stonewall. At the time I was not even aware of the absence.

3. For an eloquent statement of these two truths, see Alessandro Portelli, introduction to *The Death of Luigi Trastulli and Other Stories: Form and Meaning in Oral History* (Albany: State University of New York Press, 1991), vii–x.

4. The use of the term "empirical" is completely self-conscious and therefore in quotation marks. Having devoted my whole intellectual career to a critique of empiricism—first as an admirer of C. Wright Mills and later as a Marxist-feminist—I find it awkward to affirm or validate an "empirical" tradition. But as a feminist scholar and a lesbian historian I think it is necessary to do this. In my mind, most oral history is done to correct the historical record, to bring new experiences and new perspectives into existing historical frameworks. I am fully aware of the contradictions posed by the

implication that there is an objective record to be corrected. I agree with Sandra Harding, who argues that, at this period, the analytical categories of feminism are unstable. It is worthwhile to embrace the contradictions and move among them; perhaps from this new epistemologies will emerge. See Sandra Harding, "The Instability of the Analytical Categories of Feminist Theory," *Signs* 51, no. 4 (summer 1986): 645–64; and idem, conclusion to *Feminism and Methodology* (Bloomington: Indiana University Press, 1987), 181–90. Thus, although I agree with Joan Scott that the category of experience needs to be problematized, I do not think it is irrelevant to social history. In fact I think it is a crucial building block to expanding knowledge. Joan Scott, "The Evidence of Experience," in *The Lesbian and Gay Studies Reader,* ed. Henry Abelove, Michèle Aina Barale, and David M. Halperin (New York: Routledge, 1993), 397–415.

5. The pressure to legitimize gay and lesbian history and one's own research extended beyond the academy; it also came from family, neighbors, and political activists. In my own case, the desire for empirically sound research was intensified by my desire to receive recognition in my family. My father, a powerful patriarch and a medical doctor, has the greatest respect for the objectivity of science and conveyed this to all his children. Even after *Boots of Leather, Slippers of Gold* was published, he would still laugh at the thought of oral history being able to contribute to "real" history.

6. In the Fourth Annual Gay and Lesbian Studies Conference at Rutgers, "empirical" research was in the minority. The first issue of *GLQ: A Journal of Gay and Lesbian Studies*, of which I am a member of the advisory board, appeared with no "empirical" articles.

7. See, for instance, Luisa Passerini, "Italian Working Class Culture between the Wars," *International Journal of Oral History* 1 (1980): 4–27; Paul Thompson, *The Voice of the Past: Oral History,* 2d ed. (Oxford: Oxford University Press, 1988); Michael Frisch, *A Shared Authority* (Albany: State University of New York Press, 1990); Sherna Berger Gluck and Daphne Patai, eds., *Women's Words: The Feminist Practice of Oral History* (New York: Routledge, 1991); and Portelli, *The Death of Luigi Trastulli.*

8. Hall Carpenter Archives, Lesbian Oral History Group, *Inventing Ourselves: Lesbian Life Stories* (New York: Routledge, 1989); Newton, *Cherry Grove, Fire Island.*

9. Audre Lorde, *Zami: A New Spelling of My Name* (Trumansburg, NY: Crossing, 1982).

10. I am grateful to my colleague Masani Alexis DeVeaux for illuminating this point in one of her lectures to my gay and lesbian community seminar.

11. The analysis of storytelling style for this essay is of necessity impressionistic, based on a few selected stories. I feel I know the stories of the narrators from *Boots of Leather, Slippers of Gold* quite well and am confident that they are representative of white and black working-class Buffalo lesbians in the 1950s. We use enough stories in the book for other readers to check this. I am just beginning to work with the life history of Julia Reinstein. Although at the moment I am confident that my selection is representative, I know enough about research to be cautious about my judgments at this stage. If this kind of analysis were to be done more comprehensively, it would probably be best to arbitrarily compare one hour of tape from different narrators and chart the style of the stories told within that time period.

12. Before the 1970s, butch-fem roles were unmistakable in all working-class lesbian communities; the butch projected the masculine image of her particular time period— at least regarding dress and mannerisms—and the fem, the feminine image; and almost all members were exclusively one or the other. For a full discussion of butch-fem roles, see Kennedy and Davis, *Boots of Leather, Slippers of Gold;* and Joan Nestle, ed., *The Persistent Desire: A Femme-Butch Reader* (Boston: Alyson, 1992).

13. This is the position Davis and I take in *Boots of Leather, Slippers of Gold.* We put forward quite a complex analysis of class that differs significantly from that in

Lillian Faderman's *Odd Girls and Twilight Lovers: A History of Lesbian Life in Twenti-eth-Century America* (New York: Columbia University Press, 1991), 159–87. In a nutshell, we see working-class lesbians who frequent bars as active agents in building lesbian solidarity, creating a consciousness of kind, and expressing pride. Faderman portrays them as passive victims of circumstance who contribute little if anything to lesbian history. She implies that it is only middle-class women who shape history.

14. I am grateful to Molly McGarry's reader's report for emphasizing this point, and offering this sentence as a way of highlighting it.

15. Passerini, "Italian Working Class Culture between the Wars."

16. Some commentaries on lesbian and gay history have crystallized this division by calling those who were out before Stonewall "homosexuals" and those out afterward, "gays." See, for instance, Gilbert Herdt and Andrew Boxer, *Children of Horizons: How Gay and Lesbian Teens Are Leading a New Way Out of the Closet* (Boston: Beacon, 1993), 6. Newton comments on this distinction in *Cherry Grove, Fire Island*, 39.

17. This reference is actually to her stepfather, who lived in Silver Springs.

18. Newton, *Cherry Grove, Fire Island*, 85.

19. To say that butch and fem is part of the theater/camp tradition does not discount the position Davis and I took in "They Was No One to Mess With: The Construction of the Butch Role in the Lesbian Community of the 1940s and 1950s," in *The Persistent Desire: A Femme-Butch Reader*, ed. Nestle, 62–80. If we associate camp with the general inversion, I would agree butch and fem is part of it. I still agree with the main point of that article, that camp humor is not central to the butch persona as it is to the drag queen. The butch's performance builds lesbian community—solidarity and pride—through the serious use of the "fist," the ability of women to take care of themselves. The drag queen builds the community through the use of comedy and wit.

20. Portelli, *The Death of Luigi Trastulli.*

21. Martin Duberman, *Stonewall* (New York: Penguin Dutton, 1993), 197–98.

22. This information comes from a personal communication with Madeline Davis, who has spoken directly with the lesbian who frequented the Stonewall Inn.

23. To my knowledge Marc Stein is the only person who has written on this topic. Marc Stein, "Sex Politics in the City of Sisterly and Brotherly Love," *Radical History Review* 59 (spring 1994): 60–93. Esther Newton is also addressing this issue in her most recent work, as evidenced by her paper "Baking Ziti at the Coronation: Homophobia, Sexism, and the Subordinate Status of Lesbians in Cherry Grove" (given at the ninety-third annual meeting of the American Anthropological Association, Atlanta, Georgia, December 2, 1994).

24. Perhaps the best introduction to the dilemmas of the meaning of Stonewall, and the ongoing mythmaking, is an anecdote. In the winter of 1994 I received a call from a television producer who was polling gay and lesbian historians, asking us one question: "Was Stonewall the most important single event in gay and lesbian life (history)?" He said that Martin Duberman had suggested that he call me, and that he did not want to say any more and would explain why afterwards. In the brief minute I had to develop a strategy for responding to this question, many considerations ran through my mind: I could say "of course" and contribute to building the myth of Stonewall, or I could say "yes and no," and explain that many gay lives had been transformed by Stonewall, but others, who had fought for the right to be seen and heard before Stonewall, were made invisible by the centrality of Stonewall. Furthermore, many gays and lesbians did not feel their lives immediately transformed by Stonewall at all. I wondered why Martin Duberman had suggested he call me, what Duberman was hoping I would add to this discussion. I decided that Duberman, being a serious historian, wanted me to add some complications to gay and lesbian history, and I answered, "yes and no." I learned in the next few minutes that this was a strategic mistake: this unfortunate producer was trying

to convince his boss that their mainstream television show should do a full special on Stonewall. His strategy for doing this was to show that every historian who knew anything about gays and lesbians had said immediately and unequivocally that Stonewall was the most important event in gay and lesbian lives. Ah well!

25. And in fact there will be a new book on the subject, Ellen Lewin and William Leap, eds., *Doing Lesbian and Gay Field Work, Writing Lesbian and Gay Ethnography* (Champaign/Urbana: University of Illinois Press, forthcoming), to which I contributed a chapter.

26. Two writers have given us very effective models of how to combine homosexual and women's history, showing us that there are no shortcuts. In her book on the gay and lesbian liberation movement, Margaret Cruishank looks at women as part of all aspects of the gay movement and then has a separate chapter on lesbian feminism that focuses exclusively on lesbians. Margaret Cruishank, *The Gay and Lesbian Liberation Movement* (New York: Routledge, Chapman and Hall, 1992). Esther Newton employs a similar method for studying Cherry Grove, including women amply in each chapter on the community as a whole, and then having two chapters devoted exclusively to the lesbian subcommunity.

27. A framework that prioritizes fixed identity also simplifies the meaning of identity. When Davis and I began the writing of *Boots of Leather, Slippers of Gold,* we never expected to have a chapter on identity, partly because the Stonewall conceptual framework did not lead us to expect how interesting and complicated the issue of identity is in lesbian history. (Partly, we were so concerned to do legitimate history that we ignored all the clues that life stories provide on how people think about their identities.) In the 1940s, butch and fem expressed most people's identities; inherent in this formulation was an understanding that the butch, a woman who took on male characteristics, was the "real" lesbian, the real deviant. By the 1950s, although butch and fem were still used by some, gay was also current, and narrators conceptualized themselves as gay because they wanted sexual relations with women. Thus, in one set of ideas both the butch and the fem were gay, while in another the butch remained the real lesbian. The changing forms of self-identity crystallize the problems raised by assuming a self-identified lesbian as the core of lesbian history. See chapter 9, *Boots of Leather, Slippers of Gold,* for a full discussion of this issue.

Joan Nestle, in writing the biography of Mabel Hampton, also problematizes the framework of fixed lesbian identity. She argues that we need to set aside the habit of defining lesbian unidimensionally. Research has already shown how the creation of a lesbian identity is important in twentieth-century lesbian history; now we can go on to look at identity in the context of particular lives. On the basis of items that Mabel left to be opened after her death, Joan suggest that Mabel, an unquestionably proud lesbian and African American, saw herself as a worker, a citizen, and a lover of music and theater as well. "I Lift Up My Eyes to the Hill: The Life of Mabel Hampton as Told to a White Woman" (paper presented at the first annual David R. Kessler Lecture in Lesbian and Gay Studies, Center for Gay and Lesbian Studies, CUNY Graduate Center, November 1992).

28. See, for instance, Cherríe Moraga and Gloria Anzaldúa, eds., *This Bridge Called My Back: Writings by Radical Women of Color* (Watertown, MA: Persephone Press, 1981); Barbara Smith, ed., *Home Girls: A Black Feminist Anthology* (New York: Kitchen Table: Women of Color Press, 1983); Audre Lorde, *Sister Outsider: Essays and Speeches* (Trumansburg, NY: Crossing, 1984); and Gloria Anzaldúa, *Borderlands, La Frontera: The New Mestiza* (San Francisco: Spinsters/Aunt Lute, 1987).

15

Looking for Lesbians in Chinese History

Vivien Ng

Several summers ago, I picked up a copy of Paula Martinac's *Out of Time*[1] and read it from cover to cover in one sitting. In this delightful lesbian ghost story (of sorts), strange things began to happen to Susan Van Dine, a perennial graduate student, after she "lifted" an old photo album from an antique store in New York City. I was especially taken by the way Susan was able to reconstruct gradually the lives of the four women whose photographs made up the album. At the time, I had just started my research on early Chinese feminists, a daunting task that involves lifting the layers of neglect and distortion that had shrouded their lives for so long. I could not help but fantasize, "If only 'my' women would communicate with me the way Harriet and Lucy did with Susan!"

"My" women founded *New Chinese Women Magazine*, a Chinese-language monthly that was published in 1906–7 in Tokyo, Japan. The founding editor, Yan Bin, was enrolled at Waseda University, one of the most prestigious institutions in Japan. Chinese students began studying in Japan in ever increasing numbers from 1900 on, after the disastrous Boxer Rebellion, which ended with the sacking of Beijing by the combined forces of eight imperialist powers. After this humiliation, even the conservative Manchu government conceded the need for the young minds of China to receive Western-style education. Japan was favored by many Chinese students for a number of reasons, among them the more or less hands-off policy adopted by the Japanese government toward anti-Manchu political activities of the Chinese residing there. In 1900, the number had burgeoned to almost ten thousand. *New Chinese Women Magazine* estimated that in 1907, at least one hundred Chinese women were enrolled in various schools in Tokyo.

Unlike Yan Bin, who opted for medical education, the majority of Chinese women were enrolled at the Aoyama Girls' Practical School, which was founded by Shimoda Utako, an ardent proponent of women's education who once had an audience with Queen Victoria. Regardless of their differing life goals, there was a strong sense of community and sisterhood among the Chinese women living in Japan. As early as 1903, they formed the all-female Mutual Love Society, with about twenty charter members. Their stated mission was ambitious: "To rescue the 200,000,000 Chinese women, to restore their basic and fundamental rights, to enable them to possess the idea of nationhood, so that they may ultimately perform their duty as women citizens." In 1904, in response to Russia's occupation of Manchuria, members of Mutual Love Society organized the "Resist Russia Volunteer Brigade." Thus, very quickly, Mutual Love Society expanded its embrace of women's rights to include anti-imperialist struggle.

The militantly nationalistic orientation of Mutual Love Society was probably shaped by one of its members, the dashing Qiu Jin, who self-identified as a swordswoman, and who wore men's clothes as a political statement. Much has been written about Qiu Jin's anti-Manchu revolutionary work in Japan and China, as well as her subsequent arrest and execution by the Manchu government in 1907. In recent years, there has been a burgeoning interest in China and Taiwan in Qiu Jin. Hong Kong television even aired a miniseries based loosely on her life. Even so, there are gaps in our knowledge about this dynamic woman.

As a lesbian historian, I am eager to identify and write about "lesbians" in modern Chinese history. Ever since I published "Homosexuality and the State in Late Imperial China,"[2] which deals mainly with male homosexuality in seventeenth- and eighteenth-century China, I have been on a single-minded mission to write about Chinese lesbians. I became even more determined after I met a graduate student from China who was pursuing a Ph.D. degree in Chinese history at New York University. She confessed to me that after having been assigned Adrienne Rich's essay on compulsory heterosexuality in a Chinese history seminar, she complained to another student from Asia about the relevance of their reading assignment. She declared at the time, "There were no lesbians in China!" Her categorical declaration could not be dismissed as a mark of utter ignorance or homophobia, because in one crucial aspect, she was absolutely correct: there is no lesbian counterpart to the richly documented male homosexual tradition in China. Dorothy Ko's analysis of erotically evocative poems written by several seventeenth-century women poets about female bodies suggests the existence of a female homoerotic literary tradition, but it remains unclear whether the poets were following the male-centered poetic convention or writing about themselves.[3] Even if they were expressing their own feelings, were they "lesbians"? Is it possible to apply the term to "non-Western" cultures?

My search for lesbians in Chinese history has led me to my project on early

Chinese feminists, on "my" women. One promising area of investigation is the nature of the friendships that bonded so many of the early Chinese feminists together. One noteworthy example is Qiu Jin's relationship with Wu Zheying, who was a poet, renowned calligrapher, and reformer in her own right. The two met in 1903 shortly after Qiu Jin's arrival in Beijing with her husband, and quickly became inseparable. Both lamented the fact that they had met too late and their time together was too short (Qiu Jin was already seriously contemplating leaving China for Japan). The following year, on the seventh day of the Chinese New Year, Qiu Jin and Wu Zheying exchanged a formal pledge of eternal friendship, an occasion that Qiu Jin marked with a poem called "Orchid Verse." The next day, Qiu Jin appeared before Wu Zheying in a man's suit and presented her with a pair of shoes and a skirt, explaining to her dear friend that "These items were part of my trousseau. Now that I have decided to wear men's clothes, I have no need for them. Please keep them in remembrance of me after we part." In 1907, after Qiu Jin was executed, Wu Zheying, at great risk to herself, collected Qiu Jin's remains so she could give them a proper burial.

Were Qiu Jin and Wu Zheying lovers? June Chan, a Chinese American lesbian activist in New York City, includes pictures of Qiu Jin in her famous slide show on Asian lesbians. However, historian Mary Rankin, who has written the most extensive biography of Qiu Jin in the English language, does not explore the nature of the Qiu-Wu friendship. It is perhaps telling that she rendered the name of the all-female Chinese organization in Japan Gong ai hui as Humanitarian Society, rather than Mutual Love Society.[4] No other historian of modern China has dared to address the possibility of a lesbian relationship between Qiu Jin and Wu Zheying. No doubt, they are wary of being accused of imposing Western constructs on China. In other words, they succumb to the belief that lesbianism is a Western cultural invention, and that to label a Chinese woman "lesbian" is tantamount to forcing on her a Western identity. In my opinion, their "caution" stems not from theoretical considerations similar to those articulated by Gloria Anzaldúa in "To(o) Queer the Writer—*Loca, escritora y chicana*," but from their reluctance to face the thorny methodological and ideological challenge of writing about lesbians in Chinese history.[5]

What do I think? Have I found the necessary "proof"? Take, for example, the formal pledge of friendship. Can I call it a "commitment ceremony"? What about the "Orchid Verse"? Was it inspired by the Golden Orchid Society of marriage resisters in south China? Anthropologists Marjorie Topley and Andrea Sankar estimate that marriage resistance arose in three districts in the Pearl River Delta from approximately 1865 to 1935.[6] However, Janice Stockard reports a reference to it in the 1853 edition of *Shunde County Gazetteer*: "Girls in the county form very close sisterhood with others of the same village. They don't want to marry, and if forced to marry, they stay in their own families, where they enjoy few restrictions. They don't want to return to the husband's family, and some, if forced to return, commit suicide by drowning or hanging."[7] In the 1904 lay Buddhist publication *Nüren jing* (Canon for women), the section on filial piety includes a denunciation of marriage resistance (the compiler's commentary is indicated here by the use of brackets):

> Recently, there has developed a custom [this custom is deplorable] that is passed on from woman to woman. [Imitating and learning every step; forming Golden Orchid bonded sisterhood.] These women practice celibacy, vowing never to marry. [Blasphemous!] They refer to the husband's family as "cocoons." [They believe that father-in-law, mother-in-law, husband, children, etc. bind their bodies and deprive them of their freedom. The analogy "cocoon" therefore signifies suffocating bondage until death!][8]

What was the nature of the relationship between women in the sworn sisterhoods? Sankar, Stockard, and Topley all acknowledged the presence of "lesbianism" among the sisters, but only Sankar has offered more than cursory treatment of this reality:

> Sometimes sexual relationships formed among two or three sisters, creating physical as well as emotional bonds. Larger sisterhoods may have contained several couples or ménage à trois. . . . Although lesbian relationships may not have been subjected to outside social pressures, they faced serious problems. The relationships I observed were often unstable. The ménage à trois was the most problematic form, and tended to become increasingly difficult as women aged. Two of the partners would gradually draw closer together and move away from the third.[9]

Among Chinese sources, a graphic description of the sexual nature of Golden Orchid coupling is found in the 1923 publication, *Zhonghua chuanguo fengsu zhi* (Compendium of Chinese customs): " Although the cohabiting women do not possess the form of male-female sexual relationship, they do possess the pleasure of such relationship. Suffice to say that they use friction and/or mechanical means; to say more requires the use of inelegant language which gentlemen cannot use."[10]

When Qiu Jin wrote her "Orchid Verse," was she aware of the Golden Orchid sworn sisterhood of marriage resisters? More important, did she choose "orchid" for her title to describe a particular kind of friendship with Wu Zheying? This is impossible to answer fully. I know that in 1908, in the Paris-based Chinese magazine *New Century*, a short piece about the marriage resistance movement/custom was published, indicating a degree of interest in the subject by radical intellectuals at the time. But it may be impossible to prove conclusively that Qiu Jin had personal knowledge about the Golden Orchid sworn sisterhood. In the early autumn of 1905, Qiu Jin convened an emergency meeting of Chinese female students in Tokyo, to pressure her friend Chen Xiefen to resist her father's arrangement to have her marry a wealthy Cantonese merchant as his concubine. At that meeting, when Chen protested that she could not violate her father's wishes, Qiu Jin answered her sharply: "A man who forces his daughter to become a concubine violates life itself. Moreover, this matter affects the reputation of all of us here. You have got to cancel your engagement!" Such strong language was received with great enthusiasm and, in the midst of an eruption of thunderous applause, Chen quietly withdrew from the meeting. (She later did indeed break her engagement.)[11] Qiu Jin herself had divorced her husband and given up custody of her children before she left China for Japan. Does this make her a "marriage resister"?

Qiu Jin returned to China in 1906 to take a more direct part in the revolutionary movement to overthrow the Manchu dynasty. Later that same year, a number of Chinese women, under the vigorous leadership of Yan Bin, founded in Tokyo the *New Chinese Women Magazine.* This radical publication saw only six issues—it was shut down by the Japanese government when the entire sixth issue was confiscated because one of its articles supported the use of political assassinations. But during its short life, the magazine was able to sustain a large circulation (estimated at ten thousand copies per issue and circulated throughout East Asia and even Southeast Asia), thus proving its timeliness and popularity.[12]

The cosmopolitan orientation of the founding editors and the keen interest they had in the feminist movement in the United States and Europe are clearly evident in the pages of the magazine. Each issue contained news about developments concerning women in other countries, and at least one prominent Euro-American woman was featured in every issue. These biographical profiles reveal much about the types of women the editors wanted their Chinese readers to emulate: Margaret Fuller (presented as a journalist), George Eliot (novelist), Mary Lyon (college president), Florence Nightingale (nurse), Lucretia Mott (abolitionist), Mary Livermore (public speaker), and Joan of Arc (national savior). My imagination runs rampant with possible scenarios. Did Yan Bin and her coeditors pick Margaret Fuller only because she was a journalist and therefore a role model for them? Were there other, unstated reasons? Had they read the *Memoirs of Margaret Fuller Ossoli,* published in 1852, two years after Fuller's death? Did they know about Fuller's close friendship with Anna Barker? There are many questions but too few answers.

Yan Bin was clearly the driving force behind this successful magazine. Her signature was everywhere. I often wonder how this remarkable woman managed to find the time to be a medical student, editor, essayist, polemicist, playwright, and feminist agitator all at once. I feel privileged to catch glimpses of her public persona through her writings, but what was she really like? What happened to her after the magazine was shut down? Did she finish her medical training? Did she manage to track down and reunite with her "dearest and most intimate" friend, Lo Ying, about whom she had written a moving biographical sketch? I have come across only a brief reference to the fact that Yan Bin did return to China (date unknown) and became the headmistress of a girls' school in Shanxi province (another possible lesbian scenario?). Very little else is known. What about the other writers for the magazine? Alas, I need supernatural help, of the kind Susan Van Dine received in Paula Martinac's *Out of Time,* to reconstruct as fully as possible the lives of this first generation of Chinese feminists, some of whom may well have been lesbians. Perhaps, in the end, it is enough that what I try to do is not to establish beyond a reasonable doubt whether Qiu Jin "slept" with Wu Zheying or whether Yan Bin did so with Lo Ying, but to reclaim the bonded nature of their emotional lives.

Notes

1. Paula Martinac, *Out of Time* (Seattle: Seal, 1990).
2. Vivien Ng, "Homosexuality and the State in Late Imperial China," in *Hidden from History: Reclaiming the Gay and Lesbian Past*, eds. Martin Duberman, Martha Vicinus, and George Chauncey, Jr. (New York: New American Library, 1989), 76–89.
3. Dorothy Ko, *Teachers of the Inner Chamber* (Stanford: Stanford University Press, 1994).
4. See Mary Rankin, *Early Chinese Revolutionaries: Radical Intellectuals in Shanghai and Chekiang, 1902–1911* (Cambridge: Harvard University Press, 1971); and idem, "The Emergence of Women at the End of the Ch'ing: The Case of Ch'iu Chin," in *Women in Chinese Society*, ed. Margery Wolf and Roxane Witke (Stanford: Stanford University Press, 1975), 39–66.
5. Gloria Anzaldúa, "To(o) Queer the Writer—*Loca, escritora y chicana*," in *Inversions: Writings by Dykes, Queers and Lesbians*, ed. Betsy Warland (Vancouver, BC: Press Gang, 1991), 249–63.
6. See Marjorie Topley, "Marriage Resistance in Rural Kwangtung," in *Women in Chinese Society*, ed. Wolf and Witke, 67–88; and Andrea Sankar, "The Evolution of the Sisterhood in Traditional Chinese Society: From Village Girls' Houses to Chai T'angs in Hong Kong" (Ph. D. diss., University of Michigan, 1979).
7. Janice Stockard, *Daughters of the Canton Delta: Marriage Patterns and Economic Strategies in South China, 1860–1930* (Stanford: Stanford University Press, 1986), 160.
8. *Nüren jing* (1971 Taibei reprint ed.), *juan* 1, p. 21b.
9. Andrea Sankar, "Sisters and Brothers, Lovers and Enemies: Marriage Resistance in Southern Kwangtung," *Journal of Homosexuality* 11, 3–4 (summer 1985): 69–81, esp. 78–79.
10. *Zhonghua chuanguo fengsu zhi* (Compendium of Chinese customs), ed. Zheng Xiaokuang (Shanghai: Guangyi Book Company), *Xiapian, juan* 7, p. 34.
11. Guo Yanli, *Qiu Jin Nianpu* (Chronological biography of Qiu Jin) (Jinan: Jilu Press, 1983), 77 n. 48.
12. Li Yuning, "Zhongguo xinüjie zazhi ti chuang kan zhi nei han" (The founding of New Chinese Women Magazine and its contents), in *Zhongguo funü shi lun wen ji* (Essays on the history of women in China), ed. Li Yuning and Zhang Yufa (Taibei: Commercial Press, 1981), 179–241, esp. 241 n. 71.

16

The Curious Case of
Michael Wigglesworth

Alan Bray

In this essay I propose to look at the reactions of certain individuals in early modern society to the fact of their male homosexual desires. The compass of my material is therefore very small, suggestive rather than definitive; and at first sight the material may well appear to be decidedly odd. There is, however, I believe, a pattern to be discerned in the reactions of these men and a cultural context, which illuminates much of what it was in that society to be a man. In conclusion I will make a suggestion as to the wider role such attitudes may have had in the changing social and economic history of England at the close of the seventeenth century.

Desires

The first such reaction is in the diary of Michael Wigglesworth as a young tutor at Harvard in the 1650s, prompted by the sexual dreams and fantasies that so troubled him. Michael Wigglesworth's diary is a document that is far from easy to unravel. Cautiously, he writes in guarded generalities and especially so around the details of these troubling desires. There is, however, one important occasion when he speaks more directly. On a Sabbath in the summer of 1653 he found comfort in his reflections, but that assurance was painfully shattered as he was teaching his pupils some two days later when, in the warm afternoon, the troubling sexual desires returned. In an unusually clear entry he tells us that the troubling sexual thoughts were directed to the male pupils he lived with so closely. "Such filthy lust," he writes, "flowing from my fond affection to my pupils whiles in their presence on the third day after noon that

I confess myself an object of God's loathing as my sin is of my own; and pray God make it no more to me." For a devout man like Michael Wigglesworth, such "unnatural filthy lust," as he put it, troubled him deeply and was a disturbing sign of God's dealings with him. We might in any case have guessed the object of his sexual desires even without the help of this passage, for these young men were unmistakably at this time the focus of his emotional life. In his diary his introspection turns and turns again to the "love I bear to these which thou hast given me" as he worries over the spiritual state of his charges, their progress in their studies, and also the pain they gave him by their disregard of his solemn warnings, those "unloving carriages of my pupils" that "can go so to my heart." These concerns and his sexual desires were directed to the same insistent object.[1]

Yet although *we* might be ready to see this connection, it was not one that Michael Wigglesworth was at all willing to recognize. That phrase "fond affection" ("such filthy lust also flowing from my fond affection to my pupils") is misleading to the twentieth-century eye. It did not attribute his lust for his pupils to an excess of loving concern for them. An "affection" in a common seventeenth-century sense was rather a passion or a lust, and a "fond" affection made explicit what the word implied: that it was a mad, an unreasoning passion. Certainly, he recognizes the love in his anxious cares for his students. But throughout this diary, one looks without success for any recognition of an equivalent involvement of his will in his *sexual* feelings as there is in his loving concern. The effect is rather to hold these two apart and to treat his daytime fantasies like his sexual dreams, as things that for him were unbidden. Nor is there any suggestion, as a European or North American today might assume, that these were homosexual desires nevertheless and whether he wished it or not a reflection of his nature. When we look for any assumptions equivalent to that, there is rather an echoing silence.

Of course one might argue that this is merely a trick of the eye. He did not *say* such things, but surely he recognized his desires as *his* feelings, in one way or another, even if he did not spell that out for us? I suggest rather that we read that absence as it appears, as part of the diary, without writing into it a gloss derived from our own culture. Michael Wigglesworth saw a reason for this, as we shall see, but it proves first easier to follow if one is aware from the onset that Michael Wigglesworth's reaction was by no means unique to him. We see, for example, the same assumptions in the surviving documents concerning Casiodoro de Reina, a minister of the Spanish Protestant church in London in the early 1560s, who in 1563 was alleged to have sexually abused the boy who acted as his servant and with whom he shared a bed. Reina's defense to this when first confronted was that he *had* had several emissions when the boy was in his bed but that what had happened had happened when he was asleep; and what a man does in his sleep he cannot be guilty of. It was a thing, as Reina put it, "without the agreement of the will," a thing "without decision," and the same assumptions appear to have been shared by the boy. In the first interviews the boy was adamant that he had indeed been abused. But he added crucially that he did not know whether at the time Reina was awake or asleep, and later when he apparently adjusted the evidence he had given, he said that at the time he had not known that it was a matter of Reina being alleged *to be a sodomite*. That charge, he said, was put up out of hatred. The twists in the boy's evidence reflect the assumptions of Reina's own defense. Reina, like Michael Wigglesworth, places the sodomitical desire he was accused of outside his own will and personality. The sodomite willed such things; he did not.[2]

No more did Michael Wigglesworth. Why then did he, unlike Reina, remain guilty? Curiously, we know the answer, from a visit Michael Wigglesworth paid to a doctor in 1655 when he was considering marriage and which he recorded in his diary in the spring of that year. From this, one can see that the purpose of the visit was to discuss what Michael Wigglesworth believed was the origin of these sodomitical dreams and unwelcome fantasies: a venereal disease he believed he had acquired in the time before his conversion, the mysterious "weakness" he repeatedly refers to in his diary; here lay his sin. It was indeed an orthodox view of how dreams could be sinful. As the Calvinist theologian Richard Baxter explained in his *Christian Directory*,

> Dreams are neither good nor sinful simply in themselves, because they are not rational and voluntary, nor in our power: but they are often made sinful by some other voluntary act: they may be sinful by participation and consequently. And the acts that make them sinful are either such as go before or such as follow after.

And the "antecedent causes," as Baxter puts it in this account of the matter, include "any sinful act which distempers the body." Michael Wigglesworth's dreams were rooted, or so he believed, in just such an "antecedent cause": this sexual sin of his youth. Thus in a desperate mood in February 1655, when considering the "hard morsel I have had to chew upon all the winter," he wrote in his diary that

> A 3d exercise hath been my weakness, which sure is an affliction many ways. As first because it exposeth to sin and temptations by day which are too hard for me at some times in some degree. 21y it exposeth unto dreams and self pollution by night, which my soul abhors and mourns for. 31y were it nothing else but shame and fear lest it should be judged to arise from wantonness rather than weakness by those that know not the true cause, that were some trial. But 41y and principally because it driveth me to such a strait as I think few were ever in the like.[3]

It was in this "weakness," he believed—not in his own choice or nature—that the origin of these sodomitical sins lay. It was a result of "rebellious nature" in his body, something *he* was "overborne" by, the result of a wound inflicted on him by his sin. The reason Michael Wigglesworth was guilty when Reina apparently was not is that while one attributes the sodomitical behavior of his bed merely to the sleep of reason, the other attributes his sodomitical dreams and those equally unwilled (and unwelcome) daytime fantasies to his supposed venereal disease. It is his physical weakness brought on by his youthful sin that he believes has brought him to this. But each has in common the same assumption that this sodomitical behavior was invasive of his personality.[4]

Michael Wigglesworth had good reason, of course, to distance himself from such (to him) abhorrent desires. One might well wonder whether his reaction was indeed a trick of the mind to achieve that. Certainly it is the explanation most readily to hand, but I would like to raise by that possible explanation a very large question mark. Rather, what I propose to do in the rest of this essay is to stand back from the curious case of Michael Wigglesworth and attempt to place it in its wider cultural context, on the basis of a number of documents from this period that I believe turn radically on what is at issue in Michael Wigglesworth's reaction to his desires. In this context his reaction proves to be neither eccentric nor unexpected; in fact, it had a great deal to do with manliness.

Manliness

In his autobiography, the Catholic scholar and convert Augustine Baker urges his readers to send their sons not to the universities but to study at the Inns of Court (where lawyers trained), where, he says, in these days of Protestantism and decay they will now find a more "manly" education. Augustine Baker was no enemy to the universities, and he is careful to distinguish what the universities should represent from their present languishing state; and as a testimony to this the catalogue of sins he recalls sharing in when he was a student in Oxford in the 1590s includes gluttony, theft, and sodomy. Why was it unmanly to be a glutton, a thief, or a sodomite? The answer was the lack of control they had over their appetites, appetites run wild, of which the sodomitical appetite that troubled Michael Wigglesworth so was a part, but no more. It is why Augustine Baker's sodomitical companions are also described as gluttons, why those in Thomas Shepard's similar memoir of his university days are described as both sodomites and drunkards, and also why Michael Wigglesworth's contemporaries seem at times so loose in the terms they apply to the sexual appetite more generally, as when Elias Pledger, the Puritan diarist, described a would-be seducer of his young female cousin as a "Beastly Sodomite." The looseness of the object the "sodomite" chooses is a ready indication of how little of the term was in the object chosen and how much in the uncontrolled appetite, of which the sodomitical appetite of Michael Wigglesworth was a ready part, but no more. It is also equally evident in the characteristic detail that when the Casiodoro de Reina was accused of sexually assaulting his servant boy, he was also accused of scandalous conduct with the boy's mother: the two sins seemed quite akin.[5]

The sharp point is nicely put in this respect in John Donne's epigram,

> Thou call'st me effeminate, for I love women's joys;
> I call not thee manly, though thou follow boys.

The speaker is being accused of being a womanizer and becoming womanlike because of it. The trick in the epigram is to turn the accuser's words back on himself by implying that, though he does not follow women, he does follow boys and to the same end. In this culture sexuality itself, whatever its object, makes a man effeminate. It is "wantonness" itself, "whereby occasions are sought to stir up lust" (according to William Perkins's commentary on the seventh commandment) that is "effeminate." But sexuality was not neatly distinguished in this cluster of ideas either in itself or from the other fruits of sensuality that an unrestrained and thus unmanly appetite could lust for. What these avowedly unmasculine figures share, drunkard, glutton, fornicator, and sodomite alike, is a ruinously unrestrained appetite, an appetite without "masculine" restraint; and the sodomite's improper sexual appetite is but one expression of this.[6]

And such an unmanly, consuming appetite could destroy its possessors; this is the point I want to draw out here, as a gloss on Michael Wigglesworth's fears. Most evidently to their neighbors, it could destroy them financially and in the end as likely as not make thieves of them, for such unappeasable appetites, it was assumed, needed financing. Augustine Baker described his sodomitical and gluttonous friends as thieves, so that they could eat the meat in Lent their colleges did not provide but their appetites lusted for. Casiodoro de Reina, the sodomite and seducer of mothers, was accused also of embezzlement.[7]

But his unrestrained appetites could destroy the unmanly man in less evident ways also. One of these was in his body. When Augustine Baker urged his readers to keep their sons from these unmanly sins, his argument is that they should do so if they wish to have heirs in "that the youth is in danger to become so far corrupted that he will never be able to get a child." The fear is not that he will not *desire* to father a child but that he will not be *able* to do so. It is a physical degeneracy such an appetite could bring them to that is the object in focus here.[8]

Is it then surprising that Michael Wigglesworth saw the same destructiveness at work in his mind? In the end an unmanly, consuming appetite could consume its owner. It was this his unmanly "weakness" had brought him to. It was the coherence of Michael Wigglesworth's personality that he believed was being undermined by his weakness, that seemed to be pushed aside by the dreams and involuntary fantasies from outside himself that his venereal disease, or so he believed, had brought.

The Scourge of Villainy

Michael Wigglesworth's reaction reveals a manliness that recognized itself as frighteningly open to being undermined. This was no eccentricity, and indeed we can see the same assumptions set out at length in Satire VII of *The Scourge of Villainy*, by the Elizabethan social satirist John Marston. In the poem the author searches for a man, as Diogenes once did, about the streets of Marston's London; but can find none. "These are no men," he says, but mere "resemblances": the wealthy man has lost his manliness to the pleasures of the table; the soldier has lost his to drunkenness and whoring; and the young man enamored of effeminate fashion—and indeed of "riot, lust, and fleshly seeming sweetness"—is the same. In losing their manliness, in this account these figures have also lost something that now may not seem at all a matter of gender. They have lost their souls. In Marston's Aristotelian terms, such figures have lost the rational part of their souls that distinguished them from the beasts, the same loss seen in Michael Wigglesworth's frightened reference to his "fond affection," his unreasoning passion:

> He hath no soul, the which the Stagirite [Aristotle]
> Term'd rational, for beastly appetite,
> Base dunghill thoughts, and sensual action
> Hath made him lose that fair creation.
> Only the misleading appearance of men is left.
> That lustre wherewith nature's Nature decked
> Our intellectual part, that gloss is soiled
> With staining spots of vile impiety
> And muddy dirt of sensuality.
> These are no man but apparitions
> Ignes fatui, glow-worms, fictions,
> Meteors, rats of Nilus, fantasies,
> Colosses, pictures, shades, resemblances

Marston is using "meteors" in the once more common sense of the insubstantial phenomena of the air, like lightning, the rainbow, or the ignes fatui, the deceptive lights that appear to hover over the marshes and mislead unwary travelers. Such men, he tells us, have no more true substance than the seeming animals produced by the flooding of the Nile, mere confections of mud. To the eye, they may seem to possess the endurance of a colossal statue (before it falls); but in truth they are no more than pictures, insubstantial images, mere resemblances.[9]

Clearly neither Marston nor his readers thought London was populated wholly by ghosts. A "satirist" was expected to exaggerate and rail, but satires were expected also to sting and to do so had to make sense in the assumptions of their readers. Marston's *Scourge of Villainy* did, for Satire VII was the logical conclusion of much of what this culture believed about manliness.

It was not necessarily what everyone thought, however; indeed, I think that unlikely. What we have here seems to me rather the language of the magistrate and the minister and those who followed them: a fear of an aggressive manliness, fighting drunk, and the prospect of the social disorder such an unrestrained manliness could conjure up. But for a moment it gives us a glimpse into the private fears of a man of Michael Wigglesworth's time and culture. It says something of the fear that for a man might accompany the pleasure of a sexual act: immensely desired and yet potentially carrying a terrible price. It also says something of the (to our contemporaries) unsettling lack of distinction there could be in the pleasures of the senses, where sexuality lacks the carefully labeled categories of a later period and is scarcely distinguished from other sensual pleasures, of eating or of getting drunk or dressing up, perhaps even of fighting or going to bed. But perhaps most of all it gives us an understanding of how a sense of masculine gender in that culture might be thought of not as something that exists of itself, but rather as something that was always threatened and contingent.[10]

The assumptions about consumption evident in Michael Wigglesworth's diary were a way of thinking that would not find it easy to survive in England in common credence much beyond the end of the century. The birth of a "consumer society" in eighteenth-century England and the effect on economic growth of new and positive attitudes to consumption have been part of a much visited debate among historians since the publication by Neil McKendrick, John Brewer, and J. H. Plumb in 1982 of their work *The Birth of a Consumer Society: The Commercialization of Eighteenth-Century England*. The ultimate origins of this thesis lie in the economic statistics collected by Phyllis Deane and W. A. Cole in their *British Economic Growth, 1688–1959*, published in 1962, and in the highly influential paper by Elizabeth Waterman Gilboy "Demand as a Factor in the Industrial Revolution," first published in 1932. The model in this argument is that the takeoff in England's eighteenth-century economy was fired by an increase in *demand*. Cultural change—a rise in consumption standards and a spread of new wants through the population—would have played a major role in bringing about such a changing economic environment; and much persuasive work has since appeared arguing along these lines, notably the major collection of essays *Consumption and the World of Goods* in 1993, edited by John Brewer and Roy Porter.

Only recently has consideration been given to the effect changing gender differences might have had on these changes: in work such as that of Lorna Weatherill, Amanda Vickery, and the literary critic Laura Brown on patterns of distinctively female consumption and the meanings these could impart to the objects women collected and preserved. Illuminating though this work certainly is in bringing out the distinctive ways women consumed and to what ends, a difficulty with generalizing from this work to England's eighteenth-century economic growth is that the behavior and meanings we see being brought out by this work are not necessarily *new*. In the stereotypes of eighteenth-century satire, women remained fully as much consumers as they had been in social satire a century or more before. Pope's poetical description of the enticing contents of Belinda's female toilet, with its "Puffs, Powders, Patches, Bibles, Billet-doux," with its Arabian perfumes and Indian gems, its suggestive disorder and hints of sexuality, would have been familiar material to any seventeenth-century satirist.

The question I would like to raise is the possibly distinctive (and changing) role played by men in this economic change. In the consumer economy of eighteenth-century England, would not that image of the unmanly consuming man ultimately destroying himself, the image that has been at the heart of this essay, have become a curious and outmoded object? Would a change in comparison to what came before not have lain rather elsewhere, in the idea that now a *man* might also be a consumer and still be a man and in doing so know nothing of that old crisis that had arisen when a man had been perceived as a consumer? This is not of course to say that men in the sixteenth and seventeenth centuries did not get drunk, celebrate violence, dress extravagantly, eat to excess when they could, and fornicate. They certainly did all these things. Rather, my point is that for men in that period there could be a cultural fear accompanying consumption—one of an undifferentiated and potentially apocalyptic nature—in which the feared outcome of the lack of self-control such things risked could be a man's radical undoing. Part of the necessary test of manliness had been successfully to essay that risk.

By the eighteenth century in England that set of ideas had fallen into history, and they would have been ill placed in England's eighteenth-century consumer economy. This was an economy created in substantial part by its distinctive new skills of advertising and its creation of the art of "puffing" in the hands of promotional geniuses like the entrepreneur Josiah Wedgwood. But such promotion turned on a different and now positive language of consumption and aesthetics, in terms of choice and discerning taste. Did the positive distinction it encouraged in consumption not free the consuming man from an old fear? Was the new consumer of eighteenth-century England specifically a man?[11]

Notes

This essay has been given in a number of earlier versions as a seminar paper, and I have greatly benefited from the discussion of the participants. I owe a particular debt to Margaret Hunt, who commented on the paper at an early stage, and to the trustees of the Georges Lurcy Fund at Amherst College, Massachusetts, who generously assisted me with my visit to the United States to present this paper. It is reprinted here, in adapted form, with permission from *History Workshop Journal* 41 (spring 1996).

1. I have used the edition of "The Diary of Michael Wigglesworth" in *Publications of the Colonial Society of Massachusetts*, vol. 35, Transactions 1942–1946, ed. Edmund S. Morgan, Boston, 1951, 311–444. This is cited below as "Diary." There is also *The Diary of Michael Wigglesworth, 1653–1657; The Conscience of a Puritan*, ed. Edmund S. Morgan, New York, 1965. The manuscript is in the care of the Massachusetts Historical Society: Wigglesworth papers, 15.7. Dreams: "Diary," 369, 324. Fantasies: "Diary," 322, 323, 350, 399, 406. Both are referred to in more general terms at "Diary," 398, quoted below. The quotations in this paragraph are to "Diary," 350, 322, 323, 322.

Quotations, whether from modern or original editions, are given according to the following rules. Spelling and obsolete forms of words generally (other than verb forms) have been modernized, as have punctuation and the use of capitals. Abbreviations have been expanded, except where they serve a metrical purpose. Dates are given with the year beginning on 1 January. I have not preserved italic type. Titles of books have been similarly modernized in the text but not in the notes. Documents not in English are given in translation.

Richard Crowder was strictly right in his claim that Wigglesworth nowhere details the subject matter of his sexual dreams. Richard Crowder, *No Featherbed to Heaven: A Biography of Michael Wigglesworth, 1631–1705*, East Lansing, MI, 1962, 62. Wigglesworth *did*, however, detail the contents of his worrying sexual fantasies (or perhaps part of them), both at "Diary," 350, as I discuss (and in the phrase "unnatural filthy lust" at "Diary," 322); and it is not unreasonable to link the two, as Wigglesworth does at "Diary," 398. My attention was first drawn to the sodomitical nature of these comments by Jonathan Ned Katz, *Gay/Lesbian Almanac*, New York, 1983, 94–100.

2. The main sources for this are transcribed by A. Gordon Kinder, *Casiodoro de Reina: Spanish Reformer of the Sixteenth Century*, London, 1975, appendix 3 pp. 99–112 (discussed by him at 27–36).

"Without the agreement of the will": absque consensu voluntatis, Kinder, 105. "Without decision": absque determinatione, Kinder, 109. The boy on whether Reina was asleep: Kinder, 106. The boy's later evidence: Kinder, 33 n. 66.

3. Doctor: "Diary," 405. Baxter: Richard Baxter, *A Christian Directory*, London, 1673, 407 (pt. 1, chap. 8, pt. 7, pars. 1 and 2.1). Also in Cynthia Griffin Wolff, "Literary Reflections of the Puritan Character," *Journal of the History of Ideas* 29, no. 1 (January–March 1968): 20. February 1655 quotation: "Diary," 398.

4. "Diary," 406, 399.

5. *Memorials of Father Augustine Baker*, ed. Dom Justin McCann and Dom Hugh Connolly, London, 1933, 41–44. At 34–35 he adds fornication and drunkenness to the list of the sins of the universities and contrasts the present state of the universities with what they ought to be: "the seed or fountain of all virtue for the whole kingdom."

The principal source for Thomas Shepard's life is his autobiography, "The Autobiography of Thomas Shepard," in *Publications of the Colonial Society of Massachusetts*, vol. 27 (1927–1930), 343–400, cited below as "Autobiography"; also in *God's Plot: The Paradoxes of Puritan Piety*, ed. Michael McGiffert, Manchester, 1972. pp 33–77. Thomas Shepard's memoir is the piece entitled "An: 1639," which begins, "The good things I have received of the Lord," written in the same manuscript as that containing his autobiography. It is an account of his conversion and vocation, and is given in "Autobiography," 393–95 (and in McGiffert's version also, 71–74). The passage I am referring to is in "Autobiography," 393:

> He is the God that began to strive with me . . . although I oft resisted the Lord and neglected secret prayer and care of his ways a long time and . . . followed my bowling loose company until I came to that height of pride that for their sakes I was once or twice dead drunk and lived in unnatural uncleannesses not to be named and in speculative wantonness and filthiness with all sorts of persons which pleased my eye (yet still restrained from the gross act of whoredom which some of my own familiars were to their horror and shame overtaken with).

"Bowling": in the obsolete sense of excessive drinking. "Loose": unchaste. Shepard then goes on to illustrate first the one and then the other; "unnatural uncleannesses not to be named" is an indirect expression for sodomy, as in Edward Coke, "Of Buggery, or Sodomy," in *The Third Part of the Institutes of the Laws of England*, London, 1644, 58: "a detestable and abominable sin amongst Christians not to be named." In this last, the reference is to his intimate friends ("familiars"). "Gross" cannot be a defining adjective; Shepard would scarcely have recognized degrees of wickedness in whoredom. It serves to intensify the disapproval of whoredom rather than restrict the term to any particular act. The contrast is between the actions of his friends and his easy acceptance of what he saw ("speculative" [obsolete]: in vision), something that pleased his eye. There is a parallel passage to this in "Autobiography," 361 (and in McGiffert, 40–41).

Pledger: Wolff, "Literary Reflections of the Puritan Character," 18. The boy's mother: Kinder, 105; see also 35.

6. John Donne, *The Satires, Epigrams and Verse Letters*, ed. W. Milgate, Oxford, 1967, 52. On the wordplay in Donne's epigrams, see Frank S. Caricato, *John Donne and the Epigram Tradition*, Ph. D. diss., Fordham University, 1973, although I have read the sexual innuendos here differently; and see M. Thomas Hester, "Donne's Epigrams: A Little World Made Cunningly," in *The Eagle and the Dove: Reassessing John Donne*, ed. Claude J. Summers and Ted-Larry Pebworth, New York, 1986, 80–91, on the verbal tension in the epigrams, which problematizes their material. Perkins: William Perkins, *A Golden Chaine: Or, The Description of Theologie*, in *The Workes of ... M. W. Perkins*, vol. 1, Cambridge, 1608, 60.

7. Baker: *Memorials of Father Augustine Baker*, 43. Reina and embezzlement: Kinder, 113–14.

8. *Memorials of Father Augustine Baker*, 34–35.

9. *The Poems of John Marston*, ed. Arnold Davenport, Liverpool, 1961, 140–46. My comments on individual words are partly derived from Davenport's excellent notes. I have modernized the quotations following the rules in note 1. "Effeminate invention": "invention" in the now obsolete sense of his unmanly love of fashion; "He's nought but clothes." There is a perceptive discussion of the place of the sodomitical in Satire VII in this respect in Bruce R. Smith, *Homosexual Desire in Shakespeare's England: A Cultural Poetics*, Chicago, 1991, chap. 5, esp. 180–81.

The woman who appears in the poem is the very epitome of deceitful appearance that the other figures have been reduced to. But while they have fallen to this state, she has not; the woman *is* what they have *become*.

10. The ideas about manliness I have described in this essay are related to those in Thomas Laqueur's discussion of the reaction in the Renaissance to effeminacy in a man as entailing a sort of phantasmagoric dissolution of his being. Thomas Laqueur, *Making Sex: Body and Gender from the Greeks to Freud*, Cambridge, MA, 1990, esp. 125–26 and 123. I am much more wary, however, in drawing conclusions about femininity from the material I have used for this essay, in line with the conclusions Thomas Laqueur drew about femininity from his material: in such a culture a woman did not exist as an ontologically distinct category; she was in effect an incomplete male. Although I appreciate that much of the material I have used can be read in this way, I think this would be mistaken, because these texts are concerned with the nature of manliness and therefore make a very shaky basis for drawing indirect conclusions about femininity. The source of the tension I see in them is rather between manliness and unmanliness generally than between being a man and being a woman. The force of Laqueur's book lies rather in its effective implicit criticism of sociobiological assumptions about the nature of sexual difference. A more nuanced account of gender in Renaissance physiology is given in Stephen Orgel's crucial *Impersonations: The Performance of Gender in Shakespeare's England* (Cambridge, 1996). As he shows, the Galenic single-sex model that Laqueur discusses coexisted, even within the same work, with a two-sex model. These models were not in competition but rather were alternative explanations: the first directed to the nature of man, the second to that of women.

11. Neil McKendrick, John Brewer, and J. H. Plumb, *The Birth of a Consumer Society: The Commercialization of Eighteenth-Century England*, London, 1982. Phyllis Deane and W. A. Cole, *British Economic Growth, 1688–1959*, Cambridge, 1962. Elizabeth Waterman Gilbody, "Demand as a Factor in the Industrial Revolution," in *Facts and Factors in Economic History: Articles by Former Students of Edwin Francis Gay*, ed. Arthur H. Cole et al., Cambridge, MA, 1932, 620–39: reprinted in *The Causes of the Industrial Revolution*, ed. R. M. Hartwell, London, 1967, 121–38. John Brewer and Roy Porter, eds., *Consumption and the World of Goods*, London, 1993.

The views in these works have subsequently been significantly modified in detail; of particular relevance here is the tendency to shift the perspective from the last quarter of the eighteenth century to the later seventeenth century and the early part of the eighteenth. This was raised in the initial reception of *The Birth of a Consumer Society* in reviews by B. A. Holderness, *English Historical Review* 99 (1984): 122–24; and Peter Borsay, *British Journal for Eighteenth-Century Studies* 8 (1985): 235–36; and later reinforced by Lorna Weatherill, *Consumer Behaviour and Material Culture in Britain, 1660–1760*, London, 1988; and Beverly Lemire, "Consumerism in Preindustrial and Early Industrial England: The Trade in Secondhand Clothes," *Journal of British Studies* 27, no. 1 (January 1988): 1–24. There is a valuable review of the continuing debate at that time in Joseph P. Ward, "Reinterpreting the Consumer Revolution," *Journal of British Studies* 29 (1990): 408–14; and there are still dissenting voices on the fundamental economics: Joel Mokyr, "Demand vs. Supply in the Industrial Revolution," *Journal of Economic History* 37, no. 4 (1977): 981–1008; there is a response to Mokyr's article by Ari Y. Ben-Shachar, *Journal of Economic History* 44, no. 3 (1984): 801–5 (and a reply on pp. 806–9).

Lorna Weatherill, "A Possession of One's Own: Women and Consumer Behaviour in England, 1660–1740," *Journal of British Studies* 25, no. 2 (April 1986): 131–56. Amanda Vickery, "Women and the World of Goods: A Lancashire Consumer and Her Possessions, 1751–81," in *Consumption and the World of Goods*, ed. Brewer and Porter, 274–301. Laura Brown, *Alexander Pope*, Oxford, 1985, esp. chap. 3, "The Ideology of Neo-Classical Aesthetics in *Epistles to Several Persons* (1731–5)," 94–127; and idem, "Reading Race and Gender: Jonathan Swift," *Eighteenth-Century Studies* 23, no. 4 (1989–90): 425–43. These authors have not suggested that the "consumer economy" was prompted by female consumption alone, but rather that there were differences in the way men and women consumed. This is particularly so of Amanda Vickery. I was prompted to some of these thoughts by a talk Roy Porter gave at the Institute of Historical Research in London in January 1990, when in commenting on eighteenth-century English medicine, he contrasted the eighteenth-century concern with the disease of "consumption" with the negative attitude of the Christian humanism of the previous century to consumption as excess. This talk was later reproduced in *Consumption and the World of Goods*, ed. Brewer and Porter, 58–81.

Belinda: "The Rape of the Lock" Canto I, line 138, in *Pope: Poetical Works*, ed. Herbert Davis, Oxford, 1966, 91.

I have concentrated largely (although not entirely) in this essay on masculine consumption in terms of consumables rather than durable objects. These were at least as important as durable objects in the eighteenth century's economic takeoff, as Carole Schammas has argued persuasively in "Change in English and Anglo-American Consumption from 1550 to 1800," in *Consumption and the World of Goods*, ed. Brewer and Porter, 177–205.

17

Coming to Terms: Conceptualizing Men's Erotic and Affectional Relations with Men in the United States, 1820–1892

Jonathan Ned Katz

In the United States, the term "homosexual" was not in use—nor was "heterosexual"—before 1892. Those categories were widely distributed only in the first quarter of the twentieth century. Before that, a medically modeled, gender-divided "homosexuality" and "heterosexuality" had not yet cleaved and conquered. Carnal pleasure was not yet organized on a same-sex/different-sex axis. Sexual acts were judged, first of all, by whether they served reproduction. By that standard, nonprocreative different-sex erotic acts were just as perverted as same-sex erotic acts.[1]

Between 1820 and 1892, then, what words did Americans use to name, conceptualize, and judge men's erotic and affectional relationships with men?[2] And what does their language and other evidence suggest about men's self-conceptions (if any), their relationships with men, and the particular historical organization of man-to-man eroticism and affection?

To avoid a basic misunderstanding, I would like to immediately counter an assumption that many readers will bring to this essay—the supposition that I am setting out to study early forms of "homosexuality." To the contrary, I do not assume that my object of research is an essential, unchanging same-sex eroticism that takes different historical forms.[3]

I do start with a present interest in men's erotic and affectional relationships with men. I also assume that such relationships existed in some form in this past era. But I assume, as well, that I do not know the particular historical character of these relationships *as they existed and functioned within the sexual and gender systems of the nineteenth-century United States.* Back then, they may have been socially organized, named, and perceived in ways quite foreign to us. This essay begins, then, to study the specific historical names for, the ideas and judgments about, and the social configurations of men's lust and love for men in another America.

Not surprisingly, "love" was one of the major terms used by nineteenth-century men to name and affirm their sexual and affectional feelings for men. When the semiliterate, twenty-five-year-old farm laborer Ed Cattell writes in 1877 to "my loving old friend" Walt Whitman, Cattell stresses, "i love you Walt and all ways will." [4]

Cattell was not *necessarily* expressing an erotic love, and Whitman probably saved this letter because the love it expressed could pass as incorporeal. The dominant nineteenth-century idea of "true love" distinguished emphatically between that good "spiritual" emotion and bad "sensual" feeling. Love and lust were segregated, consigned to separate spheres, like middle-class women and men. [5] Many nineteenth-century men, therefore, could speak of their intense "love" for other men without anyone realizing that this love included any hint (sometimes even a strong hint) of sensuality.

However, Whitman's diary and a second 1877 letter from Cattell to Whitman suggest that the two had shared a number of moonlight meetings, and that this farm lad's "love" had been actively expressed in erotic and romantic encounters. Cattell writes to Whitman,

> it seems an age Since i last met With you down at the pond and a lovely time We had of it too old man. i would like to Com up Som Saterday afternoon and Stay all night With you. . . . i love you Walt and Know that my love is returned. [6]

Though the dominant nineteenth-century idea of love was cordoned off from lust, love was not, surprisingly, restricted to a particular sex. Oddly, in this intensely sex-stratified society, love was not yet thought of as sexed. The idea of a love proper to a particular sex, aimed properly at a different sex, only became dominant with the invention and distribution of the "heterosexual" norm and "homosexual" anti-norm. [7]

"Friendship" was another of the prominent terms used by men in the early and mid-nineteenth century for naming and conceptualizing intense, sometimes erotic relationships of men with men.

The letters of the working-class Fred Vaughan suggest that he was, in 1860, trying to maintain an intimate friendship with Walt Whitman, with whom he may have earlier lived. [8] Vaughan writes to the poet after attending a New York lecture by Ralph Waldo Emerson, whose strained delivery he criticizes. But, Vaughan adds, Emerson "has *that* in him which makes men capable of strong friendships."[9] Emerson, says Vaughan, spoke of such relationships, saying "that a man whose heart was filled with a warm, ever-enduring *not to be shaken by anything* Friendship was one to be set on one side apart from other men, and almost to be worshipped as a saint." Vaughan asks, "There Walt, how do you like that? What do you think of them setting you & myself, and one or two others we know up in some public place, with an immense placard on our breast, reading *Sincere Friends!!!*"[10] Vaughan's reference to "one or two" other "Sincere Friends" identifies himself and Whitman as such friends and names and classifies a small group of other men, known to himself and the poet, by their deep feelings for men.

Vaughan's reference to "Sincere Friends" is typical of his age. Men of this era placed great stress on authenticity and depth of friendly feeling. They distinguished not between "same-sex" or "different-sex" friends, but between "true" friends and "false," based on the integrity and durability of feeling.[11]

Whitman did not respond to Vaughan's demand for closeness, and the two became estranged. But fourteen years later, Vaughan writes to the poet, still calling him "my friend," still stressing "the part though occupiest in my spiritual nature." He adds, "My love my Walt—is with you always."[12] Vaughan perceived his intense, friendly feelings for Whitman as "spiritual," though his letters to the poet express an intense, possessive yearning for intimacy now associated with sexual love.

Vaughan's thinking of friendship as spiritual was also typical of its time. The age's friendship ideal (like its love ideal) opposed the spiritual and sensual, imagining a clear distinction between friendship and erotic feeling, mind and body, spirit and flesh, purity and carnality.[13]

The working-class Vaughan's attendance at a public talk by the genteel, middle-class Emerson also shows how the friendship ideal of a famous, influential, college-educated man was distributed to a less-educated, lower-class man, who used it to frame his fervent feelings for Whitman.

Love and friendship, two kinds of feeling, provided major ways of categorizing and conceptualizing the intimate, sometimes erotic relationships of men with men.

The relationship of a "youth" and an "old man," or a "boy" and a "man," terms focusing on age, were other prominent nineteenth-century words for avowing intimate and erotic relationships between males.[14]

In 1877, the twenty-five-year-old farmworker Edward Cattell, in his first letter to his "loving old friend," the fifty-one-year-old Whitman, calls himself Whitman's "young frand." Cattell mobilizes the terms "young" and "old" to affectionately stress his and Whitman's age difference and affirm their intimacy.

The term "boy friend" did not in the nineteenth-century commonly refer to a sexual lover, so a former soldier, Benton Wilson, could, in 1867, sign a letter to Whitman "your Boy Friend with Love."[15] But men who did participate in an erotic attraction between younger and older might employ the same language to express their feelings. In 1881, the sixty-two-year-old Whitman writes to his beloved, twenty-two-year-old Harry Stafford. When he recalls past times, says Whitman, "*you, my darling boy, are the central figure of them all.*"[16] In 1883, Stafford signs a letter to Whitman, "With lots of love and a good old time kiss I am ever your boy Harry."[17] For Whitman and Stafford, "boy" and "man" named and authorized an intimacy that the evidence suggests was suffused with eroticism.[18]

On board the U.S. navy ships sailed by Philip Van Buskirk, many sailors rejected in practice the dominant reproductive ethic and justified boys' and men's—and boys' and boys'—sexual relationships.[19]

In 1853, the judgmental, Catholic Van Buskirk asked Old White, an experienced mainmastman, "what's your opinion of those men who have to do with boys? If you were King, wouldn't you kill every one of 'em?" The old salt answered, "Every feller that lives ashore and does *that*, I'd shoot him." But Old White applied a different standard to sailors: "what can a feller do? three years at sea—and hardly any chance to have a woman. I tell you . . . , a feller *must do so*. Biles and pimples and corruption will come out all over his body if he don't."[20] Sailor folklore stressing the health consequences of erotic abstinence helped Old White justify the sexual expression of men and boys.

Writing between 1851 and 1855, Van Buskirk reports that boys and men seeking erotic encounters with each other on U.S. navy ships found them under the boom cover, which protected stored masts. This sexual interaction was so common it had a name—the "boom cover trade."[21]

In the U.S. navy, Van Buskirk reports, erotic interactions between boys and men, or between older boys and younger ones, were so common that the junior partners had a name, "chickens," and the relationship was dubbed "chickenship"—language suggesting an institutionalized practice.[22]

Familial labels—child/parent, father/son, brother/brother, uncle/nephew—were used often in the nineteenth century to conceptualize and legitimate affectional and erotic feelings of otherwise unrelated men and men, men and boys, and boys and boys.

Writing to Whitman in 1863, a soldier, Elijah Fox, addresses him as "Dear Father," adding,

> You will allow me to call you Father wont you. I do not know that I told you that both my parents were dead but it is true and now Walt you will be a second Father to me wont you, for my love for you is hardly less than my love for my natural parents. I never before met with a man that I could love as I do you still there is nothing strange about it for "to know you is to love you."[23]

Fox's "there is nothing strange about it" suggests the opposite, his feeling that the intensity of his love for this older man was unusual enough to seem "strange."

Whitman, answering Fox, calls him "son." And Whitman, pursuing his fantasy of a live-in intimacy with the soldiers Tom Sawyer and Lewy Brown, repeatedly calls both "son," as he later does Peter Doyle. The poet's erotic feelings for these younger men are clear in his letters.[24]

In 1876, planning a trip to New York with Harry Stafford, the current love of his life, Whitman writes to his future host, "My (adopted) son, a young man of 18, is with me now. . . . Could I bring him with me to share my room?" Five days later the forgetful Whitman tells his future host, "My nephew & I when traveling always share the same room together & the same bed, & would like to do so here."[25] The binaries uncle/nephew, father/son were working hard here to explain to an outsider the close relationship of younger and older man.[26]

Whitman's metaphorical adoption of a son was one nineteenth-century way of conceptualizing an intense intimacy between men of different ages. When Whitman, near the end of his life, refused to publicly support the decriminalization of men's sex acts with men, and defensively claimed to have fathered *six* children, metaphorical parenting was already a long-established tradition in his life. His false paternal claim, I have suggested, was a private joke affirming his loving relations with his six most beloved "sons."[27]

Van Buskirk's diary indicates that in the mid-nineteenth century the terms "masturbation" and "onanism" named not only a "solitary vice"—a "self-abuse" or "self-pollution"—but at least four different varieties of erotic interactions between or among males.

In one case, a man or boy would, by publicly practicing on himself, teach other men or boys to masturbate—a learning experience that itself constituted an erotically charged relationship of males.[28] Van Buskirk reports in 1855 that a military man called Rio Grande spent evenings with young sailor boys, telling them about

> the mysteries of *having to do with women* and *doing for yourself.* He explained . . . how by masturbation . . . all of the pleasure that a woman yields by her embrace [could be obtained]. It was this man's wont to practice masturbation on himself in the presence of all the smaller boys in order to teach them the *modus operandi.*[29]

In a second kind of act, men or boys might join in simultaneous, mutual masturbation. Sailors had a name for this: "going chaw for chaw."[30] Whatever the fantasies and desires of the participants, we can view it as an act involving men with men.

A third kind of act that Van Buskirk thought of as self-abuse involved one man actively using another passive man or boy for the active man's pleasure.

In 1844, when Van Buskirk was ten, an old soldier named Scott persuaded him one evening to stand against a tree and (in Van Buskirk's later description) used him for "the abusing of himself." Van Buskirk thought of Scott's act as masturbation, though we can view it as a same-sex erotic act.[31]

In a fourth kind of act perceived as masturbation, one man would offer to "do it" for another, or ask to have it done, without necessarily doing it for himself. In one case, in 1852, the censorious Van Buskirk charged a sailor, Andrew Milne, with masturbating. Milne indignantly replied, "I acknowledge doing it for other men, but, 'pon my word, I haven't done it to myself since I been on the ship but once."[32] Milne apparently considered "doing it for other men" much less of an offense than doing it to himself.[33] In another case, around 1855, a sailor named Charley Evans spread gossip that Van Buskirk had asked him for a "yankum"—sailor slang for masturbation.[34] In the nineteenth century, the rhetoric of onanism provided an important language for categorizing and identifying what from our perspective were erotic relations between and among males.

For college-educated men of the middle and upper classes, references to ancient Greece and Rome and to famous ancient historical and mythological male couples provided another set of terms for signifying affectionate and erotic relationships between men. (Achilles and Patroclus, Damon and Pythias, and Orestes and Pylades were favorite couples.)[35] Such names might reach an uneducated man via an enthralled educated man: alone at Walden Pond with a hunky French-Canadian woodchopper, Alek Therien, Henry David Thoreau tells him about the deep friendship of Achilles and Patroclus.[36]

We need always, of course, to ask exactly how nineteenth-century men understood references to ancient Greek and Roman sexuality. The semieducated van Buskirk first read of "pederasty" in Gibbon's *Decline and Fall of the Roman Empire*. But the marine understood pederasty to mean a form of mutual masturbation in which the hand of one man was used to "pollute the other," either serially or simultaneously.[37]

References to biblical names and passages and to famous saints or Christian theologians were another common premedical way of signifying erotic and affectional relationships between men.

The theological reference to a "crime not to be mentioned among Christians" was invoked by a reverend who atypically, but astutely, comments on (and condemns) the first edition (1855) of *Leaves of Grass*.[38]

In 1874, the English sex-radical Edward Carpenter thanks Whitman for having "given me a ground for the love of men," adding that, for some men, "there is that which passes the love of women"—echoing a biblical passage about David and Jonathan.[39]

In 1890, Whitman writes to a friend about John Addington Symonds, "sometimes I wonder whether J A S don't come under St. Paul's famous category." (The reference is to men who, "leaving the natural use of women, burned in their lust one toward another; men with men working that which is unseemly.")[40]

The theological term "sodomy" and the secular terms "buggery" and "crime against nature" were used in legal and nonlegal parlance to refer to the act of anal intercourse between men. In 1846 Henry Watson, commander of the U.S. marines on the *Portsmouth*, explained that a midshipman resigned after being "charged with a most unnatural, and diabolical crime." The charge, Watson says, "was Arson, or in nautical parlance it is called buggering." "Arson" was also apparently sailor slang punning on "arse" and the associated sex act.[41]

Writing about his navy experience in 1847, Van Buskirk boasts that he had not "once consented to participate in sodomy with any one"—apparently, a fairly remarkable achievement. He explains, "no boy or man can ever remain a year on board of an American man-of-war without being led or forced to commit this crime (which, by the way, is not regarded as a crime in a man-of-war)."[42]

In 1855, referring to the youths in a dormitory at marine headquarters in Washington, DC, Van Buskirk says, "There is so much sodomy carried on . . . I felt it my duty to sleep there to prevent or restrain the spreading of the contagion by every means in my power."[43] His era's conceptual segregation of moral motives and carnal urges allowed him to believe that his sleeping with the boys was motivated by duty, not desire.[44]

Van Buskirk several times uses the term "sodomites" to identify men (plural) by their participation in sodomy. In 1855, he warns the fourteen-year-old Charley Evans to avoid brandy, chewing tobacco, smoking, lying, and associating with "noted sodomites."[45] That a number of men were identified by Van Buskirk and others as "sodomites" is significant in the history of identifying labels.[46] In the 1840s and 1850s, it seems, the sodomite group arrived on the American scene.

"Already Do the Beastly Sodomites of Gotham Quake"

One of the earliest known U.S. references to a *group* of men identified, negatively and collectively, as "sodomites" occurs in a series of articles in 1842, in the *Whip* and the *Rake*, papers directed at a New York City audience of "sporting men." Such men participated in the "sporting" culture that emerged in the city after 1820, openly encouraging men's sexual intercourse with female prostitutes. But this same culture strongly condemned men's "sodomy"—and the "sodomites" named after that act. By passionately attacking sodomites, proponents of the sporting culture distinguished, within the terms of their own pleasure ethic, between good men and bad, and between permissible and impermissible enjoyments.

One of these newspapers refers to "sodomites" as a "set" of persons.[47] Another report refers to "the numerous names" of those "who follow that unhallowed practice of Sodomy."[48] Here, sodomy no longer signified the temporary, aberrant act of a single individual—it named a sinister, sinful collectivity.

Sodomites, in these reports, are a "beastly crew," a group closer to the animal than human.[49] Sodomites are repeatedly referred to as "beasts" and "fiends," animals and monsters, the evil opposites of men and humans.

The first report in the *Whip* also characterizes sodomites by their youth, gentility, and effeminacy: they are "nearly all young men of rather genteel address, and of feminine appearance and manners." But sodomites also include "one or two old and lechrous villains"—not mentioned for any deviation from masculinity.[50]

One of these older men, the *Whip* charges, has "murdered" a "youth of our acquaintance, who was so unfortunate as to fall within the snare of this old sodomite." This youth fell into a decline "which emaciated his form."[51]

This report is the first of several to describe the sodomite as an older, powerful, wealthy exploiter of a poor youth.[52] The class hostility of sporting men against wealthy men was mobilized here against sodomites.

In a later story the *Whip* explicitly names and calls "the attention of the police" to the alleged murderer. He is "an Englishman," a Captain Collins, who had once "kept the Star House in Reade street" (outing was clearly one early form of anti-sodomite activity).

The *Whip* stresses,

> There is no language . . . severe enough . . . to expose the fiendish enormity of this *brute*, who has been the instrumental cause of the death of a young man, who was employed by the monster as barkeeper; who was forced to nightly lie with beasts in the shape of men, by the order of his employer. Though horrid as this may seem, we can prove it by a number of young men who are now in the city, and who have also felt the inhuman embrace of this monster.

The *Whip* calls Captain Collins "king of the Sodomites."

Among those who follow the "unhallowed practice" of sodomy, says the *Whip*, "we find no Americans, as yet—they are all Englishmen or French."[53] The acts of sodomites, the paper stresses, are not native to America, or natural to Americans: these "horrible offences [are] foreign to our shores—to our nature they certainly are—yet they are growing a pace in New York."[54] Attributing sodomy to foreigners simultaneously affirmed the purity of Americans and the young American nation's need to guard against foreign sources of moral corruption. Anti-sodomite discourse supported the nationalistic rhetoric of young America.

"Among the worst of these miscreants," says one story, "is Johnny L'Epine, of No.————Cedar street, a man whose hair has the impress of seventy winters' snow. . . . The man is a Frenchman, we believe, by birth, and has lived in this city from an early age, a walking libel on his country and his kind."[55]

L'Epine's offense is "to perambulate the west side of Broadway and, whenever he can meet a youth of prepossessing appearance to accost and entice him with proffers of employment."[56] The "victims" of sodomites, it is said, "are generally young men of most prepossessing looks."[57] Such youths swarm about New York, says the *Whip*, and "one or another" is "daily allured" (!) into L'Epine's office.[58] The youth's subsequent fate, it is reported, "is best known to the parties concerned. After Johnny has kept a boy a week he may be known in the street by his pallid countenance, his effeminate lip and his mincing gait."[59] (It is surprising to learn how long "mincing" has been associated with effeminate males who commit sodomy.)[60]

The sodomite's influence is apparently quick to work its destructive way on the manhood of impressionable youths. The young man forced into sodomy by Captain Collins was drained of his vital energy and died. The idea of the sodomite as vampire was in construction. The "pallid" look of Johnny L'Epine's victim also closely resembles the drained appearance of masturbators, described in the large, popular nineteenth-century literature against "self-abuse."

The sodomy/masturbation connection is made explicit in 1842 in the *Rake*, another New York sporting paper. This prints a letter claiming that a

> vile wretch in this city . . . makes it his daily practice to entice boys and young men to his hotel and office, and tries all means to perform Sodomy and Masturbation. In some cases he has succeeded; but through the medium of your columns this wretch will be compelled to cease his horrid crimes.

The writer warns this wretch to "Repent!"[61]

The sodomite in these accounts is, surprisingly, the active figure, the one "to perform Sodomy and Masturbation" upon a youth, presented as passive, compliant, and victimized.

One of the "nondescript victims of a morbid appetite" described in the *Whip* is named Sally Binns—a male identified publicly by a female name (apparently, a self-chosen name). This Sally Binns, it is said, is "usually to be seen on the 'four shilling side' of Broadway"—each side apparently had prostitutes of a specific price.

Binns's hair, the paper reports, "is curled down his neck; he straddles [wiggles] as he walks and if any one speaks to him, he drops a curtsy." He also

> puts on female attire and enacts feminine parts in the Thespian Association over St. John's Hall, in Frankfort street. [The association of sodomites with cross-dressing, performance, and theater has a long history.][62] He wears a snuff colored frock and fashionable pantaloons, with watch, rings and *bijouterie*. He has lost all sense and feeling of manhood, and is described by the poet as
> "Not quite a woman; by no means a man."[63]

The distinction in these reports is between "sodomites" and "men," or "sodomites" and "youths," though all these assigned identities are fluid. Men and youths, it is suggested, join the sodomite "crew" by giving in to their seductive "allure." By indulging repeatedly in sodomy, anyone can take on the identity of "sodomite"—it is not congenitally given. "Sodomite" is an attributed group identity. Whether it also served as a self-conception we as yet have no evidence.

The "diabolic enticements" of sodomites are presented as exerting a powerful "allure" for non-sodomites. "Fear seizes the mind of the moral man" when he is "accosted" by a sodomite, says the paper. The moral man's "first impulse is to escape."[64] But his second impulse, it is hinted, makes escape difficult.

The *Whip* claims to "have the names of men who have been acted upon by these fiends."[65] The phrase "acted upon" again makes "men" the passive, powerless victims of active, powerful "sodomites."

Sodomites are said to often blackmail proper, well-bred men innocent of sodomy: "Men of respectability are frequently made the victims of extortion" by sodomites, says the *Whip*, "for even death is preferable to the remotest connection with such a charge."[66] A passage in Herman Melville's novel *Redburn* (1849) also suggests that a handsome youth will not, without recompense, quietly depart the room of an older, wealthier man.[67]

Because the relationship between sodomites and moral men is fluid, it is rather easily sullied, it seems, by any association with sodomites. No respectable men, says the *Whip*, are willing to "appear at the police office . . . to prefer a charge against one of these abominable sinners."[68]

In 1842, the paper suggests, sodomites have staked out their own space in the sexual geography of New York City: "we know where these felons resort for the purpose of meeting and making appointments with their victims."[69] The *Whip* locates sodomites on Broadway and in the vicinity of City Hall Park, as do some other early reports.[70] Such established meeting places suggest a fairly well developed sodomite culture.

Discussing the behavior of sodomites, the *Whip* suggests that "abominable and horrid stews are kept, in which these enormities are committed."[71] The existence. of whorehouses devoted, at least in part, to sodomitical activities is hinted at in this and at least one other known document.[72] It seems, however, that the nineteenth-century term "male prostitute" referred not to men who had sex with men, but to men who had sex with or pimped for female prostitutes.

The *Whip* reporter appropriates moral reform rhetoric to his own ends, claiming to write in order to expose the "inhuman enormities" of the sodomites—to expel them from their jobs and "to rout from our city these monsters."[73] Employment discrimination was clearly an early form of sodomite persecution.

This anti-sodomite crusader threatens to enlist state aid (in the form of the city's judicial authorities): when the time comes, he says, sodomites "will be called upon by a tribunal that they dare not refuse to obey—the Law."[74]

The writer names a particular sodomite, Johnson, who is said to perform nightly in one of the city's "Concert Rooms"—saloons or halls presenting a varied entertainment "of music, drink, and sex."[75] The *Whip* warns, "even if the task is left to us alone, we will drive his filthy carcass from the place." The paper addresses this performer and his fellow sodomites: "we intend to single you out one by one—and you are the first."

The same performer is warned not to open his mouth in public again, for his breath is "death to inhale"—sodomite and contagion are linked.[76] Another account entreats "every honest man to point the finger of scorn" at the sodomites' "polluted persons and shun them" as he would "a pestilence."[77] The association of sodomites and metaphorical disease long preceded the medical model that constructed "inversion" and "homosexuality" as mental diseases.

Ferdinand Palmo, a founder of New York City concert halls, is warned that he has among his performers one "who . . . carries the soul of [a] hell-engendered Sodomite" (seemingly, the same performer mentioned above). Palmo is asked "to discharge him," and the performers who work with this sodomite are asked to refuse to go on unless he is fired. Palmo's customers are also asked "to aid us in driving this monster . . . from the city."[78] The *Whip* warns this sodomite "to quit the life you are leading, or shortly you will receive a thunder-bolt from us that will make you curse the hour you were born."[79]

The *Whip*'s 1842 linking of this sodomite with Palmo's concert hall tallies with a scene in Melville's satiric novel *Redburn*. Outside a fashionable hotel in Liverpool, young Redburn and his "courtly," "feminine" friend Harry Bolton suddenly come upon a "Lord Lovely," who Bolton calls his "old chum." (Bolton's work as a male prostitute is earlier hinted at, and "chum" was a nineteenth-century term for an intimate male friend.)[80]

The innocent young Redburn describes Lord Lovely as "not much of a Lord to behold; very thin and limber about the legs, with small feet like a doll's, and a small glossy head like a seal's. I had seen just such looking lords standing in sentimental attitudes in front of Palmo's on Broadway." Outside Palmo's, in Melville's New York, there apparently lounged numbers of doll-like men with aristocratic airs. Melville hints here at the nineteenth-century American existence of the "queen," the effeminate, man-loving man, whom Randolph Trumbach and Alan Bray have identified as a type in eighteenth-century London.

After its first exposé, The *Whip* reports that its sodomite hunting is having an effect: "Already do the beastly Sodomites of Gotham quake; they feel their brute souls quiver with fear."[81]

By its third exposé, however, the paper reports that it has "received a number of letters from the friends of these brutes threatening us with violence, if we persisted in our strictures upon these *harmless* young men." Those letters constitute the earliest U.S. report of resistance to the persecution of sodomites.[82]

The *Whip*'s reports do not indicate whether those denounced as "sodomites" found some way to use that term as an identity tag of their own. But the attributed group identity "sodomites" and the act "sodomy" were certainly major categories with which men engaging in sex with men had to come to terms. That they did find ways of coming to terms is suggested by those letters to the *Whip* defending sodomites as "*harmless*."

These accounts also provide clues to the ideas and values of the *Whip* writer who so vociferously condemned sodomites, as well as to the views of his readers. As "sporting papers," the *Whip* and the *Rake* upheld a culture whose "most conspicuous sexual ethic," says historian Timothy Gilfoyle, was its defense of men's freedom to have intercourse with female prostitutes. The *Sporting Whip* declared, "Man is endowed by nature with passions that must be gratified." That theory of imperative male "passions" meant that "no blame can be attached to him, who for that purpose occasionally seeks the woman of pleasure." [83]

The sporting press's defense of men's pleasure-sex with women, says Gilfoyle, "challenged the emerging 'respectable,' bourgeois, Christian morality" upheld "by Protestant and Catholic clergy, male and female moral reformers, and entrepreneurs and small merchants." [84] These respectables denounced sex for pleasure and upheld sex for reproduction—within the institutions of true love and legal marriage.

The intensity of the *Whip* writer's attack on sodomites can thus be understood as a way he clearly distinguished, within the terms of a pleasure ethic, between permissible and impermissible enjoyments, anticipating a major project of twentieth-century sex modernists.

Among the sexual pleasures denounced by the *Whip* was the erotic "intercourse" of white women and black men, which the paper deemed "a practice worse, by far, than sodomy!" [85] The copulation of different races (and different sexes) was apparently far worse than "sodomy" between men (of the same race).

The *Whip*'s pleasure norm did not, then, view all different-sex erotic acts as good. It upheld no heterosexual ideal. Forced by its pleasure principle to distinguish between licit and illicit satisfactions, *The Whip* mobilized race differences and a specific sodomy between men, to condemn such pleasures, thereby honoring white men's pleasure-sex with white female prostitutes.

"Mary Jones"

In New York City, about ten o'clock on the night of Tuesday, June 11, 1836, a master mason named Robert Haslem, a white man, was walking home after a liaison with a white woman he had picked up earlier that evening.

On a corner of Bleeker Street, Haslem met a black woman, Mary Jones, dressed "elegantly and in perfect style," with white earrings and gilt comb in her hair—as the *New York Herald* reported. [86] Haslem or Jones initiated a conversation—the newspapers differ.

Haslem asked Jones, "*Where are you going my pretty maid?*" and volunteered to go with her. Before they set off "on this tour of pleasure," says the *Herald*, she "lovingly threw her arms around him and strained him to her heart." Then, "these delicate preludes having ended, they proceeded onwards, until they arrived at an alley in Green street, which having entered * *." Here, a string of asterixes in the *Herald*'s report suggest, almost as clearly as the missing words, an erotic act.

Afterward, on his way home, Haslem discovered that he was missing his wallet and ninety-nine dollars; in their place he unaccountably found the wallet of a man he did not know, with a bank order for $200.

Haslem sought out the man, who at first denied ownership of the wallet. He then admitted he had had his pocket picked under the same circumstances as Haslem. He had been "too wise," however, "to expose himself" by reporting the theft to the police.

Next morning the determined Haslem confessed his story to constable Bowyer who, that evening, set out to find Mary Jones. At eleven or twelve that night, on the Bowery, Bowyer passed a black woman and, according to the *Herald*, "thinking that this might be the one he sought," looked at her face and "made up his mind that he was right."

"Where are you going at this time of night?" he demanded. She answered, "I am going home, will you go too?" He agreed, and "she conducted him to her house in Green Street, and invited him in." He declined, "with great regret," but later walked her to an alley where she asked him to have sex — "to reenact the scene of the previous evening" is how the paper put it. She then "proceeded to be very affectionate," and Bowyer arrested her.

"A tussle ensued," the *Sun* reports, during which the prisoner took two wallets from her bosom and threw them away. One turned out to be Haslem's. On the way to the "watch house" (jail), Jones apparently tried to ditch another wallet, but was caught. With Jones locked up, the constable took her key, searched her apartment, and found a number of other wallets.

Bowyer then searched Mary Jones, and, says the *Sun*, "for the first time discovered that he [Jones] was a man." Until this moment, says the paper, neither Bowyer nor Haslem had any doubts about Jones's sex.

"Bowyer also discovered," says the *Sun*, that the prisoner, "to sustain his pretension, and impose upon men"—here seventeen words in bad Latin complete the sentence. Translated, the Latin says that the woman impersonator "had been fitted with a piece of cow [leather?] pierced and opened like a woman's womb ["vagina" is likely the intended word], held up with a girdle." [87] Latin-reading upper-class men could apparently contemplate such details without harm; women and lower-class persons of either sex could not.

On June 16, five days after Haslem's fateful meeting with Jones, the prisoner was tried for stealing Haslem's wallet and money, a grand larceny.

The accused appeared in court, the *Sun* reported, "neatly dressed in female attire. . ., his head covered with a female wig." (It seems unlikely the prisoner chose to be tried in drag; this was probably the court's doing.) The spectacle of a cross-dressed black man—and his and Haslem's ensuing testimony—the *Herald* reports, provided "the greatest merriment in the court, and his Honor the Recorder, the sedate grave Recorder laughed till he cried."

During the trial, the *Sun* reports, a spectator "seated behind the prisoner's box, snatched the flowing wig from the head of the prisoner." This "excited a tremendous roar of laughter throughout the room."

A legal affidavit—seemingly, a fairly accurate transcription—relates the words the prisoner uttered in his own defense.[88]

Asked his age, place of birth, business, and residence, he answered, "I will be thirty three Years of age on the 12th day of December next, was born in this City, and get a living by Cooking, Waiting &c and live No. 108 Green St." "What is your right name?" he was asked. "Peter Sewally," he answered. "I am a man."

"What induced you to dress yourself in Women's Clothes?" He replied,

> I have been in the practice of waiting upon Girls of ill fame and made up their Beds and received the Company at the door and received the money for Rooms &c and they induced me to dress in Women's Clothes, saying I looked so much better in them and I have always attended parties among the people of my own Colour dressed in this way—and in New Orleans I always dressed in this way.

He added, "I have been in the State service"—his military duty was offered as an implicit plea for leniency.

Asked if he had stolen Haslem's wallet and money, Sewally answered, "No Sir and I never saw the Gentleman nor laid eyes upon him. I threw no Pocket Book from me last night, and had none to throw away, and the Pocket Books now Shown me I never Saw before.—" The illiterate Sewally signed his statement with an X.

The following day, June 17, two New York papers carried detailed stories of the case. The *Herald* was fairly open about the sex acts associated with the prisoner's cross-dressing and pickpocketing: "Sewally has for a long time past been doing a fair business, both in money making, and *practical* amalgamation, under the cognomen of *Mary Jones*." The word "amalgamation" was used often in the nineteenth century to refer to sexual contacts between whites and African Americans.

During the daytime, added the *Sun*, Sewally

> generally promenades the street, dressed in a dashing suit of male apparel, and at night prowls about the five points and other similar [disreputable] parts of the city, in the disguise of a female, for the purpose of enticing men into the dens of prostitution, where he picks their pockets if practicable, an art in which he is a great adept. Numerous complaints of robberies so perpetrated by him had been made at the police office at sundry times; but owing to the scruples of the complainants against exposing themselves in the Court . . . , on trial, they have generally abandoned their complaints, and their stolen money, watches, &c. On this occasion, however, the complainant, to recover his money, mustered courage enough to stand the brunt of the trial.[89]

The *Herald* reports, "The jury[,] after consulting a few moments, returned a verdict of guilty of grand larceny." The *Herald* later reports that Sewally was sentenced to five years in the state prison.[90]

Just a week or so after Sewally's trial a color print of him dressed as a woman, and titled " 'The Man Monster,' Peter Sewally, Alias Mary Jones," was printed in New York City by a well-known lithographer.[91] Despite its title, the print portrays Sewally as a rather ordinary-looking, unstereotyped, and unthreatening black woman in a clean white dress with pretty blue flowers. The prosaic image counters the monstrousness invoked by the title. The lithograph and newspaper accounts suggest that Sewally's cross-dressing, theft, and sexual conduct were sensational in 1836, but not as upsetting or terrifying as they would have been in the early colonial era.

Nine years later, in 1845, a New York paper reports that "A notorious character, known as *Beefsteak Pete*," had been arrested for "perambulating the streets in woman's attire" with an object of a "villainous character."[92]

The following year, a New York paper reports that "Pete Sevanley, alias 'beef steak Pete,' a notorious black rascal, who dresses in female attire and parades about the street," and who had been "liberated from Blackwell's Island" a short time earlier, had been arrested for "playing up his old game, sailing along the street in the full rig of a female." He had been sent back to prison for six months, "to finish some blocks of stone."[93]

Sewally's first-person statement of 1836 provides the earliest U.S. evidence of a supportive link between female prostitutes and a man who, dressed as a woman, sometimes had intercourse with men. His testimony is also the earliest account of African American parties in New York City and New Orleans attended—peacefully, it seems—by a cross-dressed black man. The story of Sewally's arrest shows us an African American man working the race, class, sexuality, and gender systems to appropriate for himself a little of the wealth of white men.

The newspapers document the white judge's and white jury's response to Sewally. They punish him quite severely for a theft accomplished via a masquerade, and they have a good laugh at his and his white victim's expense. The papers' need to maintain a "respectable" level of discourse meant that his sex acts with men were given less explicit coverage than his cross-dressing and theft.

In these documents, the exact character of Sewally's erotic desire remains ambiguous, though his pecuniary motive is clear. But his unusual, defiant, long-term cross-dressing and streetwalking provide evidence of a man appropriating for his own a particular model of illicit womanhood, female prostitutes, or "Girls of ill fame," as he calls them. The stories of Peter Sewally and Sally Binns, mentioned earlier, show that enacting this sort of "woman" was another option available to men in the nineteenth century who, for whatever reason, desired intimate contact with men.[94]

"Love," "friendship," "friend," "chickenship," "chicken," the "boom cover trade," "boy"/"man," "child"/"parent," "son"/"father," "brother"/"brother," "nephew"/"uncle," "masturbation," "onanism," "arson," "buggery," "sodomy," "sodomite" (and "sodomites"), "crime against nature," the "girl of ill fame," "pederasty," words associated with ancient Greece and Rome, the Bible, and Christian theology—all provided numbers of nineteenth-century ways of naming and, sometimes, coming to terms with men's and youths' desire for men and youths. At the nineteenth century's end, these terms—and many others—would be subordinated under one single, powerful, unifying medical sign: "homosexuality." Before "homosexuality," the abundance of nineteenth-century American terms for men's affectional and sexual relations with men suggests the possibility of an equally large, unmapped variety of relationships.

Notes

This essay was begun in 1994 under a Ken Dawson Award from the Center for Lesbian and Gay Studies (CLAGS); I am grateful to the CLAGS jury for the award, and to Martin Duberman for initiating CLAGS. This essay is indebted to the earlier research of many people, especially Timothy Gilfoyle, who published brief references to the 1842 attack on New York City "sodomites" and the 1836 case of "Mary Jones" in *City of Eros: New York City, Prostitution, and the Commercialization of Sex, 1790–1920* (New York: W. W. Norton, 1992). I am also personally indebted to Gilfoyle for many leads to other sources. For his publication of excerpts from the diary of Philip Van Buskirk I am indebted to B. R. Burg, *An American Seafarer in the Age of Sail: The Erotic Diaries of Philip C. Van Buskirk, 1851–1870* (New Haven: Yale University Press, 1994). For his publication of the letters of numbers of working men to Walt Whitman I am indebted to the two volumes edited by Charley Shively, *Calamus Lovers: Walt Whitman's Working Class Camerados* (San Francisco: Gay Sunshine Press, 1987), and *Drum Beats: Walt Whitman's Civil War Boy Lovers* (San Francisco: Gay Sunshine Press, 1989). For their research on this and earlier eras I am also grateful to Alan Bray, Martin Duberman, the late Michael Lynch, Robert K. Martin, and Randolph Trumbach. George Austin Thompson of the New York University Library and David Kahn, director of the Brooklyn Historical Society, shared valuable finds, Beert Verstraet translated a Latin passage, and many discussions with Allan Bérubé and Carole S. Vance were great fun and helped clarify my ideas. This essay is dedicated to the memory of the Walt Whitman lover Michael Lynch.

1. See Jonathan Ned Katz, "The Invention of the Homosexual," in *Gay/Lesbian Almanac* (New York: Harper and Row, 1983); and idem, *The Invention of Heterosexuality* (New York: Dutton, 1995).

2. I focus on men in this chapter as a pragmatic way of narrowing down the research task. I also focus, as often as possible, on the class of laboring men, urban and rural, about whose love and lust lives little is known.

3. At the end of this hetero- and homosexualized twentieth century, it also seems wise to warn readers against a second common assumption—about erotic "identities." Whether men who lusted after and loved men in the early and mid-nineteenth century had self-conceptions based on their lusting and loving is another question to be answered by reference to empirical research and careful analysis of the evidence.

With one major exception (discussed later in this essay), most of the nineteenth-century men about whom I and others have so far discovered evidence were "white," though bits of evidence refer to men of color. My future research will take affirmative action to locate more evidence about men of color and to analyze the historical construction of "whiteness," "blackness," and "race."

4. Charley Shively, *Calamus Lovers: Walt Whitman's Working Class Camerados* (San Francisco, Gay Sunshine Press, 1987), 156.

5. Only at the end of the century did the term "sex-love" emerge to signify a new ideal of erotic love. See my comments on "sex-love" in *Gay/Lesbian Almanac*, 141–42, 250–51, 254, and my discussion of the early nineteenth-century separation of lust and love in *The Invention of Heterosexuality*, 40–55.

6. Shively, *Calamus Lovers*, 160.

7. The historical construction of the hetero/homo binary is discussed in my books *Gay/Lesbian Almanac* and *The Invention of Heterosexuality*.

8. Vaughan's relation with Whitman and his family is discussed by Shively, *Calamus Lovers*, 14, 36–50.

9. Vaughan was right on target; Emerson's diaries of his college days document his intense fascination with another student, Martin Gay. See Jonathan Ned Katz, *Gay American History: Lesbians and Gay Men in the U.S.A.* (New York: T. Y. Crowell, 1976), 445, 456–60.

10. Shively, *Calamus Lovers*, 43. After his "Sincere Friends" comment Vaughan adds, "Good doctrine that but I think the theory preferable to the practice"—a dig at Whitman's not living up, in his relationship with Vaughan, to the poet's professed ideal of friendship.

11. On the role of sincerity and depth of feeling in nineteenth-century relationships, see Karen Lystra, *Searching the Heart: Women, Men, and Romantic Love in Nineteenth Century America* (New York: Oxford University Press, 1989).

12. Shively, *Calamus Lovers*, 50.

13. Whitman's many references, in poems and essays, to "friends" and "friendship" show him rejecting the genteel, spiritual friendship ideal to affirm a specifically erotic intimacy between men. When Whitman spoke in his poems and essays for the erotic love of men and women—and men and men—he spoke against the grain. In his preface to the second edition (1856) of *Leaves of Grass*, Whitman is already criticizing "the filthy law" that "sex" and "desires, lusty animations, organs, acts, are unmentionable and to be ashamed of, to be driven to skulk out of literature." He adds, "as to manly friendship, everywhere observed in The States, there is not the first breath of it to be observed in print." He promises to end that literary silence. And in the next edition (1860) of *Leaves of Grass*, in the new "Calamus" section on men's erotic intimacy with men, Whitman envisions a "new friendship" and a "new City of Friends." See Walt Whitman, *Leaves of Grass*, Comprehensive Reader's Edition, Harold W. Blodgett and Sculley Bradly (New York: New York University Press, 1965); for "new friendship," see David S. Reynolds, *Walt Whitman's America: A Cultural Biography* (New York: Knopf, 1995), 402.

14. Later in this essay I discuss a parallel, condemnatory concept, which stressed the age difference between an old "sodomite" and his young victim.

15. Shively, *Calamus Lovers*, 16, 70.

16. Shively, *Calamus Lovers*, 147, 169.

17. Shively, *Calamus Lovers*, 170, 171.

18. On Whitman and Stafford's relationship being suffused with eros, see Whitman's letters to Stafford and Stafford's to him in Shively, *Calamus Lovers*, 137–71, and Edwin Haviland Miller's discussion in *The Correspondence of Walt Whitman* (New York: New York University Press, 1964), 3: 2–9.

19. The diaries of Philip Van Buskirk, discussed and quoted from by Burg, provide a rich source of clues to the language, conceptions, and erotic and affectional interactions of American sailors in the 1850s and 1860s. Van Buskirk, born in 1834, into a Southern,

Catholic, middle-class family, was catapulted out of his class by his father's bankruptcy and suicide, to land at age twelve in the U.S. Marines. There, he became a meticulous diarist and participant-observer in the affectional and sexual lives of sailors. B. R. Burg, *An American Seafarer in the Age of Soil* (New Haven: Yale University Press, 1994).

20. Burg, 78.

21. Burg, 75. "Boom cover trade" seems to include an early use of "trade" in connection with male–male erotic encounters.

22. Burg, 79.

23. Charley Shively, *Drum Beats: Walt Whitman's Civil War Boy Lovers* (San Francisco: Gay Sunshine Press, 1989), 144.

24. For Whitman's calling young men "son," see his correspondence with Elijah Fox, Thomas Sawyer, Louis Brown, Harry Stafford, and Peter Doyle, indexed in *A Supplement to the Correspondence of Walt Whitman with a Composite Index*, vol. 6 of *The Collected Writings of Walt Whitman*, ed. Edwin Haviland Miller (New York: New York University Press, 1977).

25. Whitman, *Correspondence*, 3: 67–68.

26. In a letter of 1863, Whitman calls the soldier Tom Sawyer "my dear darling brother" and asks Sawyer "to call me the same" (Whitman, *Correspondence*, 1:93). In the manuscript version of a poem, Whitman's narrator "dreamed in a dream of a city where all the men were like brothers, O I saw them tenderly love each other." (Shively, *Calamus Lovers*, 39). During the Civil War the term "comrade" and "comradeship" took on a new poignancy as the term by which Witman fondly named numbers of young fighting men, and by which they named him. In the 1860 edition of *Leaves of Grass*, Whitman is already celebrating the "need of comrades" (Shively, *Calamus Lovers*, 35). In 1863, Elijah Fox addressed the poet as "Dear Father & Comrade" (Shively, *Drum Beats*, 145). Commenting in 1889 on one of these war letters, Whitman said, "Comradeship—yes, that's the thing: getting one and one together to make two—getting two together everywhere to make all: that's the only bond we should accept and that's the only freedom we should desire: comradeship, comradeship" (Shively, *Drum Beats*, 54).

27. Katz, *Gay American History*, 628 n. 32.

28. Van Buskirk reports that when he enlisted in the Marines as a drummer, in 1846, a fellow music boy, Dorell, practiced masturbation publicly, and taught it by example (Burg, 24).

29. Burg, 24.

30. Burg, 77.

31. Burg, 74. On another occasion, between 1849 and 1851, in New Orleans, a Spaniard offered the teenaged Van Buskirk lodging, and, he says, "had a fancy to handle my person indelicately—more plainly to play with my pene—which I had to submit to; in the morning he gave me a half-dime or a dime to buy something to eat." Van Buskirk's matter-of-fact report of the Spaniard's behavior suggests that he thought of his own passivity as saving him from being a party to onanism, which he considered a grave sin (Burg, 91).

32. Burg, 40.

33. This evidence does not document the "confusion" of masturbation and same-sex sex acts (or "homosexuality"), as two researchers have suggested (see my comments in *Gay/Lesbian Almanac*, 2–3). It is just that today's "homosexuality" is confronted here by a radically different, but equally valid, sexual system.

34. Burg, 114.

35. Reynolds, 578.

36. Katz, *Gay American History*, 490.

37. Burg, 77, 54, 117.

38. The Reverend Rufus Griswold reviewed *Leaves of Grass* in *The Criterion*, Nov. 10, 1855.

39. Katz, *Gay American History*, 359.

40. Katz, *Gay/Lesbian Almanac*, 59.

41. Burg, 75, 186 n. 8.

42. Burg, 74.

43. Burg, 113.

44. In the 1850s Van Buskirk characterizes his ship's storeroom as a "Sodomy den," the name also of a dormitory at the Annapolis Naval Academy in 1869 (Burg, 79, 154).

45. Burg, 114.

46. This contrasts with the American colonial era, when acts of sodomy did *not* constitute a sodomite, a person defined by the practice of sodomy (see Katz, *Gay/Lesbian Almanac*). "Certainly," Van Buskirk says that same year, "ninety per cent of the white boys in the Navy of this day . . . are, to an extent that would make you shudder, blasphemers and sodomites" (Burg, xi).

47. "The Sodomites," *Whip*, Jan. 29, 1842, 2.

48. "Morbid Appetite," *Whip*, Feb. 12, 1842, 2. A typo in this sentence has been silently corrected.

49. *Whip*, Jan. 29, 1842, 2.

50. *Whip*, Jan. 29, 1842, 2. Three sodomites are here cited by name: Johnson, Adly, and Captain Collins.

51. *Whip*, Jan. 29, 1842, 2.

52. *Whip*, Feb. 12, 1842, 2.

53. *Whip*, Feb. 12, 1842, 2.

54. *Whip*, Jan. 29, 1842, 2.

55. "Sodomites," *Whip*, Feb. 26, 1842, 3. The report adds of L'Epine: "He is a wholesale importer."

56. *Whip*, Feb. 26, 1842, 3.

57. *Whip*, Jan. 29, 1842, 2.

58. "Allured" is an interesting word, suggesting, more than "lured," an active attraction on the part of the one "allured."

59. *Whip*, Feb. 26, 1842, 3.

60. For a 1933 reference to a "street corner 'fairy' of Times Square" who was "rouged, lisping, [and] mincing," see George Chauncey, *Gay New York: Gender, Urban Culture, and the Making of the Gay Male World* (New York: Basic Books/HarperCollins, 1994), 67.

61. "Awful Depravity! Sodomy!," *Rake*, July 30, 1842, 2.

62. See Laurence Senelick, "Mollies or Men of Mode? Sodomy and the Eighteenth-Century London Stage," *Journal of the History of Sexuality* 1:1, July 1990, 33–67.

63. *Whip*, Feb. 26, 1842, 3. A typo in the original has been silently corrected.

64. *Whip*, Jan. 29, 1842, 2.

65. *Whip*, Jan. 29, 1842, 2.

66. *Whip*, Jan. 29, 1842, 2.

67. Jonathan Ned Katz, "Melville's Secret Sex Text," *Village Voice Literary Supplement*, Apr. 1982, 10–12.

68. *Whip*, Jan. 29, 1842, 2.

69. *Whip*, Jan. 29, 1842, 2.

70. *Whip*, Jan. 29, 1842, 2.

71. A typo in "horrid" has been silently corrected.

72. In 1846, an editorial in a New York City working-class newspaper calls on the police of the Sixth Precinct to close up a "male brothel," described as "a den of infamy kept in the Bowery not far from Pell street, which is a notorious resort for the vilest

characters of men, and courtezan lovers, who deserve not the name of men." Although the wording is ambiguous, this does sound like a place where effeminate men had sex with manly men for money. See "Robbers Cave," *Subterranean*, Dec. 26, 1846. I thank Timothy Gilfoyle for this document.

73. *Whip*, Jan. 29, 1842, 2.

74. *Whip*, Jan. 29, 1842, 2.

75. "Our Arrow Has Hit the Mark!" *Whip*, Feb. 5, 1842, 2. Historian Timothy Gilfoyle identifies Concert Rooms in *City of Eros* (New York: W. W. Norton, 1992), 129. "Johnson" is named in *Whip*, Feb. 12, 1842, 2.

76. *Whip*, Feb. 5, 1842, 2.

77. *Whip*, Feb. 12, 1842, 2.

78. *Whip*, Feb. 5, 1842, 2.

79. *Whip*, Feb. 12, 1842, 2.

80. For "chum" see Robert K. Martin, "Chums: The Search for a Friend," in *Hero, Captain, and Stranger: Male Friendships, Social Critique, and Literary Form in the Sea Novels of Herman Melville* (Chapel Hill: University of North Carolina Press, 1986), 40–66. For "chummying" (in Melville's *White-Jacket*), see 40; for "chummy" (in Melville's *Pierre*), see 62.

81. *Whip*, Feb. 5, 1842, 2.

82. The defenders of sodomites are warned by the *Whip*'s writer, "we will never hold our peace until we have rid the city of these vagabonds" (*Whip*, Feb. 12, 1842, 2).

83. Gilfoyle, 99.

84. Gilfoyle, 98. Middle-class Christian morality, says Gilfoyle, espoused "the values of self-control, chastity, domesticity, sobriety, and frugality."

85. *Whip*, March 12, 1842, 2.

86. "General Sessions, Thursday," *New York Herald*, June 17, 1836, 1. All the quotations in the following section come from this source, unless otherwise noted.

87. "Reported for the Sun: Court of Sessions—Yesterday," *New York Sun*, June 17, 1836, 2. Bowyer, says the *Sun*, "also discovered that the prisoner, to sustain his pretension, and impose upon men as sexus femineus, fabrefactus fuerat pertio bovillis, (cara bubulu) terebratus et apertus similis matrix muliebris, circumligio cum cingulum!!!"

88. "People v. Sewally," June 16, 1836, District Attorney Indictment Papers, Court of General Sessions, New York City Municipal Archives and Records Center.

89. The *New York Sun*, cited above, reported that in addition to Mary Jones, Sewally used the aliases Miss Ophelia, Miss June, and Eliza Smith.

90. The *New York Sun* of June 17, 1836, says that the court sentenced Sewally to the state prison for three years. But an item headed "Court of General Session," in the *New York Herald*, June 20, 1836, 2, says he was sentenced to five years.

91. An original of this color print is in the New York Historical Society, "Crime" Folder, Prints Division, Negative no. 40697. It is reproduced in black and white in Gilfoyle, 137.

92. "City News," *Commercial Advertiser*, Aug. 9, 1845, 2. I am indebted to George Thompson for this reference and the next.

93. "Police Intelligence," *New York Herald*, Feb. 14, 1846, 2.

94. Whether Sewally also fulfilled his emotional needs in this manner we can only guess.

18

Invisible Women: Retracing the Lives of French Working-Class Lesbians, 1880–1930

Francesca Canadé Sautman

Defining the Territory

The cultural archaeology of lesbians within the French working class from 1880 to 1930 brings us into contact with a world relentlessly subsumed. It is a community history conducted after the informants are, for the most part, no longer alive. It is a struggle to make visible a world that had every reason to insure its survival through invisibility. It seeks to speak *of* but not *for* voices that have been traditionally ignored, silenced, or distorted from all sides because they were the voices of women, of lesbians, and of working-class people all at once.[1] It means straining our ears to hear those voices emerge in the discordant orchestra whose score they did not, for the most part, write.

The public expression of French lesbian culture has been boxed in for decades by a discourse on homosexuality written by men about men. French texts on homosexuality commonly refer to "female homosexuality" when discussing lesbianism[2] and afford it a few scant pages, if any at all. A general vulgarization work on homosexuality, coauthored by André Baudry, one of the organizers of the gay political group Arcadie, devoted 6 pages out of 140 to women. It claimed that lesbians were never able to generate the sort of aesthetic and artistic fervor that men did, and that as a consequence, were less readily condemned than men.[3] In the 1970s, according to lesbians who were interviewed,[4] and also according to a historical evaluation of the lesbian movement,[5] Arcadie, albeit mixed, offered little to attract women's participation.

The figures of the "Left Bank women" of the 1920s loom large in the history of the French lesbian community. Scholars have trained their lenses on these highly accomplished, artistic women, many of them foreigners, who lived at the higher rungs of the social ladder, with strong connections to men of the intelligentsia but independent enough to live their own lives as they wished, enclosed behind the walls of their comfortable homes. Scholars turn their attention to the fascinating figures of Colette, Renée Vivien, Adrienne Monnier, Djuna Barnes, Nathalie Barney, Romaine Brooks, and others of the same milieu.[6] Yet an enormous void is still felt: what do we know of the lives of lesbians of more modest means, and of poor and working-class lesbians?

Written documents about the lives of working-class lesbians are almost nonexistent, partially because lesbian lives have been traditionally overlooked by male writers, and partially because the truism that working-class people in general tend to remain shadowy players on a stage set by academics, mostly educated in middle-class values, holds very true in French gay history.

While among lesbian writers and scholars in the United States there has been some commitment to preserving material about lesbian working-class life,[7] similar studies are still wanting with respect to France. A factor may be that the relationship between French lesbian culture and working-class culture is a great deal less obvious than in the United States, while upper-middle-class and even upper-class or aristocratic lesbians are well known. And while extreme-right parties—in the prewar period[8] as well as more recently[9]—have vehemently condemned feminism and the struggle for women's rights as spawning lesbianism and "other ills," at the same time, class-conscious right-wing lesbians have been an acceptable representation in politically explicit lesbian writing.[10]

The archaeology of lesbian working-class life requires that we blend the methods of oral history with quantifiable historical data, by patiently piecing together fragments of information and, regardless of how resilient they are, prying at them to "bring out" the "unsaid." In this respect, every scrap of testimony garnered from autobiographies and interviews is precious. The study of gay life also can tap a literature, which is often lurid and homophobic but sometimes grudgingly sympathetic, depicting homosexual life in the 1890s, 1920s, and 1930s, written by *littérateurs* like Willy, Charles Etienne, Jean Lorrain, Jean du Coglay, Jacques de Lacretelle, Suzanne de Callias, and René Crevel.[11] This period in French literary production also witnessed a number of journalistic exposés (by Maryse Choisy, Francis Carco, and Raymond Boucard) that straddled an uneasy frontier with fiction, since the authors did not always hesitate to embellish the material collected in the field with literary flourishes, picturesque colorations, or personal impressions. At the same time, all these works have been relied on heavily by historians of gay culture such as Barbedette and Carassou,[12] because they contain so much detail about social spaces, manner of dress, speech, and sexual activities, although historians have traditionally harbored a legitimate suspicion toward fiction as documentation.

Iconography, whose reading presents its own difficulties, can be very helpful: the paintings of Toulouse-Lautrec and Brassai's photographs, accompanied by the text of his own recollections, are witnesses to a culture that does not always surface in texts. Reliance on the contemporary press for information contained in crime, gossip, or local news columns is also not free from distortion and falsification. Problematic again, not to say downright unsavory, are the case studies and textbooks produced by criminologists, sexologists, and moral crusaders of the time, dealing with sexuality, prostitution, and jail life. Police chiefs also wax eloquent in their memoirs on these matters, but leave out as much as they put in, often in their zealous efforts to justify their subordinates' behavior. In short, engaging such a study requires a preliminary acknowledgment that many of the sources available are unsatisfactory in and of themselves, that they need to be juxtaposed to and confronted with each other.

If a working-class lesbian has not left a memoir of her own, been written about by others, or was not already known for activities in the public sphere (whether political or artistic), her only chance of being known to posterity was through some form of official record, such as an arrest, or being involved in an incident reported in the scandal columns of the press. But during this period, the law acted only against public obscenity or molestation, and being a lesbian in itself was not illegal, as the moral crusader Taxil found out when he pressured the préfecture to stem the tide of growing lesbianism. *Monsieur*, he was told, in substance, we deplore the situation too, but the offense was not foreseen by the Code Napoléon, and furthermore, the *tribades* do not accost young girls or get caught in obscene acts in public. The prefect added an interesting detail about cruising patterns: it was indeed an offense in a thicket or a railway car, but not in the privacy of one's home.[13]

The laissez-faire attitude expressed by this Paris prefect prevailed in France until the Pétain regime began to actively harass homosexuals, who were soon to be deported under Nazi laws. It was in 1934, the year several new fascist parties were founded, after an anti-Parlementarian rightist riot, that the drag queens of Paris were molested and the balls shut down. In 1942, a Vichy law increased the consent age for homosexuals only and was confirmed by de Gaulle in 1945. In the 1950s, arrests for various homosexual offenses picked up; 61 percent of the men arrested were from the working class.[14] Women who routinely wore pants, a tie, and a man's jacket to clubs had their papers checked by the police.[15]

In this context, working-class lesbians have fared poorly. Historians, inside and outside the academy, have indeed applied themselves to documenting workers' lives. However, women workers are rarely the focus of French labor history, which deals with the social conditions or political culture of the working class, and rarely with its sexuality, unless it is grounded in studies of the family. A nonheterosexist discussion of the sexuality of working-class women is also irreparably hindered by the presupposition of repugnance to homosexuality and of hegemonic aggressive heterosexuality among workers.

This position has remained dear to a sizable portion of the left, in particular, the French Communist Party, founded in 1920, which exercised a durable influence on the organized section of the French working class and has historically followed a strictly Stalinist line. Thus, it has contributed to raising to dogma status the axiom that homosexuality is a luxury—and a vice—only the idle rich can afford. Nor were communists alone in taking this position.[16] Anarchists, who might have been expected to accept homosexuality, understood lesbianism no better. The "sexual liberation" they advocated remained an exclusively heterosexual affair, nor was "free love" always enthusiastically endorsed by the women in the movement as emancipation.[17] When Louise Michel was "accused" of being a lesbian by her right-wing detractors, her anarchist brothers strove to clear her name by constructing the myth of the "Red Virgin" whose passion for workers' rights transcended sexuality, and subsequent left-wing historians, such as Edith Thomas, a Communist Party historian of the women of the Commune, reinforced this notion.[18]

In this silence, against all odds, isolated figures of working-class lesbians do surface. These are the domestic workers, the cook Delphine and the maid Marie, whose amorous nocturnal noise troubled a confused ten-year-old Gide in his parents' house, or again, Colette's cook, who aggressively pursued the other female domestics in the neighborhood, writing them tersely negotiated billets-doux, and was fired by the embarrassed writer, known herself to have tasted same-sex love.[19] These are, in the household of an unnamed duchess, two servants who were lesbian lovers, and were found in the mistress's bedroom, arrested, taken to the infirmary, and diagnosed as suffering from "manic hysteria."[20] These are two very young millinery workers, in the Riom region in 1898, an orphan and a married woman, who fell in love in the shop and, overwhelmed with grief at the harshness of life, made a suicide pact and inhaled charcoal fumes. In what she intended to be her farewell letter, the married woman—who survived—wrote, "unable to live one without the other, we prefer to die together. We are happy at the thought." She concluded, "Before entering our last sleep, we ask to be buried side by side. We should love to have flowers on our grave."[21] Some working-class women who engaged in lesbian relationships were even famous for a time, such as Manet's model Victorine Meurent,[22] or Louise Weber, better known as La Goulue, who for years ruled the stage of the Moulin Rouge.[23]

Lesbians and the Sex Industry

It would be simple to blame the left alone for the silence surrounding lesbians within the French working class. Yet that apparent absence has also been constructed as a very significant presence in the classist and patriarchal terms of bourgeois discourses. Bourgeois conservatives or liberal reformers, from the nineteenth century to well into the twentieth century, repeatedly equated "sapphism" and prostitution, making the female sex worker a central figure in the story of poor lesbians and as well, establishing that to be a lesbian, a woman had to be a whore.

Some moral ideologues insisted on the "sexual purity" of working-class

people and made a considerable ideological investment in the purported innocence of the "folk" in all areas of sexuality, a problem familiar to folklorists,
because even the raunchy (heterosexual) content of folk literature was consistently expurgated until not so long ago.[24] Thus, characterizations of the sexual
mores of the working class oscillated between accusations of inbred immorality
and vice, evidenced foremost by prostitution, and the postulate of its inherent
childish innocence, which meant that "unnatural" vices such as homosexuality
and lesbianism were foreign to it and had to be induced in weak constitutions
by the debauched example and corruption of the upper classes.[25]

Taxil, however, like Fiaux and other writers of his time, was convinced that
"tribadism" completely infected the brothel world, and he suggested that if
prostitutes were questioned "in their own environment" (i.e., inside the
brothel), they would admit to their lesbian lifestyle without shame. Taxil
claimed that only the "lowest class" of prostitutes (i.e., those who cater to
workers) stuck to male pimp-lovers, while women in the higher echelons of
brothel hierarchy had female lovers only.[26] The implication that sexual preference is linked to class hierarchy within prostitution reinforced the floating
assumption that homosexuality—including lesbianism—is strictly a vice of
the rich. Fiaux, on the contrary, was convinced that few brothel inmates could
escape recruitment into tribadism and the "bi-uterine" relations he railed
against; in fact, he felt that prostitutes were corrupted a lot earlier than others
believed.[27] These remarks underscored the fact that "lesbianism" was not as
"acceptable" to (male) bourgeois society as has been claimed,[28] especially when
operating in "lower-class" contexts.

Invisible and yet visible: such was the paradox in the subsumed existence of
lesbian sex workers. While the day-to-day lives of these early lesbians seldom
reach us, "lesbian acts" fantasized or even invented by the broader culture were
made quite visible and enjoyed widespread popularity. The public exploitation
of titillating lesbian images and acts by a male-oriented sex industry was the
flip side of the invisibility coin, which the moralists did not fail to lay at
the doorstep of the "wealthy lesbian" brothel patrons, whom they excoriated
consistently.[29] The publicizing in the 1890s of lesbian scenes and clubs in
pleasure guides to Paris aimed at tourists has been documented.[30] Nor was it
always necessary for people seeking such entertainment to visit secret night-
spots. During the sudden fashion of nudity on stage in Paris in 1907, the Little
Palace theater produced a spectacular "scene of intoxication and lesbian passion," which had a great success, even though it landed its owner an original
sentence of three months in jail, with fifteen days each for the actresses, a
sentence subsequently doubled by a higher court. The judge had deemed the
performance entirely devoid of artistic feeling, stating that "because of its
brutal realism and revolting obscenity," it was simply "pornography."[31] This
type of "pornography" had become, by the early 1900s, standard fare at the
"better-class" brothels, which made their largest profits on the viewing of the
assorted "tableaux vivants," along with sadomasochistic practices and "lesbian

scenes" staged for the customers.[32] Its more popular and "soft-core" version was still available in the 1920s in the form of "tableaux vivants" in fair booths, such as the "Her Majesty, Woman" display seen by Brassai, which included a "Lesbos."[33]

Several famous incidents in the crime annals of the fin de siècle document without a doubt the existence and complexities of lesbian relationships among sex workers. Mélie Hélie, or la Grande Mélie, better known to posterity as "Casque d'Or," was a star of the crime columns of the early 1900s. A journalist convinced her to give him her story, which he rendered in flowery words for the paper Fin de Siècle.[34] Chautard, a typographer turned populist historian, gave a less flattering version of her as a prostitute, animal trainer, wrestler, and actress whose portrait almost made it to the 1902 Salon, who left her male lovers to live with female concubines.[35] Mélie consorted, for instance, with Hélène de la Courtille, a tough streetwalker who had definite same-sex preferences; she took the young Mélie under her protection and did not hesitate to fight with men who approached her friend too closely.[36]

In another case, Jeanne P., also known as La Mascotte, lived maritally with a certain Louise and knifed her in a fit of jealousy, provoked by her suspicion that Louise actually experienced pleasure with the men who paid her for sex, one among many of the violent scenes that made bar and hotel owners eject the women, often sustaining injuries at the hands of these combative women of the street.[37]

The most dramatic case may have been the story of Thérèse V., which covered the pages of the tabloid press in the 1890s. Thérèse was the sister of a burglar who died on his way to New Caledonia, a mother at fifteen, locked up in a penitentiary colony until the age of eighteen. She initially married but soon left home and became a prostitute to survive. She met Berthe, whose life story closely resembled her own, and they lived together as lovers. Again, both women were jealous and frequently fought, injuring each other with knives. After Berthe died of illness, Thérèse lived for two years with another woman. She then took up for five years with this woman's pimp, named Sylvain, after she had broken up with the woman. When Thérèse left him for another pimp, Sylvain, in the tradition of the milieu, hunted her down all over Paris and stabbed her to death. The response to Thérèse's death is as significant for our subject as her harsh life: her coffin was carried in a public procession through the neighborhood she had frequented, and, at the corner of the rue de Flandre and the boulevard de la Villette, it stopped in front of a group of women who placed a crown of flowers on it.[38] Thérèse had not been killed, however, for "her passions against nature," but rather for the classic crime of deserting her official exploiter. Significantly, it was women, not men, who placed flowers on the casket of one of their own who had defied the male order of the streets. The underworld, male and female, could thus accept lesbians in its ranks, closing around them the folds of its secret ways.

Lesbians in Jail Culture

Sex workers, as well as many other working-class women, spent a considerable amount of time in jail, for uncontrolled prostitution, various types of theft, abortion, infanticide, and, occasionally, homicide. By the early nineteenth century, crowded jail conditions were accused by doctors, reformers, and journalists of promoting the "ravages of lesbianism." Same-sex sexual activity and relationships were indeed frequent among women in jails and brothels, and characteristically lesbian attitudes about men and women, love and sex, the attendant rituals and social customs practiced by jail inmates, documented by these hostile but at times fastidious observers are striking. Police reports, journalistic exposés, and extensive collections of jail letters attest to social self-regulations among jail inmates, often marked by strictly defined and coded male/female roles. For instance, when a woman assaulted another for making advances to her lover and was locked up and chained as a result, she would say that her girlfriend "lui a fait un enfant" (made her pregnant).[39]

The account of one professional investigative reporter was distinctly hostile. Robert Boucard's *Les Dessous des prisons de femmes* (completed in 1929), promises, by its very title (*dessous* meaning at once the "hidden side" and "underwear"), a lurid description of women left to themselves. He depicts nights during which women were subject to "odious contacts," and wild women attacked others, sometimes to contaminate them. In the custom of the "prison baptism," every newcomer was subjected to the desires of the whole group, then, officially "married" to an inmate, blessed by all, and subjected to terrible punishment if she left her appointed consort. Boucard provided no explanation for the apparent contradiction between this custom of collectively enforced "marriage" and the complicated courting process described in letters sent to freely chosen lovers. At the same time, he mentioned more benign customs, such as the trade in flowers, which was allowed for a time at Saint-Lazare: flower girls from the outside plied romantic lovers with roses, violets, or carnations, which were strewn on the bed of the woman they wished to woo; this practice ended when competition for specific women turned the flower language into fistfights.[40]

An important consequence of Boucard's exposé is a plea for jail reform, making a case for solitary reclusion rather than communal internment and its "repulsive nocturnal promiscuity." One of the rampant themes of this exposé is that women are bearers of disease and contamination. Many inmates indeed suffered from venereal disease, and "venereals" were accused of spreading their infection on purpose, by sexually assaulting other women. These women, "caged" in the "Ménagerie" (wild animal farm or zoo), remained raucously rebellious. They scribbled in the sand of their cages inscriptions like "death to man, death to all men," The Great Panther of the Boul'Mich has been caged here for the fifth time," and "You can't tame the Tigress from Belleville."[41]

Carco's observations about women who loved other women, recorded in the late 1920s but published later, were slightly more sympathetic. He claimed that women committed suicide, for instance by swallowing broken glass, when they were separated too long from their lovers. Some simply showed a willingness to suffer physical harm for their lover's sake: they would stick long, sharp needles in their arms. He also reported that women were divided along strictly gendered roles, although laws governing female dress created specific obstacles to gendered dress: pants could be worn only by special permission. The women who took on the role of men had to arrange their clothes with pins to resemble pants, and they wore an embroidered insignia, a heart and dagger, on their jail shoes. These public displays of cultural codes "for women" did not fail to attract harsh punishments, but the women remained intractable.[42]

Women's jails were often subject to extremely harsh rules of absolute silence. Yet women broke that silence by initiating a vast system of correspondence, the *biftons,* notes passed to lovers inside and friends outside with the complicity of guards, networks of friends in jail, or the jail hierarchy of newer inmates working for older ones. Ingenious methods to evade detection included hiding letters behind official notice boards or inside the vagina,[43] but these letters were constantly being seized by the authorities. The substantial collections we can read today are but a fraction of the extensive communications between women throughout prisons.

Letters to female lovers emphasized several consistent themes: the pain of separation from the lover, sexual desire, the woes of imprisonment, the bad treatment at the hands of the guards and occasional retaliation, hatred and contempt for men, especially their lovers' "men," and threats and warnings against adultery.[44] In some letters, the expression of love borrowed from the rhetoric of maternal love, but it quickly added correctives. Some expressed the wish to build a culture of separatism, devoid of men. Some of the letters exposed to a hesitant noninitiate, in rather fine rhetoric, the advantages and pleasures of love with a woman. Many letters expressed the conviction that the women were formally married, stating, for instance, "although we haven't gone to bed, we are married," "signed: your legitimate wife."[45]

For women of those days, the step from working class to underclass was often short. Job scarcity and professional limits kept young working-class girls out of many trades, and unions even participated in this exclusion. Workers' political parties inveighed against the destruction of the family by the bourgeois industrial machine and extolled traditional roles for women, and the absence of independent means of support made it difficult for many women to face life alone.

For working-class women who wanted to live a life dedicated to same-sex love, the imperatives of economic survival were overwhelming. It is significant that in an interview, a young lesbian factory worker in the 1970s stated that she could handle the taunts and jeers from her coworkers on the job but found her low pay and the impossibility to be promoted or to advance professionally as a woman worse than periodic harassment.[46] Thus, the history of French working-class lesbians remains inscribed even today in the uneasy fortunes of women.

Should social background and education make it possible to live in ways not consonant with mainstream norms, the meaning of crossing class barriers was very different for men and for women. Two homosexual men, for instance, one the salon anarchist and social conservative, anti-dreyfusard Jean Lorrain (1855–1906), the other, the anticolonialist, anarchist, and socialist Daniel Guérin (1904–1988), enjoyed contacts, social and sexual, with young working-class men that they saw as indispensable. Lorrain died from health problems due to the abuse of ether, and Guérin died of old age.[47]

How telling is the contrast with the story of the enigmatic Madeleine Pelletier. Pelletier was born in a milieu of very lower-middle-class, impoverished shopkeepers and grew up humiliated and resentful of her poverty, which she actively sought to escape. Through a university system newly opened to women, she obtained her degree as a doctor of medicine. Suffocating under the constraints of her sex, Pelletier dressed habitually as a man, a task facilitated by a rotund physique that did not necessarily identify her as feminine. In this manner of dress, she stormed political meetings and attended conventions. Curious spectators asked, "What is *that*? A man or a woman?" She donned her male clothes to walk the streets, alone at night, perplexed and fascinated at being taken for a man, entreated by streetwalkers who called, "tu viens, mon gros?" Pelletier professed complete disdain for sex, advocated virginity, and asserted that she did not seek Lesbos at all. Yet her correspondence with her closest friend, Arria Ly (another mannishly dressed woman who denied being a lesbian), indicated unrequited erotic feelings toward her. In her correspondence with Caroline Kauffman, she admitted that she found same-sex relations perfectly normal and would have liked to have a girlfriend, if she were sure of her discretion. She would have even written a sonnet on the topic, including the verse "When, with a knowing hand/I caress your lovely breast, My sweet friend."

What Lorrain and Guérin lived freely, and spoke about occasionally, Pelletier was unable even to articulate. Rather than deal with issues of sexuality, she put all her energy into public action, as a socialist and a feminist. She took risks, fought for unpopular causes, and courted danger. During the war, dressed as a man, she came close to being lynched by a crowd in Nancy comprising many women, as the police checked her papers, taking her for a spy. In an ironic twist, Pelletier, a pacifist, had unsuccessfully attempted to serve in the French army's medical corps during World War I. She decided to travel alone to the front, in the midst of the battle of the Marne, and watched, in the silence of battlefields void of combatants but strewn with corpses. When she had seen it all, and had faced down fear, she went home, embittered again. Pelletier's life ended tragically. She was interned for insanity, in actuality as punishment for performing abortions, and died of a broken heart.[48] Pelletier's missed opportunities, contrasted with Lorrain or Guérin, are a brutal reminder of the discrepancies in social conditions wrought by class and aggravated by gender.

Today, historical research provides the texture of community memories that are eroded by indifference and even violently erased. Every shred of this memory, the very process of gathering it, takes on, for lesbian and gay historians, special meaning. The women and men of the past whose lives we study moved at times painfully, at times gracefully through their own layers of invisibility. They force us to think of their lives around same-sex desire as more than a poorly developed blueprint for the present, to acknowledge their courage and their affirmation of agency. To reach for the "invisible women" of working-class France is to confront and challenge silence, to seek survival—theirs and ours—in the continuum of recovered memory.

Notes

1. These layers of silence evoke Diana Collecott's discussion of the "silence of lesbian erasure": lesbians can be heard only if one learns to listen to the "double talk" particular to the oppressed, historically used by slaves, women, and homosexuals. "What Is Not Said: A Study in Textual Inversion," in *Sexual Sameness: Textual Differences in Lesbian and Gay Writing*, ed. Joseph Bristow (London: Routledge, 1992), 91–110.

2. Marie-Jo Bonnet, for instance, takes vigorously to task those writers who constantly assume that they can simply infer lesbian sexuality from knowledge of male homosexuality by merely inverting the gender terms. Marie-Jo Bonnet, *Un Choix sans équivoque* (Paris: Denoël-Gonthier, 1981), 184–85.

3. Marc Daniel and André Baudry, *Les Homosexuels* (Paris: Casterman, 1973), 135–36. The authors even assert that a few lesbians were burned in the Middle Ages but in no common measure with sodomites "because they cannot physically commit the abominable act of anal penetration."

4. Catherine Valabrègue, *Le Droit de vivre autrement: Modes de vie inhabituels, enquêtes et témoignages* (Paris: Denoël-Gonthier, 1975), interview, 109–20.

5. Claudie Lesselier, "Silenced Resistance and Conflictual Identities: Lesbians in France, 1930–1968," *Journal of Homosexuality* 25, no. 3 (1993): 105–25.

6. See in particular Shari Benstock, *Women of the Left Bank: Paris, 1900–1940* (Austin: University of Texas Press, 1986); and also Catherine Van Casselaer, *Lot's Wife: Lesbian Paris, 1880–1914* (London: Janus Press, 1986).

7. Elizabeth Lapovsky Kennedy and Madeline Davis, *Boots of Leather, Slippers of Gold: The History of a Lesbian Community* (New York: Routledge, 1993) is a model for this type of scholarship within the academy. Personal histories and testimonies about lesbian working-class life have been preserved by Joan Nestle in several works, *A Restricted Country* (Ithaca, Firebrand, 1987) and *The Persistent Desire* (Boston: Alyson, 1992), while Audre Lorde's autobiography, *Zami: A New Spelling of My Name* New York: Persephone, 1982, devoted substantial sections to factory life and political organizing. Community history projects such as the Lesbian Herstory Archives and the San Francisco Lesbian and Gay History Project have taken painstaking care in documenting the lives of working-class lesbians.

8. Anne-Marie Sohn, "*La Garçonne* face à l'opinion publique," *Le Mouvement Social* 80 (July–September 1972): 3–27, 13–14.

9. Claudie Lesselier, "The Woman's Movement and the Extreme Right in France," in *The Nature of the Right: A Feminist Analysis of Order Patterns,* ed. Gill Seide (Amsterdam: Benjamins, 1988), 173–85.

10. See, for instance, Hélène de Monferrand's (very soft) lesbian pulp novel *Les Amies d'Héloïse* (Paris: Editions de Fallois, 1990), whose main character is a supporter of the OAS. Nor is this novel particularly marginal: it was published in the widely distributed French paperback series Le Livre de Poche and received the Prix Goncourt for a first novel in 1990.

11. Along with the woman poet-artist Claude Cahun, Crevel was the only other openly homosexual member of the surrealist movement; he killed himself at the age of thirty-five.

12. Gilles Barbedette and Michel Carassou, *Paris Gay 1925* (Paris: Presses de la Renaissance, 1981).

13. Léo Taxil, *La Corruption fin de siècle* (Paris: Henri Noirot, 1891), 262.

14. Daniel Guérin, interview, in Gérard Bach, *Homosexualités: Expression-répression* (Paris: Le Sycomore, 1982), 99–103.

15. Interview in Valabrègue, *Le Droit de vivre autrement,* 120.

16. For the shifting communist position on sex, sexuality, and homosexuality in the 1930s, see François Delpia, "Les Communistes français et la sexualité (1932–36)," *Le Mouvement Social* 91 (1975): 121–52.

17. Claire Auzias, *Mémoires libertaires, Lyon, 1919–1939* (Paris: Editions de l'Harmattan, 1993), 253–55.

18. Marie Marmo Mullaney, "Sexual Politics in the Career and Legend of Louise Michel," *Signs* 15 (1990): 300–322.

19. Colette, *Mes Apprentissages* (Paris: Hachette, 1972), 127–28, quoted in Van Casselaer, *Lot's Wife,* 112.

20. Ali Coffignon, *Paris vivant: La Corruption à Paris* (Paris: Kolb, 1889), 303–4.

21. Louis Proal, *Le Crime et le suicide passionnels* (Paris: Felix Alcan, 1990), 80–81.

22. See Eunice Lipton's study of Meurent, *Alias Olympia: A Woman's Search for Manet's Notorious Model and Her Own Desire* (New York: Scribner, 1992).

23. La Goulue's long-standing involvement with a woman was acknowledged by Yvette Guilbert, *La Chanson de ma vie: Mémoires* (Paris: Grasset, 1927), 61–63, and virtuously denied by a recent biographer, Michel Souvais, *Les Cancans de la Goulue* (Paris: Les Compagnons de Montmartre, 1991). For a more extensive discussion of her life, see Francesca Canadé Sautman, "Invisible Women: Lesbian Working-Class Culture in France, 1880–1930" in *Homosexuality in Modern France,* ed. Jeffrey Merrick and Bryant T. Ragan, Jr. (New York: Oxford University Press, 1996) On La Goulue as entrepreneur and orientalism in Paris see Zeynep Çelik and Leila Kinney, "Ethnography and exhibitionism at the Expositions Universelle Assemblage 13 (Dec. 1990). 35–59, 50–55.

24. On the erasure or erotic and obscene folklore by the academy, see Claude Gaignebet, *Art profane et religion populaire au moyen âge* (Paris: Presses Universitaires de France, 1985), 19–31.

25. Julien Chevalier, *Une Maladie de la personnalité: L'Inversion sexuelle* (Lyon: A. Storck, 1893), 228–229.

26. Gabriel Antoine Jogand-Pagès [Leo Taxil, pseudo.], *La Prostitution contemporaine* (Paris: Librairie Populaire, 1884), 172. Taxil used the pseudonym to avoid problems with censorship but was still fined for the few explicit engravings contained in the book.

27. Louis Fiaux, *Les Maisons de tolérance* (Paris: Georges Carré, 1892), 137–48.

28. Van Casselaer, *Lot's Wife,* 8, 115.

29. Taxil, *Corruption,* 254–58; Fiaux, *Maisons,* 144–47; Chevalier, *Une Maladie,* 235.

30. Michael Wilson, " 'Sans les femmes, qu'est-ce qui nous resterait?': Gender and Transgression in Bohemian Montmartre," in *Body Guards: The Cultural Politics of*

Gender Ambiguity, ed. Julia Epstein and Kristina Straub (New York: Routledge, 1991), 195–222; 221 n. 58.

31. G. J. Witkowski and L. Nass, *Le Nu au theâtre depuis l'Antiquité jusqu'à nos jours* (Paris: Darangon, 1909), 272–84.

32. Alain Corbin, *Women for Hire,* translated from the French (Cambridge: Harvard University Press, 1990), 81.

33. Brassaï [Gyula Hacász], *Le Paris secret des années trente* (Paris: Gallimard, 1976), "La Fête foraine," 16–23.

34. Pierre Drachline and Claude Petit-Castelli, *Casque d'or et les Apaches* (Paris: Renaudot, 1990).

35. E. Chautard, *Goualantes de la Villete et d'ailleurs* (Paris: Marcel Seheur, 1929), 86–87.

36. Drachline and Petit-Castelli, *Casque d'or,* 21–25, 44–45.

37. Chautard, *Goualantes,* 89.

38. Ibid., 94–98.

39. Chevalier, *Une Maladie,* 242.

40. Robert Boucard, *Les Dessous des prisons de femmes: Des documents, des faits: Comment elles vivent, se pervertissent, expient* (Paris: Editions de France, 1930), 6, 78–9, 194–95, 54–55. We might note that the publisher is the same one who produced Carco's reportage.

41. Ibid., 6, 197, 70–79.

42. Francis Carco, *Prisons de femmes* (Paris: Editions de France, 1938), 6–17.

43. A. Galopin, *Les Enracinées* (Paris: Fayard, 1903), 203–4, 244–45, 245–46, 280, 255, 202, 58–60, 262–63, 285–87, 238–41, 272–73.

44. The sexual content of these letters is guite explicit, notwithstanding commentary on women in jails that seeks to negate it. Gisele Ginsberg, for instance, in *Des prisons et des femmes* (Paris: Ramsay, 1992), 154–61, suggests that female "homosexuality" is not "sexual," that sex between women in jail is merely one more form of oppression, or sex is presented as "male" while women supposedly seek only maternal love and nurturing tenderness.

45. Galopin, *Les Enracinées,* 216–18; in French, "la légitimate" is the legally married wife, as opposed to the common-law wife.

46. Interview in Valabrègue, *Le Droit de vivre autrement,* 109–15.

47. Guérin is being rediscovered by the French gay community. An exhibit at the Centre gai et lesbien in Paris in June 1995 and an essay ("Hommage à Daniel Guérin," 3 *Keller: Le Mensuel du Centre gai et lesbien,* June 1995, 41–47) were dedicated to him; a video *(Daniel Guérin ou l'art de la dissidence: Combats dans le siècle)* is also being made about his life and work by Laurent Muhlheisen, Patrice Spadoni, and Jan-louis Touton.

48. She also traveled unofficially to the Soviet Union, walking and crawling under barbed wires at the border with Estonia to enter. For Pelletier's biography, see Claude Maignien and Charles Sowerwine, *Madeleine Pelletier, une féministe dans l'arène politique* (Paris: Editions Ouvrières, 1992), 140–51.

19

Homosexuality and the Sociological Imagination: The 1950s and 1960s

Jeffrey Escoffier

Perhaps the fruitful distinction with which the sociological imagination works is between "the personal troubles of milieu" and the "public issues of social structure."

No social study that does not come back to the problems of biography, of history and of their intersections within society has completed its intellectual journey.

—C. Wright Mills, *The Sociological Imagination*

For me, the process of discovering "the gay world"—it was another part of coming out—started with reading. By searching through the available knowledge I needed in order to identify myself as "a homosexual," I adopted positive representations and rejected homophobic ones. In the late 1950s and early 1960s there were no maps to guide an earnest young homosexual through the quagmire of discourses dominated by medical and psychiatric theories. I have begun to see the map of discourses only now, some thirty years later, as I try to understand the role played by the popular sociological books on homosexuality.

At the time, during the early 1960s, I read everything I could lay my hands on. While I read my way through the literature on homosexuality, new ideas about homosexuality were circulating through the hodgepodge of discourses regulating interpretations of homosexuality—popular, psychological, legal, or literary—that reported on the discovery that homosexuals had a social world of their own, a community even. This "discovery" of the homosexual subculture was increasingly accompanied by the idea that homosexuality was a benign variation of sexual behavior. Thus the process of my socialization into "the homosexual role" (as sociologist Mary McIntosh called it) can only be understood by locating the historically specific conjuncture of the hegemonic discourses on homosexuality, the circulation through the interlocking net of these discourses of new ideas about homosexual identity and community, and my own rather idiosyncratic process of reading.

One of the most important developments for lesbians and gay men in the 1950s and 1960s was the increasing appearance of public representations that revealed the *social* dimension of gay life. The existence of a homosexual social world implied that lesbians and gay men could lead a life (even if it was a secret to the nonhomosexuals in their lives) that included friends, durable relationships, and a social and cultural life.

It is almost impossible to get any idea of what effect the popular sociology literature had on homosexuals themselves—there were no surveys, and no one collected readership statistics or sales figures to tell us who or how many people read these books. So I have decided to use myself, as a young man in this period coming to terms with my homosexuality, as a piece of evidence, a way of gauging the significance of this small body of publications.

The Discovery of the Social

In the years before Stonewall the psychiatric discourse on homosexuality was hegemonic: Edmund Bergler, *Homosexuality: Disease or a Way of Life* (1957); Irving Bieber, *Homosexuality* (1962); Albert Ellis, *Homosexuality: Its Causes and Cure* (1964); Charles Socarides, *The Overt Homosexual* (1968); Lionel Ovesey, *Homosexuality and Pseudo-homosexuality* (1969); and Lawrence Hatterer, *Changing Homosexuality in the Male* (1970). "The only pro-gay book of the 1950s, Donald Cory's *The Homosexual in America*, was published by a tiny publishing house and was generally unavailable."[1]

The emergence of a discourse of popular sociology about homosexuality initiated a process that potentially disrupted the hegemony of the psychiatric discourse of individual pathology. The refashioning of homosexuality as a social phenomenon, rather than a purely psychological or individual one, was established by two means—first, by the definition of *homosexuality as a social problem* (ambiguously framed as a problem of the social adjustment of homosexuals or the elimination of prejudice against homosexuals), and second, the public recognition of *the existence of a homosexual social world*. Starting in the immediate postwar period and up through the 1960s, homosexuality emerged as a social issue in a number of different bodies of discourse.[2]

In the immediate period after World War II homosexuality emerged into the American public consciousness with an unanticipated vigor. Homosexuality as a public issue was firmly established by the controversy that followed in the wake of Alfred Kinsey's findings on the widespread prevalence of homosexual experience.[3] This was later reinforced by Senator Joseph McCarthy's highly publicized witchhunt in the early 1950s to fire homosexuals as well as communists from government employment. These two events alone probably had more to do with making homosexuality an issue in American public life than any other source.

In addition to the 1948 publication of the Kinsey report on male sexual behavior, most of the fiction of the 1940s that dealt with male homosexuality was published in only two years—1948 and 1949.[4] The threat of homosexuality to the postwar social order as well as the plight of homosexuals were extensively examined in novels, plays, and popular magazines.[5] Images of the gay social world also began to surface in the mass media in the 1960s. Three of the more notable examples were the famous gay bar scene in the popular Hollywood movie *Advise and Consent* (1962), one of the first representations of gay life in movies since the Production Code was adopted in the 1930s; the 1964 *Life* magazine article "Homosexuality in America"; and finally the *Esquire* article "The New Homosexuality" in December 1969.[6]

Nevertheless, throughout the 1950s and early 1960s, the literary and popular sociology discourses on homosexuality were situated within a network of discursive formations in which psychoanalysis remained the hegemonic discourse on homosexuality.[7] The Kinsey reports, for example, had almost no impact on psychoanalytic discussions. In fact, the psychoanalytic profession's writing on male homosexuality throughout the 1950s and early 1960s took on an ever more moralistic tone and tended increasingly to reflect conventional social values.[8] The conformism of the postwar era emphasized the norm and stigmatized the deviant. It is in this period that an academic literature on the sociology of deviance also emerged. Initially the problem of deviance was interpreted as one of psychological maladjustment.

One of the strongest and most articulate voices opposed to attributing deviance to psychological maladjustment was that of psychoanalyst Robert Lindner, best known as the author of a booklength case history called *Rebel without a Cause: The Story of a Criminal Psychopath* (the movie of the same title shares little more than the title itself). In a series of essays first published in 1956 under the title *Must You Conform?* Lindner explored the issues of rebellious youth, political dissent, educational theory, *and* homosexuality.[9] Lindner saw homosexuality as a "solution to the conflict between the urgency of the sexual instincts and repressive efforts brought to bear upon sexual expression by the reigning sex morality."[10] Yet while Robert Lindner promoted rebellion against conformity and criticized prejudice against homosexuals, he also claimed that "the proposal that homosexuality is directly related to sex-conformance pressure offers the hope that it can be eradicated." He believed that "homosexuality is the source of immense quantities of unhappiness and frustration of individuals and a chronically irritating generator of intrahuman hostility."[11] He saw the emergence of a homosexual movement, however admirable as a form of rebellion, as evidence that "culture, the maker of man ... now threatens to unman him. ... at this point culture, now designated Society, abandons humanity."[12] Lindner's style of discourse owes a great deal to the radical psychoanalyst Wilhelm Reich, and like Reich's thinking on homosexuality it implied that heterosexuality and standard forms of gender behavior were biological norms. Nevertheless Lindner's work offers an interesting attempt to identify the role of social processes and the repression by those processes of homosexuality. But Lindner, along with other radicals, was unable to acknowledge the positive role of sociation and institutionalized social life in the gay community.[13]

The ambivalence of the discourse constituted by the critique of conformism provided no useful way for most homosexuals to distinguish between the possibility of actively acknowledging one's homosexuality (thereby rejecting the repressive effects of conformism) and accepting oneself as a homosexual, an unhappy and frustrated kind of rebel, who should be willing to give up such a hopelessly negative form of revolt.[14]

Discussions of homosexuality in the critical discourse on conformity and alienation or in mainstream journalism and the mass media were not able to escape the power of the psychological and cultural norms that dominated American social life in this period. Nor did the acknowledgment of homosexuality as a social problem immediately provide the symbolic capital necessary to banish the stigmatizing norms of mainstream American culture; only the exploration of the already existing social life of homosexuals could provide public categories of social knowledge that demonstrated the possibility of homosexual life as an everyday reality.

A Popular Sociology of Homosexuality

During the 1950s and 1960s popular sociology books frequently made the best-seller list: *The Lonely Crowd* (1950) by David Reisman, *The Organization Man* (1956) by William Whyte, C. Wright Mills's *Power Elite* (1956), Robert Lindner's *Must You Conform?* (1956), Vance Packard's *Hidden Persuaders* (1957), Paul Goodman's *Growing Up Absurd* (1960). These books—all profoundly critical of the status quo and the culture of conformism—were highly influential on the American politics and culture of the period. They all grew out of a deep sense of frustration and were motivated by the possibility of social change. They all recognized the growing desire for social reform in American life.

Homosexuality was ripe for popular sociology. From 1951 and continuing up through 1968, the year before the Stonewall riots, almost a dozen books were published that sought to portray the social world of the homosexual.[15] This series of books presented a new genre of works addressed to the general public; they were books of popular sociology that explored homosexuality as a *social* problem—in the words of Martin Hoffman, author of *The Gay World*, "perhaps *the most serious undiscussed problem* in the United States today."[16]

It is not at all clear whether academic sociology had any influence whatsoever on these books of popular sociology.[17] But several authors—Donald Webster Cory[18] and Martin Hoffman, for example—may have been aware of the interactionist tradition in American sociology, which influenced the sociology of deviance during the 1960s.[19] Whether they were aware of it or not, their books would easily have fit into that tradition. The interactionist tradition in sociology seeks to explain human action as the result of the meanings that interacting social actors attach to actions and things. For example, members of the symbolic interactionist school (one of the most influential schools in this tradition) interpreted deviance "*not* [as] a quality of the act a person commits but rather [as] the consequence of the application by others of rules and sanctions to an 'offender'."[20]

The interactionist tradition (going back to Georg Simmel, pragmatism, and George Herbert Mead) emphasizes sociation and interaction as the constitutive acts of the social.[21] This contrasts sharply with the implied concept of society found in other authors, like Robert Lindner, who believed that all postwar forms of social life repressed "healthy" instinctual energies, or like Jess Stern, who seemed to believe that social life represented an ideal moral order that was being destroyed from within by antisocial or decadent behavior. Throughout this period psychological works that often treated homosexuality as an individualized pathological form of sexual behavior remained the most influential genre of nonfiction works dealing with homosexuality for a general audience.[22]

The new popular sociology approach marked a growing awareness of the *social existence of homosexual communities* in American cities. Among these authors, both Donald Cory and Martin Hoffman knew that the existence and development of a gay social world implied something new and important about homosexuality. While two of the popular sociology books explored lesbian life, this discourse was preoccupied with male homosexuality.

An obsessive interest in effeminacy and its significance in gay male life runs through most of the books that deal with male homosexuality. Homosexual desires were widely experienced as a threat to a man's masculinity. Cory emphatically downplays the cultural presence of flamboyant effeminacy. The queen, he states, "is a rarity even in gay circles."[23] But he does go on to give a loving portrait of drag balls.[24] Stern, however, constantly uses words like "mincing," "swishing," and "sashaying" as if they were objective terms of description. We know that effeminacy, camp humor, and drag were prominent aspects of gay life in the 1950s and early 1960s. And we also know that fear of effeminacy prohibited many men from acknowledging their homosexuality and entering the gay social world.

The first work to reveal the social world of homosexuals came naturally enough from within the homosexual community itself. Under the pseudonym Donald Webster Cory, Edward Sagarin (who later, ironically, became an extremely homophobic critic of gay liberation) published the first exploration of homosexual society in 1951. Between 1951 and 1964 Cory and his occasional collaborator, John P. LeRoy, published the four most thorough and sophisticated books about homosexual life to appear before Stonewall. Cory's books covered the full range of gay life—relationships, the social origins of homophobia, the role of gay bars, the significance of the gay contribution to culture, and a critique of the psychological theory of homosexuality. Cory's books probably never reached a very large public because they were all published by small publishing houses, although at least one, *The Lesbian in America*, was reprinted in mass-market paperback form by MacFadden Books in 1965.

It would be interesting to know about the concrete social situation that enabled Donald Webster Cory to write and publish *The Homosexual in America* in 1951—the first work of American popular sociology on homosexuality. Cory's book, an ambitious defense of the homosexual way of life, derives its strength from Cory's fundamental belief that homosexual patterns of behavior are socially constructed. Moreover, Cory quite self-consciously views the existence of a gay social world as the necessary foundation of the happiness of homosexuals.[25] In his concluding chapter he directly addresses his fellow homosexuals, and one of his most ardent pleas is "Do not fear the group life of the gay world." "In the gay life," he urges us, "you can be yourself and form friendships with those who know what you are and who accept you and love you. . . . The group life is not a thing of shame, a den of iniquity. It is a circle of protection, a necessary part of a minority society."[26]

But even such a profoundly sociological approach could not escape the hegemony of psychiatric discourse. Over and over again Cory takes on those notions about homosexuals that are derived from psychiatry—the causes of homosexuality, whether it is possible to cure homosexuals, whether sublimation offers a way to avoid a homosexual way of life—and offers many strong and cogent criticisms of the psychiatric arguments.

If Cory displays any ambivalence it is in the way he dismisses certain aspects of gay life that he believes throw a bad light on it. One of the most significant is his discussion of effeminacy; another is his dismissal of the significance of alcoholism. In addition, there is no discussion at all of "really embarrassing" topics like sexually transmitted diseases or sex in public restrooms (tearooms). His discussion of effeminacy overlooks the cultural centrality of camp, and he dismisses as a stereotype the importance of queens in the gay life of the 1940s and 1950s. The major tragedy of gay life, in Cory's view, is the need for concealment. He interprets many of the psychological characteristics and social patterns of gay life as resulting from the power of the stigma and the protective need for concealment.

In the middle of this twenty-year publishing arc there appeared *The Sixth Man* (on male homosexuality) and *The Grapevine* (on lesbians), two books by Jess Stern, a former reporter for the *New York Daily News* and an editor of *Newsweek*. They were published by Doubleday, as well as in mass-market paperback form. Jess Stern claims that his study of male homosexuals, *The Sixth Man*, "is as unbiased a report . . . as a disinterested reporter could make it."[27] But despite his stated intention to present a neutral, journalistic approach,

Stern's books display ambivalence, hypocrisy, and contempt. Homosexuality in Stern's view is a tragedy for homosexuals and society. The homosexual world, he writes, is "a glittering make-believe world—at times tragic, sometimes ludicrous, even comical." The tragic aspect of gay lives is so apparent to him that he announces, "I had yet to meet a truly happy homosexual."[28] It is this very idea of tragedy that encapsulates the liberal moralist's expression of sympathy and contempt.

Stern's exploration of the new gay social world is set within the grand narrative of "the Decline of the West."[29] Virtually every chapter recounts the negative impact of homosexuality on American life. Stern devotes several chapters—the most vicious ones in the book—to the role of homosexuals in the fashion industry. He believes that homosexuals are an overwhelmingly bad influence on the fashion industry and that they are responsible for promoting fashion models who are beautiful but too thin and flat chested, because homosexuals hate women and want women to look like boys.[30] Other chapters examine the impact of homosexuals on the entertainment industry, office work, and gyms and the marriages of closeted gay men to unsuspecting women. Everywhere the presence of homosexuals undermines the norms of gender roles and sexual decency—because homosexuals are secretive and vindictive.

One of the most important contributions to the new discourse that built on the discovery of the social was Hendrik Ruitenbeek's anthology *The Problem of Homosexuality in Modern Society*, published as a widely available quality paperback original by E. P. Dutton. It captured perfectly the ambivalent mix of psychoanalysis and sociology. Ruitenbeek's anthology republished a series of classic psychoanalytic essays by Sandor Ferenczi, Abram Kardiner, and Clara Thompson on the theory of homosexuality. It also included Freud's famous and very sympathetic "Letter to an American Mother" and Simone de Beauvoir's chapter from *The Second Sex* on "The Lesbian," and it was one of the only books (if not *the* only book) that made available to a broad public Evelyn Hooker's pathbreaking article on the psychologically well adjusted homosexual. It also included a number of articles of neutral sociological description of the homosexual community by sociologists like Albert Reiss, Maurice Leznoff, and William Westley, as well as a number of pieces on hustlers and George Devereaux's classic study of institutionalized homosexuality among the Mohave Indians. While it had a more intellectual tone than any of the others, the anthology was widely available in paperback.

Toward the end of the period Martin Hoffman's book *The Gay World* appeared. In addition to being the first and only one of these books to use the term "gay" in the title, it also was published in a widely circulated mass-market paperback format that still can be easily found in secondhand bookstores. Like the work of Robert Lindner and many of these books (except the work of Donald Cory), *The Gay World* is an amalgam of sociological observation and psychiatric expertise, yet it offers a fairly positive account of gay social life, tinged only with a concern for the difficult and sad state of affairs that homosexuals must experience.

Popular sociology represented the discovery by both homosexuals and non-homosexuals of an image of the gay social world—an imagined community. Both kinds of readers read these books and articles "to find themselves" through either a process of identification or one of counteridentification. They read these works to sort out their relation to the imagined homosexual world of American society in the 1950s and 1960s. In many of these works, the lives of homosexuals were presented as tortured and unfulfilled, even if only because of the social oppression. Such an ambivalent discourse made the process of individual identity formation fraught with misrecognitions.[31] There were several different types of gay readers. Those who were already familiar with the gay social world had found it by going to the bars, cruising in the parks and toilets, and through friends. But the vast majority of homosexuals were isolated and asocial members of the homosexual minority—they were in the closet. The popular sociology discourse, the literary discourse, and the psychoanalytic discourse were encountered by closeted gay men who used these discourses to name themselves, describe themselves, judge themselves—and by these means homosexualize themselves.

My Own Private Discourse: Reading in the Closet

By the time I graduated from college in 1964 I was twenty-one. I had come to see myself as homosexual—"queer," as I often thought with a certain vacillating mixture of acceptance and self-contempt. I still had had no experience of the homosexual world itself, although I did have a number of homosexual affairs while I was at college. But I had put together my own representation of the homosexual world primarily from literary works and books like Hendrik Ruitenbeek's anthology.

My main strategy of "consciousness-raising" (or as we might say now, identity formation) was reading.[32] This was an essential way of learning about homosexuality for a young college student who had little contact with (or even initially, little idea of how to contact) other homosexual men or the gay community. As Roland Barthes observed, "reading is steeped in Desire (or Disgust)." Later, during my summer vacations, I supplemented my reading by cruising in Washington Square Park. Reading and cruising are not such dissimilar techniques. Both require the "reading" of signs and the construction of a discourse that opened oneself to a knowledge of homosexualities and a constant reconstruction of one's sense of self.[33] Responsiveness to or identification with other cultural themes and figures has significantly affected the crystalization of homosexual identities—for men, interest in opera, female popular singers, artistic sensibility, or even a strong disinterest in sports. The role of cultural media has been often extremely important to the personal development of homosexuals. Reading also always involves the "double misreading of [the reader's] unconscious and of his ideology," and in the process discovers one's desires, fantasies, and even one's imagined place in society.[34]

My own private discourse started when I had my first homosexual affair, during the summer between my sophomore and junior years of high school. I remember that Richie and I decided that we weren't fags as long as we didn't kiss—although we fucked, sucked, and rimmed. Did I really believe that I wasn't a fag if we didn't kiss? I don't think so, but I thought agreeing with that statement would reassure Richie.

I have no memory of what led me to James Baldwin's *Giovanni's Room*.[35] It may have been an accident that I discovered it at the main library on Staten Island.[36] *Giovanni's Room* was the most explicit rendering of homosexual love I had ever encountered. I still have a vivid memory of some of its scenes that date from my first reading. In *Giovanni's Room*, Baldwin recounts the main character David's first romantic homosexual affair as an adolescent as a transfigurative experience of love, but one that also opened up a "cavern . . . in my mind, black, full of rumor, suggestion . . . I could have cried, cried for shame and terror, cried for not understanding how this could have happened to me."[37] After repeated flights from homosexual relationships David becomes involved with a woman, Hella, only to fall in love once more with a man, Giovanni. Baldwin's novel showed the prefigurative hope of homosexual love, but that love is undermined by what he portrayed as the nightmarish homosexual underworld of desperate sex. The image of homosexuality that Baldwin created forced me to recognize myself as "queer," but it did nothing to reconcile me to the gay world. In fact, Baldwin offered a picture of homosexual love that was doomed to fail, largely because the gay social world could not sustain it.

I began to look for other books that would help me understand myself. Soon I found Norman Mailer's *Advertisements for Myself*.[38] It contained two essays, "The White Negro" and "The Homosexual Villain," that gave me license to think more adventurously about my homosexuality.

The essay "The Homosexual Villain" was a modest and candid piece that Mailer wrote for the homosexual rights magazine *One*. It is a self-examination of Mailer's use of homosexuality as a character trait of several villains in his novels. But what particularly impressed me was his laudatory discussion of Donald Webster Cory's *Homosexual in America*. "I can think of few books," Mailer wrote, "which cut so radically at my prejudices and altered my ideas so profoundly." Mailer realized that he had been closing himself off from understanding a very large part of life.[39] He also acknowledged that the insight Cory's book had given him had helped him realize that anxieties about "latent homosexuality" had disappeared with acceptance of homosexuals: "Close friendships with homosexuals had become possible without sexual desire for even sexual nuance—at least no more sexual nuance than is present in all human relations."[40]

The other essay, "The White Negro," became my credo; it was my political manifesto. The essay was full of foolish, even repugnant things, but it also enunciated a philosophy of risk and psychological growth. It synthesized existentialism, the liberatory potential of jazz and black culture, sexual radicalism, and the violence of the psychopath. How often would I examine myself and strive to be one of those with the "knowledge that what is happening at each instant of the electric present is . . . good or bad for their cause, their love, their action, their need," and recognize that I was "moving through each moment of life forward into growth or backward into death."

"The White Negro" was a direct descendant of Robert Lindner's *Rebel without a Cause* (which Mailer quoted at length), for the white Negro was the hipster, the psychopath, the American existentialist.[41] But where Lindner had been unwilling to endorse homosexuality as rebellion against conformity, Mailer wholeheartedly included homosexuality as one possible form of sexual radicalism. Mailer's discussions in these two essays of the sexual radicalism of black culture and of homosexuality contributed to my growing consciousness of the social implications of homosexuality.

Norman Mailer's vision of the pivotal role of black culture and its sexual radicalism encouraged me to look to the black experience for lessons relevant to my situation as a homosexual. This was further reinforced by my discovery, through Leslie Fiedler's *Love and Death in the American Novel*, of the homoerotic tradition in American literature that paired a white man with a man of color—for example, Ishmael and Queequeg, Huck Finn and Nigger Jim. Fiedler's book was rather homophobic (which I was quite aware of at the time) because his Freudian analysis of American fiction emphasized the paucity of "mature" heterosexual relationships, but I was grateful for his identification of the homoerotic themes in American fiction.

The homoerotic tradition in American literature provided a romantic counterpoint to the process of *thinking through* and politicizing homosexual issues by reading about black civil rights and black cultural politics. Baldwin's homosexuality and then the publication in 1962 of the essays that later made up *The Fire Next Time* made him the perfect guide into my new homosexual "identity politics" (as it later came to be called). This awareness of the politics of identity was soon reinforced by the appearance of "black power."

Baldwin's work in those years was devoted to exploration of the tragedy of difference, of divisions created by power and violence, of "definitions" of black and white, male and female that we cannot transcend. In the novels and essays I read in this period Baldwin seemed to explore the possibility of love and the difference that love might make in the racial conflicts of America and in our sexual lives. He reaches for "a region where there were no definitions of any kind, neither of color nor of male and female."[42]

While Baldwin rejected any relationship to "the gay community,"[43] he did believe that homosexuality was a legitimate form of love. Baldwin's relationship to homosexuality was deeply ambivalent. Yet for me his ambivalence was productive. He helped me situate my thinking about it in the context of the most important social issues of the day. Coming to terms with it was part of my relationship to politics and society. Baldwin's vision of love, Mailer's sexual politics, and the homoerotic romance of American literature encouraged me to enter into relationships with black men, which I pursued, off and on again, for fifteen years.[44] Through my identification with Baldwin and my new sexual experiences I began to think of myself as part of a minority, and the struggles of African Americans were linked to my own.

My process of reading as a way to acquire self-knowledge and shape my identity was filled out by other experiences and by reading the fiction of Jean Genet and John Rechy. On a more abstract level I also read André Gide's defense of homosexuality, *Corydon*, Jean-Paul Sartre's famous discussion in *Being and Nothingness* of bad faith and authenticity, which used the homosexual as its example, and the radical Freudian books of Herbert Marcuse and Norman O. Brown.

The "private" discourse of reading eventually opens up into social life.[45] Roland Barthes pointed out that "to read is to decode: letters, words, meanings, structures, . . . but by accumulating decodings . . . the reader is caught up in a dialectical reversal: finally he does not decode, he *overcodes*."[46] The homosexual reader emancipates himself or herself by coding-over the guilty knowledge acquired by growing up in a homophobic society and potentially transforms the knowledge of homosexuals living-in-community discovered by reading into the practical knowledge of a collective identity.

At some point as a homosexual reader I began to accept my task as a historical actor. My intellectual development found no outlet until I moved to New York City upon graduation in 1964 and began to expand my sexual experience. During the "Summer of Love" in 1967 I first walked hand in hand with a man on the Lower East Side, hung out at Max's Kansas City, went to the Stonewall Inn, and publicly socialized with other gay and straight people in the social circles around Andy Warhol. I vividly remember reading the July 3, 1969, issue of the *Village Voice* with its account of the Stonewall riots. In the following months I began to come out to my friends, and when I moved to Philadelphia in 1970 I went as an openly gay man and was active in the gay movement there. I had finally entered the gay social world.

The Social in the Heart of the Individual

We do not have the empirical evidence that would let us evaluate the effect that the popular sociology discourse about homosexuality may have had on lesbians and gay men in the 1950s and 1960s. However, the appearance of that discourse, in conjunction with the growing public discussion of homosexuality as a social problem, made, I believe, a very significant contribution. The very fact that *the social* was discovered and elaborated in a number of homosexual discourses made explicit the unconscious assumptions that were thought to govern the constitution of a homosexual social world. The public representation of a homosexual social world entered the network of homosexual discourses and altered the equilibrium psychiatry had created as the dominant discourse on homosexuality.

It was precisely the difficulty of really evaluating the empirical effect of the discovery of the social and its representation in the popular literature that raised the question of my own process of homosexualization. The popular sociology discourse emerged during the period in which I struggled to come to terms with my homosexual desire. It is as a comparative exercise that I offer the history of my reading and sexuality against the backdrop of the discovery of the social. *The social* entered "my own private discourse" through many tributary streams: Mailer's radical sexual politics, the homoerotic tradition in American literature, Ruitenbeek's collection of social-psychoanalytical essays, and Baldwin's personal encounter with and rejection of the homosexual social world.[47] By means of this personally constructed discourse, one can find the social in the very heart of the individual.[48]

The gap between the privatized discourses of the closet and the public discourses of the social was dramatically reduced by the new political discourses of gay liberation. The homosexual political movement that emerged in the wake of the Stonewall riots and feminism was thoroughly grounded in a social perspective. The gay liberation movement made one of its major priorities the dismantling of psychiatry's dominance over homosexual discourse.

Notes

1. Allen Young, "Out of the Closets, into the Streets," in *Out of the Closets*, ed. Karla Jay and Allen Young (New York: Douglas/Links, 1972), 17–20.

2. The appearance of Gunnar Myrdal's book *The American Dilemma* in 1944 marked the renewed recognition of race as a social issue in American life.

3. Alfred M. Kinsey et al., *Sexual Behaviour in the Human Male* (Philadelphia: W. B. Saunders Co., 1948). See the useful commentaries on the Kinsey report by Morris Ernst and David Loth, *American Sexual Behaviour and the Kinsey Report* (New York: Educational Book Co., 1948); and Donald P. Geddes, ed., *An Analysis of the Kinsey Reports on the Human Male and Female* (New York: New American Library, 1954).

4. Roger Austen, *Playing the Game: The Homosexual Novel in America* (Indianapolis: Bobbs-Merrill, 1977), 93–94.

5. For a survey of the fiction that explored homosexuality in this period, see the studies by John W. Aldridge, *After the Lost Generation: A Critical Study of the Writers of Two Wars* (New York: Noonday Press, 1951); Austen, *Playing the Game;* and Georges-Michel Sarotte, *Like a Brother, Like a Lover: Male Homosexuality in the American Novel and Theatre from Herman Melville to James Baldwin* (New York: Anchor Press/Doubleday, 1978).

6. "Homosexuality in America," *Life*, June 26, 1964, xi; Vito Russo, *The Celluloid Closet: Homosexuality in the Movies*, rev. ed. (New York: Harper and Row, 1987), 120–22, 140–43; Tom Burke, "The New Homosexuality," *Esquire*, December 1969.

7. Kenneth Lewes, *The Psychoanalytic Theory of Male Homosexuality* (New York: Simon and Schuster, 1988).

8. Ibid., 122–73.

9. The essay on homosexuality was reprinted in the important and influential collection of sociological and psychological articles edited by Hendrik M. Ruitenbeek, *The Problem of Homosexuality in Modern Society* (New York: E. P. Dutton, 1963).

10. Robert Lindner, *Must You Conform?* (New York: Grove, 1961), 40–41.

11. Ibid., 42.

12. Ibid., 75.

13. It was in this same period that the social constructionist approach to homosexuality was first elaborated in academic sociology by Mary McIntosh in her influential article "The Homosexual Role," *Social Problems*, 1957. McIntosh was very much influenced by the interactionist tradition in sociology called "symbolic interactionism."

14. For a useful discussion of the effects of a discursive formation on the individual, see Michel Pecheux, "The Subject-Form of Discourse in the Subjective Appropriation of Scientific Knowledges and Political Practice," in *Language, Semantics, and Ideology*, trans. Harbens Nagpal (London: Macmillan, 1982), 155–70.

15. Donald Webster Cory, *The Homosexual in America: A Subjective Approach* (New York: Castle Books, 1951); A. M. Krich, ed., *The Homosexuals: As Seen by Themselves and Thirty Authorities* (New York: Citadel, 1954); J. Mercer, *They Walk in Shadow* (New York: Comet Books, 1959); Jess Stern, *The Sixth Man* (New York: Doubleday, 1961); Alfred A. Gross, *Strangers in Our Midst* (Washington, DC: Public Affairs Press, 1962); R. E. L. Masters, *The Homosexual Revolution: A Challenging Exposé of the Social and Political Directions of a Minority Group* (New York: Julian Press, 1962); Donald Webster Cory and John P. LeRoy, *The Homosexual and His Society: A View from Within* (New York: Citadel, 1963); Ruitenbeek, *The Problem of Homosexuality in Modern Society*: Jess Stern, *The Grapevine: A Report on the Secret World of the Lesbian* (New York: Doubleday, 1964); Donald Webster Cory and John P. LeRoy, *The Lesbian in America* (New York: Citadel, 1964); Martin Hoffman, *The Gay World: Male Homosexuality and the Social Creation of Evil* (New York: Basic Books, 1968). There were also several works that used a cross-cultural approach.

16. Hoffman, *The Gay World*, 3.

17. The literature of popular sociology was paralleled by the growth of an academic sociology in the interactionist tradition that treated homosexuality (without any moralism) as a social phenomenon. Howard Becker, *Outsiders: Studies in the Sociology of Deviance* (Glencoe: Free Press, 1963); Erving Goffman, *Stigma: Notes on the Management of Spoiled Identity* (Englewood Cliffs, NJ: Prentice-Hall, 1963); Edwin Schur, *Crimes without Victims* (Englewood Cliffs, NJ: Prentice-Hall, 1965); William Simon and John Gagnon, eds., *Sexual Deviance* (New York: Harper and Row, 1967).

18. Edward Sagarin, who wrote under the name Donald Webster Cory, eventually became a sociologist specializing in the sociology of deviance and criminology. He completed his dissertation, *Structure and Ideology in an Association of Deviants* in 1966. It was later published by Arno Press in 1975.

19. For a brief history of the interactionist perspective, see Randall Collins, *Three Sociological Traditions* (New York: Oxford University Press, 1985), 180–222; and also Nicholas C. Mullins with Carolyn J. Mullins, *Theories and Theory Groups in Contemporary American Sociology* (New York: Harper and Row, 1973), 75–104. By 1963 two of the most influential "symbolic interactionist" books on "deviant identities" appeared: Becker's *Outsiders: Studies in the Sociology of Deviance* and Goffman's *Stigma: Notes on the Management of Spoiled Identity*.

20. Becker's famous definition from *Outsiders: Studies in the Sociology of Deviance*, quoted in David Jary and Julia Jary, *The HarperCollins Dictionary of Sociology* (New York: HarperCollins, 1991), 263.

21. Georg Simmel, "The Problem of Sociology," in *Essays on Sociology, Philosophy, and Aesthetics*, ed. Georg Simmel and K. H. Wolff (Columbus: Ohio State University Press, 1959), 327–40; George Herbert Mead, *Mind, Self and Society* (Chicago: University of Chicago Press 1932).

22. Frank Caprio, *Female Homosexuality* (New York: Citadel, 1954); George Henry, *All the Sexes* (New York: Rinehart, 1955); Edmund Bergler, *Homosexuality: Disease or a Way of Life* (New York: Hill and Wang, 1957); idem, *1000 Homosexuals* (Paterson:

Pageant Books, 1957); Irving Bieber, *Homosexuality* (New York: Basic Books, 1962); Albert Ellis, *Homosexuality: Its Causes and Cure* (New York: Lyle Stewart, 1965); Charles Socarides, *The Overt Homosexual* (New York: Grune & Stratton, 1968); Lionel Ovesey, *Homosexuality and Pseudo-homosexuality* (New York: Science House, 1969); and Lawrence Hatterer, *Changing Homosexuality in the Male* (New York: McGraw-Hill, 1970).

23. Cory, *The Homosexual in America*, 63. Cory's most extended discussion of effeminacy takes place on at 62–64.

24. Ibid., 129–34.

25. Ibid., 230–31, 258–59.

26. Ibid., 264.

27. Stern, *The Sixth Man*, 13.

28. Ibid., 13–18.

29. Ibid., 16.

30. Ibid., 76–92.

31. For a discussion of this process, see Pechaux, "The Subject-Form of Discourse," 110–29.

32. Michel de Certeau discusses reading as an active process in *The Practice of Everyday Life* (Berkeley: University of California Press, 1984), 165–76.

33. See Roland Barthes's thoughtful and suggestive essay "On Reading," in *The Rustle of Language*, trans. Richard Howard (New York: Hill and Wang, 1986), 33–43.

34. Ibid., 42–43.

35. James Baldwin, *Giovanni's Room* (New York: Dial Press, 1956).

36. Somewhere along here I came across an essay by liberal newspaper columnist Max Lerner called "The Gay Crucifixation," reprinted in *The Unfinished Country* (New York: Simon and Schuster, 1959).

37. Baldwin, *Giovanni's Room*, 12.

38. Norman Mailer, *Advertisements for Myself* (New York: G. P. Putnam, 1959).

39. Norman Mailer, "The Homosexual Villain," in *Advertisements for Myself*, 194.

40. Ibid., 196.

41. For James Baldwin's contemptuous dismissal of "The White Negro," see "The Black Boy Looks at the White Boy," in *Nobody Knows My Name* (New York: Doubleday, 1961); for Eldridge Cleaver's praise of Mailer's essay and his attack on Baldwin for his homosexuality, see Eldridge Cleaver, *Soul on Ice* (New York: McGraw-Hill, 1968).

42. James Baldwin, *Another Country* (New York: Dial Press, 1962), 301–2.

43. See Richard Goldstein's interview with Baldwin. Asked whether he felt like "a stranger in gay America," Baldwin responded, "Well, first of all I feel like a stranger in America from almost any conceivable angle except, oddly enough, as a black person. The word 'gay' has always rubbed me the wrong way. . . . I simply feel it's a world that has very little to do with me, with where I did my growing up. I was never at home with it." Richard Goldstein, "Go the Way Your Blood Beats," in *James Baldwin: The Legacy*, ed. Quincy Troup (New York: Simon and Schuster, 1989), 174.

44. And no doubt influenced my choice of pursuing a graduate degree in African studies.

45. The relatively private experience of reading was socialized during the early years of the women's and gay movements by participation in consciousness-raising groups and study groups.

46. Roland Barthes, "On Reading," 42.

47. It is necessary to remember that Baldwin's rejection is always compensated for by his deep commitment to the African American historical experience.

48. Pierre Bourdieu and Loïc J. D. Wacquant, *An Invitation to Reflexive Sociology* (Chicago: University of Chicago Press, 1992), 44.

20

Twenty-five Years after Stonewall: Looking Backward, Moving Forward

A Symposium with Cheryl Clarke, Martin Duberman, Jim Kepner, Karl Bruce Knapper, Joan Nestle, and Carmen Vazquez

KARL BRUCE KNAPPER (MODERATOR): I work at the Martin Luther King Jr. Papers Project at Stanford, where we are putting together a fourteen-volume edition of King's speeches, papers, and correspondence. I am also the president of the board of directors of Frameline, sponsor of the San Francisco International Lesbian and Gay Film Festival. I am also on the editorial collective of the *Socialist Review*, and was on the national steering committee for last year's march on Washington.

The other panelists are Carmen Vazquez, who is originally from Puerto Rico. She is the founding director of the San Francisco Women's Building, and former executive director of the National Network for Immigrant and Refugee Rights. She has now moved to New York City and is currently the director of public policy for the Lesbian and Gay Community Services Center here.

To my immediate left is Martin Duberman, who is a professor of history at CUNY, the founder and director of CLAGS, and the author of, among other books, *Paul Robeson, Cures,* and *Stonewall.*

To my right is Cheryl Clarke. She is an African American lesbian feminist poet and the author of four books of poetry. She is currently director of the Office of Diverse Community Affairs and Lesbian and Gay Concerns for Rutgers University.

On her right is Joan Nestle. She is the cofounder of the Lesbian Herstory Archives and, until her recent retirement, a teacher in the SEEK program at Queens College of CUNY. She is also the author and editor of a number of books, including *A Restricted Country* and *The Persistent Desire*.

And on the far right we have Jim Kepner, who has been a pioneering gay activist since 1952. He is a writer, as well as cofounder and curator of the International Gay and Lesbian Archives.

One of the sobering effects for me of the march on Washington was looking around at the one million people and realizing that, other than our sexual orientations, I had very little in common with many of them, and I probably had more in common with progressive straight people in San Francisco.

And that is a sobering thought when you try to think about building a coalition in—among—such a diverse group. I would also like to say that we need to learn how to build alliances with people in other communities, particularly since many of us belong to them—which is something a lot of people don't get. Fighting for progressive change means fighting for more than just lesbian and gay rights. That is not the only thing which informs our existence. When we get lesbian and gay rights, the rest of us will still have problems.

JIM KEPNER: I left Galveston when I was twenty. I looked up the word "homosexual" in the dictionary after having heard a perfectly loathsome description of the term. But the dictionary didn't say much.

I moved shortly to San Francisco—I had heard rumors about San Francisco—and began hunting for the doorway to come out through. I made my confession to a fellow worker at Southern Pacific General Headquarters in the freight accounts department, and she told me about the Black Cat Bar up on Montgomery, an old, old bar. And I waltzed up the street at least six inches above the sidewalk going to join my brothers and sisters for the first time.

The San Francisco police force beat me to the door. Now, I had romantic visions of going to save my brothers and sisters, but what I actually did was hide in the doorway across the street, cursing myself for being a coward. And I saw about fifteen or twenty handsome, husky types, of the kind that would later be called "San Francisco clones," as if that was something new, and about twelve or fifteen others that I thought were my sisters at first.

Well, I guess they were, in a sense [laughter]. The handsome, husky ones were all going like guilty sheep led to the slaughter they so richly deserved for being what they were. And the queens—my "sisters"—were all struggling, albeit individually, and one of them let out a yell to the officer behind, "Don't shove, you bastard, or I'll bite your fucking balls off."

And it took me over a year to understand why that made me feel good [laughter]—somewhat, at least. It was a way of fighting back. That poor queen paid dearly, but many of those queens had been paying dearly for a long time.

There were, before Stonewall, and before the Mattachine Society had its first beginnings on November 11, 1950, in Los Angeles—although it took a number of months before they actually came up with that name—several earlier organizations in New York, in Chicago, in Philadelphia, in Boston; it was rumored that there was one even in 1925 in Los Angeles, as well as a Black gay businessmen's group that apparently started in Detroit about 1946, and was still going when I spoke there in 1974. But in general, there is no evidence that I found—and if someone has the evidence please come up with it—that any of these groups had a direct, significant effect on the movement later.

Stonewall and the Mattachine Society had that direct, significant effect. And part of that effect—a small part—is in the fact that there are still people and individuals active in the movement ever since, who came out of those two turning points. Another effect, possibly more important, was that each of those two incidents led directly to a redefinition of who we are and how we relate to society.

For ten years I had talked to various people—not often, because the response was so negative it was discouraging—about "when do we organize?" And over and over I got the same answer: "But we're sick. What is the point of organizing? We are sinners. We are going to Hell. What is the point of organizing? We are silly. We are immature. We couldn't possibly get together on anything. And besides, if we tried, the police would arrest us all right away." Those attitudes I heard over and over, and it was a miracle that several organizations did get together.

Now getting together isn't enough. You have to have some level of agreement on what the objectives are and how the hell to get to them. So it was a miracle that in Los Angeles on November 11, 1950, five men got together who had a common radical background—even though it was against the grain of the times: this was during the McCarthy period. They had the chutzpah to try to organize when everybody knew it was "impossible." And they brought with them, also, a certain theory about what minority groups need. Calling homosexuals—white homosexuals, at least—a "minority group" then was not popular: "We don't want to be a minority group. We are just like everybody else except for what we do in bed. And we don't talk about that."

So the Mattachine people realized that in order to develop a minority group strength, before you could even talk about changing the law, you have to begin to build a positive sense of identity, which most gays did not have. And you have to begin to build a community and some of the institutions of that community. Not necessarily a ghetto. Not with a wall around it. Now because Harry Hay, the chief founder who gets all the credit, was a philosophizer, the others did the organizing [laughter]. Because Harry Hay could outtalk the others, their agreement was much more an appearance than reality. And most of the rest of them didn't really buy this idea of the "community."

Now, when the new people came into the movement, most of them were very conformist, very conservative, very scared, and when they heard rumors that there were some communists involved in the leadership, they decided that they had to get rid of them. Actually they didn't throw them out: Harry resigned for the founders, though the official view is that the founders were thrown out (of course they would have been anyhow). And the Mattachine Society became very conservative, even to the point of having members sign a loyalty oath—not just to the country, but to the neighborhood church and the supermarket. And we ripped one another apart. We went into that organization thinking we were marching to Armageddon, that it was going to be easy, that within a month or two, or two years at the most, we would win our rights in a hostile society, and then we could go back to just enjoying ourselves.

And in the tearing apart what appeared was the fact that we don't all want the same things. Some want only to change the sodomy laws and get the vice cops off our backs. Some want gay identity and gay community. Some want radical social or sexual freedom. Some assume, beautifully, that a good sex education program will get rid of all the problems we have, and Archie Bunker will be a nice guy and will accept us. Some want to get on the revolutionary bus, whichever particular sect happens to be running that bus, or the salvation bus—and I don't necessarily mean to disparage any of these terribly [laughter]. Let's say I don't agree equally with all of them. And some want respectability, which happens to be a very different thing from self-respect.

Those activists in the early period who were most hell-bound for respectability were the ones who had the worst self-images. Respectability is a pasting-over. It is a PR job. "Clean up our image, and let everybody else think we are just like them." But we are not just like them. Which does not mean that we are all alike. And people get hung up on that just as they get hung up on the concept that the term "community" means that we are all alike. It doesn't.

Our movement has had a constant history of swinging sharply back and forth between some of these contrary, and some of these mutually exclusive, goals. Not all of them are mutually exclusive. But it took about till 1977, by my measure, after the Dade County vote, when most of us began to realize—I noticed this earlier—that we don't all want the same thing, and when most of us began to realize that diversity isn't just a curse. We had a lot of generals in our movement in the early days, who figured that "if you don't agree with my opinion, it is just a matter of my banging it over your head so that you 'get right.' "

Well, our diversity at least gives us one advantage. I feel that the potential for holocaust is never totally absent. Our movement, in thirty-five or forty years, made about the same degree of progress that the German homosexual movement did, which got wiped out overnight. I am not predicting that that is going to happen. I certainly hope it doesn't, but we have the advantage of being able to build bridges back—because of our diversity—to every section of the community we come from, and we damn well better be about that business. We are being about that business, but not adequately.

I think that we must begin to look at the meaning of our gayness deeper than just our sexuality, without in any way negating our sexuality, and that we look into our spirit. Each of us will define it differently—and that becomes our biggest task, along with looking after our health and looking after the Mother Earth. Some of us will dance in the moonlight; others of us will need to go to the moon and beyond. We must move on, and we must serve the world. A multifaceted society requires the interchangeable talents that I think we are very equipped for.

JOAN NESTLE: In the late 1950s, I entered the public life of the Village lesbian bar community. Walking through the heavy, single-wooden door of the Sea Colony on Abingdon Square, I entered a world that would become a milestone in a people's history, but I did not know that then. What I did know was that I was a freak, a pervert, a "lezzie," and that I had to be in that bar to find women who would hold me in their arms. I soon learned the price of my desire: the humiliations of the bathroom line, the police visits, the flashing red lights warning us of surveillance, women's faces bloodied by the fists of angry men, and sometimes by our own. In that smoke-filled, drink-pushing place, with Tony at the door sitting heavily on his barstool, and Maria endlessly wiping the bar top while she exchanged words with every customer, I lost all other distinctions of character, other than I was a queer, and here was where queers lived.

On weekends, when hundreds of women passed through the Colony, slow-dancing their way into a hot weekend, teachers greeted students, secretaries and hookers took turns at the jukebox, telephone operators and hairdressers flashed their pinky rings, longtime butch-femme couples shared their tables with young women still learning the ropes. Hate and ridicule waited for us in the streets. But many times we outlasted them, pouring out into the dawn, a tired crew of women going for breakfast as the morning light came up.

In those bars, I got what I had come for. I found the touch and taking that I had yearned for. But I found an even more lasting legacy: a wonder at, and a belief in, what desire could engender, what a community of women deemed powerless by the society could call into being, without money, without social position, without connections. I also learned to question prevailing historical narratives. We were a different kind of "fifties woman," risking all for our need to touch each other.

And yet the same old drone about America in the 1950s goes on and on. Marginal peoples do not only die on the margins. They live and struggle and create. They create legacies of understanding, resistance, and celebration. When we tell our stories, we are not revising history, as we have been accused of, but we are revealing it. A part of my life's work has been putting working-class lesbian narratives, stories, into history. And grassroots women speaking are as analytical as any academic professor.

[Nestle reads from archival materials]:

The speaker is a Jewish woman, then in her late sixties: "I had a chance to read a copy of the *Well of Loneliness* that had been translated into Polish before

I was taken into the camps. I was a young girl at the time, around twelve or thirteen, and one of the ways I survived in the camp was by remembering that book. I wanted to live long enough to kiss a woman."

The speaker is Jeanette Flash Gray, writing about gay Harlem in the 1930s: "I'm glad I had a chance to go to Blind Churls' and Mister Rivers and similar places in Harlem. I'm glad I had a chance to be a bull-dagger before it became fashionable to be a lesbian."

The speaker: a butch woman, living in Buffalo in the 1950s: "Things back then were horrible, and I think that because I fought like a man to survive, I made it somehow easier for the kids coming out today. I did all their fighting for them. I'm not a rich person. I don't have a lot of money. I don't even have a little money. I would have nothing to leave anybody in this world, but I have that I can leave to the kids who are coming out now, who will come out into the future, that I left them a better place to come out into, and that's all I have to offer, to leave them. But I wouldn't deny it, even though I was getting my brains beaten out, I would never stand up and say, 'No, don't hit me. I'm not gay. I'm not gay.' I wouldn't do that."

Now another voice, the voice of the government, 1950. Headline: *Sexual Perverts in Government Employ:* "Mister Speaker, I have just read an article about the number of sexual perverts in the employ of the government. I never thought there were so many homosexuals in the whole United States." The article goes, "on the committee that has been investigating this matter has found that 574 such persons have quit their jobs, and that 420 have been fired. What we need is a thorough house-cleaning, the sooner the better."

The speaker, a femme from the 1950s: "But the most searing reminder of our colonized world was the bathroom line. Now I know it stands for all the pain and glory of my time. And I carry that line and the women who endured it deep within me. Because we were labeled 'deviants,' our bathroom habits had to be watched. Only one woman at a time was allowed into the toilet because we could not be trusted. Thus, the 'toilet line' was born, a twisting horizon of lesbian women waiting for permission to urinate, to shit. The line flowed past the far wall, past the bar, the front room tables, and reached into the back room. Guarding the entrance to the toilet was a short, square, handsome butch woman, the same every night, whose job it was to twist around her hand our allotted amount of toilet paper. She was us, an obscenity, doing the man's trick so we could breathe. The line awaited all of us every night, and we developed a line act. We joked, we cruised, we commented on the length of time one of us took. We made special pleas to allow hot and heavy lovers in together, knowing full well that our lady would not permit it. I stood, a femme, loving the women on either side of me, loving my comrades for their style, the power of their stance, the hair hitting the collar, the thrown-out hip, the hand encircling the beer can. Our eye played the line. Subtle touches, gentle shyness, weaved under the blaring jokes, the music, the surveillance. We lived on that line, restricted and judged. We took deep breaths and played. But buried deep in our endurance was our fury. That line was practice and theory seared into one. We wove our freedoms, our culture, around their obstacles of hatred, but we also paid our price. Every time I took the fistful of toilet paper, I swore eventual liberation. It would be, however, liberation with a memory. And I want to thank my community for remembering with me all these years."

CHERYL CLARKE: I'll begin with a line from a poem by Gwendolyn Brooks. "It is brave to be involved, to be not fearful, to be unresolved."

When I was asked by Ellie Bulkin and Joan Larkin in 1979 to submit to something called *Lesbian Poetry*, which was published in 1981 by the now-defunct Persephone Press, I had already realized the potency of a rebellious literature and orality, and would not have been able to nourish myself on feminist and lesbian-feminist writing had I not first found my anger and voice in the poetry of the Black Power/Black Arts movement ten years before then. Coming out as a lesbian was light action compared to coming out as a Black person. In 1973, I came out as a lesbian. Twenty years later, I am still evaluating what taking on that identity means to me, and the various communities I find myself in.

Today, as we know, taking on any construction as an identity is a highly charged and contested act. Lesbianism, for me, is not a floating signifier, nor is it a pure uncontaminated fixed state [laughter]. My question from the very beginning was always, "Of what use is it to be a lesbian?" And I mean that in a very positive sense. My usefulness, as a lesbian, was enabled first by a small group of Black lesbian feminists in the 1970s, and then later, by a very multicultural community of hardworking, focused, and serious women involved in producing a literature for the post-Stonewall lesbian-feminist world.

Finding that feminist voice, however, was greatly shaped and clarified by Black women novelists, historic and contemporary. Barbara Smith's "Toward a Black Feminist Criticism" was a groundbreaking piece of work which opened a whole new approach to reading and learning from Black women's writing. *Conditions 5: The Black Women's Issue*, coedited by Smith and Lorraine Bethel in 1979, was the first work to publish the writings of self-identified Black feminists, and Black and lesbian feminists, and opened up the field to other women of color.

As I wrote recently, for a publication celebrating the twenty-fifth anniversary of Stonewall,

The decade of the eighties changed the color of the lesbian and gay movement. For the first time since Stonewall, lesbians and gays of color began asserting their contributions to the overall movement in the U.S. Publications like *This Bridge Called My Back: Writings by Radical Women of Color* edited by Cherríe Moraga and Gloria Anzaldúa in 1981, and *Homegirls: A Black Feminist Anthology*, edited by Barbara Smith, were clarion calls to lesbian feminist communities that it was in our best interest to solve the problems posed by monocultural leadership. Issues of race, class and ethnicity were placed at the top of the agendas of all the women's organizations I found myself a part of by 1986. Antisemitism in the lesbian community was challenged in the writings of Ellie Bulkin, Irena Klepfisz,

Melanie Kaye Kantrowitz, Adrienne Rich, Evelyn Torton Beck. All of us, no matter what our backgrounds, were expected to examine our heritage of prejudice, our class positions, and the ways in which we acted out of our privilege. Being "out" was not enough. One's anti-heterosexist practice needed to be defined in relationship to one's diverse anti-oppression stances. Lesbian leadership at all levels was visible in pursuit of multi-cultural leadership and community.

I learned firsthand, along with a whole lesbians-in-print movement, how crucial it is to create books. We learned how to shape ourselves and to imagine our audiences. Through our work on journals, occasional publications, independent alternative press anthologies—which haven't all been taken over by university presses and major presses—we learned that lesbians are a palpable audience, and we wanted them as much as and more than they wanted us.

I call myself a lesbian from vantage points that may or may not be available to women who love women in other cultures and countries and classes. My lesbianism must be constantly mediated by my racial, gender, political, class, and poet positions. My own "house of difference" (Lorde) provides me with the strategies necessary to traverse and reconstruct the world I live in and the space I occupy. As Walt Whitman said, "I resist anything better than my own diversity. And breathe the air and leave plenty after me. And I'm not stuck-up and I'm in my place."

Looking back, I see that, when I chose to be a lesbian poet, I did not want to claim a middle ground or a mainstream—and still don't. However, a lesbian public is both inside and outside that mainstream, decentered from and central to it, resisting literacy and orality. Looking forward, I still see lesbianism as an act of resistance. The late Ella Baker, a formidable organizer in the Black Freedom Movement for five decades, says she saw herself not as a, quote, "leader," but as a facilitator. By "facilitator," she meant that she saw herself as someone who made it possible for other people who wanted to, to take leadership in their communities.

That is the way I experience my own entry into the world of lesbian feminist writers, editors, publishers, and booksellers—lesbians, period. And that is also how I see myself, though I would not be so hesitant as Baker to call myself a "leader." There was, and is, plenty of work to be done.

MARTIN DUBERMAN: When people talk about "how little has changed in gay and lesbian life," it seems to me you had to be alive in those years to fully understand just how much *has* changed. Perhaps there has been more change for our social movement in a shorter period of time than for any other. That doesn't mean that the change and the progress aren't reversible. Obviously they are. But the difference between the late 1960s and the mid 1990s is extraordinary. Let me give you just one or two examples of what I mean.

Often of an evening when we went out bar-ing or cruising, we would carry with us in our wallets the names of one of the three lawyers, who knew how to get us out of jail if we were entrapped that night by a plainclothes policeman.

Entrapment was a commonplace. The cops would choose their youngest, hunkiest policemen, dress them in the going gay uniform of the day—chinos, tight T-shirt, sneakers—and would send them out on the streets to entice gay men. Often the cops made the first approach, and as soon as a gay man responded to it, he was arrested. Rumor has it that the arrests were sometimes delayed until after the sex act was completed [laughter].

At Fire Island, in those same years—a gay resort, mind you—the police also entrapped on the boardwalks at night. After they arrested a gay man, they would take him down to the dock, where they would chain him to the telephone pole. They would then go back on the boardwalk, make another arrest, chain that man to the telephone pole. Four or five hours later—meaning at dawn—when a dozen or so gay men were chained to this pole, the police would call for the patrol boat to come over from Sayville, and the gay men would be taken across the bay, subject to a kangaroo court and extortionate fines, then released—though their names were often published in their local newspapers, so that subsequently they sometimes lost their jobs and apartments as well.

But I've been instructed *not* to linger on the memory track tonight, and instead to talk to you about the more prosaic nuts and bolts development of gay and lesbian studies on our college campuses. I can summarize that development simply by saying that none of us would have dreamed a mere fifteen years ago, even ten years ago, that anything remotely like the phenomenon we are currently seeing on the campuses would take place. At San Francisco State, there is now an undergraduate major in gay and lesbian studies. Several other places—most recently and most startlingly (given its setting in a rural, conservative area) Allegheny College in Meadsville, Pennsylvania—now have a minor in gay and lesbian studies. At Allegheny, the minor came about as a result of four or five open, determined, gay and lesbian faculty members banding together, approaching the administration and insisting that this, in fact, happen.

The lesbian/gay studies movement is not confined to the United States. It is, in fact, international. Probably the two largest centers of scholarship at the moment are the United States and the Netherlands. But, in fact, international conferences have been held in several other countries, and academic journals are being published in a variety of places—such as Italy, West Germany, and England.

Here at the CUNY Graduate School, as I'm sure most of you know, there is the Center for Lesbian and Gay Studies (CLAGS). CLAGS—which I direct [I stepped down as director in 1996]—is a good example, I think, of just how rapidly everything has happened. CLAGS was only officially established here in April 1991. Yet our mailing list is now over nine thousand, and we are inundated, in our tiny office, with telephone inquiries and letters.

CLAGS has also been involved over the past three years is an attempt to create a new Ph.D. called "Studies in Multiculturalism." The six constituent groups taking part in these discussions—African American studies, Asian

American studies, women's studies, Latino/a studies, cultural studies, and lesbian and gay studies—are trying, even beyond getting the new Ph.D. on its feet, to find out exactly what it is that we *do* have in common, politically and intellectually. One offspring of these discussions has been a decision to try and clarify the ways in which our families differ one from the other: what kind of values emanate from our different ethnic and racial backgrounds, what values are inculcated in our young. We have had two mini-conferences already on the theme "Families and Values."

One might well ask, "Why this sudden efflorescence of activity on the university level?" I think the primary reason is that a political movement preceded. (The same has been true, of course, for African American studies and women's studies.) First came Stonewall, then the organization of the Gay Liberation Front, then later, considerably later, came the development of gay and lesbian scholarship. I think those of us who are scholars—though some of us regard ourselves as activists as well—need to acknowledge more than we do that there never would have been any such thing as the Center for Lesbian and Gay Studies had it not been for the brave activists who put their lives on the line early on. Gay activism began this whole process. Gay scholarship, as scholars are wont, has subsequently brought up the rear.

The process of institutionalizing lesbian and gay studies can be problematic. Once a subject matter, a set of events and experiences, receive scholarly attention, a real danger arises that the experience will be over-rationalized and presented in lifeless form. Academics are specialists in that: they know how to take the juice out of a life narrative [laughter]. But we lesbian and gay scholars are *trying* not to do it in the same old way. It will be up to you to judge whether or not, and to what extent, we succeed.

In saying all this, I am not implying for a minute that the battle is won, even on the university level. Homophobia is very much alive and well on our college campuses. It tends to be homophobia of the subtle, liberal variety, just as is racism on the college campus. Academics—or most of them—like to think of themselves as progressive people who do not harbor the crude prejudices of their less fortunate fellow citizens [laughter]. But, of course, they do. And because they believe they *don't*, their racism and their homophobia are even more insidious; academics tend to be out of touch with their own prejudice, unaware that their hidden values need policing. And so when it comes time, for example, to hire or to promote, if the candidate is openly gay or lesbian, the professional discussion is almost never explicitly about sexual orientation but rather about whether the candidate is really "a good enough scholar or teacher," or "a good enough citizen of the community," or whether he or she has published enough.

And where the will exists to be negative, the way can always be found. The result is that many gay and lesbian academics never get a chance to work their way up the ladder because they are turned down on grounds entirely different from the real source of objection to them—namely, their sexual orientation.

All this is changing, but openly gay and lesbian graduate students are well aware that they are taking extraordinary career risks in devoting themselves to lesbian and gay studies, that they are, in a real sense, marginalizing themselves, putting themselves at risk in terms of securing a future in the academic world. We hope that the climate will continue to change, but there are no guarantees. Every revolution, as we know, can be stopped dead in its tracks.

Finally, I would like to emphasize that when gay and lesbian scholarship is done properly, it *is* a form of activism. By which I mean, scholarship can and does change stereotypic, mainstream images. And once public imagery gets changed, what follows thereafter—though not always quickly—are changes in legislative and judicial opinion.

But I, for one, do not justify gay and lesbian studies solely on the basis of what it does for gays and lesbians themselves. Clearly we gays and lesbians need this new scholarship because we have been kept out of the textbooks and do not even have alternate family traditions to fall back on, as do other oppressed minority groups. Many—most—gays and lesbians are desperate for some sense of belonging, for roots, for a feeling of continity with what has come before.

On the other hand, the new scholarship creates some unease, because what we have been finding is that same-gender sexuality and bonding, like everything else in human history, changes through time and across cultures. Sexuality and gender have been differently configured in different settings. If we look to the past in order to find people exactly like ourselves, we are dooming ourselves to disappointment—because the past never provides exact duplicates of what we find around us in the present (which, as a non-historical people, we equate with the universal).

Nonetheless, in a mere twenty years, gay and lesbian scholarship has produced basic information of enormous importance—to *everybody*. For example: information about how identity is formed on both an individual and communal level; information about the relationship between gender and sexuality; information about the purported nature of "male" or "female" desire that centrally challenges standard notions; information about how minority cultures interact with the mainstream; information about how minority groups make themselves visible, make their demands heard, make their presence known.

Above all, I think, gay and lesbian scholarship is important to *everybody* because it tells a story of survival, a story of how individuals—and then "a people"—who are "different," developed strategies for coping with oppression. I believe *all* of us—regardless of our sexual preference—are, in our fantastical heads, deeply idiosyncratic—and that all of us can therefore learn from the experience of any marginalized group that has managed to endure in a conformist society, and even command respect for its differentness.

CARMEN VAZQUEZ: I want to start by sharing a journal entry with you, because my Mommy taught me that it is impolite to start talking with people unless you give them a chance to know a little bit about you. And the journal entry says, "I want to realize the possibility of playing with double-scoop, chubby chocolate-fisted kids who grow up loving the boy and the girl in themselves. I want to live in a country that assures warm beds and warm meals on cold, damp mornings for everyone, everywhere, every day. I want to run the edge of a blade across my lover's breasts and thighs, to free her of her garter-belt and stockings with one clean move as we make love under a silver night moon in the Arizona desert. I want to catch fat trout in clean California running waters when the mountains sing the morning. I want to someday work on the election of an African American butch lesbian from Louisiana to the Senate of the United States" [whooping and laughter]. And, you know, a while back I met her, in Texas actually, [laughter]. "I dream of being alive for the cure to AIDS, of knowing just one joyous moment in this unrelenting grief for brothers and sisters lost to this pandemic, lost forever. I dream of the day when Puerto Rico will be a free and sovereign nation. I dream of claiming my birthright to citizenship in that nation. I dream of having the health and strength to enjoy a martini in front of a roaring fire and loving my partner when I'm 84." End of journal entry.

These waking dreams of mine are, in very broad strokes, who I am: a butch Puerto Rican socialist, with dreams of a world where I and those I love can be free and whole people, a woman with faith in a moment of freedom that isn't here yet. I believe that the central tenet for a progressive lesbian/gay liberation movement has to be individual human autonomy in sexuality. Because it is our sexuality, no matter what we say, it is our sexuality which has been the source of our vilification, our sexuality which has been termed "sick," illegal, and "immoral." It is through the denial of our sexuality and the free expression of our desire that we have been denied our humanity and our souls. And, you know, if we are to reclaim our souls, which is what a liberation movement has to be about, then we have to have the right to name our desire and to freely express our love for one another.

Our sexuality, whatever expression we might give it, is not outside our class and race experience. It is shaped by them. And if this struggle is to carry the force of a moral imperative, then it has to be larger than us. It must speak to the human condition, to individual human freedom denied anywhere. There is no moral imperative when we act only in our own interests, when we posit the end of discrimination based on sexual orientation as the high priest or high priestess of our movement, with race and class concerns relegated to strategic issues to which we have to pay lip service when we need more colored or female votes at the polls in order to defeat an antigay initiative.

As I grew up in the projects of Harlem, right here in this city—that's General Grant projects, up on 125th Street—I learned to spare my mom's pride by editing the social worker's insults out of my translation. I learned to take care of my father when he reverted to living out the terror of war in a South Pacific island. I learned to take care of my sisters and brothers. I learned to stay one step ahead of the pride and shame game by not telling my neighbors that I was hungry, because there was shame in hunger. I learned about my butch self, about romance and flirting and passion and desire and love within a familial and cultural context. I learned how to flirt with, and how to love, women from my father and uncles and boy cousins. I learned how to please women from my mother and my aunts and my girl cousins. I learned me some values. I learned from my mother that nothing would ever be more important in my life than speaking the truth of my experience. I learned that the way to have honor in my life was to defend the honor of my people, my family and my community however they came to be defined. I learned, when I was thirteen or so, that who I loved the most, who I wanted to be with, in that secret and sometimes tortured way that the young of any orientation know so well, was women. I learned about passion and communion and desire from a woman seven years my senior when I was fifteen. I learned what sex meant. I learned how taking Eva in my arms, and kissing her, and rolling around with her on a couch, or a bed, or on the floor was to find and touch the very deepest part of me. I learned about the joy of imagination, about the unbelievable relief of surrendering myself to my desire.

And I think that we are not going to win full civil rights protection, much less liberation, until we understand that the dialogue we must engage hetero-sexual America in is not whether we are born gay or chose it. Rather, the dialogue must be—the dialogue has to be—about how to bridge the chasm that has been socially and politically constructed between ourselves and other human beings, other Americans, who also know the joyous truth about the power of erotic desire in their lives.

We have to stop ceding the terms of the debate to the right by pretending that sex and desire haven't anything to do with our identity. They have every-thing to do with our identity. Everything. They call us "immoral" and "child molesters." And we dodge the challenge presented to us by responding with "Well, the overwhelming percentage of child molesters are heterosexual." What does that mean? The percentage of queer child molesters is so teeny we shouldn't worry about it, so let's go on to talk about what great parents we are?

It doesn't translate. It's not honest. We are not responding to the ethical and moral challenge being presented to us. What we should be saying is "Look, Bubba, the use of power, control, and violence to violate the integrity, whole-ness, and autonomy of another human being is not okay anywhere by anyone." Individual human autonomy and sexuality are ethical standards no one has the right to violate. No one. Ours is—or ought to be, I think—a movement dedicated to defending those ethical standards.

I truly believe that no movement for human liberation has ever been led forward, or won, by apologists. We must learn to make our case to the American public with our hearts and minds firmly rooted in the truth of who we are, without shame. That truth owes no one any apologies. No one. We owe our-selves the cleansing clarity of our rage: rage for a people burned and tortured, silenced and dehumanized for centuries; rage against the violence and harassment two lesbians have to endure in Mississippi in order to live and work on their land; rage against the HIV killer that keeps claiming the lives of our sisters and brothers while our politicians tell us that we can't be sexually explicit in our prevention messages; rage for the rape of our homes, and our sisters, and our brothers, and our souls; rage for the children torn from our lives; rage for being made to suffer the ridicule of our name in silence. No longer. No longer. No longer. And we owe ourselves enough love to transform our rage into the work of liberation; into the work of reclaiming our humanity; into the work of building community among ourselves in relationships of respect and unwavering alliance with others who struggle to rebuild their communities and win their liberation.

If it feels like we are being scapegoated, well, that's because we are. America is a wounded nation, a nation of alienated people, a nation desperately in need of spiritual and mental transformation. And I think we need to begin to think of ourselves as a people who can provide some of that healing. We have to stop pretending that we are just like everybody else and learn to say, "God bless the difference!" "God bless the difference!"

KARL BRUCE KNAPPER: Well, we have about half an hour left. I'd like to begin with each of the panelists talking about their vision for the future, and how they think that we can make this twenty-fifth anniversary of Stonewall count, and where we go from here.

JIM KEPNER: We certainly have to deal with the question of AIDS. And we may be dealing with that for a long time.

We have to build our community more strongly. We have to build those bridges to the nongay community while building our own community and not apologizing for that.

We have to deal with this question of whether investigating, searching for our spiritual element is somehow a negation of our sexual element. We've grown up in a dualistic society where spirit and sex are seen as two separate things, and if you deal with one, you are somehow negating the other. The philosopher Gerald Heard suggested that maybe we'd get around this by simply using a different term. Let the term "sexuality"—now, I don't necessarily buy this—but let the term "sexuality" apply to what the heteros do, and to the question of procreation, and that what we do together with one another, exciting as it is, moist as it is, emotional as it is, is something else, something like "recharging our batteries" [laughter], lining up those energy zones within ourselves in such a way that we get a burst of synergy. That I think we need to explore [laughter]. Right now, I guess, safely.

JOAN NESTLE: I do have some issues, or some warnings. For instance, the relationship between capitalism and our starring on the stage, and that is something to really watch out for, because we know that this is how the society works: that if it can make money off of a people, then it will, but that doesn't really mean a transformative change for those people in the society.

The other thing—and this comes from my work with the Lesbian Herstory Archives—when we started the archives twenty-three years ago, we had some early discussion with the New York Public Library about whether they wanted to sort of be cosponsors with the project, or something. And they said no. They said they weren't interested in collecting "unknown people." And now they are.

And I think it is wonderful. The NYPL exhibit ["Becoming Visible"] is tremendously powerful. It isn't now anymore that there is only one archive in the United States, or the world. There are many. But my challenge to you is, no matter how wonderful the exhibits are in the marble museums along Fifth Avenue, no matter how many universities offer to take your money for courses—and I taught one here at the CUNY Graduate School and I know how exciting it is—don't turn your backs on the grassroots institutions that did this before and will do it afterwards; they will need you desperately. University libraries are going around this country offering hundreds of thousands of dollars for people's papers to put in their, you know, "treasured archives." So I say this. This is very self-serving: the Lesbian Herstory Archives will need you more than ever. But go there. Go there and see what a grassroots dream built in Park Slope. Okay?

CHERYL CLARKE: We have to continue to build bridges to the nongay community as well as fighting heterosexism and homophobia where we are. We have to continue to assume—and push others to assume—leadership around AIDS; particularly, I would say, AIDS as it is affecting women, and women of color, and people in poor communities, as well as people in lesbian and gay communities. I think, in keeping with what Carmen said, in terms of lesbian and gay people being a people who can provide some healing, I think that we must take some—as many of us have—some leadership around the violence that is also epidemic in our culture, and not just the violence against us. And all of us, I think, have to really play a role with our youth. More and more of them are coming out at younger and younger ages. And often there is not a lot of support for them. I think it is extremely important for us to work with our young people. And, as Joan said, I think it is very important for us to still support our grassroots institutions, as well as our other institutions—I guess I'm thinking of our bookstores, of our presses. So, I guess, that's what I have to offer.

MARTIN DUBERMAN: I also have a few warnings. They can be summed up by two words: "celebration" and "patience." I see much more infighting than I do mutual celebration. Lateral hostility has always characterized our movement, and I don't know—no one knows how to measure this—whether it's more characteristic of our movement than other movements for social change. All such movements are, by their nature, expressive, and the more diverse a movement is (such as ours), the more need there will be for diverse expression—and that can lead to recrimination.

But what I'm hearing lately is something more worrisome. And that is: "You shouldn't be doing *this* kind of work. You should be doing *that* kind of work.

And if you're not doing the work that *I'm* doing, you're not doing work that matters at all." The fact is, a lot of different kinds of work need doing. And people are differently qualified to do it. If we genuinely believe in the rhetoric of diversity, we should also understand that different individuals are better qualified for some kinds of work than others. The radicals in our movement—and I count myself one—can, for example, sometimes be scornful of those gay and lesbian lawyers, who are "merely" engaged in civil rights work.

But we desperately need our civil rights, and the struggle for them is essential to our well-being. Not everyone can do that work. Not everyone has the given temperament and the given skills. So the first thing I would like to see is more respect for and more celebration of the diversity of our talents and contributions. As far as I'm concerned, so long as someone *is* making a contribution, that is sufficient reason for applauding them.

And that leads me to my second point, which is that not enough people are. Our organizations remain understaffed and underfunded. For many gays and lesbians, the struggle just to come out to themselves sexually—and then the next step, to friends, families, coworkers, employers—seems fully to drain their energy, at least temporarily. Coming out seems about all most people are able to do because life, for most people, is a difficult daily struggle; there just isn't much energy left over beyond that.

But somehow more of us have to find the energy, because the way things now stand, this is a David and Goliath contest that Goliath might win this time around. The religious right has prepared brilliantly. They've been at this for years. They know how to organize on the local level. They know how to build from local strength to state strength to national strength; and the gay movement has not understood that well enough so far.

In part, this is not simply a gay-lesbian issue. It is an American left issue. The history of the left in this country is not a history of sustained commitment. What has happened over and over again is that in a crisis situation, legions will turn out for a given march, possibly even for a weeklong set of organizing events. But if the revolution doesn't happen next Friday—and, of course, it never does—then, "Well, you know, we've got careers to build and we've got families to take care of, and we've got relationships to tend."

This is, I think, peculiarly American. It contrasts vividly with the European left, where it seems to be better understood that struggle is a matter of many generations, and that one generation builds on the work that precedes. But in this country the generations tend to turn on and consume each other, rather than to build on each other's work. And I'm not sure what explains this cannibalism between the generations and within the movement. I am very sure, though, that it saps what strength we have.

CARMEN VAZQUEZ: For me there are two really critical pieces that we keep sliding around on. One is class. Class, class, class. What is that? No, it's not the classroom, and it's not the lower-, middle-, upper-class stuff that we learned in civics. But it is the piece of our work as a movement that, I think, we have not grappled with. We have not grappled with the very different places that we come from economically. We have not grappled with the fact that for an awful lot of us all of this "Stonewall 25" business is like, "I can't come near it, because it doesn't speak to my reality, because I still have too much to lose if I come anywhere near close to it."

So I think that it is important for us to look at our own issues with money, with economic injustice, and with why that is still such a hard thing for us to address. We have begun to talk about racism—and I'm not saying that we've made tremendous strides in terms of addressing it in our movement—but I do think that it is an issue that we are a little bit more willing to look at, as we have been willing to look at sexism. Class becomes that closet thing that nobody wants to talk about because "of course, we are all the same and nobody came from this place and that place, and nobody's rich, and nobody's really poor."

And I think the other issue is the creation of intergenerational life. The *real* creation of intergenerational life. Because I think what Marty is saying is true about generations consuming each other. And that for us particularly there is a real sort of sadness sometimes, and anguish, that we have about sort of being stuck in the middle all the time. And historically, that is where we have been stuck. Although many of us have children. Many of us have parents. Many of us are old enough to now be elders, and gettin' there real fast if we're not. So I think that we need to create special places in our communities where our youth and our elders can be as visible and involved a part of who we are and what we do and the fun that we have as everybody else in between.

And I guess the last thing is that I think we really need to pay attention to supporting our institutions. You know, it is a long struggle. And from our institutions will consistently come the leadership—even if we are critical and disagree with it—the strategies, the money, the organizing campaigns. You can't have a movement without leadership and you can't have a movement without institutions that are supported, and supported over many, many, many years by its people.

KARL BRUCE KNAPPER: I'd like to end by saying that one thing we can do when we leave here, in carrying on the memory of Stonewall, is individually to try and make a difference. We do count and we *can* make a difference.

The biggest influence in my life has been my mother. She raised me to believe that I came from a race of survivors, and that I had to carry on the tradition that generations of people—Black people in this country—had done before me. And that is why I had to vote. And that is why I had to go to college. And that is why I had to do a lot of other things that didn't necessarily make sense to me, because I had to build on the efforts of those who had gone before me—my foremothers and my forefathers. And that is something we can do. Because if we really do intend to change the world and make it a better place, not just for a few privileged members of our community, but for all of us, that is what we are going to need to do. And, you know, that old feminist parable about "the personal is political" is very true. You don't have to get out in the street and scream and yell. But if you can make a difference in your individual personal life with the people that you impact, then that is the biggest change you can cause.

Three

Mind/Body Relations: Science and Psychology

A. Genes, Hormones, and the Brain

21

Psychobiologic Research on Homosexuality

Heino F. L. Meyer-Bahlburg

Despite its gradual depathologization by the American Psychiatric Association since 1974, homosexuality continues to be a topic of clinical relevance in child and adolescent psychiatry. The reason is that homosexuality has remained a difficult issue for parents and their children, especially during adolescence, and the identification of male homosexuals as a high-risk group for acquired immunodeficiency syndrome (AIDS) has added to the concerns.[51] Mental health professionals continue to receive questions about homosexuality and requests for its treatment; therefore they need to be abreast of current developments in the field.

In research work on homosexuality, three aspects are distinguished. Homosexual *behavior* refers to overt sexual activities between two partners of the same gender. Such activities are not uncommon as part of the sexual interactions of children or adolescents. By contrast, homosexual *orientation* refers to the overall sexual responsiveness of a person to men or women. It is specified for limited life periods and assessed on the basis of (1) sexual imagery (e.g., daydreams, nighttime dreams, masturbation fantasies), (2) erotica use, (3) erotic attractions, and (4) actual sexual partner experience. A crude but useful measure of sexual orientation is the Kinsey scale, a seven-point scale ranging from zero (exclusively heterosexual) to six (exclusively homosexual), with three being the approximate bisexual midpoint.[36,37] Some laboratories combine interview-based and self-report measures of sexual orientation with psychophysiologic measures of sexual arousal in response to visual or auditory presentations of men or women in erotic situations.[52] Sexual orientation is usually not assessed before puberty, and despite some anecdotal retrospective accounts, there is no well-established empiric base to decide the question of whether and to what extent a sexual orientation can be defined for prepubertal children. The third concept of homosexuality, homosexual *identity*, that is, labeling oneself *gay, lesbian,* or *bisexual,* is the result of a gradual *coming out* process: the recognition of one's own homosexual orientation and its partial or complete disclosure to others.

An adolescent's sexual orientation may contrast with his or her sexual identity as *straight, bisexual,* or *gay* or lesbian, especially at the developmental stage when the adolescent first starts noticing sexual feelings toward people of the same sex. Also, one's sexual orientation may not parallel actual sexual partner experience, for instance, when the adolescent is not yet sexually active, when he or she is experimenting with partners of both sexes, or when he or she is in an institutional situation where sexual partners of the other sex are not available. In fact, many more adolescents engage transiently and sporadically in overt homosexual behavior than ever become homosexually oriented.[20]

It is the aspect of homosexuality as a sexual orientation that is addressed by most etiologic research on homosexuality. In the last few years, psychobiologic research on homosexual orientation has come forward with a number of highly publicized findings in the areas of genetics, endocrinology, and neuroanatomy. The purpose of this essay is to summarize briefly these findings, put them in a wider perspective, and outline their limitations.

Genetic Studies

Soon after karyotyping had become available, several studies showed that the answer to the etiologic question concerning homosexuality did not lie in sex chromosome abnormalities.[50] Instead, most genetic studies to date have focused on the question of heritability using the twin-study approach. The first startling results of a very high concordance of forty monozygotic (MZ) twin pairs for homosexuality (thirty-seven of forty in contrast to a very modest concordance of twenty-six dizygotic (DZ) twin pairs four of twenty six) had been presented by Kallmann,[33,34] but his studies suffered from serious methodologic biases. The subsequent decades saw mostly scattered reports on individual twin pairs discordant for sexual orientation or on small groups of twin pairs showing higher concordance among MZ twins than among DZ twins, although the MZ concordance rates were far below those of Kallmann's (for references, see Buhrich et al.).[9]

The most recent reports concern samples of somewhat larger size. Pillard and Weinrich[49] conducted a family study of male homosexuality. Contrasting fifty-one predominantly homosexual index subjects and fifty predominantly heterosexual index subjects, they found that the homosexual index men had about four times as many homosexual brothers as the heterosexual index men did; there was no significant difference in the number of homosexual sisters. The authors concluded that there is a significant familial component to male homosexuality, but the data do not permit a further analysis of the question to what extent *familial* covers social rather than genetic influences.

Buhrich et al.[9] assessed sexual orientation and related variables in ninety-five pairs of male MZ twins and sixty-three pairs of male DZ twins recruited from a general twin registry. They found a significantly higher rate of adult homosexuality among the MZ than among DZ twins but did not provide concordance rates. (By the current author's calculations, the differences between MZ and DZ twins in concordance are not statistically significant.) Instead of calculating concordance rates, Buhrich et al. used sophisticated statistical analyses of sexual orientation as a dimensional continuous variable. A univariate analysis confirmed the presence of familial factors, but the authors were unable to distinguish shared environmental from genetic influence. Hierarchical tests of multivariate models supported the existence of a significant genetic influence on sexual orientation.

Bailey and Pillard[5] studied homosexual male probands with MZ cotwins, DZ cotwins, or adoptive brothers; the homosexual probands were recruited using homophile publications. Researchers assessed the sexual orientation of relatives either by asking relatives directly or, when this was impossible, asking the probands, using a seven-point Kinsey scale. Of the relatives whose sexual orientation could be rated, 52 percent (twenty-nine of fifty-six) of MZ cotwins, 22 percent (twelve of fifty-four) of DZ cotwins, and 11 percent (six of fifty-seven) of adoptive brothers were homosexual. The calculation of heritabilities (similar to the approach by Buhrich et al.)[9] resulted in substantial heritability estimates under a wide range of assumptions about the population base rate of homosexuality and about ascertainment bias.

King and McDonald[35] presented data on a sample of forty-five homosexual index cases recruited through homophile publications who reported on their cotwin's sexual orientation. Five of twenty MZ twins reported homosexuality or bisexuality in their cotwin as compared with three of twenty-five DZ twins. Unfortunately, this study combined males and females.

All these studies suffer from significant methodologic problems, among these ascertainment bias, nonoptimal assessment of sexual orientation (e.g., focus on behavior rather than imagery) and of zygosity (by questionnaire rather than direct measurement), and modest sample sizes. Nevertheless, the genetic data available permit two conclusions: (1) The rather consistent findings that concordance rates are higher for MZ twins than for DZ twins suggest a genetic contribution to sexual orientation, but differences between MZ and DZ twins in the effect of social influences cannot be excluded. (2) The variable and often high nonconcordance rates among MZ pairs exclude a single-gene effect.

Supplementing or replacing the analysis of concordance rates in twins with the assessment of heritability by means of quantitative genetic modeling techniques that are suited for continuously distributed phenotypes with a multifactorial cause may constitute an important advancement. Yet this new method relies on a number of highly controversial assumptions, and it requires sample sizes far beyond those used in the studies available. A detailed critique of this method is provided in McGuire.[42]

Psychoendocrine Studies

It was only in the late nineteenth century that a medical-biologic view of homosexuality gradually began to replace religious and criminal interpretations. Ever since, empiric research into its psychobiology has considered sexual orientation mostly in the context of sexual and psychosexual differentiation, that is, the development of physical and behavioral differences between the sexes. This research was based on the notion that an individual's homosexual orientation constitutes an aspect of cross-gender behavior, that is, behavior that is more typical of the other gender than of the person's own. Empirically this notion has found partial support in the demonstration of neuropsychologic differences between homosexual and heterosexual men that to some extent are similar to those found between the sexes.[22, 41]

Additional support comes from a number of data sets that show atypical gender role behavior (by history) in about two-thirds of homosexuals.[8, 62] For many homosexuals, this finding implies only a history of relatively low masculinity or femininity;[19] for a small minority, it implies having crossed—during childhood—the line into the other gender's role behavior and identity.[27] The remaining one-third of homosexuals report histories of gender-typical behavior. Thus from the outset, one has to note that psychoendocrine theories based on the concept of psychosexual differentiation, if they are validated at all, may apply only to the two-thirds of homosexuals who have a history of atypical gender role behavior. (Animal models indicate that, under certain experimental circumstances, hormonal factors may affect some specific aspects of sex-dimorphic behavior independently of others, but it will be very difficult to demonstrate such effects in human investigation, where strict experimentation with hormones is not possible.)

If male homosexuals are conceptualized as feminine and lesbians as masculine, it makes sense to search for an explanation in the sex hormones as the major biologic factor that underlies sexual differentiation and the development of the secondary sex characteristics. Consequently, in the last twenty years, numerous studies have investigated systemic hormone levels in—mostly adult—males and females differing in sexual orientation.[43, 44] For males, the evidence for differences between homosexual and heterosexual individuals in systemic hormone levels after puberty is essentially negative. The majority of females with homosexual orientation also appear to have testosterone and estrogen levels within the range typical of their sex. There seems to be a significant subgroup of about one-third, however, who have elevated testosterone levels, in a range comparable to what is commonly seen in hirsute women but still far below the normal male range. Recent studies by Dörner et al.[14]

suggest that such findings may relate to adrenal enzyme abnormalities (see below).

Because of the largely negative results from studies of systemic hormone levels in adolescence and adulthood, most of the psychoendocrine research on homosexuality is currently focused on prenatal hormones. A decisive role of prenatal or perinatal sex hormones in the development of sex-specific repertoires of both reproductive and nonreproductive behaviors has been demonstrated in many mammalian species,[21] and this includes the development of sexual preference in several species of lower mammals (for a critical review, see Adkins-Regan)[1]. Based on the scattered human data in this area, a number of biologically oriented researchers have formulated an analogous prenatal hormone theory of human sexual orientation. The evidence linking prenatal hormone variations to variations in human sexual orientation comes in part from endocrine disorders involving major variations in the fetal production or use of androgens; the syndromes of prenatal androgen excess in genetic females and the syndromes of androgen insensitivity in genetic males are particularly pertinent.

An increase in bisexual and homosexual orientation has been found in follow-up studies of prenatally hyperandrogenized females with congenital adrenal hyperplasia (CAH).[11, 15, 48, 63] The classic form of this syndrome, a result of 21-hydroxylase deficiency, is the most prevalent syndrome of fetal androgen excess in genetic females.[55] CAH females are born with varying degrees of external genital ambiguity, but their ovaries, fallopian tubes, and uteri are normal. Although the majority of these patients seem to be heterosexual, the finding of increased bisexuality and homosexuality suggests that high prenatal levels of circulating androgens in women contribute to the development of a nonheterosexual orientation.

Genetic males with complete androgen insensitivity (originally known as testicular feminization), when evaluated in adolescence or adulthood, are found to be erotically attracted to men.[39, 40] These patients have normal testes and make at least normal amounts of testosterone and its primary metabolite dihydrotestosterone but are unable to respond to either. At birth, their external genitalia appear feminine, and consequently these infants are raised as girls. Thus their sexual orientation to men may reflect social effects as well as insensitivity to androgens.

Genetic males with partial androgen insensitivity who make normal amounts of testosterone and dihydrotestosterone and respond with partial genital masculinization usually become erotically attracted to females.[47] Most are raised as males, but at least some of those raised female also develop sexual attractions to other females and may even undergo gender change later.[26]

Genetic males with 5-alpha-reductase deficiency[31, 32] or 17-beta-hydroxysteroid-dehydrogenase deficiency[53] secrete normal amounts of testosterone but cannot make dihydrotestosterone. Consequently their external genitalia look female at birth, and they are apparently raised as girls. They virilize strongly in response to pubertal increases in circulating testosterone. If they remain untreated, they tend to develop sexual feelings toward women and many seem to adopt a male gender role in later adolescence or adulthood. The behavioral method of these studies is highly problematic, however.[30,43]

The evidence from human intersex research suggests that, in either genetic males or females (i.e., independently of chromosomal sex), at least some degree of prenatal exposure to and use of androgens seems to "facilitate" (Money),[46] but certainly not determine, the development of erotic attraction to females as postulated by the prenatal hormone theory. By contrast, complete nonresponsiveness to androgens is associated with the development of erotic attraction to males.

Estrogens are also interesting in this context. Increased bisexuality is reported in women with a history of prenatal exposure to diethylstilbestrol (DES) that had been prescribed to their pregnant mothers.[16,17] DES is a nonsteroidal estrogen that bypasses the biochemical mechanisms that usually inactivate circulating estradiol in the fetus. Animal research has indicated that some effects of prenatal and perinatal androgens on the central nervous system (e.g., the "defeminization" of gonadotropin regulation and copulatory behavior of rats) are at least partially mediated by estrogens derived from testosterone by aromatization inside the target cells. To induce such effects by exogenous estrogen administration, one has to use DES or pharmacologic doses of steroidal estrogens. The pertinent research data indicate that estrogen-mediated developmental effects on sexual orientation may have to be taken into consideration. Thus human studies of the effects of altering the prenatal hormonal milieu by the administration of exogenous hormones lend support to a prenatal hormone theory that implicates both androgens and estrogens in the development of sexual orientation.

If one wants to generalize the prenatal hormone theory of sexual orientation from patients with known prenatal hormone abnormalities to the general population, one needs to search for indications of a difference in the prenatal hormonal milieu between homosexuals and heterosexuals. Here the evidence is insufficient. Homosexuals usually do not have somatic symptoms of intersexuality, and the fact that their adult sex hormone levels are in the normal range also does not suggest prenatal hormone abnormalities.

An interesting functional sign of prenatal or perinatal sex hormone variations, the positive estrogen feedback effect on luteinizing hormone (LH), has been derived from rodent research. In the mature female, rising estrogen levels typically trigger an LH surge associated with ovulation, but in rodents who have been prenatally or perinatally exposed to androgens, the LH surge is blocked. Owing to prenatal or perinatal exposure to their own androgens, genetic males usually do not show this phenomenon unless they have been castrated early in development.

In the search for corresponding functional signs of intersexuality in human homosexuals, Dörner and his team[12,13] have found that homosexual and transsexual men are more likely to react to estrogen administration with a delayed increase of LH. The authors interpreted the delayed LH response as an effect of positive estrogen feedback and a sign of deficient prenatal androgenization.

It can be argued, however, that the delayed LH response does not meet usually accepted criteria of a positive estrogen feedback effect and is a mere rebound phenomenon (e.g., see Gooren).[24,25] Also, in contrast to rodents, Rhesus monkeys do not show a marked effect of their prenatal androgen levels on their pattern of LH regulation; instead their positive estrogen feedback effect on LH depends exclusively on their systemic androgen levels. Finally, attempts at replicating the findings of Dörner's team by other laboratories brought conflicting results.[23,24,27,29,54] Studies of other features of gonadotropin regulation, such as pulse frequency and amplitude, also yielded mixed results.[56]

Therefore other explanations of Dörner's LH rebound findings must be considered. For example, the LH rebound effect could be due to increased rates of testicular impairment resulting from a high rate of sexually transmitted diseases in homosexuals.[29] This interpretation is plausible because men (regardless of sexual orientation) who show a marked LH rebound after estrogen administration also have a decreased testicular capacity to release testosterone after priming with human chorionic gonadotropin.[24] This controversy will be difficult to settle during the current human immunodeficiency virus (HIV) epidemic, when the study of LH regulation in human homosexuals has been complicated by findings of lowered testosterone and elevated LH levels in homosexual men who have advanced stages of HIV disease.[10]

Assuming for a moment that a definitive functional indicator of a particular prenatal hormonal milieu had been found in homosexuals, how could neuroendocrine intersexuality develop without genital intersexuality? Detailed developmental studies in animals have shown that the sex hormone–dependent differentiation of the genitals has a different time course than the sexual differentiation of the brain. In animal experiments, drugs or severe stress can influence the prenatal hormonal milieu and can affect brain and behavior, without signs of genital abnormalities (e.g., see Ward).[61]

Human research on the effects of prenatal stress has led to inconsistent results. Dörner's group[14] has summarized several of their studies that suggest a prenatal stress interpretation for human homosexuality, but these studies suffer from problems of sampling and assessment, and alternative psychosocial interpretations of the findings appear plausible. Of two prenatal stress studies in the United States, one has been positive (Ellis et al.),[18] and the other, methodologically very carefully done, has been negative (Bailey).[5]

In a recent new development, Dörner et al.[14] have formulated a new version of the prenatal hormone theory of homosexual orientation by combining the prenatal stress hypothesis with a genetic vulnerability to hormonal stress effects; the genetic vulnerability is based on deficiencies of enzymes involved in steroid synthesis. The authors developed this theory when they found the cortisol (F) precursor 21-deoxycortisol (21-DOF) to be significantly increased after adrenocorticotropic hormone (ACTH) stimulation in homosexual males and females as compared with heterosexual controls; a similar increase was found in the mothers of homosexual men. In female-to-male transsexuals, 21-DOF was increased significantly already before ACTH stimulation and even more after. The authors concluded from these data that "heterozygous and homozygous forms, respectively, of 21-hydroxylase deficiency represent a genetic predisposition to androgen-dependent development of homosexuality and transsexualism in females." They suggest that, in genetic males, testicular androgen deficiency "may be induced by prenatal stress and/or maternal or fetal genetic alterations." In addition, the authors found increased basal levels of dehydroepiandrosterone in male-to-female transsexuals as compared with normal males (and in one homosexual male who did not show the 21-DOF increase) and concluded that "partial 3beta-ol hydroxysteroid dehydrogenase deficiency may be a predisposing factor for the development of male-to-female transsexualism." (Transsexuals are of interest here because at least half of these persons have a history of predominantly to exclusively homosexual orientation relative to their original gender.) This bold and complex theory and the data it is based on are in urgent need of independent testing and replication. Even if replication should be successful, there is at least one significant problem: the theory by itself fails to explain why the majority of women with classic CAH (which is due to 21-hydroxylase deficiency in homozygous) do not develop homosexuality or transsexualism.

It is too early to conclude definitively that there is a contribution of prenatal or perinatal sex hormone levels to the development of homosexuality in general except perhaps in persons with clear-cut physical signs of intersexuality. Also, there are other potential avenues to a psychoendocrine explanation of homosexuality,[44] which have not yet been exhausted.

Neuroanatomic Studies

During the last three decades, a variety of sex hormone–dependent structural sex differences, ranging from dendritic branching patterns of neurons to the size of nerve cell nuclei, have been determined in the brain of several avian and mammalian species.[4, 60] More recently, structural sex differences have also been reported for the human brain, in terms of both large brain structures and specific cell nuclei.[4, 38, 58] The available data must be considered tentative at best, however, given that for most of these findings replications by independent laboratories have not yet been attempted or have failed.

In line with the fact that the psychobiologic theory of sexual orientation constitutes a specific application of the general psychobiologic theory of psychosexual differentiation, several researchers have searched for differences in sex-dimorphic structures between homosexual and heterosexual individuals. Swaab and Hofman[59] performed a morphometric analysis of the human hypothalamus and determined that the volume of the suprachiasmatic nucleus

(SCN) in a sample of homosexual men was 1.7 times as large as that of a reference group of male subjects and contained 2.1 times as many cells; however, the sex difference they had noted previously had pertained only to the shape of the SCN, not its volume or cell number. Nonetheless, the observation of a similarly enlarged SCN in a woman with Prader-Willi syndrome, whose features include a congenital LH-releasing hormone deficiency in which sex hormone levels are very low, suggests that the interaction with sex hormones at some stage of development of the SCN might be involved. In general, the SCN is involved in the regulation of physiologic rhythms; the specific role it may have for sexual orientation is unknown. A nearby nucleus, called the *sexually dimorphic nucleus*, for which Swaab and Fliers[57] have previously reported a marked sex difference in volume and cell number, did not yield differences between homosexual men and controls. Working independently of Swaab's team, LeVay[38] reported that one of two sex-dimorphic interstitial nuclei of the anterior hypothalamus (INAH 3), out of a total of four INAHs, was more than twice as large in heterosexual men as in women and also more than twice as large in heterosexual men as in homosexual men. Using the same samples, however, LeVay could not replicate the sexual dimorphism of the sexually dimorphic nucleus described by Swaab and Hofman.

A third paper was published by Allen and Gorski,[2] who found a larger brain structure that was dimorphic for both sex and sexual orientation. In this case, however, the homosexual men did not fit in a continuum with heterosexual men and women at the two poles but surpassed both groups: the anterior commissure in homosexual men was 18 percent larger in its midsagittal area than in heterosexual women and 34 percent larger than in heterosexual men. The anterior commissure is thought to be related to cognitive function and cerebral lateralization but not to reproductive function; it is of interest in this context that there are several (inconsistent) reports of increased rates of non–right-handed men in homosexuals in the literature. The authors interpret their anterior commissive finding—somewhat vaguely—as supporting the hypothesis that factors operating early in development differentiate sexually dimorphic structures and functions of the brain in a global fashion.

It is important to keep in mind that the findings of brain structural differences between homosexuals and heterosexuals have to be considered even more tentative than the respective findings of differences between the sexes. None of the findings on sexual orientation have yet been replicated by independent laboratories, and the published studies differ markedly in the neuroanatomic techniques employed and in important characteristics, such as age at death and AIDS status, of the persons whose brains were analyzed.

Practical Implications

Summarizing the evidence for a psychobiologic basis of sexual orientation, the last two decades of research have generated provocative data and substantial controversy. Yet the evidence available to date is still inconsistent, most studies are methodologically questionable or outright unsatisfactory, and alternative interpretations of the results cannot be ruled out. The genetic studies suggest a polygenic contribution to the development of homosexuality. Psychoendocrine findings indicate that variations in prenatal sex hormone levels may also be involved, at least in intersex individuals, and may underlie the neuroanatomic findings described. Yet it is quite conceivable and seems highly likely to this author that variations in prenatal hormone levels may be only one among several factors—both biologic and social—that interact in the development of sexual orientation.

The fact that homosexuality per se is not a psychiatric diagnosis implies that treatment with the goal of changing homosexual orientation is inappropriate, although the complex theoretical question of behavioral "normalcy" and the corresponding ethical issues of treatment cannot be discussed in the context of this brief overview (for a historical review, see Bayer).[7] Yet even the scientific basis alone as provided by the current state of psychobiologic research on homosexual orientation is insufficient to justify the assessment of sex chromosomes or sex hormones or the performance of brain-imaging procedures on adolescents or adults with emerging homosexual orientation. Much less so does it justify the treatment of homosexuality with sex hormones or psychosurgery as performed in the past or the prevention of homosexuality by prenatal endocrine screening and intrauterine sex hormone treatment of fetuses with inappropriate sex hormone levels, as advocated by some (for references, see Meyer-Bahlburg).[44]

When an adolescent or his or her parents come with a concern about homosexuality, the inquiry usually represents a composite of several issues: for example, difficulties in communication between parent and adolescent, a power struggle between parent and adolescent, homophobia of the parent, worries about the adolescent's future without family and children, fears about AIDS, religious norms, and the "diagnostic" question of whether the adolescent is actually developing a homosexual orientation. I usually try to get a sense of what the major issues are and how serious they may be. Apart from the concerns around sexuality, there are often problems that would profit from intervention. I offer evaluation and counseling, ranging from a telephone consultation to multisession brief therapy, with a focus on the family where indicated. In the course of my involvement with them, I give all families the explicit message that there are many opinions in our society about homosexuality, both negative and positive; that the mental health professions do not consider homosexuality a mental illness; and that we do not recommend any treatment for homosexuality itself. It is generally better to present this message after good rapport has been established, or a homophobic inquirer may just break off the contact and shop around for a mental health professional who offers an antihomosexual stance. If the adolescent or parents are interested, I give a brief overview of the status of psychobiologic findings and their limitations.

References

1. Adkins-Regan E; Sex hormones and sexual orientation in animals. *Psychobiology* 16:335–47, 1988.
2. Allen LS, Gorski RA: Sexual orientation and the size of the anterior commissure in the human brain. *Proc Natl Acad Sci USA* 89:7199–202, 1992.
3. Allen LS, Hines M, Shryne JE, et al: Two sexually dimorphic cell groups in the human brain. *J Neurosci* 9:497–506, 1989.
4. Bailey JM: A test of the maternal stress hypothesis for human male homosexuality. Unpublished doctoral dissertation. University of Texas at Austin, 1989.
5. Bailey JM, Pillard RC: A genetic study of male sexual orientation. *Arch Gen Psychiatry* 48:1089–96, 1991.
6. Bailey JM, Pillard RC, Neale MC, et al: Heritable factors influence sexual orientation in women. *Arch Gen Psychiatry* 50:217, 1993.
7. Bayer R: *Homosexuality and American Psychiatry. The Politics of Diagnosis.* New York, Basic Books, 1981.
8. Bell AP, Weinberg MS, Hammersmith SK: *Sexual Preference. Its Development in Men and Women.* Bloomington, Indiana University Press, 1981.
9. Buhrich N, Bailey JM, Martin NG: Sexual orientation, sexual identity, and sex-dimorphic behaviors in male twins. *Behav Genet* 21:75–96, 1991.
10. Croxson TS, Chapman WE, Miller LK, et al: Changes in the hypothalamic-pituitary-gonadal axis in human immunodeficiency virus-infected homosexual men. *J Clin Endocrinol Metab* 68:317–21, 1989.
11. Dittmann RW, Kappes ME, Kappes MH: Sexual behavior in adolescent and adult females with congenital adrenal hyperplasia. *Psychoneuroendocrinology* 17:153–70, 1992.
12. Dörner G: Neuroendocrine response to estrogen and brain differentiation in heterosexuals, homosexuals, and transsexuals. *Arch Sex Behav* 17:57–75, 1988.
13. Dörner G, Döcke F, Götz F, et al: Sexual differentiation of gonadotrophin secretion, sexual orientation and gender role behavior. *J Steroid Biochem* 27:1081–87, 1987.
14. Dörner G, Poppe I, Stahl F, et al: Gene- and environment-dependent neuroendocrine etiogenesis of homosexuality and transsexualism. *Exp Clin Endocrinol* 98:141–50, 1991.
15. Ehrhardt AA, Evers K, Money J: Influence of androgen and some aspects of sexually dimorphic behavior in women with the late-treated adrenogenital syndrome. *Johns Hopkins Med J* 123:115–22, 1968.
16. Ehrhardt AA, Meyer-Bahlburg HFL: Influence of in utero exposure to hormones on mood and behavior in adulthood [abstr.]. *Neuroendocrinol Lett* 12:216, 1990.
17. Ehrhardt AA, Meyer-Bahlburg HFL, Rosen LR, et al: Sexual orientation after prenatal exposure to exogenous estrogen. *Arch Sex Behav* 14:57–77, 1985.
18. Ellis L, Ames MA, Peckham W, et al: Sexual orientation of human offspring may be altered by severe maternal stress during pregnancy. *J Sex Res* 25:152–57, 1988.
19. Friedman RC: *Male Homosexuality. A Contemporary Psychoanalytic Perspective.* New Haven, Yale University Press, 1988.
20. Gagnon JH, Simon W: *Sexual Conduct.* Chicago, Aldine, 1973.
21. Gerall AA, Moltz H, Ward IL (eds): *Handbook of Behavioral Neurobiology. Vol 11. Sexual Differentiation.* New York, Plenum, 1992.
22. Gladue BA, Beatty WW, Larson J, et al: Sexual orientation and spatial ability in men and women. *Psychobiology* 18:101–8, 1990.
23. Gladue BA, Green R, Hellman RE: Neuroendocrine response to estrogen and sexual orientation. *Science* 225:1496–99, 1984.
24. Gooren L: The neuroendocrine response of luteinizing hormone to estrogen

administration in heterosexual, homosexual, and transsexual subjects. *J Clin Endocrinol Metab* 63:583–88, 1986.

25. Gooren L: The neuroendocrine response of luteinizing hormone to estrogen administration in the human is not sex specific but dependent on the hormonal environment. *J Clin Endocrinol Metab* 63:589–93, 1986.

26. Gooren L, Cohen-Kettenis PT: Development of male gender identity/role and a sexual orientation towards women in a 46,XY subject with an incomplete form of the androgen insensitivity syndrome. *Arch Sex Behav* 20:459–70, 1991.

27. Gooren LJG, Rao BR, van Kessel H, et al: Estrogen positive feedback on LH secretion in transsexuality. *Psychoneuroendocrinology* 9:249–59, 1984.

28. Green R: *The "Sissy Boy Syndrome" and the Development of Homosexuality.* New Haven, Yale University Press, 1987.

29. Hendricks SE, Graber B, Rodriguez-Sierra JF: Neuroendocrine responses to exogenous estrogen: No differences between heterosexual and homosexual men. *Psychoneuroendocrinology* 14:177–85, 1989.

30. Herdt GH, Davidson J: The Sambia "turnim-man": Sociocultural and clinical aspects of gender formation in male pseudohermaphrodites with 5-alpha-reductase deficiency in Papua New Guinea. *Arch Sex Behav* 17:33–56, 1988.

31. Imperato-McGinley J, Gautier T: Inherited 5a-reductase deficiency in man. *Trends Genet* 2:130–33, 1986.

32. Imperato-McGinley J, Peterson RE, Gautier T, et al: Androgens and the evolution of male-gender identity among male pseudohermaphrodites with 5a-reductase deficiency. *N Engl J Med* 300:1233–37, 1979.

33. Kallmann FJ: Comparative twin study on the genetic aspects of male homosexuality. *J Nerv Ment Dis* 115:283–98, 1952.

34. Kallmann FJ: Twin and sibship study of overt male homosexuality. *Am J Hum Genet* 4:136–46, 1952.

35. King M, McDonald E: Homosexuals who are twins. *Br J Psych* 160:407–9, 1992.

36. Kinsey AC, Pomeroy WB, Martin CE: *Sexual Behavior in the Human Male.* Philadelphia, WB Saunders, 1948.

37. Kinsey AC, Pomeroy WB, Martin CE, et al: *Sexual Behavior in the Human Female.* Philadelphia, WB Saunders, 1953.

38. LeVay S: A difference in hypothalamic structure between heterosexual and homosexual men. *Science* 253:1034–37, 1991.

39. Lewis VG, Money J: Gender-identity/role: G-I/R Part A: XY (androgen-insensitivity) syndrome and XX (Rokitansky) syndrome of vaginal atresia compared. *In* Dennerstein L, Burrows GD (eds): *Handbook of Psychosomatic Obstetrics and Gynaecology.* Amsterdam, Elsevier Biomedical Press, 1983, p 51.

40. Masica DN, Money J, Ehrhardt AA: Fetal feminization and female gender identity in the testicular feminizing syndrome of androgen insensitivity. *Arch Sex Behav* 1:131–42, 1971.

41. McCormick CM, Witelson SF: A cognitive profile of homosexual men compared to heterosexual men and women. *Psychoneuroendocrinology* 16:459–73, 1991.

42. McGuire TR: Is homosexuality genetic? A critical review and some suggestions. *J Homosexuality;* in press.

43. Meyer-Bahlburg HFL: Hormones and psychosexual differentiation: Implications for the management of intersexuality, homosexuality, and transsexuality. *Clin Endocrinol Metab* 11:681–701, 1982.

44. Meyer-Bahlburg HFL: Psychoendocrine research on sexual orientation: Current status and future options. *Prog Brain Res* 61:375–98, 1984.

45. Meyer-Bahlburg HFL: Can homosexuality in adolescents be treated by sex hormones? *J Child Adol Psychopharmacol* 1:231–35, 1990–91.

46. Money J: *Gay, Straight, and In-between. The Sexology of Erotic Orientation.* New York, Oxford University Press, 1988.

47. Money J, Ogunro C: Behavioral sexology: Ten cases of genetic male intersexuality with impaired prenatal and pubertal androgenization. *Arch Sex Behav* 3:181–205, 1974.

48. Money J, Schwartz M, Lewis VG: Adult erotosexual status and fetal hormonal masculinization and demasculinization: 46XX congenital virilizing adrenal hyperplasia (CVAH) and 46XY androgen insensitivity syndrome (AIS) compared. *Psychoneuroendocrinology* 9:405–15, 1984.

49. Pillard RC, Weinrich JD: Evidence of familial nature of male homosexuality. *Arch Gen Psych* 43:808–12, 1986.

50. Pritchard M: Homosexuality and genetic sex. *J Ment Sci* 108:616–23, 1962.

51. Robinson BE, Walters LH, Skeen P: Response of parents to learning that their child is homosexual and concern over AIDS: A national study. *J Homosex* 18:59–80, 1989.

52. Rosen RC, Beck JG: *Patterns of Sexual Arousal. Psychophysiological Processes and Clinical Applications.* New York, Guilford, 1988.

53. Rösler A, Kohn G: Male pseudohermaphroditism due to 17β-hydroxysteroid dehydrogenase deficiency: Studies on the natural history of the defect and effect of androgens on gender role. *J Steroid Biochem* 19:663–74, 1983.

54. Seyler LE, Canalis E, Spare S, et al: Abnormal gonadotropin secretory responses to LRH in transsexual women after diethylstilbestrol priming. *J Clin Endocrinol Metab* 47:176–83, 1978.

55. Speiser PW, New MI: An update of congenital adrenal hyperplasia. *In* Lifshitz F (ed): *Pediatric Endocrinology. A Clinical Guide,* ed 2. New York, Marcel Dekker, 1990, p 307.

56. Spijkstra JJ, Spinder T, Gooren LJG: Short-term patterns of pulsatile luteinizing hormone secretion do not differ between male-to-female transsexuals and heterosexual men. *Psychoneuroendocrinology* 13:279–83, 1988.

57. Swaab DF, Fliers E: A sexually dimorphic nucleus in the human brain. *Science* 228:1112–15, 1985.

58. Swaab DF, Gooren LJG, Hofman MA: The human hypothalamus in relation to gender and sexual orientation. *Prog Brain Res* 93:205, 1992.

59. Swaab DF, Hofman MA: An enlarged suprachiasmatic nucleus in homosexual men. *Brain Res* 537:141–48, 1990.

60. Tobet SA, Fox TO: Sex differences in neuronal morphology influenced hormonally throughout life. *Prog Brain Res* 93:205, 1992.

61. Ward IL: Sexual behavior. The product of perinatal hormonal and prepubertal social factors. *In* Gerall AA, Moltz H, Ward IL (eds): *Handbook of Behavioral Neurobiology.* Vol 11. Sexual Differentiation. New York, Plenum, 1992, p 157.

62. Whitam FL, Zent M: A cross-cultural assessment of early cross gender behavior and familial factors in male homosexuality. *Arch Sex Behav* 13:427–41, 1984.

63. Zucker KJ, Bradley SJ, Oliver G, et al: Psychosexual assessment of women with congenital adrenal hyperplasia: Preliminary analyses. In *Abstracts of the 18th Annual Meeting, International Academy of Sex Research,* Prague, CSSR, 1992.

22

Scientific Authority and the Search for Sex Hormones

Diana E. Long

Those who cannot remember the past are condemned to repeat it. —George Santayana

A science that hesitates to forget its founders is lost. —A. N. Whitehead

The research of Simon LeVay is the occasion for this essay. As a historian of science, I am intrigued by his "discovery" that there are anatomical differences in the hypothalami of men and women, of gays and straights, and I want him to get ahead with his research and tell me more. But as a historian I am alarmed by his belief that this single piece of information will modify our society's judgment of women and gays as bad, pathological, or dangerous. Women and gays can feel some assurance, perhaps, that our sense of being as good, normal, and safe as men and straights is backed by science, but this essay is a warning that the track record of physiological science as friend of the underdog is highly ambiguous. Earlier hopes of liberation through single factor hypotheses of biomedical science had outcomes that force us to think of all the politics and psychology that intervene between the scientist's hopes for doing good and the social outcomes.

In this essay I will relate a story with direct relevance to LeVay's research, the establishment in the 1920s of an optimistic Committee for Research in Problems of Sex, the CRPS, and the political fate of that reform effort. I present this as a cautionary tale not only about reductionism but also about the limits of the scientist's power to make liberating change in our society. My story concludes that scientists do not get to act alone as arbiters of our sexual mores, but have a cultural authority rooted in an American system for doing science. Is this story relevant? The quotations with which I began this essay offer two answers, quotations that warn us about the dangers of knowing, or not knowing, the past.

The CRPS: Its Goals, Successes, and Participation in the American Health Care System

In the beginning, as William O'Neill told us, everyone was brave.[1] The CRPS began as a typical progressive move to shed rational light on the troubling failure of traditional sexual mores in modern times. This sense of failure was the shared concern of social hygienists, the medical elite, and natural and social scientists who saw good social uses for their discoveries. Two institutions created in 1916 (J. D. Rockefeller Jr.'s Bureau of Social Hygiene and the federal government's National Research Council) saw the potential in this alliance for a sexology that might really solve the fundamental social problems of sex. Their leaders brought together, in 1921, a group of men and women to plan the reform of sex education, sex legislation, and medical sexology by a study of the root problems of human sexuality, reproduction, and sex differences. At their planning meeting, the social hygienists talked about the need for more effective understanding *and* regulation of prostitutes, and the need to develop birth control. Typically, at this meeting, reformers saw birth control in terms of both eugenics (they feared "the fertile womb of the Italian") and feminism, meaning the just need of "these modern women" to control their own reproduction in order to be free to seek a public voice and professional careers.

The social and natural scientists argued for the establishment of a sex research program on two different grounds. They thought that new scientific methods of gathering information about human sexual behavior would help modify the repressive Victorian morality by establishing norms and mores for sexual behavior that the human species could actually meet. But they also argued that their discoveries would help society control the old sinful lusts and deviations more effectively. Whether to liberate or repress sexuality, the scientists also argued that the committee should give priority to the establishment of basic facts about the development and biological control of sex and reproduction without too much concern about the applicability of these to the social problems of the time. In other words, at the start the CRPS was established for a mixture of motives—to liberate and control sex, to learn more about the reproductive system of mammals, and a variety of professional needs and interests.[2]

Staffed by prominent researchers, the CRPS was formed in 1922 as a granting agency that gave away close to two million dollars of Rockefeller money by 1952. But they could not do it all, and they quickly set some telling priorities. At first it looked as though the reform program, with the help of an interdisciplinary approach called "psychobiology," would determine the priorities.[3] But the psychobiologists were soon forced to concede that they did not have the staff or defensible methods of doing all those surveys, consulting with all those people, or taking on established ideologies like the church.[4]

And besides, by the mid-1920s the biologists, who had claims to be the best basic researchers, as they were beginning to be called, had an appealing alternative approach. Borrowing their reductionism and their standards from the physical sciences, these researchers thought that good biosocial science had to start with simple correlations established in animal studies before medical, educational, and legislative experts could translate these discoveries into policy. This way of dividing up the labor of expertise emerged in stages and resulted in a new, very American way of organizing the relations of science and culture around interlocking institutions of medicine and health care.[5]

First came the decision, in 1921, to place the CRPS in the Medical Science Division, not the Psychology and Anthropology Division, of the National Research Council. This was done, they said, because the social scientists, in a newly organized group, were too timid and too limited in their organizational expertise to take on this controversial topic.[6] Those who know the history of the medical establishment in the United States know that, after the Flexner Report of 1910 and funding by the Rockefeller Foundation of "scientific" medical education and research in academic centers, the medical establishment was anything but timid. It was becoming highly organized and confident in its ability to medicalize all aspects of human life.[7]

The second stage was the decision to fund grantees on the basis of "best research," not social need. The Rockefeller mantra on this was "promising lead not pressing need."[8] This was an opportunity for several ambitious biomedical researchers. Chicago embryologist Frank R. Lillie argued from the beginning of the meetings of the CRPS that his biological sex research program not only had panache (being based on the newly established facts of "female" and "male" sex hormones), but also had staying power in science policy as a causal model in which research could be planned in terms of the rippling effect of those hormones in the physiological and "psychobiological" systems.[9] Parts of this program, which was chosen by the committee, included the role of these new substances in determining the dimorphic form, function, and behavior of the mammalian organism, including, as they said, man. They said "man," but they mainly studied women as the "different" sex.[10]

The endocrinological program was adopted by the CRPS and received most of the funds in the 1920s and 1930s, with which it produced, successively, three research paradigms and research communities in medical sexology. While each paradigm was more sophisticated than the last, each basically argued that the amount and type of sex hormones was the fundamental fact of the distinct biology, biochemistry, and behavior of males and females. Productivity in advancing this kind of science was rewarded with intellectual, professional, and social "credit" that became the third hallmark of this field along with its commitment to medicine and to "promising leads." These three decisions ensured not only that this field became credible as a science, but also that it had an audience and a social impact.[11]

The CRPS group developed an intellectual rationale for their system of first developing the basic science and then sending it out into established medicine to do its good work, but this approach depended on having clinical as well as laboratory sexologists in place, and in the right place. The Rockefeller Foundation and the CRPS gave great attention to the "dissemination" of the scientific results to the public along the proper institutional paths. In the interwar period, the Rockefeller Foundation was able to establish several aspects of this organizational system, funding as it did not only the basic research program at the CRPS, but new medical centers of research and education. The foundation during this period was also supporting a new, relevant social science industry in the universities. We know the importance of this to the actors because the big controversies surrounding the CRPS had to do not only with programs that were open to social criticism (like Alfred Kinsey's in the 1940s), but also programs that were not represented by sufficiently powerful institutions (like George Hamilton's study of marriage in the 1920s). By the 1950s, the Rockefeller had turned the organizing and funding role over to the government, which had a scope and scale of powers (and funds) that no private endowment could match. Since then the National Institutes of Health and the National Science Foundation have stood at the center of a far more complex and deeply rooted science establishment in government, business, medicine, and science. And by the 1950s the clinical and social agencies had lined up to educate Americans about sex in a medical discourse validated by this "American system" of sexology.

This system, as it rested on a productive scientific community, was the vision of Warren Weaver, a creative organizer who was the head of the Division of Natural Sciences at the Rockefeller Foundation after 1933. Weaver was the one who persuaded the foundation that its role was to set up a certain kind of process for getting research done, a division of labor along specialized lines that would insure an open-ended growth of scientifically based expertise and technology. I will give just one example of his rhetoric and plan. In the 1930s, Weaver began funding, in a big way, the biochemists who were determining the precise molecular structure and functioning of the sex hormones. Frederick Hisaw at Harvard was a member of this scientific "stable of horses," a star competitor, and inexpensive too. In a memo to the Rockefeller Foundation after visiting Harvard in 1935, Weaver wrote, "it will cost only 3500 dollars to put the machine in place and $600 a year to run it."[12]

Well-funded scientists, like the CRPS beneficiaries, produced wonderful paradigms that were productive in science, medicine, and pharmaceutical business. All these partners did their job in bringing the new technologies to market as powerful pills whose specific actions are increasingly well known. The dangers in the system, the side effects of these powerful pills, and the often equally hidden and harmful ideological effects were sometimes able to slip between the cracks of this organization because those who could detect them did not have responsibility for them. In the case of Diethylstilbestrol, DES, the scientists who did the basic research on the synthetic female hormone were not asked, and did not volunteer, to argue the case for or against its clinical use in 1941.[13]

Separating scientists from the consequences of their work is only one social problem in this system. A second problem is that the system has been a collaboration of experts. While the lab and clinical scientists, the drug companies, and the government's Food and Drug Administration all represent different professional interests, they do not represent a very wide spectrum of social interests, including those of consumers. Inevitably interlocking, specialized institutions that represent the same vested interests and social identities were and are insensitive to their research subjects, patients, or customers. We have already heard from Jennifer Terry of the ideological baggage that influenced both the research approaches and social uses of the study of homosexuality in the last century.[14] Compatible ideological interests and social identities also ensured that the endocrine sex program fit in with the prevailing social mores and patterns of thought.

I want to emphasize, however, that these interests were powerful in science because they were compatible with the preferences within the science itself for reductionist approaches to nature and "nonpolitical" approaches to society.

Reductionist Models and Their Consequences for Sex Research

Given their place in a network of institutions responsible for developing and applying new discoveries, scientists can only make statements about the part of the problem on which they are experts and, most credibly, in the kind of reductionist terms that they use as scientists. We have become used to their assumption that they are searching for the cause of sex form, function, and behavior in endocrine organs and processes, and their claim that such discoveries alone justify society's support of their research. Hence the belief that what LeVay is saying is that the cellular differences he has discovered in the hypothalamus are *the* cause of homosexuality.

This view of science as a struggle to define and defend one's hypothesis has lasted because it has succeeded so well technologically. It has not had to succeed morally or socially in the way the founders of the CRPS first suggested, with the consequence that the various social agendas built into their research never got argued or tested. The only critics of a new experimental hypothesis have been peers in science whose job it is to try to challenge the claims of the researcher. In this adversarial system, it is the scientist's job to try to take that hypothesis as far as he can, modify it if it runs into obstacles, and compete with alternative models of sexuality in the other sciences.

This approach to science encourages a reductionism that I will again illustrate with the story of the search for sex hormones since 1920. The history of hormonal hypotheses about sex began in the 1920s with what seemed the simplest (and traditional) model that there are separate and opposite sexes and sex hormones. Because the research was being selected for funding on the basis of its "doability" as science, not on the basis of its social implications, none challenged that idea of sex exclusivity and "sex antagonism." The substance that Allen and Doisy discovered in the sow ovary, "Female Sex Hormone," was assumed to be the exclusive property of such females, and what Lillie's group discovered in male animals, "Male Sex Hormone," was assumed to be exclusive to cocks, bulls, and stallions. This assumption was very important for scientists who felt that "you can only study differences" in the search for sex hormones.[15] Hence the importance to the researchers (whatever their political beliefs about sexual orientation) of finding some way to fit homosexuals into the simple model (with results Jennifer Terry has described). And hence their profound discomfort with the discovery of stallion estrogen in the mid-1930s. What was so potent a symbol of masculinity doing with all that hormone of femininity? They reacted in private with predictable jokes and anxieties. A colleague of mine in biology at Boston University recalled that "this seemed like the beginning of the end for us men." In public they said it was "just some peculiarity of the metabolism of the horse testis." [16]

Not likely. Stallion estrogen was not their only source of suspicion that the simple model was wrong: consistently their experiments showed that the male and female sex hormones were not regulating reproductive cycles as if they were lonely actors and the sole cause of sexuality and sex difference.

In the 1930s, therefore, Dorothy Price and Carl Moore recast the endocrine paradigm on a different level. Instead of envisioning the testis and ovary (the gonad) as the source of sex difference and reproductive function, scientists imagined a feedback system between gonad and pituitary as the source of control. This more complex model allowed them to account for their observations without giving up the endocrine model or giving up their way of doing science by testing simple hypotheses What resulted was in fact the first negative feedback model for a system, one that Norbert Wiener acknowledged as a source of his new science of cybernetics.[17]

The young scientists watching this revolutionary work were not the only ones who were anxious about its implications for conservative sexual values. The 1940s and 1950s saw the development of a new sexism based supposedly on these scientific findings and the reification of old binaries about manliness and womanliness in the language of the new research. The scientists did not challenge those binaries or the reductionism of their statements, which allowed the put-down of women as bad, pathological, and dangerous.[18] They needed the binaries and reductionism to do their research. They counted on the enlarging sphere of cognitive light generated by science to eventually reveal more realistic definitions of the functions and behaviors of women and men. In the meantime, they left the interpretation of what they were doing to others and, amply supported by the American system in their own realm, did not protest against those interpretations. In the light of the potential they correctly saw in sex hormones for the control and management of sex in all its aspects, they trusted the system to use this power wisely.

Conclusion: The Social Role of the Scientist

Because this arrangement has been so successful in providing medical benefits, because it has created such seductive new sciences as cybernetics,[19] and because it has immunized our comfortable cultural assumptions about sex from direct scientific scrutiny, this system has been very hard for scientists to criticize.

As the creators of new knowledge, researchers found themselves feared and admired, and yet at the same time treated as children playing charming new games with little social relevance. Lay people are unclear whether or not to take seriously their claims about the powers, or potential powers, of the substances they offer to us as facts.

The scientists themselves often used, and use, this metaphor of play, a metaphor that deserves some serious attention,[20] as a way of resolving their paradoxical position of both having and lacking power. They have tended rather to tell jokes that reveal their stress and their insights.[21] Just walk down the corridor of any research science department and you will see evidence in the cartoons on their doors of the social insights and profound psychological anxiety of scientists who are brokering either the "secrets of life" or the "secrets of death."[22]

This has been a condition of life for scientists in our system of sex research at least since the 1930s. The 1920s was a time when the popular press had a field day with jokes about "gland doctors" and about aging, anxious old men being turned into monkeys when they tried the new monkey gland cures.[23] By the 1930s these works were updated with new material on the public anxieties about being chased by doctors bearing syringes labeled "hormone of maternal instinct."[24] The public fears reflected the fact that the scientists were indeed locked into the search for such simple correlations.

Even as their paradigms became more complex, the scientists explained what they were doing to themselves and to others in terms of their discovery of the key substrate for important aspects of human sexuality. CRPS member C. N. H. Long, for example, was a prominent biochemical researcher who helped show how the sex hormones are not profoundly different, but only slight modifications of a common (steroid) molecule. He considered it entirely beyond his responsibilities as a scientist to tackle what we would call the gender implications of his work, but his conversations with colleagues and family made it clear that he assumed that these should be in line with the secrets hidden in the endocrine hypothesis. But were they? He told a joke. Seeing an attractive woman walk down the hall one day in the 1930s shortly after the new molecular structure had been revealed, Long quipped to a colleague, "There but for one hydroxyl group go I."[25]

What did he mean by this? Was he reinforcing or challenging the binary construction of male and female? These implications were not discussed, and in fact this joke was one that his colleague thought should not even be made public.[26] Long himself maintained an agnostic attitude whenever he could on public issues; he "left to one side those things he could not approach as a scientist," the Reverend Sidney Lovett said at his memorial service. And he did this as the biochemist chosen to be dean of the Yale Medical School from 1947 to 1952.

This choice was typical of scientists of his generation, those who came of age in the 1930s. They agreed with the scientific ban on ideas that could only confuse; researchers who got involved with politics or history were indeed "lost for science." This dilemma was characteristic of a certain generation, but its effects have been persistent. Everett Mendelsohn summarized them in the 1970s as the choice that science constantly avoids in our society.[27] The question he raised is pertinent. Is science a moral and artistic endeavor, like symphony orchestras, that do not expect social criticism of their choice of composition? Fine, but then science should be supported with levels of funding similar to those of orchestras. Or is science a political and cultural actor, one whose risk taking and material effects we reward financially? Fine, but then it must be accountable for its effects. Between these two moral poles hangs a good deal of scientific history.

The two quotations with which I began this short essay represent also the two poles in our attitude toward the past; and they can be reconciled. Scientists, I have argued, do indeed know their past and the success that "tunnel vision" has had in bringing material benefits. They know the trade-off of leaving the hard social questions to one side in exchange for getting ahead with their cognitive work. They choose to repeat or not to repeat that past. And they may well choose to repeat even a bad past in the belief that the science comes first.

LeVay's insistence that the public consider the link of his research to the question of homosexual identity suggests that he has questioned the traditional division of labor between science and nonscience. But his assertion that the research will be used for liberatory ends cannot stand by itself. More questions than that of the biological basis for gay sex will be raised—and answered—using "his" research as evidence. Is he prepared to take these on? That is not what he is being paid to do, in our system of scientific research. He is being paid to maximize his claims about the hypothalamus, to test how far his hypothesis can go. To warn the public that this is just a game that should not be taken seriously is to invite the government to reduce its support of science—a Hobson's choice that keeps scientists in their place.

Hobson's or Mendelsohn's, the choice is a real one and it has a long past. In sex research we can trace this peculiar situation of scientists back to the very establishment of the new science of sex endocrinology. LeVay's research, which goes far beyond the cognitive content of that original field, nevertheless is successor to its professional-social dilemma.

Notes

This essay was originally presented at the Graduate Center, City University of New York panel on "The Brain and Homosexuality: A Symposium," sponsored by the Center for Lesbian and Gay Studies (CLAGS), December 9, 1991. I began by saying, "Before I begin, I want to welcome, as the director of the women's studies program at the University of South Maine, the opening of the Center for Lesbian and Gay Studies. The CUNY Graduate Center and all the friends of CLAGS deserve our thanks for their support of this important center for research on a subject our society has too long chosen to ignore."

1. William L. O'Neill, *Everyone Was Brave* (Chicago: University of Chicago Press, 1969).

2. All these views were expressed at the conference convened by the National Research Council and Bureau of Social Hygiene on October 27–28, 1921. Transcript in the paper of the CRPS, NRC Archives at the National Academy of Sciences, Washington, DC, File "1921 Conference." I have written briefly on their place in the history of sex research in Diana E. Long, "The Social Implications of the Scientific Study of Sex," *The Scholar and the Feminist IV: Connecting Theory, Practice, and Values*, 1977.

3. Donna Haraway has a fine deconstruction of the politics and psychology of sex according to the chair of the CRPS, Robert Yerkes, in *Primate Visions: Gender, Race, and Nature in the World of Modern Science* (New York: Routledge, 1989), 71.

4. Sophie B. de Aberle and George Washington Corner were participants who wrote the history of these *Twenty-Five Years of Sex Research: History of the National Research Council's Committee for Research in the Problems of Sex, 1922–1947* (Baltimore: W. B. Saunders, 1953). See also Adele Clarke's analysis of this example of scientific controversy in "Controversy and the Development of the Reproductive Sciences," *Social Problems*, 1990, 37: 18–37.

5. On the political dynamics that formed this powerful alliance of medicine, government, and business, see Paul Starr, *The Transformation of American Medicine* (New York: Basic Books, 1982). Starr's book, however, does not address the place of science and the scientist in this amalgam, nor the political dilemmas of the American system for the public.

6. Aberle and Corner, *Twenty Five Years*, note 4 above.

7. The detailed story of the formation of that confident profession is told in Rosemary Stevens, *American Medicine and the Public Interest* (New Haven: Yale University Press, 1971).

8. This philosophy is enthusiastically represented in Raymond Fosdick, *The Story of the Rockefeller Foundation* (New York: Harper, 1951); and in Wilder Penfield, *The Difficult Art of Giving: The Epic of Alan Gregg* (Boston: Little Brown, 1967), 225 and passim.

9. Diana E. Long, "Biology, Sex Hormones, and Sexism in the 1920s," *Philosophical Forum* 1974, 5: 81–94; and Nelly Oudshorrn, *Beyond the Natural Body: An Archaeology of the Sex Hormones* (London: Routledge, 1994).

10. In Victorian Anglo-American culture, women were "the sex." In the mid-twentieth century, however, the female became the "different sex" amenable to deconstruction by medical science. Caroll Smith-Rosenberg, *Disorderly Conduct: Visions of Gender in Victorian America* (New York: Knopf, 1985).

11. Bruno Latour introduced the important metaphors of credit and scientific trials to represent *Science in Action: How to Follow Scientists and Engineers through Society* (Cambridge: Harvard University Press, 1987), esp. 71 ff.

12. I tell this story of discipline formation around sex research in Diana E. Long, "The 'Physiological' Identity of American Sex Researchers between the Two World Wars," in *Physiology in the American Context, 1850–1940*, ed. Gerald L. Geison (Baltimore: American Physiological Society, 1987), ch. 11, 263–78. The best study of the new alliance between philanthropists and scientists in the 1930s is Robert Okhler, *Partners in Science: Foundations and Natural Scientists, 1900–1945* (Chicago: University of Chicago Press, 1991).

13. Susan Bell has written extensively on the dilemmas and tragedies of Diethylstilbestrol (DES) that arose from the constraints on the scientists, clinicians, and FDA personnel who approved that drug for clinical use in 1941. "A New Model of Medical Technology Development: A Case Study of DES," *Research in the Sociology of Health Care*, 1986, 4: 1–33.

14. Jennifer Terry, "Will We Know One if We See One? Constitutional and Anthropometric Studies of Sex Variant Bodies" (paper given at the CLAGS symposium on "The Brain and Homosexuality," December 9, 1991). See also idem, "Lesbians under the Medical Gaze: Scientists Search for Remarkable Differences," on research conducted under the auspices of the Committee for the Study of Sex Variants during the 1930s in New York City in *Journal of Sex Research*, 1990, 27: 317–39.

15. I tell this story in Long, "Biology, Sex Hormones, and Sexism in the 1920s," as does Oudshoorn, *Beyond the Natural Body*, note 9 above.

16. Oudshoorn, *Beyond the Natural Body*, note 9 above.

17. Diana E. Long, "Moving Reprints: An Historian Looks at Sex Research Publications of the 1930s," *Journal of the History of Medicine* 1990, 45 (3): 452–68.

18. Emily Martin has recently approached these insults and untruths from another perspective, contrasting the destructive medical narratives about women's bodies with the stories women tell themselves. *The Woman and the Body: A Cultural Analysis of Reproduction* (Boston: Beacon, 1987).

19. Adele Clarke tells the story of sex research as part of the new reproductive science expertise in America in *Disciplining Reproduction: Modernity, American Life Sciences and the "Problem of Sex"* (Berkeley: University of California Press, 1996).

20. The idea that science, like all creative work, has the freedom of play dates back at least to J. Huizinga and has been popular with twentieth-century scientists, including C. N. H. Long, "The Selection, Care and Preservation of Research Scientists," *Pediatrics*, 1955: 203–11. I described this metaphor as an anxious counter to the growing organization of science in Diana E. Long, " 'The Selection, Care and Preservation of Research Scientists' at the Committee for Research in Problems of Sex, 1922–1941" (lecture given at the Yale University Beaumont Club, February 1982).

21. Michael Mulkay, *On Humor: Its Nature and Place in Modern Society* (Oxford: Blackwell, 1988).

22. Evelyn Fox Keller, *Secrets of Life, Secrets of Death: Essays in Language, Gender, and Science* (New York: Routledge, 1992).

23. David Hamilton, *The Monkey Gland Affair* (London: Chatto and Windus, 1986); and Jessica Jahiel, "The Development of a Scientific Idea: Male Sex Hormone Therapy" (Ph.D. diss., Boston University, 1991).

24. A cartoon on this theme appeared in 1935, when C. N. H. Long's associate Abraham White had isolated prolactin at Yale University.

25. I know this story because I am his daughter and heard it *privately*. I explore the ambiguities of this private/professional relationship to my work as a historian in Long, "Moving Reprints," note 17 above.

26. In my interview on the history of endocrinology with F. D. Lukens, Long's

colleague, this clinical scientist asked me to turn off the tape recorder when he told me this story of their research days together in the 1930s at the University of Pennsylvania.

27. Mendelssohn discussed this issue at a conference, chaired by Stephen Toulmin, on the "Past, Present, and Future of the Biomedical and Behavioral Sciences," Santa Fe, New Mexico, 1978, which was published as the "Report of the Scholarly Adjuncts, National Commission for the Protection of Human Subjects," in the *Congressional Report*, December 1976.

23

Creating Natural Distinctions

Dorothy Nelkin and M. Susan Lindee

At the 1991 CLAGS conference on "The Homosexual Brain," Dorothy Nelkin argued that linking homosexual behavior to brain structure reflects in part the growing preoccupation with biological determinism in American culture. Responding to the expectation that defining homosexuality as a biological status will reduce prejudice, she suggested that genetic explanations in fact can serve multiple social agendas. In particular, they have in the past been used to justify social stereotypes and persistent inequities as "natural" and therefore inevitable. Thus, while biological claims could lead to greater tolerance for human differences, they can also lead to pernicious abuse. Ultimately, it is not biology but common beliefs and social biases that shape social policies.

The appropriation of genetic explanations is the subject of a book by Dorothy Nelkin and M. Susan Lindee, *The DNA Mystique: The Gene as a Cultural Icon.* The following material, excerpted from this book, contains the core of Nelkin's 1991 remarks.

Biological explanations have long served to justify social inequalities by casting the differential treatment and status of particular groups as a natural consequence of essential, immutable traits. In the 1990s the language of genetic essentialism has given new legitimacy to such explanations. Group differences are appearing in popular culture as genetically driven, encouraging stereotyped images of the nurturing female, the violent African American male, and the promiscuous homosexual. But the images of pathology have moved from gross to hidden body systems. Once blacks were portrayed with large genitalia and women with small brains: today the differences lie in their genes.

The belief in essential differences has been reinforced by scientific studies of body parts such as genes or neurons that seem to explain behavior, as well as by scientific theories about evolution that seem to biologically ground social practices. Molecular genetics, behavioral genetics, neurobiology, and sociobiology have provided a language through which group differences can be interpreted as biologically determined. These sciences have encouraged the increasing acceptability of genetic explanations and their strategic role in the continuing debates over gender, race, and sexual orientation.

Current interest in the genetic basis of group differences coincides with extraordinary concern about gender roles, ethnic identity, and sexual orientation. Genetic explanations can be used to marginalize groups or—as in the case of some feminists, African Americans, and homosexuals—to celebrate group differences. Some who have traditionally suffered from prevailing biological theories are now embracing biological difference as a source of legitimacy and as evidence of their own superiority.

They shrewdly exploit the discursive power of biological boundaries to promote reformist agendas. Some feminists have celebrated biological difference as a source of special identity or a rationale for equal protection, citing the "creative power that is associated with female biology" and the "native talent and superiority of women."[1] Controversial Afrocentrist Leonard Jeffries, a professor at City College in New York, has claimed that melanin is "responsible for brain development, the neurosystem and the spinal column"; since African Americans have more of it, they are more creative.[2] Meanwhile gay activist Simon LeVay has promoted the idea that homosexuality is inborn and unchangeable, for such a claim seems to transform nonconformist sexual behavior from a "lifestyle choice" to a natural imperative.[3] These individuals, despite radically different perspectives and conflicting social policy agendas, seem to agree about one thing: in contests over social worth, biology matters. Whoever can successfully argue that biology—and more specifically DNA—supports their particular political viewpoint has a tactical advantage in the public debate.

Neither biological nor environmental explanations of human behavior have an inherent social meaning. Both forms of explanation can be used to justify liberal or conservative causes; both can be applied oppressively, and each can be used to promote greater human freedom. In the last two decades biological determinism has been the target of several well-publicized attacks by leading academic biologists and philosophers. But environmental determinism, too, can be used to limit human rights and constrict groups identified as inferior. In the 1950s and 1960s, for instance, popular interest in the power of the environment reinforced women's traditional roles as caregivers. It justified the 1950s "back to the home" movement for mothers who had been employed during the war years: if the achievements of children were finely calibrated to their training and environment, then mothers were needed at home and entirely responsible for their children's behavior.

Biological explanations may reassure threatened groups that they possess special skills and advantages, thereby demonstrating their inherent superiority or worth. When feminist texts promote caring or intuition as unique feminine skills, they are effectively depicting their readers as advantaged. When men's movement texts celebrate male aggression as biological strength, they are elevating a presumed necessary evil to the status of a positive social good. Both groups are engaged in setting boundaries of identity and delineating criteria of social worth. Here, as in other forums, genes have become a way to establish the legitimacy of social groupings. This function is even more overt in the public debate over the meaning of race.

In the 1980s, growing concerns about domestic problems—the cost of welfare programs, the changing ethnic composition of major cities, and the growing "underclass"—encouraged speculation about the role of genetics in perpetuating poverty and violence. Code phrases like "welfare mother," "teenage pregnancy," "inner-city crime," and "urban underclass" were often indirect references to race. But some public figures did not hesitate to make the connection explicit. Marianne Mele Hall, a Reagan administration appointee, announced in 1992 that African Americans were "conditioned by 10,000 years of selective breeding for personal combat and the anti-work ethic of jungle freedoms."[4] Columnist George Will, in a 1991 *Newsweek* column inspired by a speech by Harvard professor James Q. Wilson, proposed that a black "warrior class" in the inner city was a consequence of nature "blunder[ing] badly in designing males." Men are innately uncivilized, he said, and though socialization has often constrained biology, two "epochal events" have changed this picture: "the great migration of Southern rural blacks to Northern cities and the creation of a welfare state that made survival not dependent on work or charity."[5]

In the 1990s, race theorists are more and more willing to publicly express their views about genetic differences between ethnic groups and to suggest the significance of such differences for social policy. Michael Levin of City College in New York has not only argued that blacks are less intelligent than whites, but also used his theories to oppose affirmative action. He has asserted that differences in average SAT test scores (which unquestionably exist) are self-evident proof of genetic differences—as though such scores directly reflect inmate intelligence. Genetic images appeal to these writers as a way of resisting cultural imperialism and establishing collective identity on the basis of shared identification with a common ethnic heritage.

Afrocentrists are effectively attempting to transform their differences into positive biological strengths. But they share with racist critics the assumption that race is a biological reality with some meaning for this debate.[6] For gay rights activists, the problems are different; they face the daunting task of redefining a "sin" or a "lifestyle choice" as a biological access to DNA. By 1994, the extravagant publicity launching Herrnstein and Murray's book *The Bell Curve*—an immediate best-seller—moved the debate over genetic differences to center stage.

To protest such constructions, some African Americans have proposed a counternarrative drawn from a long history of Pan-African ideology, in which black skin is a sign of superiority. In public lectures, Leonard Jeffries presents a view of world history and race biology that celebrates biological differences. "Black Africans of the Nile Valley," he claims, are the source of all science, mathematics, and religion. And melanin, the pigment that makes skin dark, is a crucial biological need. "You have to have melanin to be human. Whites are deficient in it . . . it appears that the creative instinct is affected."[7] Distinguishing sun people (blacks) from ice people (whites), he is interested in promoting collective identity on the basis of a biological construction of "race."[8]

In the debates over the "homosexual brain" or the "gay gene," nature and nurture have even more complicated meanings.

In August 1991, Simon LeVay, a neuroscientist at the Salk Institute, published a paper in *Science* that linked homosexual behavior to brain structure. LeVay said that homosexual males, like all women, had a smaller hypothalamus than heterosexual males. The hypothalamus is a part of the brain between the brain stem and the cerebral hemispheres, believed to play some role in emotions. It is too small to be effectively examined through contemporary brain imaging techniques such as Positron Emission Tomography (PET scans). LeVay needed, therefore, to study the brains of cadavers. His conclusions were based primarily on the postmortem examination of the brains of forty-one persons, nineteen of them homosexual males who had died of AIDS. He has acknowledged that his findings were open to several interpretations. The size differences in the hypothalamus could indicate a genetic basis of sexual orientation, but they could also be a consequence of behavior; or they could be coincidental, reflecting neither cause nor effect but the presence of some other condition (such as AIDS).

LeVay preferred the genetic explanation, describing his "belief," his "faith" in the biological basis of behavior. Indeed, LeVay's research followed from his personal conviction that "I was born gay." He has stated that virtually all human variation, including detailed personality differences and such cultural preferences as musical taste (Mahler over Bruckner, for example), are biological. LeVay is convinced that children are entirely genetic products. Some children are, from the moment of conception, fated to become gay; if parents have any influence at all, LeVay argues, it is only in the way they respond to the inevitable.

LeVay's claims were later supported by the findings of a team of geneticists led by Dean Hamer at the National Cancer Institute. In 1993 they claimed to locate genes on the X chromosome that predisposed some men toward homosexuality. The X chromosome is inherited in boys, of course, only from the mother. This report and Hamer's popular book on the subject received extensive media coverage and attracted significant public interest.[9]

The research constructing homosexuality as biological had a tactical advantage; it shifted responsibility from the person to the genes. Individual homosexuals had no choice but to behave as they did. It would therefore be unjust for society to discriminate against them, for the Constitution, demanding equal protection, prohibits discrimination on the basis of immutable characteristics.

LeVay thus sought publicity for his research, and his conclusions became a media event, discussed in popular magazines, major newspapers, and television talk shows. The hypothalamus, a little-known organ deep within the brain, became a popular symbol of virility. A Calvin Klein advertising campaign referred to a "hypothalamus-numbing host of imitators." A *Newsweek* article titled "Born or Bred?" explored the implications of the "new research that suggests that homosexuality may be a matter of genetics not parenting." The magazine's cover photo featured the face of an infant, with the headline "Is This Child Gay?"[10] "Is Lesbianism a Matter of Genetics?" asked the headline of another 1993 article. "Little girls are made of sugar and spice and everything nice, and some of them may have a dollop of genetic frosting that increases the likelihood they'll grow up gay."[11] Vice President Dan Quayle publicly disagreed, however, insisting that homosexuality "is more of a choice than a natural situation. . . . It is a wrong choice."[12]

The debate was joined on television's *Nightline* in a program on homosexuality. The topic was whether "a newborn infant may already have certain physical differences in the brain that could be distinguished from the brain of an infant that will grow up to be a heterosexual." A leader of the religious right, Jerry Falwell, appeared on the show to insist that homosexuality was not innate but a learned and chosen lifestyle; he worried that the research would be used to legitimate homosexual practices. Meanwhile, host Ted Koppel, referring to a "potentially gay fetus," asked, "Will people abort?" (Extending this idea, a 1993 Broadway play called *Twilight of the Golds* featured a geneticist and his wife who learn through prenatal tests that their unborn son will be gay. After much soul-searching, they abort the fetus; the family is torn apart.)[13]

The media also speculated on the potential effect of genetic research on homophobia. On a segment of the prime-time news show "20/20," Barbara Walters asked, "I wonder if it were proven that homosexuality was biological if there would be less prejudice?"[14] *Newsweek* presented the views of homosexuals who welcomed the research, anticipating that it could reduce animosity. "It would reduce being gay to something like being left-handed, which in fact is all that it is," said Randy Shilts.

But the gay community has been divided about the consequences of genetic identification. Some anticipate abortion of "gay fetuses," increased discrimination empowered by genetic information, or the use of biotechnology to control homosexuality, for example, with excision of the "gay gene" from embryos before implantation.[15] Janet Halley, a law professor, has predicted that essentialist arguments of biological causation will work against constitutional rights and encourage "the development of anti-gay eugenics."[16] The *National Enquirer* responded to research on the "gay gene" with the headline "Simple Injection

Will Let Gay Men Turn Straight, Doctors Report."[17] And a spokesman for the National Gay and Lesbian Task Force suggested that genetic thinking would give rise to the idea that "by tweaking or zapping our chromosomes and rearranging our cells, presto, we'd no longer be gay."[18]

There is some historical justification for these concerns, since Nazi extermination of homosexuals was grounded in their presumed biological status. And other campaigns by gay activists have had unexpected consequences. The 1973 American Psychiatric Association decision to change the classification in the Diagnostic and Statistical Manual failed to produce the social legitimation anticipated by those who had advocated the change. LeVay himself dismisses such historical precedents. "Those who look to history are condemned to repeat it."[19]

If "Dear Abby" is any indication, however, the biological narrative has influenced popular beliefs about homosexuality. In 1992, when a reader complained about the columnist's suggestion that homosexuality was a consequence of both nature and nurture, Abigail van Buren responded, "I have always believed that one's sexuality is not a matter of choice—that homosexuals, like heterosexuals, are born that way. I apologize for my lapse in judgment in buying that nature-nurture theory. I knew better and am profoundly contrite."[20] This strong statement in such a visible source suggests that in the short term, at least, biological explanations have gained ground in the popular understanding.

In the public debates over human differences—for example, the meaning of gender, race, and sexual orientation—genetic images are strategically employed in an effort to delineate boundaries, justify rights, or legitimate inequalities. Genes can be understood in this debate as rhetorical devices that can be utilized in many different ways. They have been used to identify biological differences and give them social meaning—by those, for example, who believe education will make no difference in the social status of black Americans; by those who favor homosexual marriage; by those who promote equality of the sexes; and by those who oppose equality in general.

Biological differences in themselves have no intrinsic social meaning. Skin color is genetic—it is a real biological property—but it became a sign of political and economic difference for specific historical reasons, including the European colonization and exploitation of Africa. Due to the vagaries of evolution and population genetics, African populations happened to have skin that was uniformly darker than that of European populations. If both Africans and Europeans had instead manifested equivalent variation in skin color (displaying skin tones within each group ranging from very light to very dark), skin color would not have been a reliable sign of Continental origin and therefore could not have served as a visible mark of social or economic status. (Perhaps some other biological trait, such as eye color, would have come to stand for racial difference.) Certainly racial classifications vary across cultures. For example, Brazilian ideas about race, the anthropologist Marvin Harris has observed, would be "inconceivable in the cognitive frame of descent rule" that guides American ideas. Full siblings in Brazil can be assigned to different racial categories if they differ in physical appearance.[21]

Sex, too, has a complicated history as a social category. Thomas Laqueur's work has demonstrated that for much of human history, from classical antiquity to the end of the seventeenth century, men and women functioned in two different social roles but were seen as variations on essentially one biological sex. The boundaries between male and female were understood to be "of degree and not of kind." To Galen, for example, the sex organs of both men and women were basically "the same," the uterus seen as a form of penis, the ovaries a form of the testicles.[22] The biological story of difference was rewritten in the midst of the scientific revolution, Laqueur has argued, and two distinct biological sexes became a political necessity by the late eighteenth century on account of economic and social changes.[23] From another perspective, the biologist Anne Fausto-Sterling has noted that people do, biologically, come in more than two sexual forms—some experts estimate that hermaphrodites (individuals who have some combination of both male and female genitalia) account for one in every twenty-five births, or 4 percent of the human population. These intersex individuals are socially invisible because of medical management: such infants are promptly designated male or female and their genitals surgically transformed.[24]

The existence of the homosexual body, too, depends on culture. In Greece in the fourth and fifth centuries B.C. there was no culturally recognized distinction between heterosexuality and homosexuality. Greek thinkers found nothing surprising in the coexistence of desire for both male and female sexual partners. They were, however, concerned about the control of desire and the uses of pleasure, and Greek texts devote significant attention to questions of control and power, though virtually none to sexual orientation.[25]

The biological groupings that appear in the contemporary debate, then, are specific historical products. not necessary biological categories. The meaning of these groups as genetically constructed is likewise flexible. Biological differences can become a source of stigmatization (extra math study for girls) or regressive social policy (expecting all mothers to stay home with their children). They can also be a source of political power (legal recognition of homosexual marriage with all attendant benefits, for example). When defined as an unchangeable and fundamental biological attribute, race, sex, or sexual preference can become a source of social support and authenticity that may be particularly valued by groups that have been the focus of past discrimination.

Biological narratives do not inherently oppress. But we argue that they are dangerous precisely because of the cultural importance attached to DNA. These narratives, attributing social differences to genetic differences, are especially problematic in a society that tends to overstate the powers of the gene. Charged with cultural meaning as the essence of the person, the gene appears to be a powerful, deterministic, and fundamental entity. And genetic explanations—of gender, race, or sexual orientation—construct difference as central to identity, definitive of the self. Such explanations thereby amplify the differences that divide society.

It is especially ironic that DNA has become a cultural resource for the construction of differences, for one of the insights of contemporary genomics research is the profound similarity, at the level of the DNA, among human beings and, indeed, between humans and other species. We differ from the chimpanzee by only one base pair out of a hundred—1 percent—and from each other by less than 0.1 percent. The cultural lesson of the Human Genome Project could be that we are all very much alike, but instead contemporary molecular genetics has been folded into enduring debates about group inferiority. Scientists have participated in these debates by seeking genes for homosexuality and alcoholism, genes for caring, and genes for criminality. This research and the ideological narratives that undergird it have significant social meaning and policy implications.

Notes

1. Alison Jagger, *Feminist Politics and Human Nature* (Sussex: Harvester Press, 1983). See also Deborah L. Rhodes, "The No-Problem Problem: Feminist Challenges and Cultural Change," *Yale Law Journal* 100, 1 (1991):1–62.

2. Jeffries, who has published little scholarly work, is well known because of his work with the New York City Board of Education on curricular reform and his public speeches in the late 1980s and early 1990s. See Eric Pooley, "Doctor J: The Rise of Afrocentric Conspiracy Theories: Leonard Jeffries and His Odd Ideas about Blacks and Whites," *New York Magazine*, 2 September 1991.

3. Simon LeVay, *The Sexual Brain* (Cambridge: MIT Press, 1993).

4. Cited in Micaela di Leonardo, "White Lies, Black Myths," *Village Voice*, 22 September 1992, 31.

5. George F. Will, "Nature and the Male Sex," *Newsweek*, 17 June 1991, 70.

6. David Layzer, "Affirmative Action Is at Least on the Right Track," *New York Times*, 23 June 1990.

7. Pooley, "Dr. J," 34.

8. James Traub, "Professor Whiff," *Village Voice*, 1 October 1991.

9. Dean Hamer et al., "Androgen Involvement in Homosexuality," *American Journal of Human Genetics* 53 (1993): 844–52. Also see Robert Pool, "Evidence for a Homosexuality Gene," *Science* 261 (16 July 1993): 221–91; Dean Hamer, *The Science of Desire* (New York: Simon and Schuster, 1994).

10. David Gelman, "Born or Bred?" *Newsweek*, 24 February 1992, 48–53.

11. This was based on a report of a study published in the *Archives of General Psychiatry* that focused on 108 lesbians with identical and nonidentical twin sisters, plus 32 lesbians with adoptive sisters. The study suggested that sexual preference depended on biology. Identical twins were much more likely to both be lesbians than were fraternal twins or sisters with no genetic relationship. "Most lesbians feel they were born gay," the report said. *Newsweek*, 22 March 1993, 53.

12. Quoted in Karen DeWitt, "Quayle Contends Homosexuality Is a Matter of Choice, Not Biology," *New York Times,* 14 September 1992."

13. The play, by Jonathan Tollins, starred Jennifer Gray.

14. *Twenty/Twenty,* 24 April 1992.

15. See letters to the editor, *New York Times,* 27 July 1993.

16. Janet E. Halley, "Biological Causation of Homosexuality and Constitutional Rights" (public lecture, New York University Law School, 11 October 1993).

17. *National Enquirer,* 10 August 1993.

18. Ron Wilson, "Study Raises Issue of Biological Basis for Homosexuality," *Wall Street Journal,* 30 August 1991.

19. Speech at a CLAGS symposium on "The Homosexual Brain," CUNY Graduate School, New York, 9 December 1991.

20. "Dear Abby" column, "Genes Are Key in Sexual Orientation," *Delaware County Daily Times,* 21 January 1992.

21. Marvin Harris, "Referential Ambiguity in the Calculus of Brazilian Racial Identity," in ed. Norman Whitten Jr. and John Szwed. *Africo-American Anthropology,* (New York: Free Press, 1970), 75–86.

22. Thomas Laqueur, *Making Sex: Body and Gender from the Greeks to Freud* (Cambridge: Harvard University Press, 1990), 25–27.

23. Ibid., 201–27.

24. Anne Fausto-Sterling, "The Five Sexes: Why Male and Female Are Not Enough," *Sciences,* March–April 1993, 20–25.

25. We are indebted to Sheila Murnaghan, who, in her talk "Was Sex Different in the Ancient World?" (University of Pennsylvania, 17 February 1994), brought to our attention the extensive recent literature on sex and sexuality in ancient Greece. See also David M. Halperin, John J. Winkler, and Froma Zeitlin, eds., *Before Sexuality* (Princeton: Princeton University Press, 1990).

24

LeVay's Thesis Reconsidered

William Byne

Dr. Simon LeVay claims to demonstrate a correlation between sexual orientation in men and the structure of a portion of the hypothalamus (1). His study has been highly publicized by both the news media and the scientific press. Most of the discussion has focused on the implications of the findings and has paid little attention to their reliability and validity. Criticism has been limited by and large to a few technical issues such as the fact that the number of brains examined was relatively small, and the fact that all of the brains from homosexuals came from men who had died from AIDS. I want to discuss both the scientific and political aspects of Levay's work from a perspective that has received scant coverage in the scientific press and the news media.

The fact of the matter is that every few years a study is published that claims to demonstrate a sex difference in the brain or a biological correlate of sexual orientation. Almost without exception, these studies have been subsequently discredited because of their inability to be reproduced by independent laboratories (2). Whether or not LeVay's study will join this long tradition of irreproducible results remains to be seen. Unfortunately, even if his study fails to be replicated, it will continue to have tremendous impact for years to come owing to the publicity it has already received.

In support of this assertion, I will offer an example from the sex differences literature. If you ask what relevance this has to the issue of sexual orientation, the answer is simple. According to the biologically deterministic theories, gay men are merely women with male genitals, while gay women are men with female genitals. While many would object to this characterization as simplistic, it is supported by the historical record. As soon as any sex difference in brain structure or physiology is reported, biological determinists rush to see whether that particular attribute is sex-reversed in homosexuals. Thus, any report of sex differences in the brain becomes relevant to the issue of sexual orientation.

I would like to make it clear from the beginning that I am open to the possibility of sex differences in the human brain. Indeed, it would be surprising if there were none, since there are sex differences in virtually every other organ system. Nevertheless, I am not convinced that any structural sex difference has been demonstrated unequivocally in the human brain—with one exception: men's brains, like their bodies, tend to be larger than those of women. Even if other sex differences in brain structure were conclusively proven, our current knowledge of the brain would not allow us to interpret their significance with any degree of confidence. Historically, however, as documented in the writings of Stephen J. Gould, Elizabeth Fee, Ruth Bleier, and other feminist scholars, alleged sex differences in the human brain have always been interpreted in a manner that tends to justify the existence of sexual inequalities in our society.

In 1982, de Lacoste-Utamsing and Holloway at Columbia University claimed to provide the first reliable evidence for a sex difference in human brain structure—a larger and more bulbous splenium of the corpus callosum in women than in men (3). The corpus callosum is a sheet of nerve fibers that connects the two halves of the brain. It is one of the most, if not *the* most, clearly defined structures on the medial bank of the brain. The splenium is the posterior portion of the callosum. Despite the fact that this study involved only nine male and five female brains, and that the reported sex difference in the size of the splenium did not meet even the minimal conventional standard of statistical significance, this study was published by *Science*, publicized by the news media, and rapidly incorporated into the medical literature, including its authoritative textbooks, where it is cited as "a clear-cut sex difference in the human brain" (4). Furthermore, the supposedly larger splenium in females has been interpreted as the biological explanation for presumed sex differences in mathematical ability, and hence for the relative absence of women in scientific and engineering disciplines.

Over the past decade not a single study has been able to replicate the finding of a larger splenium in women, even though at least thirteen studies have attempted to do so, and most of these used advanced imaging techniques and living subjects (2). Most of these thirteen studies, however, found some variation in the callosum correlated with whatever variable the authors chose to study, but no study has fully replicated the results of any other (5).

Thus it is legitimate to ask, if scientists cannot even agree on the presence or absence of a sex difference in an entity as concrete and well defined as the corpus callosum, how can we even begin to grapple with issues as complex as sexual orientation? Furthermore, given the degree of conflicting results generated from measurements of this well-defined structure, what level of controversy can we expect to result from the inevitable attempts to replicate LeVay's study, which involves a relatively ill defined cell group in the hypothalamus?

While many have expressed skepticism about Levay's study, most have adopted a wait and see attitude, thinking that replication studies will tell whether or not he is right. But thirteen failures of replication have failed to convince many that there is no sex difference in the size of the splenium. [See "Note."] The example of the splenium, then, should serve as a warning about hasty interpretations of findings based on limited sample sizes and limited knowledge about the function of particular brain structures.

Before turning specifically to LeVay's thesis, I would like to say a little about the assumptions on which most biological studies of sexual orientation are based.

Most research into the development of sexual orientation has been based on two assumptions. The first of these is that homosexuals fall at an intermediate point on a continuum between pure maleness and pure femaleness. This is evident in the literature in the equation of male homosexuality with failed masculinity. In the biobehavioral literature, this equation has led to the concept of homosexuality as central nervous system hermaphroditism and to the search in male homosexuals for female mating centers and for feminized hormonal profiles and neuroendocrine responses (6–8). The parochial nature of this assumption is revealed by modern cultures such as the Sambia of New Guinea in which homosexual behavior among males has been viewed as essential to the attainment of strength and virility, and by ancient cultures whose history, art, literature, and myths were filled with the homosexual exploits of archetypally masculine figures such as Achilles, Hercules, Zeus, and Julius Caesar (9, 10).

The second assumption is that homosexuality results from some defect in either biological constitution or socialization. This assumption not only poses a false dichotomy, but also limits the range of possible etiologies to various alternatives of pathology. However, in 1951 Ford and Beach described cultures in which homosexual behavior was required of all males and suggested that the widespread incidence of this behavior in such cultures argues against the notion that it regularly arises from some pathological context (11). Moreover, the fact that exclusive homosexuality is exceedingly rare or unknown in such cultures (12) suggests that homosexuality as popularly understood in our society may be a largely cultural phenomenon. That is, essentially exclusive homosexuality throughout most of one's adulthood may occur more commonly in societies—such as our own—that expect one to choose between homosexual and heterosexual lifestyles.

Currently, the major impetus for speculation on a constitutional basis for sexual preference comes from studies in laboratory animals showing that reproductive behavioral capabilities are determined by sex hormones in early development (13). According to the hypothesis derived from these studies, which I will refer to as the prenatal hormonal hypothesis, the intrinsic pattern of mammalian brain development is female, and the production of hormones by the male fetus is necessary for masculinization to occur. By masculinization, I am referring to the processes by which the rodent brain acquires the ability to regulate male behaviors and loses the ability to regulate female behaviors.

According to the prenatal hormonal hypothesis, male heterosexuality and female homosexuality are thought to result from prenatal exposure to high levels of male hormones, while male homosexuality and female heterosexuality are thought to result from exposure to low levels. This speculation in based on the observation that one can produce female-type mating postures in male rats by experimentally inducing a testosterone deficiency during a critical phase of early development; conversely, mounting, a stereotypical male mating behavior, is displayed with increased frequency in female rats that were treated with testosterone in early development (13).

The problems inherent in extrapolating from mating behaviors and postures in rodents to psychological processes in humans are numerous. Nevertheless, some authors seem to regard any procedure that increases lordosis responses in male rodents as a model for the origins of homosexuality in men, while any procedure that increases mounting behavior in female rodents is viewed as a model for the origins of lesbianism. In these laboratory situations, the neonatally castrated male rat displaying lordosis when mounted by another male is considered the homosexual, while the male that mounts another male escapes scientific scrutiny and labeling, as does the female that displays lordosis when mounted by another female. Thus, in these laboratory models it is what you do and not who you do it with that defines sexual orientation, whereas in humans, sexual orientation is defined not by the motor patterns of copulation but by the gender of the individuals that arouse one's erotic interest.

A final but salient objection to the prenatal hormonal hypothesis must be addressed. One of the most striking aspects of the organization of reproductive behaviors in rodents is the stereotypic nature of the lordosis reflex and the mounting response. In fact, the frequency with which a female rat will display receptive sexual behavior can be predicted by the number of estrogen-induced progestin receptors in her brain (14). It is difficult to imagine that the gamut of human sexual behavior can be reduced to factors as simple as this.

Now I would like to turn my attention to sex differences in the structure of the hypothalamus. The hypothalamus is a small—about three cubic centimeters—segment of the brain located just above the pituitary gland. In addition to influencing the secretion of hormones from the pituitary, it also influences various functions such as the maintenance of body temperature and blood pressure. But more relevant to this discussion, it also influences various drives, including hunger, thirst, aggression, and sex. Over the past twelve years, various types of structural sex differences have been demonstrated in the hypothalamus of various laboratory rodents. The significance of this lies in the fact that the regions displaying the sex differences participate in the regulation of a number of endocrinological and behavioral functions that, in rodents, show differences between males and females.

The best studied of these anatomical sex differences was described by Dr. Roger Gorski's laboratory at UCLA in 1978 and involves a cell group—or nucleus—that is approximately eight times larger in male rats than in female rats (15). Gorski called this nucleus the sexually dimorphic nucleus of the preoptic area, or SDN-POA. Shortly thereafter, Dr. Ruth Bleier and I examined the hypothalamus of several rodent species and discovered that the SDN-POA is merely the midportion of a more extensive complex of sexually dimorphic nuclei (16). Thus, the term "*the* sexually dimorphic nucleus" is a misnomer. Nevertheless when I use the terms "sexually dimorphic nucleus" or "SDN-POA" I will be referring specifically to the cell group described in the rat by Gorski or its presumed counterpart in other species.

These sex differences have now been replicated in several laboratories and extended to other species, including guinea pigs, rats, hamsters, ferrets, and mice. Interestingly, however, while it has been found in all other rodents examined, anatomists have been unable to identify a cell group comparable to the rat's SDN-POA in mice (16, 17). And if mice do not have such a nucleus, why should we automatically expect humans to have one?

Nevertheless, Dr. Dick Swaab in the Netherlands looked in human brains for the counterpart of the rat's SDN-POA, and reported in *Science* that he had found it (18). The nucleus that Swaab reported to be sexually dimorphic had since 1942 been known as the intermediate nucleus. Swaab reported that it is larger in men than in women and suggested that it is the counterpart of rats' SDN-POA. He therefore designated it the "sexually dimorphic nucleus." Swaab also provided evidence that the size of the human "sexually dimorphic nucleus" does not vary with sexual orientation. Two subsequent studies, including Le-Vay's were unable to demonstrate a sex difference in the human "sexually dimorphic nucleus."

The first of these studies was conducted by Gorski's group at UCLA. While they did not find a sex difference in the "sexually dimorphic nucleus," they described three hitherto undescribed nuclei and reported that two of these demonstrated sex differences. They designated these newly described nuclei as the second, third, and fourth interstitial nuclei of the anterior hypothalamus, and reported that the second and third nuclei were larger in men than in women. The name "first interstitial nucleus" was then given to Swaab's sexually dimorphic nucleus. (If it is not sexually dimorphic, then "sexually dimorphic nucleus" is a misnomer.)

LeVay has provided evidence that the third interstitial nucleus demonstrates dimorphism not only with sex but also with sexual orientation in men. Specifically, he suggests that gay men, like heterosexual women, have a smaller third nucleus than heterosexual men. If we refer back to the example of the corpus callosum, it may be at least a decade before we have any idea whether or not his findings are reliable.

In the meantime, I would like to question LeVay's suggestion that the third interstitial nucleus influences sexual orientation. The evidence he provides for this is that, in rats, experimentally induced lesions in the region of the SDN-POA disrupt mounting behavior in males. Aside from the fact that we now have two reputable scientists, LeVay and Swaab, suggesting that two different nuclei are the counterpart of the SDN-POA in the rat, it is crucial to note that destruction of the rat's SDN-POA does not impair mounting or any other sexually dimorphic mating behavior or endocrinological function (19). The effective lesion site within the anterior hypothalamus lies above, not within, this cell group. Moreover, as noted previously, extrapolating from mounting behavior in rats to homosexuality in men shifts the emphasis from erotic responsiveness to the motor patterns of copulation.

Why are biological theories of sexual orientation so widely accepted on the basis of such paltry evidence? According to Dr. Heino Meyer-Bahlburg at Columbia University, the hormonal theory enjoys widespread acceptance by behavioral scientists dissatisfied with the status of psychosocial explanations (13). For example, researchers at the Kinsey Institute for Sex Research go as far as to suggest that the familial factors commonly thought to be associated with homosexuality might themselves be the result of a pre-homosexual son or daughter being "different" to begin with (20). While they acknowledge that their own data do not speak to the issue of biological causation, they nonetheless suggest that their failure to identify psychosocial causes justifies turning to biology. Thus, the popularity of the belief in early hormonal influences leading to homosexuality seems to be sustained largely by default.

Perhaps another reason for the ready acceptance of the hormonal theory is related to the strength of the cultural conviction that homosexuality is undesirable or pathological. In a recent survey of 1,009 physicians, 30 percent were opposed to qualified homosexual candidates gaining admission to medical school, while 45 percent and 39 percent, respectively, were opposed to homosexuals entering pediatric or psychiatric residencies (21). The hormonal theory may serve to legitimize such social prejudice by perpetuating the stigmatization of homosexuals as abnormal or defective in the absence of evidence linking homosexuality to psychopathology.

Alternatively, Dr. Bell at the Kinsey Institute has argued that if sexual orientation is a biological matter, "society would do well to reexamine its expectations of those who cannot conform" (20). One might question, however, whether we want to establish an immutable biological basis as a criterion for granting civil liberties. Any form of gay rights premised on the assumptions of biological determination and immutability would be impoverished at best. Furthermore, the protections offered by purported biological causes are ephemeral.

Within the neuropsychiatric literature the biologically deterministic theories are almost invariably stated in pejorative terms. For example, in a study guide widely used by psychiatric residents preparing for their board exams, homosexuality is referred to as a "gene controlled disarrangement in psychosexual maturation patterns," and elsewhere, in some of the most authoritative reviews of the subject, homosexuality is described as resulting from a hormonal "disorder," "defect," "deficiency," "failure," and "aberration" (22). The danger here lies in the fact that states perceived as undesirable and of biological origin have traditionally been assigned to the medical domain.

Modern physicians have used a variety of methods in attempting to "cure" homosexuality. These include not only psychoanalysis, but also hormone injections, antidepressants, insulin shock, and even psychosurgery—that is, surgery on the brain. The rationale of these operations was to destroy the hypothetical "female mating center," which is no longer believed to exist (8). More recently, there has been discussion of amniocentesis during the midtrimester of pregnancy so that androgen deficiencies in male fetuses can be detected and corrected in order to prevent homosexuality in men (23).

Even if one were to agree that the prevention of homosexuality is a desirable goal, such a suggestion is clearly premature in the absence of direct evidence that the human brain *has* androgen receptors during the midtrimester (24). In the absence of these receptors, the brain could not respond to the hormones if they were given. Clearly, it is imperative that behavioral scientists and physicians begin to appreciate the psychosocial complexity of sexual orientation and resist the temptation to hastily embrace simplistic biological explanations.

Now what if LeVay's study *is* replicable? Even then, it would be naive to assume that sexual orientation is genetically or hormonally determined. This is because the human brain is relatively immature at birth, doubling in size during the first year of life and quadrupling by the end of the fourth. The major growth of the human brain, therefore, occurs at a time when it is in constant interaction with the external world. This postnatal maturation of the brain is particularly significant in light of research on laboratory animals showing that early social experiences influence the size, anatomy, and chemistry of the brain (22). The biology of the brain itself, therefore, is influenced by the early environment and experiences of the individual. Thus, efforts to tease apart and measure biological and social influences on personality characteristics may be based on a dichotomy that is scientifically meaningless. Perhaps society would be better served if research efforts in the biobehavioral sciences focused less on biological constraints and more on the malleability and plasticity of human behavior.

Postscript

It has now been six years since LeVay published his study. Contrary to my predictions, there has not been a rush to replicate his findings. This is undoubtedly due to the difficulties in obtaining suitable autopsy specimens and preparing them for microscopic analysis. Unlike the corpus callosum, hypothalamic nuclei cannot be visualized by magnetic resonance imaging (MRI). The ease with which MRI brain scans can be obtained and analyzed may account for the plethora of studies examining the corpus callosum for sex and sexual orientation differences. As of this writing, there have been over forty studies examining the callosum for sex differences, and not a single one has replicated the initial findings of de Lacoste-Utamsing and Holloway, including a study by

LeVay (25). LeVay also failed to find variation in the callosum with sexual orientation.

My own studies of the interstitial nuclei of the anterior hypothalamus suggest that the third nucleus in humans may indeed be comparable to the SDN-POA of rats—at least with respect to the localization of particular cellular markers. My studies also suggest that the third nucleus may be larger in men than in women. However, my preliminary studies have been based on archival brain material. Because my samples from women had been in fixative longer, on average, than the samples from men, and because fixatives can cause tissue to shrink, the apparent sex difference in my preliminary studies may merely be a fixation shrinkage artifact. I am currently obtaining hypothalamic material at the time of autopsy so that measurements can be obtained on male and female samples that were subjected to identical periods of fixation.

I am also collecting samples from gay men and heterosexual intravenous drug users who died with AIDS in order to address the possibility that the third nucleus varies with sexual orientation as reported by LeVay. In order to address this possibility, researchers must take HIV-related hormonal abnormalities into account. This is because in some species, the size of sexually dimorphic nuclei varies with the amount of testosterone in the circulation (26), and testosterone levels decline with HIV infection as a result of the illness itself and the side effects of particular treatments (27). Thus, it is entirely possible that the effects on the size of the third nucleus that LeVay attributed to sexual orientation were actually due to some hormonal abnormality resulting from AIDS or its treatment. His inclusion of a few heterosexual men who died with AIDS did not adequately control for this possibility.

Note

In reviewing the aforementioned thirteen studies in *Psychoneuroendocrinology*, Sandra Witelson concludes that "splenial areas tended to be larger in men" (5). That is, even if there *were* a sex difference, it would be opposite to that claimed by the original authors. Had there been any scientific rationale for linking a large splenium to mathematical ability to begin with, we might now argue that women should have superior mathematical ability. Seriously, however, the literature clearly does not allow one to conclude that the splenium is larger in women. Nevertheless, that claim—and its interpretation regarding mathematical ability—remains prominent in the literature. Recently LeVay speculated that the splenium of gay men may be structurally feminized (letter, *New York Times*, October 7, 1991).

References

1. LeVay, S. 1991. A difference in hypothalamic structure between heterosexual and homosexual men. *Science* 253:1034–37.

2. Byne, W. 1995. Science and belief: Psychobiological research on sexual orientation. *Journal of Homosexuality* 28:303–44.

3. de Lacoste-Utamsing, M. C., & R. L. Holloway. 1982. Sexual dimorphism in the human corpus callosum. *Science* 216:1431–32.

4. Kelly, D. D. 1986. Sexual differentiation of the nervous system. In ed. E. R. Kandel and J. H. Schwartz, *Principles of Neural Science,* 771–83. New York: Elsevier.

5. Witelson, S. F. 1991. Neural sexual mosacaicism: Sexual differentiation of the human tempero-parietal region for functional asymmetry. *Psychoneuroendocrinology* 16:131–53.

6. Dorner, G., W. Rhode, F. Stahl, L. Krell, and W. G. Masius. 1975. A neuroendocrine predisposition for homosexuality in men. *Archives of Sexual Behavior,* 4:1–8.

7. Gladue, B. A., R. Green, and R. E. Hellman. 1984. Neuroendocrine response to estrogen and sexual orientation. *Science* 225:1496–99.

8. Medical News Staff. Stereotaxic surgery results in "cures" of German sex offenders. *Journal of the American Medical Association* 229:718.

9. Herdt, G. H. 1984. Semen transactions in Sambia culture. In *Ritualized Homosexuality in Melanesia,* ed. G. H. Herdt, 167–210. Berkeley: University of California Press.

10. Boswell, J. 1980. *Social Tolerance, Christianity and Homosexuality.* Chicago: University of Chicago Press.

11. Ford, C. S., and F. A. Beach. 1951. *Patterns of Sexual Behavior.* New York: Harper and Bros.

12. Money, J., and A. A. Ehrhardt. 1972. *Man and Woman, Boy and Girl.* Baltimore: Johns Hopkins University Press.

13. Meyer-Bahlburg, H.F.L. 1984. Psychoendocrine research on sexual orientation: Current status and future options. *Progress in Brain Research* 71:375–97.

14. Parsons, B., T. C. Rainbow, D. W. Pfaff, and B. S. McEwen. 1981. Oestradiol, sexual receptivity and cytosol progestin receptors in the hypothalamus. *Nature* 292:58–59.

15. Gorski, R. A., J. H. Gordon, J. E. Shryne, and A. M. Southam. 1978. Evidence for a morphological sex difference in the medial preoptic area of the rat brain. *Brain Research* 148:333–46.

16. Bleier, R., W. Byne, and I. Siggelkow. 1982. Cytoarchitectonic sexual dimorphisms of the medial preoptic and anterior hypothalamic areas in guinea pig, rat, hamster and mouse. *Journal of Comparative Neurology.* 212:118–30.

17. Young, J. K. 1982. A comparison of the hypothalami of rats and mice: Lack of a gross sexual dimorphism in the mouse. *Brain Research* 239:233–39.

18. Swaab, D. F., and E. Fliers. 1985. A sexually dimorphic nucleus in the human brain. *Science* 228:1112–14.

19. Arendash, G. W., and R. A. Gorski. 1983. Effects of discrete lesions of the sexually dimorphic nucleus of the preoptic area or other medial preoptic regions on the sexual behavior of male rats. *Brain Research Bulletin* 10:147–54.

20. Bell, A. P., M. S. Weinberg, and S. K. Hammersmith. 1981. *Sexual Preference: Its Development in Men and Women.* Bloomington: Indiana University Press.

21. Matthews, W. C., M. W. Booth, J. D. Turner, and L. Kessler. 1986. Physicians' attitudes toward homosexuality: Survey of a California county medical society. *Western Journal of Medicine* 144:106–10.

22. Byne, W., and B. Parsons. 1993. Sexual orientation: The biological theories reappraised. *Archives of General Psychiatry* 50:228–39.

23. Goy, R. W., and B. S. McEwen. 1980. *Sexual Differentiation of the Brain.* Cambridge: MIT Press, p. 69.

24. Abramovich, D. R., I. A. Davidson, A. Longstaff, and C. K. Pearson. 1987. Sexual differentiation of the human midtrimester brain. *European Journal of Obstetrics, Gynecology and Reproductive Biology* 25:7–14.

25. LeVay, S. 1993. *The Sexual Brain.* Cambridge: MIT Press.

26. Commins, D., and P. Yahr. 1984. Adult testosterone levels influence the morphology of a sexually dimorphic area in the Mongolian gerbil brain. *Journal of Comparative Neurology* 224:132–40.

27. Croxson, T. S., W. E. Chapman, L. K. Miller, C. D. Levit, R. Senie, and B. Zumoff. 1989. Changes in the hypothalamic-pituitary-gonadal axis in human immunodeficiency virus-infected men. *Journal of Clinical Endocrinology and Metabolism* 89:317–21.

B. Psychology and Sexual Orientation

25

Heterosexuals' Attitudes toward Lesbians and Gay Men: Does Coming Out Make a Difference?

Gregory M. Herek

In the past quarter century, scientific research on homosexuality has undergone a sea change. Breaking with past studies that defined gay men and lesbians as mentally ill and sought a cure for homosexuality, social and behavioral scientists have instead turned their attention to the many problems and challenges that gay people face in a heterosexist society. These include the problems created by individual and institutional prejudice, often labeled homophobia or heterosexism.

One of the most consistent findings in this research area has been that heterosexuals who personally know a lesbian or a gay man manifest more positive general attitudes toward gay people as a group. This finding is consistent with a long-standing social psychological theory of prejudice called the *contact hypothesis*. As formulated by Gordon Allport, the contact hypothesis states that

> Prejudice (unless deeply rooted in the character structure of the individual) may be reduced by equal status contact between majority and minority groups in the pursuit of common goals. The effect is greatly enhanced if this contact is sanctioned by institutional supports (i.e., by law, custom, or local atmosphere), and if it is of a sort that leads to the perception of common interests and common humanity between members of the two groups. (Allport 1954, 267)

Unfortunately, most empirical research on the association between heterosexuals' attitudes and their personal contact with gay men or lesbians has not moved beyond simply demonstrating that such a correlation exists. The research described here was designed to explore in greater depth the role that contact plays in shaping heterosexuals' attitudes toward gay people. I shall report findings obtained from a two-wave probability sample in a national telephone survey concerning AIDS and stigma. Because of time limitations and other constraints, only the second wave of the survey (conducted in 1991–92) included questions about attitudes toward both lesbians and gay men. The first wave (conducted approximately one year earlier) included questions only about attitudes toward gay men.

With my collaborator, John Capitanio, I sought to replicate the previously reported finding of a correlation between having contact and professing favorable attitudes toward gay people. We also tested three hypotheses, based on the contact hypothesis. First, we hypothesized that contact experiences with two or more gay individuals are associated with more favorable attitudes than are contact experiences with only one person. Because gay people inevitably differ on characteristics irrelevant to their category membership, heterosexuals with multiple contact experiences have increased opportunities for observing such variation and, consequently, individuating out-group members. Such individuation (i.e., thinking of a group as consisting of varied individuals rather than as a monolithic entity) is likely to reduce intergroup prejudice.

Second, we hypothesized that contact with gay close friends or immediate family members is more likely to be associated with favorable intergroup attitudes than is contact with mere acquaintances or distant family members who are gay. Close relationships with gay men or lesbians can provide heterosexuals with intimate, personally relevant information about gay people. They are likely to foster personalization of gay people—that is, thinking of gay people as complex human beings rather than abstract symbols or unidimensional caricatures—which helps reduce prejudice.

Third, we hypothesized that a lesbian or gay person's management of information concerning her or his sexual orientation (which, in most cases, is concealable) has important implications for heterosexuals' attitudes. We predicted that heterosexuals who have been told directly by another person that he or she is gay are more likely to have positive attitudes toward gay people generally than are heterosexuals who acquired such information about a friend or relative indirectly (e.g., from a third party). In part, this prediction is based on previous findings that self-disclosure of personal information often leads to greater liking of an individual. In addition, we assumed that most heterosexuals—as a consequence of living in a society in which homosexuality is stigmatized—possess relatively little knowledge about gay people and hold attitudes toward gay people that are more negative than favorable. Upon learning that a friend, relative, or acquaintance is homosexual, they are likely to follow one of three courses: (1) attach their preexisting antigay stereotypes and attitudes to that person, and possibly reinterpret past experiences with her or him in a way that is consistent with those prejudices; (2) maintain positive feelings toward the person while regarding her or him as an atypical case that is not representative of the larger population of gay people; or (3) maintain positive feelings toward the person and, on the basis of those positive feelings, individuate and personalize the larger category of gay and lesbian people.

Whereas many factors could determine which of these outcomes occurs, we assumed that the third course, which involves changing long-standing beliefs and deeply felt attitudes, requires the greatest cognitive effort and is therefore the least likely. We hypothesized, however, that one or more direct discussions with a friend or relative about the latter's homosexuality can help motivate the heterosexual person both to maintain the relationship and to change her or his attitudes toward gay people generally. In addition, such conversations can provide the heterosexual person with information that will assist her or him in regarding the friend or relative as representative (or not atypical) of gay men or lesbians while also individuating the category of *gay people.*

In addition to testing these hypotheses about the possible effects of contact on attitudes, we also wished to replicate and extend a finding from my previous research with Eric Glunt (Herek and Glunt 1993). In that earlier study, we found that heterosexuals are more likely to report contact to the extent that they belong to demographic groups that (1) have more opportunities for contact (e.g., heterosexuals living in urban settings) and (2) are perceived by gay men and lesbians as more accepting of gay people (e.g., women, the well educated) than is society as a whole. This pattern suggests the possibility of a reciprocal relationship between contact and attitudes: not only might intergroup contact reduce prejudice, as predicted by the contact hypothesis, but individuals low in prejudice might also have more opportunities for contact.

Method

The methods used in the national survey are briefly described here. Readers desiring more detailed information should consult my published papers with John Capitanio (Herek and Capitanio 1993, 1994, 1995, 1996). The Wave 1 sample was drawn from the population of all English-speaking adults (at least eighteen years of age) residing in households with telephones within the forty-eight contiguous states. Telephone numbers were generated using random-digit dialing, or RDD. Interviews were conducted by the staff of the Survey Research Center at the University of California at Berkeley between 12 September 1990 and 13 February 1991, using their computer-assisted telephone interviewing (CATI) system.

Wave 1 interviews were completed with 538 respondents, which represented a response rate of 70 percent. Interviews lasted an average of thirty-nine minutes. Approximately one year later, we attempted to recontact all Wave 1 respondents. We were able to complete follow-up interviews with 382 (71 percent) of the original respondents. The Wave 2 interviews lasted an average of forty minutes. All the findings reported here are based on data from respondents who self-identified as heterosexual (506 in Wave 1, and 363 in Wave 2).

Measures

The survey included a large number of questions about AIDS-related attitudes and beliefs, as well as respondents' demographic characteristics. Only the items relevant to the present chapter are described here.

Attitudes toward gay men (Waves 1 and 2). Attitudes toward gay men were measured with a three-item short form of the Attitudes toward Gay Men (ATG) scale, which has been shown to be a reliable and valid measure of heterosexuals' attitudes toward gay men when administered by telephone and in paper-and-pencil format (see Herek 1994). For each statement, respondents were provided with four response alternatives (*agree strongly, agree somewhat, disagree somewhat, disagree strongly*), which were scored on a four-point scale. Item responses were reversed as necessary and summed to yield a scale score that could range from three to twelve, with higher scale scores indicating more unfavorable attitudes. The items are listed in table 1.

Attitudes toward lesbians (Wave 2 only). In the Wave 2 survey, a three-item short form of the Attitudes toward Lesbians (ATL) scale was included in the survey protocol. It comprised the same three ATG items, reworded to apply to

TABLE 1
Heterosexuals' Attitudes toward Gay Men
(Waves 1 and 2) and Lesbians (Wave 2)

	1990–91	1991–92
Sex between two men is just plain wrong.		
% Agree (somewhat/strongly)	69.8	68.3
% Disagree (somewhat/strongly)	28.7	31.4
I think male homosexuals are disgusting.		
% Agree (somewhat/strongly)	54.1	59.9
% Disagree (somewhat/strongly)	44.8	39.7
Male homosexuality is a natural expression of sexuality in men.		
% Agree (somewhat/strongly)	23.6	24.6
% Disagree (somewhat/strongly)	74.4	75.4
Sex between two women is just plain wrong.		
% Agree (somewhat/strongly)	N.A.	64.3
% Disagree (somewhat/strongly)	N.A.	35.3
I think lesbians are disgusting.		
% Agree (somewhat/strongly)	N.A.	59.9
% Disagree (somewhat/strongly)	N.A.	39.7
Female homosexuality is a natural expression of sexuality in women.		
% Agree (somewhat/strongly)	N.A.	26.6
% Disagree (somewhat/strongly)	N.A.	73.2

SOURCE: N.A.: item was not administered in that wave of the study. Reprinted from Herek 1994.

lesbians. Response alternatives and scoring were the same as for the ATG items. The items are listed in table 1.

Contact experiences. Personal contact was assessed through a series of questions. First, respondents were asked whether they had "any male or female friends, relatives, or close acquaintances who are gay or homosexual" and, for those answering in the affirmative, how many. Respondents reporting only one relationship were asked to describe the gay person's gender, how she/he was related to the respondent (immediate family, other family, close friend, other friend, close acquaintance), and how the respondent first learned about the other person's sexual orientation (were told directly by her/him, were told by someone else, just guessed that the person is gay). Those who chose either of the last two alternatives were asked, "Has he/she ever told you directly that he/she is gay?" Respondents who reported knowing two or more gay people were asked the same series of questions about each of "the two gay people you feel closest to."

Results

Wave 1

Of the 538 respondents with complete Wave 1 interviews, 46 percent were male and 54 percent were female. Racially, the sample was 81 percent White, 10 percent Black, 5 percent Hispanic, and 3 percent Asian (less than 1 percent of respondents did not use one of these labels). The mean age was 43.8 years; median annual household income was between $30,000 and $40,000; and the median level of educational attainment was "some college."

Attitudes toward gay men. As shown in Table 1, most respondents expressed negative attitudes toward gay men; a majority agreed that "Sex between two men is just plain wrong" and "I think male homosexuals are disgusting." Only a minority agreed that "Male homosexuality is a natural expression of sexuality in men." When we summed responses to these three items into an ATG score, the overall mean score was 9.08.

Interpersonal contact. Almost one-third of the sample (31 percent) reported that they knew at least one person who is gay or lesbian. Within this subgroup, roughly one-third knew one gay person, whereas two-thirds knew two or more. Both male and female respondents were more likely to report that their closest relationships were with gay men rather than lesbians. Of the 263 reported relationships (55 respondents described one relationship and 104 described two), only 27 percent were with a lesbian. Shifting the unit of analysis from the relationship to the respondent, only 34 percent of those who knew one or more gay people described at least one relationship with a lesbian.[1] Female respondents were more likely than males to know a gay person (of those who knew any gay people, 67 percent were women).

Respondents were more likely to describe contact with gay or lesbian friends rather than relatives. Of the 263 reported relationships, 75 percent were with a friend or acquaintance (21 percent with a close friend, and 54 percent with an acquaintance or more distant friend), whereas only 23 percent were with a relative (4 percent with immediate family, and 19 percent with more distant relatives.)[2]

In slightly more than one-third (38 percent) of the relationships reported, the heterosexual person learned directly from the friend or relative about the latter's homosexuality. In the other relationships, the heterosexual was told by a third party (32 percent) or guessed that the person was gay (30 percent). In one-fourth of the latter situations (told by third party, guessed), the heterosexual subsequently was told directly by the gay person about her or his sexual orientation. Thus 53 percent of the relationships described by respondents included direct disclosure, either initially or after the heterosexual person learned through another route that the person was gay (note that respondents could describe up to two relationships).

Interpersonal contact and attitudes. As expected, heterosexuals reporting contact with a gay person had significantly more favorable attitudes toward gay men than those without contact. Moreover, respondents manifested progressively more favorable attitudes to the extent that they knew more gay people. We also found that intimate contact was more likely than superficial contact to be associated with favorable attitudes. As shown in figure 1, the most favorable attitudes were manifested by respondents with a gay close friend, whereas the least favorable attitudes were manifested by respondents with a gay distant relative. Scores for those with an immediate family member or gay acquaintance were intermediate between these two extremes. Figure 1 also displays the tendency for respondents with multiple relationships to manifest more positive attitudes than those with only one gay friend, relative, or acquaintance.

Receiving direct disclosure of another's homosexuality was more likely to be associated with positive attitudes toward gay people than was having acquired such information indirectly. Of the 153 respondents with contact, 33 percent reported disclosure from one friend or relative, 28 percent reported disclosure from two friends or relatives, and 38 percent reported no direct disclosure. Respondents who had been told directly by a friend or relative about her or his homosexuality manifested significantly lower ATG scores (more favorable attitudes) than did those who had guessed or had been told by a third party; the effect was even stronger if respondents had received disclosure from two gay men or lesbians.

We observed that whether or not heterosexuals were recipients of direct disclosure was strongly related to the closeness of their relationship with the gay person. Almost all (93 percent) of the respondents with a gay close friend were recipients of direct disclosure, compared to 86 percent of those in the immediate family group, 57 percent in the other friend group, and 9 percent of

Figure 1: Heterosexuals ATG Scores, by Number and
Closeness of Relationships (Wave 1)

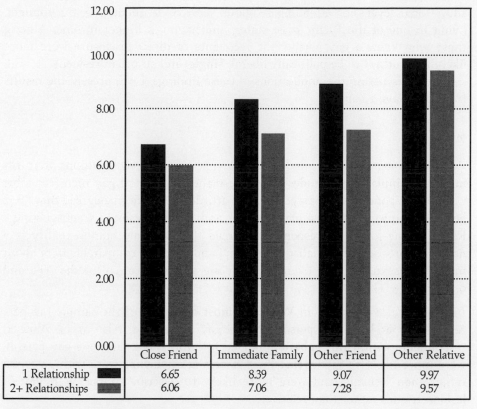

	Close Friend	Immediate Family	Other Friend	Other Relative
1 Relationship ▰	6.65	8.39	9.07	9.97
2+ Relationships ▰	6.06	7.06	7.28	9.57

ATG: Attitudes toward Gay Men.
Higher scores = more negative attitudes.

those in the distant relative group. Because of this strong association, the observed intergroup differences in ATG scores may have resulted from the closeness of relationships rather than from receiving disclosure. Statistically disentangling the disclosure and relationship variables was not possible with the current data set. However, one category of relationships—acquaintances and friends who were not described as "close"—included roughly equal numbers of respondents with and without disclosure experiences (57 percent and 43 percent, respectively). ATG scores for respondents in this group differed significantly according to disclosure category, with the lowest (most favorable) scores manifested by those reporting two or more disclosures. Thus, disclosure appears to be associated with more favorable attitudes independently of its association with type of relationship—at least among respondents with two or more gay acquaintances.

Who has contact? We found that certain groups of heterosexuals were more likely than others to experience contact and direct disclosure. Having contact with a gay man or woman was predicted by being female, having a higher educational level, *not* attending religious services frequently, being younger, living in one of the Pacific coast states, and having a higher income. Among those who knew a gay person, the recipients of direct disclosure were more likely than others to be politically liberal, single, and an urban resident.

Before discussing the implications of these findings, I will present the results from the Wave 2 survey.

Wave 2

Attitudes toward lesbians and gay men. The response distributions were remarkably similar for attitudes toward lesbians and toward gay men (see table 1). Most respondents expressed negative attitudes. A majority agreed that "Sex between two women is just plain wrong" and "I think lesbians are disgusting." Roughly one-fourth of respondents agreed that "Female homosexuality is a natural expression of sexuality in women" and with the comparable item about male homosexuality. The overall mean scale scores were 9.0 for the ATL and 9.1 for the ATG.

Interpersonal contact. As in Wave 1, almost one-third of the sample (32 percent) knew at least one person who is gay or lesbian. Also as in Wave 1, respondents within this subgroup tended to know more than one gay person, were more likely to report that their closest relationships were with gay men rather than lesbians, and were more likely to describe contact with gay or lesbian friends rather than relatives.

Interpersonal contact and attitudes. As in Wave 1, contact with a gay person was associated with significantly more favorable attitudes toward lesbians and gay men. Once again, respondents manifested progressively more favorable attitudes to the extent that they knew multiple gay people. This relationship is shown in figure 2, which displays mean ATG and ATL scores for respondents reporting one, two, three or more, and no relationships with gay people. As in Wave 1, we also observed that intimacy of the relationship was related to attitudes; the least favorable attitudes were manifested by respondents reporting a gay distant relative. As in Wave 1, respondents reporting direct disclosure had more favorable attitudes than did respondents reporting contact without disclosure (see figure 3). The difference was statistically significant, however, only for respondents who reported disclosures from at least two friends or relatives.

Discussion

Heterosexuals who had experienced interpersonal contact with gay men or lesbians expressed significantly more favorable general attitudes toward gay

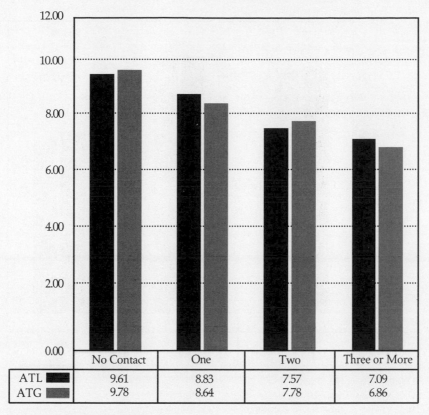

Figure 2: Heterosexuals ATL and ATG Scores, by
Number of Relationships (Wave 2)

	No Contact	One	Two	Three or More
ATL	9.61	8.83	7.57	7.09
ATG	9.78	8.64	7.78	6.86

ATG: Attitudes toward Gay Men.
ATL: Attitudes toward Lesbians.
Higher scores = more negative attitudes.

people than did heterosexuals without contact. This pattern was generally consistent across both waves of data collection, and for attitudes toward lesbians and gay men alike. Because most previous research in this area has not directly assessed heterosexuals' attitudes toward lesbians, the extent to which findings about attitudes toward gay men or toward "homosexuals" (a term likely to evoke attitudes toward gay men) could be generalized to attitudes toward lesbians has been in doubt. The present research suggests that such attitudes closely resemble attitudes toward gay men.

The relationship between contact and attitudes was affected by three different aspects of the contact experience. First, favorable attitudes were more likely among heterosexuals who reported multiple contacts with lesbians or gay men. Although knowing one gay person was associated with more positive attitudes than was knowing none, only respondents who knew at least two gay people were consistently significantly different from those with no contacts. Perhaps

Figure 3: Heterosexuals' ATL and ATG Scores, by Number of
Relationships Involving Direct Disclosure

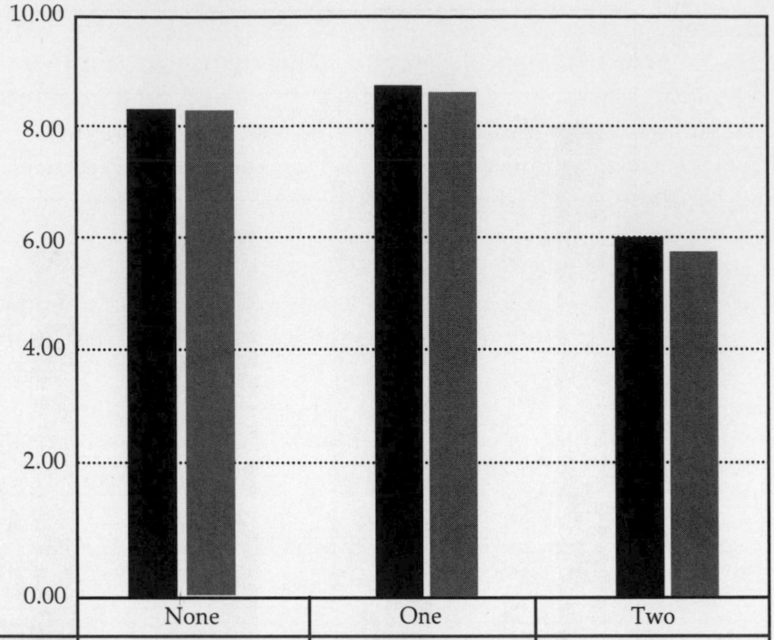

	None	One	Two
ATL	8.29	8.51	6.01
ATG	8.27	8.45	5.68

ATG: Attitudes toward Gay Men.
ATL: Attitudes toward Lesbians.
Higher scores = more negative attitudes.

knowing multiple members of a stigmatized group is more likely to foster recognition of that group's variability than is knowing only one group member. Knowing multiple members of a group may also reduce the likelihood that their behavior can be discounted as atypical.

The two other dimensions of contact examined here—degree of intimacy and direct disclosure—were highly correlated. Having a close gay or lesbian friend was almost always associated with direct disclosure, whereas heterosexuals who knew lesbians or gay men only as distant relatives were likely to have learned about the individual's sexual orientation indirectly. One interpretation of this pattern is that gay people come out to their close friends but not to distant relatives or acquaintances (with whom their homosexuality may be common knowledge but not openly discussed). Alternatively, disclosing one's stigmatized sexual orientation may strengthen a relationship, whereas not disclosing—despite the heterosexual's knowledge that one is homosexual— may weaken a relationship. In either case, the results are consistent with the contact hypothesis: Interpersonal relationships characterized by intimacy, shared values, and common goals are more likely to be associated with favorable attitudes toward gay people as a group than are superficial or distant relationships.

Although the strong correlation between closeness of relationship and receipt of disclosure makes it difficult to evaluate the individual contribution of each, both variables appear to affect intergroup attitudes. Closer relationships were consistently associated with more favorable attitudes. Furthermore, in the one relationship category for which disclosure experiences were nearly equally divided (acquaintances/distant friends), respondents reporting at least two disclosure experiences had significantly more favorable attitudes toward gay men than did other respondents.

The importance of disclosure and relationship type is also highlighted by our analysis of ATG scores among the twenty-six respondents who reported knowing one or more gay people at Wave 2 but none at Wave 1. This group did not manifest a significant attitude change across waves, a finding that could be interpreted as disconfirming the contact hypothesis. I believe, however, that this pattern is better understood as demonstrating that type of contact, not contact per se, shapes intergroup attitudes. For all but one of the twenty-six respondents, the relationship newly described at Wave 2 was distant: with a distant relative, an acquaintance, or a friend described as "not close." Furthermore, two-thirds of the twenty-six respondents did not report direct disclosure. Thus, although this subsample experienced new intergroup contact between Waves 1 and 2, that contact was of the sort least likely to reduce prejudice. Consequently, the subsample does not provide an adequate test of the contact hypothesis.

When we examined trends across the two waves of data collection, we found that heterosexuals who knew a gay man or lesbian when we first interviewed them subsequently tended to develop more positive attitudes toward gay people as a group, a conclusion that is consistent with the contact hypothesis. Yet we also observed that heterosexuals with favorable attitudes at Wave 1 were subsequently more likely than others to experience contact. Lesbians and gay men appear to be selective, when possible, in associating with heterosexuals and revealing their sexual orientation.

Another theoretically interesting finding concerns the apparent relationship between intergroup attitudes and receipt of disclosure. In a close relationship, we speculate that a minority individual's direct disclosure about her or his concealable stigma can provide the majority group member with the necessary information and motivation to restructure her or his attitudes toward the entire minority group. This seems most likely to occur when the gay man or lesbian carefully manages the disclosure process so that the heterosexual can receive information (e.g., about what it means to be gay, about the gay person's similarity to other gay people) in the context of a committed relationship. For example, the gay person may disclose in a series of gradual stages, frame the disclosure in a context of trust and caring, explain why she or he did not disclose earlier, answer the heterosexual person's questions, and reassure the heterosexual that her or his past positive feelings and favorable judgments about the gay friend or relative are still valid.

Such interactions may assist the heterosexual person in keeping salient the relevant in-group–out-group distinction (i.e., heterosexual-homosexual) while observing behaviors that are inconsistent with her or his stereotypic beliefs, thereby facilitating the rejection of those stereotypes while fostering attitude change. If this experience leads the heterosexual person to accept that the friend or relative is indeed representative of the larger community of gay people (i.e., the friend or relative is not regarded as an anomaly), the heterosexual is likely to experience cognitive dissonance: on the one hand, she or he has strong positive feelings toward the gay friend or relative; on the other hand, she or he probably has internalized society's negative attitudes toward homosexuality. If the dissonance is resolved in favor of the friend or relative—an outcome that is more likely when the gay person plays an active role in imparting information about her or his stigmatized status—the heterosexual's attitudes toward gay people as a group are likely to become more favorable.

In contrast, a readily apparent stigma (such as race or physical disability) can usually be detected without such disclosure. Consequently, contact between the bearers of such stigma and members of the majority group may be less likely to reduce the latter's prejudice than when a stigma is concealable. This is exemplified in the assertion by a White person that "Some of my best friends are Black." Although having a best friend from a minority group should be associated with an absence of prejudice toward the group, making such a statement is commonly perceived as a defensive attempt to disavow racist attitudes. Rather than simply dismissing the statement (many individuals who make such a statement probably do not actually have best friends from the minority group), we can draw a potentially important insight from it. Because of the visible nature of race, a White person can have a Black friend but never discuss issues related to race in any depth. Without such discussion, even a White who personally knows Blacks might still retain negative stereotypes and attitudes toward African Americans as a group (e.g., if her or his Black friends are not perceived as representative of African Americans generally). In contrast, because homosexuality represents a concealable stigma, knowing that some of one's best friends are gay probably means that a heterosexual has directly discussed homosexuality with gay individuals and consequently has acquired greater insight and empathy for their situation, which can be generalized to gay people as a group. Rather than concluding that her or his friends are unlike other gay people, for example, a heterosexual who has discussed the issue may come to regard sexual orientation as irrelevant to one's qualities as a human being.

The results reported here suggest directions for future studies. Collecting heterosexuals' first-person accounts of their contact experiences with gay people would be useful for identifying different patterns of contact and developing hypotheses about their role in attitude change. Similarly, descriptions by gay men and lesbians of their coming out experiences could be useful for describing how gay people decide to disclose to others, how they manage the disclosure process, and what happens when they lose control of that process. Controlled field experiments and longitudinal survey studies of heterosexuals' attitudes will be important for understanding the causal relationships between contact and attitude change. They also will permit description of the cognitive processes that underlie these relationships.

The findings also have important policy implications. At the most basic level, they demonstrate that heterosexuals can and do establish close relationships with openly gay people. This conclusion is contrary to one of the U.S. government's principal objections to allowing gay people in the military, namely, that heterosexual personnel cannot overcome their prejudices against homosexuality. A second implication of the findings is that heterosexuals' antigay prejudices are likely to be reduced in the course of close, ongoing contact that involves direct disclosure about sexual orientation. Thus, institutional policies are more likely to reduce prejudice to the extent that they encourage gay people to disclose their homosexual orientation to heterosexual peers. Conversely, policies that discourage or punish such disclosure may perpetuate prejudice.

Recognizing the ongoing dangers posed by societal prejudice, lesbian and gay activists nevertheless have often called on gay people to disclose their sexual orientation publicly, that is, to come out of the closet. Perhaps the most noted political leader to advocate this strategy was Harvey Milk, San Francisco's first openly gay supervisor, who was assassinated in 1978. For example, in a message that he had recorded to be played in the event of his death, Milk expressed the belief that coming out would eliminate prejudice: "I would like to see every gay lawyer, every gay architect come out, stand up and let the world know. That would do more to end prejudice overnight than anybody could imagine" (Shilts 1982, 374).

Such calls to come out reflect a conviction that the tenets of the contact hypothesis are applicable to heterosexuals' attitudes toward lesbians and gay men. Although not definitive, the findings of the present study suggest that this belief is fundamentally correct. Coming out to heterosexuals—especially to close friends and immediate family—appears to reduce prejudice against gay people as a group. Furthermore, the finding that heterosexuals with multiple contacts and disclosures hold the most favorable attitudes of any group suggests that coming out will be most effective as a strategy for reducing prejudice when it is practiced by large numbers of lesbians and gay men. Thus, although coming out to loved ones exposes gay men and lesbians individually to the possibility of ostracism, discrimination, and even violence, it appears to be one of the most promising strategies for promoting the kind of societal change that will ultimately end such prejudice.

Notes

1. Because respondents were asked to describe their two *closest* relationships with a gay/lesbian person (rather than all relationships), more distant relationships may have manifested a different gender distribution. Respondents' closest relationships, however, tended to be with gay men.

2. A few individuals reported that they knew at least one gay man or lesbian in response to the initial screening question, but then declined to answer subsequent questions about the relationship(s). Consequently, the numbers described here do not total 100 percent.

References

Allport, G. 1954. *The Nature of Prejudice.* New York: Addison Wesley.

Herek, G. M. 1994. Assessing heterosexuals' attitudes toward lesbians and gay men: A review of empirical research with the ATLG scale. In *Contemporary Perspectives in Lesbian and Gay Psychology,* ed. B. Greene and G. Herek, vol. 1, 206–28. Newbury Park, CA: Sage.

Herek, G. M., and J. P. Capitanio. 1993. Public reactions to AIDS in the United States: A second decade of stigma. *American Journal of Public Health* 83:574–77.

———. 1994. Conspiracies, contagion, and compassion: Trust and public reactions to AIDS. *AIDS Education and Prevention* 6:367–77.

———. 1995. Black heterosexuals' attitudes toward lesbians and gay men. *Journal of Sex Research* 32:95–105.

———. 1996. "Some of My Best Friends . . ." Heterosexuals' attitudes toward Gay men and Lesbians. *Personality and Social Psychology Bulletin.* 22:412–24.

Herek, G. M., and E. K. Glunt. 1993. Interpersonal contact and heterosexuals' attitudes toward gay men: Results from a national survey. *Journal of Sex Research* 30:239–44.

Shilts, R. 1982. *The Mayor of Castro Street: The life and times of Harvey Milk.* New York: St. Martin's.

26

Difference and Diversity: Gay and Lesbian Couples

Bianca Cody Murphy

Some therapists believe that they should treat gay and lesbian couples "just like heterosexual couples." Others hold the view that gay and lesbian couples are completely different from heterosexual couples and that only specially trained professionals can work with them. This essay is an attempt to overcome the lack of information about gay and lesbian couples by focusing on the question of differences. What are the differences between heterosexual couples and homosexual couples? How do gay couples and lesbian couples differ from each other? What are the differences among lesbian couples and among gay couples? And what are the therapeutic implications of these differences?

Any discussion of differences between heterosexual and homosexual couples and between gay couples and lesbian couples is necessarily embedded within a larger context of belief systems about gender and sexual orientation. Our society currently divides people into gender categories and sexual orientation categories. Both categories are treated as if they are dichotomous. One is either male or female, heterosexual or homosexual. The categories are often described as opposites; they are defined in relation to each other and as different from each other. Furthermore, we act in society "as if" there is an essential difference between men and women and between heterosexuals and homosexuals. Finally, these "differences" have powerful political implications. Difference can be used to pathologize, normalize, or valorize. It is no wonder that many gay men and lesbian women in reaction to the pathologizing of their lives and relationships attempt to downplay the issue of difference. Attempts to normalize their experiences result in many gay and lesbian people saying, "We are just like you."

On the other hand, the creation of difference can be used by the minority group to valorize its experiences. Rather than being "too emotional and dependent," women can revel in their empathic and relational abilities. Similarly, gay men and lesbian women can take pride in their freedom from the bonds of gender role constraints and their ability to create new forms of relationships.[1]

Furthermore, gay men and lesbian women may contribute to these overgeneralizations and to the maximizing of differences between heterosexual and homosexual. Because gay men and lesbian women often feel outside the dominant group, their longing for a place where they can feel "in" may lead them to deny their unique experiences and emphasize their similarities with other gay and lesbian couples.

Another important political implication is that while focusing on gender or sexual orientation, we may ignore other meaningful contexts such as age, class, race, and ability. The experiences of African American gay and lesbian couples may be quite different from those of Caucasian lesbian or gay couples. A working-class gay male couple in an isolated rural area are confronted with different issues than a white professional male couple in San Francisco. The adolescent gay couple who came out in the 1980s after both the gay liberation movement and the AIDS epidemic face different developmental and cultural challenges than the seventy-year-old gay male couple who came out in the 1950s. Further, in the course of looking at the impact of the broader social contexts, therapists must attend to the areas of traditional concern—the role of the family of origin, specific couple dynamics, and individual issues.

Gay and lesbian couples differ from heterosexual couples in that both members of the homosexual couple are of the same biological sex and share the same gender socialization. They also differ from heterosexual couples because of the adversity they face in a sexist, heterosexist, and homophobic society. In the past, lesbian women have often been subsumed under the generic concept of "homosexuals." However, biology and the gender socialization of women present lesbian couples with issues different from those faced by gay male couples.[2] The following discussion focuses on two kinds of differences—the differences between homosexual and heterosexual couples, and the differences between gay and lesbian couples.

Although it is often difficult for all people—heterosexual, gay, or lesbian—to form a couple, gay men and lesbian women face the additional burden of the developmental consequences of universal heterosociality.[3] First, there are few places to meet other gay and lesbian singles. Although there are some gay or lesbian dating services, they do not compare in number to the dating services for heterosexual people. In addition to formal dating and introduction services, many heterosexuals have access to the "informal dating services" of friends and family members who are eager to match single people.

Most places for dating and socializing assume heterosexuality—two men would be jeered at (or worse) if they danced together in a nightclub; two women might be stared at if they held hands at the country club. Thus, even if they have met in other ways, a large part of gay and lesbian couple socialization takes place in the relative "safety" of the gay and lesbian bars. In large urban areas there are a growing number of alternative places to meet and socialize. These include gay or lesbian organized sports, hiking trips, vacation tours, dancing lessons, and bridge clubs. However, for those outside the large cities, the bars may be the only alternative, and in some communities there may be no "public" places for same-sex couples to socialize.

Homosexuality has been called "the love that dares not speak its name," and, in fact, gay men and lesbian women frequently have no name or term with which to refer to the person with whom they are in a couple. Some same-sex couples use the word "lover"; however, this may sound too sexual, placing the emphasis on the sexual relationship when the emotional component may be more, or at least equally significant. Some prefer to use the term "boyfriend" or "girlfriend," but this can be particularly confusing for a lesbian woman who, for example, says she went to the movies with her "girlfriend," because she may also use this term to describe other women friends. Others use the term "partner," yet another term with multiple uses: work partner, tennis partner, life partner. Other common terms include "significant other," "spousal equivalent," and "domestic partner."

Once same-sex couples begin their relationships, some studies suggest that they may be quicker than their heterosexual counterparts to move in together. Berger found that almost a quarter of the gay male couples in his sample moved in together within one month of meeting; the median time between first meeting and moving in together was just under four months.[4] Mendola found that almost half of the couples in her sample moved in together within six months of meeting.[5] Berger suggests that the relative speed with which the subjects in his sample moved in together may be due to the lack of external validation for their couple status—living together may be an attempt to solidify the relationship. Seeking couples counseling is another way of validating the "couple" relationship.

Empirical studies on gay and lesbian couples frequently use "living together" as one of the criteria for the definition of the "couple relationship."[6] This is particularly true when the researcher is attempting to compare gay or lesbian couples with heterosexual married or cohabiting couples.[7] However, it should also be noted that almost half of gay and lesbian couples do not live with each other.[8]

In general, heterosexual marriages are approved of, supported, and cushioned by the larger society. The therapist can help the gay and lesbian couple grieve the loss of heterosexual privilege. For many, this grieving process occurs at the time the gay man or lesbian woman first comes out. However, it often reappears when one makes a commitment to a same-sex partner. At the same time that there is excitement about the beginning of the new relationship, one or both members of the couple may experience disappointment and sadness at the lack of societal recognition and support for their couple status. If the partners are at different stages of grieving the loss, one partner may feel surprise and anger at the other's sadness.

Although not all heterosexual couples marry, all heterosexual couples do have the choice to marry. Gay and lesbian couples in the United States have no choice—they are denied the legal right to marry. Because they cannot marry, gay and lesbian couples cannot file joint income tax returns; they can be denied the opportunity to provide health insurance for one another; and they can be prevented from visiting each other in the intensive care unit of the hospital. The clinician might help the couple explore other ways of protecting and supporting their couple relationship. Gay and lesbian couples can give each other health care proxies or power of attorney agreements. They can protect each other through wills and relationship contracts.[9] A growing number of gay and lesbian couples choose to create a ceremony to validate and celebrate their commitment to each other. Although almost all lesbian and gay couples would like to have their relationships validated, legally recognized, and supported, the majority of gay and lesbian couples would not choose to be "married" even if they had that as a legal option.[10] Many same-sex couples, particularly lesbian-feminist couples, reject what they perceive to be the "patriarchal institution" of marriage with its overtones of "ownership" of the partner. It has been suggested that same-sex couples may be more likely than married heterosexual couples to leave unsatisfying relationships because they do not have social or institutional barriers to separation.[11] Some gay and lesbian couples come to therapy to have the therapist officiate over the separation. The end of therapy may be the official marker that the relationship is over.

Gay and lesbian couples are not only denied support for their relationships, they are discriminated against and may become victims of violence and hate crimes. Gay men and lesbian women can be fired from their jobs, evicted from their homes, and lose custody of and visitation rights to their children. In their most severe form, prejudice and hostility result in violence that ranges from verbal harassment to murder. In recent surveys as many as 92 percent of lesbians and gay men responded that they have been the targets of antigay verbal abuse or threats, and as many as 24 percent report physical attacks because of their sexual orientation.[12] It should be noted that many gay men and lesbian women do not report verbal harassment or physical violence against them to the authorities because they fear that they will be subjected to secondary victimization at the hands of police or others who may learn of their sexual orientation as a result of their having reported the original attack.

Lesbian women are victims of violence both as women in a sexist society and as lesbians in a homophobic society. Lesbian women, although less likely than gay men to be physically attacked because of their sexual orientation, are more likely to be attacked because of their gender. There is a 25 percent chance that a woman in this country will be a victim of rape in her lifetime and a 50 percent chance that she will be subjected to some sexually coercive act.[13] Lesbian women are also likely to be victims of sexual abuse. Thirty-eight percent of the lesbian women in a recent survey reported that they were victims of childhood sexual abuse.[14] Because the members of the lesbian couple are both women, there is greater likelihood that one or both members of the lesbian couple will be sexual abuse or assault survivors. When each woman is at a different stage of dealing with her abuse or assault history, the therapist should help the couple negotiate how much information they want to share with each other and how they wish to handle their sexual relationship.

Stage differences in coming out affect the relationships of same-sex couples. Each of the partners may make what feels like a personal decision about coming out, but the consequences of such a decision affect the couple.[15] One partner's decision to disclose her/his orientation may be threatening to her/his partner, whereas another partner's decision to hide his/her orientation may be perceived as a rejection or devaluation of the relationship. The literature on coming out indicates that disclosing one's sexual orientation fosters the development of a cohesive self-identity. Having an open identity as a gay man or lesbian woman across life contexts is related to positive self-esteem[16] as well as overall psychological adjustment.[17]

Members of a gay or lesbian relationship who are closeted will frequently be invited to family gatherings, weddings, bar mitzvahs, and holidays without their partners. Not knowing that they are coupled, many people assume that they are single. But being out does not always ensure the recognition of the couple. As mentioned earlier, some family members and heterosexual friends invade the couple boundary and treat the partners as if they were single. Many same-sex couples report being given separate rooms when visiting their families, having their partner's name left off cards and invitations, and having family members ask them when they will be getting married.

The repeated invalidation of the same-sex couple and the negative reaction of society may lead the gay or lesbian couple to tighten its boundaries in what has been described as a "two-against-a-threatening-world" posture or fusion.[18] Any couple that is attacked from outside and withdraws into itself may be subject to distance regulation problems. Because this pulling together is a reaction against society's lack of recognition, moves toward individuation by one of the partners can be perceived by the other partner as steps toward dissolving the couple.[19] Since much socializing is gender-based, it is easier for heterosexual couples to separate—for the man to have a "boys' night out" or for the woman to have an evening with women friends. In gay and lesbian couples there are no gender-based reasons to spend time apart. And separate socializing with same-sex friends can be seen as a sexual threat. Thus, the members of many gay and lesbian couples do most of their socializing with their partner.

The potential for fusion, for the losing of individual boundaries, is stronger in lesbian than in gay or heterosexual couples because both the participants in the lesbian relationship have been socialized as women.[20] McCandlish maintains that in heterosexual relationships, it is the woman who, because of her socialization, usually expresses the need for openness and communication, whereas the man creates emotional distance.[21] Chodorow states that because women mother in our society, women have less-differentiated ego boundaries and lack separateness.[22] However, many lesbian women reject the notion of "fusion" and speak instead of the greater ability for emotional closeness and empathy in female couples. Lesbian couples' strengths are often in the area of closeness, whereas their difficulties are more often in the area of separation. Male gender socialization often leads gay male couples to emphasize autonomy and competition rather than closeness and intimacy.[23]

Gay and lesbian couples do not have role models for their relationships. The models of intimate relationships in our society are heterosexual couples—those portrayed on television, written about in books, and discussed in advice columns. When same-sex couples do appear in the media, they are often presented quite negatively. If we are to believe the movies, lesbian couple relationships seldom survive.[24] In almost every popular American film in which there is a lesbian couple, the relationship ends—often painfully. McWhirter and Mattison and Brown have suggested that the lack of traditional role models is good for gay and lesbian couples because it affords an opportunity to create new kinds of relationships.[25] Although this may be a liberating experience, it can also be difficult and lead to confusion and conflict between the members of the couple as they struggle to define a relationship pattern.

Most intimate relationships are evaluated in terms of sex roles and gender differences.[26] The members of heterosexual couples assume roles in relation to each other that are frequently based on sex roles. The gay or lesbian couple, composed of two members of the same gender, cannot resort to sex roles as a way of deciding how to handle relationship issues. People sometimes ask same-sex couples which partner is in the "male" role. This is an example of heterosexual bias. Although, like all couples, gay and lesbian partners may relate to each other in patterned ways, it is inaccurate to overlay heterosexual sex roles on the same-sex couple. Studies of gay and lesbian couples show that the butch/femme pattern is extremely rare.[27]

Furthermore, same-sex couples are more likely than heterosexual couples to have a relationship pattern based on role flexibility, equality, and shared decision making.[28] For gay male couples, if there is a power imbalance it may be based on age, with the older partner having more power than the younger partner.[29] Lesbian couples, in which both partners are socialized as women to be nurturant, care-taking, and relationship oriented, are likely to emphasize the importance of power equality, intimacy, closeness, and communication in their couple relationships.[30]

Same-sex and heterosexual couples report similar amounts of satisfaction in their sexual relationships.[31] However, differential patterns of genital sexual contact emerge. Gay men have more frequent sex, have more sexual variety, and are less sexually exclusive than heterosexual men and either heterosexual or lesbian women.[32]

In the initial stages of their relationships, gay male couples have sex more often than heterosexual cohabiting, married, and lesbian couples. However, once the relationship has existed for ten years or more, gay male couples report having sex less frequently than married couples.[33] Blumstein and Schwartz suggest that although sexual activity with the partner may decline for gay men, sexual activity outside the relationship increases.[34] Thus, although married couples have more sex within the couple, gay men have more sex in general.

Lesbian couples have less sex than heterosexual or gay male couples throughout their relationship. However, they experience more nongenital sexual contact—hugging, holding, kissing, and cuddling.[35] There are two possible explanations why lesbian couples have less genital sex—internalized homophobia and female socialization. Because it is the sexual act with a same-gendered partner, not the affectional ties, that is considered taboo, some women who have internalized society's antihomosexual beliefs think that if they do not have sex with each other they are not bad, sick, or lesbian. However, gay men are exposed to as strong antihomosexual attitudes as lesbian women, and they have more genital sex than both lesbian and heterosexual counterparts. For gay male couples, internalized homophobia (and misogyny) may be reflected in the sex behaviors they feel comfortable choosing. For example, some gay men are unwilling to engage in receptive anal intercourse, believing that to be receptive makes them submissive, effeminate, and/or stigmatized.

Although internalized homophobia affects the sexual relationships of both gay and lesbian couples, the differences in amount of sexual activity and sexual exclusivity may be seen as reflections of gender socialization. Men are most often the sexual initiators in heterosexual couples.[36] Women are taught to deny or downplay their sexual needs, to be passive and noninitiating, to subjugate their pleasure to that of their partners. Blumstein and Schwartz suggest that the heterosexual pattern represents a compromise between differences in men and women's desire for genital sex.[37]

Furthermore, lesbian women may experience difficulties in the actual mechanics of sex. The most frequent form of heterosexual sex is vaginal intercourse. In this method of sex, the woman can, if she chooses, be passive and receptive while still providing stimulation to her partner. Lesbian sex requires more action. The most common form of genital sex for lesbian couples is manual stimulation, whereas the most preferred is oral-genital stimulation.[38] Both require that women learn to feel comfortable with active involvement in the stimulation of their partners and take pleasure in the female body, its appearance, its feel, its smell, and its taste. This goes against the social dictate that has trained women to hide, cover, and deodorize their bodies.

Lesbian women report that they are happy with their amount of sexual activity and that they have more affectionate and nongenital sexual contact than heterosexual and gay male couples. In addition, lesbian women report more orgasms than heterosexual women. Rather than just asking why lesbian women have less genital sex, we also might ask why heterosexual and gay couples have less affectionate touching and nongenital sex.

Therapists often feel uncomfortable talking about sex. This may be particularly true for the heterosexual therapist working with lesbian or gay couples. For their part, the members of a gay or lesbian couple may feel uncomfortable talking about sexual issues with a therapist who they may feel is not knowledgeable about common gay and lesbian sexual behaviors. The term "having sex" is usually used to describe heterosexual intercourse. What is meant by gay or lesbian "sexual contact" can be unclear. The couples therapist must feel comfortable talking explicitly about gay and lesbian sex and should be familiar with information about common sexual practices and sex therapy for gay and lesbian couples.[39]

In terms of sexual exclusivity, gay male couples are more likely to be nonmonogamous than either heterosexual or lesbian couples;[40] sexual exclusivity is more important to heterosexual than to gay or lesbian couples;[41] gay men do not expect sexual exclusivity in their couples;[42] and gay men are less jealous than heterosexual men.[43] In fact, in some parts of the gay community, gay men may feel pressured to be nonexclusive.[44] (It should be noted that most studies on gay male sexual behavior were conducted before the AIDS crisis.)

It has often been suggested that the lack of sexual exclusiveness in gay male couples—pejoratively referred to as "promiscuity"—reflects some depraved and essential immorality. However, Blumstein and Schwartz suggest that the relatively high levels of gay male nonexclusivity reflect the differing meaning that women and men place on sexual relationships outside the couple.[45] For men, the emphasis is on sex. Many men report seeking outside sex to experience variety in their sex lives, and both gay and heterosexual men frequently report having sex with strangers. Women, however, emphasize the "relationship" and often have sex with people with whom they have an emotional connection.[46]

The AIDS epidemic affects all couples, but none as much as gay male couples. Clearly when one or both partners are either HIV positive or have AIDS, the couple is affected.[47] Living with the fear of HIV infection and coping with the ongoing stresses of caring for the sick or the trauma of having so many friends, acquaintances, and ex-lovers die also currently affect gay male couples disproportionately.[48]

One of the effects of the AIDS epidemic is that more gay male couples are becoming monogamous, and the range of sexual activity is changing.[49] However, many gay male couples are not practicing safer sex, they rely instead on monogamy as protection. Gay couples (and heterosexual and lesbian couples as well) need to be informed that due to the long incubation period of the virus, monogamy alone is not a protection against the spread of the disease.[50]

There is a common belief that AIDS is not an issue for lesbian couples. However, although it is true that lesbian women are in the lowest risk category and there has not been much information about the spread of AIDS through lesbian sexual activity, lesbian couples also need information about AIDS prevention.[51] As greater numbers of lesbian couples choose to parent, AIDS prevention can become an important issue for those who are seeking to get pregnant either through heterosexual intercourse or through artificial insemination.[52]

Despite the value of recognizing differences, one of the dilemmas of focusing on differences is that the therapist may ignore the ways all couples—heterosexual, gay, and lesbian—are similar. Studies have shown that same-sex and cross-sex couples seek similar things in relationships, report similar amounts of relationship satisfaction, get into fights about similar issues, and end their relationships in similar ways.[53] The clinician working with same-sex couples should not assume that they are completely different and should recognize that many clinical intervention strategies used with heterosexual couples are also appropriate to gay and lesbian couples.[54] In addition to the common issues that affect all couples, the clinician working with gay and lesbian couples also must attend to the ways that gender socialization, coming out, discrimination, and stigmatization affect same-sex couples.

There is a second dilemma. Focusing on "gay couples" or "lesbian couples" as a group in order to distinguish them from "heterosexual couples" obscures the variety among gay and lesbian couples. There are few empirical studies of same-sex couples, and most of these are limited to white, middle-class, urban, able-bodied, young participants and rely on self reports and small samples.[55] There is a serious limitation on the ability to generalize from such data. For example, one of the frequently cited "differences" between gay couples and lesbian couples is that gay men are more interested in sex than lesbian women. However, Bell and Weinberg, in one of the few studies that included a large number of African American participants, found that male and female sexual interest was not significantly different for black homosexual respondents.[56] Although heterosexism, homophobia, and sexism affect the dynamics of all gay and lesbian couples, it is important to recognize that age, class, race, ethnicity, and physical ability, as well as the dynamics of each individual couple, make each relationship unique.

A number of clinicians have suggested that the cultural expectations of Asian, African American, Latino/Latina, and Jewish gay men and lesbian women present them (and the couples in which they are members) with unique stresses.[57] Ethnic and racial minority gay men and lesbian women live in three communities: the gay and lesbian community, the racial/ethnic community, and the dominant mainstream society. Although each community offers some support, each has its own expectations and demands, which often conflict. The tension of living in these three communities, in all of which one feels marginalized, adds to identity difficulties, which can be particularly troublesome if there are racial and cultural differences between the partners.[58]

Gay and lesbian couples in which one or both partners have a physical disability are also faced with additional challenges and dual minority membership. Those living in a rural area may be more isolated than those in urban centers. Furthermore, gay and lesbian couples at different ages have different issues. Older gay men and lesbians are, in general, less likely to disclose their sexual orientation to others,[59] perhaps because many remember the oppression of their youth.[60] Thus, older gay and lesbian couples may have difficulty confronting a nursing home that does not recognize them as married; they may receive little recognition or support in dealing with the death of their partner; and they may be isolated and have few social activities.

Finally, the therapist must remember that every couple is composed of two unique individuals. With a lesbian couple, for example, the assumption that the two women are similar in certain relational capacities because of their socialization as women may prevent the therapist from seeing their individual differences. Although it is important to acknowledge and explore the effects of their shared experience of being both female and lesbian in a sexist, homophobic culture, the clinician must not lose sight of the distinctness and the unique impacts of their specific families of origin and individual issues.

Notes

1. L. Brown, New voices, new vision: Toward a lesbian/gay paradigm for psychology, *Psychology of Women Quarterly* 13 (1989): 445–58; and N. S. Eldridge, Gender issues in counseling same-sex couples, *Professional Psychology: Research and Practice* 18 (1987): 567–72.

2. C. Browning, A. Reynolds, and S. Dworkin, Affirmative psychotherapy for lesbian women, *Counseling Psychologist* 19 (1991): 177–96; B. McCandlish, Therapeutic issues with lesbian couples, in *Homosexuality and Psychotherapy*, ed. J. C. Gonsiorek (New York: Haworth 1982), 71–78; B. C. Murphy, Counseling lesbian couples: Sexism, heterosexism and homophobia, in *Counseling Gay Men and Lesbians: Journey to the End of the Rainbow*, ed. S. H. Dworkin and F. Gutierrez (Alexandria, VA: AACD Press, 1992), 63–79; S. Roth, Psychotherapy with lesbian couples: Individual issues, female socialization and the social context, in *Women in Families: A Framework for Family Therapy*, ed. M. McGoldrick, C. Anderson, and F. Walsh (New York: Norton, 1989), 286–307; S. Vargo. The effects of women's socialization on lesbian couples, in *Lesbian Psychologies*, ed. Boston Lesbian Psychologies Collective, (Chicago: University of Illinois Press, 1987), 161–73.

3. R. Friedman, Couple therapy with gay couples, *Psychiatric Annals.* 21 (1991): 485–90.

4. R. M. Berger, Men together: Understanding the gay couple, *Journal of Homosexuality* 19, 3 (1990): 31–49.

5. M. Mendola, *The Mendola Report* (New York: Crown, 1980).

6. Berger, Men together; M. E. Reilly, and J. M. Lynch, Power-sharing in lesbian partnerships, *Journal of Homosexuality* 19, 3 (1990): 1–30; D. M. Tanner, *The Lesbian Couple* (Lexington, MA: Lexington Books, 1978).

7. P. Blumstein and P. Schwartz, *American couples: Money, Work and Sex* (New York: PocketBooks, 1983), M. Cardell, S. Finn, and J. Marecek, Sex-role identity, sex role behavior and satisfaction in heterosexual, lesbian and gay male couples, *Psychology of Women Quarterly* 5 (1981): 488–95; L. A. Kurdek and J. A. Schmitt, Relationship quality of partners in heterosexual married, heterosexual cohabitating, and gay and lesbian relationships, *Journal of Personality and Social Psychology* 51 (1986): 711–20; B. C. Murphy, Lesbian couples and their parents, *Journal of Counseling and Development* 68 (1989): 46–51.

8. K. Jay and A. Young, *The Gay Report* (New York: Summit Books, 1979).

9. H. Curry and A. Clifford, *A Legal Guide for Lesbian and Gay Couples* (Berkeley: Nolo Press, 1986).

10. Berger, Men together; Mendola, *Mendola Report.*

11. Kurdek and Schmitt, Relationship quality; L. A. Peplau and S. Cochran, A relational perspective on homosexuality, in *Homosexuality/heterosexuality: Concepts of Sexual Orientation*, ed. D. P. McWhirter, S. A. Sanders, and J. M. Reinisch (New York: Oxford University Press, 1990), 321–49.

12. G. Herek, Hate crimes against lesbians and gay men, *American Psychologist* 44 (1989): 948–55.

13. P. DeVasto, A. Kaufman, L. Rosner, R. Jackson, J. Christy, S. Pearson, and T. Burgett, The prevalence of sexually stressful events among females in the general population, *Archives of Sexual Behavior* 13 (1984): 59–67; F. Mims and A. Chang, Unwanted sexual experiences of young women, *Psychosocial Nursing* 22 (1984): 7–14; D. Russell and N. Howell, The prevalence of rape in the United States revisited, *Signs* 8 (1983): 688–95.

14. J. Loulan, *Lesbian Passion* (San Francisco: Spinsters, 1987).

15. B. Decker, Counseling gay and lesbian couples, in *Homosexuality and social work*, ed. R. Schoenberb, R. S. Goldberg, and D. Shore (New York: Haworth, 1984), 39–52; S. Roth. and B. C. Murphy, Therapeutic work with lesbian clients. A systemic therapy view, in *Women and Family Therapy*, ed. M. Ault-Riche (Rockville, MD: Aspen Press, 1986), 78–89.

16. V. Cass, Homosexual identity formation: A theoretical model, *Journal of Homosexuality* 4 (1979): 219–35; J. D. Hencken and W. T. O'Dowd, Coming out as an aspect of identity formation, *Gai Saber* 1 (1977): 18–22; B. Ponse, *Identities in the Lesbian World* (Westport, CT: Greenwood, 1978).

17. E. Coleman, Developmental stages of the coming out process, *Journal of Homosexuality* 7, 2–3 (1981–82): 31–43; J. C. Gonsiorek, An introduction to mental health issues and homosexuality, *American Behavioral Scientist* 25, 4 (1982): 367–84; Murphy, Lesbian Couples.

18. Krestan and C. Bepko, The problem of fusion in the lesbian relationship, *Family Process* 19 (1980): 277–89.

19. Roth, Psychotherapy; Roth and Murphy, Therapeutic Work.

20. Krestan and Bepko, Problem of fusion; B. Burch, Psychological merger in lesbian couples: A joint ego psychological and systems approach, *Family Therapy* 9 (1982): 201–8.

21. McCandlish, Therapeutic Issues.

22. N. Chodorow, *The Reproduction of Mothering: Psychoanalysis and the Sociology of Gender* (Berkeley: University of California Press, 1978).

23. D. Elise, Lesbian couples: The implications of sex differences in separation-individuation, *Psychotherapy* 23 (1986): 305–10: L. A. Peplau and S. Cochran, Value orientations in the intimate relationships of gay men, *Journal of Homosexuality* 6, 3 (1981): 1–19.

24. B. C. Murphy, "The portrayal of lesbians in film: Reflections of lesbian relationships". (Paper presented at the annual meeting of the American Psychological Association, San Francisco, August 1991).

25. D. P. McWhirter and A. M. Mattison, *The Male Couple: How Relationships Develop* (Englewood Cliffs, NJ: Prentice-Hall 1984); Brown, New voices.

26. Eldridge, Gender issues.

27. J. Marecek, S. Finn, and M. Cardell, Gender roles in the relationships of lesbians and gay men, in *Gay Relationships*, ed. J. DeCecco (New York: Harrington Park, 1988); J. M. Lynch and M. E. Reilly, Role relationships: Lesbian perspectives, *Journal of Homosexuality* 12, 2 (1985–86): 53–69.

28. Blumstein and Schwartz, *American Couples*; J. Harry, Gay male and lesbian relationships, in *Contemporary Families and Alternative Lifestyles*, ed. E. Macklin and R. Rubin (Beverly Hills: Sage, 1983), 216–34.

29. Blumstein and Schwartz, *American Couples*; J. Harry, Decision making and age differences among gay male couples, *Journal of Homosexuality* 8, 2 (1982): 9–22.

30. N. S. Eldridge and L. A. Gilbert, Correlates of relationship satisfaction in lesbian couples, *Psychology of Women Quarterly* 14 (1990): 43–62; L. A. Peplau, S. Cochran, K. Rook, and C. Padesky, Loving women: Attachment and autonomy in lesbian relationships, *Journal of Social Issues* 34, 3 (1978): 7–27; Reilly and Lynch, Power-sharing.

31. W. Masters and V. Johnson, *Homosexuality in Perspective* (Boston: Little, Brown, 1979).

32. A. Bell and M. Weinberg, *Homosexualities: A Study of Diversity among Men and Women* (New York: Simon and Schuster, 1978); Blumstein and Schwartz, *American Couples*.

33. Blumstein and Schwartz, *American Couples*.

34. P. Blumstein and P. Schwartz, Intimate relationships and the creation of sexuality, in *Homosexuality/Heterosexuality*, ed. McWhirter, Sanders, and Reinisch, 307–20.

35. Loulan, *Lesbian Passion*.

36. Blumstein and Schwartz, *American Couples*.

37. Blumstein and Schwartz, Intimate relationships.

38. Bell and Weinberg, *Homosexualities*.

39. K. A. George and A. E. Behrendt, Therapy for male couples experiencing relationship problems and sexual problems, *Journal of Homosexuality* 14, 1–2 (1987): 77–89; H. L. Gochros, The sexuality of gay men with HIV infection, *Social Work* 37 (1992): 105–9; M. Hall, Sex therapy with lesbian couples: A four stage approach, *Journal of Homosexuality* 14, 1–2 (1987): 137–56; J. Loulan, *Lesbian Sex* (San Francisco, Spinsters, 1984); idem, *Lesbian passion*; D. P. McWhirter and A. M. Mattison, Treatment of sexual dysfunction in homosexual male couples, in *Principles and Practices of Sex Therapy*, ed. S. Leiblum and L. Pervin (New York, Guilford, 1980), 321–45; M. Nichols, Doing sex therapy with lesbians: Bending a heterosexual paradigm to fit a gay life-style, in *Lesbian Psychologies*, ed. Boston Lesbian Psychologies Collective, 242–60.

40. Bell and Weinberg, *Homosexualities*; Blumstein and Schwartz, *American Couples*; Mendola, *Mendola Report*.

41. L. A. Peplau, Lesbian and gay relationships, in *Homosexuality: Research Implications for Public Policy*, ed. J. C. Gonsiorek and J. D. Weinrich (Newbury Park, CA: Sage, 1991), 177–96.

42. McWhirter and Mattison, *The Male Couple*.

43. R. O. Hawkins, The relationship between culture, personality, and sexual jealousy in men in heterosexual and homosexual relationships, *Journal of Homosexuality* 19, 3 (1990): 67–84.

44. J. M. Ussher, Couples therapy with gay clients: Issues facing counselors, *Counselling Psychology Quarterly* 3, 1 (1990): 109–16.

45. Blumstein and Schwartz, *American Couples*.

46. Ibid.

47. S. B. Geis, R. L. Fuller, and J. Rish, Lovers of AIDS victims: Psychosocial stresses and counseling needs, *Death Studies* 10 (1986): 43–53.

48. R. Bor, N. Prior, and R. Miller, Complementarity in relationships of couples affected by HIV, *Counselling Psychology Quarterly* 3, 2 (1990): 217–20; S. Morin, R. Charles, and A. Maylon, The psychological impact of AIDS on gay men, *American Psychologist* 11 (1984): 1288–93; J. W. Shannon and W. J. Woods, Affirmative psychotherapy for gay men, *Counseling Psychologist* 19 (1991): 197–215.

49. Berger, Men Together.

50. Ibid.

51. Loulan, *Lesbian Passion.*

52. Browning, Reynolds, and Dworkin, Affirmative psychotherapy.

53. Bell and Weinberg, *Homosexualities;* Blumstein and Schwartz, *American Couples;* S. M. Duffy and C. E. Rusbult, Satisfaction and commitment in homosexual and heterosexual relationships, *Journal of Homosexuality* 12, 2 (1985–86): 1–23: L. A. Kurdek, The dissolution of gay and lesbian couples, *Journal of Social and Personal Relationships* 8 (1991): 265–78; Kurdek and Schmitt, Relationship quality.

54. Kurdek, Dissolution.

55. Peplau, Lesbian and gay relationships.

56. Bell and Weinberg, *Homosexualities.*

57. E. T. Beck, *Nice Jewish Girls: A Lesbian Anthology* (Watertown, MA: Persephone (1982); C. S. Chan, Cultural considerations in counseling Asian American lesbians and gay men, in *Counseling Gay Men and Lesbians,* ed. Dworkin and Gutierrez, 115–24; O. Espin, Latina lesbian women, in *Lesbian Psychologies,* ed. Boston Lesbian Psychologies Collective, 35–55; D. K. Loiacano, Gay identity issues among Black Americans: Racism, homophobia, and the need for validation, *Journal of Counseling and Development* 68 (1989): 21–25; V. M. Mays, "The black women's relationship project: A national survey of black lesbians" (Paper presented at the annual meeting of the American Psychological Association, Washington, DC, August 1986); E. S. Morales, Counseling Latino gays and Latina lesbians, in *Counseling Gay Men and Lesbians,* ed. Dworkin and Gutierrez, 125–40.

58. N. Garcia, C. Kennedy, S. Pearlman, and J. Perez, The impact of race and cultural differences: Challenges to lesbian relationships, in *Lesbian Psychologies,* ed. Boston Lesbian Psychologies Collective, 142–60.

59. C. T. Tully, Caregiving: What do midlife lesbians view as important, *Journal of Gay and Lesbian Psychotherapy* 1 (1989): 87–104.

60. D. Kimmel, Psychotherapy and the older gay male, *Psychotherapy: Theory, Research and Practice* 14 (1977): 386–93.

The Origin of the Gay Psychotherapy Movement

Charles Silverstein

On December 15, 1973, a ray of sunlight rose above the horizon, a historic change in the psychiatric and psychological professions providing warmth to gay people who, because of their homosexuality, had been long forced to live a cold, closeted life. It was on that date that the Board of Trustees of the American Psychiatric Association announced that homosexuality had been removed as a mental disorder per se from the *Diagnostic and Statistical Manual (DSM II)* (APA 1968).

It had been a long night. In the previous decades, gay people walked in the shadows of society, splitting their public and private lives, terrified that exposure of their homosexuality would result in family rejection, imprisonment, and job loss. Like many men in my generation, I too had been in the closet for much of my adult life. I therefore felt rather proud of my contribution to the December day's event.

The nomenclature change was the result of serendipity. In 1972, the Association for the Advancement of Behavior Therapy (AABT) was holding its annual meeting in New York City. There was a panel on homosexuality chaired by Helen Singer Kaplan. Kaplan invited Bernice Goodman and me, as representatives of Identity House, to speak on the panel (Silverstein 1972). It was the first time openly gay people spoke at an AABT convention, and the meeting room was filled to capacity.

The convention program also listed lectures by behaviorists noted for their use of electrical aversion therapy on gay men. The Gay Activist Alliance (GAA), New York's most militant gay rights organization, voted to "zap" (demonstrate against) AABT and the professionals who used aversion therapy.[1]

Members of GAA walked into the meeting room and politely informed the speaker that he would be allowed fifteen minutes in which to make his presentation, after which gay activists would take over the meeting, which we did. We spoke about the harm done to gay people through the use of aversion therapy. Behaviorists at the meeting were outraged at the interruption.[2]

In the audience was Robert Spitzer, a psychiatrist and member of the Nomenclature Committee of the American Psychiatric Association. This committee is the group that formulates and makes changes in the diagnostic system. At the time, homosexuality was listed in the *Diagnostic and Statistical Manual* as a "sexual deviation."

Spitzer suggested that gay activists take their complaint to the Nomenclature Committee. An ad hoc committee of gay activists, mostly from GAA, was formed to organize the presentation. The committee consisted of Ron Gold (chairman), Jean O'Leary, Rose Jordan, Ray Prada, Brad Wilson, Bernice Goodman, and myself. A preparatory written report citing recent psychological research on homosexuality was prepared by Brad Wilson (1972) and Rose Jordan, and sent to the APA committee.

The ad hoc committee, which was ruled with an iron hand by Ron Gold, elected to make two presentations at the meeting with the psychiatrists. Jean O'Leary was assigned the first of these, an oral presentation about the harmful effects of pejorative labeling on gay people. I was asked to discuss the diagnosis of homosexuality from the professional point of view.

Our committee met often. At these meetings, each member was assigned the responsibility of fielding potential questions from the psychiatrists. Jean and I were asked to read our presentations, so that they could be critiqued by others. At each of these meetings I reported that I had not yet finished mine. This was met by displeasure, particularly from Gold, who insisted that my presentation be sufficiently militant and confronting. It was precisely because of these demands of militancy that I willfully avoided informing them about my preparations.

I had decided to spend my available time reading about all the diagnostic systems that had been invented to classify human behavior. I found that they went back to the ancient Greeks. With particular interest I read through the American diagnostic systems, which began in 1871 (Association of Medical Superintendents of American Institutions for the Insane), right through the various editions of the *Diagnostic and Statistical Manual*. My intention was to understand their structure and point of view, to understand them as social documents that reflected the worries and fears of their ages. I began to look on them as spotlighting people whose behavior was inexplicable and therefore condemned. The last thing I wanted to do, at least at that point, was to write something. Nor did I want to play the role of the gay activist at the meeting with the Nomenclature Committee; I did not want to be their antagonist or accuser.[3] I knew they were expecting that, and I thought it the better strategy to take a different approach. But what approach?

I found that it was not possible to read through the diagnostic systems without starting to chuckle. They could all have been subtitled "Miss Manners Meets the Psychiatrists." Most of the diagnostic categories consisted of socially disapproved behavior. Examples in *DSM II* included lying, stealing, the fear of getting syphilis, or simply being a cranky person.[4] I decided to use humor to point out the unscientific nature of diagnostic systems.

It was on the evening of February 7, 1973, that I wrote the paper (Silverstein 1976–77). The first part of it highlighted the humor one can find within the pages of diagnostic systems. The second part chastised the Nomenclature Committee for the role the psychiatric profession played in the disenfranchisement of, discrimination against, and legal penalties imposed on gay people because we had been diagnosed as psychopathic and sexually deviant.

The presentation to the committee was held at the Psychiatric Institute on February 8, 1973. It was quite clear that at least one member of the Nomenclature Committee was gay. I wondered how he would feel during the committee discussions after we left. I wondered whether he felt any sense of rage at the demeaning prospect of discussing whether or not he (as a representative gay man) should be diagnosed as sexually deviant. I knew that if I were in his place, constraint would be difficult. (I later learned that it presented no problem for him.)

The committee received us cordially. They had read the written report, and they listened carefully to what we had to say. During lunch, Henry Brill, the committee chair, mentioned some of the impediments to removing homosexuality as a mental disorder. He first cited problems with the Russians. The psychiatric diagnostic system becomes part of the International Classification of Diseases, which includes all the physical diseases of the body. He claimed that the Russians were opposed to the removal of homosexuality. He thought, however, that they could probably negotiate it.

The psychoanalysts, on the other hand, formed the biggest roadblock. Psychoanalysts were adamant in their belief that homosexual behavior was aberrant, and doomed a gay person to a life of loneliness, depression, and ultimately suicide. Only psychoanalysis could save the homosexual from himself, said the most pompous of the analysts (Socarides 1978). Brill and I also gossiped about famous gay psychoanalysts such as Anna Freud and Harry Stack Sullivan.[5]

After many months, and quite a bit of political wrangling from many directions, the Nomenclature Committee voted to recommend the removal of homosexuality as a mental disorder in the next edition of the *Diagnostic and Statistical Manual* (APA 1980). Their recommendation, however, had to be approved by the Board of Trustees of the American Psychiatric Association. I was not directly privy to these discussions, but my understanding from those who were is the following: Most members of the board were sympathetic to the request by the Nomenclature Committee. On the other hand, the removal of homosexuality as a mental disorder represented conflicting moral, ethical, political, and economic values. There was sympathy with the idea that gay people had been discriminated against in our society, and that the medical/psychological profession had contributed to that sorry state of affairs. But many members of the association, in particular psychoanalytically oriented psychiatrists, had built their reputations on "curing" homosexuals, and an affirmative action by the board would have been a slap in their professional faces. It would also have an economic effect on the psychoanalysts, since many gay men would no longer feel justified in going to them for treatment. We gay activists had always maintained that trying to change the sexual orientation of gay people was fueled by economics as much as by psychological theory. The board of trustees was forced to face that problem, and they feared a rebellion by the psychoanalytic members of the association, who were lobbying very hard and circulating petitions against the nomenclature change.

In March 1973 Richard Pillard, a Boston psychiatrist, was able to get the Northeastern New England District Branch to endorse the nomenclature change, making them the first APA affiliate to do so. This was an important step, since it demonstrated that local associations would support a decision to remove homosexuality from the list of disorders.

The board decided that the issue was so explosive that a unanimous vote was required for the sake of solidarity. In consultation with the Nomenclature Committee, particularly Robert Spitzer, the board tried to satisfy both sides in the conflict. They finally asserted that some homosexuals are happy with their lives and have no wish to change their sexual orientation. These homosexuals were "ego syntonic." They were "normal" (although they never used that word publicly) and therefore not in need of psychiatric treatment. On the other hand, there were homosexuals who were unhappy with their lot, that is, "ego dystonic," and these homosexuals were in need of treatment, and could remain on the list of mental disorders. It was a compromise that infuriated the recalcitrant psychoanalysts, who raised a petition to force a vote on the nomenclature change by the whole association.

Gay activists were cognizant that a referendum of the APA membership might overturn the nomenclature change. The psychoanalytic group, led by Charles Socarides (Bayer 1981), sent out a letter to the entire membership challenging the board decision, claiming that the association was being taken over by gay activists and that untold harm would be done to homosexuals who would be deprived of treatment for their unfortunate sexual adjustment if the decision was not overturned. To counter this letter, another one was sent out, this time written by Robert Spitzer and Ron Gold, and paid for by The National Gay Task Force, which had been organized after Gold and Bruce Voeller left GAA.

The strategy of the activist letter was clever. It argued that a professional organization should support the actions of its board of trustees. To reject the decision, after it had been carefully considered by both the Nomenclature Committee and the board of trustees, would be an insult to the organization. They also cited many examples of civil rights violations against gay people that had been justified by psychiatric diagnosis. The issue of homosexuality was left in the background since we were under no illusions about the conservative nature of most psychiatrists in the country. Many prominent psychiatrists signed the letter, including the then present and all the candidates for the future president of APA. The letter did not divulge that it was paid for by a gay activist organization.

Socarides and his psychoanalytic colleagues howled when they learned about the letter. They claimed fraud and demanded an investigation of APA officers, which could not have endeared them to these officials. The investigation did not support Socarides.

About ten thousand psychiatrists voted in the referendum. Fifty-eight percent supported the actions of the board, while 37 percent voted against it (5 percent not responding). One wonders why the majority of voters supported the deletion of homosexuality as a mental disorder, besides a belief that homosexuality is not abnormal.[6] I think there are three reasons. For some, it was a matter of supporting the officers of their organization, regardless of the wisdom of the action. Others voted their conscience, understanding that discrimination against gay people was a very real problem, and they wanted to help remove the stigma. I suspect that hostility toward Socarides was a third reason. Many psychiatrists were embarrassed by his bull in a china shop approach to conflict, his arrogance, and his inability to negotiate or compromise. They simply did not want to be on any side that included him.[7]

One of the criticisms leveled against the APA for removing homosexuality as a disorder is that science does not advance by a vote of hands. These critics forget that any list is produced by a group of people who vote for or against it. "Science," I learned from my reading of diagnostic systems, has little to do with it.

About a month later, the television program *Sixty Minutes* decided to do a segment on the nomenclature change, and asked to interview me. It was an excellent way of publicizing the event and the services of our organization. There was one problem, however: I was not "out" to my mother, who lived in Miami. She had to be told before I appeared on national television. It was just by chance that she decided to visit and stay with me on the same day *Sixty Minutes* was scheduled to do the taping. Unfortunately, her plane was late and she arrived at my office just an hour before the camera crew was scheduled to arrive.

She was obviously very curious, and rather proud, that her son was to appear on *Sixty Minutes*, one of her favorite programs. I told her that the program was about homosexuality. "But why do they want to interview you?" she asked. "Because," I said, "I'm a homosexual." First there was a gasp, then a sense of shock. Then the television crew walked in (early), bringing along with them huge floodlights, cameras, and coils of thick electrical wire. Dazed, my mother sat in the chair as the crew set up their equipment; then, without a word, she retired to my quarters and refused to budge.[8] The taping consumed the next few hours, the airing of the program gave gay people all over the country an important psychological boost, and my mother, who by that time had gotten over the shock, instructed all her "girlfriends" in her Miami condominium to watch "my son, the doctor."

The effect of the nomenclature change was electric. On the most obvious level, the diagnostic status of homosexuality, the change meant that the psychiatric/psychological profession had no justification to continue "curing" sexual orientation. There had been sodomy laws in almost all the states that depended on the medical opinion that homosexuality was perverse. The APA decision laid the groundwork to challenge these laws, a process that is still incomplete. The publicity around the event also encouraged many gay people to come out, as if the APA gave them permission to disclose their sexuality to friends and family. For gay men who hated their homosexuality, the announcement was like an elixir that restored self-esteem and confidence.

The announcement was also profound on a meta-level of analysis. It was not only the pathologization of homosexuality that had been attacked by the gay liberationists and gay professionals. On a deeper level, the campaign to change the diagnostic status of homosexuality challenged the foundation on which the psychiatric/psychological professions judged sexual behavior. Before 1973, the foundation was simply the moral code of our society. That which was immoral was invariably also illegal, and, hence, pathological. That is why homosexuality was categorized as a sexual deviation in the *Diagnostic and Statistical Manual II* (1968), along with the paraphilias—for example, fetishism, exhibitionism, voyeurism, sadism, and masochism.

The removal of homosexuality from the list was an attack on the use of morality as the basis for diagnosing sexual behavior. But if the moral code was no longer the standard for judging the pathology of a sexual behavior, then what would replace it? The foundation for the diagnosis of sexual disorders fell apart like a house of cards (Spitzer 1981). Why couldn't the same standard of internal conflict be used with all the other sexual deviations (now called mental disorders)? A shoe fetishist may be quite happy with his sexual experiences. Is he no longer suffering from a pathology (Silverstein 1984; Suppe 1984)?

The result of the 1973 decision to remove homosexuality from the list of disorders has brought about a more relaxed attitude toward those who are involved in "kinky sex." While these behaviors are still classified as mental disorders, they no longer carry the degree of heinousness they were associated with in the past.

The Early History of Gay Psychology

How did organized psychiatry get turned around from condemning homosexuality to approving of it? There were a number of factors that coalesced in the early 1970s. There was first of all the diminution of the psychoanalytic movement's power to control psychiatric thinking. Another factor was the rise of multidisciplinary sex research, unfettered by the cliché beliefs of the psychoanalysts. A third reason was the drive among gay psychiatrists and psychologists to come out of the closet and work for the common good of gay people. I played a role in some of these factors, but I began working for the gay movement in earnest first by joining the gay rights movement, then by working as a psychologist in the gay community.

Before the 1970s, there was no established alternative treatment for gay people in New York City. Virtually every therapist set the goal of changing the patient's sexual orientation from homosexual to heterosexual. This goal was not necessarily imposed on the patient. Gay people were a distinctly unhappy group, suffering from significant depression and loneliness, which subsequently led to a higher than average suicide rate (Bell and Weinberg 1978).

The origins of gay psychotherapy begin in the fertile soil of the 1970s political movements. Previous to that date, gay organizations such as the Mattachine Society and the Daughters of Bilitis aimed at fitting into society. Their goal was to be accepted by the heterosexual majority. They acted like ladies and gentlemen, watchful of their manners, respectful to authority, and conservative in dress (they wore suits and dresses to demonstrations).

The 1969 riot at the Stonewall Inn galvanized a younger group of gay people into organizing the Gay Liberation Front (GLF), which identified with left-wing ideologies, liberation movements such as the Black and women's movements, and confrontation tactics. Their members believed that social activism was required to counter prejudice against gay people. Unlike the earlier gay organizations, they were not good boys and girls. They were spoiling for a fight.

GLF self-destructed due to internal conflict. It was replaced by the Gay Activist Alliance (GAA) an equally militant but more efficient organization. One of its most popular slogans was "The cure for homosexuality is rebellion." Its popularity was based in part on anger against the psychiatric establishment for the psychological harm they had done to gay people. The GAA subscribed to the popular left-wing notion of the day that "elitism" contributed to the oppression of gay people. Elitism was reflected in what were described as "vertical hierarchies," an organizational structure in which important decisions were made by executives, officers, or "professionals." The ideal organization was "horizontal," whereby every member of the group had an equal say in the setting of goals and tactics. "Participatory democracy" was the name given to this early 1970s idealistic form of democracy. It was not an efficient system of decision making. In fact, meetings of the GAA and other organizations built on participatory democracy (such as early gay counseling centers) resembled something between a lunatic asylum and trench warfare.

Gay psychotherapy was an offspring of the gay rights movement. A group of activists, some of whom were young gay professionals, dedicated themselves to changing the psychiatric/psychological profession's attitude toward, and treatment of, homosexuals. This group had two goals in mind: to provide counseling services to gay people in emotional crisis, and to work politically toward removing the stigma from society. With regard to the first of these goals, they knew that many gay people preferred to see a homosexual rather than a heterosexual counselor. Many gay people liked, even preferred, their sexual orientation, and resented a heterosexual therapist's assumption that they should become heterosexual. "I don't want my homosexuality to become the center of treatment" was an often heard comment by gays who sought psychological help.

In 1971, Identity House (called "I House") was opened as a weekend walk-in center in the rectory of the Church of the Holy Apostle in Chelsea. Its founding members were Sidney Abbott, Bernice Goodman, Barbara Love, Tina Mandel, and myself. Goodman was a social worker and I a graduate student in psychology. The other three were socially concerned lesbians who were active in both the women's movement and the gay movement. The five founders sat as members of the steering committee, and I was asked to serve as director. No one received a salary. The walk-in center was staffed each evening by a male and female peer counselor who provided support to gay men and women who "walked in" (no appointment necessary) and wanted to talk about their emotional problems. The peers were supervised by professionals who volunteered their time. Gay people who needed long-term therapy were referred to therapists on the staff who supervised the peers.

As an organization, I House was far ahead of its time. It started serving gay people two years before the APA nomenclature decision removing homosexuality from the list of mental disorders. We had no other models of gay counseling on which to base out services, nor were there public or private funds available to us. Our only source of income was donations contributed by gay people counseled in the walk-in clinic. With that small sum, the organization had to pay rent, advertising, and the phone bill.

I House, though it had a director and a steering committee, operated on the basis of "participatory democracy," and so believed that a consensus of the entire group was required to formulate policy, rules, and procedures. Virtually all the founders and charter peer counselors of the group were veterans of the gay rights and the women's movement, and they knew from the experience of their own lives about the pain gay people suffered. Even though they were deeply committed to providing the best possible services, the organizational structure led to an extraordinary number of internal conflicts between the members, and between members and officers.

The seeds of dissension were sown the first day I House opened its doors. In retrospect one can see that the conflict was unavoidable. In the early 1970s, gay people mistrusted professional therapists, accusing them, not without justification, of using their power against homosexuals. Professionals had not only diagnosed homosexuality as a mental illness, but had often justified legal sanctions against gay people. The nonprofessional founders of the organization were suspicious of and feared the intentions of any professional, including those who helped found the organization. At the same time, however, they were dependent on these same homosexual therapists to train and supervise them. The internal conflict of being dependent on people they did not trust simmered for over a year.

The professionals, who numbered only a few, believed that peer counseling was in the best interest of gay people. At the same time, they mistrusted the intentions of the peer counselors, believing, not without justification, that some of them wanted to be therapists, even without academic credentials. While a few of the peers returned to graduate school for training, others believed that compassion for gay people and proper supervision were all that were necessary to be a "therapist" in the clinic as well as in private practice. The professionals were adamantly opposed to that view.

It was only a matter of time until suspicion and conflicting intentions had a profound effect both in the steering committee and during meetings of the membership. General meetings were already peppered with strife. Angry outbursts were common, and because "elitism" was frowned on, the chair was prevented from curtailing discussion. The undercurrent of hostility between professionals and peers finally erupted, and the future of the organization and its services was in jeopardy. Neither side saw any room for compromise.

In 1973, the two professionals on the steering committee, Bernice Goodman and I, and Don Sussman, the director of the walk-in service, decided to resign. We believed that the gay community needed a full-time counseling center, staffed with legally qualified professionals and administered by a full-time director. We wanted an "elitist" organization with efficiently chaired meetings. "Seed money" was found to rent a large Upper West Side apartment, and in June 1973, it opened to the public with a full-time director and administrative assistant. We were each given a salary of fifty dollars a week. As director, and because of the inadequate salary, I and my lover took the master bedroom for our quarters. Many gay and lesbian therapists volunteered three or more hours a week, without remuneration, and provided therapy for gay people. Therapy fees were turned over to the organization to pay expenses. The organization was called the Institute for Human Identity (IHI), unfortunately creating some confusion in the public mind between IHI and I House.

Within the first few months, all available therapy hours were fully booked. Though IHI was the first full-time gay counseling center to open in New York City, it was not the first in the country. That honor goes to the Homophile Community Health Center, directed by Don McGaw in Boston. Counseling centers opened later in Seattle, Los Angeles, Philadelphia, and Pittsburgh.

There were a number of ways in which we tried to inform the gay community about our services. Perhaps the most humorous of our strategies were the nightime forays to "the trucks." The area called "the trucks" was located in Greenwich Village only a couple of blocks from the Hudson River. During the day, huge food trucks occupied the space. At night gay men wandered into the trucks to have sex. During weekend nights one might find hundreds of men having sex or watching others.

Don Sussman and I decided to advertise the new therapeutic services of IHI by going to the trucks. On a number of Friday and Saturday nights, we drove there, opened up a folding table on the sidewalk, and served coffee to the gay males milling about. Along with every cup of coffee went an IHI brochure. Serving coffee led to continuous conversations and discussions about the counseling needs of gay people—just what we wanted. We were very amused when we later saw "the trucks" listed on intake forms as the referral source for new clients.

Some of the IHI services were unique in the city. For instance, we offered a natural childbirth class for pregnant lesbians and their lovers. The class was advertised in the *Village Voice,* and the ad drew a large number of homophobic phone calls. But it also piqued the interest of some news reporters, who wrote about the class and the counseling center.[9]

There was a therapy group for lesbian couples led by a lesbian, and one for male couples led by a gay man. IHI also advertised a group for heterosexually married gay men, and our phones did not stop ringing for two weeks, suggesting the high incidence of gay married men. Unfortunately, almost all of them were looking for sex with another gay married man, not for a support group. "What do you do in this group?" was the most common question asked over the phone. "What!" most of them exclaimed after a description of the support group, "You just talk?" Click. We then advertised for a unique group composed of couples in which one member of the pair was homosexual and the other heterosexual. That group was very successful.

It was during my tenure as director of IHI that I started writing and publishing, and again it happened by chance. In 1974 I received a phone call from Bill Cohen, who requested a meeting with me. He and his partner wanted to start a new company, called Haworth Press, which would specialize in publishing professional journals. Since Bill was gay, he wanted his first venture to be the *Journal of Homosexuality,* a professional journal that would publish the latest social science research about homosexuality. He asked me to be its founding editor. There were very few gay psychologists who were out of the closet in those days, and he came to me because of my affiliation with a gay counseling center. Given that Bill and his partner were investing their own money in the company, beginning their venture with a gay journal was a very brave act on their part.

It seemed ironic to me then (and still does) that someone who never got a grade better than a C in English should be asked to edit a journal. There were only two journals devoted to sex research at the time, the *Journal of Sex Research,* published by the Society for the Scientific Study of Sex, and the *Archives of Sexual Behavior,* not affiliated with a professional organization.

With the encouragement of friends, particularly Cyril Franks, editor of *Behavior Therapy,* the research journal for the Association for the Advancement of Behavior Therapy, I agreed to serve as editor. I was alotted the sum of twenty-five dollars a month for expenses, which included phone bills, stationery, envelopes, and postage.[10]

I intended to announce the publication of the journal during the annual meeting of the American Psychological Association in Hawaii. There was a panel on homosexuality scheduled for the conference. Sitting on the panel were four psychologists, two of whom were friends, Harold Greenwald and Albert Ellis. There was no openly gay person on it, which was typical for the time. Just before the panel discussion began, a gay friend mentioned to me that he heard the panel chair say to friends, "I have to leave now and chair the fag panel."

In the audience were quite a number of gay psychologists, although we did not know each other yet. The panel members made their presentations, describing gay life in the usual pejorative ways. At the end of the panel, the chair asked whether there were any questions. Furious, I jumped to the microphone and asked why there were no gay psychologists on the panel. The chair said, "There aren't any in APA."

"Well, you're looking at one," I responded, becoming the first gay psychologist to come out on the floor of the APA. I then gave a critique of the bias of the panel and asked both Howard and Al to tell us whether they had had any homosexual experiences, and how they felt about them.[11] Howard replied that he did, but did not like it, while Al said that he enjoyed the experience— although neither statement was very descriptive.

In the audience were Marty Rogers and Steve Morin, psychologists from California who had been talking together about the formation of a gay group within APA. It was after the confrontation at this panel that they organized the Association of Gay Psychologists, and held their first meeting at the APA convention in Montreal the next year.

That evening I attended a cocktail party hosted by Howard. "Why did you tell people you are a homosexual?" he asked. I gave the obvious reply. "But I've known you for years," he said, "and I know you're heterosexual." There was nothing I could say that would convince him. Finally, he came to the conclusion that my statement was a ploy to seduce women! This bizarre reasoning made me aware of how painful it must have been for him to learn of my sexual orientation.

In 1976, while still director of IHI, I was approached by Frank Taylor, formerly editor in chief at McGraw-Hill Publishing Company, to write a book for parents who learn that a son or daughter is gay. He sought me out because of my affiliation with IHI and the fact that I was so public about my homosexuality. *A Family Matter: A Parents' Guide to Homosexuality* (1977a) was the first book published for parents of gay children.

Taylor was also the representative of the English firm that had published *The Joy of Sex*. It sold an enormous number of copies worldwide, and the publisher, Mitchell-Beazley (London), made a fortune from it. They thought they could repeat the financial success with *The Joy of Gay Sex*. The publishers and Taylor (given the times) agreed that only Americans could write that kind of book, and of Americans, only New Yorkers. Taylor asked me whether I would write the book. We agreed that my strength was as a psychologist and counselor to the gay community, and that the book demanded a coauthor who was, among other qualifications, a skilled writer (which I was not), and whose sex life was more catholic[12] than my own.

The next part of this story has never been discussed openly before. One of the writers being interviewed was Edmund White, who was struggling to publish his novels. He was a patient of mine in psychotherapy. Ed faithfully reported his conversations with Taylor (who knew nothing about my relationship with White) about the writing job. I was in quite a dilemma, since Ed did not know that I was the other coauthor. I said nothing to him until he informed me that he had been chosen ("in the debutante contest," I think he said) to cowrite *The Joy of Gay Sex* (1977b), and was trying to find out who the other writer would be. It was then that I told him. The news obviously came as a shock. I also stated that the ethics (and common sense) of my profession prevented me from being both his therapist and his colleague. If he accepted the job, which I encouraged him to do, we would have to terminate the therapeutic relationship. He could seek therapy with someone else.

At first, as one might expect, Ed was upset and angry that he was forced into the choice of losing either badly needed income or his therapy, which he felt was productive. Ed now jokes about his dilemma, saying, "The need to pay my rent exceeded my need for therapy."

It turned out to be an excellent collaboration. We were very different; Ed was a Midwestern WASP with a strong literary background, and I, a Brooklyn assimilated Jew, with expertise in psychology. Fortunately, though different in ethnicity, we were very similar in terms of our gay political beliefs. Ed claimed to have been at the Stonewall the night of the riot, and I admitted to some envy because of it. We wanted to write the kind of book that we would have wanted to read ourselves as adolescents, a book that would be a guide to help men come out. We reasoned, therefore, that the book should have a wider focus than just sex. We set as our goal to advise the reader about life in the gay community. Eventually the majority of passages in the book were of a nonsexual nature. Ed and I lived just a few blocks from each other in those days, so it was easy for us to meet frequently, talk over our strategies for the book, and trade essays for critiquing.

We agreed that the book should be sexually stimulating. Toward that end we wrote six masturbation stories and spaced them throughout the book. We also wrote rather openly about the "kinkier" varieties of sex, such as bondage and water sports, and we tried to serve as "wise older brother" to teenagers struggling with their feelings and their homophobic families.

We did not have so easy a relationship with the publishers, who we perceived to be quite horrible. They were an English firm, Mitchell-Beazley Publishers, and exuded contempt for writers as well as for homosexuals. This seemed odd to us, since the publisher and the art director were gay. They were also married to women, and buried deep in the closet; we believed they used their trips to New York City to vent their sexual frustrations.

This was also early 1977, when Anita Bryant had begun railing against homosexuals.[13] The publishers were very worried that the public outcry against gay people would seriously affect sales, and that books might be confiscated by local officials and governmental customs services. Many people are under the impression that publishers like to have their books confiscated or burned. Nothing could be further from the truth. It is very expensive to fight censorship battles, and it is a rare publisher who is willing to do so. It was made quite clear to us that Mitchell-Beazley would not defend *Joy* in court.

The manuscript was therefore scrutinized with a magnifying glass by attorneys on both sides of the Atlantic (Crown became the U.S. publisher).[14] Ed and I were forced to defend our text on many occasions. For instance, the publishers objected to a section on sexually transmitted diseases, maintaining that information about disease is a turn-off. Ed and I would not relent on this issue. After discussions with the Centers for Disease Control and with local physicians, we wrote an informative essay on STDs. At the next conference with the English publisher, we were given a written critique of the section in the form of questions. The questions were off the wall. For instance, one of them asked, "Why haven't you included a section on Dobbie's Itch?"[15] Upon inquiry Ed and I learned that the list had been prepared by the publisher's dentist, a man raised in South Africa. The essay was never submitted to a physician.

Worries about censorship and confiscation of copies ultimately led to the removal of all the masturbation fantasies that Ed and I had enjoyed writing. The lawyers also objected to the word "shit," and went ballistic over our essay on "bondage," which they pared down to only a short paragraph. Then, one day, the editor in chief at Crown Publishers summoned me to his office to ask why Ed and I insisted on writing the word "cock" rather than "penis." By this time we had been through many hours of censorship and our patience was wearing thin. "Because a cock and a penis are not the same," I responded with hostility. "Your penis is part of your anatomy, while your cock is something you fuck your wife with." "Cock" stayed in the book.

More serious was the problem over the essay on teenagers. The publishers rejected our essay out of hand because it did not condemn sex between teenagers and adults. They insisted that the essay label such men abnormal and immoral, and that we advise teenagers against sex with older men. The publishers may have been overreacting to the Anita Bryant scare, but Ed and I agreed that we could not condone a blanket condemnation of sex between teenagers and older men, as the publishers were demanding. In the end, we agreed that it was better to drop the essay in its entirety rather than publish faulty information. This is why there is no essay on teenagers in the original *Joy of Gay Sex*.[16]

Ed and I reacted to the publishers' interference in our own characteristic ways. As the New York Jewish, gay militant, I was confrontational, while Ed, the Midwestern WASP, was more subtle in his reactions (and perhaps more effective). One evening, while at dinner with the Mitchell-Beazley mafia, I told them I did not want to have dinner with them anymore. When asked why, I simply told the truth, which was that I did not like them, and saw no reason to suffer through a long meal with people I do not like. Ed thanked me profusely afterward.

One day, the English editor of the book (in contrast to the American editor), who was heterosexual, said that he wanted to learn more about what homosexuals were like. He wondered whether he might go somewhere and observe them. I was not sympathetic to his request, which I interpreted as either condescension or an indication that he was in the closet. Ed had no such reservations. "I know just the place you should visit," he said, laying a trap for the editor, but flashing the WASP charm Ed is rightly noted for. "It's called 'The Toilet,' but don't worry about the name, it's not so bad." Ed then gave him instructions on how to get there. I could never have done that. Those readers old enough to remember "The Toilet" can imagine the shock this proper English editor experienced when he entered that foul-smelling place. He faithfully reported to us what happened while he was there, but he never asked for our advice again.

There were bitter arguments over the drawings for the book. They were made from photographs taken by the art director (a closeted married gay man) of two naked, straight men simulating gay sex.[17] The heterosexuality of the models was quite obvious, since their naked bodies were so far apart one could have placed a complete set of the *Encyclopedia Britannica* between them. Things got even worse when the photos were transformed into line drawings. The drawings badly stereotyped sex roles. Using today's gay argot, the "tops" were always either big black men or muscular, hairy white men. The "bottoms" were always rather thin, blondish, passive, fey-looking men. "Well, that's the way homosexuals are," said the art director when he heard our criticism. At the most bitter of these meetings, Ed declared that if they were not redone, he would not support the finished book, and then he left for Fire Island, leaving me with the mafia. I threatened to sue to have my name taken off the book, and I left to speak to a literary attorney. In the end the publishers made a number of drawing changes that were satisfactory to us, but they were very angry. I never received any more Christmas cards from them.

The publishers' fear of legal troubles over the book were not unfounded. Even though the publishers were English, no British press would publish it in England. The chain bookstores in the United States carried the book "under the counter" and out of sight so that straight customers would not be offended. If you wanted it, you had to ask for it. Some libraries bought the book, to a chorus of objections by the religious right about "immorality" and demands that it be hidden from the eager eyes of children.[18]

A French Canadian firm published the book and sent thousands of copies to Paris, where the French customs seized and shredded the books. Thousands of English edition books were seized by Her Majesty's customs in London and burned.[19]

Jearold Moldenhauer, owner of Glad Day Book Shop in Toronto, ordered copies of the book. Her Majesty's customs confiscated the book because it had descriptions and drawings of anal intercourse. It is prohibited to import such materials into Canada.[20] Moldenhauer, at great financial risk, decided to sue for the return of the books. I volunteered to appear at the trial. The customs officer testified that anal intercourse was on the prohibited list for entry into Canada. When asked whether he considered the educational or cultural value of the book, he said, "That's not my business."

My own testimony was rather straightforward. I gave the history of the book, the reasons for writing it, and the goals we set for it. I also noted that the book was part sex manual and part counsel for young people entering the gay world. The cross-examination consisted of asking me about the pictures and descriptions of anal intercourse. The crown asked whether I knew that there were nine pictures of anal intercourse in the book. "I've never counted them," I said, "but I'll be willing to accept your count." It was all quite polite, the Canadians not taken to dramatics in the courtroom as we are here.

The judge's verdict was a model of fairness and sensibility. In what must be counted as one of the finest legal decisions for gay people, Judge Hawkins wrote, "To write about homosexual practices, without dealing with anal intercourse, would be equivalent to writing a history of music and omitting Mozart" (Hawkins 1987). The books were ordered returned to Glad Day Book Shop.

My writing and administrative work at IHI continued for the next few years. Unfortunately, because of the previous conflicts at I House, there was no communication between them and myself during this time. They continued to function as a separate organization. I House remained a mainly peer counseling organization (with referrals to therapists), helping a large number of men and women cope with the coming out process and the stresses of living in a homophobic society. IHI emphasized the professional nature of psychotherapy, and it provided a safe place for gay therapists to work as openly gay people. Both these organizations continue to serve the gay community of New York City, each in its own way—and still without public funds.

Our goal had been to change the negative attitude of the "helping professions" toward homosexuality. The psychiatric/psychological professions were viewed as "gatekeepers" of society's attitudes. They instructed society as to normal and abnormal behavior, and their opinions carried great weight with lawmakers, the courts, and the general public. A concerted campaign went on to change those opinions through a number of grassroots actions.

One of these actions was the organization of gay caucuses within professional and semiprofessional organizations. Probably the first of these was the formation of a caucus in the Association for Humanistic Psychology in 1972. An informal caucus was also formed at the Association for the Advancement of Behavior Therapy the same year. This was followed by the Committee for Lesbian and Gay Concerns in the American Psychological Association in 1973. In the next ten years, gay and lesbian support groups coalesced in almost every professional organization in the country.

Psychoanalytic organizations, on the other hand, fiercely resisted any change in the party line that homosexuality was abnormal. Though the ranks of analysts probably contained as high a percentage of gay people as any other profession, they were all in the closet and feared exposure. This was true even though Anna Freud was a lesbian and lived with another woman for most of her life. (Her lesbianism is denied by many analysts even to this day.) New York's William Alan White Institute trained psychoanalysts based on the work of Harry Stack Sullivan, yet their trainees were not told that Sullivan was a gay man who lived with another man for over twenty years.

A second technique for bringing about change was giving talks to local hospital and clinic staffs. These discussions, sometimes instigated by gay professionals on the staff who were closeted due to fear of reprisal, opened up dialogue about the treatment of homosexuality in their institutions. The greatest value, however, was to make contact with closeted gay people on staff, and to recruit them as staff members for IHI. It should be noted that there were a number of heterosexual professionals who were sympathetic to gay people and who also volunteered to help. For instance, the first clinical director at I House was a female heterosexual.

I House and IHI were safe havens for gay professionals. They were the only places where professionals could relax the vigilance required at their usual workplaces. Many of these same professionals in their daytime jobs were forced to subscribe to the notion of gay people as abnormal or face dismissal (or, if in private practice, to face the shutting off of referrals). Both the caucuses and the speaking engagements provided yet two other venues for them to meet and form informal support groups.

By the mid-1970s the tide had turned against participatory democracy and nonprofessional control of counseling centers. Professionals were too busy to participate in endless meetings and internal conflict. They expected efficiency from administrators who handled the day-to-day operation of the clinics. Peer counseling was still the mainstay at I House, but it took a backseat role at IHI and at most other gay clinics in the country. Eventually peer counseling ceased to be offered at IHI.

In 1978, I resigned as director of IHI. Anyone who has held an administrative post will understand my reasons. I had simply become tired of the nitpicking details of the job, the lack of funds, the incessant problem of juggling different ideological subgroups within the organization, and the attention I was forced to give to matters that were petty, fueled by envy or jealousy, or just plain stupid.

Here's an example. One of the female therapists suggested that we have sanitary napkins in the bathroom, just in case a woman needed one in an emergency. I asked her to buy a box, leave it in the medicine chest, and get reimbursed from petty cash. "Who put the box of sanitary napkins in the bathroom?" asked another therapist at the next staff meeting. A heated argument then ensued between two opposing camps, those who thought it acceptable to provide sanitary napkins, and those who insisted that women in need of them should carry their own. During the fracas, in which I took no part for obvious reasons, I kept thinking about Swift's *Gulliver's Travels* and the battle between the "Big Endies" and the "Little Endies." If my memory serves me right, the sanitary napkins were removed.

Then there were the constant problems connected with organizing a board of directors. We were very naive and inexperienced in those days about the task of raising money. Nor did fund-raisers want to help us, believing, quite rightly, that gay people would not support a gay organization financially.[21] The task of raising money fell to the board, but since we did not know wealthy people, its members were well-meaning but incompetent as fund-raisers. Before each meeting of the board, which took place one Sunday morning each month, I bought Danish and bagels, then made the coffee. The meetings were useless, board members not having the slightest idea of how to raise money for us. Then, one day, one of the board members complained that I had not bought enough prune Danish! In response, I suggested that they either take out their checkbooks and make contributions to IHI or not come back. That was the end of IHI's first board of directors. Subsequent boards were no different.

After I left IHI, my writing and private practice took up most of my time. It also allowed my lover and me to spend more time together. William and I would ultimately share our lives for twenty years. He was with me the night of February 7, 1973, when I wrote the presentation for the APA Nomenclature Committee. He watched the growth of IHI and the gay movement, and he proofread all my books.

The New Medical Attacks on Gay People

The war over the mental status of gay people has now entered a new phase. Threats have come from two quarters. The first, and more important from both a theoretical and practical point of view, is the rise of up-to-date biological theories to explain the origin of homosexual desire.[22] These explanations are hotly contested in the gay community. For the most part, gay men view them favorably for both personal and political reasons. Their argument is similar to that over Paragraph 175 of the German penal code in the last century (Schmidt 1984). The code declared homosexual behavior a crime, based on the belief that homosexual behavior was voluntary, therefore perverse. Critics, following the theories promulgated by Ulrich (Kennedy 1988) and Hirschfeld (Schmidt 1984), argued that homosexuals are born, not made, so that their sexual behavior is neither voluntary nor willful.[23] The proposed biological explanation in Germany repudiated criminal sanctions against homosexuals and at the same time reduced their sense of personal guilt. The same arguments are made today by gay men who are in favor of biological rather than psychological theories of etiology. For those gay men who feel guilty over their sexual desire, a biological causation relieves the feeling of culpability.

Many lesbians, on the other hand, reject biological explanations of human behavior, particularly sexual orientation. They argue that sexuality is a social construction unfettered by biological influences, one that is learned through society's demands for a strict dichotomy between male and female behavior.

One important biological proponent is Dörner (1980), who believes that homosexuality results from prenatal hormonal changes in the brain of the fetus before the fourth month of gestation. He further states (unfortunately) that it might be possible to prevent the development of homosexuality by interfering with this process during pregnancy (Dörner 1983).

There have been a rash of new studies on the genetic and physiological differences between homosexuals and heterosexuals (see Hamer et al. 1993; LeVay 1991; Pillard and Weinrich 1986; and Whitam et al. 1993). These studies have looked at two aspects of biology: genetic comparisons of twins and differences in anatomical cerebral structures between gay and straight men. (Readers should consult other chapters in this volume for reviews and critiques of this literature.) The twin studies demonstrate that concordance of sexual orientation runs about 50 percent or more in identical twins, but only about 20 percent in other siblings, so that biology plays a significant role in the determination of sexual orientation. But why only 50 percent? Doesn't that mean that psychological factors contribute to sexual orientation as much as biological ones? ask social constructionists who eschew physiological explanations.

I can state my belief while at the same time acknowledging that it is unprovable at this time. I am an unashamed, remorseless biological determinist.[24] I have yet to hear a psychological theory or social constructionist idea that can explain why little boys and girls violate the rules of sex role behavior taught by family and society. A very high percentage of gay men were sissies during their childhoods. They were teased and beaten by siblings and other children, and depreciated by their own parents. They were criticized for walking the wrong way (like a girl), throwing a ball wrong (if they were willing to throw the ball in the first place), and being too close to their mothers rather than their fathers (domestic rather than aggressive).

In my experience as a psychologist, I have heard countless gay men reflect on the pain of those early years, and how much they wanted to please their parents (particularly their fathers) and peers. Were these children stupid? Were they unaware of what was expected of them? So many of them would have jumped at the opportunity to trade their depreciated tea sets for the enviable jocks' uniform.[25] I cannot fathom how social conditioning theory can explain this behavior.

I believe that sexual orientation will be found to be wholly biological in origin, and I say that even though current research does not yet support this conclusion. How one behaves sexually and romantically, on the other hand, seems to me to be a function of growing up in a particular society at a certain period of history. Biology provides the template; social learning the human behavior. Time will tell.

Biology also presents some problems for those who champion politically correct behavior. Let us suppose, just for the sake of argument, that biologists conclusively find a physiological mechanism for sexual orientation. Let us also assume that through prenatal testing, physicians can identify the future sexual orientation of the child. It is inevitable that some prospective parents will decide to abort a gay or lesbian fetus. Wouldn't those who believe in abortion rights on demand be required to support a woman's right to abort a child because she doesn't want a fag or dyke in the family? Those gay people who support abortion on demand would find themselves in the hypocritical position of supporting abortion for one reason but condemning it for another.

Even more ticklish, from the point of view of politically correct behavior, is the question of sex roles (if one is biologically biased) or gender roles (if one is social learning biased). They gay movement is politically allied with the women's movement. It therefore accepts the belief that one learns male and female behavior in a process of social conditioning, unalloyed by biological factors. There is more faith here than evidence. In the early days of the gay movement, we used to say that sexual identity and gender identity are orthogonal (independent). I am not so sure anymore. I have come to believe that there is a correlation between these two variables. While the gay movement avoids discussing the possibility that male and female behavior may be influenced physiologically, biologists are moving ahead with the idea and publishing interesting studies (Imperato-McGinley 1994). This is an issue that may further divide gay men and lesbians.

The concept of "sexual addiction" (Carnes 1983), also called "sexual compulsion" (Quadland 1985), is the second new attack on the mental status of homosexuality, this time by some gay psychologists. They maintain, in this controversial form of treatment, that the model of addiction to drugs is analogous to "addiction" to sex, and every bit as harmful. Levine and Troiden (1988) have stated their opposition to that model. What is noteworthy is that all the symptoms of "sexual compulsion" are behaviors still frowned on by society at large, for example, masturbation or frequent sexual partners, or sex outside the primary relationship. Gay men who volunteer for treatment are motivated by guilt over their sexual behavior. In previous decades, homosexual behavior was classified as "compulsive" by psychoanalytic writers, and many gay men (including this one) confessed their sins and went for the "cure." Many gay men still feel guilty about their sexual desire, and this may be the wellspring for allowing the label of "sexual compulsive" to be pinned on them. It is for this reason that many gay professionals look on the sexual compulsion movement as driven by homophobic ideology.

It is difficult to fully understand why we condemn certain forms of sexual behavior—like "promiscuity." But I am certain that when we condemn the behavior of others there is a strong component of envy of the other person's freedom and abandon, of their indifference to what people think, and of their ability to smash into smithereens the propaganda about romance, love, and intimacy that our society values over sex. Those who would suppress sexual expression, it seems to me, are acting like cops, not social scientists.

A Final Note

Living and working in New York City gives one a distorted view of the acceptance of homosexuality. Here, one can easily find gay therapists or heterosexual ones who respect the sexual identity of their gay patients. The city is filled with highly publicized gay organizations that cater to almost every conceivable need of gay people. But other sections of the country are not so liberal in their attitudes and still make life difficult for gay people. Gay liberationists and professionals still need to work together to change that, just as they did in the 1970s.

Notes

1. There were two presentations about aversion therapy that day. GAA had excellent communication with the press, who always knew about our demonstrations beforehand. The choice of who to zap was based on the time of the presentation, so that reporters could get their copy into the newspapers on time.

2. Many members of AABT disapproved of aversion therapy, but were shocked at the sight of gay activists interfering with their meeting. Gerald Davison (1976) later asked for a complete prohibition against changing sexual orientation on moral grounds.

3. It was not as if I objected to being a gay activist. At GAA I was a member of the "suicide squad," whose task it was to jump over police barricades during demonstrations and get arrested by the police while photographers took pictures for the newspapers. Unfortunately, I had the propensity to trip over the barricades rather than sail over them, and my career with the "squad" lasted only one evening.

4. *DSM II* also listed a diagnosis called "Cephalalgia." *DSM III* (APA 1980) dropped it with the statement "It is not clear what was included within this DSM II category" (384). In *DMS IV* (APA 1994), a child may have a "reading disorder," and an adult a "nicotine disorder."

5. There is a story, perhaps apocryphal, that Anna Freud was rejected for membership in the American Psychoanalytic Association on the grounds that she was "not a Freudian." They meant she did not have an M.D., but apparently they did not notice the absurdity of that reasoning.

6. A few years later, due to the lobbying of a number of psychiatrists, particularly Richard Pillard in Boston, homosexuality was removed completely from *DSM*.

7. Socarides invited a few of his medical students for dinner one night and revealed to them his ability to spot a homosexual instantly, "the result," he said, "of my many years of clinical acumen." After dinner, the three students went out dancing to a gay bar! He has never forgiven me for my role in the APA decision. I recently tried to join the National Association of Research and Therapy on Homosexuality (NARTH) (which claims to be a professional association), an antihomosexual organization of which he is president. In a letter from Joseph Nicolosi, executive director, I was rejected for membership because "We consider your professional views and objectives as too radically opposed to ours."

Bayer (1981) has superbly documented the scientific and political battles that were fought within the psychiatric community over the nomenclature change. It is a fascinating story to read. If Spitzer had not been in the audience that day, the nomenclature change might not have occurred for many years.

8. In time she became a great fan of my lover, and the two of them talked for hours, mostly comparing notes about my liabilities.

9. One evening, a new client was looking for the bathroom. She opened one door and saw a pregnant lesbian on the floor with a nurse standing over her. She opened a second door and found my lover, who had just taken a shower, standing stark naked in the room. "What kind of place are you running here?" she asked the receptionist.

10. And all the stamps I could steal in Bill Cohen's office.

11. In retrospect, I am shocked at the rudeness of my demand.

12. The pun is perhaps mean-spirited.

13. One of her claims was that homosexuals kill children. When asked how, she said by swallowing semen. She may not have been one of the brightest bulbs on the block, but her accusation that homosexuals molest children was very damaging to the fight for gay rights.

14. Mitchell-Beazley, in London, printed the books and sold the bound copies to Crown Publishers, who distributed them in the United States. Attorneys for both firms read and raised questions about sections of the manuscript.

15. I later learned that Dobbie's Itch is a South African disease and a cousin to syphilis.

16. In the *New Joy of Gay Sex* (1992), coauthored with Felice Picano, one will find a lengthy essay on teenagers. There were no attempts at censorship, but then again, that was 1992, not 1977.

17. I remember that one of them was called "Mr. Grease," but I never learned why.

18. As this essay is written in December 1995, the presence of the *Joy of Gay Sex* in the Clifton, New Jersey, library has been challenged by the religious right.

19. Two of my books have been banned in England. The other is *Man to Man: Gay Couples in America* (1981).

20. However, homosexuality and anal intercourse are legal in Canada, and one can publish pictures of anal intercourse. Customs operates from a different set of laws, independent of the civil law that governs the country.

21. I remember one fund-raising party at IHI where I talked about the day when the gay community would have its own "Community Chest" to raise funds for gay organizations. People actually laughed at it. One person wrote a pledge for twenty-five dollars, but never paid it, and we ended up in the red. Today the Network in New York City is somewhat like the Community Chest.

22. Biological theories go back to the ancient Greeks. In this century, Steinach was the first to suggest a biological treatment for homosexuality (Schmidt 1984).

23. This was the concept of the "third sex," making homosexuals a categorically different group from either males or females.

24. Some friends call me a biological "reductionist," which is the closest they get to calling someone a profane word in print.

25. As they age, many of them will develop a sexual attachment for especially masculine men, perhaps due to a depreciated image of their own masculinity.

References

American Psychiatric Association. 1968. *Diagnostic and Statistical Manual of Mental Disorders*. 2d ed. Washington, DC: American Psychiatric Association Press.

———. 1973. Press release. December 15.

———. 1980. *Diagnostic and Statistical Manual of Mental Disorders*. 3d ed. Washington, DC: American Psychiatric Association Press.

———. 1994. *Diagnostic and Statistical Manual of Mental Disorders.* 4th ed. Washington, DC: American Psychiatric Association Press.

Association of Medical Superintendents of American Institutions for the Insane. 1871. *Statistical Tables.* Harrisburg: T. F. Scheffer.

Bayer, R. 1981. *Homosexuality and American Psychiatry.* New York: Basic Books.

Bell, A. P., and M. M. Weinberg. 1978. *Homosexualities: A Study of Diversity among Men and Women.* New York: Simon and Schuster.

Carnes, P. 1983. *Out of the shadows: Understanding sexual addiction.* Minneapolis: CompCare.

Davison, G. C. 1976. Homosexuality: The ethical challenge. *Journal of Consulting and Clinical Psychology* 44:157–62.

Dörner, G. 1980. Sexual differentiation of the brain. *Vitamins and Hormones* 38:325–81.

———. 1983. Letter to the editor. *Archives of Sexual Behavior* 12:577–82.

Hamer, D. H., S. Hu, V. L. Magnuson, N. Hu, and A. M. Pattatucci. 1993. A linkage between DNA markers on the X chromosome and male sexual orientation. *Science* 261:321–27.

Hawkins, D.C.J. 1987. Reasons for judgment. *The glad day bookshop, Inc., appellant, and, the deputy minister of the department of national revenue (customs and excise).* Court file no. 300/86. March 20.

Imperato-McGinley, J. 1994. 5-alpha-reductase deficiency. *Current Therapy in Endocrinology and Metabolism,* 351–54.

Kennedy, H. 1988. *Ulrichs: The Life and Works of Karl Ulrichs, Pioneer of the Modern Gay Movement.* Boston: Alyson.

LeVay, S. 1991. A difference in hypothalamic structure between heterosexual and homosexual men. *Science* 253:1034–37.

———. 1993. *The Sexual Brain.* Cambridge: MIT Press.

Levine, M. P., and R. R. Troiden. 1988. The myth of sexual compulsivity. *Journal of Sex Research* 25:347–64.

Pillard, R. C., and J. D. Weinrich. 1986. Evidence of familial nature of male homosexuality. *Archives of General Psychiatry* 43:808–12.

Quadland, M. C. 1985. Compulsive sexual behavior: Definition of a problem and an approach to treatment. *Journal of Sex and Marital Therapy* 11:121–32.

Schmidt, G. 1984. Allies and persecutors: Science and medicine in the homosexual issue. *Journal of Homosexuality* 10(3–4):127–40.

Silverstein, C. 1972. Behavior modification and the gay community. Paper presented at the Annual Convention of the Association for the Advancement of Behavior Therapy. New York City, October.

———. 1976–77. Even psychiatry can profit from its past mistakes. *Journal of Homosexuality* 2:153–58.

———. 1977a. *A Family Matter: A Parents' Guide to Homosexuality.* New York: McGraw-Hill.

———, and Edmund White. 1977b. *The Joy of Gay Sex.* New York: Crown.

———. 1981. *Man to Man: Gay Couples in America.* New York: William Morrow.

———. 1984. The ethical and moral implications of sexual classification: A commentary. *Journal of Homosexuality* 9:29–38.

Silverstein, C., and F. Picano. 1992. *The New Joy of Gay Sex.* New York: HarperCollins.

Socarides, C. 1978. *Homosexuality.* New York: Jason Aronson.

Spitzer, R. 1981. The diagnostic status of homosexuality in *DSM-III:* A reformulation of the issues. *American Journal of Psychiatry* 138:210–15.

Suppe, F. 1984. Classifying sexual disorders: The *Diagnostic and Statistical Manual* of the American Psychiatric Association. *Journal of Homosexuality* 9:9–28.

Whitam, F. L., M. Diamond, and J. Martin. 1993. Homosexual orientation in twins: A report on 61 pairs and three triplet sets. *Archives of Sexual Behavior* 22:187–205.

Wilson, B. 1972. Memorandum to the committee on nomenclature of the American Psychiatric Association: Should homosexuality be in the A.P.A. nomenclature. Gay Activist Alliance, New York.

28

Media, Science, and Sexual Ideology: The Promotion of Sexual Stability

Gilbert Zicklin

In March 1994, the Gay and Lesbian Association of the Cornell University Medical College organized a conference boldly called "The Biological Nature of Homosexuality." Among the guest speakers were Laura Allen, Dean Hamer, and Simon LeVay, all of whom have published research reports contributing to the proposition that homosexuality has a biological basis. No one on the panel argued that there is no biological basis to homosexuality, or that whatever biological factors are associated with homosexuality, they are of minimal significance in the material development of homosexual desire. No one on the panel commented critically on the biological position or on the research that has been deemed to support it.

I begin by mentioning this conference, which followed upon wide media dissemination of the reports of biologically oriented research into the origins of homosexuality, because its bias is illustrative of the currency recently gained for discussing homosexuality as a biological phenomenon. I intend to argue the following:

1. that the relationship between the data and the conclusions about a biological basis to homosexuality that some researchers assert, and the media have highlighted, is largely without scientific merit;

2. that the media's treatment of the research as "discoveries" offers the public a distorted view of the state of scientific knowledge on this subject;

3. that the narrative about sexuality underlying both the media's and the scientific community's interest in biological explanations for erotic attraction ignores the socially constructed, highly symbolic codes that make sexual desire and desirability meaningful.

To show this I will first describe a sample of studies published since 1990 that assume a biological perspective on sexual desire. I will present a critical analysis of the methodological problems of each of these studies, contrasting my critique with the print media's portrayal of the research findings. I will then focus on an exemplary journalist's coverage of the issue for the *New York Times*. I conclude with an analysis of what lies behind both the researchers' and the media's tendency to see homosexuality as a fixed condition that is set at birth or very shortly thereafter, rather than viewing it more sociologically, the way we do kinship or religious ties.

The biologically oriented research I will examine flows from two streams: neuroanatomical studies of the structural similarities and differences in the brains of male and female laboratory animals, and in humans, among samples that differ by gender and by sexual orientation; and studies that purport to show a chromosomal basis for homosexual desire, or from whose data such a chromosomal basis can logically be inferred. In the interests of space, I will not consider the line of study looking at brain-mediated neuroendocrine effects on sexual behavior, though I believe the logic works the same.

I will sample this research by considering the reports of Simon LeVay, Michael Bailey and Richard Pillard, Roger Gorski and Laura Allen, and Dean Hamer et al.[1] First, a snapshot of these studies.

Simon LeVay, a biologist formerly at the Salk Institute in La Jolla, reported that he found a difference in the size of the INAH-3 region of the hypothalamus in brains identified as belonging to gay males compared with those of nongay males. The size of the gay males' region was similar to that of the females in the study (who were not identified with respect to sexual orientation).

Michael Bailey, a psychologist at Northwestern University, and Richard Pillard, a professor of psychiatry at Boston University School of Medicine, compared concordance rates for homosexuality in a sample of male identical co-twins, nonidentical co-twins, and adoptive brothers. They found that about half of the identical, or monozygotic, twins in their sample shared the trait of homosexuality, while for the dizygotic twins the concordance figure was between one-fourth and one-fifth. This translates into the highest concordance rates for the closest genetic relationship, that of monozygotic twins. Bailey and Pillard carried out a comparable study of females and reported similar results.[2]

Roger Gorski and Laura Allen, researchers at UCLA, reported a difference between homosexually and heterosexually identified males, and between males and females, in the size of the anterior commissure, an area that binds the two hemispheres of the brain. They reported that homosexual males had the largest commissures, heterosexual males the smallest.

Dean Hamer et al., of the National Cancer Institute, studied the distribution of homosexual relatives among a sample of homosexual subjects, and examined DNA samples of forty pairs of self-identified gay brothers. Subjects reported more homosexuals among their maternal relatives, and the researchers found similar DNA sequences in thirty-three out of the forty pairs of gay brothers in a region of the X chromosome known as Xq25. These findings led Hamer et al. to hypothesize the genetic transmission of homosexuality through the maternal line.

In the LeVay study, three problems stand out.[3] First, and most important, LeVay relies on hospital records for the measure of a key variable, the sexual orientation of the subjects whose brains he is dissecting. The ethnomethodology of record keeping tells us that these official designations are liable to be off the mark. What one decides to reveal to a record keeper, what the record keeper surmises one does not want to reveal but thinks should be included, what the record keeper decides is meant by certain signs the person exhibits—all these may go into the act of fixing a label on a person. The designation of a sexual orientation that is made in a hospital setting in situations of extremis may bear only a tangential relationship to the truth of a person's sexual life. LeVay relied *solely* on such hospital designations for the determination of a principal variable in his study. It is therefore unclear that sexual orientation differentiated LeVay's subjects, whatever other factors may have been involved.

The second problem with the LeVay study involves a likely confounding of independent variables. There was a disproportionate number of deaths from HIV infection among his homosexual subjects. HIV infection is known to damage brain cells directly, as well as through the lowering of testosterone levels in males, which in turn affects brain tissue. This, in itself, may account for an observed correlation between homosexual orientation and the smaller size of the INAH-3 region. If death by HIV infection is not controlled for, the cause of observed differences in brain structure is uninterpretable.

LeVay engaged in the unusual practice of measuring the size of the INAH-3 area himself; scientists more commonly use additional or other researchers for this task. The absence of blind raters, coupled with his well-known desire to find a biological basis for homosexuality, leaves his work open to the charge of experimenter bias.[4] Since his findings have not been replicated, and given the methodological problems with his research, the reliability of his data as well as his interpretation of them can be questioned.

The other anatomical study, that of Gorski and Allen, also suffers from the designation of research subjects' brains as belonging to "homosexuals" or "heterosexuals," without clear operational definitions for these terms. But even if this were not so, there is a larger problem with the research. Gorski and Allen found a larger anterior commissure in the brains of "gay" males than in those of "straight" males, those of the former being comparable to that found in females' brains. But the anterior commissure has not been shown to have any relationship to sexuality; rather, it is thought to aid communication between the two brain hemispheres. Why compare this particular structure among samples with different sexual orientations, if you have no theoretical reason for looking for this difference? It is on a par with recent research reporting that the finger whorls, testicular laterality, and so forth of gay males differ in direction from those of straight males. Since we are given no theoretical basis for these associations, they have little meaning for a study of sexual orientation. In fact, this pig-in-a-poke way of searching for neuroanatomical correlates of behavior increases the risk of false positives, since five times out of one hundred, observed correlations will occur by chance and mean nothing.

Bailey and Pillard's research method included asking male monozygotic (MZ) and dizygotic (DZ) twins and biological and nonbiological nontwin siblings about their sexual orientation. They acquired their subjects through advertisements placed in gay publications in several cities in the Midwest and Southwest. The authors conclude from their data that there is a genetic basis to sexual orientation. They base their claim on the significantly higher percentage of MZ twins concordant for sexual orientation than the other, less genetically connected siblings.

But the method of subject selection undermines the study's validity. Self-selection of subjects, that is, using volunteers, introduces the possibility of a very particular bias in the case of a disapproved behavior: if more homosexual monozygotic twins with homosexual co-twins volunteered for the study than a random sample would find, or as Bailey and Pillard recognize, "if discordant MZ twins were less likely to participate than discordant DZ twins," then the difference in concordance rates for these two types of relatives could not be attributed to genetic differences but rather to the peculiarity of the sample. The overrepresentation of concordant MZ twins is quite possible, since gay MZ twins are likely to be more interested in studies that highlight the special meaning of close biological connections, and they might also have less trepidation about participating since there is a greater likelihood that they would be "out" with one another than would any other pair of male siblings. Conversely, some twins who perceive themselves as discordant on sexual orientation may be motivated to avoid studies wherein this difference may be revealed. Thus, Bailey and Pillard have a double problem: they attract the kind of twins who fit their hypothesis and deter the ones who might weaken it.

At least Bailey and Pillard do recognize that even when heritability might account for phenotypic variance, what is inherited could be a physical trait, an intervening variable, and not necessarily a gene for sexual orientation. In the authors' words.

> given any heritability estimate, there are a variety of possible developmental mechanisms. For instance, these data are consistent with heritable variation in prenatal brain development or in some aspect of physical appearance that, by way of differential parental treatment, leads to differences in sexual orientation.[5]

While Bailey and Pillard say this, they write as if their data can and do show that homosexuality is genetically transmitted. But no matter what concordance rates Bailey and Pillard had found, it would be impossible to establish a direct causal role for the genetic material itself, a point whose significance is often ignored as researchers imagine they are moving toward uncovering biological causes.[6]

The authors do not take into account the possibility that MZ twin relationships create a unique psychosocial environment that in itself can account for higher rates of concordance. The intensely shared life of identical twins, including the phenomena of identification, mirroring, and imitation, might plausibly constitute fertile ground for the development of same-sex erotics.

Parenthetically, while there has been no report of a reliable replication of the Bailey and Pillard study, it is worth noting that King and McDonald recently reported far less concordance for identical twin pairs than did Bailey and Pillard.[7]

The study reported by Hamer et al. has been presented as making the most convincing case for the role of heredity. Its problems of methodology are different, but quite serious. Hamer and his colleagues recruited seventy-six homosexual men for a pedigree study to determine which other members of the families of these men were also homosexual. They reported homosexuality to be significantly more common among the maternal relatives and concluded that a putative gene for homosexuality is passed through female family members. Yet the sociology of family life in the United States suggests that women are more likely than men to keep in touch with relatives, so a son might well know more about his mother's side of the family than his father's. Moreover, in this culture as a function of gender politics, a homosexual son might be closer to his mother than to his father and might therefore be more identified with and knowledgeable about his mother's relatives, including the question of their sexual preferences. American gender and family patterns, not genes, may account for the data.

Postulating genetic transmission of homosexuality through the maternal line, Hamer et al. examined the X chromosome in forty pairs of gay brothers recruited through advertisements in homophile publications. They report finding a region of the X chromosome that was shared in thirty-three of the forty pairs. They took this to mean that a linkage was established between a region of the X chromosome and homosexuality, that is, that the gay concordant brothers received the same X chromosome from the mother significantly more often than by chance. But we do not know whether it was more often than their straight siblings, for they did not examine the X chromosome of any heterosexual brothers of the homosexual sib-pair subjects. Only in this way could we have been assured that the shared markers actually distinguish the homosexual brothers from their heterosexual siblings. Without such a control group, we cannot speak of any correlation between the genotype, in this case the Xq28 locus, and the phenotype, sexual orientation. In order to have a correlation, we must demonstrate that the variation in that region of the X chromosome is associated with changes in the variable, sexual orientation. But since the X chromosome of the heterosexual brothers of the gay sib subjects was not examined, no actual correlation of variables can be shown.

Why didn't Hamer et al. look at these brothers' DNA? Hamer says it was because of a supposed difficulty in being sure that a heterosexually identified brother was not a secret homosexual, since if such "faux heterosexuals" were in the sample it would distort—that is, weaken—the anticipated results of the study. He suggests that since homosexual desire is morally questionable in our culture, a heterosexual would be loath to confess his homosexual desires, while someone who already experiences the opprobrium of being known as a homosexual would be unlikely to be hiding significant heterosexual desires. This *may* be true, but surely skilled researchers could have elicited the existence of homosexual desire and practice from heterosexually identified brothers with appropriate open-ended interviews. Eliminating these brothers from the study did more to undermine its validity than including them would have, even with the possible concealment of their homosexual desires. For in the latter instance, the association between the variables would have been weakened but maintained, whereas in the former instance, the relevant association cannot be shown or known about. Hamer et al. understand the relevance of the heterosexual brothers' DNA. Failure to examine it renders the data almost meaningless.

Finally, and most tellingly for the direct genetic transmission hypothesis, Hamer et al. cannot specify that what they found in the genotype actually is expressed in the pertinent phenotypical behavior. That is to say, they cannot state that the presence of a certain DNA pattern or gene in the Xq28 region of the X chromosome actually influences sexual desire. (This is the same logical problem encountered in the work of Bailey and Pillard.) The authors imply that it does, either by affecting the prenatal development of the hypothalamus or through another biochemical route. Now, again, even if it could be shown that this area of the X chromosome varies reliably with a person's object of desire, such a correlation could result if that gene influences a trait that might be related to the development of homosexuality in a given cultural setting. Such might be the case were the Xq28 locus related to certain temperamental traits, like intense curiosity, rebelliousness, or the need for autonomy, for example. We would then have an intervening variable through which homosexuality would be associated with the Xq28 allele. The actual trait expressed by the allele would not be related directly to sexual desire, but to an element of personality that itself is correlated imperfectly with the development of sexual orientation. Thus, a child who is very curious, rebellious, or defiant who might be more likely to have had pleasurable sexual experience with persons of the same sex might find the expectations that a male in this culture be exclusively heterosexually oriented a fit basis around which to establish an opposing psychoerotics. Of course a parent may contribute to the structuring of this environment as she or he defines for the child what will constitute the transgressive, the rebellious, the conforming, the submissive. Such an explanation, which takes cognizance of social, psychological, and even political factors shaping erotic development, goes unrecognized by these researchers, although such explanations are at least as well documented as any physical mechanisms for establishing sexual preference.[8]

Research that appears to accept the direct biological basis of sexual orientation has drawn criticism from many quarters in the biological and social sciences. R. Hubbard, D. Nelkin, E. Balaban, W. Byne, T. McGuire, R. Lewontin, H. Fingarette, and J. N. Katz, among others, have expressed serious reservations about the claims of biological causation of what are seen as complex social behaviors. Yet when the research of LeVay, Gorski and Allen, Bailey and Pillard, and Hamer et al. has been reported in the popular press, it is almost always represented as contributing to *"mounting evidence"* that homosexuality is biologically based.

These scientific reports have generated a great deal of attention from the popular media. From front-page stories in the *New York Times* to feature articles in *Time, Newsweek,* and *U.S. News and World Report,* from a lead article in the *Atlantic Monthly* to pieces in the *Chronicle of Higher Education, Mother Jones, Discover, National Review,* and the *Nation,* the coverage of purported anatomical and genetic findings with respect to homosexuality has been robust. I searched a select group of newspapers, news magazines, journals of opinion, and monthlies for the years 1990–93 and found dozens of articles, feature stories, personal essays, and editorial page commentaries about this work. The periodicals I searched included only the most prestigious newspapers such as the *New York Times,* the *Washington Post,* the *Los Angeles Times,* the *Houston Post,* and so on; they did not include the thousands of local newspapers, unindexed in library catalogues, that may have carried stories about this research as well.

Overwhelmingly, the articles reporting on this research tend to stress the likely validity of asserted biological bases to sexual orientation. The titles of some of these newspaper and magazine articles suggest the tilt: "Brain Differences Linked to Sexual Preferences." "Are Some Men Born to Be Gay?" "Brain Feature Linked to Sexual Orientation," "Are Some Men Born to Be Homosexual?" "Are Gay Men Born That Way?" "Study Ties Part of Brain to Men's Sexual Orientation," "Exploring the Brain for Secrets of Sexuality," "Study Shows Homosexuality Is Innate," "Report Suggests Homosexuality Is Linked to Genes," "X Marks the Spot: Male Homosexuality May Be Linked to a Gene," "Study of Gay Men and Their Brothers Links Homosexuality to Genetics," "Study Suggests Genes Sway Lesbians' Sexual Orientation," "Genes Tied to Sexual Orientation," "The Search for Sexual Identity: Genes vs. Hormones," "Study Links Genes to Homosexuality," "Research Points toward a 'Gay' Gene," "Born or Bred: The Origins of Homosexuality," "Born Gay? Studies of Family Trees and DNA Make the Case that Male Homosexuality Is in the Genes," "Opening a Window: Genes May Play a Role in Homosexuality," "The Gay Science of Genes and Brains," "Evidence for Homosexuality Gene," and finally, "Genetic Clue to Male Homosexuality Emerges." For these journalists, the mystery of homosexuality is thus solved.

While one reads the occasional dubious headline, such as "Media Hype about the 'Gay Gene,' " and "The Search for Sexual Identity: False Genetic Markers," the media tend mainly to follow a pattern in reporting on this subject. The pattern is (1) repeat claims made by the researchers about the findings; (2)

quote them or a couple of friendly experts about the *import* of their findings; (3) quote one or two sources who issue a caveat about the validity of the study; and (4) imply that, caveats notwithstanding, a biological basis for sexual orientation is likely, if not yet proved. This sequence, lacking as it does any developed critical viewpoint, is seen often. While there appear to be systematic differences between the newsmagazines and newspapers, with the former even less likely to pay serious attention to any critique of these studies, on the whole, media representation of this research depicts it as a cumulative body of scientific work. It accepts the assumption of a fixed, unchanging "sexual orientation" that is biologically rooted.

Let us move beyond the headlines for a moment and see *how* the reporting of a *New York Times* journalist uses this structure in her reportage. The *Times* reporter, Natalie Angier, is by now one of the most sophisticated covering this story. Her work is untypically inclusive of criticism from expert sources about both the methods and the claims of the biological research. Yet her work still illustrates the distorting media paradigm described above.

An article that illustrates her approach comes from the July 16, 1993, edition of the *Times.* It begins with an attempt to characterize the significance of the Hamer study: "Ushering the politically explosive study of the origins of sexual orientation into a new and *perhaps* more scientifically rigorous phase, researchers report that they have linked male homosexuality to a small region of one human chromosome" (my italics). Then the caveat: this is "just a single chapter in the intricate story of sexual orientation and behavior," followed by a repeat of the "importance" of the findings. The "findings" are then further elaborated, followed by another caveat: "But researchers warn against overinterpreting the work, or in taking it to mean anything as simplistic as that the 'gay gene' had been found" (Angier's quotation marks around *gay gene*). Are we then to think that the idea of a "gay gene" is a function of simplistic thinking? Or is it that believing a *single* gene could control sexual orientation is simplistic? Or is it rather that concluding from the Hamer study, alone, that the gay gene has already been found is simplistic? In her very *next* sentence Angier writes, "The researchers emphasized that they do not yet have a gene isolated, but merely know the rough location of where the gene or genes may sit.—" The air is cleared: there *are* gay genes. Only where they are is a mystery.

Angier continues in a cautionary style, reporting that even if they do pinpoint this gene there are probably other genes on other chromosomes involved in sexual orientation. She then speculates about how "the gene" could work, using that term now without any quotation marks that might convey doubt. It could work either by directly influencing "sexual proclivity" or by doing so indirectly, through affecting temperament. Thus, Angier has now fully envisioned the existence and operation of a "gay gene," when only some paragraphs before she had signaled the wrongheadedness of such a concept.

When toward the very end of the article Angier turns to some of the methodological problems of the study, for example the lack of a control, she says, "So far the study has been limited to men who said they were gay, eliminating the ambiguity that would come from considering the genes of men who called themselves heterosexual." Instead of actually clarifying why the heterosexual brothers were not part of the DNA study—a very serious problem, as I indicated—Angier has merely restated the researchers' unconvincing explanation, which she now treats as self-explanatory. She concludes her article with the prospect of the work ahead for these scientists, who must sort out "which gene or genes is relevant." Her apparent caveat about the complex nature of sexual desire and whether it could be accounted for by a "gay gene" has now vanished; she has adopted the researchers' account of their work and their perspective on sexual orientation, namely, that it is biologically given.

Though I focus on Angier, her method is an instance of what is actually a widespread tendency in the reportage on this research. It is the use of a rhetoric that subtly inserts the belief that sexual orientation is caused by a biological condition, in gradual steps, amid all-too-stillable doubts. Despite the ambiguous, often equivocal findings that result from the studies' methodologically faulty designs, we have seen dozens of news articles proclaiming supposedly valid, reliable findings.

Questions naturally arise: (1) How is it that this bandwagon has gotten rolling, in the media and even in the lesbian/gay community, for a biological explanation of sexual desire, with so little evidence? (2) What in the scientists' perspective accounts for their persistence in pursuing the biological basis of homosexuality, despite both the experimental impossibility of showing that it is *directly* biologically caused, and the pile of equivocal findings? and (3) What are the ramifications of promoting such a perspective?

To amplify the first question, especially for this audience, we might ask why no such media attention has been showered on scholarly work in the *social sciences* that conceptualizes in a sociocultural framework: the sociological analyses of Bell and Weinberg, of Klassen, Williams, and Levitt, or of Ira Reiss; the work in history of Trumbach, Bray, or Faderman; in social psychology, Herek; in anthropology, Herdt and Williams—just to name a few of the scholars doing notable research bearing on issues related to the nature of homosexuality. Among many other things, this research has examined what sociological factors, if any, a homosexual preference is related to; what are the prevalent beliefs of the U.S. population about what causes homosexuality, what should be done about it, what is its current moral status, how prevalent is it; historically, when did our current ideas and practices first appear and why; what factors are associated with homophobic attitudes; how do other cultures organize sexual practices, and how do they explain these arrangements; how does gender intersect with homosexual preference, both in this culture and in non-Western cultures, and so forth.

An answer to why the media play up the biological studies as opposed to the sociocultural is that the former are appealing because they present themselves as having solved "the riddle of sexual desire," that is, they offer something akin to certainty. Moreover, researchers themselves have encouraged this attitude toward their studies by making grandiose claims for their findings. For example, in a *New York Times* article of December 17, 1991, one scientist, asked to comment on the first Bailey and Pillard study, asserted that "Some of the earlier evidence suggested there was a genetic effect, but the studies were not well done. This is something that really sort of clinches it." Bailey and Pillard themselves write in a *New York Times* op-ed piece, "Our own research *has shown* [my italics] that male sexual orientation is substantially genetic."[9] A reporter for the *Chronicle of Higher Education*, referring to an unnamed scientist, writes, "He found the results [of the Bailey and Pillard study] so compelling that he has decided to start a search for the gene or genes that may cause homosexuality."[10] Natalie Angier reports that Gorski and Allen "believe the[ir] finding supports the idea that brains of homosexuals differ in many subtle ways from those of heterosexuals, and that sexual orientation has *a deep biological basis*" (my italics).[11] Reporters are able to hype these studies in good conscience, since in this enterprise they apparently have the assistance of some scientists.

Interestingly, some of the researchers themselves quite consciously want the public to subscribe to a biological model of sexual orientation. LeVay talks of how he hoped to get the results he did because he thought it would be good for the gay population, both in terms of legal outcomes in civil rights cases and with respect to reducing prejudice should biological explanations come to replace moral ones in the public's understanding of homosexuality. Like LeVay, Bailey and Pillard also believe that if sexual orientation is innate, "it is," in their words "good news for homosexuals and their advocates."[12] Richard Green, another sex researcher with a biological model of homosexuality, commented to a *New York Times* reporter that "if sexual orientation were demonstrated to be essentially inborn, most laws that discriminate against gays and lesbians, including sodomy laws, housing and employment discrimination laws, all would fall."[13] Thus, there is a politics at play in this scientific quest. It is a *liberal* politics, based on the impulse to normalize and include. However, I will argue that what biologistic politics ends up including is a relatively innocuous, not quite normal, population.

I will make that argument by offering another answer to the question of why the media have given this story so much play. I suggest that the assumptions behind the biological research are part of a particular politico/cultural framework for understanding erotic life. It is a framework that seeks to allay the fear of the "normals" by allowing them to believe that one is given an essential sexual orientation at birth. This can reduce some of a heterosexually identified person's fears about whether he or she is sufficiently masculine or feminine, with which fear the modern erotic is so bound up. For if sexuality is in one's genetic makeup, then in a heterosexually identified person, any erotic interest in one's *own* sex can be dismissed as small potatoes, clearly not adding up to the main thing, the *real* thing, biological homosexuality. Dichotomizing the erotic into two biologically based identities reduces the anxiety of those who might worry about being "possibly homosexual" because they experience some sexual interest in and desire for the same sex: "After all," they can reason, "to be a homosexual you've got to be born one, and if I were born one, I probably wouldn't have any heterosexual desire; I would only be attracted to my own sex, and I'm not." Klassen, Williams, and Levitt found that a fairly large minority of Americans (about 40 percent in their sample) agree "strongly" or "somewhat" with the statement that "there is some homosexuality in everyone." At the same time, large majorities believe homosexuality is morally wrong. A sizable group, then, is precariously positioned with respect to the meaning of whatever homosexual desire they experience.[14]

As such, the situation represents a classic instance of cognitive dissonance. The dissonance may be reducible if we accept the model of erotic life that says that if you are strongly disposed, in your brain, to the same sex and not much, if at all, disposed to the opposite sex, are you *really*, that is, *bodily* queer. By advancing the cut-and-dried biological model of sexual orientation, the media fulfill the hidden wishes of the public (and here I would include some of the gay public) to be free from the taint of possible perversity with respect to their sexual desires and, *within each group*, free from the deviant status to which these desires might consign them. Gays are always and only erotically interested in their own gender; the same goes in reverse for straights. In this way, identities are formed that anchor individuals in subcommunities of like-desiring persons, and a culture and politics are built around those identities that function as part of their reification. This, in turn, protects those who hold to the reified identity from the uncomfortable oscillation of erotic interest and desire. For hitherto scorned, isolated, and therefore individually often defenseless persons, the opportunity to now identify with a large and significant community that claims normal social and psychological status has strong appeal, an appeal understood early on by sociologists.

Thus genetic explanations of the gender we are sexually attracted to appeal to us and make prima facie sense in part because they do provide certain and unchanging identities (gay, straight, even bisexual) on which a supportive community can be built. We learn not to pay attention to discrepant feelings that might jeopardize our hard-won identities. And we feel under attack by those who would destabilize sexual orientations, who would see them as a complex but socially learned praxis rather than a biologically given destiny.

But our sexuality is not genetically coded. Human sexual desire long ago became unloosed from the reproductive cycle. For us, sexual contact is a richly textured experience suffused, as are all signifying acts, with culturally created meanings. We see this clearly when we look at the cross-cultural and historical studies of sexuality, but it is equally the case with the mundane heterosexual and homosexual practice of our own day. It is elementary sociology to state that far more is at stake in sexual interplay than the accomplishment of a genetically coded act, though it may be more comfortable for people to think of themselves as infra-human sexual animals, and unsociologically place responsibility for their sexual attractions on their genes, than to imagine and claim the freedom humans actually enjoy in the sexual realm.

In this sense, the biological approach to sexual orientation is a conservative one. By imagining sexual desire as akin to a biological trait like eye color or left-handedness, we neutralize the spontaneous and inventive in sexual relations, and create an essential grid of strictly coded sexual identities. Handedness is a genetically coded trait, and while it can be modified by sociocultural prescription, the underlying organization of right and left hemispheres will not be rearranged, nor will it shift apparently without warning, the way desire does. This is the framework imagined by the biologist model. It is an approach grounded in the view that "gays" are biologically, in effect categorically, different from "straights," a difference sealed by nature in hormone and brain, and ultimately, in DNA.

While the adoption of such a point of view by self-identified gay men and lesbians can be the basis for a separatist model of political and civic association, accepting marginal status as its basis (and, in turn, marginalizing "promiscuity," transvestites, transsexuals, effeminate men, butch women, fetishists, child lovers, SMers, etc.) comes at the price of accepting the framework of majoritarian contempt, at the least. It allows for all the trimmings of religio-ethnic identity: parades, holidays, customs, literature, organizations, leadership cadre. It is concerned with respectability rather than expressive freedom, with conforming to, rather than transgressing, boundaries; in a word, with normality rather than perversity. In the absence of convincing scientific evidence, choosing one view of sex and identity over the other is mainly a political choice, with consequences for how power and resources are organized and distributed in society, and for what cultural values gain or lose ascendancy.

The choice scientists make in looking for *the biological causes* of homosexuality reflects both sociopolitical and epistemological pressures. Historically, it is associated with a number of sociologically relevant conditions: the decline of the psychoanalytic model of homosexuality as an illness; the chance for medically oriented researchers to obtain research funds; the initiative and momentum created by massive spending of money and human capital on the Human Genome Project; a significant weakening of older sexual values and norms, and the consequent anxiety attendant on normlessness. Epistemologically, the conviction that the best understanding of numerous human behavioral and experiential phenomena is one that reduces them to biological, physiological, tissue-bound, and cellular etiologies is obviously pre-sociological. Such a reductionist and anti-sociological tack accounts for the persistent pursuit of biological causes for many behaviors that are politically and interpersonally quite complex—madness of various sorts, repeated violations of law, heavy drinking, individual and group differences on IQ and achievement tests, all sorts of gender-coded behaviors, and now, sexual attraction.

The biological model functions conservatively to restore stability in sexual life: it fixes sex in an ahistorical order, resolves certain tensions and ambiguities of desire, and reinforces the gender system (males do not desire other males; females do not desire other females, unless they are born that way [in which case they are forgivable]: heterosexuals have no homosexual desire; homosexuals have no heterosexual interests). It makes for a neater view of the erotic universe. But it is a retrograde choice from the point of view of a sociological model of sexuality and gender. It would be far more consonant with a sociological view of self and identity for the gay community to proclaim the message of the early gay liberation movement, that "we must free the homosexual (and the heterosexual) in all of us, and the woman and the man, and the fetishist, and the pervert . . ." And thus, the community would better remember one of the sociological lessons of Stonewall, to honor the transvestite prostitutes who threw the first rocks.

Notes

I thank David Schwartz for his inestimable help in the preparation of this essay. I would also like to thank Bill Byne for starting me thinking about the shortcomings of the new biological research into sexuality. Of course, neither one bears responsibility for the final product.

1. S. LeVay. A difference in hypothalamic structure between heterosexual and homosexual men, *Science* 253 (1991): 1034–37; M. J. Bailey and R. C. Pillard, A genetic study of male sexual orientation, *Archives of General Psychiatry* 48 (1991): 1089–96; L. S. Allen and R. Gorski. Sexual orientation and the size of the anterior commissure in the human brain, *Proceedings of the National Academy of Science* 89 (1992): 7199–7202; D. H. Hamer, S. Hu, V. L. Magnuson, N. Hu, and A. M. L. Pattatucci, A linkage between DNA markers on the X chromosome and male sexual orientation, *Science* 261 (1993): 321–27.

2. J. M. Bailey and D. S. Benishay, Familial aggregation of female sexual orientation, *American Journal of Psychiatry* 150 (1993): 272; J. M. Bailey, R. C. Pillard, M. C. Nealem, and Y. Agyei, Heritable factors influence sexual orientation in women, *Archives of General Psychiatry* 50 (1993): 217.

3. Others have noted some of these as well. See W. Byne and B. Parsons, Human sexual orientation: The biologic theories reappraised, *Archives of General Psychiatry* 50 (1993): 228–39 for an excellent review article.

4. See E. Marshall, *Science* 257 (1992): 620–21. It makes LeVay's rejection of an offer from a reputable neuroanatomist to undertake a reexamination of his brain samples, as reported by Marshall, somewhat questionable.

5. Bailey and Pillard, *op. cit.*

6. We will have more to say about this in the discussion of the Hamer et al. research.

7. M. King and E. McDonald, Homosexuals who are twins: A study of 46 probands, *British Journal of Psychiatry* 160 (1992): 407–9.

8. One recent example of such work is that of M. S. Weinberg, C. J. Williams, and D. W. Pryor (*Dual Attraction: Understanding Bisexuality*, [New York: Oxford University Press, 1989]), who link bisexuality to an "open gender schema." "Among self-identified bisexuals," they write, "gender-role prescriptions have been revised to accept erotic attraction to one's own sex as something positive."

9. *New York Times,* December 17, 1991.

10. *Chronicle of Higher Education,* December 18, 1991.

11. *New York Times,* August 1, 1992.

12. *New York Times,* December 17, 1991.

13. *New York Times,* July 18, 1993.

14. A. D. Klassen, C. J. Williams, and E. E. Levitt, *Sex and Morality in the U. S.* (Middletown: Wesleyan University Press, 1989).

Four

Laws and Markets

A. Under Law

29

Homosexual Identity and Gay Rights

Anne B. Goldstein

The law acts on people and things directly and powerfully: criminal law, for example, confines and punishes some people in order to protect others; property law secures some uses of property by excluding others. But what makes these exercises of power "law" rather than merely force is not simply that they are done by or through the sovereign; they are also "law" because they are done and justified with reference to rules and principles that apply generally and not just to one particular case.

The law—by which I mean both the making and the use of such general rules and principles—cannot, and does not, operate in a vacuum. The law is a part of our society and culture, and it is shaped by the ways its makers, interpreters, and enforcers understand our world. To get right down to the specific case at hand, decisions about how to interpret existing laws affecting gay people, and about what new laws to make, depend on the relevant decision makers' understanding of what it means "to be gay," in at least two distinct senses: first, their understanding of who is gay, and second, their understanding of what homosexuality is.

My essay focuses on some ways we go about answering these two interrelated questions.

Who Is Gay?

First, who is gay? I expect that each of us has our own understanding of what it means to be gay, compounded from various sources—reading, watching movies, personal experience, talking with other people, thinking about it on our own. If we have spent any appreciable time on the question, we can hardly have failed to notice that, whatever our personal beliefs, there are those who differ from us. Here are a few basic questions:

- Is there one truth about each person—gay or straight—for an entire lifetime, or even for part of a lifetime?
- And, if there is, is it a truth about experience or about desire?
- If desire alone is dispositive, what sorts of desires are important, and which irrelevant?
- If experience in dispositive what kind, and how much?
- Does it matter whether the experiences occurred throughout a lifetime or during a more limited period?
- How important, if at all, is it for sexual behavior to be "transgressive"?
- What about cross-gender behavior, in or out of bed—is that important?
- Is conscious adoption of a gay identity necessary? Sufficient?

Any one of us can answer such questions, and by answering them construct a category that contains some people and excludes others, but we can do so only idiosyncratically. We simply have no clear, recognized, unambiguous meaning to resort to. The concept is contested, and our usage is therefore pervaded by ambiguity and multiple meanings, across the issues I have identified and many others as well.

Notwithstanding these ambiguities and multiple meanings, whenever the law acts on gay people as such, it needs, and it uses, the idea that some people are gay and others are not—often without recognizing the inconsistencies and contradictions in the various ideas we have about what it means to be gay.

A good example of this—an easy target, really—is the U.S. military's attempts to exclude homosexuals from its ranks. These regulations have a long and shameful history, but I will focus here only on the last two chapters of it. The most recently abandoned regulations—the ones superseded by the new "don't ask, don't tell" policy—categorized people by their desires. People who did "homosexual acts"—that is, who engaged in "bodily contact, actively undertaken or passively permitted, between [persons] of the same sex for the purpose of satisfying sexual desires"—were only presumed to be homosexuals. They could refute this conclusion by showing that their homosexual acts were "a departure from [their] usual and customary behavior" and "unlikely to recur." In contrast, if the discharge board decided that a person, however virginal or celibate, nevertheless desired or intended to engage in homosexual acts, he or she would be discharged as a homosexual.[1]

This regulation was open to challenge on many different levels. Some people challenged their discharges by arguing that they had been misidentified—that the discharge board or court martial had incorrectly assessed their desires. Other people argued that mere desire, in the absence of any proof of action or intention to act, was not enough. Joseph Steffan, for example, at first won the right to graduate from Annapolis and be commissioned as a naval officer on this ground,[2] although that decision was later reversed because the court reasoned that "the military may reasonably assume that when a member states that he is a homosexual, that member means that he either engages or is likely to engage in homosexual conduct."[3] Still other service members challenged the regulations as irrational because they were unrelated to any legitimate need of the armed services. Keith Meinhold's reinstatement to the navy was ordered on this ground.[4]

In the 1992 campaign, Bill Clinton seemed to be criticizing the military's policy for its irrationality. But although President Clinton's campaign promise was to "end restrictions on gays in the military," after the election, in response to Defense Department and congressional resistance, this promise segued into a statement that "the issue ought to be conduct," without any discussion of what conduct would matter, and then to the much weaker promise that nobody would be discharged on account of his or her "status" alone.

As the new policy itself makes clear, however, "homosexual conduct" is so elastic a concept that it can be stretched into virtual equivalence with homosexual status. The new rules still require discharge for "homosexual acts"[5]—that is, for "bodily contact . . . for the purpose of satisfying sexual desires"[6]—but now discharge is required as well for much lesser touchings, such as "[b]odily contact which a reasonable person would understand to demonstrate a propensity or intent to engage in [homosexual] acts."[7]

Consider for a moment the person who is immunized from discharge by these new regulations. Is he or she really, meaningfully gay? To be safe, he or she must be not merely celibate but wholly untouching and untouched. Mere desire is formally permitted, but only so long as the desiring subject gives no hint of the fires within.[8]

What understanding of homosexuality could justify such a regime? One reason these new rules may be struck down by the courts,[9] as their predecessors sometimes have been, is that the Defense Department has not been able to articulate very good reasons for its own regulations. After all, its own studies show that gay people make, if anything, better soldiers and sailors than straight people.[10] Instead of dropping the ban, however, the Defense Department has fallen back on the argument that gay people must be excluded from the armed services because some straight service members are prejudiced against them. This argument has the virtue of frankness, if nothing else.[11]

Whether or not such a shameful argument can withstand constitutional attack is beyond the scope of this essay, as are the deepest sources of such prejudices themselves. But I can discuss how the various ways we think about homosexuality shape particular expressions of and justifications for these prejudices, and indeed shape all our arguments about homosexuality.

What Is Homosexuality?

So far I have talked about disagreements over criteria for inclusion in the group of gay people, and about how people within the group ought to be treated. Now I want to shift levels and talk about ideas concerning homosexuality itself.

Many of us write and speak as if "homosexuality" has some invariant core meaning, independent of history and culture, the reality of which could be subject to rigorous verification. Whether or not this is true—and I suspect it is not—I submit that it can be useful to recognize that, like most ways of understanding and describing aspects of the human condition, "homosexuality" is also a cultural and historical artifact.

In the first volume of his *History of Sexuality*, Michel Foucault famously claimed that "homosexuality" was invented in approximately 1870. Of course, Foucault knew that before 1870 some men made love with other men, that some men did so predominantly, that some men even did so exclusively. He knew, too, that some of these men, and some of their peers, noticed these preferences. When he nevertheless claimed that homosexuality was invented in 1870, he was speaking not about such raw facts and how *we* would interpret them, but about how the pre-1870 world was understood by its people themselves.

Here is the distinction that Foucault noticed and articulated:

> [Before 1870, a]s defined by the ancient civil or canonical codes, sodomy was a category of forbidden acts; their perpetrator was nothing more than the juridical subject of them. The nineteenth-century homosexual became a personage, a past, a case history, and a childhood, in addition to being a type of life, a life form, and a morphology, with an indiscreet anatomy and possibly a mysterious physiology. Nothing that went into his total composition was unaffected by his sexuality.[12]

Before the invention of "homosexuality," sexual touchings between men were judged according to criteria that applied equally to heterosexual practices, such as the parts of the body involved, the relative status of the parties, and whether the sexual drama conformed to sex role stereotypes. Although illicit sexual acts were seen as sinful, immoral, criminal, or all three, before the 1870s illicit sexual acts between men, or between women, were not seen as fundamentally different from, or even necessarily worse than, illicit acts between a man and a woman. What was new, then, was an understanding of sex not merely as behavior, some of which might be criminal or sinful, but as *sexuality:* pervasive throughout a person's entire life, character, and being. Sexual acts might be mere incidents within a life, but sexuality was constitutive of identity.[13]

This idea, new in the 1870s, is today our dominant assumption. Indeed, it is so dominant that it inflects our interpretations of the much older notions that sex between men or between women is a sin or a crime. Those ideas certainly persist, but not quite in their original form. Originally ideas about acts, they now often elide into ideas about the people who do those acts. No longer is the doer of such acts merely the "juridical subject" of them; he or she has become, at least in some eyes, the quintessential sinner or criminal, whose very existence is a wrong.

The most well known 1870s understanding of homosexuality was medical: it was seen as an illness. Early sexologists searched their subjects' bodies for physical signs of degeneracy, and their histories for excessive masturbation or indulgence in alcohol, either their own or an ancestor's. Over the years, ideas about the causes of homosexuality have continued to evolve, but the assumption that sexual inclinations toward a person of one's own sex are beyond one's control (at least without professional treatment) remains at the core of the medical model. Thus, the idea of homosexuality as illness could from the beginning be counterposed against the ideas that sex between men or between women could be either sinful or criminal.

History has shown the weaknesses of this approach. Illnesses may be contagious; infected people should be isolated or cured. The history of well-meaning attempts to cure people of their homosexuality is fully as horrifying as the history of outright punishment for sin or crime. Moreover, legislatures and courts that understand homosexuality as an illness are much more likely, for example, to prohibit homosexuals from being adoptive or foster parents, for fear the children will "catch" it,[14] than to repeal or overturn their sodomy statutes. Especially in this age of AIDS, the idea that homosexuality is an illness is plainly no friend of gay rights.

The doctors' ideas about homosexuality as a medical category were an adaptation of ideas developed by Karl Heinrich Ulrichs, rightly called "the grandfather of gay liberation."[15] Ulrichs, a German lawyer, developed his theories both to understand his own life and to campaign for societal tolerance and law reform. In its origin and at its core, Ulrichs's was a theory of desire: his construct, the "Urning," the man who desires other men, is recognized and defined by desires, natural for him, which in turn explain and justify his behavior. Ulrichs posited that the Urning's defining desires were inborn and immutable; he claimed that individuals with all the defining characteristics could be found at all times and in all culture.[16] The modern gay liberation and gay rights movements may be seen as being in this tradition, from Mattachine and the Daughters of Bilitis to Queer Nation, especially when they claim that there is more to being gay than what you do in bed, or with whom—that there is a gay culture, a gay sensibility. Such ideas underlie, I think, arguments that homosexuality should be seen as a suspect category, entitled to special protection under the equal protection clause of the Constitution. They also provide one source of arguments that gay people have the right to come out, to find one another and form organizations, to march, to live lives that are not just open but even public. Such arguments counter what Nan Hunter calls the No Promo Homo movement, exemplified by the Briggs Initiative in California and, more recently, the Colorado constitutional amendment—attempts to restrict public expression and public advocacy by gays.[17]

The most recent idea about homosexuality is that it is just one manifestation of normal human sexuality, one variation among many. This idea combines the pre–nineteenth-century assumption that a person's sexuality should be evaluated without consideration of the gender of his or her object choice with the twentieth-century notion that sexual expression is good and sexual repression, bad. This idea undergirded the opinions of the four dissenting justices in *Bowers v. Hardwick*—the ones who would have held that Georgia's sodomy statute was unconstitutional.[18] I think this idea underlies the Kentucky Supreme Court's decision that Kentucky's sodomy statute violates that state's constitution,[19] and recent decisions that the Department of Defense regulations excluding gays from military service lack any rational basis.

Notes

1. *See, e.g.*, Steffan v. Aspen, 8 F.3d 57, 65 (D.C. Cir. 1994), *vacated and rehearing en banc granted* (D.C. Cir. Jan. 7, 1994); *rev'd sub nom* Steffan v. Perry, 41 F.3d 677 (reserving question of whether dismissal of celibate, merely desiring, homosexual would be constitutional).

2. Steffan v. Perry, 8 F.3d 57, 65.

3. Steffan v. Perry, 41 F.3d at 686.

4. Meinhold v. U.S. Dept. of Defense, 808 F. Supp 1455 (C.D. Cal. 1983), *aff'd on other grounds* 34 F.3d 1469 (9th Cir.) (policy does not apply to sailor who merely said, "I am gay" on television, but would apply to one who demonstrated a concrete desire or intent to engage in homosexual acts); *see also* Pruitt v. Cheney, 963 F.2d 1160 (9th Cir. 1992) (complaint states equal protection grounds for relief); Dahl v. Secretary of the Navy, 830 F. Supp 1319 (E.D. Cal. 1993) (prejudice alone cannot justify policy).

5. 10 U.S.C. § 654(b)(1) (1995).

6. 10 U.S.C. § 654(f)(3) (A) (1995).

7. 10 U.S.C. § 654(f)(3) (B) (1995). The earliest-released version of this language was more explicit: "[b]odily contact between persons of the same sex that a reasonable person would understand to demonstrate a propensity or intent to engage in homosexual acts (e.g., hand-holding or kissing in most circumstances." Text of Pentagon's New Policy Guidelines on Homosexuality in the Military, *New York Times*, July 20, 1993, at A16.

8. According to the earlier formulation of these rules, he or she may, it is true, visit a gay bar, march in a gay rights rally in civilian clothes, and list a person of the same gender as an insurance beneficiary or the person to be contacted in an emergency. See Text of Pentagon's New Policy Guidelines, *supra* n. 7.

9. One lower court has already suspended the operation of "don't ask, don't tell" as to six service members who were threatened with discharge for openly stating that they were gay: see Able v. U.S. Dept. of Defense, 880 F. Supp. 968 (E.D. N.Y. 1995).

10. See studies cited in Meinhold v. U.S. Dept. of Defense, 808 F. Supp. at 1457–58.

11. See, e.g., Debbie Howlett, Keep Ban, Schwarzkopf Testifies: Openly Gay Troops Pose "a Problem," *USA Today*, May 12, 1993, at 3A (quoting retired General Norman Schwarzkopf as saying, "Homosexuals have served in the past and done a great job serving their country, and I feel they can in the future," but that "it's open homosexuality in a unit that causes this breakdown in unit cohesion."); *accord*, Capitol Hill Hearing with Defense Department Personnel, *Federal News Service*, July 20, 1993 (testimony of chairman of the Joint Chiefs of Staff General Colin Powell). The authors of the Senate report repudiated such frankness when providing a rationale for enacting the "don't ask, don't tell" rules, 10 U.S.C. § 654; see testimony of Sam Nunn before the senate, 141 *Cong. Rec.* S.5171-01, S.5173 et seq.

12. Michel Foucault, *The History of Sexuality, vol. 1, An Introduction* 43 (R. Hurley trans., 1978).

13. And not just sexuality—the observation applies, for example, to mental illness, where a person suffering from schizophrenia *becomes* a schizophrenic, and so forth.

14. *See, e.g.*, Opinion of the Justices, 129 N.H. 290, 530 A.2d 21 (1987) (holding that proposed law prohibiting homosexuals from adopting children or being foster parents is constitutional; then-Judge now Justice, Souter voted with majority). The court reasoned as follows:

The rationale underlying the role model theory is that persons in the position of parents are the primary role models after whom children consciously or unconsciously pattern themselves. Although opponents of the bill have cited a number of studies that find no correlation between a homosexual orientation of parents and the sexual orientation of their children, the source of sexual orientation is still inadequately understood and is thought to be a combination of genetic and environmental influences. Given the reasonable possibility of environmental influences, we believe that the legislature can rationally act on the theory that a role model can influence the child's developing sexual identity.

Opinion of the Justices, *supra*, 129 N.H. at 296, 530 A.2d at 25 (citations omitted).

15. Vern Bullough, introduction to *The Riddle of "Man-Manly" Love: The Pioneering Work on Male Homosexuality*, by Karl Heinrich Ulrichs (trans. Michael A. Lombardi-Nash, 1994); *accord*, Martin Danecker, *Theories of Homosexuality* 33 (trans. David Fernbach, 1981); John Addington Symonds, letter to Edward Carpenter, February 7, 1893, published in John Addington Symonds, *Male Love: A Problem in Greek Ethics and Other Writings* 152 (John Lauritsen ed., 1983).

16. This work was carried on by others; see, e.g., Edward Carpenter, *Intermediate Types among Primitive Folk: A Study in Social Evolution* (1921).

17. Nan D. Hunter, Identity, Speech and Equality, 79 *Va. L. Rev.* 1695, 1702–06 (1993). Hunter makes this point more strongly, claiming that "[t]he Briggs Initiative referendum campaign [in 1978] marked the moment when American politics began to treat homosexuality as something more than deviance, conduct, or lifestyle; it marked the emergence of homosexuality as an openly political claim and a viewpoint," at 1704.

18. See Anne B. Goldstein, History, Homosexuality and Political Values: Searching for the Hidden Determinants of *Bowers v. Hardwick*, 97 *Yale L.J.* 1073, 1088–91 (1988).

19. Commonwealth v. Wasson, 842 S.W.2d 487 (Ky. 1992).

30

Sexual Preference as a Suspect Classification

David A. J. Richards

The Equal Protection Clause of the Fourteenth Amendment speaks in terms of an abstract normative concept, equal protection. Consistent with its abstract normative character, the Supreme Court has extended forms of suspect classification analysis from the historical paradigm of suspectness (race) to ethnic origin,[1] alienage,[2] illegitimacy,[3] and gender;[4] it has refused to extend it to poverty[5] and apparently would not extend it to sexual preference.[6] My concern here, consistent with comparable treatments of this issue by others,[7] is with the best interpretive understanding of our traditions, which includes, when necessary, a critical theory of interpretive judicial mistake.

In my judgment, the refusal to accord suspect classification status to discrimination on grounds of sexual preference is a grave interpretive mistake, a mistake at least as grave as the refusal to extend constitutional privacy analysis to homosexual sodomy in the now justly infamous *Bowers v. Hardwick*.[8] I will some remarks about the relationship of the two mistakes in the course of my argument, but my main goal is to offer a plausible view of why the former is a mistake. The issue is of central importance not only to the integrity of American constitutional law but to the integrity of gay persons, both as individuals and as a community. We must get these arguments right, because so much turns on them in terms of our legitimate place in American constitutional culture among those groups whose claims for simple justice have transformed the interpretive understanding of American public law as a community of principle. I argue that we should resist various alternative attempts to ground the suspectness of sexual preference on either political powerlessness or the alleged immutability of sexual preference (on analogy to race and gender), and focus rather on the suspectness of the attempt to discriminate against the public claims to justice central to gay public and private identity (on analogy to religion).

Political Powerlessness

A plausible general theory of suspect classification analysis must unify, on grounds of principle, the claims to such analysis of African Americans, women, and gays. Political powerlessness alone cannot do so. Lack of political power—measured either by some statistical norm[9] or by the utilitarian principle[10]—does not function at the level of rights-based ethical discourse fundamental to suspect classification analysis. It wrongly suggests, as Bruce Ackerman does, that the gains in political solidarity of groups subjected to deep racist, sexist, or religious prejudice (in view of resistance to such prejudice) disentitle them from constitutional protection, as if the often meager political gains blacks, women, and gays have achieved (when measured against their claims of justice) are the measure of constitutional justice; and it preposterously denies constitutional protection to women, as Ely does, because they are, statistically, a majority of voters. The view also proves too much: it extends protection to any political group (though subject to no history of rights-denying prejudice) solely because it has not been as politically successful as it might have been (say, dentists). Procedural models of suspect classification analysis suppress the underlying substantive rights-based normative judgments that determine how equal protection has been and should be interpreted.

Suspect classification analysis focuses, rather, on the political expression of irrational prejudices of a certain sort, namely, those rooted in a history and culture of unjust exclusion of a certain group from the scope of political community required by respect for their basic rights of conscience, speech, and association. The fundamental wrong of racism and sexism has been the intolerant exclusion of blacks and women from the rights of public culture; they have been exiled to cultural marginality in supposedly morally inferior realms. Such unjust cultural marginalization has, in my judgment, also victimized homosexuals, and its rectification entitles sexual preference to be recognized as a suspect entitles sexual preference to be recognized as a suspect classification.

Immutability

The fact that sexual preference is not, like race or gender, an immutable and salient personal characteristic has sometimes been taken to disqualify sexual preference from treatment as a suspect classification.[11] The argument is controversial even on its own empirical and ethical terms.

Sexual preference may be a largely settled and irreversible erotic preference for most people long before the age of responsibility.[12] The possible concealment or even repression of the preference—as a reason for disqualifying it from treatment as a suspect classification—is not a reasonable condition of political respect if sexual preference is integral to the authenticity of moral personality and the prejudice against it as politically unreasonable as racism and sexism. The sacrifice of moral authenticity is not a demand any person could reasonably be asked to accept as the price for freedom from irrational prejudice; and homosexual persons can no more be reasonably asked to make such a crippling sacrifice of self than any other person.

In fact, immutability and salience do not coherently explain even the historical paradigm of a suspect classification, namely, race, and therefore cannot normatively define the terms of principle reasonably applicable to other claims to suspect classification analysis. The principle of *Brown v. Board of Education*[13] itself cannot reasonably be understood in terms of the abstract ethical ideal that state benefits and burdens should never turn on an immutable and salient characteristic as such. Many cases show that this is not a reasonable ideal or principle. Handicapped persons are born with handicaps that often cannot be changed; nonetheless, people with such handicaps are certainly owed, on grounds of justice, a distinctive measure of concern aimed to accord them some fair approximation of the opportunities of nonhandicapped persons. It is no moral objection to such measures that they turn on immutable characteristics, because the larger theory of distributive justice has identified such factors as here reasonably relevant to its concerns.

The example is not an isolated one; its principle pervades the justice of rewards and of fair distribution more generally. For example, we reward certain athletic achievements very highly, and do not finely calibrate the component of our rewards attributable to acts of self-disciplined will from those based on natural endowments. Achievement itself suffices to elicit reward, even though some significant part of it turns on immutable physical endowments that some have and others lack. Or we allocate scarce places in institutions of higher learning on the basis of an immutable factor such as geographic distribution, an educational policy we properly regard as sensible and not unfair. The point can be reasonably generalized to include that part of the theory of distributive justice concerned with both maintaining an economic and social minimum and creating some structure of differential rewards to elicit better performance for the public good. The idea of a just minimum turns on certain facts about levels of subsistence, not on acts of will; we would not regard such a minimum as any the less justly due if some component of it turned on immutable factors. Differential rewards perform the role of incentives for the kind of performance required by modern industrial market economies such as the United States and Western Europe; immutable factors such as genetic endowment may play some significant role in such performance. Nonetheless, we do not regard it as unjust to reward such performance so long as the incentives work out with the consequences specified by our theory of distributive justice. Our conclusion, from a wide range of diverse examples, must be that immutability and salience do not identify an ethically reasonable principle of suspect classification analysis. Race is a suspect classification, when it is, not on these grounds, but when it expresses a rights-denying culture of irrational political prejudice.

From this perspective, the issue of the immutability of sexual preference should be irrelevant to its constitutional examination as a suspect classification, and the issue of irrational political prejudice (which does not turn on salience) should be central. The insistence on immutability and salience as requirements for suspect classification analysis in the case of sexual preference would be and is unprincipled. It is not a requirement we impose elsewhere, and there is no good argument of principle why we should impose it here.

Against this background, there are good reasons why gay persons might and should resist interpreting their claims to suspect classification analysis in the biological and genetic terms that some gay scientists have recently proposed.[14] To claim a mode of argument not required for other claimants to suspect classification analysis ethically undercuts the integrity of the arguments of principle that gays may, can, and should make as arguments available on fair terms to all persons. It also falsely and malignly biologizes what is essentially a principled argument for the just ethical emancipation of gay persons in terms that subvert its emancipatory potential. Biological reductionism was central to the unjust cultural subjugation of African Americans, women, and gays as separate species, and will wreak comparable havoc with gays today, confirming, rather than challenging, unjust cultural stereotypes of biologically rooted inferiority.

The contemporary constitutional issue of principle is precisely to highlight the devastating impact on the basic rights of gay people of a heretofore unchallenged homophobic cultural orthodoxy, the ways it has stunted and stultified the range of human and moral imagination that gay persons, as individuals, may reasonably bring to the diverse patterns of a well-lived and ethical life. We need an interpretation of suspect classification analysis adequate to our indignation at the force this unjust culture has uncritically enjoyed.

The Suspectness of Sexual Preference as Religious Persecution

The most precise and illuminating constitutional analogy for the suspectness of sexual preference today is neither race nor gender, but the oldest suspect classification under American public law, namely, religion.[15] The constitutional protection of religion never turned on its immutable and salient character (people can and do convert, and can and do conceal their religious convictions), but on the traditional place of religion in the conscientious and reasonable formation of one's moral identity in public and private life and the need for protection, consistent with respect for the inalienable right of conscience, of persons against state impositions of sectarian religious views. Normative claims by gay persons today have exactly the same ethical and constitutional force:

they are in their nature claims to a self-respecting moral identity in public and private life through which gay persons may reasonably express and realize their ethical convictions of the moral powers of sexual love in a good, fulfilled, and responsible life against the background of an unjust and now quite conspicuously sectarian tradition of moral subjugation.[16] Sexual preference should be a suspect classification on the most traditional and conservative readings of American constitutional principles. Gay persons have as much right to make claims on the basis of such principles as any persons and citizens in America. It is time that they reclaimed America's traditions of toleration from the bigoted religious sectarians of the right who have so degraded and abused them.

The essential points of the suspect classification analysis of sexual preference are (1) a history and culture of unjust moral subjugation of homosexuals, and (2) the political legitimation of such subjugation by the exclusion of homosexuals from the constitutional community of equal rights in the unreasonable way that gives rise to intolerance and the irrational political prejudice of homophobia.

The history and culture of the moral subjugation of homosexuals are ancient. Plato in *The Laws* gave influential expression to the moral condemnation of homosexuality in terms of two arguments: its nonprocreative character and (in its male homosexual forms) its degradation of the passive male partner to the status of a woman.[17] Homosexuality was, on this view, an immoral and unnatural abuse of the proper human function of sexuality, marking the homosexual as subhuman and therefore wholly outside the moral community of persons. The exile of homosexuals from any just claim on moral community was given expression by the striking moral idea of homosexuality as unspeakable. It was, in Blackstone's terms, "a crime not fit to be named: *peccatum illud horribile, inter christianos non nominandum*"—not mentionable, let alone discussed or assessed.[18] Such total silencing of any reasonable discussion rendered homosexuality into a kind of cultural death, naturally thus understood and indeed condemned as a kind of ultimate heresy against essential moral values.[19]

The traditional moral condemnation of homosexuality was thus, in its historical nature, a form of intolerance that should have been subject to appropriate political and constitutional assessment in light of the argument for toleration.[20] However, liberal political theory, as in the related area of gender, not only failed reasonably to extend its analysis to sexual preference; it indulged irrationalist intolerance by accepting an unreasonable conception of constitutional community excluding homosexuals as subhuman and thus unworthy of the rights of conscience, free speech, and association central to the exercise of their moral powers.[21] The same defective political epistemology of gender and sexuality that unleashed the long-standing cultural intolerance against women applied, a fortiori, to homosexuals, a group whose sexuality was, because morally unspeakable, even less well understood, fairly discussed, or empirically assessed. The vacuum of fair discussion and assessment was filled by the fears and irrationalist stereotypes reflective of the long moral tradition that exiled homosexuals from moral community.

It is consistent with this argument about homophobia as a culturally constructed irrational prejudice (an insult to culture-creating rights) to observe the extraordinarily important role homosexuals have played in the construction of Western culture, including its arts.[22] An argument of essential human rights is not directed at saints, heroes, or persons of genius, who can find creative redemption in circumstances that crush the moral powers of other people. The cultural tradition of the West may honor its women and men of genius who are homosexuals, but not as homosexuals, and not homosexuals as such. The bitter, plain truth is that ordinary people of good will whose sexual preference was homosexual could find in their culture only their denial as unspeakable, voiceless, dead.

The persisting political force of irrationalist homophobia, as an independent political evil, is quite apparent today when persons feel free to indulge their prejudices against homosexuals although neither of the two traditional moral reasons for condemning homosexuality can any longer be legitimately and indeed constitutionally imposed on society at large.

One such moral reason (the condemnation of nonprocreational sex) can, for example, no longer constitutionally justify laws against the sale to and use of contraceptives by married and unmarried heterosexual couples.[23] The mandatory enforcement at large of the procreational model of sexuality is, in circumstances of overpopulation and declining infant and adult mortality, a sectarian ideal lacking adequate secular basis in the general goods that can alone reasonably justify state power; accordingly, contraceptive-using heterosexuals have the constitutional right to decide when and whether their sexual lives shall be pursued to procreate or as an independent expression of mutual love, affection, and companionship.[24] Gay persons should, on grounds of principle, equally be entitled to this basic right of all persons.

And the other moral reason for condemning homosexual sex (the degradation of a man to the passive status of a woman) rests on the sexist premise of the degraded nature of women, which has been properly rejected as a reasonable basis for laws or policies on grounds of suspect classification analysis.

Nonetheless, although each moral ground for the condemnation of homosexuality has been independently reflected as a reasonable justification for coercive laws enforceable on society at large, they unreasonably retain their force when brought into specific relationship to the claims of homosexuals.

These claims are today in their basic nature arguments of principle made by homosexuals for the same respect for their intimate love life, free of unreasonable procreational and sexist requirements, now rather generously accorded heterosexual couples. Empirical issues relating to sexuality and gender are now subjected to more impartial critical assessment than they were previously; and the resulting light of public reason about issues of sexuality and gender should be available to all persons on fair terms. However, such a claim of fair treatment (an argument of basic constitutional principle if any argument is) was contemptuously dismissed by a majority of the Supreme Court of the United States in *Bowers v. Hardwick*.[25]

Traditional moral arguments, now clearly reasonably rejected in their application to heterosexuals, were uncritically applied to a group much more exi-
gently in need of constitutional protection on grounds of principle.[26] Reasonable
advances in the public understanding of sexuality and gender, now constitutionally available to all heterosexuals, were suspended in favor of an appeal to the
sexual mythology of the Middle Ages.[27] The transparently unprincipled character of *Bowers* confirms the unjust continuing complicity of American constitutionalism with the legitimation of the cultural construction of the morally
subjugated status of homosexuals. If the *Plessy* court illegitimately fostered the
construction of American racism,[28] the *Bowers* court has illegitimately advanced the construction of homophobia.

The issue in *Bowers* (the illegitimate criminalization of homosexual sex acts)
is not the same issue as suspect classification analysis. Not all acts that should
enjoy protection by the constitutional right to privacy would also call for
suspect classification analysis; contraceptive-using heterosexual adults, who enjoy and should enjoy protection by the constitutional right to privacy, are not
reasonably understood as a suspect class. And the scope of protection of groups
properly regarded as suspect classes cannot be limited to the right to privacy or
indeed to any fundamental right; it extends to all laws or policies actuated by
irrational prejudice. Correspondingly, the issue of sexual preference as a suspect
classification is much larger than the issue of *Bowers*. *Bowers* is an interpretive
mistake as an analysis of the constitutional right to privacy. But even if *Bowers*
had been rightly decided, the issue of sexual preference as a suspect classification would remain.[29]

The moral insult of homophobia, like that of racism and sexism, cannot be
limited to any particular right; it denigrates one's status as a bearer of rights
within the moral community of equal rights. Suspect classification analysis
arose from the study of the radical political evil of a political culture, ostensibly
committed to toleration on the basis of universal human rights, that unjustly
denied a class of persons the cultural space in the political community that is
their inalienable human right as persons with moral powers. To deny such a
group, already the subject of a long history and culture of moral degradation,
their culture-creating rights is to silence in them the very voice of their moral
freedom, rendering unspoken and unspeakable the sentiments, experience, and
reason that authenticate the moral personality that a political culture of human
rights owes each and every person. Sexual preference is a suspect classification
because homosexuals are today victimized by irrational political prejudices
rooted in this radical political evil, denying them the cultural resources of free
moral personality.

Such political prejudice is an evil, subject to suspect classification analysis,
whatever the form of erotic life in which a gay person finds fulfillment.[30] Such
erotic life may be embedded in complex, symbolically elaborated and idealized
forms of intense, deeply loving relationships in which the sex acts that concern
Bowers v. Hardwick are not in play. The political prejudice of homophobia

remains the same evil of radical cultural intolerance, whatever the sex life in question, because it denies the cultural space through which persons of homosexual preference may reasonably define a life of personal and ethical self-respect on whatever terms best give expression to their free moral powers.

Another way of making the same point is to observe that homophobic prejudice, like sexism, unjustly distorts the idea of human rights applicable to both public and private life. If the political evil of sexism expressed itself in a morally degraded interpretation of private life (to which women, as morally inferior, were confined), the evil of homophobic prejudice is its degradation of homosexual love to the unspeakably private and secretive not only politically but intra-psychically in the person whose sexuality is homosexual. The political evil of this prejudice, based on the compulsory secrecy of the preference, is not always ameliorated and may indeed sometimes be aggravated by the growing practice of either not enforcing or repealing or otherwise invalidating criminal laws against homosexual sex. Such developments—without comparable anti-discrimination guarantees against homophobic prejudice—legitimate the ancient idea of something unspeakably and properly private, something all the more outrageous if given any public expression whatsoever (thus legitimating sexist violence against forms of public expression of homosexual preference). But such compulsory privatization insults homosexuals in the same way it traditionally insulted women; it deprives them as moral persons of their right to speak and feel and live as whole persons on the terms of public and private life best expressive of their free moral powers. That is the moral right of every person in a free society, and homosexual persons have a right to it on equal terms.

It is for this reason that, in my judgment, appropriate constitutional remedies for homophobic prejudice include the range of remedies now available in the case of race and gender. I include among these remedies, in contrast to some commentators,[31] affirmative action, because the underlying constitutional concern should be the deconstruction of the compulsory privatization of homosexual preference. Homosexuals cannot justly be required to be secretive as the condition of fair access to public goods; to the extent they are so required, they suffer unjust discrimination on grounds of prejudice. Such prejudice can, as in the case of race and gender, be remedied by appropriate affirmative action plans that insure that the qualifications of public homosexuals are fairly assessed and that the presence of such homosexuals in various positions undermines political prejudice in society at large.

Homophobia may be best understood today as a form of residual gender discrimination, in particular, sexist discrimination focusing on the terms of intimate life. The nonprocreative character of homosexual sexuality may be of relatively little concern, but its cultural symbolism of disordered gender roles excites anxieties in a political culture still quite sexist in its understanding of gender roles. Homosexuals—both lesbians and gay men—are, on this view, in revolt against what many still suppose to be the "natural" order of gender hierarchy: women or men, as the case may be, undertaking sexual roles improper to their gender (for example, dominance in women, passivity in men). It is plainly unjust to displace such sexist views, no longer publicly justifiable against heterosexual women, against a much more culturally marginalized and despised group—symbolic scapegoats of the feeble and cowardly sense of self that seeks self-respect in the unjust degradation of morally innocent people of good will. Homosexuals have the right, on grounds of suspect classification analysis, to be protected from such irrational prejudice.

It is prejudice of this sort that accounts, in my judgment, for the area of our national public life that is most conspicuously and unashamedly homophobic, the American military.[32] In the area of gender, many note the damage that liberal political theory's complicity with sexism inflicted on the political culture's interpretation of basic human rights, that is, a hypermasculinized vision of the content and scope of human rights.[33] Exclusion of women from the military surely reflects this misinterpretation,[34] and the exclusion of homosexuals is a variation on the same sexist theme.

People serving in the military must satisfy the reasonable requirements such service calls for, but these requirements have little to do with gender as such[35] and nothing to do with sexual preference.[36] The confusion of the military virtues of courage and competence with traditional ideas of manliness (including aggressive heterosexual virility) is, at bottom, transparently sexist (as if a woman or homosexual in the military must be either the perpetrator or victim of sexual harassment); it morally insults both women and homosexuals to ascribe to them incapacities of moral control or susceptibilities that reflect and reinforce irrational prejudice in this way. It also disfigures what military service is and should be in the defense of a constitutional culture of human rights.

Military service is a part of that culture and should reflect its best values and aspirations. However, instead of distributing rights and responsibilities on terms that respect all persons as equal members of the political community, the military has cordoned itself off from the larger fabric of constitutional principle, a judicially protected bastion of sexist prejudice exempt from reasonable constitutional analysis.[37] This is to make of military service not the defense of constitutional values, but their subversion in this last sectarian sanctuary of a corruptly hypermasculinized interpretation of political liberalism.

Notes

This essay is a development of the interpretation of suspect classification analysis in general and the suspectness of sexual preference in particular offered in David A. J. Richards, *Conscience and the Constitution: History, Theory, and Law of the Reconstruction Amendments* (Princeton: Princeton University Press, 1993), esp. chap. 5. Some of the arguments in the article are further developed in idem, "Sexual Preference as a Suspect (Religion) Classification: An Alternative Perspective on the Unconstitutionality of Anti-Lesbian/Gay Initiative," 55 *Ohio State L.J.* (1994).

1. See, for example, *Hernandez v. Texas,* 347 U.S. 475 (1954) (discrimination against Mexican Americans in jury selection).

2. See, for example, *Graham v. Richardson,* 403 U.S. 365 (1971) (state cannot deny welfare benefits to aliens).

3. See, for example, *Trimble v. Gordon,* 430 U.S. 762 (1977) (state law struck down governing intestate succession that barred inheritance by illegitimate children from their fathers).

4. See, for example, *Frontiero v. Richardson,* 411 U.S. 677 (1973) (federal law struck down on equal protection grounds permitting male, but not female, members of the armed services an automatic dependency allowance for their spouses); *Craig v. Boren,* 429 U.S. 190 (1976) (state law struck down prohibiting sale of beer to males under age twenty-one and to females under age eighteen).

5. See, for example, *James v. Valtierra,* 402 U.S. 137 (1971) (state constitutional amendment involving wealth classification—special local referenda for low-rent housing projects—not suspect, and therefore constitutional).

6. For two considered rejections of the claim on this ground by the Court of Appeals for the District of Columbia, see *Dronenberg v. Zech,* 741 F.2d 1388 (D.C. Cir. 1984) (Navy policy of mandatory discharge for homosexuality held constitutional); *Padula v. Webster,* 822 F.2d 97 (D.C. Cir. 1987) (FBI rejection of lesbian as special agent held constitutional). For a good overview, see "Developments in the Law: Sexual Orientation and the Law," 102 *Harv. L. Rev.* 1509 (1989).

7. See, for example, Note, "The Constitutional Status of Sexual Orientation: Homosexuality as a Suspect Classification," 98 *Harv. L. Rev.* 1285 (1985); Comment, "An Argument for the Application of Equal Protection Heightened Scrutiny to Classifications Based on Homosexuality," 57 *S. Cal. L. Rev.* 797 (1984); Seth Harris, Note, "Permitting Prejudice to Govern: Equal Protection, Military Deference, and the Exclusion of Lesbians and Gay Men from the Military," 17 *NYU Rev. L. & Soc. Change* 171 (1989–90).

8. 478 U.S 186 (1986). I examine the interpretive illegitimacy of this decision in David A. J. Richards, "Constitutional Legitimacy and Constitutional Privacy," 61 *NYU L. Rev.* 800 (1986), a discussion developed at greater length in idem, *Foundations of American Constitutionalism* (New York: Oxford University Press, 1989).

9. See Bruce Ackerman, "Beyond *Carolene Products,*" 98 *Harv. L. Rev.* 713 (1985).

10. See John Ely, *Democracy and Distrust: A Theory of Judicial Review* (Cambridge: Harvard University Press, 1980).

11. See, for example, Michael J. Perry, "Modern Equal Protection: A Conceptualization and Appraisal," 79 *Colum. L. Rev.* 1023, 1066–67 (1979).

12. On irreversibility, see Wainwright Churchill, *Homosexual Behavior among Males* (New York: Hawthorn, 1967), 283–91; C. A. Tripp, *The Homosexual Matrix* (New York: McGraw-Hill, 1975), 251; D. J. West, *Homosexuality* (Chicago: Aldine, 1968), 266; Michael Ruse, *Homosexuality* (Oxford: Basil Blackwell, 1988), 59–62. On the early age of its formation, see John Money and A. Ehrhardt, *Man and Woman, Boy and Girl* (Baltimore: Johns Hopkins University Press, 1972), 153–201. One study hypothesizes that gender identity and sexual object choice coincide with the development of language, that is, from eighteen to twenty-four months of age. See J. Money, J. G. Hampson, and J. L. Hampson, "An Examination of Some Basic Sexual Concepts: The Evidence of Human Hermaphroditism," 97 *Bull. Johns Hopkins Hosp.* 301 (1955). Cf. Alan P. Bell, Martin S. Weinberg, and Sue K. Hammersmith, *Sexual Preference* (New York: Simon and Schuster, 1978). For a recent judicious review of the relevant scientific literature, see Richard Green, *Sexual Science and the Law* (Cambridge: Harvard University Press, 1992), chap. 4.

13. 347 U.S. 483 (1954).

14. For further developments of this skeptical theme, see Janet E. Halley, "Sexual Orientation and the Politics of Biology: A Critique of the Argument from Immutability," forthcoming, *Stanford L. Rev.;* Edward Stein, "The Relevance of Scientific Research about Sexual Orientation to Lesbian and Gay Rights," forthcoming, *Journal of Homosexuality.*

15. See Richards, *Foundations of American Constitutionalism,* 260, 280.

16. I develop this theme of moral subjugation as a form of moral slavery (relevant to claims of African Americans, women, and gays) in a work in progress, "Abolitionist Feminism, Moral Slavery, and the Constitution: 'On the Same Platform of Human Rights.' " For a related argument to similar effect, see Janet E. Halley, "The Politics of the Closet: Towards Equal Protection for Gay, Lesbian, and Bisexual Identity," 37 *UCLA L. Rev.* 915 (1989).

17. See Plato, *The Laws,* book 8, 835d-842a, in *The Collected Dialogues of Plato,* ed. Edith Hamilton and Huntington Cairns (New York: Panthenon, 1961), pp. 1401–2. On the moral condemnation of the passive role in homosexuality in both Greek and early Christian moral thought, see Peter Brown, *The Body and Society: Men, Women, and Sexual Renunciation in Early Christianity* (New York: Columbia University Press, 1988), 30, 382–83.

18. See William Blackstone, *Commentaries on the Laws of England,* vol. 4 (Chicago: University of Chicago Press, 1979), 216.

19. For further discussion of this point, see David A. J. Richards, *Toleration and the Constitution* (New York: Oxford University Press, 1989) 278–79. For a useful historical view on the social construction of homosexuality, see David Greenberg, *The Construction of Homosexuality* (Chicago: University of Chicago Press, 1988).

20. For further elaboration of this argument and its implications for American constitutional law, see Richards, *Toleration and the Constitution;* idem, *Conscience and the Constitution: History, Theory, and Law of the Reconstruction Amendments* (Princeton: Princeton University Press, 1993).

21. For relevant historical background, see David A. J. Richards, *The Moral Criticism of Law* (Encino, CA: Dickenson-Wadsworth, 1977), 78–82.

22. See, in general, Wayne R. Dynes, ed., *Encyclopedia of Homosexuality,* 2 vols. (New York: Garland, 1990).

23. See *Griswold v. Connecticut,* 381 U.S. 479 (1965); *Eisenstadt v. Baird,* 405 U.S. 438 (1972).

24. For further discussion, see Richards, *Toleration and the Constitution,* 256–61.

25. *Bowers v. Hardwick,* 478 U.S. 186 (1986).

26. For further criticism, see Richards, *Foundations of American Constitutionalism,* 209–47.

27. Justice Blackmun put the point acidly: "Like Justice Holmes, I believe that 'it is revolting to have no better reason for a rule of law than that so it was laid down in the time of Henry IV. It is still more revolting if the grounds upon which it persists [result] from blind imitation of the past.' " *Bowers,* 478 U.S. at 199 (quoting Oliver Wendell Holmes, "The Path of the Laws," 10 *Harv. L. Rev.* 457, 469 (1897)).

28. See *Plessy v. Ferguson,* 163 U.S. 537 (1896) (racial segregation held consistent with equal protection).

29. For development of this analysis, see Halley, "The Politics of the Closet."

30. See, in general, Halley, "The Politics of the Closet."

31. See Ruse, *Homosexuality,* 265–67. For a good general treatment of the need for antidiscrimination protection for homosexuals, see Richard D. Mohr, *Gays/Justice: A Study of Ethics, Society, and Law* (New York: Columbia University Press, 1988), 137–211.

32. For an excellent and probing analysis of this issue, see Harris, Note, "Permitting

Prejudice to Govern; and Kenneth I. Karst, "The Pursuit of Manhood and the Desegregation of the Armed Forces," 38 *UCLA L. Rev.* 499 (1991).

33. See Richards, *Conscience and the Constitution*, 178–91.

34. For the Supreme Court's insensitivity to this issue, see *Rostker v. Goldberg*, 453 U.S. 57 (1981) (gender-based statute, authorizing the registration for the draft of men but not of women, held constitutional).

35. Even the gender-based combat exclusion of women may in contemporary circumstances be largely unreasonable, as Kenneth Karst has recently argued with great force; see Karst, "The Pursuit of Manhood," 529–45.

36. See Karst, "The Pursuit of Manhood," 545–63.

37. See, for example, *Rostker v. Goldberg*.

31

Convictions: Theorizing Lesbians and Criminal Justice

Ruthann Robson

Those of us engaged in lesbian legal theorizing have been disinclined to address the multitude of issues provoked by the lesbian as criminal defendant. In the explicitly sexual context, the dominant assumption has been that lesbians were rarely, if ever, prosecuted for sexual crimes; I have elsewhere argued that this assumption is mistaken.[1] In the nonexplicitly sexual context, two contradictory assumptions coexist. First, the pairing of "lesbians" and "criminal" is metaphorical at best,[2] lesbians inhabiting a gendered realm of privatized tranquility. Second, the pairing of "lesbians" and "criminal" is stereotypical at worst, lesbians being stock characters in films and fiction about vampires, prisons, and ax murders. Yet these assumptions are not the only deterrents to theorizing lesbians as criminal defendants. More important, conceptualizations of equality and identity often operate as obstacles to theorizing lesbians accused or convicted of nonsexual crimes. This essay is an attempt to articulate and confront these obstacles, as well as to begin a specifically lesbian legal theorizing of the relationships between lesbianism and criminal justice.

The Politics of Equality

Politically, it has seemed most urgent for lesbian/gay/bisexual legal theorists to theorize equality, so that many other projects are relegated to a subordinate status. But the political importance of theorizing equality is not only an obstacle in terms of allocating energies and resources. The theorizing of lesbians as criminal defendants may be incompatible with a political agenda of achieving equality.

To theorize legal equality is to theorize the necessity of a departure from legal censure, especially the criminal penalties that have attached to lesbianism. The criminalization of lesbians through statutes that outlaw our sexual expressions is often considered the foundation on which our discrimination rests. In cases involving the custody of children, for example, the existence of a sodomy statute supports cross-examination of the lesbian parent regarding her sexual conduct and a judicial finding that she is an "admitted felon" as well as a "sexual deviant." Repeal of the so-called sodomy statutes has thus been an explicit goal of the lesbian/gay legal reform movement: distance from criminality is a necessary condition of equality.

The pursuit of equality has a rhetorical inconsistency with criminality. Focusing on equality, the lesbian and gay civil rights movement has sought to present images of what I call "but for" lesbians, who, "but for" their lesbianism, are "perfect." These "but for" images of lesbians are intended to contradict the pathological depictions of lesbians advanced by conservatives. However, conservatives have evinced the ability to pathologize even these "but for" images, often relying on lesbian- and gay-produced theorizing, cultural production, and research. For example, lesbian and gay work on the economic status and political power of our communities is routinely harnessed against antidiscrimination laws in a strategy with disturbing similarities to stereotypical anti-Semitism.[3] Such a climate understandably produces a reluctance to theorize on issues so easily manipulated by conservatives. While our own theorizing might attribute the disproportionate number of lesbians on death row in the United States[4] to social biases and discrimination, conservative explanations would certainly link lesbianism and murder as social—and moral—pathologies, both deserving state condemnation through legal mechanisms.

The "but for" lesbian is not merely a rhetorical strategy; she is necessary doctrinally, especially as discrimination theory has developed in the United States. In the relatively rare event that there exists a legal bar to discrimination on the basis of sexual orientation, a discrimination plaintiff must demonstrate that "but for" her lesbianism, she would have been granted the benefit, such as housing or employment. The lesbian with a criminal conviction is not a preferred plaintiff under these circumstances. As employers and others become more sophisticated, the articulation of an acceptable reason to "discriminate" becomes more important. A criminal conviction is not only socially unacceptable, it is enshrined in the positive law of many jurisdictions: conviction of a felony can foreclose the right to vote or own a firearm and is admissible as evidence of veracity. Thus, the lesbian "criminal" is inconsistent with particular litigation to achieve equality, just as a more general focus on lesbian criminality is inconsistent with the overall rhetorical strategy of normalization to achieve equality.

The overarching nature of equality discourse is also implicated in a propensity to conceptualize lesbians as victims (subjected to homophobic violence) rather than possible perpetrators of violence: rights for "innocent victims" are much more palatable than "special rights" for morally culpable actors. Even violence between lesbians is often articulated in terms of equality: the battered lesbian is entitled to the same social services, legal remedies, and criminal defenses as her heterosexual counterpart. The lesbian perpetrator remains relatively untheorized, except to the extent that she is implicitly subjected to an equality claim that she should be treated as *her* heterosexual counterpart—the male batterer—and prosecuted to the full extent of the law. She must thus be de-lesbianized: she is a "common criminal," a "stranger," a "man." In the context of criminal justice, our theoretical and political energy is directed almost exclusively to the lesbian we can valorize as the victim.

Even when a lesbian perpetrator is theorized, she tends to be recast as a victim. The case of Annette Green is illustrative. Green is reportedly the first American lesbian allowed to raise a battering defense in the prosecution for the murder of her lover. The judge accepted the defense argument that battered "woman" meant battered "person," thus allowing evidence of battering. The prosecutor argued that the battering defense was inappropriate, despite his admission that Green had been "battered. She was shot at before by the victim. She had a broken nose, broken ribs." The jury rejected the battering defense summarily, taking only two and a half hours to deliberate, which included the time necessary to agree on a jury foreperson. One interpretation is that the failure of the battering defense in the case of a lesbian is due to a reluctance to believe that lesbians can be victims.[5]

The lack of success of victimization as a trial strategy for individual lesbians is certainly worth exploring. However, I am here interested in the import of the strategy's insistence on a formal and neutral version of equality—as well as further reifying the already rigid American model of equality—that rejects (or hopelessly distorts) previous theoretical formulations of domestic violence that rely on a gendered dynamic of power. In the convoluted scenario exemplified by Annette Green, the perpetrator—this time the lesbian who has been murdered—is again relegated to the realm of the untheorizable.

The situation of Annette Green as well as many other lesbian criminal defendants demonstrates the disjuncture at the meta-theoretical level between equality paradigms and criminal justice concerns. Theorizing lesbians involved in the criminal justice system does not fit neatly into equality structures because there is no congenial category of similarly situated persons who are consistently being afforded more favorable treatment. Feminists have confronted a similar problem in attempting to theorize female criminals; the male criminal is not an appealing normative category and may even be afforded less favorable treatment in some circumstances.[6] Further, many feminists have correctly identified equality itself as a problem, rather than a solution, for women. For example, women accused of murdering their male partners could rarely meet the classic male-defined criteria for self-defense. In response, feminists developed the battered woman syndrome defense, the same defense Green unsuccessfully sought to translate into the lesbian context.

Despite its problems, equality retains a fundamental appeal. Some feminist legal theorists have, for example, criticized the battered woman syndrome defense on the basis that it is predicated on (and therefore perpetuates) female inequality.[7] Some feminist criminologists have posited an "equality" or "liberation" theory of female criminality linking women's claims for equality with hypothesized increases in women's criminal activity. Empirical findings that women are prone to be convicted more frequently, receive harsher sentences, and remain incarcerated for longer periods validate the theoretical subject, as do similar empirical findings regarding lesbians in comparison to nonlesbian women. Such invocations of equality suggest their own problems: the battered woman's syndrome defense has assisted some women; the liberation theory is consistent with an anti-equality backlash; contrary or inconclusive empirical data trivialize any theoretical inquiry.

The problems and appeals of theorizing equality have been articulated by feminists as the sameness/difference conundrum. This conundrum also structures lesbian/gay legal theorizing and strategizing.[8] As many have argued, this conundrum, with its concomitant requirement of "rights," often rigidifies our theorizing and stalls our activism. Such arguments have a magnified resonance in the criminal justice context. In criminal law, the other side of the "equality" equation is always the state—not other criminal defendants.[9] Thus, we need to be especially skeptical of the capacity of "civil" rights equality discourse to dominate our theorizing and our ultimate goals in the criminal context.

In one circumstance, however, the politics of equality should be given more attention rather than less in the criminal justice context. The theorizer and the theorized subject occupy a vexing relation of inequality. By theorizing, we risk exploiting and sensationalizing real lesbians involved in ugly and tragic events who often face prolonged incarceration. Such theorizing works to the benefit of the relatively insulated and privileged academic or other writer and ultimately entertains (often through educative pleasure) the audience.

The most flagrant example is Aileen Wuornos, known (incorrectly) as the first female serial killer.[10] To even attempt to theorize about her is to risk further exploiting and sensationalizing a person who has been so repetitiously exploited and sensationalized that her very exploitation is sufficiently notorious to warrant a documentary film: *Aileen Wuornos: The Selling of a Serial Killer*. Most media accounts are not so self-conscious, of course. The media frenzy over Wuornos produced a superficially fictionalized American made-for-television movie, *Overkill: The Aileen Wuornos Story*, as well as segments on U.S. television tabloid shows such as *Hard Copy*, *Dateline*, and *Inside Edition*, a segment on Court TV, talk show interviews, and pieces in popular magazines such as *People*, *Glamour*, and *Vanity Fair*.

Such media exploitation and sensationalization are not independent of the legal process. In the Wournos case, for example, how is the legal process affected when sheriffs and an (ex)lover/codefendant are marketing the story; a public defender is negotiating a deal with a producer; a producer is paying childhood acquaintances for exclusive rights to their memories; and an "adopted mother" and new attorney are negotiating interviews from death row? Given such events, the court proceedings not only become secondary, but may also become more subject to the forces of the market than the interests of justice.[11] Unfortunately, Wuornos's situation is not unique.[12]

I am not suggesting that lesbian theorists occupy exactly the same position as those betraying confidences for movie deals. Neither am I suggesting that defendants or prisoners possess no agency, personality, or power, nor am I suggesting that lesbian theorists should refrain from theorizing about lesbian criminal defendants. What does worry me, however, is that our treatments of lesbians accused or convicted of murder will be distinct but not sufficiently different from more obvious types of exploitation. The power differentials between theorist and inmate are vast.

Our possible exploitation of theorized subjects is related to the political dangers of promoting an aestheticization of violence through sensationalization. This aestheticization has attached to our cultural notions of serial killers in particular, and murderers in general.[13] The social problems derived from being a woman, from being a lesbian, and from being economically disadvantaged are sublimated into a romanticized version of the "outlaw." The outlaw is supremely individual, effectively erasing the "social" aspects of her condition. She can then be romanticized through true crime books, media reports, and even theories. She becomes an excitingly individual problem solved through resort to the rationalized procedures of criminal investigation and prosecution. Even as we criticize and theorize these criminal justice processes, her peril may still become our profit.

Conceptualizing Identities

In addition to the political and ethical problems with theorizing lesbians and criminal justice, there are methodological ones. These methodological problems are concretized versions of the postmodernist problematics of identity that have so preoccupied lesbian and "queer" theorizing. The first layer is the problem of identifying a lesbian presence in newspaper reports, trial transcripts, and appellate opinions; what criteria do we use? For example, the identification of lesbians on death row in the United States depends on an (implicit) articulation and application of operative criteria. Of the seventeen women who are "implicated as lesbians" by Victoria Brownworth, only a few have consistently maintained a lesbian self-identity before the circumstances leading to their conviction and during the trial and related proceedings, and continue to do so as prisoners on death row. While sexual identity is arguably always socially constructed, it is difficult to fathom more "constructing" circumstances than the threat of being executed. In other words, if one's very life is at stake, it seems one might reconceptualize one's identity to comport with identities that maximize the chance of survival. At the very least, living on death row isolated from previous communities and intimacies might cause one to change one's sexual identity.

Any self-identity must always be evaluated in the context of the relevance of lesbian identity at trial. Lesbian identity can be important as part of the prosecution's theory of the case. In the example of murder, the importance of the defendant's lesbian identity can vary with the gender identity of the victim. If the victim is a woman, then the (lesbian) defendant committed the crime out of sexual passion: the victim was the defendant's lover, former lover, or sexual threat to the defendant's relationship. If the victim is male, then the (lesbian) defendant committed the crime out of her antipathy for men.

A few recent murder prosecutions in the United States demonstrate this. In Annette Green's case, the prosecutor secured her conviction for the murder of her lover by stressing the intimate relationship of the defendant to the victim, alluding to sexual jealousy rather than self-defense as the motive for Green's violence. In the cases of Aileen Wuornos and Ana Cardona, both presently on Florida's death row for murdering males, the lesbian-as-man-hater is never explicitly articulated but virtually floats from the transcript pages. Thus, sexualized banalities of lesbians—and women in general—as jealously possessive ("hell hath no fury") or man-haters may fluctuate with the gender identity of the victim but can be marshaled toward a finding of guilt.

Another problematic aspect of lesbian identity as deployed in prosecutions is its proof. In the cases of Green, Wuornos, and Cardona, the defendant's lesbianism was not contested by the defense. In cases in which the defendant does contest her lesbian identity, the prosecutor must prove it in order to sustain that portion of the theory of its case. In the absence of a living lesbian lover who can testify to the existence of her relationship with the defendant (an issue discussed below), the evidence used to prove lesbianism is extremely troublesome and clichéd. One type of evidence is gender conformity. The defendant "dressed like a man, kept her hair cut like a man, wore men's clothing, including men's shoes."[14] While this strategy may become less effective in contemporary urban courtrooms, many women remain imprisoned for crimes proved in part by such references. Another type of evidence is nonheterosexuality. The defendant has no apparent heterosexual activity—no "boyfriend"—so must therefore be a lesbian. This strategy may be gaining ascendancy, if its popularity outside the criminal context is any indication.[15]

Defining and applying criteria for lesbian identity do not entirely resolve the methodological issues posed by identity problems. An additional methodological difficulty arises when an attempt is made to determine the relevance of lesbian identity. This question is usually posed to me as "Are you saying that these women are convicted *because* they are lesbians?" While I cannot sustain any claim of legal causation, it would also strain credulity to maintain that lesbianism plays no role in convictions. One of the few empirical studies that have been done concludes that lesbians are more likely than heterosexual women to be convicted and serve longer sentences.[16] The statistical abnormality of the number of women "implicated as lesbians" on death row in the United States is also probative.[17] As one death row expert has cautiously opined, "all other things being equal, a female offender's lesbianism would be a disadvantage rather than an advantage in the capital punishment process."[18]

Nevertheless, numerical correlations are ultimately unsatisfactory for the purposes of theorizing lesbians in the criminal justice system. Problems of methodology include not only defining lesbian identity, but isolating lesbianism as a factor. Like other lesbians, a lesbian criminal defendant is not exclusively a lesbian. Statistically, a lesbian who is a criminal defendant is probably also a woman of color and disadvantaged economically.[19] Positing ethnic, racial, or class status as the *cause* of prosecution and conviction is facile; however, empirical data that point to the statistical overrepresentation of disempowered groups within the criminal justice system confirm a social observation. There is little reason to suspect that lesbianism operates radically differently from other minority identities as a derationalizing, dehumanizing wedge between the criminal defendant and the criminal justice system as embodied by prosecutor, judge, and jury.

Another reason for the difficulty in isolating lesbianism as a consistent factor within the criminal justice system is that crimes and their trials are exceedingly particularized. Variables include the circumstances of the crime, the situations of the defendant and victim, and the location of the trial. The manner in which lesbianism is deployed may be inconsistent with its deployment in a different trial, or even within the same trial. The criminal defendant may not be the only incarnation of lesbian identity, and the prosecution may also have to grapple with lesbianism. In some instances, the victim may be implicated as a lesbian; the prosecutor must thus maintain that a crime against such a person is worth punishing. In other instances, the prosecution's star witness may be a lesbian, in which case the prosecution must maintain that she is credible. In such situations, neither the prosecution nor the defense strategy can consist of a simple condemnation (or valorization) of lesbian existence. Thus it becomes necessary to differentiate between good lesbians (worthy of protection and believable) and bad lesbians (worthy of punishment and disbelief).

As used by the prosecution, the tropes manipulated to differentiate between good lesbians and bad lesbians demonstrate an amazing versatility.[20] One of the most interesting manipulations occurs in the prosecution of Ana Cardona for the murder of her child. Cardona is portrayed as a feminized, attractive, and popular lesbian as contrasted with her (former) lover, Olivia Gonzalez-Mendoza, who is portrayed as mesmerized by Cardona. Such a construction reverses the stereotypical one in which the "bad" lesbian is identified as the more "male"-identified partner, lack of gender conformity being a sign of deviance and maleness being an indicator of a propensity toward violence.[21] Interestingly, however, the construction of Ana Cardona is consistent with the "femme fatale" trope so prominent in murder prosecutions of heterosexual women. Further, the "femme fatale" construction is conjoined in the Cardona case with another trope prominent in murder prosecutions of heterosexual women: the bad mother.[22] Although the defense argued that the actual murderer of the child was Olivia Gonzalez-Mendoza and there was testimony to support such an argument (especially at the separate penalty phase of the trial, in which the jury considered the imposition of the death penalty), Ana Cardona, as the biological mother of the victim, was the person prosecuted for a capital crime, convicted, and sentenced to death. The state attorney offered Olivia Gonzalez-Mendoza a relatively generous plea bargain in exchange for her agreement to testify against Ana Cardona. As an editorial from the *Miami Herald*, entitled "Deserved the Death Penalty," opined, "Cardona may have been the weaker partner in this union, but she was something that Gonzalez was not. She was Baby Lazaro's mother. She had the moral, legal, and every other responsibility for his welfare. She was not too weak to call the police, or HRS [the state agency responsible for child welfare], or somebody to come and get the baby."[23] In a similar case in California, the court held that the biological mother's "legal duty" to protect the child from the behavior of her lesbian lover satisfied the requirements for first degree murder although there was no evidence the biological mother ever physically harmed the child.[24]

Yet lesbianism itself may be understood as a trope in the murder prosecution of Ana Cardona. From a different perspective, centering the trope of "bad mother," lesbianism becomes an enhancement of that category. Especially in the press accounts of Ana Cardona's trial, "lesbian" functions as a suppressed intensifier, not unlike "cocaine-user" or "selfish." Similarly, in the prosecution and press coverage of Aileen Wuornos, "lesbian" functions as an adjective for "prostitute," negating the possibility that Wuornos is any storybook "heart of gold" streetwalker. In both the Cardona and Wuornos cases, the lesbian identity amplifies another identity—(bad) mother or prostitute—and becomes submerged into it.

This submersion of lesbian identity into another disparaged identity renders methodological purity impossible. Perhaps this submersion is a testament to the progress—or at least superficial shift—in contemporary life that renders it publicly treacherous to link lesbianism and murder as correlated pathologies. From a prosecutor's perspective, such an explicit linkage could risk losing the conviction (depending on the attitudes of the jurors, judge, or appellate judges) or some political prestige (depending on the attitudes of one's superiors, the local press, and the voter population). Thus, as in discrimination discourse, legal actions that are detrimental to lesbians can appear to be only coincidentally related to their lesbian identities. The assertion of the irrelevance of lesbianism can serve the state's interest.[25]

The danger for lesbian legal theorists, reformers, and activists is we will be daunted by methodological complications. Theorizing lesbians within the criminal justice system is a rather messy project, given the blurring of lesbian identities and the relevance of such identities. Despite these methodological obstacles, and despite the political and ethical problems previously discussed, I believe we must move toward theorizing the connections between lesbianism and criminal justice systems.

Toward a Lesbian Legal Theory of Criminal Justice

Identifying the obstacles to theorizing lesbians and criminal justice marks a preliminary path. Some of the equality-related problems of theorizing lesbians as criminals can be surmounted by a more expansive and radical interpretation of equality. The adages about a society being appropriately judged by its treatment of its criminals and freedom being realized only when the least fortunate are free are applicable to lesbian legal theorizing. Theorizing for the exclusive benefit of "but for" lesbians is partial at best. Thus I maintain that we must attempt to theorize—and incorporate in our legal reform agendas—lesbians accused or convicted of crimes, including violent crimes. While the project of theorizing lesbians and criminal justice with "lesbian" as its centrifugal force arguably reinstates the previously discussed obstacles to theorizing, lesbian legal theory must take up the case of criminal justice in general, and criminal defendants in particular. If it does not, then it risks being a "but for" theoretical position, which "but for" its lesbian emphasis, could be a normalized theory. Lesbian legal theory in this regard should take heed of feminist legal theory's history, a history considered by many to be marred by its accentuation of legal issues important to professional women. Nevertheless, in making criminal justice an important subject of inquiry and advocacy, we should not make equality a shibboleth that obscures the differences between civil rights and criminal justice.

Our ambitions of equality should also appropriately extend to our own work. Our theorizing must not only address but pay particular attention to the possibilities of exploitation of criminal subjects. Further, we must be wary of the sensationalization and aestheticization of violence. Lesbians convicted of murder should not be glamorized as outlaws just as they should not be dismissed as irrelevant. Both options tempt the theorist, who can make particular crimes into a "sexy" presentation at a prestigious conference, or who can decide that the issue of crime is not one that deserves attention in the present scholarly climate. The issue of advocacy in cases in which lesbianism is implicated also merits examination. While I believe our practical intercession in the area is important, I remain uncertain about the terms and conditions of that intercession. As always, it seems to me that subjecting our own involvements to rigorous reflection is extremely vital. I am not suggesting a spectacle of mutual trashing, or even self-flagellation. Instead, I believe we can aspire to (if not always achieve) an ethical consciousness about the impact and consequences of our own stake as theorizers in the realm of criminal justice.

By adopting expansive definitions, we can surmount methodological obstacles resulting from the imposition of identity criteria. I suggest that we be less interested in consistent or even articulated self-identified lesbian identifies of various actors than in the specter of lesbianism whenever it is introduced into criminal justice proceedings, however obliquely. Ultimately, I am less concerned with whether or not an individual defendant is "really" a lesbian than with the manner in which her "lesbianism" becomes pertinent. The question I am thus interested in interrogating is to what effect is lesbianism—as trope, stereotype, theory of the case, prejudice—articulated during the criminal process?

This expansive definition of identity also means that combinations of identities, be they ethnic, racial, economic, or constructed like "prostitute" or "bad mother," also merit attention. Nevertheless, I believe we must be wary of the way other identities are utilized to "trump" lesbian identity. Lesbianism becomes irrelevant for those who argue that a particular case is "really about" prostitution, or mothering, or economic status. My wariness extends to the manner in which theories of the female offender can suppress considerations of lesbianism. My argument is certainly not that prostitution, or mothering, or economic status, or gender is irrelevant. My argument is simply that we must consistently entertain the relevance of lesbianism.

Further, we must expand our methodologies. We must address complicated and particularized situations as such. While statistics can be useful, we must be wary of reasoning from statistics. We should also be wary of adopting criminal justice definitions as our own. The very definition of "crime" needs to be vigorously questioned. Given the erratic and bizarre ways our sexual acts have been and continue to be "crimes," we have more than sufficient cause to be similarly distrustful of other constructions of crime. In terms of our inquiries, we must also expand our concerns from the more easily researched and potentially glamorous crimes such as murder to the more mundane crimes of shoplifting, fraud, and drug offenses. We must also expand the subject positions to be theorized. While the purpose of this piece has been to focus on lesbians as criminal defendants, the positions of all lesbians within the criminal justice system merit interrogation. The position of the lesbian as victim of a crime has received the most previous attention, and we should not abandon that project. But I believe further expansion is necessary. For example, what does it mean for a lesbian to prosecute other lesbians within the criminal justice system?

Theorizing lesbians and criminal justice as a matter of lesbian legal theory must put lesbians at the center of its theoretical perspective. In this regard, such theorizing is no different from theorizing child custody or immigration as a matter of lesbian legal theory. At least as I conceptualize it, lesbian legal theory allows lesbian to become the centrifugal force around which all else is problematized.[26] Thus, in the criminal justice system context it requires an examination of the entire system in light of its impact on lesbians and its use of "lesbianism" in the achievement of its own goals. Such a project can benefit from the extensive work done by criminal justice critics, including feminist criminologists who continue to examine the complicated impact of criminal justice systems on women and its use of gendered stereotypes. If we consider the criminal justice system from the perspective of lesbianism—and more particularly the survival of lesbians and lesbianism—what theoretical conceptualizations of criminal justice do we develop? If we apply our politics of equality and our interrogations of identity to the categories of "criminal" and "justice" as rigorously as we have applied them to the category "lesbian," how do our theories of crime and punishment alter? Once we begin the serious task of taking criminal justice as a subject for lesbian legal theory, perhaps we will be able to intervene in actual criminal trials in ways that promote lesbian survival.

Notes

I am grateful to Victoria Brownworth for sharing her work, information, and insights on lesbians and murder. I am also grateful to participants who commented on earlier portions of this work during presentations at CUSH (Columbia University Seminar on Homosexualities) and CLAGS (Center for Lesbian and Gay Studies, City University of New York), as well as at the CLAGS Conference on "Homosexualities and Social Sciences," New York. I am also grateful for the editorial comments of Didi Herman and Carl Stychin.

1. Ruthann Robson, *Lesbian (Out)Law: Survival under the Rule of Law* (Ithaca, NY: Firebrand, 1992), 29–45.

2. The power of this perception was demonstrated to me by another gay/lesbian legal scholar who assumed that my presentation entitled "Lesbians as Criminals" concerned "lesbians and child custody."

3. In the legal literature, this argument was recently made in Robert Duncan, "Who Wants to Stop the Church: Homosexual Rights Legislation, Public Policy, and Religious Freedom," *Notre Dame Law Review* 69:393, 407–11 (1994).

4. There are approximately 2,887 persons on death row—convicted of a capital crime and sentenced to death—in the United States. Of this number, forty-one are women (approximately 1.4 percent); however, of the forty-one women, approximately seventeen are "implicated" as lesbians (approximately forty-one percent). See Victoria Brownworth, "Dykes on Death Row," *Advocate*, June 15, 1992, 62–64. I discuss the problem of implicated identity below.

5. Green's defense attorney, William Lasley, believes that the verdict is explainable by homophobia. Lasley also reports that prospective jurors were heard expressing the desire to be selected as jurors in order to "hang that lesbian bitch," and she was subjected to homophobic treatment by state personnel.

The statements of the prosecutor, Assistant State Attorney Bob Johnson, are quoted in *Gay Community News*, September 17–23, 1989, 1. The prosecutor also charged Annette Green with the highest degree of murder allowable under the applicable law, despite circumstances that comprise classic examples of lower degrees of murder, such as battering, mutual fighting, intimate relation, and diminished capacity (because of alcohol). I further discuss this case in Robson, *Lesbian (Out)law*, 158–60.

6. The feminist literature on female offenders is vast. Important works include Freda Alder, *Sisters in Crime: The Rise of the New Female Criminal* (New York: McGraw-Hill, 1975); Susan S. M. Edwards, *Women on Trial* (Manchester: Manchester University Press, 1984); Coramae Richey Mann, *Female Crime and Deliquency* (Birmingham: University of Alabama Press, 1984); and Anne Worrall, *Offending Women: Female Lawbreakers and the Criminal Justice System* (New York: Routledge, 1990). A compre-

hensive anthology including women as offenders, victims, and workers is Barbara Raffel Price and Natalie J. Sokoloff, eds., *The Criminal Justice System and Women*, 2d ed. (New York: McGraw-Hill, 1995). A useful overview of two decades of the literature occurs in Sally S. Simpson, "Feminist Theory, Crime, and Justice," *Criminology* 27 (4): 605–31 (1989).

7. See, e.g., Phyllis Crocker, "The Meaning of Equality for Battered Women Who Kill Men in Self-Defense," *Harvard Women's Law Journal* 8:121 (1985); Elizabeth M. Schneider, "Describing and Changing: Women's Self-Defense Work and the Problem of Expert Testimony on Battering," *Women's Rights Law Reporter* 9:195, 207 (1986).

8. For a discussion of this conundrum in the context of "family," see Brenda Cossman, "Family Inside/Out," *University of Toronto Law Journal* 44:1 (1994).

9. There is an argument that the other side of the equality equation is always the state, even in civil litigation. However, even to the extent that we recognize the state's implicit position with regard to civil litigation, such a recognition undergirds rather than diminishes any recognition of the power of the state's explicit position in criminal law.

10. For a discussion of whether Aileen Wuornos fits any criteria of a serial killer, such as killing for pleasure, see Phyllis Chesler, "A Woman's Right to Self Defense: The Case of Aileen Carol Wuornos," *St. John's Law Review* 66:933, 946–48 (1993). Even if Wuornos does fit the criteria, she is certainly not the first woman to do so. Chesler, 946, citing Eric Hickey, *Serial Murderers and Their Victims* (Pacific Grove, CA: Brooks/Cole, 1991), 86 (between 1800 and 1988 a total of thirty-four female serial killers have existed). See also Ann Jones, *Women Who Kill* (New York: Holt, Rhinehart and Winston, 1980), esp. 129–39 (discussing many cases, including Belle Paulson, a woman who lured a succession of men to her farm and murdered them for pecuniary gain).

11. Phyllis Chesler outlines some of these events, "A Woman's Right to Self Defense," 961–62. Chesler's most damaging observation is that because childhood acquaintances were offered payments for exclusive interviews with a producer, they may have interpreted the terms of these deals to include not cooperating with Wuornos's defense attorneys.

12. In a case involving a death sentence of a woman for the kidnapping and murder of a young girl with whom she had sex, the defendant argued at trial that she suffered from battered woman syndrome and had procured the girl and killed her at the insistence of her husband. In a recent appeal, she contended that her attorney's negotiation of publicity contracts directly influenced his trial strategy. At trial, the attorney conducted a four-day direct examination of the defendant, eliciting "lurid facts" previously ruled inadmissible. Such facts were central to his "copyrighted, 400-plus page 'appellate brief' which he has attempted to market as the basis of a book or movie." Neelley v. State, 1994 West Law 248245 (Ala. June 10, 1994).

13. The work of Jane Caputi, *The Age of the Sex Crime* (Bowling Green, Oh: Bowling Green University Press, 1987) articulates this point with relation to male serial murderers whose victims are predominantly women.

14. Perez v. State, 491 S.W.2d 672, 673, 675 (Tex. Crim. App. 1973).

15. As I discuss elsewhere, this strategy was employed in recent U. S. politics to raise the specter of lesbianism on unmarried women nominated for political office. See Ruthann Robson, "The Specter of a Lesbian Supreme Court Justice: Problems of Identity in Lesbian Legal Theorizing," *St. Thomas Law Review* 5:4398 (1993).

16. Robert Leger, "Lesbianism among Women Prisoners: Participants and Nonparticipants," *Criminal Justice and Behavior* 14 (4): 448 (1987).

17. See Brownworth, "Dykes on Death Row," 62.

18. Victor Streib, "Death Penalty for Lesbians," *National Journal of Sexual Orientation Law* 1 (1994) (an electronic journal).

19. See Pat Carlen, *Women, Crime and Poverty* (Milton Keynes, England: Open University Press, 1988); Coramae Richey Mann, "Minority and Female: A Criminal Justice Double Bind," *Social Justice* 16 (3): 160–72 (1989).

20. Defense strategies have been less explicit because of the burden of the prosecution to prove its case and the complementary lack of burden on the part of the defense.

21. This stereotyped construction is most operative in cases in which the "bad" lesbian is accused of murdering her lesbian partner.

22. The work of Marie Ashe examines the legal construction of "bad mother." Marie Ashe, "The 'Bad Mother' in Law and Literature: A Problem of Representation," *Hastings Law Journal* 43:1017 (1992). For a discussion of how the criminal law "enforces the subordinating aspects of motherhood and punishes women's resistance," see Dorothy E. Roberts, "Motherhood and Crime," *Iowa Law Review* 79:95 (1993).

23. Editorial, *Miami Herald*, April 3, 1992, 26A.

24. People v. Martin, 4 Cal. Rptr.2d 660 (5th Dist. 1992).

25. For example, the state objected to the National Center for Lesbian Rights' motion for leave to file an amicus brief on behalf on Aileen Wuornos relating to the homophobia that may have denied her a fair trial. The state argued that lesbianism was irrelevant.

26. My notions of lesbian legal theory here depend on my earlier work, notably Robson, *Lesbian (Out)Law.*

32

Colin Powell's Reflection: Status, Behavior, and Discrimination

David Chang

Proponents of civil rights for homosexuals long have sought to draw a parallel between race and sexual orientation. As race is a characteristic of birth and largely immutable, so sexual orientation has been proclaimed a characteristic of birth and largely immutable. Advocates on both sides seize the latest bits of scientific study that might support or undermine the idea that a person's sexual orientation is set at birth. The issue is important, because drawing connections—or denying connections—between racism and homophobia has been widely viewed as providing—or denying—the critical moral context in which discrimination because of sexual orientation can be deemed contrary to the nation's higher constitutional ideals.

Indeed, during the debate about lifting the ban on gays and lesbians in the military, a central question concerned the comparability between discrimination because of race and discrimination because of sexual orientation. A key figure in this debate was General Colin Powell. On the comparability of race and sexual orientation, Powell said,

> Skin color is a benign, nonbehavioral characteristic. Sexual orientation is perhaps the most profound of behavioral characteristics. Comparison of the two is a convenient but invalid argument. As Chairman of the Joint Chiefs of Staff, as well as an African-American fully conversant with history, I believe the policy we have adopted is consistent with the necessary standards of order and discipline required of the armed forces.[1]

Debates about the origin and immutability of sexual orientation—as well as focus on the choices made by homosexuals—miss the mark and preclude a

431

rigorous understanding of the relationship between discrimination because of race and discrimination because of sexual orientation. Discrimination because of sexual orientation is not so different from racial discrimination as opponents of gay rights would believe, nor is it so similar to racial discrimination as proponents of gay rights might believe.

There was a germ of truth in Powell's attempt to distinguish between race and sexual orientation. Race is, indeed, not a behavioral characteristic; physical gender, as well, is a nonbehavioral characteristic. Although not always about behavior, sexual orientation is at least defined by thoughts—thoughts that frequently are transformed through choices into action.[2] Perhaps recognizing this, some seek to draw a parallel between race and sexual orientation by arguing that homosexuality is innate and immutable. If people are born gay, as people are born black, the argument goes, then discrimination because of sexual orientation is as immoral as racial discrimination.

On closer analysis, however, whether people are born gay is beside the point. There are claims that all sorts of thoughts have innate roots. Opponents of rights for gay men and lesbians forcefully argue that rape, for example, is not less a social evil if a person has an innate inclination to rape because he was born with an XYY chromosome. Child molestation is no less a social blight if the molester's inclination was formed by genetics, childhood experience, or a combination. Furthermore, it is undeniably true that the decision to transform thoughts—whether innate or not—into action involves choice. This choice to act is the basis for many to distinguish discrimination against gays, who choose to act on their sexual orientation, from discrimination against blacks or women, who obviously make no choice in being black or female.

But here is where opponents of gay rights overstate their claim. Contrary to Powell's analysis, the issue is not simply how closely analogous are race or skin color and sexual orientation or behavior. Rather, the question concerns *discrimination* because of race and *discrimination* because of sexual orientation. Racial discrimination is frequently about choices, not simply the status of race. Once slavery ended, blacks were branded criminals not simply for being black, but for *choosing* to breach some social code of ritual manners signifying subordination.

For example, there was a time, not so long ago, when interracial marriage and sex were criminal in many states. Indeed, society's racism was particularly virulent in these contexts of marriage and sex. Under many miscegenation laws, blacks who married or had sex with whites were branded criminal. Some were lynched. This is not discrimination based on race alone—as slavery might be viewed as imprisonment at hard labor simply for being black. Rather, this was discrimination triggered by a *choice* deemed inappropriate for a black person. Despite the fact that blacks could insulate themselves from punishment by choosing not to breach social restrictions, this is a paradigm of what anyone would view as pure racial discrimination. A choice deemed appropriate for a white person—to marry a white person—is deemed inappropriate for a black person. The essence of racial discrimination is the prohibition of *choice* for one race that another race is permitted to make.

So choice is involved, whether one chooses interracial marriage or chooses to rape. But society's prohibitions of these choices are distinguishable, because the prohibition of rape is a universal prohibition. Rape is a choice prohibited to all, by virtue of being human. In contrast, the miscegenation law's prohibition of marriage is partial. Only nonwhite people are prohibited from marrying white people. Only white people are prohibited from marrying nonwhite people. The prohibited choices are not universal, and the discrimination as to who makes the various choices is a function of race.

This discrimination because of race is morally significant because it violates principles of human equality fundamental in America's post–Civil War constitutional tradition. It violates the idea that every individual has an equal birthright to pursue society's opportunities—that it is wrong to look at a newborn baby and conclude that there are certain choices some people are permitted to make that this baby, when grown, should be prohibited from making, because of some physical characteristic with which this baby was born. In contrast, a universal prohibition—such as the criminalization of rape—defines a choice that no one may make. Denying a choice to everyone, unlike denying a choice because of racist judgments about race, does not violate the principle that every individual has an equal birthright to pursue society's opportunities.

Understanding the prohibition of interracial marriage as racial discrimination, even though interracial marriage is chosen, can help us better understand both the commonality and differences between discrimination because of race and discrimination because of sexual orientation. Consider the paradigmatic discrimination against lesbians and gay men. The discrimination against men marrying men, or having sex with men, and similar discrimination against women with women are structurally gender discrimination.[3] The essence of gender discrimination is the prohibition of a *choice* for one gender that the other gender is permitted to make. This is parallel to the structural essence of racial discrimination—the prohibition of a *choice* by a person of one race that a person of another race is permitted to make. As a matter of logic, therefore, the prohibition of homosexual marriage or sex is as much gender discrimination as the prohibition of interracial marriage or sex is racial discrimination. This is so despite the fact that choice is involved. Indeed, this is so because the choice to marry or have sex that is allowed to some is denied to others *because of their gender.*

Although the prohibition of marriage and sex between people of the same gender is, indeed, pure gender discrimination, discrimination against gays in other contexts—for example, employment in the military—is a step removed from pure gender discrimination. The ban on lesbians in the military is not pure gender discrimination, because some women are permitted to choose a career in the military. Similarly, the military ban on gay men is not pure gender discrimination, as men who make one *choice* deemed inappropriate for their gender—same-sex intimacy—are prohibited from making the further *choice* of serving in the military.[4]

Is it significant as a matter of social justice—and ultimately as a matter of constitutional law—that employment, housing, and other forms of discrimination against lesbians and gay men are not pure gender discrimination, but derived from gender discrimination? To address this question we must return to the context of race. The following analogy is a speculative modification of America's social experience, but might be essential for an understanding of the structural relationship between discrimination because of race and discrimination because of sexual orientation.

Suppose that society's mores against interracial sex and marriage were more lasting and more intense than they actually have been. Suppose that people sexually attracted to people of other races were perceived as a discrete class of person—a wholly different kind of person. *Their sexual orientation is deemed wrong for a person of their race.* They are called interracialsexuals.[5] Where this sexual orientation comes from is a matter of debate. But interracialsexuals are targets of public scorn and discrimination. Not only are they prohibited from marrying and having sex, they are subject to employment discrimination, housing discrimination, and the full range of discrimination of which people who hate are capable.[6]

The prohibition of interracial marriage and sex involves pure racial discrimination, as previously discussed. But further discrimination against interracialsexuals—in employment and housing—is a step removed from pure racial discrimination. People who are black are not prohibited from choosing to be, say, teachers. Rather, black people *who choose to marry white people* are prohibited from choosing to be teachers.

Although such employment discrimination against interracialsexuals is not pure racial discrimination, but derived from pure racial discrimination in a particularly virulent context, Colin Powell, and others who are *fully committed to racial equality*, probably would not say that employment discrimination against blacks who choose to marry whites does not amount to immoral racial discrimination. For those fully committed to racial equality, it probably would not matter that race is nonbehavioral, while interracial sexuality is behavioral. Rather, the morality of this discrimination depends on the morality of the foundational discrimination, which is purely racial—the prohibition of interracial sexual liaisons.

Similarly, homosexuality, like interracialsexuality, might be behavioral, but gender, like race, is not. Although employment discrimination against homosexuals is not *pure* gender discrimination, but is derived from gender discrimination in a particularly virulent context, a society that is *fully committed to gender equality* would not say that discrimination against women who choose to have relationships with women does not amount to *immoral* gender discrimination. For people fully committed to gender equality, it would not matter that gender is nonbehavioral, while homosexuality is behavioral. Rather, the morality of discrimination against lesbians and gay men depends on the morality of the underlying discrimination, which is purely because of gender—the prohibition of homosexual liaisons.

What are the legal and political implications of the observations that (1) discrimination against gay men and lesbians in rights of marriage and sexual activity is *gender* discrimination in a particularly enduring and intense context; and (2) other forms of discrimination against lesbians and gay men are not gender discrimination per se, but are derived from this foundational gender discrimination?

First, *derivative* discrimination against gay men and lesbians—in employment, housing, and other contexts—perhaps cannot be squarely confronted until the definitional discrimination against homosexuals is first, understood as gender discrimination, and second, condemned as gender discrimination. Otherwise, opponents of gay rights will retain the forceful arguments that race (and, indeed, gender) is a matter of physical status, while homosexuality is a matter of thoughts (whether voluntary or not) and chosen actions. The moral principle that identifies *why* the state should not deny certain choices to certain people that it allows to others—the principle defining the immorality of discrimination because of gender—remains hidden. The basis for distinguishing homosexual liaisons from rape or child molestation remains hidden. The moral common ground linking the ideas that racism is wrong, sexism is wrong, and heterosexism is wrong remains obscured.

Second, because discrimination against homosexuals in the contexts of marriage and sexual activity truly is a matter of gender discrimination, *political* considerations of its propriety will be informed by society's feelings about gender discrimination and gender roles. However committed to racial equality our political culture claims to be, its understanding of and commitment to principles of gender equality is more tenuous. The Equal Rights Amendment was not ratified. The nation's ideological conscience has not yet grasped the moral parallel between racial discrimination and gender discrimination—that both racist discrimination and sexist discrimination violate the principle that each individual has an equal birthright to pursue society's opportunities.[7]

Thus one's expectations from America's legal/political community must be limited because of its ambivalent commitment to gender equality. Because discrimination against homosexuals is gender discrimination in such an intense and enduring context, widespread (i.e., national) changes in law and society will require protracted political struggle, debate, and education. Gay rights advocates must strongly articulate the principle that equal opportunity for all humans must not be restricted by prescriptions that some people should not pursue goals of which they are fully capable because of the body with which they were born—when others are permitted to pursue those goals because of the body with which they were born.

No wonder, then, that advocates of rights for gay men and lesbians have had so much difficulty persuading opponents that traditional condemnations of homosexuality as immoral are themselves immoral. The fundamental point, it seems to me, is that people will not understand why homophobia is immoral until they understand why sexism is immoral. And they will not understand why sexism is immoral until they understand not simply that racism is immoral, but *why* racism is immoral.

Lazy thinking can lead one to right conclusions as well as to wrong. Our first task is to ensure that social truths that have been achieved through years of struggle become not thoughtless platitudes, but the product of moral understanding capable of growth. It is not enough to know that racism is wrong. The important point is to know *why*.

Notes

1. Scott Tucker, Panic in the Pentagon, *Humanist* 53 (May–June 1993): 41–45 (quoting Powell letter to Rep. Pat Schroeder). Powell also said, "The presence of homosexuals in the force would be detrimental to good order and discipline, for a variety of reasons, principally relating around the issue of privacy. I think it would be very, very difficult to accommodate [homosexuality] into the armed forces." Transcript of Question and Answer Session at U.S. Naval Academy, Jan. 11, 1993.

2. Cf. Andrew Sullivan, The Politics of Homosexuality: A New Case for a New Beginning, *New Republic* 208, no. 19 (May 10, 1993): 24. Sullivan stated, "Race is in no way behavioral; sexuality, though distinct from sexual activity, is profoundly linked to a settled pattern of behavior"(31).

3. See, e.g., David Chang, Conflict, Coherence, and Constitutional Intent, 72 *Iowa L. Rev.* 825–28 (1987); Sylvia A. Law, Homosexuality and the Social Meaning of Gender, 1988 *Wis. L. Rev.* 187, 230–32 ("History suggests that a primary purpose and effect of state enforcement of heterosexuality is to preserve gender differentiation and the relationships premised upon it. Thus, constitutional restraints against gender discrimination must also be applied to laws censuring homosexuality. . . . Wholly apart from the question of whether homosexuality is a constitutionally suspect classification, laws barring marriage of two people of the same sex discriminate on the basis of gender."). Rex Lee, A Lawyer Looks at the Equal Rights Amendment 65 (1980).

4. It is perhaps more accurate to say that under the "don't ask, don't tell" policy, men who make the choice to reveal their sexual orientation are prohibited from making the further choice of serving in the military.

5. Cf. Samuel Marcossen, Harassment on the Basis of Sexual Orientation: A Claim of Sexual Discrimination under Title VII, 81 *Geo L. Rev* 1, 6 (1992) (arguing that a "state law which criminalizes an individual's 'preference' for sexual relations with persons of a race other than her own—we may call such persons 'miscegenosexuals'— would fall on equal protection grounds as readily as did the law banning interracial marriages.").

6. A social construct of interracialsexuality and its condemnation is not so far removed from historical reality as might at first appear. Fear of interracial sexual liaison has been declared "the principle around which the whole structure of segregation of the Negroes—down to disenfranchisement and denial of equal opportunities on the labor market—is organized. . . . Every single measure is defended as necessary to block 'social equality' which in turn is necessary to prevent 'intermarriage.' " Gunnar Myrdal, *An American Dilemma* 587 (1944).

7. Furthermore, many might reject the notion that discrimination against homosexuals in contexts of marriage and sexual liberty is, in fact, discrimination because of gender. The American polity has a history of similar lapses in rationality in understanding the prohibition of interracial marriages as racial discrimination. When roles are so deeply entrenched that they seem part of nature's order or God's Will, whether those roles were of racial homogeneity or sexual heterogeneity, many fail to see that discrimination based on race or gender is, indeed, *because of* race or gender.

33

Corpus Juris (Hetero)Sexualis: Doctrine, Discourse, and Desire in *Bowers v. Hardwick*

Kendall Thomas

Heterosexuals don't practice sodomy.
—Senator Strom Thurmond

In *Bowers v. Hardwick*,[1] the U.S. Supreme Court was asked to consider the constitutionality of a Georgia criminal statute prohibiting "sodomy"; the "anti-sodomy" law covered a broad range of private sexual practices between consenting adults, including, but not limited to, those involving individuals of the same sex.[2] Michael Hardwick, the Georgia citizen who challenged the statute, sought a broad judgment from the Supreme Court regarding the "facial" constitutionality of the law; that is, Hardwick argued that the federal Constitution precluded the Georgia legislature from punishing *any* private consensual instance of the sexual activities interdicted by its "anti-sodomy" statute, regardless of the marital status or sex of those who violated it. The Supreme Court, however, resolutely avoided judgment on that broad issue The Court took the view that the only question properly before it in *Hardwick* went to the constitutionality of the Georgia law as applied to private sexual practices between consenting adults of the same sex, which the Court denominated "homosexual sodomy." Having thus narrowed the scope of its inquiry, the Court went on to uphold the constitutionality of Georgia's "anti-sodomy" law, at least as it had been applied to Michael Hardwick. The closely divided Court concluded in an opinion by Associate Justice Byron R. White that the federal Constitution does not "[confer] a fundamental right upon homosexuals to engage in sodomy," and thus cannot support judicial invalidation of "the laws of many States" that "make such conduct illegal and have done so for a very long time."[3]

The decision in *Hardwick* has given rise to a considerable body of critical commentary in legal circles. Most of these discussions have centered around the question of whether the Court's refusal to declare the Georgia statute unconstitutional comports with or contradicts its earlier decisions regarding state regulation of private sexual conduct.[4] However, this focus on the Court's refusal to extend the doctrine of constitutional privacy has obscured another, equally important dimension of the *Hardwick* opinion: its place in the broader archive of cultural texts about the meaning of legal identity and sexual difference. Attention to the larger social significance of the *Hardwick* case requires analysis not so much of the doctrine as of the discursive strategies the Court employed to explain the doctrinal grounds on which the decision rests. In my view, the failure of academic lawyers to attend to the rhetorical register of *Hardwick* may be traced to the undertheorized and ultimately incomplete understanding of the rhetorical forms in which Supreme Court opinions are cast.

It is fair to say that until quite recently, professional students of the Supreme Court have been conditioned to train their interpretive energies on the logic, rather than the language, of the Court's opinions; in short, they have viewed the rhetoric of Supreme Court analysis and argument mainly as a tool for communicating rules of constitutional law, which are taken to be separate and distinct from that rhetoric itself. Happily, a number of legal scholars have come to reject this orthodox view of the relation between legal discourse and legal doctrine.[5] Against the standard view, proponents of the "linguistic" turn in legal scholarship have sought to demonstrate that a judicial opinion (or for that matter, any legal text) is something more (and other) than its juridic propositions. In this critical perspective, a judicial decision is a complex combination of rules and rhetoric that cannot be understood without rigorous attention to its discursive dimensions, to what might loosely be termed its "figural" or "metaphorical" elements.

Our understanding of any particular legal judgment will remain incomplete unless we are willing to suspend the traditional legal distinctions between idea and expression, between reasoning and rhetoric, between substance and style. Sustained engagement with the language of law as such alerts us to those aspects of the judicial decision that provide law with its rhetorical conditions of possibility but elude the rationalist interpretive protocols of doctrinal analysis, or more dangerously, unsettle them altogether. In the terms of Jean-François Lyotard, we must be prepared to exploit the theoretical advantages that flow from sustained investigation of the incommensurability, even antagonism, between the putatively rational "discourse" of constitutional interpretation and the pre-rational rhetorical "figures" that visibly undermine them.[6] Indeed, in seeking to overcome the conceptual and political limits imposed by rationalist doctrinal analysis, the rhetorical reading of the Court's decision in *Bowers v. Hardwick* offered here will most emphatically not approach that text "as if it were free of psychic and sexual processes, as if it operated outside the range of their effects"[7] I propose, in short, to undertake something like a psychoanalysis of juridical discourse.

I focus in this discussion on those passages in the *Hardwick* decision that, in my view, most clearly demonstrate the psychic mechanisms of identification around which the Court's interpretation and adjudication of the law of "homosexual sodomy" revolve. As I use it here, the term "identification" may be understood in something like its standard psychoanalytic sense, to refer to the "[p]sychological process whereby the subject assimilates an aspect, property or attribute of the *other* and is transformed, wholly or partially, after the model the other provides. It is by means of a series of identifications that the personality is constituted and specified."[8] My use of the concept includes the defense mechanism known in psychoanalysis as "identification with the aggressor," the transformative process whereby a subject incorporates aspects of a feared aggression in a reversal of roles in which "the aggressed turns into the aggressor."[9]

Early on in the opinion he wrote for the majority, Associate Justice Byron R. White suggests that the issue presented in *Bowers v. Hardwick* demands something more than conventional constitutional analysis. This case, he opines, "also calls for some judgment about the limits of the Court's role in carrying out its constitutional mandate."[10] After concluding that the modern privacy cases do not justify constitutional protection of consensual "homosexual sodomy," and dismissing as "at best, facetious" the idea that the asserted right can be brought within the Court's more capacious formulations protecting rights " 'deeply rooted in this Nation's history and tradition' or 'implicit in the concept of ordered liberty,' "[11] White turns from the local question of the constitutionality of the challenged statute. Responding to the felt necessity to consider the larger structural problem presented by the case, White offers the following remarks about the likely institutional consequences of a judgment in Hardwick's favor.

[We are not[inclined to take a more expansive view of our authority to discover new fundamental rights imbedded in the Due Process Clause. The Court is most vulnerable and comes nearest to illegitimacy when it deals with judge-made constitutional law having little or no cognizable roots in the language or design of the Constitution. That this is so was painfully demonstrated by the face-off between the Executive and the Court in the 1930s, which resulted in the repudiation of much of the substantive gloss that the Court had placed on the Due Process Clauses of the Fourth and Fourteenth Amendments. There should be, therefore, great resistance to expand the substantive reach of those Clauses, particularly if it requires redefining the category of rights deemed to be fundamental. Otherwise, the Judiciary necessarily takes to itself further authority to govern the country without express constitutional authority. The claimed right pressed on us today falls far short of overcoming this resistance.[12]

This passage confronts us with a complex congeries of conflicting ideas and images. Conceptually speaking, the argument made here is a familiar one; indeed, it approaches orthodoxy.[13] White plainly fears that a decision upholding the "claimed constitutional rights of homosexuals to engage in acts of sodomy that is asserted in this case"[14] would undermine the authority of the Court and erode the fragile foundations of judicial review. White's recollection of the "face-off between the Executive and the Court in the 1930s" evokes the memory of the humiliations the Court suffered as a result of its "substantive due process"[15] decisions in *Lochner v. New York*[16] and its progeny.

The unhappy history of the *Lochner* era may arguably account for the *Hardwick* Court's stated fear of the potentially catastrophic consequences that a ruling in Hardwick's favor might hold for the institution of judicial review; it does not explain the precise and peculiar linguistic means by which that fear is expressed. It is to this element of White's judicial style that I now want to turn.

Reading this passage from *Hardwick*, one cannot help but note the brutal forcefulness of the figural strategies White deploys to develop his argument against the claim "pressed" on the Court by Michael Hardwick. Several points could be made about the "ideological imagery"[17] in which White's argument unfolds, but I will confine myself to two observations that will lead to my larger thesis. The first feature of this text that commands attention is the striking dissonance between the position of principled judicial self-restraint defended in *Bowers v. Hardwick* and the passionately unrestrained terms in which that defense is conducted. The radical discontinuity between White's prudential narrative about the dangers of substantive due process doctrine and the overheated style in which that narrative and its supposed lessons are cast seems odd—especially in an opinion that begins with a promise to confine its analytic scope to the narrow issue at hand, namely, "whether the federal Constitution confers a fundamental right upon homosexuals to engage in sodomy":

> This case does *not* require a judgment on laws against sodomy between consenting adults in general. . . . It raises *no* question about the right or propriety of state legislative decisions to repeal their laws that criminalize homosexual sodomy, or of state-court decisions invalidating those laws on state constitutional grounds.[18]

The rhetorical excesses in which White indulges are all the more remarkable in light of his argument that *Hardwick* "calls for some judgment about the limits of the Court's role in carrying out its constitutional mandate."

A second and equally striking feature of the passage is its curiously apocalyptic tone. Adapting a concept made famous by the historian Richard Hofstadter, we might say that White's language is an exemplary instance of the "paranoid style" in American constitutional Law.[19] White paints an ominous picture of the "vulnerable" position in which the Court places itself: reliance on substantive due process doctrine to find rights that cannot be directly traced to the language of the Constitution would bring the Court to the brink of institutional "illegitimacy." To extend the right of privacy to "homosexual sodomy" would be to start down a primrose path of constitutional principle that can only lead to institutional perdition. The Court leaves little doubt that it is "unwilling to start down that road."[20]

To my mind, the *Hardwick* decision marks the textual site of an important institutional "representation" in the sense in which Stuart Hall has elaborated that term. For all its apparent passivity, White's stylistic strategy entails an "active work of selecting and presenting, of structuring and shaping," a productive practice of *"making things mean."*[21] What emerges from the figural field of the Court's opinion in *Hardwick* is a distinct image of heterosexuality, homosexuality, and the affective ties that bind them together. The neutered, impersonal "it" White uses to describe pronominally the position in which he and his colleagues find themselves fails to mask the libinally resonant character of the Court's rhetorical representations of "its" institutional identity. If we attend carefully to White's language in this passage, we can begin to see the operations and effects of the psychosexual fantasy that provides the legal result in *Hardwick* with its social ground.

What I am suggesting here is that the rhetorical register of White's argument may be taken as a sign that the claimed right in *Bowers v. Hardwick* (and by extension, the individual in whose name that right has been asserted) provokes fears on the part of the Supreme Court that go far beyond the perceived threat to its judicial authority. The "paranoid style" of *Bowers v. Hardwick* is a symptomatic figuration of a deeper and different anxiety. For the writer of this opinion, a decision in Hardwick's favor would somehow not only undermine the authority of the Court. A decision for Hardwick would effectively "emasculate" the Court by undermining the patriarchal (hetero) sexual ideologies and identities on which American constitutional law ultimately rests. In *Hardwick*, the claimed right to commit "homosexual sodomy" is thought (or not so much thought as phantasmatically represented) to be a threatened attack on patriarchal power. As White's reference to the shameful "face-off" during the 1930s between Franklin Roosevelt and the Supreme Court suggests, the *Hardwick* case carries a traumatic force and engenders a sense of panic among the members of the Court that may fairly be described as the judicial equivalent of castration anxiety.

Although the opinion moves rapidly through a whole series of sexually loaded images, the chief figuration by which the text of *Hardwick* gives voice to a fear that dare not (literally) speak its name may be seen in the terms of White's argument regarding the "limits of the Court's role in carrying out its constitutional mandate." In what is perhaps the most interesting aspect of the *Hardwick* decision, the Court positions itself in relation to Michael Hardwick and his constitutional claim in a series of imaginary identifications whose figural force eventually spins out of control. The images of sexual and gender identity that underwrite White's representation of the Court's institutional identity turn a perverse twist on the thesis of the great constitutionalist Alexander Bickel that judicial review "is at least potentially a deviant institution in a democratic society."[22]

We would do well to recall in this connection the legitimating role that rhetorical appeals to the ideology of fatherhood have historically played in American constitutional discourse. In America, the law of the Constitution is the "Law-of-the-(Founding)-Father(s)." Discussions of the judiciary's place in the American constitutional scheme reveal a similar reliance on "paternal metaphor": the "name' of the judge is the "Name-of-the-Father." Some sixty years ago, in one of the first efforts to apply psychoanalytic categories to the analysis of legal consciousness in America, Jerome Frank argued that the "basic myth" of American law was the myth of the "Judge-as-Infallible-Father."[23] For Frank, this myth represented a reinscription of the childhood image of the "Father-as-Infallible-Judge."

This patriarchal vision of judges and judgment informs the doctrine of "originalism" that has been so fiercely debated in American constitutional law throughout its history. According to this doctrine, the proper role of the Supreme Court is to conform its interpretations of the text of the Constitution to either the original intentions or understandings of the "Founding Fathers." If the Supreme Court is the contemporary voice of the Constitution, its legitimacy can remain secure only if the justices remain faithful to the call across the centuries of the men who wrote and ratified the document.[24]

Given this mythic backdrop, one would think that the conceptual organization of the Court's constitutional analysis in *Hardwick* would be bound to a narrative system whose chief figure would be that of stolid patriarchal identity. Remarkably, however, in *Bowers v. Hardwick* this predominant, traditional image of the Supreme Court Justice as Father undergoes a discursive sea change, or should I say sex change. For the institutional subject-position figured in the text of White's opinion begins to evoke, alongside the image of the "Judge-as-Father," a vision of the "Judge-as-Mother," in language whose logical entailments would lead the collective mind of the Court to uncomfortable conclusions.

White mobilizes "maternal metaphor" to generate a constellation of ideas and images that allow him to avoid the work of reasoned constitutional analysis and argument. The *Hardwick* decision stages a figural reversal by which the justices assume the name of Justitia. Situating itself in the place and position of a woman (or more precisely, within the cultural codes of femininity), the *Hardwick* Court seeks to persuade readers of its institutional chastity. Fidelity to the "language and design" of the "Law-of-the-(Founding)-Father(s)" demands "great resistance" to Hardwick's attempted seduction of the Court and the "illegitimacy" to which a betrayal of that law would lead. Since "homosexual activity" bears "[n]o connection" to "family, marriage, or procreation," it cannot "qualify for recognition"[25] as a species of constitutional privacy. Since Michael Hardwick's asserted "right to engage in homosexual sodomy" is "not readily identifiable in the Constitution's text," [26] judicial invalidation of Georgia's "anti-sodomy" law would represent an act of interpretive adultery, whose shameful outcome can only be the birth of a "bastard" right with no legitimate textual "roots" or claim to the "Name-of-the-(Founding)-Father(s)."

What is the meaning of this discursive transformation of the institutional image of the Supreme Court in *Bowers v. Hardwick* from a subject-positionality of "masculine" activity to "feminine" (aggressive) passivity? The beginnings of an answer to this question may be found in Leo Bersani's essay "Is the Rectum a Grave?" [27] Bersani argues there that the regnant representation of the gay male homosexual in the homophobic American mind is that of "a grown man, legs high in the air, unable to refuse the suicidal ecstasy of being a woman." [28] Bersani contends that this image is so terrifying in the patriarchal masculinist mind because it conjures up the sodomitical spectacle of a man in a passive (i.e., female) position, a position that, at least in the psychic economy of the male heterosexual, entails a horrifying abdication of power. The gay man's rectum is a "grave in which the masculine ideal . . . of proud subjectivity is buried." [29] Anal eroticism among men must therefore be repudiated (in psychoanalytic terms "sublimated"), since it poses a threat to the phallic law of masculine heterosexuality and thus (in the homophobic imaginary) to masculine identity as such. [30]

What makes *Hardwick* so fascinating a text in the juridical archive of discursive heterosexual identification is the vertiginous instability of its formation: the opinion wildly veers back and forth between masculine and feminine polarities. The Court's rhetorical contortions in *Hardwick* reveal the desperate lengths to which the paranoid judicial imagination is willing, at least figurally, to go in order to defend itself from a constitutional claim that "gnaws at the roots of [the] male heterosexual identity" [31] that subtends the Court's institutional self-image.

In order to deny Michael Hardwick's claim of constitutional privacy, the "Father-Judges" of the Supreme Court do not hesitate to abandon the paternal metaphor through which the justices have traditionally represented the Court's role in our constitutional scheme, and the patrilineal identification from which a good measure of its cultural authority has historically derived. However, the bonds between the cultural "law" of normative male heterosexuality and American constitutional law are so close that the asserted right to commit "homosexual sodomy" Michael Hardwick has "pressed" on the justices provokes nothing less than a crisis of institutional representation. This panic finds displaced expression in the wild veering of subjective standpoint(s) from which the Court's analysis of Hardwick's claim is conducted. It is as if Justice White needs to go "both ways": only a protean subject position can enable the *Hardwick* Court to manage the contradictions posed by its unwillingness to extend constitutional privacy jurisprudence to a case whose facts in many ways made it "the most private of all [the] privacy cases." [32] Over and above the rule of the case, the potentially destabilizing effects of the issue posed in *Hardwick* seem to require this presumptively heterosexual Court to perform a radical act of rhetorical dis-identification with the very figure of the male homosexual. Faced with a constitutional question that assaults its members' institutional and individual identities, the Supreme Court can only imagine or fear itself in a "vulnerable," unmanly, and perforce effeminized position. If "homosexual sodomy" is "an offense of 'deeper malignity' than rape," the Supreme Court must meet its dangers with "utmost resistance."[33] This resistance is inscribed in the rhetorical politics of the *Hardwick* opinion itself.

My contention here is not simply a negative claim. The language of the *Hardwick* Court permits it to resist Hardwick's attempt to win constitutional recognition of a right to engage in "homosexual sodomy," a refusal that flies in the face of its earlier privacy decisions. But that is not all. In a sense, the Court's effeminized posture of "weakness" is also its strength. The maternal metaphor to which White resorts allows him to reject Hardwick's attack on the Georgia "anti-sodomy" statute from a point of symbolic identification that figurally protects the Court from the dangers that simply mentioning sexual pleasure between men poses to the paternal law. If "homosexual sodomy" is a "crime not fit to be named," not even the "Father-Judges" of the Supreme Court can break that linguistic taboo without first submitting to a discursive "sex change" or "unmanning" that removes them from "the category of men" on whom the male homosexual preys.

Nonetheless, there is a sense in which the *Hardwick* Court's imaginary cross-identification across the gender divide unwittingly transposes the psychosocial difficulties raised by the case into another key. For the resistance to Hardwick that the Court's figural and phantasmagoric transsexualization into a woman makes possible cannot, by the nature of the case, fully secure its intended ratification of the masculinist heterosexual ideal. Like all acts of sexual identification, the Supreme Court's attempt to bind its institutional consciousness to the image and ideology of patriarchal male heterosexuality fails fully or finally to succeed.

The *Hardwick* Court's attempted stabilization of male heterosexual identity is doomed from its inception by the form of the figural logic by which it is governed. This is because the inaugural gesture of gender cross-identification always already entails incorporation of the very (passive) position by which the male homosexual body is phantasmagorically and, in this case, phobically conceived. In the final instance, the ideological imperatives that drive the *Hardwick* Court's decision are such that homophobic dis-identification with the aggressive male homosexual body of Michael Hardwick forces a now effeminized legal consciousness to identify with the regnant representation of the dangerous figure whose constitutional rights the decision's doctrinal contortions take such pains to deny. Homophobic dis-identification paradoxically results in homosexual "identification with the aggressor."

Moreover, the Court's construction of its identity in the text of the *Hardwick* decision may be taken as an evidentiary instance of Freud's claim that "all human beings are capable of making a homosexual object-choice and have in fact made one in their unconscious."[34] If "[the] maintenance of heterosexual identity is dependent upon active avoidance of that psychic reality,"[35] the identificatory strategy pursued in the text of the *Hardwick* decision represents a massive failure. The *Hardwick* Court cannot escape the reality that the law of heterosexuality finds its normative foothold in the very figure it views with such contempt. In the gendered "switch" from paternal to maternal metaphor, something happens: the homophobic discourse of *Hardwick* provides a dysphoric point of (re)entry for its (homosexual) repressed.

As I have argued, a careful reading of the text demonstrates that the language of the *Hardwick* opinion in fact undermines, and ultimately overtakes, the Court's putatively detached and disinterested logic. The figural "unconscious" of the text demonstrates that because of political commitments that he either cannot or will not acknowledge, Justice White is finally unable to follow through with his professed intention to avoid the dark domain of desire that a serious judicial inquiry into the legal imposition of compulsory heterosexuality would lead the Court. Obviously, I mean to evoke the expansive understanding of "desire" developed in the Freudian theory of the libido, for which the term refers to the full continuum of human emotions ranging from love to hatred. My point here is that in *Hardwick*, the voice of desire is "imbedded" in the "very delirium of metonymy"[36] by which the "Court" (itself a metonymic figure) anxiously articulates its "vulnerability" and mobilizes its powers of "resistance" to the claim "pressed" by Michael Hardwick. By the end of the *Hardwick* opinion, the text has confessed with equal insistence the very interest in homosexuality that White has so insistently disavowed: the rhetoric of *Bowers v. Hardwick* is shot through with the traces of the homophobic passion whose relevance the Court's decision has taken such great pains to deny. That passion eclipses the cool constitutional reason by which the Supreme Court claims to be bound, and belies White's contention that the *Hardwick* decision has nothing to do with the "imposition of the Justices' own choice of values" regarding the legal regulation of gay and lesbian sexuality.

In *Hardwick*, the Supreme Court does not calmly reason about homosexuality, but rather rages irrationally against it. The rhetoric of the *Hardwick* decision discursively makes and marks the sexual difference between heterosexuality and homosexuality that provides homophobia with its conditions of possibility. As a textual representation and ratification of normative heterosexuality, then, the Court's decision in *Hardwick* is not merely about the constitutional legitimacy of the politics of homophohia, but is itself an instance of the paranoid juridical forms that politics can sometimes take. I should note once again that the doctrinal step the Supreme Court was asked to take in *Hardwick* was quite conservative: Hardwick's lawyers modestly argued that the private, consensual sexual practices for which he was arrested were not different in any relevant aspect from those to which the Supreme Court had accorded constitutional protection in its earlier privacy decisions. In language to which I have already referred, White responds to this assertion of legal identity between *Hardwick* and cases such as *Griswold v. Connecticut*[37] and *Roe v. Wade*[38] by erecting a rhetorical wall of sexual difference between "family, marriage, or procreation on the one hand and homosexual activity on the other":[39] "[W]e think it evident that none of the rights announced in those cases bears any resemblance to the claimed constitutional right of homosexuals to engage in acts of sodomy that is asserted in this case."[40]

This discourse of sexual difference enables the *Hardwick* Court to sustain its doctrinal refusal to extend the protections of constitutional privacy to gay men and lesbians. A rhetorical reading of the text of *Hardwick* suggests that the sexual difference between heterosexuality and homosexuality stressed by White is not a cause, but rather an effect of the decision. As we have seen, this metalepsis produces a destabilizing effect on the very notion of heterosexual identity, without which the idea of homosexual difference makes no sense. This destabilization (or should I say devaluation) of heterosexual identity is the cost of the sexuated (ex)change in subject positions by which the Supreme Court distances itself rhetorically from Michael Hardwick and his constitutional claim, whose workings I have sought to show here.

By way of conclusion, I want to venture a few remarks about the implications that this reading of textually constructed sexual difference in *Hardwick* hold for contemporary critiques of identity politics in gay and lesbian theory. To my mind, the rhetorical reading proffered here of the (hetero)sexuated figural logic of *Hardwick* points up the need for a more precise understanding of ideologies of sexual difference than the emerging critique of gay and lesbian identity politics in American legal scholarship has thus far offered. Writing from this critical perspective, one commentator on the case has argued that the assertion of homosexual identity in *Hardwick* was "simply the flip side of the same rigidification of sexual identities by which our society simultaneously inculcates sexual roles, normalizes sexual conduct, and vilifies 'faggots' "[41] and straitjackets "those who engage in homosexual sex into a fixed identity specified by their *difference* from heterosexuals."[42] This argument holds that *Hardwick* shows the dangers of too insistent an emphasis on the "homosexuality" of the sexual practices that were prohibited by the Georgia "anti-sodomy" law upheld by the Supreme Court. According to this account, when Michael Hardwick's lawyers decided to describe their client as a "practicing homosexual" in the complaint filed on his behalf, they unwittingly undermined the force of Hardwick's essentially identitarian claim—that his interests in sexual privacy were constitutionally indistinguishable from those of heterosexuals.

I want to suggest that we should be suspicious of this strategy of argument. In my view, this critique of a rights discourse based on the assertion of homosexual identity misses the mark. I am especially troubled by the notion that the "obsessive focus"[43] in *Hardwick* on homosexual difference—on the "particularly homosexual aspect of homosexual sex"[44]—was a feature of the Supreme Court's decision for which the idea of gay and lesbian identity as such must bear the blame. The proposition that the inclusionary claims of identity politics are at base indistinguishable from those made on behalf of an exclusionary politics can be sustained only if one fails to take into account the different power positions from which, as well as the purposes for which, these appeals to identity have been made.

The emerging legal critique of the assertion of difference in gay and lesbian identity politics ignores a crucial distinction between two very different types of claims, a distinction we overlook at our peril. One could understand the assertion of homosexual difference to be an ontological claim that the physical difference between homosexual and heterosexual acts produces a difference in sexual identity. This is a categorical claim that, for my part, I think untenable. However, as I have argued elsewhere,[45] one could rest the argument for homosexual difference and its assertion on a very different ground. This argument starts from the proposition that there is an undeniable historical difference between the societal treatment and consequences of homosexual acts, a particularity that has forged a distinct social place and position for those with whom same-sex practice is identified. As a historical matter, then, the proclamation of homosexual identity does not, and need not, appeal to some common characterological essence that sets those who embrace that identity apart from those who do not; rather, this assertion of homosexual identity derives from a common historical experience of domination. This position does not contend that the "homosexual" is a "personage," or "a type of life, a life form, and a morphology";[46] it does insist that the idea of a homosexual identity be understood as a historically "entrenched contingency."[47] To state the point another way, this latter assertion of homosexual identity, as well as the pursuit of a politics based on that identity, revolves not around an essentialist claim that homosexuals are *different*, but around a historical claim that they have been treated *differently*. Viewed in this light, we might begin to think about the politics of gay and lesbian identity as a practice whose best and most basic commitments emerge in historical moments of critical calculation regarding our collective *situation*, not from a timeless metaphysical faith in our collective sensibility.

I am persuaded that the phobic figural representations by which the Supreme Court produces a hierarchical differentiation or "scaling"[48] of homosexual and heterosexual acts and agency in the *Hardwick* decision provide an indispensable map of the ideological situation with which contemporary gay and lesbian politics must now contend. The rhetorical politics of the *Hardwick* opinion suggests that we are indeed in treacherous terrain. *Hardwick* offers a textual proof from law of the social constructionist claim that the idea of a distinct "homosexual" identity (or for that matter a distinct "heterosexual" one) is a discursively constructed ideological category, and thus false. The ideological character of the "homosexual" identity fabricated in *Hardwick* resides in its constitutive "confusion of linguistic with natural reality."[49] By means of this confusion, the Court erects a thoroughly imaginary figure of the (male) "homosexual," in "willful blindness"[50] to the fact that both this figure and the act of "homosexual sodomy" of which he was accused rest on equally imaginary epistemological grounds.

This incontrovertible insight into the figural and therefore fictive foundations of "homosexual" and "heterosexual" identities is important, because it allows us to expose and attack the "regime of truth" on which the *Hardwick* opinion stands. However, the fact that the *Hardwick* Court's rhetorical representations carry the force of law should caution against the very different inference that because the "homosexual" and "heterosexual" identities the Supreme Court constructed in its decision are false, they are therefore not real. Stated bluntly, we ought not forget that conviction under the statute Michael Hardwick was charged with violating could be punished by imprisonment for up to twenty years. Nor should we ignore the fact that the *Hardwick* case took place against a backdrop of a long history of violence against "homosexuals" whose bloody consequences have been all too real.[51] The lesson I take from my reading of *Hardwick* is this: in the law, the rhetorical politics of "homosexual" and "heterosexual" identities matters. To be sure, we must remain mindful of difficulties that attend the very notion of sexual identity. At the same time, though, we must recognize that the strategic negotiation of those difficulties is a challenge that we cannot simply refuse. In *Hardwick*, the Supreme Court taught us that the assertion of sexual difference, and an oppositional politics that engages that difference, are practices that gay and lesbian Americans finally cannot do without.

To the memory of Willie L. Moore and Anthony Wayne Thomas.

Notes

1. 478 U.S. 186 (1986)

2. Ga. Code Ann. Sec. 16-6-2 (1985)

3. 478 U.S. at 191.

4. See, e.g., Daniel O. Conkle, "The Second Death of Substantive Due Process," 62 Ind. L.J. 215, 221–37 (1987); Annamay T. Sheppard, "Private Passion Public Outrage: Thoughts on *Bowers v. Hardwick*: Precedent by Personal Predilection," 54 *U. Chi. L. Rev.* 648 (1987).

5. See, e.g., the essays collected in the University of Texas Law School on "Law as Literature," 60 *Texas L. Rev.* 373 (1982); Peter Goodrich, *Legal Discourse* (1987); Stanley Sanford Levinson and Steven Mailloux, eds., *Interpreting Law and Literature: A Hermeneutic Reader* (1988); Stanley Fish, *Doing What Comes Naturally* (1989).

6. Jean-François Lyotard, *Discours, Figure* (1971).

7. Jacqueline Rose, "Margaret Thatcher and Ruth Ellis," 6 *New Formations* 3 (1988).

8. J. Laplanche and J.-B. Pontalis, *The Language of Psychoanalysis* 205 (Donald Nicholson-Smith trans., 1973).

9. Id. at 209. This is an appropriate point at which to note that my discussion of "heterosexuality" and "homosexuality" in these pages is limited to male varieties of these identities, and their identificatory expressions. This is not because I believe male

heterosexuality and homosexuality are the paradigm case of either of these two forms of sexuality; I hold no such view. I restrict my discussion to masculinist models of heterosexuality and homosexuality only because these govern the logic of the *Hardwick* Court's own analysis.

10. 478 U.S. at 190.

11. 478 U.S. at 194.

12. 478 U.S. at 194–95.

13. See, e.g., *Moore v. City of East Cleveland, Ohio,* 431 U.S. 494 at 544 (1976) (White, J., dissenting). Using almost the same language he would later employ in his opinion for the Count in *Hardwick,* Justice White condemned the *Moore* Court for overturning the criminal conviction (under a city housing ordinance) of a woman who had refused to obey an order to remove a grandson she was caring for at her home.

14. 478 U.S. at 191.

15. Broadly speaking, the doctrine of "substantive due process" is the conceptual basis for the asserted judicial power to invalidate laws that deprive individuals of life, liberty, or property without regard to the fairness or unfairness of the legal procedures by which the right in question was violated, and the absence of language in the federal Constitution explicitly protecting that right. Critics of the doctrine of substantive due process condemn it on the grounds that the doctrine allows an unelected judiciary to override the decisions of the elected members of the legislative and executive branches of government, who are deemed to be both more responsive to, and representative of, the democratic will of political society. In contemporary constitutional politics, the doctrine of "substantive due process" is at the heart of the controversies surrounding the Supreme Court's decisions with respect to contraception and abortion.

16. 198 U.S. 45 (1905). In *Lochner,* the Supreme Court struck down a New York law limiting the number of working hours of bakery employees in that state. The *Lochner* Court held that the New York law unconstitutionally infringed on the "right of free contract," although the Constitution, by its terms, does not expressly confer such a right.

17. Jay Feinman and Peter Gabel, "Contract Law as Ideology," in *The Politics of Law: A Progressive Critique* 373, 374 (David Kairys ed., 1990).

18. 478 U.S. at 190.

19. Richard Hofstadter, *The Paranoid Style in American Politics* (1965). In his classic essay, Hofstadter argues that "[catastrophe] or fear of catastrophe is most likely to elicit the syndrome of paranoid rhetoric." Id. at 39. Hofstadter further contends that the "central image" of the paranoid style "is that of a vast and sinister conspiracy, a gigantic and yet subtle machinery of influence set in motion to undermine and destroy a way of life." Id. at 29. My use of the term "paranoid style" differs from Hofstadter's in one key respect. Although some governmental officials have raised the specter of a "homosexual conspiracy" to destroy the foundations of the heterosexual "way of life" (one thinks immediately of Representatives Doran and Dannemeyer or Senator Helms), I do not find enough evidence of conspiratorial language or logic in *Bowers v. Hardwick* for an interpretation along those lines. However, as I hope to demonstrate in the text, it is difficult to deny the constitutional apocalypticism at the heart of the Court's opinion; in this respect, I found Hofstadter's concept very useful.

20. Id.

21. Stuart Hall, "The Rediscovery of 'Ideology': Return of the Repressed in Media Studies," in *Culture, Media and Society* 64 (Tony Bennett et al. eds., 1982).

22. Alexander Bickel, *The Least Dangerous Branch* 128 (1962).

23. Jerome Frank, *Law and the Modern Mind* (1930).

24. See, e.g., T. M. Cooley, *A Treatise on the Constitutional Limitations Which Rest upon the Legislative Power of the States of the American Union* 124 (Carrington's 8th

ed. 1927); H. Black, *Handbook on the Construction and Interpretation of the Laws* 20 (1911); Raoul Berger, *Government by Judiciary* (1977).

25. 478 U.S. at 195.

26. 478 U.S. at 191.

27. Leo Bersani, "Is the Rectum a Grave?" 43 *October* 297 (1984).

28. Id. at 212.

29. Id. at 222.

30. We are talking here about the meaning of the anus in the male heterosexual imagination:" [male] [h]omosexuality is always connected with the anus, even though—as Kinsey's precious statistics demonstrate—anal intercourse is still the exception even among homosexuals." Guy Hocquenghem, *Homosexual Desire* 89 (Daniella Dangoor trans., 1978).

31. Jeffrey Weeks, *Sexuality and Its Discontents: Meanings, Myths and Modern Sexualities* 191 (1985).

32. Kendall Thomas, "Beyond the Privacy Principle," 92 *Colum. L. Rev.* 1431, 1437 (1992).

33. This phrase refers to the old legal doctrine that a woman who accused a man of rape must be able to show that she responded to the threat of sexual assault with "utmost resistance." For a critical discussion of the "resistance" standard in rape law, see Note, "The Resistance Standard in Rape Legislation," 79 *Stan. L. Rev.* (1966).

34. Sigmund Freud, "Three Essays on the Theory of Sexuality" (1905), in 7 *Standard Edition of the Collected Works of Sigmund Freud* 144 (James Strachey trans. and ed., 1958).

35. Tim Dean, "The Psychoanalysis of AIDS," 63 *October* 83, 112 (1993).

36. Fredric Jameson, *Fables of Aggression: The Modernist as Fascist* 27 (1979).

37. 381 U.S. 479 (1965).

38. 410 U.S. 113 (1973).

39. 478 U.S. at 190.

40. 478 U.S. at 190–91.

41. Jed Rubenfeld, "The Right of Privacy," 102 *Harv. L. Rev.* 737, 781 (1989).

42. Id. at 779.

43. 478 U.S. at 200 (Blackmun, J., dissenting).

44. Rubenfeld, supra note 41, at 778–79.

45. Thomas, supra note 32, at 1502 n. 249.

46. Michel Foucault, *The History of Sexuality* 43 (Robert Hurley trans., 1980).

47. William E. Connolly, *Identity/Difference* 176 (1991).

48. I take this term from Iris M. Young, *Justice and the Politics of Difference* 122 (1990).

49. Paul de Man, *The Resistance to Theory* 11 (1986).

50. 478 U.S. at 205 (Blackmun, J., dissenting).

51. For a discussion of the structures of homophobic violence to which *Hardwick* in particular, and "anti-sodomy" statutes in general, lend ideological legitimacy, see Thomas, supra note 32.

34

Equal Protection and Lesbian and Gay Rights

Arthur S. Leonard

The Equal Protection Clause of the Fourteenth Amendment of the U.S. Constitution requires the *states* to afford equal protection of the laws to all their residents. Additionally, the Supreme Court interprets the Due Process Clause of the Fifth Amendment to impose an identical requirement of equal protection on the federal government. The Fourteenth Amendment requirement applies to all state and local government entities, including such bodies as school districts, public transit authorities, and the like. Thus, American society functions under a constitutional mandate to afford equal protection of the laws to all residents.

What does equal protection mean, as a practical matter, for lesbians, gay men, and bisexuals? Like all provisions of the Constitution, the guarantee acquires meaning in the context of actual cases decided by courts. Court rulings on equal protection claims create a complicated construct of classifications and tests that courts customarily use to explain whether a particular policy complies with the constitutional requirement. These rulings have only occasionally provided protection for gay people, although recent developments suggest a favorable trend.

To understand this body of law we must recognize that virtually every government rule or action may distinguish between different groups of people. Not all differential treatment violates the Constitution, or the whole system would grind to a halt. For example, Articles 1 and 2 of the Constitution as adopted in 1789 specify minimum ages for service in the Congress or as president, thus discriminating against those under the requisite age. Few would argue that the Fifth Amendment Due Process Clause (embodying the equal protection requirement), adopted as part of the Bill of Rights in 1791, should be held to alter or abolish these age requirements on the ground that they deprive younger citizens of equal protection of the laws. In this instance, age is used as a proxy for maturity and experience that would be recognized by judges as an objective difference affecting qualifications to hold office. One could conclude that younger people and older people are not "similarly situated" with respect to those qualifications relevant to elective office, so it is rational to set an age limit.

Because almost all government policies result in differential treatment, courts hold that the normal distinctions stemming from government policies comply with equal protection as long as there is a rational basis founded in legitimate governmental interests underlying the policy. Governments may make distinctions, allocate benefits, and impose burdens that affect different people differently without violating the equal protection principle, so long as there is some rational justification for the policy.[1] As to what constitutes such a justification, the Court has ruled that arguments based solely on bias, fear, or overbroad stereotypes may not be used as a rational basis to sustain legislation,[2] but justifications based on objective differences may suffice.[3]

Where a government draws distinctions in its treatment of different groups in laws or policies adopted through normal lawmaking procedures, the laws or policies enjoy a presumption of legitimacy. This means that the government incurs no obligation to articulate a justification for discrimination unless a challenger first provides convincing proof that no legitimate justification exists. For example, in *Heller v. Doe* (1993), a case in which a state had drawn distinctions between people who were mentally retarded and people who were mentally ill, the absence of an obvious reason to suspect that the state was motivated by prejudice meant that those challenging the policy bore a burden to prove that there was *no* legitimate reason for the policy distinction; only if that burden was met would the state incur any burden of justifying its policy. It is unusual in law to require somebody to prove a negative, such as the absence of a justification, and in earlier cases the Court had spoken as if the government was required at least to articulate a plausible justification for differential treatment its policies require.[4] In *Heller*, however, the Supreme Court made clear that unless the challenger met this initial burden, the government could win without submitting any evidence. Consequently, policies reviewed under the rationality standard are rarely invalidated by the courts.

However, the courts have recognized that there are circumstances in which judicial skepticism is appropriate—when differential treatment involves some "fundamental right," grounded in history and tradition, or when a classification or distinction used by the government is "suspect" because, under the circumstances, there is reason to believe that the government was motivated by bias or prejudice rather than objective, unbiased policy concerns. In such cases, the court applies "strict scrutiny" to the government policy, which means that the government must prove that the policy is narrowly tailored to achieve a compelling governmental interest.

A court's determination whether a particular policy is subjected to rationality review, the more stringent strict scrutiny, or some level of heightened scrutiny falling between the two[5] can obviously make a big difference in the outcome of a case. In a rationality review case, somebody challenging the legitimacy of government action bears the burden of persuading the court that the action violates the Constitution. Even in such cases, challenges can succeed when the only apparent justification for unequal treatment rests on bias or prejudice against the disfavored group. But in the absence of such a showing of raw prejudice, it is usually crucial that the challenger show at the outset that the government's policy affects a "fundamental right" or uses a classification that is "suspect."

Considerable controversy surrounds the methods used by the courts to identify such cases, because having passed that threshold, the challenger effectively shifts to the government the requirement to show that its discriminatory policy is objectively justifiable. The government's burden has been held to vary depending on the significance of the right at stake or the degree of "suspectness" adhering to the classification the government is using. For example, where the interest is characterized as "fundamental" (such as in voting rights cases) or the classification is "suspect" (such as in race cases), the government's burden is to show that its policy is justified by a compelling interest and that its policy is narrowly tailored to achieve that interest in the way least damaging to the fundamental interest or the equality principle. That is, in such cases the government must show that there is a "close fit" between its policy and the compelling goals the policy seeks to vindicate.

The Supreme Court has been sparing in identifying fundamental rights, although it has not always insisted that they be spelled out in the text of the Constitution. One of the problems in synthesizing rules from past decisions and attempting to project them forward to new controversies is that almost any past decision can be discussed at different levels of specificity or generality. Any particular court decision can be narrowly construed to be limited to its particular facts, or broadly construed to embody a general principle. Thus, in *Loving v. Commonwealth of Virginia,*[6] the Supreme Court invalidated under the Equal Protection and Due Process Clauses a Virginia statute banning interracial marriages. One way of reading the Court's opinion would treat it as holding that every person has a fundamental right to be free of government interference in selecting a marital partner. Because the case involved a man and a woman, however, it might be construed at a greater level of specificity as establishing that marriage between persons of the opposite sex is a fundamental right. Furthermore, one might view *Loving* as standing for the proposition that race, as a suspect classification, may not be taken into account by the state in its determination of who may marry, even if the right to select a marital partner is not otherwise deemed fundamental. The Court speaks in its written opinion of marriage as fundamental, but it is speaking within the context of a dispute involving an opposite-sex couple and at a time (1967) when it was unlikely that anyone on the Court thought their decision created a fundamental right for persons to choose marital partners of the same sex; the main portion of the opinion focuses on the racial aspect of the case.

The precedential scope of *Loving* became critically important when gay litigants began in the 1970s to challenge the refusal of states to issue marriage licenses to same-sex couples. Courts unanimously refused to find *Loving* a controlling precedent that the right of same-sex couples to marry is fundamental.[7] Even the Hawaii Supreme Court, which ruled in 1993 that the state had to show a compelling interest to justify refusing to issue marriage licenses to same-sex couples, did not use *Loving* as precedent for finding a federal or state constitutional fundamental right to marry.[8] Instead, it used an equal protection analysis based on the Hawaii Constitution, finding that just as in *Loving* the state violated equal protection by using a race classification in its marriage law, in this case the state violated its own state's constitutional equal protection requirement by using a sex classification in its marriage law; the Hawaii Constitution, unlike the U.S. Constitution, explicitly forbids sex discrimination.

Identifying suspect classifications might begin with the paradigm identified by the Court in *Loving*: race. Beginning with African slavery from early days of colonial settlement, there is a long history of racism and attendant discrimination in the United States. As a result, racial minority groups have historically wielded inadequate political power to protect themselves from discriminatory government policies through participation in electoral politics, or to rely on free market forces to prevent private race-based discrimination in jobs, education, housing, or places of public accommodation. Furthermore, although one could argue that race is a socially constructed phenomenon, the Court has tended to view it as an immutable biological characteristic, perhaps reflecting the view that however society constructs the classification of racial groups, one's membership in such a group is largely determined by factors over which one has no control. These attributes of race, that is, a history of discrimination, political powerlessness, and immutability, are frequently recited by lower courts as creating a checklist for determining whether other classifications are suspect.

In 1985, in *City of Cleburne v. Cleburne Living Center*,[9] a lawsuit challenging a zoning ordinance that erected special barriers to group homes for the mentally retarded, the Supreme Court took a somewhat different approach in describing how it identifies suspect classifications. Writing for the Court, Justice Byron R. White explained that government classifications based on race, alienage, or national origin are deemed suspect because "[t]hese factors are so seldom relevant to the achievement of any legitimate state interest that laws grounded in such considerations are deemed to reflect prejudice and antipathy—a view that those in the burdened class are not as worthy or deserving as others. For these reasons and because such discrimination is unlikely to be soon rectified by legislative means, these laws are subjected to strict scrutiny and will be sustained only if they are suitably tailored to serve a compelling state interest." White did not mention immutability as being significant in this connection.

White then explained that sex classifications call for a "heightened standard of review" because sex "generally provides no sensible ground for differential treatment." Asserting that "the sex characteristic frequently bears no relation to ability to perform or contribute to society" and that sexually discriminatory policies "very likely reflect outmoded notions of the relative capabilities of men and women," he concluded that such a classification "fails unless it is substantially related to a sufficiently important governmental interest."

On the other hand, White identified a variety of characteristics that would not constitute suspect classifications. For example, intelligence or physical disability would not be suspect classifications because they *do* bear a "relation to ability to perform or contribute to society." White asserted that age classifications were not suspect because there was no "history of purposeful unequal treatment" and no imposition of "unique disabilities on the basis of stereotyped characteristics" associated with age. Turning to the main issue in the case, the Court held that discrimination against the mentally retarded was not suspect, observing that this characteristic did bear a relation to the individual's ability to perform or contribute to society, and that much legislation on the subject was protective rather than discriminatory. Nonetheless, the Court found, using the rationality test, that the zoning ordinance in this case was unconstitutional because there was no rational justification for treating group homes for the mentally retarded differently from other group homes, apart from stereotypical fears about mentally retarded people.

Cleburne illustrates a flexible approach to identifying suspect classes. Rather than utilizing a rigid checklist on which a perfect score is necessary, the Court emphasized particular items on the list and not others in deciding to apply strict or heightened scrutiny to particular classifications. Thus it appears that the determination whether sexual orientation is a suspect classification or, to put the issue somewhat differently, whether government policies that discriminate against lesbians and gay men are subject to strict or heightened scrutiny, is not a simple matter of achieving a perfect score on a checklist based on a comparison to race.

Using the checklist approach, few judges have found that policies discriminating on the basis of sexual orientation should be subjected to strict or heightened scrutiny. One judge who has in U.S. Circuit Judge William Norris, who concluded that all the race-analogy factors were met by sexual orientation. Concurring in *Watkins v. United States Army*,[10] Norris noted that there is a long, well-documented history of antigay prejudice by government and by private actors. Sexual orientation frequently bears no relation to ability to perform or contribute to society. Gays have been saddled with unique disabilities because of prejudice or inaccurate stereotypes. The trait defining the class, in Norris's view, is for all practical purposes immutable, and despite some gains in recent years, at the relevant level of national politics for considering military policies, gays lack the ability to defend their interests. (This last point was dramatically illustrated by the 1993 battle in Congress over the military policy, which culminated in legislative codification of a ban on service by openly lesbian, gay, or bisexual individuals.)[11] Using strict scrutiny, Norris found that the military policy excluding gays from service was unconstitutional, but the majority of the court disposed of the case using a different theory, one not based on equal protection. Norris's view is definitely a minority view among federal judges who have decided sexual orientation discrimination claims.

Is sexual orientation a suspect classification when it is used by the government to distinguish between people? One might well go back one step and ask whether "sexual orientation" is even a characteristic recognizable for purposes of constitutional analysis. Sexual orientation can be defined as a characteristic based on the *direction* of erotic or emotional attraction of an individual; thus, everyone who experiences erotic attraction has a sexual orientation, whether toward members of the same sex, the opposite sex, or both. A conceptual problem emerges, however, as one looks at the myriad cases in which litigants sought to attack government policies perceived as discriminating against gay people. What exactly are we talking about in such cases, a status (state of being) or a classification defined by conduct?

For example, Colorado's Amendment 2, which was adopted by voters in 1992 and ultimately declared unconstitutional under the Equal Protection Clause by the Supreme Court in 1996,[12] does not on its face use the term "sexual orientation."[13] Rather, it speaks of "homosexual, lesbian, or bisexual orientation" when it forbids the adoption or enforcement of any policies "whereby homosexual, lesbian or bisexual orientation, conduct, practices or relationships shall constitute or otherwise be the basis of or entitle any person or class of persons to have or claim any minority status quota preferences, protected status or claim of discrimination." Is this a policy that discriminates on the basis of "sexual orientation," a status or defining characteristic, or is it, as the state of Colorado argued in defending it before the Supreme Court, only concerned with behavior?

In ruling on the constitutionality of a similarly worded city charter amendment adopted by voters in Cincinnati, Ohio, the U.S. Court of Appeals for the Sixth Circuit rejected the argument that such a policy constituted discrimination based on a personal characteristic or status.[14] Assuming for purposes of its analysis that sexual orientation, as such, is a "characteristic beyond the control of the individual" but that lesbians, gay men, and bisexuals are to all outward appearances indistinguishable from other groups in the population, the court said, "the reality remains that no law can successfully be drafted that is calculated to burden or penalize, or to benefit or protect, an unidentifiable group or class of individuals whose identity is defined by subjective and unapparent characteristics such as innate desires, drives, and thoughts." The court asserted that in terms of one's relationship with others in society, "homosexual," "lesbian," or "bisexual" orientation, as targeted by the Cincinnati policy, was relevant only in the context of behavior that would identify the individual as having such an orientation, and thus the policy could discriminate only in circumstances when a person's behavior had revealed his or her orientation to others. "Those persons having a homosexual 'orientation' simply do not, as such, comprise an identifiable class," argued the court; only those who acted on their orientation by engaging in revelatory conduct become identifiable.

The Sixth Circuit found this argument significant because of the weight it attached to *Bowers v. Hardwick*,[15] in which the Supreme Court ruled that "homosexuals" do not have a "fundamental right" to engage in sodomy with each other. Interpreting *Bowers* on a more general level, the Sixth Circuit Court characterized it as standing for the proposition that "homosexuals possess no fundamental right to engage in homosexual conduct and consequently that conduct could be criminalized." From there, it was a short logical step to asserting that any conduct that reveals an individual's "homosexual orientation" is "homosexual conduct," and because the state can criminalize "homosexual conduct," a class of people who are identifiable only by the common trait of engaging in "homosexual conduct" cannot be a "suspect class" for equal protection purposes. The Sixth Circuit's argument was not original; it has been a mainstay of federal appellate courts ever since *Bowers*, most frequently cited in cases challenging the refusal of national security agencies or the armed forces knowingly to employ lesbians, gay men, and bisexuals.[16]

The argument depends on several factors for its force, not least of which is an expansive reading of *Bowers*[17] that goes beyond its specific holding. In *Bowers*, the Supreme Court rejected the argument that homosexuals engaging in specific conduct outlawed by a Georgia statute (anal or oral sex) were within the sphere of privacy the Court had previously identified with respect to birth control and abortion. The Sixth Circuit broadened the precedential scope of *Bowers* to all "homosexual conduct" and then labeled "homosexual conduct" any conduct by which a person reveals his or her orientation as homosexual, lesbian, or bisexual, when it asserted that heightened scrutiny could not be applied to a classification that was based on criminally proscribable conduct. However, the way individuals become identifiable as lesbians, gay men, or bisexuals is not invariably by engaging in criminally proscribable conduct, but rather by speaking, engaging in nonsexual social intercourse, and associating themselves with others. Nothing in *Bowers v. Hardwick* suggests that any state could proscribe engaging in nonsexual expressive conduct that identifies one as gay, yet in most cases it seems likely that it is exactly such conduct, not engaging in anal or oral intercourse with a partner of the same sex, that renders somebody an identifiable member of the class of lesbian, gay, and bisexual people.[18]

The Sixth Circuit's approach bears striking similarity to the courts' analytical approach in cases challenging the military exclusionary policy. Under the current version of this policy,[19] Congress asserts that the "presence in the armed forces of persons who demonstrate a propensity or intent to engage in homosexual acts would create an unacceptable risk to the high standards of morale, good order and discipline, and unit cohesion that are the essence of military capability." Based on this legislative finding, Congress commands that members be separated from the service if they engage in, attempt to engage in, or solicit another to engage in homosexual acts (unless the member proves that he or she is not really homosexual, i.e., somebody who normally desires to engage in such acts), if they state that they are homosexual or bisexual (unless they prove that despite this statement they have not engaged in homosexual acts and have no propensity to do so), or if they attempt to marry a person of the same sex.

Challengers of this policy assert that it is a status-targeted policy. If Congress fears that homosexual conduct will disrupt good order and morale, why is it willing to tolerate the retention of individuals who engage in such conduct if they can demonstrate that they are not really "homosexuals"? Clearly, Congress is trying to rid the armed services of people who have a homosexual, lesbian, or bisexual *orientation* by mandating the discharge of any member whose nonheterosexual orientation comes to light as a result of any conduct, including expressive conduct or speech. The service member is not discharged because of the conduct or speech, as such, but rather because of what the speech indicates about the individual's status. The Seventh Circuit Court of Appeals first explained this distinction in *BenShalom v. Marsh*,[20] decided under the pre-1994 policy, when it rejected a First Amendment free speech argument by a service member whose discharge was based solely on her statement that she was a lesbian.[21]

The Defense Department responds that the policy has everything to do with conduct and no particular concern with status, except as status bears predictive value toward conduct. Its argument is that under *Bowers* the Defense Department is constitutionally entitled to proscribe homosexual conduct, but its main concern is with maintaining good order and morale necessary to an efficient fighting force. The department contends that the occurrence of homosexual conduct in the military will be detrimental to its mission; thus its main concern in any particular case is to determine whether the individual is likely to engage in such conduct. Anything revealing a "propensity" to engage in homosexual conduct, including a statement that one is gay, is deemed relevant for this purpose. Such speech may identify the speaker as a member of a class defined by sexual orientation[22] or it may identify the speaker as a person with a propensity to engage in homosexual conduct, a class defined by conduct. The Defense Department argues that it is concerned only with the latter; thus if the speaker can convince the department that his or her speech does not indicate such a propensity, the department will retain him or her in the service. By contrast, the military member who can persuade the Defense Department that despite his or her homosexual activity he or she is not a "homosexual" theoretically does not present a threat to the military mission, because he or she lacks the "propensity" to engage in such conduct in the future.

The level of judicial scrutiny given to Amendment 2, the Cincinnati charter amendment, or the military policy depends on whether fundamental rights or suspect classifications are involved. When courts are considering Amendment 2 or the military policy, are they considering a status classification issue or a behavioral classification issue? Is there a meaningful distinction between the two? Should it make a difference for purposes of equal protection? Is *Bowers* dispositive, as most federal courts of appeals have insisted, in rejecting equal protection claims brought by lesbian and gay litigants?

It is possible that government policies may vary with respect to the type of classifications they create. There may be times when classifications or distinctions are based solely on status, others in which behavior is the central concern, and finally those in which status and behavior are conflated so that it is difficult to disaggregate them. An example of this problem is the criminal prohibition of sodomy, an issue the Supreme Court analyzed in *Bowers* using the privacy doctrine that has evolved under the Due Process Clause but which, as Justice John Paul Stevens observed in dissent, also presented a serious equal protection issue.

Michael Hardwick challenged the constitutionality of a Georgia statute that makes oral or anal sex a felony punishable by up to twenty years in prison. The statute does not distinguish between same-sex and opposite-sex conduct. Hardwick was a gay man who was arrested in his bedroom while having oral sex with another man. His lawsuit was joined by a married heterosexual couple, who alleged that the statute violated their right to engage in oral or anal sex. The lower courts held that the heterosexual couple lacked "standing" (i.e., the requisite personal interest in the outcome) to challenge the law, because Georgia was not actively enforcing the law against married couples. A federal appeals court ruled that unless the state could show a compelling interest justifying the law, it would violate Hardwick's right of privacy, a fundamental right. The state appealed to the Supreme Court.

The Supreme Court framed the question as whether the constitutional right of privacy might prevent the state from making it a crime for homosexuals to engage in sodomy. According to Justice White, the question was thus restricted because Michael Hardwick, as a gay man, was limited to contesting the application of the law to him. At oral argument, counsel for the state conceded that it would be unconstitutional to prosecute a married couple under this statute. The Court held, by a vote of five to four, that the right of homosexuals to engage in sodomy did not "resemble" other kinds of conduct previously held to come within the right of privacy, and dismissed Hardwick's challenge.

Dissenting, Justice Stevens argued that the Court had failed to address a significant equal protection issue. If, as seemed likely, the Court would hold that Georgia could not prosecute heterosexuals for engaging in sodomy in private, then there was discrimination on the basis of sexual orientation. While the sodomy law was apparently aimed at conduct, the status of those engaging in the conduct would become crucial in a determination of whether it was prohibited. The historical factors on which the Court relied in determining that homosexuals lack a right to engage in sodomy did not support the discriminatory result of the Court's decision, because the sources cited by the Court all involved absolute, across-the-board prohibitions on sodomous conduct, regardless of the genders of participants. (The English sodomy law from which American sodomy laws initially derived, for example, outlawed all anal intercourse and disregarded lesbianism, and biblical precedents are not gender-specific.)

When the Court found that a fundamental right of privacy did not apply to Hardwick's case, it evaluated the sodomy law using rationality review, because the Due Process Clause requires that all government policies that restrict personal freedom must at least be found to serve some legitimate state interest. The Court concluded that the presumed moral judgment of Georgians that homosexual sodomy should be forbidden was sufficient justification. Stevens pointed out that Georgians had never made such a judgment, as all Georgia laws forbidding sodomy had been gender-neutral and made no sex-based distinctions. Georgia never presented any rationale for forbidding homosexuals from engaging in conduct that was, apparently, constitutionally protected when engaged in by heterosexuals. The Court's opinion makes no response to Stevens's argument.

Was *Bowers* about conduct, status, or both? In an amicus brief filed with the *Bowers* Court, which has recently taken on notoriety due to its citation and quotation by lower federal courts denying gay equal protection claims,[23] Lambda Legal Defense and Education Fund argued that "the 'regulation of same sex behavior constitutes the total prohibition of an entire way of life' because homosexuality is inexorably intertwined with 'homosexual conduct.' "[24] Expressing agreement with this view, the circuit court in *Steffan v. Perry*[25] held that the Defense Department, permitted by *Bowers* to forbid homosexual conduct, could rationally presume that any person identifying himself or herself as gay or lesbian was, in effect, admitting a "propensity" to engage in homosexual conduct.

Does the conflation of conduct and status mean, in the wake of *Bowers*, that claims of discrimination on the basis of sexual orientation must inevitably be dealt with using the relatively undemanding rationality test, as the circuit courts in the Cincinnati and *Steffan* cases suggest? Or, to the contrary, are the basic purposes of equal protection and due process so different that it is inappropriate for a court to look to *Bowers* as a precedent when evaluating a statute for compliance with equal protection? The Court's recent decision in *Romer v. Evans* did not address this question but implicitly raised doubts about the continued viability of *Bowers* as a precedent.

In *Romer*, the Colorado Supreme Court held that Amendment 2 violated equal protection because of its discriminatory treatment of a fundamental right of political participation. By removing the subject of antidiscrimination protection for lesbians, gay men, and bisexuals from the normal process of legislative and executive policy making, argued the plaintiffs in that case, the state had discriminated on the basis of sexual orientation. Because participation in the normal political process is a fundamental right, they argued, the state's discriminatory policy was subject to strict scrutiny under equal protection. The Supreme Court agreed that Amendment 2 is unconstitutional but did not directly embrace the Colorado court's fundamental rights analysis, preferring to analyze the measure as categorically discriminating on the basis of sexual orientation.

The Sixth Circuit Court of Appeals, evaluating the similarly worded Cincinnati ordinance, found that the city had several rational bases for withdrawing authority from the city government to forbid discrimination against gay men, lesbians, and bisexuals.[26] According to the court, the measure "encouraged enhanced associational liberty" by allowing individuals to refrain from associating with homosexuals; returned the city to a "position of neutrality" on the controversial issue of homosexuality; "reduced governmental regulation of the private social and economic conduct of Cincinnati residents" and thus "augmented the degree of personal autonomy and collective popular sovereignty legally permitted concerning deeply personal choices and beliefs which are necessarily imbued with questions of individual conscience, private religious convictions, and other profoundly personal and deeply fundamental moral issues"; and saved the city the expense of enforcing nondiscrimination policies. In sum, the court found that preserving the right of its residents to discriminate against homosexuals was a legitimate concern of the city of Cincinnati, making rational its decision to disempower its government from forbidding such discrimination. After deciding *Romer v. Evans*, the Supreme Court vacated the Sixth Circuit's decision and remanded the case for reconsideration.

Romer may signal an important development in equal protection doctrine and its application to governmental antigay discrimination. Although the Court never directly addressed either the question whether sexual orientation should be treated as a suspect classification or the question of what precedential weight *Bowers* should be given in an equal protection case, the Court's analysis of Amendment 2 did settle some important issues.

First, Justice Anthony Kennedy's opinion for the Court implicitly rejected the Sixth Circuit's assertion that persons having a homosexual orientation could not constitute an "identifiable class." Kennedy implicitly rejected the attempt to conflate behavior and status. By focusing exclusively on status, Kennedy avoided having to mention or deal with *Bowers*. After *Romer*, the argument that gay people are not a constitutionally cognizable class for equal protection purposes is dead.

Second, Kennedy's basis for holding Amendment 2 unconstitutional was his determination that the various justifications advanced by Colorado in its defense were pretexts for animus against homosexuals. Kennedy characterized Amendment 2 as having singled out homosexuals as virtual "strangers to the law" by categorically depriving them of any redress against discriminatory treatment by the state. The justifications offered for Amendment 2 seemed so disproportionately trivial in comparison to this extraordinary breadth of discrimination as to be blatantly pretextual. Kennedy asserted that animus against homosexuals could not, by itself, be a legitimate justification for a discriminatory policy.

In dissent, Justice Antonin Scalia asserted the inconsistency of this result with *Bowers,* which premised approval of outlawing homosexual sodomy solely on the presumed majoritarian moral disapproval of homosexuality. How could moral disapproval be sufficient to sustain criminal penalties imposed solely on homosexuals, while insufficient to sustain the apparently lesser deprivation of making it more difficult for homosexuals than for others to obtain redress for discriminatory state policies?

The Court's subsequent action vacating the Sixth Circuit's decision in the Cincinnati case and sending the matter back to the lower court for reconsideration appears to confirm this interpretation of Kennedy's opinion. Although the Court did not directly address whether sexual orientation is a suspect classification or specify that antigay measures are subject to heightened or strict scrutiny by the courts, it has established the beginnings of a new framework for analyzing equal protection claims by homosexual litigants. Policies that discriminate against homosexuals may be challenged under the Equal Protection Clause, and animus against homosexuals will not serve as an adequate sole justification to sustain discriminatory policies.

Whether this methodology will serve to strike down the current military policy or bans against same-sex marriage has yet to be determined. In both of those cases, the government will attempt to articulate justifications apart from simple animus and may well succeed in convincing courts that the requirements of *Romer* have been met. As we observed earlier, a Supreme Court decision may have different meanings depending on the level of generality at which it is described. *Romer* might be seen as sui generis, a case narrowly confined to the extraordinarily offensive measure it invalidated. On the other hand, *Romer's* apparent contradiction of some of the reasoning of *Bowers* holds out hope that future equal protection challenges to antigay government policies may fall on more fertile soul.

Notes

1. The Supreme Court has ruled that unintentional discrimination ("disparate treatment") does not violate the Constitution. Thus, policies that do not on their face require unequal treatment are not subject to constitutional attack. By contrast, in the Civil Rights Act of 1964, as most recently amended in 1991, Congress has outlawed discrimination on the basis of race, religion, national origin, or sex whether intentional or unintentional, placing on "unintentional" discriminators the burden of showing that their actions are "consistent with business necessity."

2. E.g., U.S. Dept. of Agriculture v. Moreno, 413 U.S. 5287 (1973) (denial of food stamp eligibility based solely on disapproval of "hippie communes" was unconstitutional); City of Cleburne v. Cleburne Living Center, 473 U.S. 432 (1985) (denial of permit for location of residence for mentally retarded based solely on fear and stereotypes about the retarded was unconstitutional).

3. Heller v. Doe, 113 S.Ct. 2637 (1993) (distinctions between mental illness and mental retardation justify different standards for commitment decisions).

4. See Cleburne, supra n. 2.

5. The Court has held, for example, that sex classifications are subject to an intermediate level of heightened scrutiny, requiring the government to show that its policy is justified by important government interests. See Craig v. Boren, 429 U.S. 190 (1976).

6. 388 U.S. 1 (1967).

7. See Dean v. District of Columbia, 653 A.2d 307 (D.C. App. 1995); Singer v. Hara, 522 P.2d 1187 (Wash. App. 1974); Jones v. Hallahan, 501 S.W.2d 588 (Ky. 1973); Baker v. Nelson, 191 N.W.2d 185 (Minn. 1971); Anonymous v. Anonymous, 325 N.Y.S.2d 499 (N.Y. Sup. Ct. 1971).

8. Baehr v. Lewin, 825 P.2d 44 (Hi. 1993).

9. 473 U.S. 432 (1985).

10. 875 F.2d 699 (9th Cir. en banc, 1989), cert. denied, 1112 S.Ct. 384 (1990).

11. See 10 U.S.C. § 654f, codifying § 571, National Defense Authorization Act for Fiscal Year 1994, Pub.L.No. 103–160, 107 Stat. 1670–73 (1993).

12. Romer v. Evans, 116 S.Ct. 1620 (1996).

13. The Supreme Court heard oral argument in Romer v. Evans on October 10, 1995.

14. Equality Foundation of Greater Cincinnati, Inc. v. City of Cincinnati, 54 F.3d 261 (6th Cir., May 12, 1995), 116 S.Ct. 2519.

15. 478 U.S. 186 (1986).

16. The first court to articulate a version of this theory was the U.S. Court of Appeals for the District of Columbia Circuit in Padula v. Webster, 822 F.2d 97 (1987). It has since been articulated in some form by virtually every federal circuit case rejecting an equal protection claim on the merits by a gay litigant. Although the battle over military service by openly lesbian, gay, or bisexual individuals continues, in 1995 President Clinton formally ended discrimination on the basis of sexual orientation in security clearance; the Justice Department had previously ended sexual orientation discrimination in employment by the Federal Bureau of Investigation.

17. 478 U.S. 186 (1986).

18. Shahar v. Bowers, 70 F.3d 1218 (11th Cir., 1995) vacated for rehearing en banc (1996).

19. 10 U.S.C. § 654 (1993).

20. 881 F.2d 454 (7th Cir. 1989), cert. denied, 110 S.Ct. 1296 (1990).

21. The Ninth Circuit followed the same reasoning in rejecting a First Amendment challenge to a military discharge in Pruitt v. Cheney, 963 F.2d 1160 (9th Cir.), cert. denied, 113 S.Ct. 655 (1992).

22. The Supreme Court recognized this in Hurley v. Gay, Lesbian, & Bisexual Group of Boston, 115 S.Ct. 2338 (1995).

23. See Steffan v. Perry, 41 F.3d 677 (D.C. Cir., en banc, 1994), at n. 11.

24. Id., quoting Lambda amicus brief.

25. 41 F.3d 677 (D.C. Cir., en banc, 1994).

26. Equality Foundation v. City of Cincinnati, 54 F.3d 261.

B. Homo-Economics

35

Thinking Homo/Economically

M. V. Lee Badgett

As is true of most people, a lesbian, gay, or bisexual person cannot escape his or her role as *homo economicus,* or economic human. Economic decisions and actions take up an important part of every day. Going to work, stopping off at the grocery store, preparing dinner, or helping the kids with their homework all include economic dimensions to one degree or another.

The idea that economic decisions made by gay people will be influenced by their sexual orientation is not a new idea. In the 1950s in Buffalo, lesbians may have chosen particular occupations that allowed them to dress as they chose (Kennedy and Davis 1993). The "commercialization of desire" was based on and promoted gay men's patronage of bathhouses (Altman 1982). Workplace discrimination has created and remains an ongoing issue related to economic security for many lesbians and gay men.

As the public visibility of lesbian and gay people and the movement for civil rights hit the 1990s, however, economic images and collective economic action have become increasingly important and conspicuous. A 1991 *Wall Street Journal* article called gay people "a dream market," citing marketing survey data that showed the average income of gay households as $55,430, over $23,000 a year more than the average U.S. household (Rigdon 1991). Local newspapers cover the efforts of lesbian and gay employee groups that have organized within many U.S. workplaces and have successfully lobbied for non-discrimination policies and inclusive benefits policies.

But our awakening consciousness of economic roles comes at a time when other forces outside the gay and lesbian communities have their own agendas for developing lesbian and gay Americans' economic image, whether they are businesses hoping to make money by marketing to an affluent subgroup or right-wing religious zealots anxious to portray gay people in an unpopular way.

This essay is an economist's look at some basic economic categories and the public images they represent; I ask an important strategic question for lesbian and gay people: *How should we define ourselves economically?* Like most people in our economy, we play many market roles—as producers, consumers, and investors—but when it comes to using those economic roles to promote political change, we have some choices to make about which ones are more useful and relevant. In thinking about this question, I am concerned with how particular economic identities (1) fit into our political interests and goals, such as reducing homophobia and heterosexism, and (2) help our lesbian, gay, and bisexual communities build coalitions with other progressive groups and bridges to individuals and communities that think of themselves as very different from the gay community. In this essay, I conclude that producer and investor roles best fulfill those criteria, and I argue that wielding consumer power does not require us to further develop an already dangerous tendency to see gay people primarily as consumers.

Lesbian, Gay, and Bisexual People as Producers

A focus on being a producer (or worker or employee) has long been a source of class identity and politics. For centuries workers have organized themselves into unions and other kinds of groups to exert their collective influence to force changes in the workplace or in the political realm. Workplace organizing obviously fits into political goals related to the workplace, such as nondiscrimination or domestic partner policies. In survey after survey, lesbian and gay people report experiences of employment discrimination (Badgett, Donnelly, and Kibbe 1992). In my own research, I have found evidence that discrimination against lesbian, gay, and bisexual people reduces their incomes relative to heterosexuals with the same education, experience, and other important characteristics (Badgett 1994). Within individual workplaces, even the discrimination institutionalized in benefits policies has proven vulnerable to reasoned and well-organized appeals by gay employee groups. Workplace groups—both formal and informal—have achieved some notable successes. Private employers (such as Lotus, Levi Strauss, and Ivy League universities) and public employers (including the cities of New York, Seattle, San Francisco, and Berkeley and the Universities of Iowa, Vermont, and Minnesota) have begun to offer health care and other benefits to domestic partners of gay employees.

As the organizing process continues within individual workplaces, at some point the workplace successes will contribute to the push for a broader public policy, such as a federal nondiscrimination law. Here economic reasoning will be used on both sides of the debate. Some economists will argue that the government should let the competitive labor market erode discrimination in employment, wages, and benefits: if a firm does not hire the best workers available, then discrimination will hurt that firm's competitive position, eventually driving the discriminating firm out of business. Similarly, if a firm sees a competitive advantage in offering domestic partner benefits to attract productive workers, then that firm will do so and does not need government interference. Economic counterarguments exist, of course, particularly in skepticism that markets will erode discrimination on their own (think about the persistence of discrimination against black or female workers, for instance). In the case of domestic partner policies, one could argue that individuals, employers, and society must bear large "transaction costs" in registering partnerships in many different places and ways, suggesting that one big state registry would be much more efficient.

In addition to fitting into our broad political goals, workplace activism is also an effective means of building bridges and coalitions with individuals and groups. First and foremost, workplace activism has the potential for tremendous transformations in the attitudes of heterosexual coworkers. We spend a huge part of our lives at work, and work naturally becomes a very social activity as well as an economically productive one. Being in the closet diminishes the quality and quantity of social interactions with straight coworkers, but coming out opens up many new possibilities, both personal and political (Woods 1993). Discussing gay issues at work or coming out to a boss or coworker makes gay issues much less abstract and can educate heterosexuals about many related topics that can have far-reaching effects. Heterosexual people who know gay people tend to have more progay opinions (Herek and Glunt 1993), which can be useful in campaigns to defeat antigay amendments or pass gay civil rights laws. For example, several years of work by Microsoft employees who had formed GLEAM (Gay, Lesbian, and Bisexual Employees at Microsoft) paid off in 1992 when they were able to convince the company to write letters in opposition to antigay referenda in Oregon and Colorado.

Universities have been the site of enormous gains in the effort to get domestic partner benefits and are good examples of the power of gay workplace activism to educate heterosexual people about the truth of lesbian and gay people's lives (Badgett 1994). During the effort on my own campus, we were able to turn a potentially cumbersome political process into a highly successful educational opportunity. Public hearings on a proposal to provide campus-level benefits to domestic partners (such as library cards and access to child care facilities) brought many lesbians and gay men out to tell the stories of their families, stories that many heterosexual coworkers had never imagined. After listening to these experiences of lesbian and gay coworkers, many heterosexuals told us that they had learned something important and had, in many cases, changed their initially negative opinions to support the proposal. Many of those folks became important political allies in our efforts.

A second important opportunity contained within workplaces is the potential for building coalitions with other groups fighting for fair treatment, such as unions or employee groups for women and/or for people of color. Working with other groups in coalitions might mean taking on some issues not commonly thought of as related to sexual orientation, but I would argue that coalitions improve the chances of *all* groups' goals being reached. At Microsoft, GLEAM formed a "Diversity Coalition" with groups of African American, Hispanic, Jewish, Native American, and deaf and hard of hearing employees ("Corporate Focus: Making Microsoft's Meritocracy Work," 1993). The Coalition's efforts within the company led to the empowerment of a Diversity Manager, who was able to start moving on several important diversity policies.

Finally, even in a modern market economy, work is a virtuous activity and is an important part of our political and cultural foundations as well as our economic foundation. By portraying ourselves as workers and producers to the more general public outside our workplaces, we are promoting a positive image.

Lesbian, Gay, and Bisexual People as Consumers

Of course, like all people, gay people are also consumers as well as producers. In the current market environment, however, our interests as consumers are quite complicated. Several possible relationships between consumption and political goals invite analysis: (1) creating and promoting our public identities as "queer consumers" in the U.S. marketplace; (2) targeting our consumption choices to influence corporate policies and media images of gay people (through boycotts, for example); and (3) developing separate lesbian/gay/bisexual markets, or "queer capitalism."

A "Queer Consumer" Identity

The connection between consumption and social status and opinion is, on the face of it, a clear one. As economist Thorstein Veblen (1934) wrote at the end of the last century, "The basis on which good repute in any highly organised industrial community ultimately rests is pecuniary strength; and the means of showing pecuniary strength, and so of gaining or retaining a good name, are leisure and a conspicuous consumption of goods." But is conspicuous consumption—and the attendant development of a queer consumer identity—a useful strategy for lesbian, gay, and bisexual people? Thanks in part to the efforts of marketers who portray us as an attractive and affluent group of consumers, there is a growing consciousness among gay people of being "gay consumers," and thanks to the right wing, this image has spread widely outside the lesbian, gay, and bisexual communities. But while in other circumstances this economic role could contribute to the broad political goal of "gaining or retaining a good name," consciously establishing a gay consumer identity per se is not likely to be a good strategy for building coalitions and bridges.

First, some of the assumptions behind the interest in marketing to gay people are wrong. In particular, some marketers (in inadvertent collusion with the radical right wing) portray gay people as being well educated and having high incomes (for example, Rigdon 1991). But this image comes from surveys of gay magazine and newspaper readers or from people attending gay events. Such samples of gay people are biased toward people with high incomes. Surveys of other magazines or newspapers also typically find higher than average incomes for readers, and travel and admission costs for events make it unlikely that people at gay events are economically representative of all gay people.

Other more reliable and representative surveys give a very different picture of the economic status of lesbian and gay people. Data from the Yankelovich Monitor, a random sample of U.S. households, show that self-identified gay people's household incomes are virtually the same as heterosexuals' (Elliot 1994). My own study of data from the General Social Survey from the University of Chicago makes a more detailed comparison of people with the same education, experience, occupation, and location, and I find that gay and bisexual people (who are defined by behavior) actually earn *less* than straight people (Badgett 1994).

Second, building a consumer movement based on an inaccurate portrayal of our economic clout not only is dishonest, but may actually alienate potential allies. In this era of growing economic inequality, cries of injustice coming from a supposedly prosperous group are likely to fall on resentful ears. The radical right has seized on this image to divide and conquer a potential progressive coalition. Literature in the Colorado Amendment 2 campaign reveals this strategy at work: "Are homosexuals a disadvantaged minority? You decide!" A table below that headline compares (biased) gay income figures from marketing surveys to the much lower incomes of African Americans.

Targeting Consumption Choices

We do not have to develop a consumption-based identity to wield consumer power, however. The lesbian, gay, and bisexual communities have used consumer boycotts of Coors, Cracker Barrel, and the state of Colorado, for instance, to exert economic pressure to reverse homophobic employment practices and laws. The economic effectiveness of boycotts is difficult to measure, since so many other factors influence companies' sales revenues and can hide the impact of even a well-organized boycott (certainly a difficult feat considering the national markets for most products). But regardless of whether companies are more concerned about the economic or the public relations impact of boycotts, boycotts clearly contribute to changes in policies (Snyder 1991; Putnam 1993).

Given the proliferation of boycotts in the 1990s, coalition opportunities abound. Environmentalists in particular have skillfully used consumer action, and many other groups concerned about employment fairness, animal rights, and reproductive rights include consumer action in their arsenals. Coalitions could take the form of mutual support of boycotts directed at different companies or combined forces targeting one company. And those alliances are likely to continue outside the workplace in the electoral arena, such as when gay participation in the Coors boycott in the 1970s gained the Teamsters' support for Harvey Milk's election as the first gay supervisor in San Francisco (Shilts 1982).

Although both consumers and workers can form coalitions with other groups, I would argue that consumer action works very differently from worker action when it comes to bridge building. Media campaigns, which are an integral part of many boycott strategies, are likely to increase the visibility of lesbian, gay, and bisexual people and the realities of their lives. In much gay consumer action, the image of gay people is the very issue, as in the controversy surrounding the movie *Basic Instinct*, which led to a boycott and the "Catherine did it" media campaign. The impersonality of consumption and of media images distinguishes workplace action from consumer action, however. A character who comes out in a television series might remind a viewer of a workplace friend, but a real coworker who comes out can engage her colleagues in a conversation (or struggle) about a variety of complex issues over a period of time. But this qualitative distinction is not made to denigrate the importance of gay visibility. The television character might create a natural topic for a real workplace discussion, and positive media images of gay people might make it easier for gay employees to come out at work.

Consumer action may also involve difficult choices for activists. An economically successful boycott is designed to hurt a company's management or shareholders, but that also means that the company's workers will be hurt as well. This creates the possibility of conflicting loyalties, as it would for a lesbian union member who is asked to boycott products made by members of her union, for example. Some gay employee groups have discouraged outsiders from putting direct pressure on the group's employer, preferring to work through internal political processes first.

These drawbacks to consumer activism argue for a careful selection of targets, focusing on companies that can make direct improvements in the lives of lesbian, gay, and bisexual people rather than boycotts to punish a company's failure to denounce somebody else's policy or for a company's consorting with one of our enemies. For instance, the Cracker Barrel Old Country Stores Inc. boycott targets a company that has openly fired lesbian and gay workers simply because of their sexual orientation. Successfully directing pressure against Cracker Barrel's policy of discrimination would clearly improve the lives of the fired workers and the remaining gay employees at Cracker Barrel. The more direct an attack a boycott makes on egregiously unfair behavior, the more likely gay *and* straight people are to participate and to create change.

Queer Capitalism

The first two relationships between consumption and political goals are more related to "homo economics" than to a "homo economy." Capitalism plus concentrations of gay people in large urban areas has made a queer economy possible in gay enclaves. Should gay people come together as producers *and* consumers to create a queer capitalism? A completely separate economy is difficult to imagine, but we have long had explicitly gay- and lesbian-owned businesses around, such as bookstores, bars, cafés, magazines, and newspapers, providing much-needed social and cultural bases for gay lives and organizing. In the last few years, however, a new breed of entrepreneurs (both gay and straight) have begun to market products to lesbian, gay, and bisexual people that we could already buy in their mainstream forms, such as beer, credit cards, and long-distance telephone service. Do we owe either generation of gay businesses our economic loyalties in a positive reversal of consumer action via boycott?

If we use the criteria set out earlier, the first question is whether queer capitalism promotes our political goals. The early generation of gay and/or lesbian businesses had some direct and indirect political potential. Those businesses created meeting places that facilitated political organization and the spread of important ideas, news, and information to gay people, making the further development of gay, lesbian, and bisexual culture and politics possible. Many of the newer businesses' products are more economically than culturally based, but some companies offer to donate part of their profits to gay organizations, creating a positive potential financial impact for political efforts. (Without more research, I cannot tell how gay community-centered the new gay businesses are compared to the standard profit-seeking company, particularly in terms of developing an ethic of philanthropy and more socially responsible employment practices.)

Given that they all, in at least some way, contribute to the furthering of our political goals, why not sit back and let a thousand flowers bloom? In a market economy, of course that will happen. But the marketplace is dynamic, and successful gay businesses and products will attract the attention of mainstream capitalists, who are always looking for profit-making opportunities. We have seen this happen in both the retail and publishing end of the book business, for example, as the mainstream spills over into the tributaries nurtured by small gay and lesbian presses and bookstores: large publishers offer sizable advances for books targeted at gay communities, and chain bookstores have developed large lesbian and gay sections in stores located in gay neighborhoods. Even if this competition is fair, would we want to protect gay-owned or targeted businesses from cutthroat competitors since "our" businesses support our political activities, or should we just shop at the cheapest bookstore and find the cheapest credit card available and then donate our savings ourselves (the economically "rational" decision)?

Before directly answering that question, consider the implications for promoting queer capitalism with respect to the other criteria. By definition, a separatist economy is not well suited to coalition or bridge building. Even worse, an overemphasis on developing a gay economy would be internally divisive, placing lesbian, gay, and bisexual people with competing economic loyalties, such as those based on race, ethnicity, or gender, in a tricky position. Furthermore, access to capital and credit to start a new business varies significantly by race, wealth, and gender. A queer economy is thus likely to reproduce racial, gender, and class inequality.

Given that risk, it might seem that the sink or swim approach is best suited to gay businesses. But at this point, distinctions between products offered by gay-centered businesses become important, and the difference involves whether markets, without concerted economic action by gay people, would provide the kinds of goods and services that we need in the quantities we desire. Ideally, markets are supposed to supply the goods and services that consumers want; otherwise businesses have a profit-making opportunity available. If the rate of profit is not high enough, however, mainstream companies might not shift into a gay market, as when Time Inc. canceled plans for a magazine targeted at gays and lesbians, citing a lower than expected profit potential as the reason (Carmody 1994). But other publishers of gay magazines and newspapers, presumably lesbian, gay, or bisexual themselves, have accepted losses as well as profit rates far lower than the return that Time Inc. expected from its investment. In other words, some gay-targeted products and retail establishments (e.g., bars, bookstores, and publications) constitute a basic community infrastructure that might be worth protecting because they provide and preserve something better than what other mainstream companies could supply.

Lesbian, Gay, and Bisexual People as Investors

Another way of thinking about a decision to support some lesbian and gay businesses is as an investment in the economy and the community. In economic terms, investments involve giving up something now for some future return, and investors play an important role in any economy. Gay people also make economic investments in the financial sense, particularly through retirement and pension funds. That kind of investment was used effectively as a political tool in the anti-apartheid movement, and at least one gay and lesbian group, the Wall Street Project, is trying to use the collective shareholder clout of gay people and their allies to influence corporate policies, starting with Cracker Barrel (Patron 1991). Investment advisors provide information on the gay-friendliness of corporations to allow socially conscious investors to screen out companies with poor records on policies related to lesbian and gay employees (Sullivan "Investing in change" 1993).

Lesbian, gay, and bisexual people make many other decisions that could also be thought of as investments: having children, coming out, joining political groups, renovating homes, or creating families, to name a few of the bigger decisions. In a way, those decisions are both means to facilitate larger goals about how we want to live as well as the actual achievement of goals. Along with heterosexuals, we share the goal of a better future, whether it is for our kids or for future lesbian, gay, and bisexual people. This gives us numerous opportunities for building bridges and coalitions on a wide variety of concerns, from the quality of education to crime and violence in our country. Two mothers or two fathers going to a PTA meeting can create a revolution in the attitudes of straight parents. Perhaps the best example comes from openly lesbian or gay elected officials who must represent all their constituents, regardless of sexual orientation. Both in their campaigns and in office, those officials build links across issues and communities, bringing lesbian, gay, bisexual, and heterosexual people together on a very basic human level.

All of the economic roles seen in a basic description of a market obviously fit together more tightly than their separate presentations in this overview. And just as obviously, we do not have the power to completely define our economic identity on our own: too many others want to do it for us, whether they are profit-seeking companies, the media, or the right wing. We control the political strategies that we pursue, however, and we must use economics wisely. Promoting ourselves as producers and community investors is likely to result in the perception that we are more virtuous and socially upstanding than if we collaborate in a portrayal of ourselves as hedonistic consumers. Those identities as producers and investors provide us with potential ties to other groups and promote more human contact with heterosexuals. We can mobilize our power as consumers without taking on all the economic and cultural baggage that goes along with being identified primarily as consumers. We should use our economic power in whatever way is necessary, leveraging it in coalition with other groups and using it to reach out to others who must learn to see us as fully human. Our economic clout, broadly construed, goes far beyond the money in our pockets, and we can turn our economic power into political change.

Note

An earlier version of this essay was presented at "Homo/Economics: Market and Community in Lesbian and Gay Life," Center for Lesbian and Gay Studies (CLAGS), Graduate School, City University of New York, May 7, 1994. I thank Anne Habiby, Walter Williams, Lisa Moore, and Patricia Connelly for useful conversations.

References

Altman, D. 1982. *The Homosexualization of America.* New York: St. Martin's.
Badgett, M.V.L. 1994. Equal pay for equal families. *Academe,* May–June.
———. 1995. The wage effects of sexual orientation discrimination. *Industrial and Labor Relations Review* 48 (4).
Badgett, M.V.L., C. Donnelly, and J. Kibbe. 1992. Pervasive patterns of discrimination against lesbians and gay men: Evidence from surveys across the United States. Washington, DC: National Gay and Lesbian Policy Institute.

Carmody, D. 1994. Time Inc. shelves a gay magazine. *New York Times,* June 6, C7.

Corporate focus: Making Microsoft's meritocracy work. 1993. *Gay/Lesbian/Bisexual Corporate Letter* 2 (1): 3–6.

Elliott, S. 1994. A sharper view of gay consumers. *N.Y. Times,* June 9, D1.

Herek, G. M., and E. K. Glunt. 1993. Interpersonal contact and heterosexual's attitudes toward gay men: Results from a national survey. *Journal of Sex Research* 30 (3): 239–44.

Investing in change: New investment advisory letter targets gay-friendly growth stocks. 1993. *Gay/Lesbian/Bisexual Corporate Letter* 2 (2): 4.

Kennedy, E. L., and M. D. Davis. 1993. *Boots of leather, Slippers of Gold: The History of a Lesbian Community.* New York: Routledge.

Patron, E. J. 1991. Using money to make change. *Advocate,* December 17, 70–71.

Putnam, T. 1993. Boycotts are busting out all over. *Business and Society Review,* no. 85, 47–51.

Rigdon, J. E. 1991. Overcoming a deep-rooted reluctance, more firms advertise to gay community. *Wall Street Journal,* July 18, B1.

Shilts, R. 1982. *The Mayor of Castro Street.* New York: St. Martin's.

Snyder, A. 1991. Do boycotts work? *Adweek's Marketing Week* 32 (15): 16.

Sullivan, K. 1993. Firms rated on sexual politics: Policies toward gay, lesbian employees logged in database. *San Francisco Examiner,* September 9.

Veblen, T. 1934. *The theory of the leisure class.* New York: Modern Library.

Woods, J. D. 1993. *The corporate closet: The professional lives of gay men in America.* New York: Free Press.

36

Incorporating Social Identities into Economic Theory: How Economics Can Come Out of Its Closet of Individualism

Richard R. Cornwall

My desire,
More sharp than filed steel, did spur me forth
—Shakespeare, *Twelfth Night*

The concept of social structures is foreign to economic theory. Mainstream, neoclassical economics cannot even conceive of anything other than "individuals" mattering—the vocabulary of neoclassical theory has no word for any structures other than "individual actors" and "markets." Even analysis of unions and corporations fails to get past the view that such aggregations of individuals are simply groups or "teams" of individuals each seeking to pursue his/her own self-interest with little possibility for the natures of these people to be endogenously tied together as part of the operation of these entities. The extreme individualistic bias at the deepest roots of non-Marxian theory has caused serious errors and dead ends in many aspects of economic analysis. The following are two extremes:

1. The most abstract mathematical theory of rational expectations, which took very tentative steps in the 1960s and 1970s, briefly flourished and then collapsed like a hothouse flower gone mutant in the 1980s; this theory tried to incorporate notions that people make allowance now for future consequences of the actions of others, and ended up making absurd demands on the computational abilities of humans to evaluate *all* future contingencies.

2. The study of inequality in labor markets, begun by Gary Becker forty years ago, has been continued by a long line of economists, each striving to "prove" that markets diminish inequality, if only markets are not tampered with by governments; this hegemonic analysis takes as implicitly obvious that all individuals are "equal," that is, have equal freedom to perceive all their choice options, differing only by their inborn stocks of individualistic human capital/talents.

Marxian analyses, following Marx's insightful description of the economic origin of social structures, have usefully stressed the centrality of capital and labor markets in societies spanning many types of market organization. However, rigidly tying social structures to income markets has often seemed more confusing than enlightening when issues of social identity are being addressed. Even the world of the mid-nineteenth century in Europe looked significantly distorted through Marx's lenses when the gaze shifted from the struggles of wage-laborers to create a secure social niche for themselves in their struggles with capitalists. The role of the petit bourgeois, or as many of us now would say, people with significant amounts of (individualistically conceived) human capital, running their small businesses with their own labor (selling merchandise in shops, operating a medical or legal practice, or even running a church, school, political paper, etc.) has always been an add-on to the theory despite its insights on the role of ideology, insights that neoclassical, noninstitutionalist economists steadfastly ignore.

The potential significance of this omission of any way to analyze in depth the formation of social structures and how these change over time has been recognized by many people, from Bowles and Gintis (1986) to the political philosopher Elster (1989) and sociologists like Bielby (1991) and Coleman (1990). This essay describes a new approach to the foundations of economic theory that will permit modeling the rise and change of social identities, endogenous preferences, and the social construction of "rationality." The mixture here of voices and concepts from different disciplines is queer, and few may feel fluent in all these languages, yet this *Vermischung* seems essential to initiate a *queer* political economy, since much of the most insightful thinking about shame/abjection has been done not by political economists but by literary cultural analysts—as I hope to make clear. (The cultural analysis sketched here is developed further in Cornwall 1995b and the mathematical and politically economic strands are made explicit in Cornwall 1995a.)

Self/Social-Discovery Through Markets?

The hypothesis sparking my work is that newborn homo economicus is more like Mr. Magoo than like the fully programmed robot-person economists purport to describe. Thus I assume that people start out their market-lives as economic actors who are ignorant (in the closet) about their true desires. We are then led to make choices partly via our own experience and partly via reports from other people about what is "best."

To study this social articulation of desire, I have devised simulations of individuals who make consumption-work choices and who also choose "neighbors" with whom to compare notes about which alternatives are better and which are worse. I begin with a conceit popular in the previous two centuries and now deeply ingrained in economists' thinking: the solitary individual who confronts markets completely on her/his own. I then follow Cyert and DeGroot (1980), McFadden (1981, 205), McFadden and Richter (1990, 165), Arthur (1991), Marimon, McGrattan, and Sargent (1990), and Sargent (1993)[1] in imagining this solitary individual, Robinson Crusoe (or R. C. for short), as knowing her budget constraint but not her preferences and so making choices by intelligent randomness. Thus I draw R. C. here with the face of Mr. Magoo,[2] missing his glasses and groping quite blindly for insights as to where his goodies are. Since R. C. Magoo knows he does not know how to make himself feel good—what s/he *desires*—she decides to randomly sample among all her options to discover how they work.

As a starting point with which to compare my later results on the value of social interaction for individuals trying to discover their desires,[3] table 1 shows how long (measured by how many "shopping days," or iterations) it took for everyone to find their best choice. If R. C. Magoo is a hermit with no one to pool political information with, then in ten simulations it took R. C. on average 30.1 "days" to find his/her best choice. If he was in a pool of twenty people sharing information with each other on which choices he/they found inferior, he cut that number down to only five and a half days.

This reduction in how long it takes to figure out my "true" desires is valuable because I waste fewer days and resources fumbling with alternatives that turn out to be inferior. Thus there is a significant advantage to pooling information about which choices are inferior to some other choices. Even if allowance is made for the possibility that each of us might misestimate how "good" or "bad" our experience was when we made each choice, so that we measure our happiness/utility with possible error, the gains from pooling information about which choices are inferior to which other choices remain approximately the same.

This simple result is severely complicated if we leave the homopreference

TABLE 1

Gains Achieved When More People Pool Information about Rankings

Individuals in Pool	Iterations			
	Maximum	Minimum	Average	Simulations
1	32	26	30.1	10
2	18	16	16.6	5
5	9	9	9	2
10	8	7	7.5	2
20	6	5	5.5	1

world—where everyone interacting has the same (unknown) tastes. There is a big, new difficulty when we allow for the possibility that different people have different tastes—which is the only reason for anyone to bother describing "preferences" in models of economies. In this case, if I accept the report that choice j is better than choice k from someone whose tastes are different from mine (so that I actually prefer k to j but have not discovered this yet), and if I give this report from someone else full credibility and use it in the same way I used my own experience, I would drop option k from my list of possibilities for "best" and so would *never* discover that in fact k was better for me than j. In this case of heterogeneous tastes, the pool of information about rankings of alternative choices can get seriously contaminated: *all* of us can end up making a choice that fails to be "best" for *any* of us.

The judgments each person must make in order to articulate his/her own tastes are now much more subtle. A person must not only guess how much to adjust her guess of the probability that any particular choice is best, but must also

1. guess whether each other person has the same or different tastes as she does and then

2. use this guess to decide whether or not to make use of the person's reports on a certain choice being inferior in revising her own guesses of which choice is best.

The logic starts to resemble a multiply tied pretzel, like a Möbius strip, that one follows with one's eye rather than one's finger, but models of the social construction of the articulation of desire/perception seem inevitably to lead to such thoroughly queer complexity (I *think* he saw that I saw that he saw that . . .), whether in disentangling Robert Rauschenberg from Jasper Johns—with both surrounded by macho-in-extremis Willem de Kooning and Jackson Pollock[4]—or decoding Genet from Proust and Gide.

Because of this complexity, people can be thought of as searching for clues to help them distinguish which people have the same tastes they do and with whom they can trade information about inferior/superior choices. Imagine that in this silico-society (society-on-a-silicon-chip) there is a trait each person can use easily to distinguish other people, such as having a "0-Face" versus having a "1-Face" ("0" and "1" being "traits" my computer can easily distinguish). Imagine also that in this silico-society people *do* have different tastes—two-thirds of the people have Type 1 tastes and one-third have Type 2 tastes—but that there is *no correlation between a person's type of tastes and her/his Face.* Then it turns out that if each person uses conventional statistical procedures to test whether s/he can use the trait "Face" to separate people with tastes that are apparently similar to hers from people with tastes apparently different from hers, then, in ten different simulations, the variable Face *appeared* to be a significant indicator (at the 5 percent significance level) of different tastes in 70 percent of the trials (with this percentage ranging from a low of 60 percent to a high of 87 percent in the ten simulations) even though there was actually no connection between a person's tastes and that person's Face.

A false correlation of a variable like "Face" with some other trait that in reality has no connection with Face can be called an "illusory correlation." Because people are persuaded that such an irrelevant variable as Face is helpful in their efforts to articulate their own desires through swapping information with others about which choices are better or worse, everyone can end up choosing her/his network of "friends" by excluding anyone who differs from her/himself in the variable Face. This gives a biased construction of networks that we each use to articulate our desires, networks I call *homopreference networks*.

In the ten simulations conducted, the consequence of reliance on an illusory trait was that approximately one-third (eleven out of thirty) of the people with the minority type of preferences were led into the "closet," that is, they were led to articulate a choice as being best for them that was, in fact, significantly different from what was best for them. Only one out of sixty of the people with the majority type of preferences made such an error. Further, this misarticulation of desire occurred in all ten of the simulations. This mistaken attribution of one's own tastes is what economists call pareto inefficient: it was socially feasible, in each case where someone chose as "best" a choice that was in fact inferior to another choice for this person, to rearrange this person's work-consumption combination so this person would end up better off and so no one else was affected at all.

These simple simulations lead to the conjecture that cognitive codes (e.g., different Face means different tastes) might evolve socially as people endeavor to distinguish others with the same tastes from those with different tastes in order to form homopreference networks to aid in the articulation of their desires. This evolution of shared cognitive codes is analogous to the sociologically nuanced development of linguistic variation and is akin to William Burroughs's claim that "language is a virus" (Ricco 1994, 76).[5]

This conjecture can be extended: the growth of these cognitive codes might generate structures known as "social identities," which are simply the labels that come, like game theory's focal points, to distinguish homopreference networks and that, like sociolinguistic structures, are ambiguously bordered-from/overlapping-with each other as well as being both very durable and rather plastic. When seen as a social solution to the problem of how do individuals know what they desire, these codes can be seen to be institutional "social-software" coordinating the "parallel processing" of experience by multiple individuals, which, in turn, saves people enormously in the time required to articulate their desires. This social articulation of cognitive codes, which in this model are based on the networked evolution of each person's probabilities of who is different-from-me/same-as-me, corresponds to what Dollimore (1991, 244) meant when he wrote that "identity—individual and cultural—involves a process of disavowal."

It is important to stress that this extremely simplistic and essentialist model is presented in this section *not* to offer, by itself, a model of real economies; rather, this model aims to make tangible a deep, specific criticism of neoclassical economics: The outcomes obtained with perfectly competitive market-guided economies can be ensured to have the rather minimally desirable property of not being *unanimously* judged inferior to some other allocation of tasks and consumptions (i.e., the property of being pareto efficient) *only* if the participants know their true preferences. I argue that a more useful model for political economy is that

1. we enter the world blind like Magoo about our own desires;
2. our understanding—articulation—of our desires is largely determined by the social structures in which we are ensnared;
3. important social forces of political economy mold these social structures.

We turn next to analyses of our use and formation of categories for perception and then sketch some of the forces of political economy shaping these categories.

Cognitive Processes Enabling the Social Articulation of Desire: Categories and (Illusory) Correlations

I use the phrase *socially articulated desires* to describe the process by which humans in groups categorize each other in order to recognize/express/act on their desires. This *articulation* involves both

- breaking humanity into distinct pieces, that is, forming categories for distinguishing people according to some traits; and
- joining these pieces together, that is, recognizing that society includes these different types.

To understand how we form categories we must look at human inference: how do we know? This invites epistemological complexity, but I choose queerly, instead, to follow Wittgenstein in assuming a sociolinguistic basis of "ordinary language" for "knowing" what we know.[6] Cognitive psychology has, in the last twenty years, made significant progress in mapping many contours of how individuals perceive (and also fail to perceive), encode, store, retrieve, and then express/act on perceptions. "The view that categories are invariably defined by a set of necessary and sufficient conditions for membership has by now been thoroughly discredited" (Holland et al. 1986, 182). Instead of such a discredited "positivist" epistemological approach, Wittgenstein in philosophy and Berlin and Kay (1969) in linguistics, suggested that a more useful mental model is that we form categories on the basis of prototypes and we have quite ambiguous boundaries between categories.[7]

This process for forming social categories can be thought of as the elevation of an instance of one person doing/being something into an archetype. The central metaphor/analogy here is:

figure out a problem = figuration (put a face on the problem)

The etymological roots of this linguistic associative code in English are the Latin *(figura)* and French *(la figure)* words for face. The centrality of the human face extends to more abstract domains: save face, lose face, I can't face that issue now, the buildings are face-to-face,—and so forth. The preference for the use of facial prototypes over abstract categorization may be a mere statistical regularity, as hinted in the previous section, or may be deeply embedded within our operating systems (e.g., limbic systems) of our cognitive software and hardware; that is, within the amygdala.[8] Such figuration may be supplemented only when we have had powerfully salient experience through the use of abstract categories rather than faces.

This suggests that the equation prosopopoeia = give-a-face-to/figuration-of/description by a *figure-of-speech* may be more than mere metaphor for human categorization and induction. This conjecture of a central role in human cognition for facial images is strengthened by "growing" evidence that

1. "The amygdala has a central role in social communication. . . . The direction of one's gaze signals the object of one's attention . . . while facial expression indicates how one is disposed to behave. When mutual eye contact is established, both participants know that the communication loop between them has been closed and for primates of all species this is the most potent of social situations" (Allman and Brothers 1994, 613–14).

2. Cognitive access to facial images appears to be "effortless," "a rapid, automated process" and more accurate than are "deliberative, analytic retrieval processes"; for example, sorting, matching, and elimination (Dunning and Stern 1994, 819, 832; Wells, Rydell, and Seelau 1993).

Making the blatant leap of applying this conjecture about human induction to socially mediated categorization, one may be tempted to consider the "sex/gender system" (Rubin 1975), which, from our vantage, appears to have been hegemonic until approximately the end of the last century. It was taken for granted, as "natural,"[9] that sexual object preference was determined by gender: "In the dominant turn-of-the-century cultural system governing the interpretation of homosexual behavior, especially in working-class milieus, one had a gender identity rather than a sexual identity or even a 'sexuality'; one's sexual behavior was thought to be necessarily determined by one's gender identity" (Chauncey 1994, p 48).[10] In other words, gender was determined by the dichotomy of "male" versus "female" face, and this also determined sexual object choice.

The turn of the century was a time not only of increasing urbanization in this country, but also of radical changes in the roles and extent of markets and the organization of production. The rise of wage labor in this country occurred first for men after the first third of the nineteenth century but was followed at the end of the century by dramatic changes for women as wage labor became not mono-gender but gendered and segregated. For example, at the turn of the century bank tellers switched amazingly quickly from an all-male occupation to a predominantly female category.[11] Further and equally momentous was the rise of factories with thousands of workers under one roof, which led to enormous social upheaval as new codes and occupations for imagining/running productive enterprises were developed.[12]

This blender of changing social roles created a vortex of changing social identities:

> Working-class men and boys regularly challenged the authority of middle-class men by verbally questioning the manliness of middle-class supervisors or physically attacking middle-class boys ... [One contemporary] recalled, he had "often seen [middle-class cultivation] taken by those [men] of the lower classes as 'sissy.' " The increasingly militant labor movement, the growing power of immigrant voters in urban politics, and the relatively high birthrate of certain immigrant groups established a worrisome context for such personal affronts and in themselves constituted direct challenges to the authority of Anglo-American men as a self-conceived class, race and gender. (Chauncey 1994, 112)

These struggles over where to map key social borders led

> politicians, businessmen, educators, and sportsmen alike [to protest] the dangers of "overcivilization" to American manhood. The glorification of the prizefighter and the workingman bespoke the ambivalence of middle-class men about their own gender status ... a "cult of muscularity" took root in turn-of-the-century middle-class culture.... Earlier in the nineteenth century, men had tended to constitute themselves as men by distinguishing themselves from boys.... But in the late nineteenth century, middle-class men began to define themselves more centrally on the basis of their difference from women.... gender-based terms of derision [e.g., sissy, pussy-foot] became increasingly prominent in late-nineteenth-century American culture (Chauncey 1994, 113–4)

This oversimplifies and ignores counterpressures to cover gender distinctions (e.g., Vicinus 1992 and Matthaei 1995), but this recoding of masculinity seems to have been powerful at this time.

Closely tied to this redefinition of "male"[13] in the 1890s was a redefinition of class:

> men and women of the urban middle class increasingly defined themselves as a class by the boundaries they established between the "private life" of the home and the rough-and-tumble of the city streets, between the quiet order of their neighborhoods and the noisy, overcrowded character of the working-class districts. The privacy and order of their sexual lives also became a way of defining their difference from the lower classes. (Chauncey 1994, 35)

Just as a new "face" was being put on not-male, that is, not-male became "female" instead of "boy," so "middle-class" became "clean-face-and-well-laundered/mended-clothes" versus the "dirty" faces of slums. A quickly judged face was put on people living in slums:

> The spatial segregation of openly displayed "vice" in the slums had . . . ideological consequences: it kept the most obvious streetwalkers out of middle-class neighborhoods, and it reinforced the association of such immorality with the poor. . . . Going slumming in the resorts of the Bowery and the Tenderloin was a popular activity among middle-class men (and even among some women), in part as a way to witness working-class "depravity" and to confirm their sense of superiority. (Chauncey 1994, 26)[14]

This simultaneous (re)definition of gender, class, and occupations spilled over, "infected," the definition of sexual orientation that was occurring at the turn of the century:

> In a culture in which becoming a fairy meant assuming the status of a woman or even a prostitute, many men . . . simply refused to do so. . . . The efforts of such men marked the growing differentiation and isolation of sexuality from gender in middle-class American culture. . . . The effort to forge a new kind of homosexual identity was predominantly a middle-class phenomenon, and the emergence of "homosexuals" in middle-class culture was inextricably linked to the emergence of "heterosexuals" in the culture as well. If many workingmen thought they demonstrated their sexual virility by playing the "man's part" in sexual encounters with either women or men, normal middle-class men increasingly believed that their virility depended on their exclusive sexual interest in women. Even as queer men began to define their difference from other men on the basis of their homosexuality, "normal" men began to define their difference from queers on the basis of their renunciation of any sentiments or behavior that might be marked as homosexual. (Chauncey 1994, 100)

Further, "the queers' antagonism toward the fairies was in large part a *class* antagonism. . . . the cultural stance of the queer embodied the general middle-class preference for privacy, self-restraint, and lack of self-disclosure" (Chauncey 1994, 106).

This tendency to label as "invidious" certain traits and to tie these traits to other categories is an example of errors that are typical in human categorization of both our physical environments and our social environments as we induce categories to use in sorting who is appropriate for our homopreference networks to articulate our desires. It is hard to overemphasize the enormity of the changes in the working and living conditions of most Western humans as industrial society emerged in the last century. For many people, especially those migrating from rural life, previous articulations of desires simply lacked categories to express what they were experiencing: migrating from living and working with kinfolk, typically in rural or small-town settings, to wage labor, sometimes in the new (for this millennium) institution of factories and changing fertility, all of which were engendered by and simultaneously caused reduced costs of transportation and communication—as well as more superficial changes like new commodities for consumption. This significant acceleration of the velocity of social change in the industrial era appears likely to have heightened the need for new institutions to articulate desires. This need, cutting to the heart of what it is to be human, may have contributed to perceptual errors caused by the use of new illusory variables.

It is especially notable to students of queer disciplines that the seminal as well as nomenclatory work on the phenomenon of "illusory correlation" was based on the discovery of false correlations between homosexuality and other traits. Loren Chapman and Jean Chapman (1967, 1969; Chapman 1967)[15] surveyed several dozen clinical psychologists as to which Rorschach signs they believed distinguished their gay male clients from their straight male clients. Of those surveyed, thirty-two clinicians "said that they had seen the Rorschach protocols of a number of men with homosexual problems [*sic*]" (1969, 273). The Chapmans concluded that

1. The "popularity" of signs [as indicators of homosexuality] among practicing clinicians has little relationship to the objective clinical validity of the signs. . . .

2. The most popular signs among practicing clinicians are the ones that have the strongest verbal associative connection to male homosexuality.

3. Naive observers, when presented with contrived Rorschach responses arbitrarily paired with statements of symptoms of the patient who gave each response, erroneously report observing that these same [verbally] associatively based invalid signs occur as correlates of homosexuality.

4. The naive observers report these [verbally] associatively based illusory correlations even when the materials are contrived so that other (clinically) valid correlations are present.

This work by the Chapmans has been replicated in many other scenarios where the items to be differentiated vary quite significantly and include perceptions of race and gender. Hamilton and Gifford (1976) emphasized that distinctive *and* infrequent traits often are mistakenly correlated (this is termed "paired distinctiveness"), which they conjecture is done as a simplification of the encoding process. However, as noted by Fiske and Taylor (1991, 373–76) in their good, brief overview of research on illusory correlation: "Despite the apparent importance of associate meaning [i.e., connections based merely on associations in everyday language through word-pairings: bacon and eggs or lion and tiger in contrast to the pair tiger and eggs] in stereotype-based illusory correlation effects, the majority of research has focused on paired distinctiveness."

This bias by researchers to look at a more technical variant of illusory correlation is especially striking since, although the Chapman's original work did find evidence of a role for paired distinctiveness (based on one pair of words getting illusorily paired by subjects apparently just because they were longer than all the other words even though they in fact occurred together no more often than any of the other pairs), they stressed much more (and their two later papers looked exclusively at) what they called associative connection. Thus Holland et al.'s emphasis on "prior rules" created by "semantic association" seems to be a useful and welcome insight into the origin of cognitive codes (what psychologists call "schemata").[16]

Recently, Hamilton and Sherman (1989) have been exploring other factors besides relative infrequency that can cause traits and groups to be distinctive. Among these characteristics are "self-relevance." Getting sexually high is an affective characteristic of some behavior that many humans want to be self-relevant. This leads to the conjecture that, in addition to linguistic associations, sexuality is a prime candidate for illusory correlation because of its *affective* distinctiveness, which, in turn, leads to overestimates of the frequency of queerly motivated behavior and of queer people and to the power and credibility of charges of being queer.[17]

How, one might ask, can sexual orientation be construed to be a "readily available cue" to illusorily correlate with other traits and, hence, to use for stereotyping? The intensity of the affect associated with sexual orientation leads many to pay very close attention to any clues. For example, many men, both straight and gay, are familiar with the situation experienced by Essex Hemphill at age fourteen (1992, 100):

> Crip was standing. I was sitting. It happened that from where I sat I could eye his crotch with a slight upward shift of my eyes. Well, one of the times that I peeked, Crip caught me. . . . Instantly, Crip jumped forward and got in my face. "I see you looking at my dick!" he hurled at me. I felt as though he had accused me of breaking into his house and violating his mother. Immediately, all conversation ceased and all eyes focused on me and Crip.

Hemphill survived this humiliation without getting beaten up and limped home to shut himself in his room as soon as he could break away. He learned to survive through high school by getting a girlfriend, a "good girl," who did not want to fuck.

This story highlights the role played by watching another's gaze (via our amygdalas) in making sexual orientation distinctive and suggests why sexual orientation might be a trait used in making illusory correlations that then serve as the base for the intensely believed cognitive codes underlying homophobia.[18] Feeling sexually aroused is one of the most intense affects humans ever experience. This may make distinctive anything associated with this affect, such as sexual orientation. This is somewhat similar to the tendency of European-male-dominated American culture to label African Americans outsiders by smearing both Black men and women as "hypersexual"[19] and may also be linked to the rise of the dichotomy of saint versus slut (nonsexual versus sexual) that was socially constructed for European American women in the second half of the last century.[20]

To recap: How do we know what we know—*or feel,* or *desire?* Our perceptions depend on the cognitive categories with which we articulate (i.e., perceive and express) our desires/"knowledge," and these categories have been created through the particular dynamics of the social networks we each have been in since birth. A survey of work by psychologists, sociologists, historians, philosophers, sociolinguists, and others has led to the conclusion that Wittgenstein's "ordinary language" plays an enormously important role in shaping how people induce social categories with which to perceive others and that these categories end up resembling prosopopoeic categories based on central archetypal *figures*. This use of archetypes renders this process surprisingly agile compared to other algorithms one might imagine constructing to invent categories, but also renders it very susceptible to making false—illusory—correlations of human traits.

It is important to make concrete how the false articulation of desires modeled in the first section might actually occur in our social world, how reliance on a particular social network—neighbors from a particular class and/or gender with whom to discover what choices are best for oneself—can lead one to fail to recognize one's own true preferences, for example, that one's erotic desires are overwhelmingly stronger toward people of the same sex rather than the other sex. As Bray (1982, 67–68) noted in his attempt to make comprehensible the behavior of some people in the sixteenth and seventeenth centuries at the time of the erasure of the articulation of queer.

> The individual could simply avoid making the connection; he could keep at two opposite poles the social pressures bearing down on him and his own discordant sexual behaviour, and avoid recognizing it for what it was. . . . For when one looks at the circumstantial details of how homosexuality was conceived of and how it was expressed in concrete social forms, it becomes obvious how very easy it was in Renaissance England—far more so than today—for a cleavage of this kind to exist, between an individual's behaviour and his awareness of its significance. Firstly the way homosexuality was conceived of: how possible was it to avoid identifying with the "sodomite" who was the companion of witches and Papists, of werewolves and agents of the King of Spain? When the world inhabited by the conventional image of the sodomite was so distant from everyday life, it cannot have been hard.

This quote captures well the importance of one's social network for influencing what one *can* think: "individuals prosecuted for sodomy did not necessarily identify themselves with the demonized sodomite of official discourse" (Dollimore 1991, 239). The sense of being socially of such a different caste if one were queer made it impossible for many to so position themselves in their internal cognitive maps of themselves in social space, both for many in Renaissance England and likewise for people maturing in the McCarthy-polluted 1950s. Anecdotal evidence suggests that this generation had more difficulty recognizing same-sex desire in themselves than did either those growing up before the Depression or those reaching maturity in the late 1960s, especially after Stonewall.

A useful parallel to the 1950s in the United States, which followed the two queer panics described in the following section, might be the pre–World War I period in England following the queer panic produced by the trial of Oscar Wilde. These were both times of dramatic queer cultural innovation (e.g., the Bloomsbury group's writing, painting, and historicizing in England, and Ginsberg-Burroughs-Kerouac's writing, Rauschenberg-Johns's painting, and Tennessee Williams's playwriting in the United States) and also of the dramatic social repression of queer. The ability to not articulate one's queerness in such a setting was captured well by that straddler of this sexual divide, D. H. Lawrence, writing in the suppressed prologue to *Women in Love:*

> the male physique had a fascination for him, and for the female physique he felt only a fondness . . . as for a sister. In the street it was the men who roused him by their flesh and their manly, vigorous movement. . . . He loved his friend, the beauty of whose manly limbs made him tremble with pleasure. He wanted to caress him. But reserve, which was as strong as a chain of iron in him, kept him from any demonstration. And if he were away for any length of time from the man he loved so hotly, then he forgot him. . . . He wondered very slightly at this, but dismissed it with hardly a thought. Yet every now and again, would come over him the same passionate desire to have near him some man he saw. . . . It might be any man. . . . How vividly, months afterwards, he would recall the soldier who had sat pressed up close to him on a journey from Charing Cross to Westerham. . . . [o]r a young man in flannels on the sands at Margate. . . . In his mind was a small gallery of such men: men whom he had never spoken to, but who had flashed themselves *upon* his senses unforgettably, men whom he apprehended intoxicatingly in his blood. . . . This was the one and only secret he kept to himself, this secret of his passionate and sudden, spasmodic affinity for men he saw. *He kept this secret even from himself.* He knew what he felt, but he always kept the knowledge at bay. (Lawrence 1981, 103–7, emphasis added)[21]

We have thus far developed one story for the use of prosopopoeia—of faces-as-archetypes—as the basis for our induction of social categories and of the role our social networks can play in this articulation of categories. This suggests that political and social dynamics may powerfully influence this social articulation of cognitive codes, an idea to which we now turn and which is, of course, the heart of queer political economy.

Ideology Entrepreneurs

Academic analysis of the Chapmans' work on illusory correlations has ignored the central role homosexuality played in American culture—in shaping the cognitive structures (semantic associations) of all the participants in this work. What makes this scholarly blindness so ironic is that the Chapmans' discovery was based on an "associative connection" enormously amplified by two "illusory" correlations of homosexuality with other socially feared traits—that is, two queer panics—of which they and all subsequent commentators present themselves as being blithely unaware and which transformed homosexuality from an exotic, possibly deplorable, or possibly intriguing attribute (prior to the 1930s) into the worst, most "salient" human characteristic, bar none, in the 1950s-60s, when the Chapmans did their work.

During the queer panic in the 1930s, the previously flourishing and widely known gay culture was pushed underground into invisibility. Yet

> the homosexual hardly disappeared from public view ... for police bulletins and press coverage continued to make him [*sic*] a prominent, but *increasingly sinister*, figure. As America anxiously tried to come to terms with the disruptions in the gender and sexual order caused by the Depression and exacerbated by the Second World Wan, the "sex deviant" became a symbol of the dangers posed by family instability, gender confusion, and unregulated male sexuality and violence. A number of children's murders in the late 1930s and the late 1940s, sensationalized by the local and national press and interpreted as sexual in nature by the police fanned a series of panics over sex crime. (Chauncey 1994, 359, emphasis added)

Another queer panic occurred in 1950 when, in tandem, fear of Communism was growing.

> [A] chance revelation by a State Department official during congressional hearings on the loyalty of government employees led to the entanglement of homosexuality in the politics of domestic anticommunism. Facing sharp interrogation by members of the Senate Appropriations Committee, Under Secretary John Peurifoy testified on February 28, 1950, that most of the ninety-one employees dismissed for *moral turpitude* were homosexuals. ... In the succeeding months, the danger posed by "sexual perverts" became a staple of partisan rhetoric. Senator Joseph McCarthy ... charged that an unnamed person in the State Department had forced the reinstatement of a homosexual despite the threat to the nation's safety. (D'Emilio 1983b, 41, emphasis added)

> Stricter enforcement of sanctions accompanied the attacks in print. From 1947 through April 1, 1950, when the sexual pervert issue arose, dismissals of homosexuals from civilian posts in the executive branch had averaged five per month. ... In its first sixteen months of operation, the Eisenhower program [which explicitly made "sexual perversion" sufficient grounds for disbarment from federal jobs] removed homosexuals from government at a rate of forty per month. ... Many more individuals never made it on to the federal payroll, since all applicants for government employment faced security investigations. ... States and municipalities followed the lead of the federal government in demanding from their personnel not only loyalty but traditional moral probity as well. (D'Emilio 1983b, 44–46)

Thus the first illusory correlation above tied homosexuality to sex crimes; the second amplified this hysteria by tying homosexuality to a threat to national security—a risk hard to imagine in the 1990s, when the "Evil Empire" appears totally vanquished and when the then amazingly vivid and imminent 1950s fear of atomic attack has almost totally disappeared. To understand the astounding reversal in social codes that occurred from 1930 to 1960, a seismic shift whose magnitude may well be impossible to imagine for those growing up hearing songs about a detachable penis and fistfucking, we must try to imagine 1930, when the pansy was at least as trendy as queer is now in alternative music mosh pits, New Year's Eve Exotic Erotic Balls, and so forth. Lillian Faderman (1991, esp. ch. 2), Jonathan Weinberg (1993), and George Chauncey (1994 chaps. 8–11), among others, make evident that during the 1920s a gay culture—ranging from a wide variety of baths to art, music, and Broadway shows—grew up with close connections to, and immediately succeeding, that previous modish curiosity in upscale New York, the Harlem Renaissance.

With the onset of Prohibition (enforcement under the Volstead Act beginning in 1920), this queer trend was amplified, since the "economic pressures Prohibition put on the hotel industry by depriving it of liquor-related profits . . . led some of the second-class hotels in the West Forties [of Manhattan] to begin permitting prostitutes and the speakeasies to operate out of their premises" (Chauncey 1994, 305). Further, the "speakeasies, [social reformers] feared, were dissolving the distinctions between middle-class respectability and working-class licentiousness that had long been central to the ideological self-representation of the middle class" (Chauncey 1994, 307).

It is noteworthy that much of the evolution of queer culture has been (partially inadvertently) promoted by conventional profit-seeking entrepreneurs operating small taverns, prostitution and so forth (e.g., Weeks 1979, 42; D'Emilio 1983a). But this story of the manufacture of these two pivotal illusory correlations manifests a different type of entrepreneur, one whose central roles have been detailed by numerous sociologists (just two: Michel Foucault and David Greenberg [1988]) but who has hitherto had no essential role in political economy generally, and certainly not in mainstream economics. This is the *ideology entrepreneur,* an undertaker of ventures of some personal risk and some possible personal gain—though not necessarily pecuniary gain—to reshape the margin by amplifying parts and suppressing other parts of existing cognitive codes and, occasionally, adding new inventions to existing codes.[22] This may be done somewhat unconsciously, or at least indirectly, in order to expand the entrepreneur's access to economic and other social opportunities, or it may be done with a conscious ideological goal. Further, this ideological effort may succeed or may fail to be incorporated by others in their unconscious cognitive codes.[23]

Examples of such entrepreneurship abound, but it suffices to cite a few that are relevant to the incidents described above:

1. "Joseph Pulitzer's *World* and William Randolph Hearst's *Journal* pioneered in those years a new style of journalism that portrayed itself as the nonpartisan defender (and definer) of the 'public interest,' waged campaigns on behalf of moral and municipal reform, and paid extravagant attention to local crimes, high-society scandals, and the most 'sensational' aspects of the urban underworld" (Chauncey 1994, 39).

2. "The Committee of Fifteen . . . [was] established in 1900 to suppress

female prostitution in New York's saloons (131–32). . . . The social-purity activists were also keen to prevent the violation of racial boundaries, which they imagined inevitably had a sexual element (139). . . . only twenty-two sodomy prosecutions occurred in New York City in the nearly eight decades from 1796 to 1873. The number of prosecutions increased dramatically in the 1880s, however. By the 1890s, fourteen to thirty-eight men were arrested *every year* for sodomy or the 'crime against nature.' Police arrested more than 50 men annually in the 1910s . . . and from 75 to 125 every year in the 1920s. . . . much of [the dramatic increase in arrests] stemmed from the efforts of the Society for the Prevention of Cruelty to Children, which involved itself in the cases of men suspected of sodomy with boys. The moral-reform societies' perception that [World War I] had precipitated an increase in 'perversion' in the city led them to focus on homosexual vice—and on homosexuals—as a discrete social problem for the first time (145). . . . in 1934 the [Hollywood] studios established an independent Production Code Administration, which enforced the ban for another thirty years [i.e., a prohibition on] . . . any reference whatsoever to homosexuality, or 'sex perversion' [even though it] . . . allowed the depiction of adultery, murder, and a host of other immoral practices" (353).[24]

3. " 'Degenerate disorderly conduct' . . . was the charge usually brought against gay men or lesbians found gathering on the streets or in public accommodations, or gay men trying to pick up other men. . . . In the course of its general revision of the statute in 1923, the New York state legislature, for the first time, specified homosexual solicitation . . . as a form of disorderly conduct. . . . Even the statutes against sodomy and the crime against nature, which dated from the colonial era, had criminalized a wide range of nonprocreative sexual behavior . . . without specifying male homosexual conduct or even recognizing it as a discrete sexual category" (172). "The ruling allowed bars to be patronized by homosexuals, but only so long as they did nothing to *indicate* they were homosexuals because it allowed the Liquor Authority to rule that any behavior coded as homosexual was ipso facto disorderly" (343).[25]

4. "Doctors [in the late nineteenth century] were not simply speaking up when called upon; they were actively seeking to shape society's control apparatus. Why this new involvement? Physicians came primarily from the middle class and would have shared the general sexual ideology of that class." (Greenberg 1988, 401).

These four examples illustrate the diverse type and "motives" of ideology entrepreneurs. Joseph Pulitzer and William Randolph Hearst were choosing market niches they apparently thought were more profitable than the alternatives they gave up to pursue the type of journalism they practiced. The social purity activists were, in many cases at least, pursuing ethical goals at some possible pecuniary cost to themselves. The legislators in New York who first made simple association of gay men together into "disorderly conduct" were also quite likely not seeking financial gain from this directly, though they may well have sought personal gain similar to that sought by Joseph McCarthy in the U.S. Senate in the early 1950s and by the national chairperson of the Republican Party in 1948, Guy Gabrielson, who sent seven thousand party workers a newsletter "alerting them to the new 'homosexual angle' in Washington warning [that] sexual perverts . . . have infiltrated our Government in recent years' . . . and they were 'perhaps as dangerous as the actual Communists.' " (D'Emilio 1983b, 41). Finally, the actions of the doctors (as well as numerous other new "helping" professions in the late 1800s and early 1900s) could, in many instances, have plausibly been motivated by a wish to promote "professional standards" rather than any immediate pecuniary purpose. These are not dissimilar from the ideologically entrepreneurial efforts of Western churchpeople, especially at the end of feudal times.

What appears significant about these diverse types of social ideological entrepreneurship serving to mold our cognitive codes is that

1. they often seem not to reflect monopolistic collusions of economic actors; and

2. coercive governmental actions (e.g., by Senator McCarthy or the State Liquor Authority) may arise more as rather belated responses to the social codes arising from voluntary—even, in part, libertarian—human interaction (e.g., journalism, the Committee of Fifteen, the SPCC, doctors).

Aside from environmental-pollution/epidemic "externalities," the conventional ways for both popular *and* professional economists now to conceptualize how social welfare is impaired is to appeal to

1. thinness of markets leading to distortion caused by monopolistic interaction, or

2. rent-seeking "special-interest" interference with "unbiased" government regulation and protection of property rights.

But the concept of social cognitive codes suggests that social welfare can be impaired in a new way: misleading conflations and oversimplifications in the cognitive categorizations voluntarily, but often unconsciously, adopted by people and through which they perceive, think about, and act in the world. These conflations—such as, for example, the illusory correlations illustrated simplistically in the first section—are encouraged by an aesthetics-of-simplicity for how we write our mental software, an idea called by Barbara Ponse (1978, 24–30) "the principle of consistency."

Resisting Extreme Individualism

My central thesis is that the loss of individuality in "homo"-desire is central to each individual's articulation of desire. In fact, I conjecture that this penetration of the social into the "deepest," innermost parts of the individual through the articulation of "homo"-desire is as close to a universal human phenomenon as we could imagine having the arrogance to assert. This is not characteristic only of queers, though, as John Paul Ricco (1993) has captured so well in describing the "minor architecture" of jack-off rooms, we may experience this penetration of the social into the individual especially clearly: in jack-off rooms: "individuals, as bodies-of-desire, forfeit their individual subjective selves as they are reconstituted as parts of a collective assemblage" (239).

Closely related to Ricco's assertion is Judith Butler's suggestion that performative mimetism—"Other in the self"—"constitute[s] desire" (1991, 26). Such mingling of selves is, of course, familiar if one has looked at love across other socially constructed boundaries: "love across the racial divide . . . is thoroughly public, saturated with social and political meanings. . . . the image [of interracial couples] comes to stand for a fact that none of us has any notion what to do with: the fact that each of us is a part of the other, that we are so unalterably tainted by a messy and heartbreaking history that any claim to purity or separation becomes insupportably fragile" (Scott 1994, 316–17).

This irony of the loss of individuality through the struggle to assert one's individuality by articulating her/his own desires is close to Genet's finding beauty in the *betrayal* of individual distinctness and in merger/murder/death consummating love/orgasm.[26] Indeed, *Funeral Rites* is an orgy of Genet's signifying the *in*significance of the particular person, a rite celebrating the funeral of "the individual," with its repeated, often disconcerting shifts in voice and in the frequent avowals that Jean (Genet?—he plays on an ambiguity of *who* Jean is) *writes* himself. Genets's very self-conscious articulation-of-self and his identification of writing himself/ourselves with social construction is the epitome of Oscar Wilde's "individualism as . . . 'disobedience [which] . . . is man's original virtue.' . . . There comes to be a close relationship between crime and individualism" (Dollimore 1991, 8; inner quote from Wilde 1990, 4).

Queer art, from Stéphane Dupré to Paul Stanley and David Sprigle and from Barbara Hammer to Isaac Julien in film, is driven by a post/modern awareness that makes ambiguous modernist boundaries between individuals. Steven Arnold, especially, captures with human bodies the aesthetic of isolation/merging, flowers, erections, crucifixes, and death that Genet inscribed on our queer minds.[27] As in mosh pits, there is a clear opposition to the "possessive individualism" "in which individuals are defined primarily as proprietors of their fleshy incarnation, who are consequently entitled to rights only as the owners of themselves."[28]

This ideology of the total separateness of each "rational," freely-choosing-at-all-times individual from each other, splendidly isolated by her/his libertarian shield of property rights,[29] in fact arose along with the social construction of the sanctity of property rights in the sixteenth and seventeenth centuries (coinciding with the social death of ganymedians). This evolution is the central ideological component to what is arguably the most significantly sociological innovation of the last millennium: the rise from mere social niche to social dominance of market guidance/discipline of people.[30]

Thus we are led to conclude that the roles of "ideology" are much more central to cognition, and hence to political economy, than even Marx imagined.[31] This is not mere "superstructure," frosting on the basic productive/technological relations of labor inputs to other inputs that ultimately determine the social relations of production;[32] rather, "ideology" describes the deepest patterning of human mental software and, in turn, our mental hardware.[33]

The preceding discussion suggests that the idea underlying much public policy discourse that people can "freely choose" to do or not do things would better be replaced with notions of contingent choice by individuals: each person's discovery and expression of what s/he desires is likely to be very dependent on this individual using some notion of "the other" (who has a Face different from mine). The discussion in the second and third sections gave examples of how this limitation on free choice by individuals led people to fail to percieve their sexual orientations and also contributed to recodifications of gender, class, and race in the United States.

Epilogue

Descartes's epigram *cogito ergo sum* has come to signify "Enlightenment" modernist thinking. I juxtapose instead the phrase *desidero ergo sum*.[34] This captures the post/modern notion that we, like Shakespeare's Antonio[35] and like all living organisms (birds, ants, trees, and viruses) exist in the richness of our social structures/identities because of our *desires,* and a significant goal for social disciplines, as well as for physical sciences, is to increase our understanding of the social articulation of desire.

Notes

This essay has been revised to take account of some advances I have made since presenting it at CLAGS in the spring of 1994. It is dedicated to the honor of Alan Turing and John Maynard Keynes, whose sharply contrasting social positions as intellectuals figure well the distinct possibilities for queers described here. Alan Turing's achievements birthing computers enabled the silicon simulations at the heart of this essay, and the forces I seek to conceptualize likely contributed to his death. Maynard Keynes's queer interest in arts *and* economics (see Escoffier 1995) inspire the disciplinary *Vermischung* here. I want to acknowledge sabbatical support by Middlebury College as well as access as a research associate to facilities at the University of California at Berkeley, which enabled me to conduct this queer research intensively in the Bay Area and so to recover from years of near asphyxiation in the intense heterosexism at Middlebury College and, indeed, in all of Vermont. While I was at Middlebury, my breathing was occasionally pushed above water by visits to CLAGS, early research assistance from Jeff Spencer, and supportive reactions of a number of people to my earlier efforts to endogenize the world, which they thoughtfully refrained from pointing out were a bit inadequate. These people include Lee Badgett, Marion Eppler, Rhonda Williams, Nancy Folbre, Sam Bowles, Julie Matthaei, Jeff Escoffier, Michael Jacobs, Frank Thompson, Robert Anderson, and Ellen Oxfeld. It is, *bien entendu*, important not to illusorily correlate any of these people with any foolishness the reader might find in this essay.

1. I thank Herb Gintis for these last two references, which he offered in response to an earlier version of this chapter.

2. Of course, Magoo is an especially appropriate allegorical face to put on an actor in queer political economy since Magoo, a.k.a. Jim Backus, also played the father of James Dean (in *Rebel without a Cause*).

3. R. C. Magoo's undiscovered tastes are given by the utility function u (L, B) = $L^{.66667} B^{.33333}$, where the best choice is always L = 16 regardless of the prices of L and B. For the details on how this model was set up, see Cornwall 1995a.

4. An excellent introduction is offered by Katz 1993.

5. This recalls the apparent prevalence, in any catalogue of human societies, of cultural codes in which types of homosexuality are significant, even if this was invisible to notable Western anthropologists, as surveyed by Greenberg (1988, chap. 2). It might be conjectured that the current worldwide hegemony of homophobia may be significantly due to the edge given Western homophobia-infected (Christian) culture by the rise of market-guided societies, which engendered the rise of powerful technology in the West and then contaminated other cultures (e.g., Native American, Hindu, and Muslim) that are now significant in any tabulation of world cultural patterns.

6. See also Card 1994 and Kenny 1994.

7. For a useful summary, see chap. 6 in Holland et al. 1986. This identification of categorization as being based on archetypes or typical instances has become so unproblematic for some social psychologists that it is taken as the *definition* of categorization. See, for example, Fiske and Pavelchak 1986, 171.

8. See Allman and Brothers 1994 for an excellent overview as well as Damasio 1994, esp. 133, who calls the amygdala "the key player in preorganized emotion." For work pointing to the role of the amygdala in finely perceiving social cues in our faces, see Adolphs et al. 1994 and Young et al. 1995. See also Kuhl 1993 for related research and theory. My extremely loose analogy between the limbic system and a computer's operating system would, no doubt, be contested by Damasio (1994, 250) and in no way is meant to contest his strong assertion that the whole body is an integral part of the "mind."

9. This is the Gramscian notion of "hegemony" as defined, for example, by Comaroff and Comaroff (1991, 23). See also Gramsci (1971).

10. As Foucault has powerfully argued, this too appears simplistic because it is biased by our view from our social site in North America in the 1990s, which threatens to impose a teleological reading of history so that any multiplicity of sexual identities preindustrial people might have perceived is easily lost to our view.

11. For an excellent overview of the rise of gender-segregated wage labor, see Amott and Matthaei (1991, chap. 10, 315–48).

12. This brief sketch does not indicate the magnitude of the social changes occurring then. For more detail, check Edwards 1979; Montgomery 1987; and Brody 1980.

13. This focus on "male" is revealing of our cultural categories. See also Faderman 1991; D'Emilio and Freedman 1988; Vicinus 1992; and Matthaei 1995.

14. Sounds similar to Halloween in the Castro in San Francisco, which, in 1994, had become the largest annual event in the city, with an estimated four hundred thousand people attending. It is no longer a queer event celebrating gender-fuck, but is rather a lesbian/gay-hosted party where well over half the participants appear to be straight gawkers, most not in costume and a few threateningly armed. Analogous comments apply to the social position of "street people" in our cities today as props for a middle-class sense of superiority.

15. Homosexuality was the focus of the third paper by the Chapmans (1969); the second gave great, but not exclusive, emphasis to homosexuality phrased indirectly in instructions to the experimentees ("He is worried about how manly he is"). The first,

by Loren Chapman (1967), proposed the term "illusory correlation" and looked at people's perceptions of correlations between word pairs having no connection to homosexuality. More detail on the Chapmans' work is given in Cornwall 1995b.

16. One of the more relevant such formulations is by Bem (1981), who defines a schema as a "cognitive structure, a network of associations that organizes and guides an individual's perception." Bem found that out of ninety-six Stanford University students, those with more strongly sex-differentiated semantic verbal associations with "male" and "female" (what she called "sex typed") appeared to process (encode) "schema consistent information [more] quickly" (355) than students with less clearly evident gender schema. Bem's work thus built on the Chapmans' results and exemplifies the "prior rules" created by "semantic association" as described by Holland et al. (1986). Bem acknowledges earlier work on this notion by Nisbett and Ross (1980) and Tversky and Kahneman (1973, 1974).

17. Bem (1981, 361) was also an early formulator of a role for affect in schema formation of a type of particular relevance here: "many societies, including our own, treat an exclusively heterosexual orientation as the sine qua non of adequate masculinity and femininity. Regardless of how closely an individual's attributes and behavior match the male or female prototypes stored within the gender schema, violation of the prescription to be exclusively heterosexual is sufficient by itself to call into question the individual's adequacy as a man or a woman. The society thus attaches strong *affect* to this [heterosexual] portion of the gender schema" (emphasis added). This was especially striking in Bem's test of the speed with which the subjects decided whether semantically gender-specific attributes applied to themselves (358–61).

18. Goldberg's superb introduction (1994, 1–22) offers a quick overview of the diverse distortions these codes have assumed over recent centuries as they articulated "sodometries."

19. White (1990, 76).

20. See D'Emilio and Freedman (1988).

21. Dollimore (1991, 273) led me to this picture of willful suppression of desire.

22. This conjecture of a role for conscious (possibly "self-interested") human agency in the evolution of social cognitive codes is a divergence from the analogy I have thus far drawn to sociolinguistics as formulated by William Labov, who has written that "language structure . . . is a largely mechanical system, out of the reach of conscious recognition or adjustment by its users" (1994, 604).

23. I owe this clarification to David Greenberg's response to an earlier version of this chapter.

24. This quote from Chauncey has been rearranged at the parts as indicated by ellipses.

25. This made the closet—and "don't ask, don't tell"—into official policy, stringently enforced, of which the recent spectacle in Washington over queers in the military is a clear echo.

26. This is expressed most clearly in *Funeral Rites*. See Bersani (1995) and Dollimore (1991).

27. Steven Arnold, *Lust: The Body Politic*, 81–85.

28. This is taken from Cohen (1991, 77–78).

29. For example, see Nozick (1981).

30. The synchronization of the rise of modernism and the ideology of possessive individualism together with the erasure of the social articulation of queer desire in Western cultures from the sixteenth century on is explored in Cornwall 1995a.

31. Cornwall (1995a) offers further exploration of Marx's insightful discussion of the social embeddedness of humans and of how misleading is the economists' use of the trope of "Robinson Crusoe" to represent all humans.

32. Althusser (1971) hints, but does not explicitly recognize, that ideology is much deeper than the codes promoted by what he calls "ideological state apparatuses" ("churches, parties, trade unions, families, some schools, most newspapers, cultural ventures" [137]) by arguing that ideologies represent a human's "relation to [their real] conditions of existence" in the real world (154).

33. There is evidence that patterns of perception that are learned become, rather quickly, permanent structures in our minds, which then limit/channel our subsequent perceptions: Werker 1989; Kuhl et al. 1992; and Kuhl 1993.

34. Dollimore (1991, 281) notes that Jacques Lacan made a post-psychoanalytic (post–discovery of the unconscious) reformulation of Descartes's epigram, which serves as an intermediary between Descartes's and my versions: "I think where I am not, therefore I am where I do not think. Words that render sensible to an ear properly attuned with what elusive ambiguity the ring of meaning flees from our grasp along the verbal thread. What one ought to say is: I am not wherever I am the plaything of my thought; I think of what I am where I do not think to think" (Lacan 1977, 166). Damasio (1994, 248–52) offers useful insights on Descartes's false division between thinking and feeling, but the error in this division first hit me when I read Audre Lorde (1984), that notable toiler in the laboratory of applied cognition and social articulation. Especially signficant is her piece "Poetry Is Not a Luxury" (36–39), where she juxtaposes to *cogito ergo sum* the notion that "[t]he Black mother within each of us—the poet—whispers in our dreams: I feel, there I can be free. Poetry coins the language to express . . . this revolutionary demand" (1984, 38).

35. The first line quoted in italics at the start of this piece was spoken by Antonio, whose urgent efforts to pursue Sebastian after their ship lands following a disastrous storm reflect the prominent role given by Shakespeare to clearly queer desire in *Twelfth Night*. This contrast between Shakespeare's ability to articulate queer desire and the erasure of queer articulation for several succeeding centuries is explored in Cornwall (1995a, 1995b).

References

Adolphs, R., D. Tranel, H. Damasio, and A. Damasio. 1994. "Impaired recognition of emotion in facial expressions following bilateral damage to the human amygdala." *Nature* 372 (15 December): 669–72.

Allman, John, and Leslie Brothers. 1994. "Faces, fear and the amygdala." *Nature* 372 (15 December): 613–14.

Althusser, Louis. 1971. "Ideology and ideological state apparatuses." In *Lenin and Philosophy and Other Essays*, trans. Ben Brewster, 123–73. London: NLB.

Amott, Teresa, and Julie Matthaei. 1991. *Race, Gender, and Work: A Multicultural Economic History of Women in the United States*. Boston: South End.

Arthur, W. Brian. 1991. "Designing economic agents that act like human agents: A behavioral approach to bounded rationality." *American Economic Review* 81, 2 (May): 353–59.

Bem, Sandra Lipsitz. 1981. "Gender schema theory: A cognitive account of set typing." *Psychological Review* 88, 4:354–64.

Berlin, B., and P. Kay. 1969. *Basic Color Terms: Their Universality and Evolution*. Berkeley: University of California Press.

Bersani, Leo. 1995. *Homos*. Cambridge: Harvard University Press.

Bielby, William T. 1991. "The structure and process of sex segregation." In *New Approaches to Economic and Social Analyses of Discrimination*, ed. with Phanindra Wunnava, New York: Praeger.

Bowles, Samuel, and Herbert Gintis. 1986. *Democracy and Capitalism: Property, Community, and the Contradictions of Modern Social Thought.* New York: Basic Books.

Bray, Alan. 1982. *Homosexuality in Renaissance England.* London: Gay Men's Press.

Brody, David. 1980. *Workers in Industrial America: Essays on the Twentieth Century Struggle.* New York: Oxford University Press.

Butler, Judith. 1991. "Imitation and gender insubordination." In Fuss 1991, 13–31.

Card, Celia, ed. 1994. *Adventures in Lesbian Philosophy.* Bloomington: Indiana University Press.

Chapman, Loren J. 1967. "Illusory correlation in observational report." *Journal of Verbal Learning and Verbal Behavior* 6:151–55.

Chapman, Loren J., and Jean P. Chapman. 1967. "Genesis of popular but erroneous psychodiagnostic observations." *Journal of Abnormal Psychology* 72:193–204.

———. 1969. "Illusory correlation as an obstacle to the use of valid psychodiagnostic signs." *Journal of Abnormal Psychology* 74:271–80.

Chauncey, George. 1994. *Gay New York: Gender, Urban Culture, and the Making of the Gay Male World. 1890–1940.* New York: Basic Books.

Cohen, Ed. 1991. "Who are 'we'? Gay 'identity' as political (e)motion (a theoretical rumination). In Fuss 1991, 71–92.

Coleman, James S. 1990. *Foundations of Social Theory.* Cambridge: Harvard University Press.

Comaroff, Jean, and John Comaroff. 1991. *Of Revelation and Revolution: Christianity, Colonialism, and Consciousness in South Africa.* Chicago: University of Chicago Press.

Cornwall, Richard. 1995a. "queer political economy: the social articulation of desire, political dissonance and abjection."

———. 1995b. "socially articulating queer desire: political economy and cultural analysis."

Cyert, Richard M., and Morris H. DeGroot. 1980. "Learning applied to utility functions." In *Bayesian Analysis in Econometrics and Statistics: Essays in Honor of Harold Jeffreys,* ed. Arnold Zellner, 159–68. New York: North-Holland.

Damasio, Antonio R. 1994. *Descartes' Error: Emotion, Reason, and the Human Brain.* New York: Grosset/Putnam.

D'Emilio, John. 1983a. "Capitalism and gay identity." In *Powers of Desire: The Politics of Sexuality,* ed. Ann Snitow et al. New York: Monthly Review Press.

———. 1983b. *Sexual Politics, Sexual Communities: The Making of a Homosexual Minority in the United States. 1940–1970.* Chicago: University of Chicago Press.

D'Emilio, John, and Estelle B. Freedman. 1988. *Intimate Matters: A History of Sexuality in America.* New York: Harper and Row.

Dollimore, Jonathan. 1991. *Sexual Dissidence: Augustine to Wilde, Freud to Foucault.* Oxford: Clarendon.

Dunning, David, and Lisa Beth Stern. 1994. "Distinguishing accurate from inaccurate eyewitness identifications via inquiries about decision processes." *Journal of Personality and Social Psychology* 67, 5 (November): 818–35.

Edwards, Richard. 1979. *Contested Terrain: The Transformation of the Workplace in the Twentieth Century.* New York: Basic Books.

Elster, Jon. 1989. *The Cement of Society: A Study of Social Order.* New York: Cambridge University Press.

Escoffier, Jeffrey. 1995. *John Maynard Keynes.* New York: Chelsea House.

Faderman, Lillian. 1991. *Odd Girls and Twilight Lovers: A History of Lesbian Life in Twentieth-Century America.* New York: Columbia University Press.

Fiske, Susan T., and Mark A. Pavelchak. 1986. "Category-based versus piecemeal-based affective responses: Developments in schema-triggered affect." In *Handbook of Motivation and Cognition: Foundations of Social Behavior,* ed. Richard M. Sorrentino and E. Tory Higgins, 167–203. New York: Guilford.

Fiske, Susan T., and Shelly E. Taylor. 1991. *Social Cognition.* 2d ed. New York: McGraw-Hill.

Fuss, Diana, ed. 1991. *inside/out: lesbian theories, gay theories.* New York: Routledge.

Genet, Jean. 1969. *Funeral Rites.* New York: Grove.

Goldberg, Jonathan, ed. 1994. *Reclaiming Sodom.* New York: Routledge.

Gramsci, Antonio. 1971. *Selections from the Prison Notebooks.* New York: International Publishers.

Greenberg, David F. 1988. *The Construction of Homosexuality.* Chicago: University of Chicago Press.

Hamer, Dean, and Peter Copeland. 1994. *The Science of Desire: The Search for the Gay Gene and the Biology of Behavior.* New York: Simon and Schuster.

Hamilton, David L., and R. K. Gifford. 1976. "Illusory correlation in interpersonal perception: A cognitive basis of stereotypic judgments." *Journal of Experimental Social Psychology.* 12:392–407.

Hamilton, David L., and Steven J. Sherman. 1989. "Illusory correlations: Implications for stereotype theory and research." In *Stereotyping and Prejudice: Changing Conceptions,* ed. Daniel Bar-Tal, Carl F. Graumann, Arie W. Kruglanski, and Wolfgang Stroebe, 59–82. New York: Springer-Verlag.

Hemphill, Essex. 1992. *Ceremonies: Prose and Poetry.* New York: Plume. 1986.

Holland, John H., Keith J. Holyoak, Richard E. Nisbett, and Paul R. Thagard. 1986. *Induction: Processes of Inference, Learning and Discovery.* Cambridge: MIT Press.

Katz, Jonathan. 1993. "The art of code: Jasper Johns and Robert Rauschenberg." In *Significant Others: Creativity and Intimate Partnership,* ed. Whitney Chadwick and Isabelle de Courtivron, 188–207. New York: Thames and Hudson.

Kenny, Anthony. 1994. *The Wittgenstein Reader.* Oxford: Blackwell.

Kuhl, Patricia. 1993. "Innate predispositions and the effects of experience in speech perception: The native language magnet theory." In *Developmental Neurocognition: Speech and Face Processing in the First Year of Life,* ed. Bénédicte de Boysson-Bardies, Scania de Schonen, Peter Jusczyk, Peter McNeilage, and John Morton, 259–74. Boston: Kluwer.

Kuhl, Patricia K., Karen A. Williams, Francisco Lacerda, Kenneth N. Stevens, and Björn Lindblom. 1992. "Linguistic experience alters phonetic perception in infants by 6 months of age. *Science* 255 (31 January): 606–8.

Labov, William. 1994. *Principles of Linguistic Change. Vol. 1, Internal Factors.* New York: Blackwell.

Lacan, Jacques. 1977. *Écrits: A Selection,* trans. Alan Sheridan. London: Tavistock.

Lawrence, D. H. 1981. *Phoenix II: Uncollected, Unpublished and Other Prose Works,* ed. Warren Roberts and Harry T. Moore. London: Heinemann.

LeVay, Simon. 1993. *The Sexual Brain.* Cambridge: MIT Press.

Lorde, Audre. 1984. *Sister Outsider.* Freedom, CA: Crossing.

Lust: The Body Politic. 1991. Los Angeles: Advocate (Liberation Publications).

Marimon, Ramon, Ellen McGrattan, and Thomas J. Sargent. 1990. "Money as a medium of exchange in an economy with artificially intelligent agents." *Journal of Economic Dynamics and Control* 14:329–73.

Matthaei, Julie. 1995. "The sexual division of labor, sexuality, and lesbian/gay liberation: Towards a Marxist-feminist analysis of sexuality in U.S. capitalism." *Review of Radical Political Economics* 27, 2 (June): 1–37.

McFadden, Daniel. 1981. "Econometric models of probabilistic choice." In *Structural Analysis of Discrete Data with Econometric Applications,* ed. Charles F. Manski and Daniel McFadden, 198–269. Cambridge: MIT Press.

McFadden, Daniel, and Marcel K. Richter. 1990. "Stochastic rationality and revealed stochastic preference." In *Preferences, Uncertainty, and Optimality*, ed. John S. Chipman, Daniel McFadden, and Marcel K. Richter, 161–86. Boulder, CO: Westview.

Montgomery David. 1987. *The Fall of the House of Labor: The Workplace, the State, and American Labor Activism*. Cambridge: Cambridge University Press.

Nisbett, Richard E., and L. Ross. 1980. *Human Inference Strategies and Shortcomings of Social Judgement:* Englewood Cliffs, NJ: Prentice-Hall.

Nozick, Robert. 1981. *Anarchy, State, and Utopia*. New York: Basic Books.

Ponse, Barbara. 1978. *Identities in the Lesbian World*. Westport, CT: Greenwood.

Ricco, John Paul. 1993. "Jacking off a minor architecture." *Steam* 1, 4 (winter): 236–43.

———. 1994. "Queering boundaries: Semen and visual representations from the Middle Ages and in the era of the AIDS crisis." In *Gay and Lesbian Studies in Art History*, ed. Whitney Davis, 57–80. New York: Harrington Park.

Rubin, Gayle. 1975. "The traffic in women: Notes on the 'political economy' of sex." In *Toward an Anthropology of Women*, ed. Rayna R. Reiter, 157–210. New York: Monthly Review Press.

Sargent, Thomas J. 1993. *Bounded Rationality in Macroeconomics: The Arne Ryde Memorial Lectures*. Oxford: Clarendon.

Scott, Darieck. 1994. "Jungle fever? Black gay identity politics, white dick, and the utopian bedroom." *GLQ: A Journal of Lesbian and Gay Studies* 1, 3:299–321.

Tversky, Amos, and Daniel Kahneman. 1973. "Availability: A heuristic for judging frequency and probability." *Cognitive Psychology* 5:207–32.

———. 1974. "Judgement under uncertainty: Heuristics and biases." *Science* 185:1124–31.

Vicinus, Martha. 1992. " 'They wonder to which sex I belong': The historical roots of the modern lesbian identity." *Feminist Studies* 18, 3:467–98.

Weeks, Jeffrey. 1979. *Coming Out: Homosexual Politics in Britain, from the Nineteenth Century to the Present*. New York: Quartet Books.

Weinberg, Jonathan. 1993. *Speaking for Vice: Homosexuality in the Art of Charles Demuth, Marsden Hartley, and the First American Avant-Garde*. New Haven: Yale University Press.

Wells, Gary L., Sheila M. Rydell, and Eric P. Seelau. 1993. "The selection of distractors for eyewitness lineups." *Journal of Applied Psychology* 78, 5 (October):835–44.

Werker, Janet F. 1989. "Becoming a native listener." *American Scientist* 77:54–59.

White, E. Frances. 1990. "Africa on my mind: Gender, counter discourse and African-American nationalism." *Journal of Women's History* 2, 1 (spring): 73–97.

Wilde, Oscar. 1990. *The Soul of Man and Prison Writings*, ed. Isobel Murray. Oxford: Oxford University Press.

Young, Andrew W., John P. Aggleton, Deborah J. Hellawell, Michael Johnson, Paul Broks, and J. Richard Hanley. 1995. "Face processing impairments after amygdalotomy." *Brain* 118:15–24.

Economic Identity/Sexual Identity

Michael Piore

I would like to discuss the entrance of gays and lesbians into the economic mainstream. This is difficult to think about because historically, being gay, leading a gay life, has meant being outside the mainstream. It is one of the things that has made being gay difficult. But for me, at least, it has been the best of what it meant to be gay. My life spans Stonewall, and the environment Stonewall created was for me an opportunity not only to begin to come out but also to leave behind a set of structures that I had tried, but failed, to fit into.

I associate being gay with leaving behind the attempt to fit into the mainstream of American social structures. This has also been true of my intellectual life, within the discipline of economics: I do not suppose I was ever a mainstream economist, but as I came out, I also came to see myself as pursuing an intellectual agenda more and more at odds with the structures of thought that dominate economics. This, moreover, is not just personal and idiosyncratic. Gay-identified is not a big category within economics, but those economists who are openly gay are primarily outside the mainstream of the profession.

I see these same themes playing themselves out with respect to the opening of the mainstream economy to gays and lesbians. When I grew up, the professions associated with gays and lesbians were the arts and the fashion world, definitely not corporate America. I thought that this was the case because being gay or lesbian gave you a perspective on the margin of society; that what gays and lesbians were good at—when they were out and open about it—namely, playing on what it meant to be in the center of society, and pulling society away from that center in one direction or another; and that in this way, we opened up the possibilities that were imaginable in America and made a wider space not just for ourselves but for everybody. So the idea that all of a sudden we are moving into the mainstream of the occupational world, into standard careers, challenged my own notion of what it meant, and means, to be gay and lesbian.

The basic question I ask myself is whether my idea of what it means to be gay is merely old-fashioned. Is it something that belongs to my generation, but that we should now give up? Does liberation truly mean joining the mainstream? Is it a membership card, open admission, to all the structures and institutions I used to think of as the apparatus of oppression? An invitation to manage a society I once sought to remake? Does it mean giving up the gay identity I grew up with and fashioning another? Will this new identity, whether or not it fits me personally, really mean political liberation for those who are the post-Stonewall generation and seem to have no trouble fitting into this new world? Are we gaining acceptance by giving up the core of who we really are? Are we forsaking the role we have traditionally played—deliberately or not—of widening the scope within society for diversity and heterogeneity?

Within the discipline of economics, there are basically two strong views about the relationship of the economy—or rather, a *capitalist* economy—to diversity and heterogeneity. I suppose one can trace these two views to Karl Marx and perhaps Friedrich von Hayek, but in more recent times they are associated with Kenneth Galbraith and Milton Friedman.

Friedman argued that a capitalist economy was the kind of world, among all worlds, most tolerant of diversity and heterogeneity. His basic argument was political, not economic. Capitalism, in his view, was basically about the decentralization of power, not only economic power but also, and more importantly, political power. Capitalism, for Friedman, meant a market system and, because it was a market system, everyone could pursue his or her own particular pattern of consumption. A capitalist economy was, in other words, the kind of economy most apt to produce specialty items for gays and lesbians: lube, dildos, poppers, and bathhouses. A socialist economy might have a more open ideology, but because it implied state dominance and control, every item produced was the subject of an explicit political judgment, and this led, in Friedman's view, inevitably to a uniformity in consumption. Friedman argued as well that a capitalist economy created all sorts of pockets of economic power, which could then be converted into spheres of political power resistant to control by the government. Decentralization of political power through the economy in this way was, in Friedman's view, the best possible protection for minority rights. While a capitalist economy might not actually eliminate discrimination, it created social structures that went further in that direction than any other economic system.

Kenneth Galbraith developed exactly the opposite view. In his view, capitalism is basically a mass production economy, and the engine of mass production is conformity. The search for profit, which in Friedman's view leads businesspeople to seek out market niches, leads in Galbraith's view to a continual pressure for greater and greater increases in productivity. These are to be found in the production of long runs of standardized goods. As mass production develops, such standardized goods become progressively cheaper than specialized goods for particular people and groups, because these must be made in much smaller batches. The result is that everybody is pulled toward the center, and there is less and less tolerance in the economy for diversity and heterogeneity around the edges. Galbraith himself had little to say about what this pressure toward mass markets implied for the organization of work, but Marx, from whom Galbraith borrowed much of his argument, was quite certain that the logic of mass production required a uniformity in the labor force as well, so that there would be little tolerance of diversity in capitalism in either the sphere of production or the sphere of consumption.

Until the mid-1970s, the experience in the capitalist world, at least as I saw it—I suppose I saw it partly as a gay man—was that Milton Friedman had a neat idea and a logically coherent set of arguments, but Galbraith was essentially correct. The capitalist societies—at least the ones that existed in the real world—tolerated very little diversity. But it is also true that we have since moved toward greater diversity. There has been much more tolerance in the 1970s and 1980s than there was in the earlier postwar period, indeed, more even than in the prewar period stretching back into the late nineteenth century. Has there been a sea change in capitalist economies? Have we moved into a world in which capitalism is really going to be more hospitable to diversity than it was in the past?

One supposition, of course, is that what has really changed is not capitalism but gays and lesbians, that we have actually become more like everybody else. This may indeed have happened (or be about to happen). But there are things that would lead one to believe that capitalist economies have also changed in ways that make them much more tolerant of diversity; that is, if capitalism has not been the road to liberation in the last hundred years, it will be the road to liberation in the future.

Some of what has happened to produce this change is the movement toward deregulation. Milton Friedman argued that if you did not have government regulation, you would not have the kind of mass consumption economy Galbraith described. And Friedman and his disciples among economists essentially got to dictate the program of economic reform beginning even under Carter, certainly under Reagan and Bush, and now through both Gingrich and Clinton. It is not quite the route to reform that Friedman envisaged, since what happened was a change in the political environment that led in turn to a change in the economic environment, not vice versa; but it has certainly made the business climate much more hospitable to the kind of competition Friedman advocated, and this has arguably produced a more liberated social environment.

There has also, however, been a fundamental shift in the technological trajectory of the economy. New technologies emerging today seem to be more consistent with small enterprises, less associated with economies of scale, more capable of catering profitably to niche markets. Capitalist development thus no longer seems to be driven, as it was when Marx and Galbraith were writing, by the economies of scale associated with mass production, and this technological change makes the economy much more hospitable to diversity. One can also argue that for other reasons, or possibly because of the combination of deregulation and the new technological developments, we have created in the last fifteen years a lot of new organizational forms and structures. These are most apparent in the decentralization of power and responsibility within large corporations and the reduction of managerial hierarchies. The new organizational forms are also much more tolerant of diversity and difference than the old ones.

To these changes in organizational forms, in the technology, and in the business environment, one must also add the emergence of more and more businesses catering to the gay market. It is hardly in the interest of these businesses to assimilate to the dominant culture. Thus to the extent that we are developing an entrepreneurial class, a capitalist class of our own if you like, it is a class that has an interest in preserving a distinctive gay culture and niche markets.

Nonetheless, while I think it is clear that the economy is changing in ways that make it more accepting of us on our own terms, I still believe that it is not just the economic mainstream that is widening. In moving toward acceptance within it, we are losing an important part of what, once at least, we were. Issues like gay marriage have proved to be much more radical and radicalizing than I ever believed marriage could be—especially if you were arguing in favor of it rather than against it. But I remain skeptical about the ability of economic liberation in the long run to preserve political liberation. I am skeptical in part because as we try to reach the political mainstream of society, I see the gay community more and more defined in mainstream terms and chopping off its own "fringe" elements in order to win acceptance.

This was driven home to me very personally when I agreed at the request of a friend, who is on the board of the National Gay and Lesbian Task Force, to give a reception for the national director. They wanted to use this affair as an occasion to make a pitch for the Leadership Council, which is composed of people who have each given a thousand dollars to the organization. I found myself drawing up a list of all the gays and lesbians I could think of and asking which of them could afford that thousand dollars. I find this a pretty disturbing development in the evolution of my gay identity, let alone that of the movement. It is especially disturbing because what is by common consensus the most radical of our national organizations—too radical in the eyes of many activists—has come to define "leadership" in terms of thousand-dollar contributions. If we look toward the economy as the instrument of our liberation, we are going to find ourselves more and more driven by a particular agenda. Leadership that has achieved integration into the economy in positions of the kind that enable them to part easily with one thousand dollars a year is a leadership that is bound to have a rather high stake in the status quo. To say that the problem with the whole structure is that the people with money do not give enough to the people without it seems to me an overly economic way of looking at what is involved here. The problem is that many people are not getting politically organized. So the gay community's political organizations are dominated by those people who *are* getting organized. Whatever the changes that have occurred in capitalism in recent years, I find it doubtful that they alone will guarantee that the status quo of a capitalist economy will tolerate the kind of diversity gays and lesbians used to represent.

If we look around at other groups in American society who have tried to achieve political liberation, we can see that a strategy that holds ourselves hostage politically to our economic success appears extremely problematic. The labor movement did best when it appealed to American society on the basis of a broad set of values, when it argued that the right to organize was essential to protecting the dignity of workers as human beings. It was on the basis of that appeal that American labor initially gained economic and political protection in the 1930s, and it maintained that protection in the postwar period as the leader of a political coalition that sought similar protection for economically and socially stigmatized groups, including unorganized low-income workers, racial minorities, and women. Beginning with the Vietnam War, however, American labor developed an increasingly narrow definition of itself and what it stood for and an increasingly parochial defense of its legal rights. It became wealthy and let its resources, and defense of the economic gains that generated them, substitute for a broad humanitarian appeal. Over time it has gradually lost much of the legal protection it developed in the 1930s, as well as political strength and membership. The economic gains of its members are now being lost as well.

Much the same thing has happened to the black movement. The civil rights movement made its greatest gains in the 1960s, when it was led by Martin Luther King and appealed for blacks as human beings, representatives of all oppressed peoples. In the 1970s and 1980s, however, the black movement changed. Its appeal became an increasingly narrow one, an appeal for blacks as blacks. Even Jesse Jackson's rainbow coalition is a coalition of separate groups, not of the oppressed more broadly, and other prominent African American leaders make no pretense of representing interests or concerns that extend beyond the narrow interests of their own immediate constituencies. As blacks have increasingly tried to assert their political power to protect and extend the interests of their own community in this way, the gains they had previously won in the political sphere have been increasingly called into question, and their economic gains are also in jeopardy.

Our political rights in American society are always going to be more secure, I believe, if we claim them as human beings, and if we assert the theme that, at least until quite recently, has really been true of gays and lesbians: namely, that we represent diversity. We represent the idea that to be human is to be different—that human beings are unpredictable, that what is interesting about human beings is how differently they manifest themselves. In that sense the drag queen is a kind of symbol of gay and lesbian life: she/he challenges the idea that there is one single way to be a human being. *That* is the principle that should guide our political movement, however successful we turn out to be in a capitalist economy. I believe it should guide the movement because it is *right*. But I also believe it should guide it because it is the only way we can protect the gains we have already won.

38

The Different Dilemmas of Lesbian and Gay Professionals

James Woods

My current research project has two goals. The first is to try to describe the sexual culture of the white-collar professional workplace—by "white-collar" I mean places like banks, law firms, colleges, and hospitals—and the rules and norms that operate in these sorts of settings. The second goal is to look at the strategies that first gay men and now men and women are using to navigate them and to manage their careers and their sexual identities in the workplace, and what consequences those strategy choices have. In this essay I would like to make a few preliminary observations on the results of the project to date.

One of my starting assumptions is that heterosexism, as I have come to understand it, is really built on gender oppression; it is impossible to explain it or deconstruct it without first accounting for sexism. Sexism establishes the cultural context in which heterosexism is even possible.

To date, I have interviewed only about a dozen women, so I am dealing with a small data base, and my learning curve is very steep. But I want to give you a few of my speculations. A woman I call Sigrid is a researcher at IBM who emigrated to the United States from Germany in 1987, just after she completed her Ph.D. She has been with the company now for seven years and considers herself fairly closeted, she says, although she is gradually coming out to co-workers one at a time. When I asked her why she had chosen this particular approach, she said, "I try to be more open, but it's difficult when you're in a room filled with assertive, impressive male researchers who really think they're all geniuses. It's very difficult to stand up. If I weren't a lesbian and if I had a mentor..." She pauses. "I don't have any of that, so I don't feel I can exert power in the same way. Women are less than 10 percent of the research division at IBM, so it's difficult to be, first, a minority because I'm a woman, second, a minority because I'm Jewish, and third, a minority because I'm a lesbian. That's why I keep it slow." Then Sigrid made this explicit comparison: "One of my colleagues, a gay man, a Ph.D., also German, is very militant. He's part of ACT UP. But he's in a dominant position, in a sense. As a white male engineer, he has more rights than I have. Part of me feels like an imposter here. Some of the women at IBM joke that it feels like we're working in a men's room."

Sigrid's case raises a number of points that I want to address about the differentiation of heterosexism in the workplace along gender lines. As a number of other researchers interested in organizational culture have observed, professional culture is essentially a variant of male culture, contemporary male culture. Professional norms and values, even our definitions of what constitutes professionalism are gendered. They incorporate masculine values, imagery, and norms in a variety of subtle ways. As Garreth Morgan has observed in a study called *Images of Organization,* "The links between the male stereotype and the values that dominate organizations are striking. Organizations are encouraged to be rational, analytic, strategic, decision-oriented, tough and aggressive, and so are men."

This has important implications for women who want to operate in this world, for insofar as they attempt to foster these values, they are open to criticism for being overly assertive or trying to play a male role.

The result is what has been called "sex role spillover," which is the tendency of workers to bring their expectations about gender-appropriate behavior developed *outside* the workplace to work with them, so that these behaviors become part of what we expect of each other when we are working in corporations. Sigrid, my IBM researcher, put it this way: "Think of the male stereotype. They are expected to speak up, to defend and argue, to be assertive. When a woman speaks up the same way here, she's too aggressive, a bitch. Men have been in these jobs for generations, so it's more their element. Whatever their sexuality, they're better qualified by their gender."

In short, organizational culture and norms are gendered, which means that lesbians and gay men face heterosexism at work from very different vantage points. As a lesbian engineer at Lotus told me, "Gay men ultimately have male privilege to fall back on. They experience discrimination because they're gay, but they enjoy other entitlements because they're male." Or to put it in my own words, while lesbians, gay men, and bisexuals are all sexual outcasts, we occupy very different strata on the gender hierarchy that pervades most white-collar professional organizations.

For this reason, I think workplaces are an ideal site to explore heterosexism and its differentiation. With that in mind, I want to share several brief observations about what I am seeing in this first set of interviews, a set I am calling "The Myth of the Asexual Professional." As a number of social scientists have observed, the past few centuries have witnessed the construction in Western capitalist culture of a whole series of segregations, including the segregation of work and sexuality as realms of human experience, the separation of personal and professional lives, and the creation of public and private spaces. These segregations inform corporate culture in a number of ways.

They turn up in policies on nepotism and office decor, in rules against fraternization with clients, in dress codes, in policies on sexual harassment that attempt to desexualize workers, and so forth. I am not saying all this is bad, but implicit in all such policies is the idea that work and sex can and should be kept apart. Among the gay professionals I have interviewed, the notion of professional asexuality in particular shapes deeply held beliefs about work and professionalism. At the start of each interview, I would ask a very open-ended question, something like, "What role do you think your sexuality plays at work?" Among the men, the response I got was quite predictable, usually taking the form of "My sexuality has nothing to do with my work at Company X"; or "You're going to be very disappointed with me, because I keep my professional life and my personal life totally separate"; or "It would really be unprofessional to bring sex to work."

A recent survey of Fortune 500 companies conducted by the National Gay and Lesbian Task Force found that 90 percent of companies responded that a worker's sexual orientation was unrelated to job performance. This, not so incidentally, is the same logic behind the military's "don't ask, don't tell" policy. To give one example: the *New York Times* recently quoted a gay naval commander approving the idea behind the policy, namely, that "your work life and your sex life should be kept apart. Nobody is gay or straight when they're on a ship, they're just at work."

Now, my early speculation in talking to women is that fewer lesbian professionals seem to believe this myth. Fewer women volunteer versions of it in the interviewing I have done. Let me give you two examples. Gail Murphy, fifty three years old, is an assistant vice president at a large bank headquartered in Philadelphia. During our interview she said, "You take your whole self to work, no matter where you go. I figure that my sexual orientation is so woven into who Gail Murphy is that I could never show up fully at work without it. My sexuality is very integrated in me, just as it is in people who are heterosexual or bisexual. I mean, is heterosexual stuff private? Of course not."

A woman I call Susan, a production manager for a large publishing plant in Raleigh-Durham, North Carolina, put it this way: "When you work with people, you can't help but be sensitive to their life situations, and that includes many things. For example, if I were invited to a colleague's house for dinner, I would expect him to invite my partner." When I asked her—playing the devil's advocate—why she could not simply keep things separate, Susan replied, "Because heterosexuals don't. If I'm not to talk about my personal life, then why should I have to hear about their dates, spouses, or 'private' problems? Who we are and who our partners are is a huge part of a person. You can't hack that off and leave it behind. It's part of the fabric of the workplace community."

I think there are several reasons women, and lesbians in particular, may be less likely to believe the myth of professional asexuality; I will mention them briefly. The first centers on maternity issues, which women—and lesbian parents as well—confront more directly, in a number of ways, than men do. A second reason may be sensitivity to sexual harassment, which is much more likely to victimize women than men. And the third would be, I think, the awareness among women that they are judged by appearance, or what quaintly used to be called "sex appeal," in a way that men are not, and in a way that men are fairly oblivious about. Men have enjoyed the luxury of being oblivious to how sexualized workplaces in fact are. Even as they participated in sexual horseplay and harassment of all kinds, they would nonetheless claim or believe that the workplace was asexual.

There is a second way men and women react differently, a difference involving what I call "compensation." As other researchers have shown in studies of various groups—African Americans, women, immigrants, other groups not traditionally at home in corporate America—one response to the threat of discrimination is superior job performance, extraordinary competence. Such efforts are a kind of shield against their stigmatized social identities, and in organizations dominated by white male heterosexuals—which is to say, most of corporate America—any group that deviates from that norm may feel pressure to outperform those who more clearly fit it.

Among the men I studied, this led to conspicuous displays of company loyalty, pressure to maintain the best sales record or the longest client list. Nowhere was this more acute than among nonwhite men, who felt that they already had another obstacle in their way, race. As one closeted gay Puerto Rican man put it to me, he did not want to come out at work because he did not want to put "another stone in my path."

Women as women are already familiar with these sorts of performance pressures in male-dominated organizations. To quote Gail Murphy again, "You have to do your job better than anyone else. You have to make sure that you are pristine and excellent." (Her choice of words here is really, I think, revealing.) "You spend an awful lot of energy making sure you're the best you can possibly be. I was highly respected in my work group before I came out, and I knew that I was really good at what I do. I had confidence in my work. If I weren't at the level [of vice president] and if I hadn't been really visible and successful, I don't know if I would have been taken as seriously."

Similarly, Susan, the plant manager in Raleigh-Durham, said, "I have to be perfect. My performance has to be above reproach. For example, I feel extra pressure not to have outside distractions from work. Like if my partner were sick and needed me to be home, I would be reluctant to state that as the reason for taking time off, because I don't want someone to throw it back in my face that I'm a lesbian." So one question is, Do women and lesbians face these compensation pressures more acutely? Do they feel them more acutely than gay men? And my tentative answer would be yes. Thus far, the women I have interviewed have all said that they do, in fact, feel a lot of pressure to be the superstars at their companies.

I want to mention, too, what I call "strategies for managing identity." In my study of men in corporations I created a topology of strategies, which ranged from what I called "counterfeiting"—the public tactics we're long familiar with for projecting a heterosexual identity that we know to be false—through assorted ways of integrating (and there are assorted ways), to a huge middle range of strategies that involve various devices for trying to avoid the subject altogether. Each strategy has its characteristic tactics and penalties.

I think that if we create a topology for women, we would see some significant differences, different options, different trade-offs. I will mention just a couple of examples. The first of these is the use of motherhood, in several different ways. One way is as a disguise, what I would have called "counterfeiting" when describing men. This is true for divorced women, especially. Several were using children to document their heterosexual pasts, and found it very easy at work to display that part of their history, their status as a mother, by showing photos or talking about chores—or any of the ways that motherhood becomes a sort of public event.

At the other end of the strategy spectrum, among women who were openly lesbian, motherhood is used in a quite different way, to normalize their lesbian identity. By talking about changing diapers and so on, they make coworkers comfortable. They normalize themselves. Since motherhood is a familiar cultural role, it is comfortable to coworkers. They know how to respond to it, what questions to ask, what words to use. So for open lesbians, motherhood was often an effective identity for making themselves less exotic. I saw a comparable phenomenon among men who would emphasize and talk about their monogamous relationships, or talk car payments or household chores as ways of showing how mundane their lives were with their lovers.

There are other strategies for identity management that people use to play against stereotypes. Among men, what I saw was that in many companies in which the traditional stereotype of the gay man—limp-wristed, effeminate, opera-crazed, and so on—is still very powerful, one could play against it in what might seem to us very simplistic—but effective—ways. One simply affects qualities that are explicitly coded as masculine. You talk about sports or you self-consciously adopt back-slapping mannerisms to throw coworkers off the track. Or you avoid tasks that are coded as feminine, like taking on secretarial tasks or becoming the mediator in a dispute. These strategies are surprisingly effective, because our culture continues to conflate gender conformity with sexual orientation.

In much of the country—I am not talking about New York City—that conflation is still very powerful, and playing to it proves a very effective strategy for many gay men. The strategy is not quite available to lesbians, or not available in the same way. Lesbians who do conform to expectations for their gender face different consequences, I think. Women who are very femme (which a researcher who is doing a study of lesbian professionals calls "the long hair and fingernails strategy") find that they are not taken seriously as professionals, because remember, professional culture is essentially male culture.

Lesbians who use the "femme strategy" find that they succeed in disguising their lesbianism only to be treated as sex objects. Oppositely, a lesbian who butches it up in order to be taken seriously as a professional is risking "outing" herself, especially in workplaces still dominated by men—like oil and gas companies. As my interviewee Gail, who is openly lesbian, put it, "One of the easiest ways for women to pass in the workplace is to look as feminine as possible. You know, you become a glamour dyke, a lipstick dyke. You accessorize. If you want to move up in the organization, especially, the more you can look like the traditional female heterosexual, the better. I'm personally more comfortable in slacks, and we dress casual around here, but if I were in the closet, I wouldn't dare. I'd try to look as fancy as possible."

Closeted lesbians, it seems, have to strike a middle ground: they must be sufficiently masculine to succeed in white-collar professional terms, yet feminine enough to pass as heterosexuals. In a way, this dilemma is unique to lesbians. Gay men, on the other hand, can do both; they can butch it up and find that that pulls them along professionally.

This is far from a complete typology, but my chief point has hopefully come through: when we speak of heterosexism, we must keep in mind that it is a variegated phenomenon, that it is differentiated by gender and class dynamics, and that for our analyses to be complex and rich, we need to take into account the fact that workplace life, and the strategies closeted gay men and lesbians use for coping with it, are quite different for different groups.

39

The Growth of the Gay and Lesbian Market

Sean Strub

I see some potentially very serious problems arising—warning signs for the community, if you will. Over the last fifteen years—which is the time frame in which I've been out and involved—we've gone from having one national publication, the *Advocate* (and it was, in my view, national in geography only, really not very national in a number of other areas that I'll get to), to having twelve or fifteen national titles. They're growing very dramatically—*Out, Genre, 10 Percent, Deneuve, Our World, Blk, Victory, POZ, On Our Backs*, and lots of others. There are probably going to be another six or seven national publications, with increasing specialization coming out in the next year. The local newspapers, most of which were started in the immediate post-Stonewall years, are almost all making money.

These are thriving, successful businesses, and in many cases, they're making a lot of money and are now economically viable in even the smallest communities. You can go to Des Moines, Iowa, and find a successful little gay paper. Waterloo has a gay paper. Sioux City has a gay paper.

There's a big directory of over a thousand pages that's published every month, called *The Standard Rate and Data Service Directory of Mailing Lists*. In 1985, there were no gay lists registered. Every other possible, imaginable kind of list was there, and so we wanted to register one of the gay lists we were marketing. But they wouldn't do it. And then they finally said, "Well, we could put it under Erotic Product Buyers category." And I said, "No, that's not what it is." And then after another year of letters and phone calls, they said, "Well, we'll put it under Ethnic Lists." And I said, "No, it's not that." And so then I told them I was going to put out my own directory. And they said, "Oh, well, okay, we'll establish a gay category."

Well, that gay category is now about twelve or fourteen pages. There are sixty or seventy different gay lists registered there. And in addition, they have advertisements in this directory, and in the domestic consumer list section ad for this entire year, the largest ad is Strubco's 1-800-GAYNAMES.

So we've come a long way in the list business. There's a universe of gay and lesbian lists out there, right now around two million names. These represent people who have associated themselves with a gay or lesbian cause. Ninety-six to 98 percent of the men identify as gay, and around 90 percent of the women identify as lesbian or bisexual. That universe has doubled in the last two years.

As for newsletters, there have always been some small ones around, but I think we're just beginning to see growth to the level of economic viability. There is a community of people now willing to pay a lot of money for highly specialized and timely information; and also as part of that, we're starting to see a whole directory industry as well.

One of the conventional wisdoms in telemarketing is that the younger and the more hip the audience you're telemarketing to, the shorter the call volume; that telemarketing is really geared to retired people sitting at home with nothing else to do but to speak to the telemarketer. When we call gay and lesbian lists, and it doesn't matter if whether it's for fund-raising or for commercial purposes, our call length is much longer, because people want to talk and they want to talk about the issues. Telemarketing is about to explode in this market.

I would argue that the key to successful telemarketing is first sending a lead letter in advance, or some sort of notification, so people know that you're going to do it—giving them the opportunity not to have their name marketed. We've been very aggressive over the last five years. We've sent over two million cards in our card packs, offering people the opportunity to get off our lists. The other key is calling people who are interested in what it is that you're telemarketing. If you're interested, it doesn't feel like a telemarketing call.

We've also seen the growth of local access cable shows, and some gay/lesbian television and video material. Similar to the Internet, it's a way of getting a message about the community and about our lives across the closet barriers. To get a publication, you've got to buy it or carry it into your home or pick it up at a bar; it takes a little action on the part of the closeted gay person. But logging onto the LAMBDA lounge on America Online can be done very privately. And it's a way of exposing people to the community. The same is true with public access television shows. The names that we generate through those sources are very, very few at this point, but they are new people to the community. They're not on the lists; they're not reading the gay media. And they're an exciting new point of entry.

Something that has not been written about much is the radio shows. There are probably thirty or forty regularly scheduled gay and lesbian radio shows all over the country. They are probably reaching more people than the public access cable shows.

Event marketing and sponsorship activities—like the Gay Games and Stonewall 25—are, in terms of getting corporate sponsors, leading the way in softening up the major marketers for us. Outdoor advertising is an example: things like RSVP Cruises ads in West Hollywood and in Sheridan Square are sending a message to a broad audience.

In-store marketing is, I think, about to really explode—everything from Take One stands to people doing displays in the stores and sending personnel into the stores to market and explain new products. That's all part of the growth of gay and lesbian retail establishments—like Don't Panic, which is becoming the K-Mart of rainbow flags—and it's happening everywhere.

Insertion programs—those free-standing inserts in all the local gay media—are also a powerful vehicle. Deacon MacCubbin, at Lambda Rising Bookstore in Washington, D.C., says that the gay and lesbian media have a monthly readership of sixteen million. I don't know how many different individuals that is, but in terms of advertising and reach, that's a very big number.

The growth in gay media is going to be in the direction of more specialization. We're going to see regional gay and lesbian slick, glossy magazine titles, and more diversity in the advertiser base. American Express is advertising now, and there are all sorts of major advertisers coming along—like Benetton, Perrier, and Calistoga Water. I think we're going to see some media barons buying up a lot of the local lesbian and gay papers and achieving some significant scale economies in terms of centralizing editorial marketing and business operations. Currently most of those papers are owned primarily by men who have owned them fifteen to twenty years, and are now approaching a time in their life when they're looking to do something else.

The list market is also going to grow dramatically. People in our community are getting much more sophisticated about lists and data bases and collection of data. I mentioned newsletters, directories, and telemarketing. I think we are going to see at least one full-time gay cable channel. And there are a lot of different entities and organizations with varying levels of expertise and access to capital, and they include some of the people who founded the E Network and some of Barry Diller's crew, as well as some people who are more active and visible in the community.

The event marketing of the Gay Games really broke through in a big way. The Games were maybe not as successful as they would have liked, but nonetheless are going to impact all local pride celebrations. Some places—Christopher West, in Los Angeles, in particular—have long been good at getting corporate sponsorship, but now places like Des Moines are going to be able to go to these corporate sponsors and get some support. I think you're going to see corporate sponsorship of things like the women's music festivals and conferences and seminars. The more political something is, the more difficult it will be to win sponsorship. Stonewall 25 was perceived as more political than the Gay Games, so they had a more difficult time with corporate sponsors.

Finally, in terms of growth, all sorts of buyers clubs and affinity marketing programs are emerging. Five or six different groups are creating a Gay AARP; there are travel agencies; there are long distance service or mutual funds and insurance. My company, for example, is working with an insurance company to market a same-sex partner insurance policy. We're going to actually create the marketing around that, and hopefully make some progress in the insurance industry itself.

But there are dangers and problems in all this. Some very inappropriate numbers and data have been thrown around about the demographics of the market. Moreover, the market that's reachable through lists is not "the community." For years, coming out has been a function of affluence, for the most part. That's partly because it's just easier for rich people to do whatever they want. But I think we have made it easier for other communities to come out of the closet as well; we've sold to the media and society this idea of a "gay community." But the image that has gotten out there and that is most visible is the Fire Island lifestyle, if you will. And that has eroded our credibility on Madison Avenue and with major marketers, because they look at the demographics of a very select and economically privileged group and then extrapolate to 10 percent of society; they're inevitably disappointed.

But politically, too, it's been very damaging, because those economically privileged statistics have been the fuel for the special rights charges being thrown against us in Colorado, Oregon, and other places. The public sees two gay professional white men with their BMWs and Shar Pei dogs, or whatever, and take that to be an accurate reflection of our community. I compare it to the way we all grew up seeing *Donna Reed* and *Father Knows Best* and thought those were accurate reflections of family life. Then we found out that our family wasn't like that, which creates a credibility gap that you spend the rest of your life dealing with.

Comparably, we've created a reflection of the perfect homo. And it isn't what we are; and for kids who are coming out or even for people who may already be out but feel alienated from the community, we're creating that same kind of gap: if they don't fit the "perfect homo" image, then they aren't part of the community.

I also think we are eroding the value of using the phrase "gay/lesbian owned and operated." There was a time when that had a lot of meaning, but what's happened is there are people who have come into the market in an exploitive way, and within a significant portion of the market there's developed the view that an ad saying "gay/lesbian owned and operated" *reduces* the credibility of the marketer. We don't have any system within the community of policing or regulating exploitation, yet we have been damaged by some marketers taking advantage, using phrases like "gay owned" to increase profit while abusing the consumer's expectations.

We're a very sophisticated consumer group and so when there's some sort of problem, we're going to hold a "gay owned" marketer to a different standard. I think there's a growing gap between the activist/social change community and the marketing community. There was a time when they were largely (if not entirely) synonymous. Now we're constantly hearing people say, "Well, we're not a political business." That may be inevitable, in terms of growth, but it still concerns me.

I'm concerned about the loss of control of our community's media and assets. While it is very good that Time Warner had been thinking about starting a new magazine about our community, it raises a bigger question: these businesses are evaluated on their bottom line; major corporations, without the same kind of sensitivity to the community, are coming into the marketing and fund-raising communities. The major AIDS organizations control hundreds of millions of dollars a year, and their boards are becoming increasingly straight, decreasingly HIV oriented or HIV-positive people oriented. These are institutions and assets that we created, with our dollars, and we're in risk of losing control of them.

And then, finally, there's a problem about providing infrastructure support for businesspeople in the community. As a rule, our community has not respected the contributions businesspeople have made to the movement—just as we have not done well in providing help in dealing with the unique problems of getting financing and access to capital. How do we move our wealth from one generation to another? This movement and this community *need* concentrations of wealth to accomplish certain things. And that's something we haven't addressed—not even practical matters like health insurance and the like.

40

The Gay Marketing Moment

Amy Gluckman and Betsy Reed

Since a cocky k. d. lang reveled in Cindy Crawford's feminine attentions on the cover of *Vanity Fair* in the spring of 1993, other icons of "lesbian chic" have been showing off their buzz-cuts in androgenous ads, while gay men flex their pecs in mainstream magazines and, more figuratively, in the upper echelons of the business world. *Newsweek,* having declared cuddly, cohabiting lesbians all the rage the previous year, observed a sudden bisexual moment sweeping the nation in 1995. Fashionably late, following centuries of invisibility punctuated by hostile caricatures, a conspicuous kind of gay liberation has announced its own important arrival in the 1990s.

Gay and lesbian political activists, who have toiled for decades at the grassroots level to promote a welcoming climate for gay men and lesbians, certainly deserve a large share of the credit for the proliferation of gay-positive images, both in ads and in other media. But it is not as if liberation has suddenly become the bottom line for many of those peddling glamorous pictures of lesbians, bisexuals, and gay men. Marketers, who make it a rule to tolerate their markets, have had a revelation. The profits to be reaped from treating gay men and lesbians as a trendsetting consumer group finally outweigh the financial risks of inflaming right-wing hate. As George Slowik, Jr., past publisher of the prosperous, glossy *Out* magazine, puts it, "Our demographics are more appealing than those of 80-year-old Christian ladies."

"Untold millions," as the title of one recent business book proclaims,[1] lie in the deep pockets of gay consumers, a demographic group that marketers can best tap by placing ads in outlets like *Out,* as well as in predominantly straight venues that allow tantalizing glimpses of gay life. Advertising trends indicate that corporations are cleaving to gay publications that promote a stylish, widely palatable vision of gay life, primarily mags such as *Out* and the *Advocate* that have been cleansed of the objectionable: phone sex ads, radical politics, and hard-core leather culture.

This foray into sanitized gay media is big news in the advertising business. Marketing and business publications exhibit a wary excitement, with headlines like "The Gay Market: Nothing to Fear but Fear Itself," "Untapped Niche Offers Marketers Brand Loyalty," and "Mainstream's Domino Effect: Liquor, Fragrance, Clothing Advertisers Ease into Gay Magazines." Along with Absolut, Calvin Klein, and Benetton, corporations that have taken the lead in advertising in mainstream gay publications include Philip Morris, Columbia Records, Miller beer, Seagram, and Hiram Walker.

Corporate interest in the gay market has not arisen of its own accord. Rather, it has been piqued by organizations—usually run by gays—that conduct surveys and employ selected information about gay consumers to persuade advertisers that a viable gay and lesbian market exists. Strub Media Group, for instance, distributes a flyer claiming that readers of gay publications have an average household income of $63,100, compared to $36,500 for all households. Gay marketing groups also point out that since gay men and lesbians have no children (more and more a false assumption), their disposable income is even higher than their average income would suggest. Although renowned for their gourmet capabilities in the kitchen, 80 percent of gay men eat out more than five times a month, according to well-publicized data from another such organization, Overlooked Opinions. According to a promotion used by a network of local gay newspapers, gay men and lesbians travel more, buy more CDs, use their AmEx card more, and generally spend more money on the good life than their straight counterparts. The most valuable target market—the one that is most conspicuous in the marketing literature—is white, urban, white-collar, and predominantly male.

Prime conditions exist for these notions to dictate straight Americans' view of gay men and lesbians. Unlike subgroups that could never "pass," the clearest characteristic of gay men and lesbians has been, until recently, their invisibility. There have been some stereotypes out there, focusing mostly on sexual promiscuity and mental instability. But straight Americans probably harbored few ideas about whether gay men and lesbians were rich or poor, spendthrift or frugal. Past gay invisibility has provided a blank slate of sorts, a slate that is rapidly filling up with notions that have more to do with marketing than with reality.

While anecdotes about free-spending, double-income gay households accurately represent one segment of the gay community, they have unfortunately been taken as descriptive of all gay men and lesbians, which is partly due to distortions by overzealous gay marketing groups. Eager to persuade reluctant corporations of a lucrative yet dormant gay market, Overlooked Opinions circulated misleading statistics depicting a disproportionately wealthy gay community. As M. V. Lee Badgett contends in her essay in this volume, such assertions of high gay incomes are common but inaccurate, as many have confused survey data referring to the readers of gay publications with the demographics of the community as a whole. Badgett's findings reveal that gay men earn substantially less than their straight counterparts, while lesbians are roughly even with heterosexual women in earning power.

Regardless of the truth of their impression of overall gay wealth, marketers have discovered that targeting prosperous gays can be quite lucrative. Lesbians and gay men have proven to be vulnerable to the advances of advertisers, since they have been ignored as a consumer group for so long. The makers of Absolut vodka were the first to discover and exploit the gay community's brand loyalty, which is now a veritable legend in the marketing world. Tracking consumption patterns after local ads appeared in gay media, Absolut charted dramatic jumps in specific requests for its brand name in gay bars.

But ads do not feature glamorous gays just to connect with gay consumers. Firms placing gay-themed ads are also counting on the ability of attractive gay idols to set trends for straight shoppers. It's a bet that has already paid off, in some cases. Resplendent in red, RuPaul, the queen of drag and Mac cosmetics model, has inspired hordes of genetic girls to buy the company's lipstick, through ads placed primarily in mainstream straight media. Another perk of targeting gays is the demonstrated power of ordinary gay people to establish trends followed by straights; it has become common lore, for instance, that gay men popularized Levi's button-fly jeans.

Before such money-making fads take hold in any community, media images usually introduce the novel idea. Sometimes ads alone will do it (such as vodka bottles by Keith Haring), but marketers uniformly believe that to take optimum effect, advertising has to be placed in a complementary environment. This suggests that a sort of mercenary collusion between advertising and editorial forces might have provided much of the impetus for the recent gay media moment. Circumstantial evidence abounds; flip over k. d. and Cindy and you will find Absolut. Ads for Benetton, Calvin Klein, and other companies known for their keen interest in the gay market lurk in the shadows of many of the recent gay-moment stories.

Some of the supposed attributes of the new gay target consumer group are probably harmless. *Out* magazine's media kit, for example, says that lesbians and gay men are "homemakers" and "aesthetes." The very presence of gay men and lesbians in the media—as celebrities, authors, and social actors—is a long-sought triumph, while being respected as a market often translates into political clout. In Hawaii, for instance, the argument for gay marriage has been bolstered by the prospect of a windfall from gay tourism. One economist even estimated that the first state to recognize gay marriage would reap a $4.3 billion boon.[2] And of course, with money itself a good degree of political influence can be bought. As the work of the Human Rights Campaign has shown, carefully targeted donations to political campaigns can cement the loyalty of key politicians (though the Log Cabin Republicans discovered the limits of this approach when presidential hopeful Bob Dole initially returned their carefully rendered gift in the fall of 1995). Certainly, the gay and lesbian community can wield its newly recognized market power wisely, rewarding social responsibility and punishing capitulation to the right.

To the extent that gay advances hinge on financial interests, however, they are precarious. What if a future backlash depletes gay incomes, or the right wing proves a greater economic force? Far-right boycotts have hurt progressive causes before. Fortunately, one recent attempt by the right to punish a company for gay-friendly policies flopped. The Reverend Donald Wildmon's American Family Association campaigned against Levi Strauss, which had announced that it was withdrawing its support of the Boy Scouts because of their antigay teachings, but the firm's profits soared in spite of the protest. At the same time, however, the right wing remains a formidable force in other areas of the marketplace. In 1995, for instance, when P-FLAG (Parents, Families, and Friends of Lesbians and Gays) tried to buy $1 million worth of television airtime for anti-hate public service spots, protest from Pat Robertson's Christian Broadcasting Network caused most television stations to refuse to run the ads. In general, it is companies that don't serve a substantial conservative, fundamentalist constituency—such as liquor firms—that have avidly been cultivating gay consumption. In the case of alcohol, this has made for some unpleasant bedfellows, as ads for Dewar's, Miller beer, and the like sustain mainstream gay magazines while radical gay media like *Gay Community News* struggle to survive.

In addition, there are concrete political risks in projecting a rich, powerful image to get wide attention. Overlooked Opinions admits that the religious right has appropriated its numbers. The firm received a request for evidence of the gay community's financial power from the Colorado attorney general's office, evidence that was used to support the campaign for the antigay ballot initiative Amendment 2. And the antigay group Colorado for Family Values has argued that "homosexuals are anything but disadvantaged," citing statistics that gay male households earn an average of $55,400 annually—in the same range estimated by Overlooked Opinions. This campaign, directed at lower-income communities, has succeeded in persuading some people that their own financial woes are somehow linked to gay lifestyles. In the fall of 1995, a similar attempt to convince Maine voters that gay men and lesbians were an advantaged group seeking preferential treatment was defeated by a margin of just six percentage points (ironically, this victory occurred only after progay forces outspent their opponents ten to one).

And stereotypes of gay wealth not only play into the hands of right-wing demagogues. More moderate opponents of a broad-reaching lesbian and gay agenda have seized on them as well. In the May 1993 issue of the *New Republic*, Jonathan Rauch invoked popular stereotypes about gay wealth to argue that gay men and lesbians should not consider themselves oppressed. His piece opened with chilling scenes of gay-bashing, but then proceeded to claim that gay men and lesbians are not oppressed because they meet only one of his criteria of oppression—they face direct legal discrimination. They can vote, have a right to education, and are entitled to basic human rights, but the point he returned to most is that they are also free of "impoverishment relative to the remainder of the population."[3] After citing Overlooked Opinions' income data, Rauch offered one anecdotal example after another of the wealthy gay man: a college professor friend who owns a split-level condo and a Mazda Miata; gay acquaintances with $50,000 incomes and European vacations who whine about being victims.

Not only was Rauch's analysis built on a faulty empirical foundation, it was also blind to the link between the legal discrimination that he acknowledged and economic oppression. In his discussion of whether or not gay people are economically oppressed, Rauch failed to mention the occupational segregation faced by openly gay men until literally the last few years. Like Jews throughout European history, openly gay men have been shunted into a severely limited number of occupational fields. And just as the success of the Rothschilds should never have been used to belittle the wide-ranging effects of the systematic discrimination Jews faced over many centuries in Europe, so the success of some gay figures in the arts and entertainment business (or in Rauch's circle of acquaintance) should not obscure the real effects of having to choose between being openly gay and entry into a wide range of jobs. Moreover, although discrimination against lesbians is less conspicuous because all women have faced economic oppression, it is clear that women's lower incomes place lesbian households at a unique disadvantage.

This is not to say that as a group, gay men and lesbians experience seamless economic exploitation; on the contrary, the case of gay marketing reveals the very complex relationship between gay people and the economy. We are witnessing a new stage in this relationship, and perhaps some signs of improvement in it, but gay people have always both prospered and suffered at the hands of the market. As the historian John D'Emilio has argued, gay people have enjoyed the economic freedom to build same-sex households in capitalist societies, but culturally they have served as scapegoats for the expression of various anxieties—family pressures but also class frustration, which might threaten the economic status quo were it to find its proper target. As he wrote in his 1984 essay "Capitalism and Gay Identity," "Materially, capitalism weakens the bonds that once kept families together so that their members experience a growing instability in the place they have come to expect happiness and emotional security. . . . Lesbians, gay men, and heterosexual feminists have become the scapegoats for the social instability of the system."[4] Now, suddenly, it has become useful to business interests to cultivate a narrow (and widely acceptable) definition of gay identity as a marketing tool, and to integrate gay people as gay people into a new consumer niche. The speed with which the needs of the market can steamroll the strongest of social traditions and taboos is awe-inspiring. Yet in keeping with history, the outcome for gay men and lesbians is double-edged.

Today, the sword of the market is slicing off every segment of the gay community that is not upper-middle-class, (mostly) white, and (mostly) male. Lesbians and gay men who do not see themselves in Ikea television spots or Dewar's ads feel alienated. Perhaps more important, gay politics now reflects this divide, and a growing chorus of conservative gay writers are calling for gay activism to separate itself from any broader progressive vision that might address the needs and interests of the less visible, less privileged parts of the gay community.

Just a few years ago, the AIDS crisis helped give an edge to gay politics by encouraging just those sorts of connections to develop. AIDS politicized a large group of white middle-class gay men, who suddenly discovered what it was like to live in fear of losing your housing or your medical coverage, and who had to fight the medical, insurance, and real estate establishments to survive. The crisis moved many gay men to come out, and it also prompted some of them to link the fight against homophobia to other progressive political efforts.

Fifteen minutes in the limelight, however, and this political consciousness seems to be melting away. Queer Nation's slogan, "We're here, we're queer, get used to it," was supposed to say to straight people, "We will stretch your concept of morality, of family, of politics." But many in the gay movement now seem to be saying, "We're here, we're just like you, don't worry about it." When asked about Philip Morris's gay marketing campaign for Special Kings cigarettes, the publisher of Los Angeles's *Genre* magazine responded, "*Esquire* takes tobacco ads and that is the kind of publication we want to be."

It is too early to tell whether concrete, day-to-day political action in the gay community will change as well, coming more into line with the typical politics of groups led by individuals who feel they are faring well under capitalism. But it is already clear that in some important ways, the gay moment is more of a hurdle for gay politics than a source of strength. The delicate bonds between the gay and African American communities, for example, are only being stretched closer to the breaking point. The current blitz contains hardly any images of gay African Americans or references to black gay culture or organizations. As Eric Washington pointed out in the *Village Voice*, a recent Overlooked Opinions survey asked gay New Yorkers which publications they read, listing several dailies and weeklies but omitting Harlem's *Amsterdam News*. And a question about hospital services to gays and lesbians left Harlem Hospital off the list. Such omissions not only reinforce the alienation of black lesbians and gay men from the rest of the gay community; the images of a seamlessly white middle-class gay community tap into "an undercurrent of resentment [in the African American community] . . . fed by the perception that gays are affluent and indifferent to racism."[5]

It is tempting to embrace today's recognition ecstatically and unconditionally; as Andrew Schneider, who wrote *Northern Exposure*'s lesbian episode, told *Vogue*, the network was inundated with letters from lesbians after the show aired. "They were very grateful, like starving people getting a crust of bread," he said. But seizing the gay moment even as it reinforces racial and class hierarchies will allow for limited gains. As the best feminism is sensitive to more than questions of gender, the fight against homophobia will take on its most liberating forms only if it is conceived as part of a broader vision of social and economic justice.

Notes

1. Grant Lukenbill, *Untold Millions: The Gay and Lesbian Market in America* (New York: HarperCollins, 1995).

2. "Bet on a Gay Tourism Boost in Hawaii," *Detroit News*, 1995; reprinted in *Liberal Opinion*, Sept. 18, 1995, 6.

3. Jonathan Rauch, "Beyond Oppression," *New Republic*, May 10, 1993, 18.

4. John D'Emilio, "Capitalism and Gay Identity," in *Powers of Desire*, ed. Ann Snitow, Christine Stansell, and Sharon Thompson (New York: Monthly Review Press, 1983), 100–117.

5. Eric Washington, "Freedom Rings? The Alliance between Blacks and Gays Is Threatened by Mutual Inscrutability," *Village Voice*, June 29, 1993, 25–33.

41

The Organizational Shaping of Collective Identity: The Case of Lesbian and Gay Film Festivals in New York

Joshua Gamson

Collective identity, the "agreed upon definition of membership, boundaries, and activities for the group,"[1] has recently moved into a number of intellectual spotlights. Sociological scholarship increasingly recognizes that collective identities do not precede but are actively constructed and negotiated by communities.[2] Within social movement theory, driven particularly by "new social movement" theory,[3] this insight has served to reassert, against the rational-action focus of much U.S. sociology, that "the collective search for identity is a central aspect of movement formation."[4]

That search itself, especially in the form of "identity politics," has met with increased critical scrutiny from social theorists as well. Echoing constructionist social movement research, for instance, Craig Calhoun suggests that "as lived, identity is always project, not settled accomplishment," and, moreover, is inherently problematic.[5] Drawing on criticisms that emerged from within feminist, lesbian and gay, and African American movements,[6] Calhoun argues that the tension between "identity—putatively singular, unitary, and integral—and identities—plural, cross-cutting, and divided—is inescapable at both individual and collective levels." Thus, for example, "black unity in South Africa can be understood only as a political project pushed and challenged by the ANC, Inkatha, and various factions within each. 'Black' is not a settled, pre-theoretical position." These claims that collective identity formation is an ongoing (political) process in which multiple, overlapping identities inevitably conflict run throughout current analyses of "identity movements."[7]

These approaches have spawned an increasingly sophisticated discussion of collective identity as, in Alberto Melucci's terms, "a system of relations and representations" rather than "as a 'thing,' as the monolithic unity of a subject."[8] Verta Taylor and Nancy Whittier, for instance, working from this model of identity-as-process, have made strides toward specifying the process: how groups mark the boundaries between in-group and out-group, how a political consciousness emerges from "a challenging group's struggle to define and realize its interests,"[9] and how movement actors negotiate with and resist established social definitions.

Yet the insight that identities are claimed, made, refused, and deconstructed, while rallying effectively against the view of them as preexisting characteristics or prescribed labels, has too often been taken to mean that collective identities float freely in the world. All this attention has oddly underplayed the organizational mediation of collective identity, leaving us with the thin choice between the "top-down" imposition of identities and the "bottom-up" creation of them.[10] The welcome notion that identities are "interactional accomplishments"[11] has not been met with careful regard for the question of how those interactions are structured, shaped, and limited by the organizational and institutional contexts in which they take place. The recognition in much recent writing that collective identities (e.g., "Black") are made not just by groups or factions but by groups *in organizations* (e.g., the ANC) has been largely left behind.

This essay, by uncovering that claim and pursuing it empirically not only grounds the study of a typically slippery and abstract phenomenon, but also puts on the table a misleadingly simple question: What difference does it make for collective identity construction that so much of it takes place in and through organizations? In order to begin answering that question, I import the basic analysis of organizational adaptations to the external environment, in which "both the organization's resource base and its institutional context are important."[12] Organizational analysis has focused attention on, first, the ways organizations "adjust in response to changes in the amount and type of resources available to them" and "alter their structures and goals in order to obtain the resources needed to survive."[13] Second, scholars have pointed to the ways the structure of the "sector" within which an organization is located,[14] or its "organizational field," shapes organizations.[15] Organizations respond to their "institutional environments," characterized by "the elaboration of rules and requirements to which individual organizations must conform if they are to receive support and legitimacy."[16] The question thus becomes, How do resource dependencies and the characteristics of the *institutional environment* shape collective identity articulations?

In the case of organizations claiming a community base, "support and legitimacy" do not just come from relationships to sponsors and funders. Whether based in neighborhoods or in less geographically bounded communities, such organizations are characterized by "an explicit commitment to represent the interests of their community rather than the private or professional interests of their founders."[17] Organizational survival and legitimacy depend on the maintenance of a relationship not only to sponsors but also to publics, who figure prominently in the institutional environment. A question is thus added: How does the balancing act between the roles of *community* organization and community *organization* affect the kinds of collective identities that find public homes?

Lesbian and gay film festivals provide an especially fruitful opportunity for examining these questions in the concrete, bringing collective identity theorizing face to face with organizational analysis. As organizing efforts, they operate within highly developed institutional environments (film and arts industries) and require significant financial resources. More important, film festivals are, one might say, homes or warehouses for collective identity; they involve ongoing and quite self-conscious decision making about the content and contours of the "we" being made literally visible. The festivals and the organizing behind them are significant less as tools for direct political mobilization than as "free spaces" in which the building blocks for movement cultures are consolidated and disseminated.[18] In particular, festival organizations are engaged in an ongoing process of *identity framing*, making visible particular versions of group "consciousness and character."[19] Although it is a mistake, as festival organizers often point out, to conflate the programming of works with their creation, in a very literal way these festivals provide an opportunity for emerging "cultural resources" to be publicly considered.[20] Whether these tools get picked up by other social movement actors is another question, but without an organizational sponsor and a home, they would simply not have a public life.

The relationship between these gay and lesbian cultural events and gay and lesbian social movements is also significant. These festivals are part of what Steven Buechler has termed a "social movement community," a broad range of formal and informal groups "that identify their goals with the preferences of a social movement and attempt to implement those goals."[21] As "community organizations," they remain tied to community expectations and goals, even as they operate autonomously from direct community control. Looking at them, then, can help illuminate the impact of the relationship between organizational survival, on the one hand, and survival in a social movement community, on the other.

With these issues in mind, I spent much of 1994 and 1995 investigating the New York lesbian and gay film festival scene, comprising the Experimental Festival (now Mix), founded in 1987 and exhibiting primarily experimental short film and video works, and the New Festival, founded in 1988 and exhibiting primarily feature-length narrative and documentary works.[22]

The New York Lesbian and Gay Experimental Film Festival (now Mix) was founded in 1987 by filmmaker Jim Hubbard and writer and activist Sarah Schulman, who met while putting up posters for a political event.[23] It emerged from their frustration that certain films—Hubbard's, for example—were not being shown. Simply put, the straight art-film world was not hospitable to gay and lesbian film, and the gay festival circuit emerging in the mid-1980s was not interested in experimental work, with its often radical departures from conventions of narrative film form and content.

Linked to this pragmatic motivator was both a critique of film-as-entertainment and an argument for experimental film as particularly fitting for working with and changing lesbian and gay consciousness; the festival aimed to develop what Aldon Morris calls an "oppositional consciousness," ways of thinking that emerge within struggles by subordinate groups "to dismantle systems of domination that prevent them from realizing their interests."[24] "From the dawn of cinema," a 1992 fund-raising document suggested, "gay film was synonymous with experimentation" because "dominant culture has never provided a story of homosexual life and so no formal structure was available for filmmakers to simply assume."[25] Thus, according to the notes for the first Experimental Festival:

> We organized this festival because we believe that lesbian and gay people can have an especially rich relationship to experimental film. Both avant-garde film and gay consciousness must be resolutely created in a world that insists on a homogeneous sexuality and a narrowly-defined aesthetic enforced through a stiflingly limited media. The experimental process mirrors, in many ways, the process of understanding a gay identity; both demand an endless re-imagining of the self and the world in order to envision and create what the mainstream believes should not and must not exist.[26]

This history, the organizers have argued, has been overshadowed by the "aesthetic choices of most contemporary lesbian and gay festivals,"[27] which have been in "formal and demographic lockstep with the dominant trends," pursuing a "predominantly narrative, white, male, dominant culture approved" strategy.[28]

Guided by these critiques, programming strategies early on were (and continue to be, albeit in a different way) intentionally "challenging," to take a term often thrown around among organizers. "The big concept," organizers wrote, is to "curate and structure this event so that it provokes discussion and debate within the community and so that it inspires the viewers to think and re-think for themselves."[29] So, for example, it has been the festival policy from the outset, despite the perception that there is audience resistance to it, to mix "men's" works and "women's" works consistently to create "a united vision that understands jack-off clubs and sees Annie Sprinkle's cervix, and a community that struggles against the AIDS crisis and against rape."[30] The strongest emphasis at the Experimental Festival has been on works that emphasize a "politic that isn't just around, you know, 'Let's be gay and express ourselves,' " as one programming committee member says, or, as another puts it, works that constitute a rebellion against "this is me, this is great, just these easy, continual, simplified, not thought-out portraits of identity."

The programming has thus ranged from the formally experimental to the more generally anticonventional. The 1994 festival—since 1992 the festival has been organized into named programs—included programs called *Transgressive and Redemptive Acts*, *Wet Spot* ("New York's all-new 'Hot'n'Horny' girl program"), and a collection of short films made in Brazil over the past twenty-five years ("they mix tension, guilt, heresy, sensibility, poetry, and carnival within a Brazilian social-cultural context").[31] This is programming that aims, often explicitly, to disrupt the established conventions of lesbians and gays as an ethnic-style collective, to reject the application of "straight paradigms" to un-straight lives.

The Experimental Festival's larger counterpart, the New Festival, has been anchored in quite a dissimilar model of gay and lesbian identity. Founded in 1988, it was one among the growing number of post-Stonewall efforts (parades, magazines, and so on) geared toward furthering gayness-as-ethnicity. The original impetus of the festival, as cofounder Susan Horowitz saw it, was to join grassroots community politics and film art: to bring lesbians and gays together in another public space, to increase lesbian and gay visibility, to demonstrate the pluralism of that community, and to raise lesbian and gay consciousness.

Visibility-as-politics remains central to the festival's philosophy. Board member and programmer Stephen Soba cites the late film historian Vito Russo as a strong influence on his view of the festival.

> Vito used to say that coming out was everything. It's of the utmost necessity that we be able to see ourselves, to have images of ourselves, to see ourselves in all our complexity, to see ourselves truly, to not be consigned to invisibility or stereotype, to emerge. The festival is saying we're much more complicated than you think. It's saying we are you, you're us. You're in our movies, we're in your movies. We live our lives together on the planet. It's testimony, it's documentation, it's proof that we were here. Its fundamental mandate is to provide a place and a voice and a face to gay and lesbian experience and life.

This is a broad mandate, one that allows for, even requires, a diversity of programming. In that it also draws from and attracts the lesbian and gay avant-garde, the New Festival has always included a strand of identity-disruptive content. Its definitive core has nonetheless been "a celebration and acknowledgement of who we are as Lesbians and Gay men, here and around the world," an affirmation of a stable collective.[32] The New Festival has aimed primarily to display the homoerotic subtexts of Hollywood movies, showcase independent films by and about gays and lesbians, and fight for film-industry recognition of these films. The 1994 festival, in addition to a Marlon Riggs retrospective and a presentation on "sadomasochism in contemporary life and media," for example, included the premiere of the lesbian "crossover" film *Go Fish* (a "spirited, unapologetic depiction of lesbian life in the 90s, a girl meets girl movie for the whole family"), the documentary *Coming Out under Fire* ("first-hand accounts of nine lesbian and gay veterans who joined the fight against fascism are juxtaposed with the 1993 'gays in the military' Senate hearings"), and George Cukor's *A Star Is Born* with Judy Garland.[33]

The range is broad, but what sets it apart from the Experimental Festival is the programming of celebrations of "our heritage" and "our lives," programming that assumes and advances a stable and recognizable "us." The major cultural tools with which the two festivals have worked, although they overlap, diverge both in the kind of political consciousness they express and in the solidity of the us-them boundaries they promote: the Experimental Festival sought to build a consciousness in which the oppositional "we" was always under question, and the New Festival to build a consciousness that emphasized the clarity and strength of a shared sexual status. Yet over time, both festivals have subtly turned to other cultural tools, and subtly reframed the "we" under display. To understand how and why, we need to turn to the organizational and institutional fields in which they have operated.

Despite their very different goals for "the community," and behind this their distinct working models of collective sexual identity, there is little conflict between the two festivals in New York. For one thing, New York is one of the few places where a gay and lesbian audience can be divided, and where an established avant-garde arts scene exists to provide a dependable audience for experimental work. Moreover, the New York lesbian and gay festival scene currently operates through overlapping social and professional networks, on the one hand, and a rather sharp division of labor, on the other. So, for example, the two festivals often receive many of the same submissions of video and film works, and sometimes show a few of the same pieces. The personnel of the festivals mostly know one another, and there is even direct crossover: the New Festival coordinator is also on the Experimental Festival programming committee, and the Experimental Festival organizers will on occasion curate a program for, or show their own work at, the New Festival.

Despite these overlapping networks, the two festivals maintain separate organizational profiles and largely separate audiences: the Experimental Festival serves mostly young, predominantly white, financially struggling members of the gay and lesbian art-film world; the slightly more upscale New Festival serves a more professional, also predominantly white, gay and lesbian moviegoer audience, more mixed in age, although still predominantly an under-forty crowd. On this level, the festival scene is simply structured on a division of missions serving relatively distinct and narrow lesbian and gay "taste" populations, two among a large and loose network of gatherings serving lesbian and gay populations. On another level, this division of labor between the two festivals not only reduces conflict between the festivals, but also allows each festival to go about its own business without tremendous internal conflict.[34]

Perhaps most important, this division, in which the Experimental Festival retains its distinctiveness and its avant-garde audience, and in which the New Festival retains its distinctiveness and its moviegoer audience, has been supported by a division of the institutional field in which the festivals emerged and established themselves. The Experimental Festival found a comfortable institutional home in the small, resource-poor world of avant-garde film and, physically, has been held in experimental film houses (since its third year at Anthology Film Archives).

The New Festival, on the other hand, has made the more market-oriented independent-film world its base. The early New Festival organizers, with their founding vision of a broad-based gay and lesbian visibility endeavor, built on their existing connections to feminist independent-film distribution and to market-based independent film more generally—for example, the festival has always had a tight relationship with Women Make Movies, a major distributor of independent feminist film and video.

This location in the independent-film world was a natural one. Not only did it provide ready resources—office space, personnel, and know-how, drawn from Women Make Movies—it also connected the festival to the producers and distributors of lesbian and gay films, and to networks of "film distributors, television buyers, and other mass market outlets" who, according to an early mission statement, made up a major target audience.[35] In addition to an open call for works, for example, organizers have consistently "shopped" for material at places like the Berlin International Film Festival and the Independent Feature Film Market. The festival itself, which recently found a home at the Public Theater, has been held in various rented independent movie houses: the Biograph Cinema, the Eighth Street Playhouse, the Quad Cinema.

The New Festival and the Experimental Festival have faced similar obstacles. The first organizational challenge arises primarily from the fact that both actively claim standing as lesbian and gay community organizations. Any organization attempting to culturally represent such a diverse population faces the political challenge of inclusiveness; this challenge has been felt with increasing strength in the last two decades of lesbian and gay organizing, during which lesbians and gay men of color in particular have forcefully made their voices heard within gay and lesbian organizing. As is the case in many other community-based organizations,[36] it is extremely difficult to retain legitimacy as a lesbian and gay community organization without demonstrating a commitment to gender, racial, and ethnic diversity. The festivals' sites within the organizational field, however, brought their own particular difficulties to this process.

The core of the New Festival vision, for example, has always been the notion that the festival served "the lesbian and gay community," which was being made visible in all its complexity to itself and others. Yet close as it was to necessary film-world networks, the festival's institutional location was also relatively isolated from "the community" the festival sought to organize and represent. In particular, the established lesbian and gay independent-film world, small as it has been, has been a notoriously white one—in terms of both filmmakers and audiences. Thus the New Festival faced criticisms and self-criticisms as it attempted to make good on its status as a "community event." The gay weekly *Outweek*, for example, reserved its only criticism of the first festival for its notable "lack of work by non-western, non-white film makers."[37]

The Experimental Festival faced a parallel difficulty. The goal of the Experimental Festival at its inception was to provide a space in which "gay consciousness" could be freely created, outside the constraints of commercial media and the aesthetic strategies they require. The underground-film world was, in many ways, an ideal location for such a project, supportive as it was of working outside Hollywood conventions. Yet while this institutional location made the festival possible, it also brought with it certain limitations: an often inaccessible visual and written language and, perhaps tied to this, a narrow set of practitioners interested in and able to work in that language.[38] The festival in its early years included much formalist, experimental cinema, and was a distinctly white event, despite the organizers' efforts to diversify it. This was a serious problem for an organization aiming to bring out a full range of critical "re-imaginings," and a prime target of criticism and self-criticism: like most gay and lesbian community organizations since the 1980s, the Experimental Festival was troubled by its own detachment from various segments of the population it set out to "represent," in particular lesbians and gay men of color. For a festival engaged in building a new representational language, the institutional territory of the established gay film avant-garde thus presented serious obstacles.

The difficulty in retaining legitimacy as community organizations (in the eyes not only of constituent community members, but of organizers themselves as well) has been consistently underscored by one important set of sponsors: community, state, and arts foundations. The Astraea National Lesbian Action Foundation application, for example, asks for specific numbers and percentages of leadership, staff, membership, and constituency along dimensions of gender, race, age, physical abilities, and sexual orientation; the New York State Council on the Arts asks how the needs and interests of "minorities and special constituencies" are met in programs, services, inclusion of artists, and staffing. A predominantly white organization, even one serving sexual "minorities," can address these questions only weakly.

On one level, the festivals have responded with alternate versions of the same path, successfully making large changes in the representation of people of color within them. Besides becoming more deliberate about seeking out a racially diverse array of films and filmmakers, each moved quickly to include video work, which opened up much more space for artists without the resources to work in the expensive medium of film, often women and people of color. (For example, Jim Hubbard estimates that while the percentage of films and videos by nonwhite filmmakers at the Experimental Festival was around 2 percent to 5 percent in the early years, it is now closer to 25 percent to 30 percent.) Each also opened up structurally: both eventually expanded from individual programmers to a programming committee structure, and sought out input from a racially diverse group; both began to invite guest curators, especially artists of color, to seek out and pull together programs representing experiences outside the white middle class; and each sought out people of color for inclusion in advisory and leadership positions. In fact, as of 1994, both festivals are directed by a person of color. These changes have been quite deliberate and profound.

What makes these diversification processes most interesting, however, is the ways they have been shaped by the interaction with simultaneous adaptations to the second organizational challenge: the resource environment in which the festivals began is dramatically different from the one in which they operate a short eight years later. On the one hand, state and foundation grants for the arts, always difficult for the festivals to come by, have dried up considerably. On the other hand, corporate interest in lesbian and gay films, and in lesbian and gay audiences, has picked up considerably, as has the academic consolidation of lesbian and gay studies (including lesbian and gay art). Gay-themed Holly-wood films (such as *Philadelphia*) have met with success, and independently produced films with lesbian and gay themes (such as *Go Fish*) have met with successful theatrical distribution, even as formal experimentation has been successfully commodified (on MTV, for example). These changes are part of a larger shift for the organized lesbian and gay population from, as Sarah Schul-man has put it, "an ignored community struggling to represent itself to a consumer group that is being niche marketed by the most powerful corporate influences," itself a result of the successful organizing for visibility and self-representation. Institutional changes have created new limitations and opportu-nities for the festival organizations, and their adaptations to this environment bring reframings of collective identity along with them.

Beginning in 1991, the Experimental Festival was faced with a crisis of survival. The main organizers wanted more time for their own creative work. The state arts budget, through which the festival received the bulk of its non–box office funding, was drastically reduced. Through the guest curator strate-gies they had developed to increase nonwhite representation, Hubbard and Schulman had begun to make contact with younger film and video markers of color, and in 1992 made the decision to pass the torch to two artists whose work the founders admired: Shari Frilot, a twenty-eight-year-old Black/Puerto Rican video artist, and Karim Ainouz, a twenty-seven-year-old Brazilian filmmaker.

In addition to the provision of new talent, this decision solved several organi-zational problems at once. First, it furnished the festival with new human resources, while promising to transform it into an organization more directly connected to and more adequately serving communities of color. Second, it provided the festival with new potential survival resources, not in the form of direct economic support (like most cultural workers, the festival organizers cobble together a living from a variety of jobs, often temporary), but in the form of increased cultural and social capital.[39] Frilot was educated at Harvard and in the prestigious Whitney Program; Ainouz, who was recommended to the organizers by a PBS contact, was educated at New York University's Studio Art and Cinema Studies Program and at the Whitney Program as well.

What made this move "up" in terms of "art-world currency" especially urgent were changes in the wing of the institutional sector in which the festival was located. Lesbian and gay art and film, which had until recently been operating at the margins of the art world, was becoming more central, recog-nized as a "genre" both within art-world institutions and academic institutions.

Without effective connections to these institutions, the festival would be less able to program (at a time when eligible films are coming increasingly from universities or art schools). In a subtle shift, the Experimental Festival moved from the "countercultural" worlds of traditional avant-garde film (Hubbard), with ties to grassroots politics (Schulman), toward the academic art world.

This organizational shift brought with it particular ways of speaking about and conceptualizing collective sexual identities. By 1994, having changed the name of the festival to Mix, organizers were putting out a call for work that "interrogates familiar terms used in articulating sexualities, to explore notions of hybridity, mescla, synchretism, mestizaje, samanvay, etc.," and describing their festival as one that "celebrates transgressive sexual diversity, explores hybridity within notions of queerness, takes up issues of race, class, nationality, ethnicity, and gender and critically investigates the state of lesbian and gay politics today."[40] The boundary brought into the spotlight, within this frame-work, is less between an "us" and a "them" than between "us" and "us." The framing of the "protagonist identity field"[41] moves subtly from a loose but discernible lesbian and gay "we" to a broad and fluid coalition of sex and gender transgressors.

The framing of the "antagonist identity field" shifts similarly. Where the early festival designated relatively clear enemies for opposition (state censor-ship, heterosexual conventions, and so on), the Experimental Festival began to frame itself in "postmodern" language that argues for moving "beyond the merely oppositional."[42] The change in programming content, it should be noted, is considerably more subtle than the shift toward the language of "hy-bridity" and such ("Whitneyspeak," as one committee member calls it) sug-gests. That is, although the pool of available works has expanded enormously, the principles by which films are selected now do not differ much from the selection criteria of seven years ago: interesting, challenging, transgressive. The festival, however, has put a new frame around those criteria. The move "up" in terms of cultural capital, made necessary by the consolidation of lesbian and gay art-world institutions, brings with it the frame of academic deconstruc-tionism; the notion of promoting a "transgressive" identity has begun to replace a more traditional left frame of promoting an "oppositional" one.

Indeed, this is the frame into which much of the racial diversification process has been fit: racial diversity is mobilized in the festival not so much to broaden the identity category, but to demonstrate its fluidity. Racial differences are often brought into an anti-identity politic, a rejection of "an established politic of difference," as Mix director Shari Frilot puts it, in favor of "our motivation to mix that identity up." This is a formulation of collective identity that finds its way into the Experimental Festival's organizational body not only because of its currency within some lesbian and gay populations—among lesbians and gays of color, in particular, who have long asked, as Frilot does, "Who is the 'we' here?"—but even more so because of its resonance in the organizational field. As the structure of cultural opportunities shifts (community legitimacy becomes more problematic, organizational survival seems to depend on better elite connections), new cultural tools come into play, and reframings of collective identity along with them.

The New Festival tells a different version of a similar story. At the outset, the New Festival was largely a combination of activism and entrepreneurship: attracting lesbian and gay audiences was the key to both legitimacy as a community organization and financial survival. This approach attempts to "reach as many people as possible" through "accessible" programming, in one board member's words, especially conventional narrative features with perceived commercial viability. This was not just an ideological commitment to affirmation, but an economic survival strategy that recognized the draw of affirmation for much of the consuming population.

This strategy, rooted in the entrepreneurial activism of the festival's early financers, has contended from the beginning with a vision of the festival less as a community event and more as a film event. For those coming from a film-world background (the programmers, typically), the emphasis has been less on exposure of a community to itself than, as Jeff Lunger, a central programmer of the festival until 1993, put it, on "exposure for the film makers to the gay community." The prime strategy for several years was to locate the festival firmly in the art-film market, with its greater emphasis on "inventive" (and formally experimental) work. This survival strategy involved getting "people in the film world to take the festival seriously." For that task, a festival that pleases audiences is less important than a festival that establishes its artistic seriousness.

With the "mainstreaming" of gay-themed films, however, the dynamics of the increasingly commercialized independent lesbian and gay film market have shifted the balance between community goals and survival strategies; that is, a new cultural opportunity structure has called forth shifts in organizational strategies, which themselves involve reframings of collective identity. In the early years of the festival, organizers dealt only with filmmakers and producers; films with lesbian and gay content were almost never seen as having commercial potential. As the "new queer cinema" came to be constituted as a genre,[43] and as the commercial market for gay and lesbian features increased and film companies such as New Line Cinema began appealing to specialized audiences,[44] programmers had to deal with commercial distributors. These distributors might not feel that it is in the interest of the film to premiere at the festival (they lost Gregg Araki's *Totally F***ed Up* due to distributor concerns that "too much exposure would harm the commercial release"), might have another festival in mind, or might be on a different timetable (they lost the Cuban film *Strawberry and Chocolate* when Miramax decided the festival was "too early"). The commercial success of gay-themed films has made film resources more difficult to come by, and links to the independent film market have thus become even more critical.

Two changes have been especially prominent in response to this new environment. First, the organizational struggle has become much less focused on positioning the festival as a lesbian and gay community event and more over how best to position it as a film-community event. Second, and related, as corporate interest has expanded, the community has come to be constituted less as a political group to be organized and more as a niche audience for sale.

In 1993, for example, the board fired programmers Sande Zeig and Jeff Lunger and moved to programming by committee, largely because visions of the organization's profile within the film world were at odds. As one board member explains,

> They were seeing it as this little film festival, which was perfectly fine, but we were thinking of it in bigger terms. We needed to expand. We were into making this a bigger thing and getting more corporate sponsorship and more visibility. The festival needs to be bigger in terms of profile, and more than profile, in terms of sensibility.

The need to pump up the festival's "profile" was becoming particularly acute for organizational survival, given the increased dependence on film distributors. An "artistic look" appealing to the art world would not achieve the commercial profile necessary to attract films with theatrical distributors. The charge of being "narrowly" gay also threatens resources. So, for example, the 1995 programming committee planned a "fashion series," including *Unzipped* (about designer Isaac Mizrahi); in order to score the film from its distributor, one member argued, they would have to make the show a "mainstream fashion thing" rather than a "ghettoizing thing," since the distributor apparently was not interested in pitching it as a "gay film." Many at the festival thus began to advocate for a higher profile through which to pitch the festival audience.

This "bigger thing" approach dovetails with a "niche market" appeal to corporate sponsors, in which the festival audience is consolidated and marketed for economic survival. Last year, in fact, the festival began compiling statistics on the demographics of its audience (including median income). Board member Chiqui Cartegena, herself a filmmaker, argues that "the key to the gay and lesbian film festival is that it is a market that advertisers are recognizing more and more. We do have something that is marketable." Treating the festival as constituting an audience-market for sale indeed seems to work: the festival sells its mailing list of more than fourteen thousand and has garnered sponsorship from Absolut vodka and Seagram's, *Genre, Out* and the *Advocate* magazines, worth thousands of dollars.

These attempts to market the audience and increase the festival's desirability as a springboard for commercially distributed films involve both a mainstreaming and a commercialization of the festival's articulations of identity. Attempts to diverge from that model, to destabilize the identity categories through formal and substantive challenges, take risks with organizational survival.[45] Consolidating a market niche, typically by providing "more mainstream things that will fill up five hundred seats and everything," as one programmer describes it, involves affirming that same-sex desire is a coherent, shared basis for a social grouping.

The accommodation of racial diversity takes place in this organizational context, primarily through a multiculturalism that posits a plurality of lesbian and gay experiences, but does not challenge their basic commonality. The boundaries of the collective category are expanded, the "family" enlarged; racial and ethnic differences are framed as variations on a theme rather than as demonstrations of the instability of the collective. This framing prevails not so much because organizers all share this perspective—they do not—but because the characteristics of the organizational sector favor the consolidation of an audience-as-market for survival purposes.[46]

In telling the story of these two New York film festivals, I have intended to bring the discussion of collective identity more directly into contact with organizational analysis. Between the "top-down" structural imposition and the "bottom-up" voluntaristic construction of collective identities sit their organizational bodies, filtering identity formulations. They do their filtering quite strategically, if often without conscious intent, as they attempt to strike a balance between the pressures of community standing and the pressures of their resource environment.

At the Experimental Festival, identity deconstruction, the move away from "lesbian and gay" labels, and the call for hybrid forms have flowed in large part from an organizational shift to garner connections to the elite art world while expanding racially. At the New Festival, identity affirmation has become increasingly multicultural within the limits set by dependence on independent-film world resources; the collective identity has begun a shift from political to consumer category.

This analysis pushes forward the recognition of the strategic dimensions of movement culture—it is the logic and the language of institutional sectors, rather than only of the populations whose boundaries are at stake, that account here for patterning and repatterning of collective identity. There is a danger, however, in misreading this as institutional determinism: organizational actors, as we have seen in the cases presented here, work with strong commitments to particular cultural tools, which set limits on how far within an organizational field they are willing to move. Organizational adjustments, while they rarely shift the entire direction of a group's self-definition, move some versions of identity closer to center stage.

What does it mean, then, that these organizational adjustments seem to involve a move further inside existing elite and commercial institutions? Certainly, given the exigencies of the environment, such moves make good sense. The shifting opportunities provided by the "discovery" of gay film as an artistic and commercial genre, most prominently, have made pursuits of higher cultural capital and demonstrations of consumer group status smart survival strategies. But these are not *incidental* inward moves. Success in the organizational field appears to favor identity formulations that are less explicitly oppositional—in this case, academically or commercially resonant frames—and it is tempting to assert that this trajectory is a generalizable one.

Yet the point here may be not so much that organizational survival inevitably leads away from oppositional identity frames, but that some community organizations—some identity homes—more easily detach from their community bases than others. The case of the film festivals is again instructive. They have always been, to some degree, as accountable to their film- and art-world memberships as to the breadth of lesbian and gay community members they seek to serve; the tie to "the community" is relatively remote, since community and organization meet up most prominently once a year, at the events themselves. This has made them particularly vulnerable to changes in the institutional environment, and thus their identity adaptations have more closely followed the logic of environments with which community members have little to do. Collective identities emerge from groups along this continuum of loose-to-tight relationships to a community base; it seems likely that the more detached a cultural organization is from its community base, the more prone it is to emphasize identity frames consonant with its particular cultural opportunity structure. Both activists and scholars would do well to consider not only the organizational mediation of collective identities, but also the conditions under which institutional requirements, rather than the "we" under construction, most strongly build the homes for identity.

Notes

Versions of this chapter were presented at the Colloquium Series of the Center for Lesbian and Gay Studies (CLAGS), City University of New York, in 1995, and at the annual meeting of the American Sociological Association, Washington, DC (1995). This research was supported by grants from the Program on Non-Profit Organizations and the Social Science Faculty Research Fund at Yale. I am grateful to the following people for comments, challenges, and conversations based on an earlier draft: Rikki Abzug, Courtney Bender, Cathy Cohen, William Gamson, Zelda Gamson, Jim Hubbard, Stephen Kent Jusick, Debra Minkoff, and Sarah Schulman.

1. Hank Johnston, Enrique Laraña, and Joseph R. Gusfield, "Identities, Grievances, and New Social Movements," in *New Social Movements: From Ideology to Identity*, ed. Enrique Laraña, Hank Johnston, and Joseph R. Gusfield (Philadelphia: Temple University Press, 1994), 15.

2. Verta Taylor and Nancy Whittier, "Collective Identity in Social Movement Communities," in *Social Movement Theory*, ed. Aldon Morris and Carol McClurg Mueller (New Haven: Yale University Press, 1992).

3. See, for example, Jean Cohen, "Strategy or Identity: New Theoretical Paradigms and Contemporary Social Movements," *Social Research* 52 (1985): 663–716; Alberto Melucci, *Nomads of the Present: Social Movements and Individual Needs in Contemporary Society* (Philadelphia: Temple University Press, 1989); Debra Friedman and Doug McAdam, "Collective Identity and Activism," in *Frontiers in Social Movement Theory*, ed. Aldon Morris and Carol McClurg Mueller (New Haven: Yale University Press, 1992).

4. Johnston, Laraña, and Gusfield, 10.

5. Craig Calhoun, "Social Theory and the Politics of Identity," in *Social Theory and the Politics of Identity*, ed. Craig Calhoun (Cambridge: Blackwell, 1994), 27.

6. See bell hooks, *Ain't I a Woman? Black Women and Feminism* (Boston: South End Press, 1981); Steven Seidman, "Identity Politics in a 'Postmodern' Gay Culture: Some Historical and Conceptual Notes," in *Fear of a Queer Planet*, ed. Michael Warner (Minneapolis: University of Minnesota Press, 1993), 105–42; Michael Dyson, *Reflecting Black: African American Cultural Criticism* (Minneapolis: University of Minnesota Press, 1993).

7. Calhoun, 27. See also L. A. Kaufman, "The Anti-Politics of Identity," *Socialist Review* 20 (1990): 67–80; and Taylor and Whittier.

8. Alberto Melucci, "The Process of Collective Identity," in *Social Movements and Culture*, ed. Hank Johnston and Bert Klandermans (Minneapolis: University of Minnesota Press, 1995), 50.

9. Taylor and Whittier, 111. See also Aldon D. Morris, "Political Consciousness and Collective Action," in *Frontiers in Social Movement Theory*, ed. Morris and Mueller.

10. Johnston, Laraña, and Gusfield, 18.

11. Scott Hunt, Robert Benford, and David Snow, "Identity Fields: Framing Processes and the Social Construction of Movement Identities," in *New Social Movements*, ed. Laraña, Johnston, and Gusfield, 185–208.

12. Walter W. Powell and Rebecca Friedkin, "Organizational Change in Nonprofit Organizations," in *The Non-Profit Sector: A Research Handbook*, ed. Walter W. Powell (New Haven: Yale University Press, 1987), 181.

13. Powell and Friedkin, 181–82. As Powell and Friedkin note, the idea is not that funding sources exert direct control or desire to covertly influence funded organizations, but that resource dependencies "can lead organizations to change in unanticipated ways" (191).

14. W. Richard Scott and John W. Meyer, "The Organization of Societal Sectors: Propositions and Early Evidence," in *The New Institutionalism in Organizational Analysis*, ed. Paul DiMaggio and Walter Powell (Chicago: University of Chicago Press, 1991), 108–40.

15. Paul DiMaggio and Walter W. Powell, "The Iron Cage Revisited: Institutional Isomorphism and Collective Rationality," in *The New Institutionalism in Organizational Analysis*, ed. DiMaggio and Powell, 63–82. Scott and Meyer define a societal sector as "all organizations within a society supplying a given type of product or service together with their associated organizational sets: suppliers, financiers, regulators, and so forth" (108). DiMaggio and Powell similarly define an organizational field as "those organizations that, in the aggregate, constitute a recognized area of institutional life: key suppliers, resource and product consumers, regulatory agencies, and other organizations that produce similar services or products" (64).

16. Scott and Meyer, 123.

17. Carl Milofsky, "Neighborhood-Based Organizations: A Market Analogy," in *The Non-Profit Sector*, ed. Powell, 279.

18. Sara M. Evans and Harry C. Boyte, *Free Spaces: The Sources of Democratic Change in America* (New York: Harper and Row, 1986).

19. Hunt, Benford, and Snow, 203.

20. Rhys Williams, "Constructing the Public Good: Social Movements and Cultural Resources," *Social Problems* 42 (1995): 124–44.

21. Steven M. Buechler, *Women's Movements in the United States* (New Brunswick: Rutgers University Press, 1990), 42.

22. In 1994, the Mix Festival was joined by the Lesbian and Gay Lookout Festival. Lookout, produced by the Downtown Community Television Center, has focused pri-

marily on activist documentary video. The data I draw on come primarily from participant-observation, in-depth interviews with core members of each festival, and archival research (including writings about the festivals, fund-raising documents, and other writings internal to the organizations). At the Experimental Festival, I was able to observe and participate through one full festival cycle (June–November 1994), from the beginning of organizing through the selection of works to the festival itself, serving on committees, going to meetings and screenings of potential works, working in the festival office and at the festival events themselves. At the New Festival (January–June 1995) my access was considerably more restricted (spending time in the office, attending occasional meetings, attending the festival), and I therefore depend much more heavily on interviews. In-depth interviews of one to two hours were conducted with board members, organizers, and programmers at each festival (seven at the Experimental Festival, ten at the New Festival).

23. Schulman is a founding member of the direct action group Lesbian Avengers, a novelist, and an essayist. See Sarah Schulman, *My American History* (New York: Routledge, 1995).

24. Morris, 363.

25. New York Lesbian and Gay Experimental Film Festival, fund-raising document, 1992.

26. New York Lesbian and Gay Experimental Film Festival, program flyer, 1987.

27. New York Lesbian and Gay Experimental Film Festival, fund-raising document, 1992.

28. New York Lesbian and Gay Experimental Film Festival, transition memo, 1992.

29. New York Lesbian and Gay Experimental Film Festival, transition memo, 1992.

30. New York Lesbian and Gay Experimental Film Festival, program notes, 1989. Although there are special screenings made up exclusively of women's work, at programming meetings one is likely to see "male" and "female" symbols next to potential films, as programmers consciously mix the two.

31. Mix Festival, program catalog, 1994. In 1993, Mix spawned a Brazilian counterpart, Mix Brasil, which has become its own festival, supported in 1994 by MTV Brasil, the Museum of Sound and Image, and the Sao Paulo State Council of Culture, and touring São Paulo, Campinas, Belo Horizonte, Rio de Janeiro, Brasilia, Fortaleza, Curitiba, and Salvador.

32. New Festival, program catalog, 1990.

33. New Festival, program catalog, 1994.

34. For instance, Mix organizers, despite their own objections to the idiom, sometimes use a shorthand to dismiss a film: "Not for us," they will write on their evaluation forms when screening potential work—code for "too conventional." A straightforward documentary might fall into this category, or an agitprop-style piece; those go to Lookout. (A video in which a series of young women are shown saying, or shouting, "Women are so fucking cool" gets sent there, as does a video in which a Salvadorean drag queen makes a political argument for "the emancipation of all.") A conventional narrative might also fall into that category, with the assumption being that those wanting to become commercial filmmakers should apply elsewhere—namely, to the New Festival. (In a festival committee discussion of a trailer program, one member argues that a candidate clearly "wants to be mainstream," and compares the candidate unfavorably to another, more "low down and dirty" one. Another committee member agrees, crinkling his nose in distaste. "I just thought it was a very New Festival kind of film," he says.) At planning meetings, there may be disagreements on particular films, but there is rarely dissension about the "feel" of the festival as a whole. When the Mix Festival committee, made up of about twenty people (including many people new to the process), met to divide up potential films and videos, a rating scale was discussed; not a

word, however, on the rating criteria. There is confidence that when something is "for us," enough of us will know it. Similarly, as one New Festival organizer describes it, "If something is a completely obscure formalist exercise, we say 'Send it to the Experimental.' " Exactly because there are other festivals to accommodate the "not for us" films, Mix organizers are not often faced with the question of how to evaluate film and video work that is more conventional in form—and the New Festival is not pressured by the question of experimental work.

35. New Festival, "Positive Projects" (newsletter, 1990).

36. See, for example, the discussion of women's movements in Buechler.

37. Karl Soehnlein, "The New Festival," *Outweek*, June 26, 1989, 49.

38. The first problem the organizers addressed with explanatory introductions to the works: this filmmaker likes to experiment with color for such and such a reason, this one uses silence for such and such an effect.

39. These terms are borrowed from Pierre Bourdieu, "The Forms of Capital," in *Handbook of Theory and Research in Education*, ed. John G. Richardson (New York: Greenwood, 1986). Cultural capital refers to cultivated dispositions for appropriating valued knowledge and culture, and social capital refers to connections to valued social networks.

40. Mix Festival, call for work, 1994.

41. For a general discussion of these "identity fields," see Hunt, Benford, and Snow.

42. Filmmaker Pratibha Parmar, for example, writes that "it is a condition of these postmodernist times that we all live heterogeneous realities, constructing our sense of selves through the hybridity of cultural practices, and this is inevitably reflected in the aesthetic form employed in my work. . . . This hybrid aesthetic, as it has come to be known, works with and against the 'tools of the master' because these are the tools which we, as cultural activists and artists, have appropriated and reformulated with our diasporic imaginations." Pratibha Parmar, "That Moment of Emergence," in *Queer Looks: Perspectives on Lesbian and Gay Film and Video* (New York: Routledge, 1993), 7, 10.

43. See B. Ruby Rich, "Homo Pomo: The New Queer Cinema," in *Women and Film: A Sight and Sound Reader*, ed. Pam Cook and Philip Dodd (Philadelphia: Temple University Press, 1991).

44. Daniel Mendelsohn and Bill Oliver, "Kiss or Sell? The New Market for Gay and Lesbian Film," *Off-Hollywood Report* 6 (1991): 22–27.

45. Stephen Kent Jusick, for example, who works with Mix, has organized film festivals in Baltimore and Princeton. In Baltimore, after bringing in experimental films and getting a "very hostile" audience response, he decided that "if it's a choice between no gay festival and a mainstream gay festival, I prefer that there is a mainstream festival." In Princeton, the audience "went wild, nuts, crazy, over the top" for *Pool Days*, by New York University film school graduate Brian Sloan, a film that works, in Jusick's estimation, on "melodramatic and soap opera tropes. Will he come out? Is he gay? When will he realize he's, you know, attracted to boys? It's like looking in a mirror. It's all about itself and makes you think about yourself as a commodity." Although he himself expresses disdain for these kinds of films (dismissing one gay filmmaker, with a reference to the creator of *The Brady Bunch*, as "the Sherwood Schwartz of gay film"), he was quick to realize that these were the films that would build and retain an audience.

46. Although the resolutions I have described predominate, it would oversimplify matters to paint the picture so cleanly. In fact, in their adjustments to changes in their environments, the festivals have also come to resemble one another, both structurally (as the Experimental Festival moves toward a formal board structure) and ideologically. So, for example, many at the New Festival have followed a similar path to that of the

Experimental Festival, building on ties to elite art-world organizations to provide, as Patricia White has put it, "a really, really crucial site for changing the way people see what lesbian and gay identity or sexuality or politics or potentiality or whatever is." This approach to visibility, which has always been present at the New Festival, emphasizes a curatorial strategy much closer to that of the Experimental Festival.

Similarly, the Experimental Festival has moved somewhat closer to the newly commercialized world of independent lesbian and gay film. First, detached from the traditions of formally oriented experimental film, the Experimental Festival organizers now argue that works should not be "x'd out" simply because they are narrative or documentary. "Experimental," they suggest, is not necessarily in the film or video itself, but in the programming. Narratives, even conventional narrative features, are no longer excluded by definition. Second, moves to attract corporate sponsorship have become commonplace, although limited by the organization's gay-art-world location. The organizers have pursued, so far unsuccessfully, *Out* magazine, Hiram Walker, Absolut vodka, and others; one development committee member reported a meeting in which discussion even turned to the Playboy Foundation. Mix organizers began this strategy actively in 1993, by establishing a festival catalog for which they could solicit advertising. The first year, the advertisers were mostly "alternative" businesses such as the sexually oriented journal *Steam*, nonprofit film and video companies, a "sexuality boutique created by women for women and their partners," a body piercing studio, and sex shops. By the second year, the list included Kinko's copiers, Apple Computer, the entrepreneurial gay catalog Shocking Gray, and the "party paper" *HomoXtra*. Although there is little to suggest that there are specific strings attached to advertising dollars, this strategy of "selling" the festival indicates the decreasing distance between the Experimental Festival and the "dominant culture" and "mainstream aesthetic" to which it had earlier been opposed. Seeing them through an organizational lens, we can readily interpret them as responses to a common institutional environment. As Paul DiMaggio and Walter Powell and other students of organizations have argued, this sort of "isomorphism," a "constraining process that forces one unit in a population to resemble other units that face the same set of environmental conditions," is common (DiMaggio and Powell, "Iron Cage Revisited," 66). Occupying similar resource environments (greater corporate sponsorship opportunities, new distribution arrangements for gay and lesbian films, consolidation of lesbian and gay art worlds), but each from a slightly different institutional location, the festivals come to mirror one another. This mirroring has less to do with a coming-together of models of lesbian and gay identity within the collective than with the organizational field itself.

PART Five

Sexual Policies, Sexual Politics

A. Youth

42

Teenage Narratives of Lesbian Desire

Sharon Thompson

Between 1978 and 1986, I traveled repeatedly across the United States collecting teenage girls' stories about their sexual, romantic, and reproductive experience. Throughout, I relied on a snowball technique. Beginning with narrators met through friends, family, teachers, counselors or by introducing myself in teenage hangouts (shopping malls, roller rinks, pizza parlors, as well as school and social service settings), I went on to interview as many friends and friends of friends as possible. About equal proportions of poor, working-class, and middle-class teenagers were represented in the final sample of four hundred: about 15 percent were African American, and another 15 percent were Puerto Rican, Cuban, or Chicana. Three-quarters had had sexual intercourse: about a quarter were teenage mothers.

Ten percent of the girls who spoke with me identified themselves as lesbian, and I want to focus on a subgroup of those remarkable narrators here.[1] Heirs of both the lesbian and gay rights movement and the backlash that followed, these girls came of age just as the tide turned. While the stigma against them increased before their opened eyes, feminism, which had provided a wider social context and sense of meaning for the previous generation, virtually disappeared.

Despite these erosions, a sense of collective consciousness remained, perhaps because, unlike so many of their forebears, these girls knew very well that there were others like them. In some places, teenage lesbians had even established their own cliques and customs—adolescent lesbian nations.

These girls were all lesbians from when they were like fourteen. . . . It wasn't even like they had older lesbian friends. It was like they created their own young lesbian world. It was amazing. It was incredible. I don't know where they found the strength.

If there were no visible lesbians where they were, all knew there were many somewhere else—in New York, in San Francisco.

Surprisingly, "what made me a lesbian," traditionally a highlight of coming out stories, was of little interest to these narrators. They didn't think that lesbianism needed an explanation. Somehow it seemed to come naturally. What *did* interest them was the process of coming to or upon that identity or practice: experimenting with it, becoming sexually active, making lesbianism visible, and dealing with the fallout.[2]

Jean "had an idea" that she would become involved with a woman. She "knew that would happen." Shannon "always wanted it to happen."

It was a matter of desire.

Kendra said she was

One of those people who always knew I was a lesbian. I knew that girls my own age weren't interested in girls . . . and so I had really made up in my mind when I was pretty young that I would have to play this game of, you know, boyfriends and that kind of stuff until I was a certain age and then I would be able to go out and find all the lesbians.

Eileen didn't even begin to think about herself sexually until "around fifth or sixth grade" when her friends "started playing spin-the-bottle seriously." None of the boys wanted to kiss her, "which was okay because most of them I really didn't like."

But it sort of hurt in a way. Because I really felt odd. But I could never explain to myself either why I felt odd.

As other girls recounted getting contact lenses, putting on makeup, losing weight, and acquiring trendier wardrobes, these narrators placed importance on changing physical appearance as part of the greater project of self-transformation, often detailing a series of haircuts as a prelude to coming out.

Every week I would go and get my hair cut just a little shorter until it was finally down to a crew cut, and the girls' dean called me into her office and told me if I got my hair cut any shorter I'd be kicked out.

Julie didn't discuss her appearance until near the end of her interview, when she remarked that her short hair often caused people to mistake her for a boy. (I thought her carriage, the set of her jaw, and the insinuation of her gaze probably had more to do with it.) She had cut her hair, she said, in sophomore year, right about the time when classmates reported that she began to send romantic gifts to girlfriends. As to her current minimalist haircut, her girlfriend had "cut it much shorter than she was supposed to."

All I wanted was a trim.

Her girlfriend, Lauren, spent a good half an hour describing her own physical transformation. Lauren's initial haircut gave her "real pangs." Then she "tried a whole bunch of different styles" until she ended up with an "asymmetrical" haircut, which, she declared, "I like and I'm going to keep." Very short, straight, and boyish on one side, longer and perm-curly on the other, it was as ambiguous as she.

Coming out can have several stages. Just realizing lesbian desire may take a long time, and there's a tendency to forget, to start over. Revealing desire to others—saying to another girl, "I'm attracted to you," saying to a parent, "I'm attracted to other girls or women"—frequently takes longer still. While feeling lesbian desires seemed natural, these narrators said, naming them was difficult and confusing.[3]

> I knew I was, but I didn't want to come out. I wasn't sure, you know. It was a bad time.

Others noted that as they came to think of themselves as different, they began to isolate themselves.

> I sort of like quietly withdrew from everyone—my family, my friends, everyone. And I just became friends with Gerri.

Above all, they did not want to make a mistake.

> If it is not what I was, then I don't want to be it.

To make sure, they read everything they could find.

In earlier decades, those who wanted to read up on lesbianism first had to find what little literature was available and then survive the poisonous homophobia it purveyed. Advice books for girls warned against affectionate friendships. "And don't kiss other girls!" William Lee Howard's *Confidential Chats with Girls* exclaimed in 1911. A few years later Irving David Steinhardt warned sharply against "overaffectionate girlfriends," sleepovers, even pointed compliments from girls. Counting on girls' vanity to keep them straight, Lois Pemberton's 1948 book *The Stork Didn't Bring You!* remarked that only those who were "physically unattractive" or had "grotesque disabilities" would have "unnatural sexual relations with their own sex."[4]

The enterprising few who looked to more adult texts either found psychological studies that viewed lesbianism as a mental disorder, one more sign of female masochism, or the midnight underworlds of Radclyffe Hall's *The Well of Loneliness*, Djuna Barnes's *Nightwood*, and Ann Bannon's *Women in the Shadows* and *Odd Girl Out*. As readers of true romances are trained to expect a lifetime of devotion and wealth for a first kiss, lesbian readers learned to anticipate cut wrists and nights of lamentation from this body of work. Science fiction writer Joanna Russ tells of having written a story on the basis of this kind of reading in which "a tall, strong, masculine, dark-haired girl" throws herself off a bridge after she falls in love with another girl "I couldn't imagine anything else for the two of them to do," Russ cracked.[5]

Second-wave feminism and the lesbian and gay movement gave young lesbians a lot more to read. Teenagers who looked for information on lesbianism now found feminist works like *Sappho Was a Right On Woman, Our Bodies, Ourselves, Lesbian/Woman*, and *The Joy of Lesbian Sex*; antic, erotic classics like *Ladies Almanack*; the poetry of Audre Lorde, Adrienne Rich, and many others; a growing shelf of lesbian biographies and histories; new novelists like Blanche McCrary Boyd, Jan Clausen, Bertha Harris, Kate Millet, Valerie Miner, and Jane Rule. There were also books on coming of age as a lesbian, including Catharine R. Stimpson's *Class Notes*, Rita Mae Brown's *Rubyfruit Jungle*, Nancy Garden's *Annie on My Mind*, and Sandra Scoppetone's *Happy Endings Are All Alike*, as well as Ann Heron's collection of teenage writing, *One Teenager in Ten*. The problem became how to read it all. Every narrator I spoke with had read some of this work—at least *Rubyfruit Jungle*—and become convinced that lesbianism should be an acceptable identity. They also knew a good deal about the possibilities and problems of lesbian life and something of how to talk and think through the objections they would meet.

Uncertainty ended where the body began—usually with revelatory first kisses. Hally was rapturous about her first kiss, which brought her out:

> *It was the most incredible—I knew I was gay at that minute because I had made out before and it never felt like that. . . . It was like the rockets, the fireworks, the feelings!*

Both women and girls who fall in love or lust with one another often also "fall in love with being a lesbian," as Joyce Hunter who has long counseled lesbian and gay youth, has observed. Fear and shame vanish. Confidence and happiness prevail.[6] For a moment—a month? a year?—everything is simple and clear.

> *It sort of like solved all my problems in a way—until I went home.*

"No one is more romantic than a lesbian in love," social scientist Deborah Goleman Wolf commented, and these stories support her observation—to a point.[7] These *are* very romantic histories. But they are also very hot. Often they are comic as well. Picturing themselves as suitors and seductresses excited these girls and struck them as both portentous and funny. When they found themselves taking sexual initiative and acting on passion, they were typically impressed, amused, and aroused:

> *It turned me on incredibly.*

Eager but inexperienced lovers, they found their misperceptions and mistakes—even their most successful seductions—hilarious. One account recalled how she and her girlfriend categorized "the levels of disgustingness" in preparation for becoming sexually involved.

> The mostly disgusting is like a hand job, and exceedingly disgusting is like oral sex. . . . We had decided next time one of us spent the night over at the other's, we were going to be on the next level of disgusting, and then the week after that we were going to be mostly disgusting, and then we were going to be exceedingly disgusting. And so then, um—somehow we didn't do that in stages at all. We sort of managed it all in one night and felt very much satisfied with ourselves in the morning.

When these narrators began to talk in more detail about their lives—about home, family, school—their histories became more complicated, difficult, and divided. The original plot of twentieth-century lesbian fiction, literary critic Catharine R. Stimpson has remarked, assumed damnation as the lesbian fate; the more contemporary plot has proposed an "enabling escape" from family and local restrictions. These themes still resonated for many of the young lesbians who shared their love stories with me, especially those who lived in places that lacked visible, articulate, self-conscious lesbian and gay communities. Many girls told of relying on drugs to help them through the isolation and misery of adolescence or positioned suicide as a last hope, a way out if all else failed. They planned to lay low until they were old enough to leave home, when they could search out other lesbians and live as outlaws, continuing traditions forged in the absinthe- and opium-saturated Paris nights and beery American afternoons of an earlier literature. But some of those who were fortunate enough to live in more tolerant, frank, diverse communities told a very different story, one that the lesbian and gay movement has long fought for: a story about being able to remain at home and openly integrate lesbianism and adolescent life.[8] That's the story I want to introduce here.

Shannon and Jean know each other's renditions of coming out and falling in love by heart but they aren't tired of telling it yet or of listening to each other. Their story is about coming out and becoming sexually involved. There are two loving families, a few embarrassing moments, and a happy ending.

Tall and willowy, with fluent hands, light skin, an infectious laugh, and a boyfriend, Jean began hanging out with a lesbian clique in high school when a good friend of hers came out.[9] A little after, Shannon caught her eye in chorus. Finally, Jean passed Shannon a note asking "if she had something in common" with a "mutual acquaintance" who was out.

I never actually said yes.

Shannon didn't say no either. She had not actually answered the question for herself, although she had confided her suspicions to her best friend, Sue, and consulted a therapist who "more or less" told her that she was a lesbian: "That's where I am and that's what I'll be and I should, you know, there's nothing wrong with it." Finally, Jean told Shannon what was on her mind and they started talking about becoming lovers. Shannon's main concern was her mother or best friend "finding out about anything."

"Well, why do they have to find out about anything?" Jean responded. Shannon was silent. Jean touched Shannon's hair, then kissed her.

Jean: And then she grabbed me and she threw me—!
Shannon: She always says that. I didn't throw her.
Jean: Well, you know, she responded.

Jean started to take Shannon's clothes off, but Shannon stopped her.

Jean: I don't know why!
Shannon: I was scared. It was not that I didn't want to but I was scared. Things were moving too fast, I thought.

They scheduled another meeting the next day to work on the play. Jean said,

I thought we'd get a little work done this time.

They met after school. It was raining heavily. When they got to Shannon's house, Shannon gave Jean "something to change into." From then on, sex bollixed up chronology. It wasn't easy to recall the sequence of events. They went back over their steps like detectives.

Shannon: And, uh—I don't know, some way or another, we ended up in my bedroom. I don't—I don't even remember exactly what happened, do you?
Jean: No. No. I don't remember—I knew we were in the bedroom, but I don't remember how we got in there or what led to that.
Shannon: I think my—did my mother come home? or did we—I think we thought my mother was coming and so we both jumped up and got dressed—I don't know how long? Well, it started in the living room and we went into my room because it was in the back of the house and I figured if my mother walked in we wouldn't be caught, you know right there.

Shannon's mother was "pretty open-minded" but Shannon didn't think she would appreciate walking in on a lesbian sex scene. They thought they heard something. "My dog barking probably," Shannon said wryly.

Shannon: So we both jumped up and got dressed.
Q: Which means you had gotten undressed?
Shannon: Oh, yeah, oh yeah.
Jean: We skipped that part, didn't we? We got undressed in the living room. I don't remember everything that went on but, um—I don't know. And, um, well, we were half-undressed. I have to say that I

remember that my jeans were not completely off because I had to hop into the bedroom.

It was "a little awkward" for her, Jean said,

I mean the most that I had ever done was—kiss, you know, and I don't know. It was—it was just—different—from, you know, what I had been used to and—and what I had been taught. And—I don't know—I did feel comfortable. Things were a lot softer and—I don't know.

Shannon acknowledged feeling "a little uncomfortable," because "I didn't know her that well." She also felt "a little uncomfortable" when she "thought about" what she was doing.

But—but it was nice, you know. It was something that I always wanted to do and now I could.

I asked how they knew what to do. Jean said she'd had a little more sexual experience than she had previously indicated and she'd "had friends." She asked Shannon if she had known about the kinds of things they did together before.

Shannon: I don't know. It was just—I don't know. It was just natural.

A few weeks later, they made their first visit to a gay bar.

Jean: Shannon and I had to go to the bathroom. So we got the key and, well, we started kissing in the bathroom. I thought I had the only key but . . . well, you need it explicit? Okay, this is really embarrassing. Well—well, I took Shannon's sweater off and she was wearing walking shorts. The weather was warm. It was during the summer.
Shannon: Right before the summer.
Jean: Right before the summer.
Shannon: You were going away.
Jean: Yeah, I was—this was the last day I was home. Well, yeah. . . . I sat Shannon up on the sink! And—I proceeded to, whatever—I'm very uncomfortable—and—she—you know, she had an orgasm, and right after that the door opened and someone came into the bathroom.

Luckily, Jean had just walked into one of the bathroom stalls.

In the early fall, Shannon came out to her mother, and she and Jean began spending nights together on the living room pullout couch.

She once or twice, you know, hinted that it made her a little uncomfortable but she never said, "You can't sleep together. Don't sleep together." So.

Jean confided to her sister that her friendship with Shannon was sexual. Her sister told her mother.

Now I'm glad that she did it, because it would have been a lot harder to go to my mother myself. But my mother asked me and I started to lie. So I said, "No, no, no, ma," but then I said yes, that it is true.

When Shannon met Jean's grandmother,

My grandmother asked me, "Oh, is that your girlfriend?" And I said, "Oh, yesssss," and she said, "No, no. Is that the girl you're going with?" You know, she wanted to make sure I knew what she was talking about. So I was very happy, and I heard her say, "Oh, there's nothing wrong with it. They're not doing anything bad."

In the main, stories like Shannon's and Jean's, stories about acceptance, were told by girls from tolerant families. But a few narrators recounted transforming highly conservative, homophobic parents into accepting, supportive, loving allies. Maria's family was both conservative and religious, but together with Stevie, she faced them down, rejecting the solution of enabling escape, insisting that her parents change their views and behavior. Full of the stuff of melodrama (a traitorous cousin, malicious aunts, a murderous father), this tale is nevertheless, finally, a romantic comedy.

Boasting with pleasure that they'd been together four years, Stevie and Maria proposed themselves enthusiastically as "good" interview subjects when I met them at a lesbian and gay youth group. They got along famously, aiding and abetting each other's self-presentations—funny, lovable seriocomic heroines making up a zany love affair as they went along, filling in details for each other with gusto. With the comforting distance of hindsight, even violent family scenes struck them as riotously funny.

Like Shannon's and Jean's, theirs was a match of differences—Anglo versus Hispanic; art versus business; masculine versus feminine; voluble versus reserved. (Stevie's mother, a secretary, and stepfather, a salesman, were Anglo. Maria's extended working-class family emigrated to the United States from Cuba when she was about three years old.) Throughout the interview, Maria took the first turn at most questions, looked surprised when I asked Stevie a question, and often interrupted when Stevie spoke. Stevie took Maria's preemptive strikes in stride without giving up on her side of the story. Maria spoke about feelings directly; Stevie told adventures, episodes.

Perhaps fearing that the sweetness growing between their daughter and this stolid, chivalrous Anglo girl would lead to more than friendship, Maria's parents began telling Maria tabloid horror stories about lesbian love early on in the course of the girls' friendship, long before they became sexually involved. Maria was still child enough to take these stories literally.

I actually thought that Stevie was going to kill me because my parents said, "You know what they do? They even get married and then they have jealous fights, and then they kill each other." They said, "There was once this lady, who was a lesbian, and she brought her lover home one day and her father didn't want them doing something sexual or something, and then one of the lesbians got mad and killed the father." This is what my parents told me.

One afternoon Maria came home from school and found her mementos from Stevie piled in a heap on her bed. Her mother said, "I want you to throw everything away." Maria refused. The heap remained for a few days. Then her mother put it all in the garbage.

If Maria had to engage in a decadent, stigmatized activity her father pleaded, let it be something less reprehensible:

I'd rather you be a prostitute than be a lesbian. You could be a murderer. You could be a prostitute, and that would be fine. We'd still love you.

Because her mother said, "I am going to *try* to stop loving you," not, "I *am* going to stop loving you," Maria believed that her mother would come around if she held her ground. She was right, although for months her father treated her like a stranger.

When he came home from work, I went into my room and didn't come out until the next day. We couldn't face each other. I felt ashamed for betraying the family like that, and I guess he was ashamed of me, too.

Like straight girls who prove their innocence by not planning ahead and not using contraception, Maria invoked the rule of spontaneity. Nothing was premeditated, she argued.

I wasn't looking to find, I wasn't looking to have a relationship. I just had it. It was innocent really.

Stevie supported Maria's point with another example:

I remember holding her hand from time to time, you know. But we didn't say, Oh, what are people going to think. Now we think that way.

Maria added: She used to toss me around in the air. We used to have fun.
And I never thought that it was anything wrong.
Stevie: It was wonderful. I was always making her laugh.

Maria's parents insisted she see a priest.

They figured that a priest would change me.

She replied to the priest with the same logic of love she had used with her own conscience.

I said, "There's no way I'm going to stop loving her."

Perhaps it was a sign of how Americanized Maria was that she saw love as the irrefutable answer to religion, but she was also repeating an argument that Stevie had used successfully on her after spending hours in gay bookstores looking for arguments that would advance their courtship. Stevie explained,

I would always say, If there's love, it's just love. It's not something horrible. I could understand if you were hurting somebody.

The "love" that Maria bravely defended in the face of considerable intimidation had so far consisted of Eskimo kisses, hand holding, and the occasional deliberate jostle. Maria thought,

"This is going too slow. I have to do something here." So I said to Stevie, "Well, let's become hickey sisters." She wanted to give me a hickey on my arm. I said, "That's not going to work, on my arm."

Finally, the first kiss, described by Stevie:

This was in the train station. It was bad. I don't know how many people were around. I kissed her lips and then she said, "Nooooo." And then she just walked away. I thought, Well, should I just ignore that she said no? Because in my mind, I thought, That's not no.

That night Stevie wrote Maria a note. "It just said, 'I love you.' "

That weekend they went to a movie at a central city movie theater. The illusion of privacy that movie theaters create drew them in.

Stevie: We missed the whole entire movie.

To go farther, they needed privacy. Stevie didn't have her own room. Maria's parents wouldn't let Stevie in the door. Just in time, Stevie got a house-sitting job. The first time she and Maria went there they had Stevie's little sister in tow:

Stevie: We just went into this little room and we were kissing and lying next to each other, and I touched her through, uhm—were you wearing your nightie that time?
Maria: Mmhmm.
Stevie: I bought her this little yellow nightie. This was the first time we ever did anything besides kiss. And I just put her down and then I touched her through her little yellow panties. She was soaked. [Hoots.] And I didn't realize. I didn't do anything else because my sister was banging on the door. . . . The next day . . . I had brought some wine and I put it in the refrigerator and then I pulled out this couch and put all

the air conditioning on and we were there for six hours, but it was just
   mainly hugging and kissing. . . . And then—I knew I wanted to—

Maria: Remember, you used to ask me: May I do this?

Stevie: May I do that? So our word for oral sex was kiss-kiss. So eventually I asked her may I kiss? kiss? You know, kiss-kiss. But anyway that
   first day I was just kissing her legs, you know, and the inside of her
   thighs, back and forth, and I just would sort of rush over that little area
   there, you know. I was too scared, you know. And meanwhile her little
   panties were on. And she goes, "Wouldn't it be better if my panties
   were off?"

   So then, I was like, "WOW!"

After Stevie lost her house-sitting job, Maria started staying home "sick"
when her mother and father went to church. Stevie would arrive "like ten
minutes after they left" and depart just before they were due home.

Maria: And that was so scary.

Stevie: It was like a railroad apartment. The only way to get out was
   through the kitchen and there were bars on the windows.

Giggling hysterically, they mimed how they had to hurriedly take off their
clothes, make love, and rush out.

We had it all figured out. They had to wait ten minutes for the bus.

Both Maria's aunts lived in that building. "We could have gotten caught so
many times," Maria realized. Once they rented a room:

*It was the fear, the fear. I remember one very cold winter day we were downtown
and we went to the YWCA for an hour, just to be together. And it was like—we
paid $13 and told them we were going to stay there. And then we made love and
meanwhile . . . I kept stomping on roaches, and saying, "Oh, it's nothing."*

Eventually Maria talked her mother into letting Stevie visit. Stevie was so
nervous the first day she came to the house, she turned around and left.

Stevie: I ran up the street to the flower shop and bought a rose for your
   mother. And I just gave it to you to give to your mother and I started
   crying. I was all upset. . . . Your father was at work.

Maria: My father didn't know. My mother never told my father that
   Stevie had been in the house.

Mother and daughter kept the secret of Stevie's visits for months.

*I used to be always hiding. I'd hide in the basement. I went out the back door
when he'd come home.*

Gradually even Maria's father accepted Stevie into the house, and Maria's
mother started cooking with Stevie in mind.

"She's not coming tonight?" That's what my mother says. She goes, "After I made this chicken dish?" (It's like a stew, and Stevie loves that.) She doesn't leave food out for me. She leaves it out for her.

Stevie's extraordinary determination in courting Maria's family had saved the day, but there was a catch. Once Stevie was welcome in Maria's house, even allowed to sleep over, the lovers didn't feel right about having sex there. As a result, they started making plans to live together. It would be hard for her parents to accept her leaving home, Maria said. Cuban girls weren't supposed to leave until they married, but she had thought of a way to bring her parents around: having a child by alternative insemination.

In the pell-mell of comedy and romance, it's easy to lose sight of the extent to which this group of funny love stories represents a radical departure, not just from previous lesbian experience but from much of teenage heterosexual experience as well. Love is requited and triumphant as well as balanced by work, friendship, and family. Sex is reportedly great. Color and ethnic differences are treated as immaterial, and everywhere they go, these narrators reportedly encounter—if not "out" lesbians and tolerant heterosexuals—at least people who ultimately prove ready to open their hearts.

How did these amazingly happy endings come about? Patient, stubborn, loving, and resilient, these narrators never took rejection for an answer. They insisted on their right to be lesbians and stay in the families and friendships and schools that nurtured them. But the success they had in persuading their families to keep on loving them was not just a function of their wit, determination, and compassion. True, they were diplomats and strategists of the first order, but they were also fortunate in their families' flexibility, which ultimately enabled love to become tolerance and tolerance to become love. To a large extent, this was a result of the lesbian and gay movements, but other changes were at play as well. As families have gotten smaller, for example, parents who might have banished a child had they had others to fall back on have perhaps become more likely to temporize and work at tolerance. As this takes them past the initial jolt of homophobia and they begin to watch their daughters' lovers closely, they see not murderous lesbian fiends but emotionally and financially responsible young women with a profound interest in becoming a part of the family.[10]

There are some reasons to think twice about happy endings like these, however. It's crucial not to lose the self in love, essential, especially in adolescence, to keep growing, reaching out, questioning as well as affirming the self. When women love each other, the vaunted female tendency to forge intimate connections in case-hardened steel can choke not just autonomy but also growth, individual identity, love, and desire.[11] But at the same time, fusion— bonding so tightly that individual identities are submerged either one into another or both into the couple—is a survival mechanism for lesbians—a necessary antidote to hatred and alienation and invisibility. In a less sexist, fragmented world, girls would surely not need love so much. In a less homophobic world, teenage lesbians would not need to hold each other so tightly.

Notes

A fuller account of what teenage girls who identified as lesbians told me about their experiences—including tragic stories of stigmatization, addiction, and despair—appears in "Passionate Friends: Narratives of Lesbian Desire," chap. 6 in my book, *Going All the Way: Teenage Girls' Tales of Sex, Romance, and Pregnancy* (New York: Hill and Wang/Farrar, Straus and Giroux, 1995); and in "Now You See Her, Now You Don't: The Lesbian Teenage Mother," in the Current Issues volume of the 1987 "Homosexuality, Which Homosexuality" conference papers (Amsterdam: Free University/Schorer Foundation, 1987). The comments of Lisa Duggan and Marilyn Young on an early version of the material here were extremely helpful, as was Gilda Zwerman's invitation to talk through the material at the CLAGS colloquium she chaired.

1. During the course of the general interviews I conducted, only eight teenagers told about sexual experiences with other girls. Since that was a much smaller fraction than most studies would have predicted at the time, I made additional efforts to locate teenagers with lesbian experience, interviewing participants in two lesbian and gay teenage discussion groups. The resulting sample was as demographically diverse as the general sample, but it does include some narrators who were out of high school. The oldest was nineteen.

Throughout I refer to the narrators in this essay as "lesbian" because they referred to themselves that way, not because I hold essentialist views on sexual identity. I do not.

2. It's important to note that these narrators are exceptional in that they came out in high school. Most lesbians come out after high school, several studies indicate. E. Coleman, "Developmental Stages of the Coming Out Process," *Journal of Homosexuality* 7, nos. 2–3 (1981–82): 31–43, reported age twenty for females coming out. See also Pat Califia, "Lesbian Sexuality," *Journal of Homosexuality* 4, no. 3 (spring 1971): 259. Beata E. Chapman and JoAnn C. Brannock's 1987 survey of 197 women, 96 percent of whom were lesbian, found that the mean age that the respondents thought they *might* be lesbian was 17, while the mean age reported for resolving the question of sexual identity was 21.5 years "Proposed Model of Lesbian Identity Development," *Journal of Homosexuality* 14, nos. 3–4 (1987): 73. Of course, these studies aren't synchronous with my own. It may well have become more common to come out in high school during the period of my study, but it's not my sense that it became normative to do so.

Bonnie Zimmerman, "Exiting from Patriarchy: The Lesbian Novel of Development," in Elizabeth Abel et al., *The Voyage In: Fictions of Female Development* (Hanover: University Press of New England, 1983), 244–57, notes that the autobiographical literature of feminism is replete with stories about coming out or having lesbian thoughts in high school, while the lesbian novel of development typically centers "on the heroine's adolescence, much like the traditional *Bildungsroman*" (247). Some of these are acts of narrative reconstruction, of course. Now that these speakers and writers believe that they are lesbians, they read childhood for lesbian clues and find them everywhere.

3. Barbara Ponse, "Secrecy in the Lesbian World," in *Sexuality: Encounters, Identities, and Relationships,* ed. Carol Garren (Beverly Hills: Sage, 1977) explains the term "coming out" as disclosing the gay self to an expanding series of audiences (55). Recent

theory posits a final stage in which lesbian identity is integrated with the many other aspects of the self. These narrators didn't place that stage last. Throughout coming out, they held onto the other aspects of themselves. Vivienne Cass, "Homosexual Identity Formation: A Theoretical Model," *Journal of Homosexuality* 4. no. 3 (spring 1979): 219–35.

4. Patricia J. Campbell, *Sex Education Books for Young Adults, 1892–1979* (New York: R.R. Bowker, 1979). William Lee Howard, *Confidential Chats with Girls* (New York: E. J. Clode, 1911), 41. Irving David Steinhardt, *Ten Sex Talks to Girls* (Philadelphia: Lippincott, 1914), 43. Lois Lloyd Pemberton, *The Stork Didn't Bring You!* (1948; rev. ed., New York: Nelson, 1961), 101. Evelyn Duvall's influential *Facts of Life and Love for Teenagers* (New York: Association Press, 1950; rev. ed., 1956) included same-sex crushes as one of several varieties of "love under a cloud."

5. Of course, a few lucked into Simone de Beauvoir, whose mixed review of lesbian life at least included a vision of autonomy, desire, and variability. Joanna Russ, "Not for Years but for Decades," in *The Coming Out Stories,* ed. Julia Penelope Stanley and Susan J. Wolfe (Watertown, MA: Persephone, 1980), 106. Simone de Beauvoir, *The Second Sex,* trans. H. M. Parshley (New York: Bantam, 1961), 394. See also Blanche Wiesen Cook, " 'Women Alone Stir My Imagination': Lesbianism and the Cultural Tradition," *Signs* 4, no. 4 (1979): 718–39.

6. Donald Suggs, "More Than Friends: Conversations with Lesbian and Gay Youth," *Village Voice,* March 24, 1987, 18.

7. Deborah Goleman Wolf, *The Lesbian Community* (Berkeley: University of California Press, 1979), 89.

8. Catharine R. Stimpson, "Zero Degree Deviancy: The Lesbian Novel in English," *Critical Inquiry,* winter 1981, 363–79. See also Bertha Harris, "What We Mean to Say: Notes toward Defining the Nature of Lesbian Literature," *Heresies,* fall 1977, 5–8. (Some readers will wonder why I haven't organized this chapter according to the categories of butch and fem. The answer is, they weren't narrated.)

9. Although Jean was African American, she never talked about being African American or distinguished one friend from another by color. Racism came up in her history, but when she made distinctions between friends, they had to do with who was lesbian and who wasn't.

10. Historian Marilyn Young suggested the idea that the financial contribution made by a lesbian partner may be very persuasive. Private conversation, 1987.

11. Susan Krieger, "Lesbian Identity and Community: Recent Social Science Literature," *Signs* 18, no. 1 (autumn 1982): 91–108. Chela Sandoval, "Comment on Krieger's 'Lesbian Identity and Community,' " *Signs* 9, no. 4 (summer 1984): 725–29. Ann R. Bristow and Pam Langford Pearn, "Comment on Krieger's 'Lesbian Identity and Community,' " *Signs* 9, no. 4 (summer 1984): 729–32. Susan Krieger, *The Mirror Dance: Identity in a Women's Community* (Philadelphia: Temple University Press, 1983). The fusion debate has also been reframed in terms of codependency. See Sondra Smalley, "Dependency Issues in Lesbian Relationships," *Journal of Homosexuality* 14, nos. 1–2 (1987): 125–35. Other research has suggested that feminism tempered dyadism and increased autonomy in lesbian relationships. Letitia Anne Peplau et al., "Loving Women: Attachment and Autonomy in Lesbian Relationships," *Journal of Social Issues* 34, no. 3 (summer 1978): 7–27.

43

The Lesbian Athlete: Unlearning the Culture of the Closet

Pat Griffin

I think, historically, lesbians in sport have accepted the tacit assumption that to be in athletics means you have to keep your identity a secret. That has pretty much been the pervasive norm for athletes and coaches. That assumption has been passed from generation to generation. Each new group of lesbians in sport who've come up in the ranks are apprentices, and they are socialized into the culture of the closet in insidious ways. In the course of this intergenerational socialization, young lesbians learn a confusing array of messages. They learn, on the one hand, that lesbian athletes are strong, competent, physical, and competitive. On the other hand, they learn that this information is shrouded in secrecy, that all these qualities have to be tempered and compensated for with deception and subterfuge.

I believe that we are in an interesting time right now, because there is a possibility of change in a way that I don't think has ever been present in women's athletics before, and I think the culture of the closet can begin to change. It has to do with the larger social context: many of our notions about gender, sexuality, and family are shifting. And even though there is a tremendous backlash that naturally comes whenever there is any kind of a challenge to a traditional norm, there is an opportunity in this contentious environment for real change in women's athletics. Whether or not lesbians in athletics will just slam the door tighter to the closet or whether the door will open wider remains to be seen. But I think the opportunity is there.

There are very clear and pervasive societal functions in the homophobia and heterosexism that we currently find in sports. The first one is to define and reinforce traditional conceptions of masculinity. I don't think anybody would dispute the view that athletics holds a special place for men and boys in our society. Athletics is a place where boys learn how to be men, as we define men in this culture. The ritual of sport is almost sacred in masculine culture, and boys learn that a keen interest in sport—if not aptitude, at least an interest— is essential to learning how to be a masculine man in this culture. This is particularly true of team sports, like football, basketball, ice hockey, and base-ball. I think they are popular in large measure because of their reliance on physical size, strength, power, mental toughness, competitiveness, and all the other qualities we consider important in male athletes (and all of which are also central to a traditional sense of masculinity): And far from being innate, they have to be very carefully taught and reinforced; athletics provides a major arena for learning these things.

Conversely, behaviors that are not consistent with these traits are devalued, and boys who can't reflect those behaviors comfortably learn very quickly that they don't fit in, are the last picked, and are made to feel humiliated and shunted aside. I think young male athletes learn that they need to suppress emotions that they think reflect softness—like fear, tenderness, or compas-sion—in the service of developing these traditional aspects of masculinity.

Also, sport is one of the few contexts other than the family where affection between males and the physical expression of emotional closeness are publicly accepted. Being part of an athletic team invites emotional intimacy among teammates, and athletes spend an enormous amount of time together: practic-ing, playing games, traveling to games, participating in social activities together. Athletes can hug each other after winning games, and they can cry after losing big games, and it's okay in a way that is not acceptable almost anyplace else in the traditional masculine arena.

In addition to the emotional intensity present in an athletic team, an incredi-bly high level of physical intimacy exists as well. The expression and admiration of physicality are central to athletics. Many sports require considerable physical contact among men. In addition, much time is spent in locker rooms, showers, and whirlpools, where there is not only a lot of physical closeness, but naked-ness as well.

Third, athletics is the primary arena in which young men, in particular, can achieve status among their adolescent peers. Consequently, it takes on tremen-dous importance for young men. Numerous studies of high school cultures have shown that the male jocks in a school are among the highest status groups (Palonsky 1975). That's true as well at the lower levels of junior high school and even in elementary school.

Fourth, sports is important in reinforcing male privilege. Athletics has always been a male domain in the United States, and though progress has been achieved over the last twenty years in terms of women's participation, women's athletics and women's athletic performance are still marginalized and trivial-ized.

Experiencing the body as powerful and skillful is an important part of feeling empowered, and one that our society still largely denies to girls. Athletics is one of the primary ways that boys can learn to differentiate themselves from girls and distance themselves from the qualities in themselves that they perceive to be feminine and therefore inferior. In fact, comparing a male's performance in athletics to that of a girl is the highest insult. For a boy to be beaten by a girl in an athletic game invites teasing or ridicule from male peers (and sometimes female peers as well). There have been studies of locker-room talk among men, and all of them consistently describe a high degree of the content of that talk as antiwomen and antigay (Curry 1991). More extreme examples are the number of males in team sports who participate in gang rapes and gay bashing or develop some kind of a sexual scoring system to count sexual conquests—for example, the "Spur Posse" in California a couple of years back. Such episodes are disturbing instances of the way male athletes bond around their sense of superiority to, and rejection of, what they consider "feminine" (Messner and Sabo 1994; Nelson 1994).

The last function of athletics is to reify heterosexuality. Young men and women see male team sports athletes as the embodiment of the traditional masculine image, which is presumed to be heterosexual. The idea of a gay, masculine male athlete is a contradiction for most people and runs counter to the stereotype of the effeminate, silly faggot. Because if gay men can be athletes and display all the qualities of masculinity that are valued in athletes, then how could other men confidently differentiate themselves from gay men? Studies show, also, that men have a higher level of homophobia than women (Herek 1994). In fact an integral part of the masculinity training that boys receive in athletics is the belief that to be gay is to be contemptible. Just as being called a woman or compared to a woman is an insult to most male athletes, being called a faggot is comparably insulting. In fact, I think the epithets are interchangeable, and that's part of the point.

Maintaining the myth that all male athletes are heterosexual and that sexual attractions among male athletes do not exist allows men to enjoy the physical and emotional intimacy of the athletic experience without confronting the complexity of emotional and physical ties that men can feel toward each other. These contradictions account, I believe, for the extreme homophobic atmosphere on many men's athletic teams; antigay name calling, jokes, or violence reassure an athlete and his teammates about their own masculinity and heterosexuality in an intimate, all-male context.

Athletics can serve several important functions in the maintenance of traditional gender roles and power imbalances among men and women. As Suzanne Pharr points out in her book *Homophobia as a Weapon of Sexism*, men develop a sense of entitlement, superiority, and solidarity. Fear of being perceived as gay is a powerful social control in athletics that keeps men safely within the bounds of traditional masculine and heterosexual attitudes and behaviors.

Given the function of athletics for men in the United States, the presence of women in athletics poses a challenge to the traditional gender order. If athletics is a place where boys learn how to be "masculine," develop a sense of superiority toward women, and bond with other men, acknowledging that women can participate in athletics with comparable enthusiasm, intensity, and skill threatens the special status of athletics in the men's lives. If women, as well as gay men, can be intensely competitive, tough-minded, and physically strong and competent, then our traditional conceptions of masculinity and femininity have to be reevaluated. And if women discover their own physical sense of empowerment, and bond with other women in the athletic arena, the naturalness of the traditional gender order must be reassessed.

If the special status of athletics for men is to be preserved, women must be discouraged from participation. And when they do participate, their performance must be trivialized, marginalized, or stigmatized in some way. In the early twentieth century, women were warned about all kinds of dire physiological consequences of participation: their uteruses would drop out, or they would grow facial hair. Numerous accounts were designed to scare women away from physical activity out of concern about protecting their reproductive organs—and their "real" roles as wives and mothers.

More recently, women have been discouraged from athletic participation partly by institutional barriers—lack of programs and resources, minimum coverage, and so forth—and also by the assumption of the inferiority of female performance. But the most potent strategy for discouraging female participation in athletics has always been to raise concerns about a woman athlete's "femininity." And the most threatening strategy of all has been to assume that all women athletes are lesbians. Because the lesbian label carries such a heavy negative stigma, most of the girls and women who enter sports learn to fear association with it; indeed, the association of lesbians with athletics is enough to discourage many women from considering participation in athletics at all. Women who do choose to participate, respond defensively to the lesbian label and go to great lengths to display traditional heterosexual markers, through clothing, hairstyle, and mannerisms. As long as lesbians can be stigmatized as immoral, sick, or unnatural, the label functions to control women's athletic participation. As long as women's athletic participation can be controlled, the role of athletics in defining and maintaining the traditional gender order is maintained.

Understanding the social functions of athletics in the maintenance of unequal power relations between men and women in a sexist society provides a context for understanding the socialization into the culture of the closet in women's athletics. Historically, socialization into this closet has occurred with the support of many different socializing agents operating at the cultural, institutional, and individual levels.

Some coaches have explicit policies, as did Rene Portland at Penn State a couple of years ago. Portland communicated to parents and prospective athletes that she did not allow "alcohol, drugs or lesbians" on her team. In general, lesbians on teams—if they are discovered—are eliminated in some way: they are dropped from the team or benched, or their lives are made so miserable that they quit.

The other side of that is the promotion of heterosexual images. Often college teams have promotional brochures; an extreme example, that of Southwest Missouri, had all the women basketball players dressed up like playboy bunnies in the brochure. They had little ears, little tails, and cutesy poses—on the basketball court. In the brochure they called the arena where they played "the Pleasure Palace." That is one of the most extreme examples, but you'll find women's teams in some brochures dressed in long dresses like Southern belles, and one brochure I read said, "our girls are competitors on the court and ladies everywhere else. We only recruit girls of strong moral fiber."

Then there are "conditionally tolerant" situations, usually in the form of two subtle variations. One is the "don't ask, don't tell" policy; the military adopted it officially two years ago, but it has been in operation in athletics unofficially for many years. What it basically amounts to is "You can be here, but don't ever tell anybody who you are; the only way we can coexist is if we don't have to confront the knowledge that there are lesbians on the team; and you just keep it quiet and we will collude together to keep it a secret." Lesbian visibility is the problem in the conditionally tolerant atmosphere.

What heterosexual men and women coaches and athletes get out of that strategy is that they don't have to confront issues of homophobia and hetero-sexism. What lesbian athletes get out of it is the opportunity to play. The bargain seems worth it for a lot of young women who have a passion for athletics.

In the "family secret" variation of the conditionally tolerant environment, a lesbian may come out privately to some people, maybe even to the whole team, or at least to two or three people on the team; or maybe the coach knows; or maybe the team knows that the coach is a lesbian. But it becomes a family secret, and the agreement is that no one will tell anyone outside that team context. If anybody reveals the secret, then all bets are off and we move back to the "hostile" environment, where the lesbian has to be removed from the team either directly or through some kind of subtle pressure to make her life so miserable that she will quit.

It has been my experience that almost all school athletic environments—high school and college—are either "hostile" or "conditionally tolerant." The ideal of an "open-inclusive" environment is a vision for the future but not, at this point in our history, a reality. Even in a school that has extensive program-ming for gay, lesbian, and bisexual people on a campus—for example, the University of Massachusetts—the athletic department is just as unwelcom-ing for lesbians as are most other athletic departments. Athletics is a world unto itself, even in the middle of a campus that can be quite progressive otherwise.

Women who choose to pursue sport as career athletes, teachers, or coaches challenge traditional gender and sexuality norms and power relationships. There are no better measures of how serious this violation is regarded than the pervasive use of the "lesbian" label to terrify and control women in sport, and women's defensive and timid reaction to this tactic. The nearly complete invisibility of lesbian athletes is all the more amazing in light of the fact that public suspicions are true: there are a lot of lesbians in sport. This apparent contradiction, I think, reflects the seriousness of lesbian oppression in general and in athletics in particular. Athletics is a part of lesbian subculture. Despite the stifling, soul-crushing climate in most athletic programs, lesbians have persisted in finding ways to play. But the bargain most often struck is silence and invisibility in return for limited tolerance and the opportunity to participate. The internalized oppression that most lesbians in athletics harbor is deeply rooted and paralyzing. Most of my colleagues in athletics would never consider coming out.

Lesbian survival strategies in women's athletics are passed to each successive generation of athletes and coaches. A powerful, silent socialization has created a "culture of the closet" that is familiar to any lesbian athlete or coach. The culture of the closet can be described as a set of norms that represent collusion and internalized homophobia on a grand scale. It is also true that the culture of the closet in women's athletics represents a social network of resistance that has been created as a means of survival in an extremely hostile environment.

The culture of the closet in women's athletics, as it has been constructed over the course of the last seventy years, is based on fear and pain. Lesbian athletes and coaches have internalized a profound sense of shame about who we are, and feel real powerlessness to confront and change the web of sexism, heterosexism, and homophobia that pervades athletics. This internalized homophobia has led us to become active participants in our own oppression.

Unlike many other young lesbians and gay men, lesbian athletes do have role models. Young lesbians learn by observing older lesbian athletes and coaches negotiate the athletic world. Lesbian coaches rarely disclose their identity to their athletes, but by some unspoken communication, and the absence of obvious heterosexual markers, young lesbians figure it out and learn by example how to conduct themselves in the culture of the closet. What young athletes learn is that disclosing their identity is dangerous.

The issue of lesbianism has been absent in most professional meetings, whether coaches' meetings or physical education meetings. Until the last very few years, there has been a complete blanket of silence. I did a workshop in San Francisco two or three years ago, and there were about seventy people there. I noticed, as we started the workshop, that two women got up and left the room.

My coleader went out to find out what was up, and they said they were just too scared: they couldn't stay. They had entered the room and that took everything they had; they couldn't stay. That was just a couple of years ago. So there is a persistent, private dialogue about lesbians in sport—an underground dialogue. But the public dialogue is just beginning to happen.

Passing as heterosexual, or leading others to believe that one is heterosexual, is a common strategy among lesbians in athletics. This is not easy, because the heterosexual assumption does not hold for women athletes or coaches. In women's athletics, a heterosexual image must be actively promoted to counter-act the homosexual assumption that surrounds all women in athletics. One learns to "distance" oneself from "bad," "butch," or "careless" lesbians; to avoid association with any lesbians who are too blatant, too political, or who have been publicly accused; and also to avoid places or events that are lesbian-identified.

On a college campus, it is typical for the lesbian athlete to be completely isolated from other lesbian groups on campus or lesbians who are active in gay and lesbian organizations; it is uncommon to find a lesbian athlete participating in anything on campus other than private, cliquey parties open only to lesbian athletes, lovers, and friends. So the social network of lesbians in athletics is often very hidden, suspicious, secret, and incestuous. They agree to present an acceptable and unprovocative image publicly and keep their lesbian identity discreetly hidden. Then they are tolerated. That is what I mean by being a "good lesbian."

All the strategies that maintain the culture of the closet are rooted in a profound sense of powerlessness that lesbians learn to accept as inevitable in athletics. The bargain is struck again and again, and passed from generation to generation. Silence and invisibility are maintained in return for marginal inclu-sion in a male-dominated world of athletics.

But not all is lost. Since the 1987 march on Washington, I think a real shift has started to take place. More people know someone who is lesbian or gay in their family or among coworkers, or know that there are gay and lesbian clubs on campuses. We now have Greg Louganis as well as Martina (yet another *retired* athlete; I think that is significant). And whereas the words "lesbian," "homophobia," and "heterosexism" were never mentioned in athletic confer-ences before, organizations like the Women's Basketball Coaches Association, which is a truly conservative organization, had a panel at the Final Four last year, during the coaches' meetings, during which one participant actually talked about homophobia. Moreover, newspapers from all over the country have run stories on homophobia in sports. They are mostly positive articles, or at least neutral, and that seems to be a step forward. These changes are small but real. Young gay people are developing more of a sense of entitlement than my generation ever had growing up, and they are bringing that sense of entitlement into women's athletics. I think one can identify three age-cohorts of participants in athletics now.

One I call the "Pre-Stonewall Gay-Identified" women athletes and coaches. These are women who came of age during the forties, fifties, and sixties. They mostly don't identify as feminists, though many hold feminist values. They often see identifying themselves as "gay" as a private issue that doesn't have political significance, and they are "out" only to a very small, trusted group of other gay women, mostly in the field of athletics. I think that many of these women see coming out as causing problems. They have made a home in that "conditionally tolerant" environment, and they see any attempt to change it as a real threat. In fact, some of these women can be overtly hostile to women challenging the established way. At the same time, these women have done wonderful things for athletics, in the context of where things were when they were coming of age.

The next age-cohort I call the "Post-Stonewall Lesbian-Identified" women athletes and coaches, who have come of age during the seventies and have been strongly influenced by feminism. These women typically have a strong network of lesbian friends and community. They are not professionally "out," but they regard this as a decision of professional necessity only: they feel good about who they are. They coach from the closet, basically. They may actually have a lot of empathy for the lesbians on their teams, and try to help them in any way that they can, but only from the closet, because they won't risk coming out.

Then what I see coming along is the "Post-Eighties Queer-Identified" generation of women athletes and coaches. These are young women who identify as "queer" or "lesbian" or "bisexual" or "dyke." They have come of age in the eighties or nineties, and they insist on being "out." They are proud of who they are and refuse to honor the culture of the closet. And they have a sense of entitlement that is in real contradiction to the sense of shame characteristic of the older generations of lesbians in athletics. They see the coaches and athletes who are closeted as victims of internalized homophobia, or even as assimilationists trying to fit into the dominant heterosexual culture without challenging its values.

An East Coast university was involved in a lawsuit last year. A young lesbian athlete accused her coach (who was also a lesbian—a closeted lesbian when all this happened, but not anymore) of denying her freedom of speech and her ability to be open and active in gay and lesbian campus organizations. The coach didn't object to her being a lesbian; she objected to her being an open lesbian. So this young woman, with her sense of entitlement, said, "You can't do this to me," and took it to court. There was an out-of-court settlement. The university didn't want the publicity and neither did the coach.

What this points up is the potential for sharp conflict between the new, truly new, generation of young women coming up and the "lesbian"-identified coaches whose attitude is "It's fine if you're a lesbian, and I'm glad you're here, but keep it quiet, maintain the rules." These young "queer"-identified women are pushing *all* of us. It could be that the "lesbian" coaches will get empowered by these young athletes, and will come out of the closet. Or it could be that the socialization of that closet is so strong in athletics that the young "queer"-identified women who are coming up will not be able to hang on to their sense of entitlement and will submit to the culture of the closet in order to have an opportunity to play—in the same way that so many of us have done for so long. It's hard to know which way it will go, but I do think that for the first time there is the *chance* of some real change in athletics.

References

Curry, T. 1991. Fraternal bonding in the locker room: A profeminist analysis of talk about competition and women. *Sociology of Sport Journal* 8 (2):119–35.

Herek, G. 1984. Beyond homophobia: A social psychological perspective on attitudes towards lesbians and gay men. In *Basshers, Baiters, and Bigots: Homophobia in American Society*, ed. J. De Cecco. New York: Haworth Press.

Messner, M. and Sabo, D. 1994. *Sex, Violence and Power in Sports: Rethinking Masculinity*. Freedom, CA: Crossing Press.

Nelson, M. 1994. *The Stronger Women Get, The More Men Love Football: Sexism and the American Culture of Sport*. New York: Harcourt Brace.

Pharr, S. 1988. *Homophobia: A Weapon of Sexism*. Inverness, CA: Chardon Press.

Palonsky, S. 1975. Hempies and squeaks, truckers, and cruisers: A participant observation study in a city high school. *Educational Administration Quarterly* 11 (2):86–103.

44

One Generation Post-Stonewall: Political Contests over Lesbian and Gay School Reform

Janice M. Irvine

Lesbian and gay school reform constitutes a bold strategy of the post-Stonewall movement. Marxists, feminists, and other critical theorists have noted that schools, as social institutions, serve a political function by their support of traditional arrangements of race, class, and gender. A critical scholarship has emerged that deconstructs the complexities of traditional schooling.[1] The theory and practice of lesbian and gay school reform foreground a critique of the institutional, discursive, and social production and reproduction of heterosexism by the educational system. Like schooling itself, however, lesbian and gay school reform is neither neutral nor inconsequential. Such efforts must also be scrutinized, since ideology inheres in the various strategies for their implementation.

School reform represents a contemporary political contest over social and sexual ideologies. Both supporters and opponents deploy a range of discursive strategies, or claims, in an attempt to characterize the nature of issues related to homosexuality, lesbian and gay youth, and public education. In this essay I will examine the claims-making of both school reformers and their opponents as a site in which ideas about homosexuality, sexuality, and identities are shaped and reconstituted.

Lesbian and Gay Initiatives in Public Education

School reform has assumed increasing importance for the lesbian and gay movement during the last decade, despite formidable obstacles. Many educators, for example, had to overcome the not-unreasonable fear that they would be accused of recruitment in the classroom. Activists often resisted school-based initiatives out of a reluctance to revisit the pain of their own adolescence.[2] Notwithstanding, public education has taken its place alongside the military and domestic partnership initiatives as a key site for lesbian and gay social reform.

The need for safety and tolerance propelled the first programs. Project 10 was the first major school-based program developed to provide education and counseling to students on the subject of sexual orientation.[3] Its formation in Los Angeles in 1985 was prompted by the harassment of an openly gay male student who eventually dropped out of school. This incident heightened faculty awareness of homophobia in the schools, and eventually resulted in the implementation of Project 10. Since its inception, Project 10 has been the subject of extensive publicity, and has been routinely characterized by the religious right as a program for seducing innocent children.[4]

Currently there are a range of other programs throughout the country that either teach about lesbian/gay issues or offer counseling and support to youth. Lesbian/gay content is increasingly integrated into both comprehensive sexuality education and AIDS education programs. Other initiatives mention lesbians and gay men in the context of multicultural education. Public schools have developed support groups, such as the increasingly common Gay/Straight Alliances, and Project 10 East, formed in Cambridge, Massachusetts, after the suicide of a gay youth. Massachusetts is also home to the nation's first Gay and Lesbian Youth Commission. Constituted in 1992 by Republican governor William Weld, the commission's first task was a series of projects under the rubric "Making Schools Safe for Gay and Lesbian Youth."

These educational programs are of central importance for several reasons. They represent an unprecedented opportunity for a new generation of schoolchildren to learn that lesbian/gay identities are common and viable. In effective educational systems, schools become a site for social invention, the place where "people think themselves into being."[5] The power of programs that teach about lesbian and gay issues, then, is this awareness they engender. They allow for the recognition of lesbian and gay lives and hopefully teach tolerance for diversity. For some students, such programs may facilitate the construction of lesbian or gay identities. Finally, these programs destabilize "recruitment myths" and challenge historical taboos against lesbian and gay visibility in the classroom.

The radical potential of these programs is, of course, the ground for controversy. Debates concerning the teaching of lesbian and gay content in public schools are raging across a nation that is deeply divided. The religious right, which is fully aware of the high stakes, has focused its efforts on opposing lesbian and gay programs in public schools. Critics have seized on what they call "the gay agenda in public education" to reinforce old myths about the homosexual child molester. National organizations like the Report and Focus on the Family have triggered moral panics in school districts across the country.

For example, in Des Moines, Iowa, fundamentalist Christian groups defeated a proposal to add sexual orientation to the curriculum, and in a highly contested and publicized campaign, ousted a prominent school board president who came out during the controversy.[6] California-based Traditional Values Coalition head Reverend Lou Sheldon persuaded Speaker of the House Newt Gingrich to schedule House hearings on the "promotion" of homosexuality in public schools.[7] And the children's book *Daddy's Roommate* has topped the American Library Association Office for Intellectual Freedom's Most Challenged Titles list for two years, while other gay-themed books like *Heather Has Two Mommies* and *Gloria Goes to Gay Pride* continue to generate controversy.[8]

On the national stage, then, school reform efforts are less about education and more about political contests between two opposing movements. Both sides deploy specific discursive strategies in order to launch or defeat these programs. In the following sections I will examine two pedagogic frames by which educators have made claims for programs or curricula addressing lesbian and gay issues. I call these the "culture-based model" and the "public health model." Using a case study that exemplifies each frame, I will examine its pedagogic significance, its ideological and theoretical implications, and the grounds on which opponents have attacked it.

Teaching Children about Culture

Multiculturalism has been a vehicle for the inclusion of lesbian and gay issues into public education. As schools develop curricula and programs to more accurately reflect a racially, ethnically, and gender diverse world, many educators have understandably organized for the addition of lesbian and gay content. The culture-based model discursively locates lesbians and gay men on a comparative status with racial and ethnic minorities.

The culture-based model is attractive for several reasons. First, it allows for the teaching of lesbian and gay issues in the context of education about other differences. Since multicultural curricula are the primary venue by which children learn about those who are different from themselves, it is a practical and logical vehicle in which to insert lesbian and gay lives. Second, it does not ghettoize lesbian and gay issues into a single unit or lesson. Multicultural programs, at their best, seek transformation of the curriculum and therefore broader diffusion of diverse perspectives. Third, the culture-based model is normalizing, not pathologizing. It asserts that lesbians and gay men are a minority group like many others.

Perhaps the most widely known example of the culture-based model is the Children of the Rainbow Curriculum in New York City. It is a case that exemplifies some of the common counterclaims against this discursive strategy.

In September 1992, a group of protesters gathered at City Hall Park in New York City. Holding placards that read, "No Way, Jose, Don't Teach Our Children to Be Gay," "God Made Adam and Eve, Not Adam and Steve," and "Don't Brainwash Our Children," they expressed their opposition to the implementation of the new multicultural curriculum for first-graders, Children of the Rainbow. The Rainbow Curriculum was intended to promote tolerance and facilitate an appreciation for diversity among the city's schoolchildren. Designed as a guide for teachers, it contained lessons on the artifacts, folk songs, and holidays of other cultures. It premised that children could be taught basic lessons in math, grammar, and reading by utilizing the games, songs, and dances indigenous to a wide range of cultures.

The document might have simply faded into obscurity were it not for some lessons included at the last minute. The controversy over the curriculum centered on brief sections, in fact merely six entries out of a 443-page document, that discussed lesbian and gay families. One section noted that "The issues surrounding family may be very sensitive for children. Teachers should be aware of varied family structures, including two-parent or single-parent households, gay or lesbian parents, divorced parents, adoptive parents, and guardians or foster parents. Children must be taught to acknowledge the positive aspects of each type of household and the importance of love and care in family living."[9] It goes on to note that children growing up in families headed by heterosexuals "may be experiencing contact with lesbians/gays for the first time . . . teachers of first graders have an opportunity to give children a healthy sense of identity at an early age. Classes should include references to lesbians/gay people in all curricular areas. Educators have the potential to help increase the tolerance and acceptance of the lesbian/gay community and to decrease the staggering number of hate crimes perpetrated against them." The curriculum emphasized the recognition of lesbian/gay culture; nowhere was there any mention of sex.

The opposition was fierce, preying on parents' prejudices and anxieties. Distortions and hyperbole were the weapons in what *Sixty Minutes* reporter Ed Bradley characterized as "a battle for the hearts and minds of New York City's first-graders."[10] Counterclaims in this battle, which focused almost exclusively on opposition to the inclusion of lesbian/gay content, were mobilized on two related fronts. First, critics attacked lesbians and gay men on the grounds of immorality and aberrant "lifestyle." Second, they challenged the viability of lesbian/gay culture as appropriate for a multicultural curriculum.

The moral panic assumed familiar dimensions. One assemblyman asserted that homosexuals were "a sin against mankind," while a state senator described them as "pure evil and wickedness."[11] As the controversy escalated, it became clear that the informal consensual reality shared by the opponents was that the curriculum was "homosexual/lesbian propaganda" that was "teaching sodomy to first graders."[12] Passions were inflamed by images of first-graders learning about oral and anal sex, while parents and school board members began to describe the contents of the multicultural curriculum as perverted, filthy, and deviant.

Critics of the idea of a lesbian/gay culture deployed a simple but powerful tactic to argue that it should be excluded from the multicultural curriculum. They juxtaposed the allegedly stable and indisputable cultural categories of race and ethnicity and the purportedly ridiculous and fictive notion of lesbian/gay culture. "They want to teach my kid that being gay fits in with being Italian and Puerto Rican!" one parent cried.[13] Some African American critics were incensed by comparisons of lesbian and gay politics and culture to the Black civil rights movement. At one community school board meeting, a parent and teacher said,

> Years of being thrown in jail for demonstrating against racism and being sprayed by fire hoses taught me something. I ask you where was the gay community when school children died in Mobile, Alabama? Where was the gay community when many of us were beaten at a lunch counter? Is this the only way we can be included in the curriculum—to allow the gay community to piggyback off our achievement?[14]

For others, the outrage was fueled by the contention that, unlike Blacks or presumably members of other racial groups, lesbians and gay men share no common cultural symbols or artifacts. Olivia Banks, the chair of the curriculum committee of School Board 29, was vehement during a *Sixty Minutes* broadcast on the Rainbow Curriculum:

> How dare they compare themselves to the Blacks, who've had to struggle going over—for over 250-some years? They have no special language, no special clothing, no special food, no special dress wear, so what—what makes them a culture? They don't fit into any definition of what a culture is. They are using the racial issue as a way to open doors. How dare they?[15]

When Ed Bradley suggested that lesbians and gay men have a minority identity, Banks fumed, "You're doing it again. You're putting—you're putting a sexual orientation on the same level of a race, and . . . that's unacceptable to this person sitting here."[16]

The limitations of the culture-based model emerge in the contours of this conflict. This paradigm forces the square peg of lesbian and gay identities into the round hole of fixed, essentialized definitions of culture that are common in traditional multicultural programs.[17] There are several related complications to this. First, despite widespread colloquial use of the term "gay culture," there is a vibrant debate over whether lesbians and gay men can be best described as a culture, community, ethnic group, lifestyle, or sexual minority.[18] Scholarship that contests and undermines the very notion of stable, unified cultural categories—either racial or sexual—has raised the stakes in this definitional debate.

Second, activists in the Rainbow controversy were promulgating rigidly essential definitions of both race and sexuality at a moment when theorists are destabilizing those ideas by asserting the socially constructed nature of identity categories and rejecting false universalisms and ahistorical essentialisms. Much popular opposition to the idea of gay culture rests on lingering traces of biologism from the social sciences that cast racial culture as a fixed and natural essence. From this perspective, we are all born into culture, and race and ethnicity are the quintessentially authentic cultures. One's social location in a racial culture is secured at birth, and, as Banks implies above, allows one entry into a stable system of shared language, dress, clothing, and other cultural signifiers. The popular conviction that cultural status is biologically and generationally transmitted inevitably excludes lesbians and gay men, who cannot indisputably make such claims.

Nonetheless, the bitterness of the Rainbow controversy left gay activists with no option but to vehemently argue that they *do* constitute a culture. Reminiscent of Dennis Altman's early tongue-in-cheek comment that Perrier and quiche are the gay foods,[19] one gay man earnestly insisted on *Sixty Minutes*, "We do have a culture. We do have our own literature. We have our own artworks. We have music that would be identifiable to lesbian and gay people."[20] When the paradigm of multiculturalism is the only vehicle for addressing social differences, lesbians and gay men must fit themselves, however awkwardly, into that model. However unintentionally, in this context the assertion of certain social preferences resembles a universal claim.

Third, the discursive positioning of lesbian/gay culture as equivalent to racial/ethnic culture allows for conflict when opponents exploit historical tensions among groups and fan feelings of injustice, marginality, and competition for resources. As illustrated above, critics greet the suggestion of a lesbian and gay culture not simply with opposition, but with the fear that such recognition would somehow diminish their social position or erode whatever legitimacy they have managed to garner from years of civil rights efforts.[21] The borders of identities stiffen, for example, in conflicts over the Rainbow Curriculum, where Black parents yelled "white faggots" at ACT UP members and ACT UP men yelled back, "Black racists."[22] One white school board president described how the Latino community responded to Children of the Rainbow in his district. "They said, 'We're a culture, and you [whites, liberals, gay people] are being culturally insensitive to our beliefs about sexuality, homosexuality, explicitness of sexual discussion, by pushing this curriculum.' "[23] The culture-based model, then, can generate futile and destructive political contests over who constitutes a "legitimate" culture and thereby polarize (allegedly white) lesbians and gay men against (allegedly heterosexual) communities of color.

The culture-based model has not escaped attack by the religious right. Counterclaims are mounted on several fronts. Opponents individualize and repathologize homosexuality; ridicule the notion of gay culture by making invidious comparisons; and position themselves as defenders of racial and ethnic groups.

Rainbow Curriculum opponents, such as the highly visible District 24 school board president Mary Cummins, were strategically canny in framing the debate as exclusively about the (typically male) sexually deviant individual. Cummins charged that Children of the Rainbow was "aimed at promoting acceptance of sodomy" (it was informally dubbed the sodomy curriculum). When questioned by reporter Ed Bradley, she insisted, "What is homosexuality except sodomy. . . . There's no difference. Homosexuals are sodomists."[24] Cummins's lawyer in District 24's battle against the Rainbow Curriculum, John Hartigan, extended this argument by invoking the dark specter of untold "deviants" stalking the halls of public schools.

> I do have a problem when homosexuality and lesbianism are portrayed as a culture. If homosexuality and lesbianism is a culture, then so is drug abuse. So is alcohol abuse. So is being a Nazi skinhead. There are all sorts of groups and lifestyles in the world, but it's highly misleading and I think unhealthy to treat them as cultures in the same sense as Hispanic culture or Afro American culture or Italian American culture. . . . If diversity is to be worshipped without limit, then presumably we should have Ku Klux Klan clubs in high schools, or we should have cocaine clubs in high schools. And no one should be excluded because we worship diversity and there are no limits on diversity. Ax murderers would be honored and respected.[25]

As I discuss in the next section, Hartigan supports this discursive positioning of gay people and ax murderers with data selected to depict a lethal homosexual "deathstyle."

Finally, the argument that lesbians and gay men are not a culture enabled the religious right to mobilize communities of color by arousing fear and hatred. A white organizer like Mary Cummins could cast herself as a defender of racial and ethnic minorities while simultaneously spearheading the campaign that ultimately undermined the implementation of the entire multicultural curriculum. She declared, "I will not demean our legitimate minorities, such as Blacks, Hispanics and Asians, by lumping them together with homosexuals in that curriculum."[26] Yet she ultimately not only rejected the Rainbow Curriculum but criticized the entire mandate for a multicultural curriculum. Cummins had a separate program crafted for District 24, an area that is overwhelmingly Asian American, Latino, and African American. "Reaching Out" features a story about a fictional town where all the inhabitants are squares, circles, triangles, and rectangles; the story is meant as a vehicle for diversity training. All the shapes eventually come together and form a wagon, a development that, according to Cummins and Hartigan, is "the way to teach [children] to understand about differences and getting along."[27]

In sum, the culture-based model is enormously complex in its theoretical and practical consequences. Obviously we cannot generalize to all multicultural programs on the basis of the immediate set of controversies that greeted the Rainbow Curriculum in New York City. All cities have their own unique histories of political accommodation and conflict. Yet in addition to their strengths, culture-based claims carry with them a particular configuration of vexing dilemmas. These difficulties are not necessarily resolved in what have been termed anti-bias or diversity programs, since opponents read these initiatives as thinly veiled culture-based models. In contrast, a different set of discursive strengths and limitations inheres in what I call the public health model.

Making Schools Safe: The Public Health Model

Various strategies fall under the rubric of the public health model. One common initiative is the integration of gay issues into sexuality or health education curricula, building programs around safety and danger concerns. This model also includes counseling and support programs for youth such as Project 10 in Los Angeles and its offshoots. In addition, many schools have implemented teacher trainings that emphasize the enhanced risks of gay youth for such problems as suicide, violence, or substance abuse. These myriad programs share a health promotion and risk prevention frame.

Educators in Massachusetts have most skillfully deployed public health claims-making. In the past several years the state has far surpassed any others in its institutionalization of comprehensive lesbian and gay educational reform in public schools. Emphasizing data that suggest a high rate of gay teen suicide, activists persuaded Republican governor William Weld to impanel a Commission on Lesbian and Gay Youth. In its first years, the commission held public hearings, issued widely publicized reports on the status of lesbian and gay youth in the educational and mental health systems, and implemented a state-wide program of teacher trainings on homosexuality called "Making Schools Safe." The Massachusetts success story is all the more striking in that these reforms were undertaken about the same time as New York City's Children of the Rainbow controversies.

In addition to their emphasis on suicide risk, Massachusetts educators' success with the "public health model" has been enhanced by their strategic use of claims by gay youth themselves. Through their active participation, these young people brought the issue alive, helped defuse controversy, and made a compelling case for reform. For example, they launched an extraordinary lobbying effort to enact a landmark piece of legislation, the Gay and Lesbian Student Rights Law. One thousand students descended on the State House to talk with their legislators. A seventeen-year-old senior told about the time his soccer team attacked him. "They spit on me and threw things at me and called me faggot, homo." Another student lobbied for weeks with a sign: "Gays Make up 30 Percent of Completed Teen Suicides."[28] In 1993, the legislation was passed. Massachusetts became the first state in the nation to outlaw discrimination against gay and lesbian students in the school system.

There are powerful strengths to the public health model. First, many lesbian and gay youth do face specific risks and therefore need assistance and prevention efforts. Although social worker Paul Gibson's chapter in the infamous 1989 Health and Human Services report on youth suicide was criticized as anecdotal and derivative[29] in the estimate that gay adolescents are three times more likely than heterosexuals to attempt suicide, most current research supports that figure.[30] Furthermore, studies estimate that close to half of lesbian and gay youth have experienced school victimization in the form of verbal harassment or physical violence.[31] Dropping out, substance abuse, homelessness, and HIV infection are also clear risks.[32] It is a legitimate role of the schools to educate teachers and counselors concerning these problems.

A second strength of this model lies in its ability to put a human face on discrimination. In their appearances at hearings, lobbying days, and trainings, lesbian and gay youth make educational reform vital and tangible. Ideology recedes, at least momentarily, in the face of an adolescent recounting self-hatred and victimization so extreme that it prompted a suicide attempt.

Finally, public health claims-making in Massachusetts has at least temporarily stymied opposition from the religious right. Opponents have admitted to some difficulty finding ground on which to criticize these prevention programs.[33] As an architect of the Making Schools Safe program said, "Who could be for suicide?"[34] It is reasonable to assume that opposition is inevitable. In fact, there has been town-by-town opposition,[35] as well as statewide legislative initiatives to prevent student involvement in gay-related programs without parental consent.[36] While it is too early to tell, it may be that the greatest strength of this model has been the time it allowed for mobilizing statewide grassroots support through the Making Schools Safe team-building approach. This support, sorely lacking for Children of the Rainbow, may ultimately thwart whatever opposition arises.

As with the culture-based model, the drawbacks of the public health model are the obverse of its strengths. First, lesbian and gay concerns risk being ghettoized in ancillary health education and afterschool programs. This contrasts with the culture-based model, admittedly more controversial in this respect, which effects integration throughout the curriculum. Although one teacher described curriculum reform as "the third rail of American education,"[37] educational activists ideally seek the diffusion of gay-related topics throughout the curriculum, from science to English. As one teacher proposed, "There should be, well 'Robert wants to date Pierre.' It needs to be incorporated on that level where being gay is not an issue, the issue is what is the correct conjugation of the verb 'to date.' "[38] The public health model can reinforce segregation of gay issues from the curriculum.

A second important limitation of this model is that it leaves intact, and may even strengthen, a pathologized representation of homosexuality. The overriding concentration on suicide, substance abuse, and victimization has led some gay youth and educators to speak out against the unmitigated use of what one student dubbed "the horror stories."[39] Some call for an emphasis on youths' strengths and successes.[40] Yet by definition the public health model pulls for the risks and dangers to youth, and a reformulation undermines its very strength in engendering sympathy in parents and teachers.

In fact, the safety discourse of the public health model has prompted a reciprocal danger discourse from counterclaimants. Conservative and religious opponents of these educational programs fold concern about gay youth suicide or substance abuse into their long-standing demonization of homosexuality. It serves as data to support their contention that homosexuality is a dangerous and destructive lifestyle, or as one critic put it, "deathstyle," from which children should be protected.[41] In their view, of course, it is homosexuality itself, not social oppression, that causes youth suicide or other problems.

Religious right critics mount their deathstyle arguments in a consistent and predictable fashion. This often entails a solemn recitation by an authoritative-looking older white male (sometimes a physician) of grim alleged facts about gay men and lesbians related to their disease or death. Dr. Stanley Monteith's appearance in the highly publicized propaganda video *The Gay Agenda* is a stellar example. Monteith, who once headed his local John Birch Society chapter,[42] intones a list of statistics designed to repulse Mr. and Mrs. Middle America about supposed percentages of "homosexuals" who engage in behaviors like fellatio, anal sex, fisting, golden showers, and skat. His deadpan demeanor holds throughout discussions of "rolling around in feces" and rimming, only giving way to an incredulous tone with, "And what are golden showers? Why, a man lies on the ground naked and other men stand around and urinate on him!"[43] *The Gay Agenda*, which is widely used throughout the country by opponents of gay rights initiatives, was the subject of an exposé by the *Los Angeles Times*, which reported that Monteith's statistics are derived from a study of only forty-one men conducted by the long-discredited antigay psychologist Paul Cameron.[44]

Cameron's ideologically driven and methodologically unsound research is used by many opponents of lesbian and gay educational reform. He proudly notes that he is "the wellspring of right-wing data in that area."[45] His study "The Longevity of Homosexuals," which compares obituaries from gay newspapers to those of mainstream newspapers, concludes that lesbians and gay men have an abbreviated lifespan.[46] His allegation that homosexuals die in their forties has been used by religious right critics, for example attorney John Hartigan, who spices his lectures with it to the horrified gasps of audience members.[47]

Hartigan, who played a central role in the defeat of Children of the Rainbow, is a major architect of deathstyle rhetoric. More dangerous than the discredited Cameron or Monteith, he braids together questionable data from Cameron's studies with statistics on HIV and STDs from legitimate medical journals. Another propaganda video, *The Gay Agenda in Public Education*, features Hartigan listing high HIV infection rates among gay men in urban areas as reported by the *New York Times*. He then concludes, "If that isn't dangerous, if that isn't frightening, then nothing in the world is. And it's criminal for the New York City public school's chancellor to publish a book [Children of the Rainbow] telling teachers that they should urge children not to view homosexuality as frightening when that's the medical reality."[48] This is tantamount to arguing that being Black is pathological because one of every thirty-three African American men is HIV positive.[49]

In danger discourse, then, homosexuals are cast as depraved and diseased individuals who die an early death. It is claims-making clearly designed to persuade an uninformed public to oppose lesbian and gay rights and educational reform initiatives. It is a formidable response to efforts aimed at keeping youth healthy and safe—what one critic of such programs dubbed "public safety as a Trojan Horse," a metaphor that, again, evokes warfare and destruction.[50]

The shortcomings of both the culture-based model and the public health model do not represent criticisms of either set of claims. Given both the political climate and definitional dilemmas inherent to homosexuality, there is no vehicle by which integration of lesbian and gay issues into public education is not somehow problematic. The political climate, which I discuss below, understandably fuels a defensive tone as reformers must defend cumbersome conceptualizations of homosexuality. For example: we are a legitimate culture (we have music, we have literature); we are a different kind of "different" than skinheads or ax murderers; we are born this way, your kids will not catch it; protect lesbian and gay youth or they will kill themselves. Theoretical dilemmas aside; it is the case that some critics would oppose these school reforms no matter what elegant conceptual frameworks might be crafted.

Moral Panics in the Schools

The vitriolic attacks of opponents are, in part, testimony to the enormous success of educational reformers in implementing programs nationwide. The backlash represents an irresolvable conflict not just over educational and sexual ideologies, but also over a broader social and political vision for America. These controversies reflect the widespread cultural tensions of this century. They are the inevitable result of a clash between two important movements. First, there have been rapid changes in social life and cultural values over the last hundred years, a growing secularization and liberalization sometimes labeled modernity. An increasingly sexualized society, in which sex is valued less for reproduction and more for pleasure and satisfaction, is part of this trend. Feminism, lesbian/gay liberation, and comprehensive sexuality education are emblematic of this movement. Second, religious evangelicals have coalesced throughout the century in a backlash against the changes of modernity. Although for decades they were determinedly apolitical, evangelicals have emerged as a powerful political force in the last thirty years.[51] Their opposition to lesbian/gay educational reform stems from their profound moral objection to homosexuality and sexual liberalism, but also from a recognition that such controversies serve as a potent political vehicle by which to recruit and galvanize members.

Lesbian and gay educational reform, then, is an important and volatile battleground for two competing, irreconcilable worldviews: a fundamentalist religious belief in universal, moral absolutes and a secular move toward social tolerance, diversity, and openness. In recognition of the depth of these conflicts, the board president of one Brooklyn school district that was torn apart by debates over Children of the Rainbow said, "We're going to have the equivalent of warfare for a while."[52] In this historical context, lesbian and gay educational reform is a red flag for contestation.

Controversies over teaching about sexuality and homosexuality reflect both literal and symbolic concerns. It is important to examine the very tangible questions and anxieties that inform the opposition to lesbian and gay school reform. Parents, for example, may object to what they see as the public schools' usurpation of their rights to teach children their own sexual values. Other parents worry that teachers might not be adequately trained to teach about sensitive subjects or that certain topics may be broached at an inappropriate age.

Certainly homophobia underpins some opposition to lesbian and gay school reform. Some parents, for religious or other reasons, oppose homosexuality (and sexual freedom in general) and resent that the topic is raised with their children. They fear "something sexual and deviant penetrating the school."[53] They may worry that their children will be somehow seduced or persuaded into becoming gay, or they simply believe in the hegemony of the heterosexual, nuclear family. They fear recruitment or molestation of their children, or they worry about diseases and substance abuse in what they have heard is the "deathstyle" of homosexuality. For many parents it is simply that, as journalist Anne Roiphe succinctly put it, "when it comes to their own little Heather's fate they would rather keep gender choice on the straight path."[54] There are a range of interests specific to homosexuality itself that fuel counterclaims against such education.

In many cases, however, these community controversies are driven by long-standing resentments and conflicts that have little to do with sexuality or homosexuality. It is important to understand when sexuality curriculum battles become metaphors for other problems.

Certain themes recirculate in community debates over teaching about sexuality. First, controversies over sexuality curricula often trigger familiar conflicts over the role of the public schools. These debates over whose values will be taught arise in a range of other subjects such as drug education, death education, multiculturalism, and any other "values clarification" programs. Opponents may complain that the state, in the guise of the public school, is undermining parental power and control and imposing an unacceptable value system on children. In this instance, opposition to lesbian and gay school reform is merely another plank, albeit a powerful one, in a larger platform of attack on public education.[55]

Second, frustrations over incomplete or inadequate educational reform efforts may drive opposition to gay-inclusive curricula. In New York City, for example, the efforts to introduce the Children of the Rainbow Curriculum were complicated by an unwieldy system of both local and central control. Not surprisingly, when communities viewed Chancellor Fernandez as imposing a curriculum on them, some resisted. When a local school board president, Mary Cummins, refused the curriculum, the media portrayed it as "David versus Goliath."

Third, sexuality curricula debates may be fueled by anger over inequalities in access to resources. Opposition to sexuality education may reflect a sense of powerlessness in relation to larger social institutions engendered by race, ethnicity, and social class. In the Children of the Rainbow controversies, for example, anger about unequal access was a frequent subtext of the opposition from within communities of color. Parents raged that their children were not being taught to read or write but yet they were being taught "sodomy." In addition, many members of communities of color objected to the inclusion of lesbians/gay men in a multicultural curriculum since gay people were not a "real" culture or minority. Much of this resentment flowed from the sense of a "special interest" group trying to appropriate and benefit from their years of hard work to achieve multiculturalism in the schools. Thus, competition over status and resources underpinned the debate over the curriculum.

Finally, many parents feel an overwhelming sense of powerlessness in the face of a host of potential dangers to their children. Sexuality education can be perceived as threatening in an environment in which drugs, violence, and sexual assault are constant problems. This was the sentiment shared by many opponents of Children of the Rainbow with whom Hetrick-Martin staff member Andy Humm spoke during educational workshops:

> I mean, you're already living in New York and your locus of control isn't too good, because your kid's going out in the street and you're worried about if they're going to come home alive, and now someone wants to teach faggotry to them. And you're like, "That's it, Gladys. We're going down to the school board."[56]

Simply being taught about homosexuality may serve as a metaphor for unwanted intrusion and the inability to keep children safe. It can be the last straw for the fictional Gladys and her very real counterparts, for whom a protest at the school board can represent an assertion of control.

These aspects are important in that they highlight the many different sources of support or opposition to lesbian and gay school reform. In terms of interventions or resolutions to these community controversies, it is crucial to tease out which objections are specific to lesbian and gay educational initiatives and which are symptomatic of broader social, political, and economic tensions.

Lesbian and gay educational reform faces an uphill battle in this broader context of both displaced concern and religious right opposition. Consequently, the conceptual strategies and claims that educators deploy often reflect pragmatic opportunities and political realities more than theoretical consensus. For example, many educational reformers are ambivalent about whether lesbian and gay men constitute a culture. Yet when the multicultural curriculum is the central vehicle for discussion of difference, it becomes imperative to include homosexuality. As one educator said, "You've got to go with what the system is and if [a multicultural curriculum] is going to be written, it's got to be inclusive. What are we supposed to say, 'No, go ahead, write it without us, we'll catch up later'?"[57]

Similarly, advocates for lesbian and gay initiatives in public education often mount "arguments of reassurance." In order to assuage parental fears and deep cultural anxieties about children being lured into homosexuality through programs in public schools, they insist sexual orientation is not a choice, but something we are born with. Some use research on the "gay brain" and "gay genes," studies that are deeply contested, to reassure parents that their children cannot be seduced into homosexuality.

Arguments of reassurance are difficult to resist. Even skeptics sometimes fall back on them in politically charged moments. One activist in the Children of the Rainbow controversy told me in an interview that sexual orientation is not biological and the research is inconclusive. Yet in a letter he wrote to an African-American leader at the height of the Rainbow conflict, he claimed that sexual orientation was indeed biological. "All current scientific evidence," he wrote, "points toward the fact that it is an innate human characteristic that is most certainly not chosen as you suggest." There were two unstated subtexts in this letter. First, your child will not catch it. And second, sexual orientation, since it is an immutable biological characteristic, should be accorded the same respect and protections given to racial and ethnic minorities.

At this early stage of lesbian and gay educational reform initiatives, the most pressing priority may well be simply their implementation. As I suggested earlier, however, there is no strategy that is free of the potential to generate controversy. With that in mind, it may be useful to consider the broader ideological messages in lesbian and gay school initiatives. Claims-making may either reproduce or challenge social stereotypes. They operate as assertions about "the homosexual" as a specific biological or cultural entity, and thereby reinforce particular political identities and subjectivities. As we have seen, some claims leave lesbians and gay men vulnerable to being pathologized, while others put them in a specific relationship to embattled cultural groups in ways that may generate resentments. We may do well to consider the "hidden curricula" in these various programs designed to reform the hidden heterocentric curriculum.

Notes

This article is based in part on research I conducted and a paper I presented while a Rockefeller Fellow at the Center for Lesbian and Gay Studies at the City University of New York. I am extremely grateful to Martin Duberman and everyone at CLAGS for their support during my year of research there.

1. For a very small number of examples, see Samuel Bowles and Herbert Gintis, *Schooling in Capitalist America* (New New York: Basic Books, 1976); Paulo Freire, *Pedagogy of the Oppressed* (New York: Harper and Row, 1971); Henry Giroux, *Ideology, Culture and the Process of Schooling* (Philadelphia: Temple University Press, 1981); Kathleen Weiler, *Women Teaching for Change: Gender, Class and Power* (New York: Bergin and Garvey, Pub. 1988); and Lois Weis and Michelle Fine, eds., *Beyond Silenced Voices: Class, Race, and Gender in United States Schools* (Albany: SUNY Press, 1993).

2. Many of those I interviewed cited both of these reasons as central to the hesitance of many lesbian and gay educators to take up school reform or to work on gay youth issues.

3. See Karen M. Harbeck, ed., *Coming Out of the Classroom Closet: Gay and Lesbian Students, Teachers and Curricula* (New York: Harrington Park, 1992), especially the introduction and the article by Karen Harbeck and Virginia Uribe.

4. See the video *Who's Afraid of Project 10?*

5. See Becky Thompson and Tyagi Sangeeta, eds., *Beyond a Dream Deferred: Multicultural Education and the Politics of Excellence* (Minneapolis: University of Minnesota Press, 1993), xxxi.

6. See Jose Zuniga, "Christian Right Gives Iowa's Wilson Defeat," *Washington Blade,* September 15, 1995, 24.

7. See Lou Chibbaro, Jr., "House Panel Postpones Hearing on Schools," *Washington Blade,* September 8, 1995, 21.

8. *Newsletter on Intellectual Freedom.* American Library Association, Office for Intellectual Freedom, vol. 44, no. 5 (September 1995).

9. This quote and the ones that follow are from *Children of the Rainbow: First Grade* (Board of Education of the City of New York, 1991).

10. "The Rainbow Curriculum," *Sixty Minutes,* April 4, 1993.

11. Donna Minkowitz, "It Felt Like a Nazi Rally," *New York Newsday,* October 21, 1992.

12. See, for example, Steven Lee Myers, "How a 'Rainbow Curriculum' Turned into Fighting Words," *New York Times,* December 13, 1992, 6.

13. Mary Tabor, "S. I. Drops Gay Issues from Student Guide," *New York Times,* June 9, 1992.

14. Laura D'Angelo, "Repercussions Continue after School Board Vote," *Staten Island Sunday Advance,* September 6, 1992.

15. "The Rainbow Curriculum."

16. Ibid.

17. Critics charge that some multicultural programs rely on a fixed, essentialized definition of race. These programs then become merely "add race and stir" approaches rather than transformations of the curriculum. See James Banks, *Teaching Strategies for Ethnic Studies,* 5th ed. (Boston: Allyn and Bacon, 1991).

18. See, for example, Steven Epstein, "Gay Politics, Ethnic Identity: The Limits of Social Constructionism," *Socialist Review 93/94 (1987): 9–54; Michael Warner, ed., Fear of a Queer Planet: Queer Politics and Social Theory* (Minneapolis: University of Minnesota Press, 1993), especially the introduction; and Janice M. Irvine, "A Place in the Rainbow: Theorizing Lesbian and Gay Culture," *Sociological Theory* 12, no. 2 (July 1994): 232–48.

19. Quoted in Irvine, "A Place in the Rainbow."

20. "The Rainbow Curriculum."

21. Not only people of color are voicing this threat. For example, Dolores Ayling of Concerned Parents for Educational Accountability (a religious right group that organized to oppose the curriculum) spoke of the outrage at the fact that sexual orientation is included in the Rainbow Curriculum in a way that detracts from the authenticity of

race as a cultural category (personal conversation). Many of these white advocates had not previously been known for their vigorous support of communities of color.

22. NTanya Lee, Don Murphy, and Lisa North, "Sexuality, Multicultural Education, and the New York City Public Schools," *Radical Teacher* 45 (winter 1994): 12–16.

23. Norman Fruchter, interview, October 31, 1994.

24. "The Rainbow Curriculum."

25. John Hartigan, interview, October 18, 1994.

26. Steven Lee Myers, "Queens School Board Suspended in Fight on Gay-Life Curriculum," *New York Times*, December 2, 1992.

27. Hartigan, interview.

28. Paul Gibson, "Gay Male and Lesbian Youth Suicide," in ADAMHA, *Report of the Secretary's Task Force on Youth Suicide*, DHHS publication no. ADM 89-1623, vol. 3 (Washington, D.C.; U.S. Government Printing Office, 1989), 110–42.

29. Gibson's report was widely criticized by conservatives. See Susan Okie, "Sullivan Cold-Shoulders Suicide Report," *Washington Post*, January 13, 1990. Some lesbian and gay activists and researchers also had reservations but were more circumspect about them in order to avoid fueling further criticism.

30. Conversation with Anthony D'Augelli, February 1994.

31. See, for example, Scott Hershberger and Anthony D'Augelli, "The Impact of Victimization on the Mental Health and Suicidality of Lesbian, Gay, and Bisexual Youths," *Developmental Psychology* 31, no. 1 (1995): 65–74.

32. Joyce Hunter, "Violence against Lesbian and Gay Male Youths," *Journal of Interpersonal Violence* 5 (1990): 295–300; G. Remafedi, "Adolescent Homosexuality: Psychosocial and Medical Implications," *Pediatrics* 79 (1987): 331–37.

33. Nancy Sutton, interview, November 1994.

34. Kevin Jennings, interview, November 7, 1994.

35. Sutton, interview. Sutton estimated that one-third of towns in Massachusetts have contacted her organization, Family First, about how to oppose these programs.

36. In the spring of 1995 a series of bills were introduced to the state legislature that, in actual intent, targeted gay-related school programs. The most restrictive would have seriously threatened such programs, but supporters of lesbian and gay school reform succeeded in implementing a compromise measure.

37. Jennings, interview.

38. Ibid.

39. Ibid. Jennings discussed his surprise when his student first complained about the use of "horror stories."

40. See Karen Harbeck, "Invisible No More: Addressing the Needs of Gay, Lesbian and Bisexual Youth and Their Advocates," *High School Journal* 77, nos. 1–2 (1993): 169–76. This issue was also a focus of a conference at Lesley College in Cambridge, Massachusetts, entitled "Making Schools Safe," April 3, 1993.

41. Hartigan, interview.

42. David Colker, "Anti-Gay Video Highlights Church's Agenda," *Los Angeles Times*, February 22, 1993.

43. *The Gay Agenda*, produced by The Report, 1992.

44. David Colker, "Statistics in 'Gay Agenda' Questioned," *Los Angeles Times*, February 22, 1993.

45. Paul Cameron, telephone conversation, November 9, 1994.

46. Paul Cameron, William Playfair, and Stephen Wellum, "The Longevity of Homosexuals: Before and after the AIDS Epidemic," *Omega: Journal of Death and Dying* 29, no. 3 (1994): 249–72.

47. Interfaith Coalition conference, Boston, May 15, 1994.

48. *The Gay Agenda in Public Education*, produced by The Report, 1993.

49. Lauran Neergaard, "Threat of AIDS Increases for Young," *Boston Globe*, November 24, 1995, 3.

50. Adam Pertman and Lisa Atkinson, "Some Say Gay-Pupil Policy Unneeded," *Boston Globe*, May 20, 1993.

51. There is an extensive literature on this development. See, for example, Martin Marty and R. Scott Appleby, *Fundamentalisms and Society* (Chicago: University of Chicago Press, 1993); Martin Marty and R. Scott Appleby, *Fundamentalisms Observed* (Chicago: University of Chicago Press, 1991); Robert Liebman and Robert Wuthnow, *The New Christian Right* (New York: Aldine, 1983); and Nancy Tatom Ammerman, *Bible Believers: Fundamentalists in the Modern World* (New Brunswick: Rutgers University Press, 1987).

52. Fruchter, interview.

53. Ibid.

54. Anne Roiphe, "Promoting Gayness? No—Just Basic Decency," *New York Observer*, January 11, 1992.

55. Eugene Provenzo, Jr., *Religious Fundamentalism and American Education: The Battle for the Public Schools* (Albany: State University of New York Press, 1990).

56. Andy Humm, interview, September 27, 1994.

57. Ibid.

45

Families, Values, and the Rainbow Curriculum: A Roundtable Discussion

In 1992 New York City School Chancellor Joseph Fernandez attempted to introduce a multicultural "Children of the Rainbow" Curriculum. Twenty-seven of the thirty-two community school boards soon endorsed the new curriculum, but the strongest holdout was District 24. The nine members of that Queens community board voted unanimously to reject the curriculum because it included material on gay men and lesbians. Mary Cummins, president of the District 24 board, was the most vocal opponent, claiming that the curriculum would "promote a homosexual lifestyle." Chancellor Fernandez insisted that the new curriculum was designed to instill tolerance, not to advocate any particular lifestyle.

District 24 in New York City is made up predominantly of working-class families (nearly 70 percent have minority ethnic backgrounds; Hispanics constitute nearly 45 percent), and the debate over the Rainbow Curriculum succeeded in pitting a number of African Americans and Latinos against the inclusion of lesbian and gay material. They argued that it took attention away from the long-standing struggle of "real" minorities to have their lives represented and their issues addressed.

With matters at an impasse, Fernandez suspended the District 24 board. That, in turn, led to a prolonged struggle that ended on February 11, 1993, when Fernandez was denied renewal of his contract as Chancellor.

On April 24, 1994, CLAGS cosponsored with PACE (People About Changing Education) the second of two roundtables on "Families, Values, and the Rainbow Curriculum." Both roundtables were funded by the Rockefeller Foundation and organized by Jeffrey Escoffier, the writer, editor, and CLAGS board member. The daylong discussion involved, at different points, nearly fifty people, and the transcribed tapes come to more than 150 pages. Given the sometimes rapid-fire exchanges (plus the limitations of the miking system), there are, alas, many points on the tapes where it is impossible to identify the speaker or to hear more than a few words or half sentences. Yet at least some portion of the many experiences and views recounted during the roundtable come through intact (unascribed, alas); vivid and insightful, they seem worth preserving— however fragmentary the form.

————The idea for having this kind of gathering came about out of the frustration many of us have felt ever since the defeat of the Children of the

Rainbow Curriculum here in New York last year. It's very apparent that there are a lot of committed people in this city who, on different levels, understand the need to talk about homophobia and the need to fight antigay violence in the schools. Not all those people are gay, and not all those people are in schools. Nor are all of those people in education. And so a lot of these people never talk to each other, and that has been very frustrating—like when going to meetings that were predominantly either white gay and lesbian, or predominantly gay youth, or predominantly heterosexual parents, etc. Frustrating, that is, for trying to do some coalition work. There were very few opportunities during the whole struggle over the Rainbow Curriculum last year for a diverse group of people to get together and have an honest conversation about some of the central issues involved and some of the obstacles in the schools preventing us from dealing with homophobia.

Many of us at PACE have a vision not just to do some sort of citywide coalition building but to really start talking about what local community-based strategies can or should exist for dealing with these issues. We need to be in communities doing local work, and especially in people of color communities. Curriculum issues can't be separated from all the other issues—like the alienation that parents of color and families of color feel when dealing with the schools; can't be separated from people's criticism of the schools as racist; can't be separated from some very basic systemic issues that are operating within our schools. So our strategies have to take all that into account. Our strategies can't ignore those realities.

———Memories of the school board election and the controversy during it are still very hurtful. Until the Children of the Rainbow Curriculum came along, as a school board member I had strong support in my communities, which I felt were the Latino and African American communities of Redhook and Sunset Park. I had worked hard for both of these communities. And when the attacks started, they were quite bad. . . . I still think I need to go to therapy over this stuff. I could not understand how people that I had respect for, that had respected me before this issue, that I had worked with with great success on other issues—how this issue of who you were sexually would turn them into just beasts—and this is not an overstatement. I still don't understand. . . . Why were these people, who up until that moment had been sane and respectful people, attacking me for supporting this curriculum—which basically I felt was only a curriculum that would instill in young children a common respect for every human being. That was how I defended the curriculum, and the need for it in our schools and communities. And the things that were done to me and said about me were just astounding—like the lie that I was an abusive parent. . . . That was probably the most vile thing ever said to me. The other stuff, basically, I didn't give a damn. But to attack me as a parent. . . .

When the public meeting to vote on the curriculum took place, it was one of the most personally humiliating experiences of my life. The school auditorium was jam-packed. There were people outside the auditorium; no more people could fit in. And I would say, well, about 80 to 85 percent of the people in there just yelled and screamed and cursed and threatened and made obscene gestures to us throughout the whole meeting. We couldn't even hear ourselves sitting next to each other. The police had to escort us out at the end. . . .

————For the last six years, a group of us at Bank Street School of Education started very slowly to work with some of our students, interview teachers in public schools, private schools, and Catholic schools all around the so-called greater New York area. We started working around issues of gay- and lesbian-headed families. It became immediately clear that it's about antibias work in general, and that when teachers are in classrooms, they need to not make assumptions about any family. Because the assumptions that teachers make, that most of us make, are very deep and they're colored by our own education and experience.

When we talked to the teachers and administrators of the children of gay and lesbian parents, we found that the differences between the public and private schools were not that great. The socioeconomic differences were profound, absolutely stark, in terms of the ability to come out and the ramifications of coming out. The big issue was around disclosure, and we found out just how intricate the disclosure process is, and how it looked different for each parent with a child at a different age, for parents who had two children, and so on. The complexity is overwhelming, but what came out from all of it was that disclosure is really a joint venture. That disclosure around homosexuality, around being a gay or lesbian parent isn't just the job of the parent, and it isn't just the job of the teacher. It takes both to tango.

For the most part, teachers are straight, and represent straight culture, represent it in deep ways that are hard to get at—for example, the language differences between the gay and lesbian parents and the educators around assumptions of gender nonconformity, around what's okay and what's not okay, what's a role model, what does a boy need to become a "man," and so on. Basic developmental theory is mainstreamed into this very simplistic, mechanistic formula stuff that the teachers spit out, you know, as rational. Behind that is a built-in developmental bias that what little kids do sort of "doesn't count."

————I think, especially in the Black and Latino communities, that a "family" means a father figure or a mother figure taking care of the children. A family is not two mothers. It shouldn't matter, so long as the child is loved. But society doesn't understand that. They feel like, "two mothers?—Oh, my God, the child is going to come out either gay, which they think is bad, or messed up. . . .

————Maybe some of you have heard about the Curriculum of Inclusion. That was the New York State NAACP's first direct involvement in promoting what we now call "multicultural education," or focusing on the emphasis of greater inclusion in our curriculum. Our NAACP state president was chair of the committee that put together that report, and before the report could get out to anybody, it was attacked in the media. We do have forces in the society who want us to remain a certain way, and they have control of the media and the powerful instruments to put an opinion out there or to make an issue become important.

Now, why on earth *wouldn't* any sane person want children to have more information about the history and culture of everybody? We're supposedly one country, one America, but when you hear some people talking "American values", they're not talking about all of us. They're really not, and that's why our curriculum and our educational programs have been structured the way they are: to make sure that the history, values, and issues that they know and understand are promoted. In my opinion, it makes them feel more comfortable about who they are and what has happened in this country to some of the rest of us. . . .

A lot of the white teachers felt that the Curriculum of Inclusion was threatening to their jobs, might mean in fact that they would no longer *have* jobs. So I said, "I can understand how you might feel that way, because when I look around this room, I see only one person who looks like an African American. I see no one that looks like an Asian American. I see no one that looks like a Latino. So I can understand why you might worry about being left out. Those things worry me, too." And I said, "So now you can see that we all have some reasons to worry. For years we've been talking about a global marketplace, an international workforce. Do you think any child should be denied the experience to learn more about those people that he or she will have to interface with, that he or she will have to work with in the future?"

We need to have more programs and services to train and educate parents. Because the kids can handle it. It's the adults who aren't able to handle it.

————I disagree that kids handle it well, because I'm being called left and right all over the place about tensions in schools with kids on different issues, racial, cultural, or whatever. And the research, the last time I looked, showed that children from the age of two already start building prejudices that they pick up from their parents.

————Who is this curriculum for? I mean, when you're talking about violence against young people in the public schools, there are Black and Latino young people, you know, who are being beaten up every day. . . . So in terms of this new curriculum, this was not our rainbow. We would have presented it in another way and covered other issues. That would have galvanized the base, begun to really address the issue of violence against young people and in particular violence against young people in the public schools, and link that up to the larger violence in the Black and Latino community. We would have raised up the issue in a much broader way in the Black community and built a broader coalition. We have to have a series of lead-ins in different communities. We've found that meetings *outside* the school board meetings were much more productive than those with the school board. People are afraid of schools, you know. They're seen as racist institutions. They're not teaching our kids anything. And we certainly don't trust these white people to teach our kids about sex. So, yes, there's definite homophobia, but there's so much else tied into it. You can't form any grand theory here or strategy. A lot of it is learning on the job: How to present stuff to people; what's available in terms of materials; learning how to talk with people around the issue of homophobia, because it's not been an issue that any of us have organized around in the community.

————I would like to add my two cents to this as a progressive, a revolutionary woman, working at a community service organization. When the war over the Rainbow Curriculum peaked, I was doing a lot of political work, and actually knew the sentiments, the realities, the traditional views within our community. And I was furious at first with [School Chancellor] Fernandez, the media, and who I perceived to be the white gay and lesbian community—who I felt had moved in a manner altogether disrespectful of the climate in my community. In their urgency to move forward with their agenda—which is their right—how difficult they made it for me, an activist, who was preparing to move forward by degrees. The door was shut for me even going into areas like Coney Island, where I had been working with parents, to discuss the issue. Because of other people's urgency, they just locked me out of being able to go into my community and begin to deal in degrees. And the result is that I think my community has reverted back into the complacency of not wanting to talk about the issue of homophobia at all.

————I'm a teacher at Prospect Heights High School and I would like to get help in figuring out how to confront the homophobia that exists in my classroom. I haven't been very successful at that, and would like to hear some ideas.

————In response to that, I'm involved with an organization called Greenwich Village Youth Council, where we've been dealing with youth in lower Manhattan. . . . Let me tell you about one of our youth members. He's sixteen, from a Caribbean family, and is in the New York City public school system. He said that some teachers in his school have come right out during classes and announced that they're against homosexuality; and if negative comments are made in the classroom by other students about homosexuality, the teachers often will affirm those comments and say that they agree with them. One time during a class discussion, this sixteen-year-old told me, they were talking about characteristics they all had gotten from their families, and the teacher said to this sixteen-year-old, in front of everybody, "Well, where did you get that voice from, your mother?" And he didn't say that in a positive way. I asked this sixteen-year-old what could give him some relief in the school, and he said, "Well, if there was some person identified—you know, maybe an ombudsperson—who could be trusted to handle and report those issues." But right now there is no such person. Unless an individual in a school specifically said that they were sensitive to lesbi/gay issues, nobody would know who that person was. This sixteen-year-old says that many youth cannot speak to their parents and families because they don't accept homosexuality, and so they need some kind of outlet at school. And they're not finding it there, either.

————Schools are, by their very organization, against difference. I don't think any political strategy will really deconstruct the current power structure without our unabashed support of and focus on the importance of differentness. As Audre Lorde and others have said to us for years, we either figure out how to engage with difference or it's over. We cannot disavow the importance of real, fundamental difference as the base of a multicultural democracy. And we have to figure out how to form workable coalitions and not have these bloody difficult disagreements about everything. And the schools can't or won't have these conversations. They're designed not to.

————My mother, a heterosexual black woman, right? is invested in talking about homophobia because she cares about me. There are such parents. There are folks in the community who are heterosexual, and who *are* struggling with gay, lesbian, bisexual, transgender people in their own families, and who care about them and who don't want bad things to happen to them. Think about that in terms of alliances—which is not the same as thinking about what people have in common. There is a potential for progressive heterosexuals to organize each other and do some of this work—though I don't know exactly how that ties into more explicitly political strategies.

————What I don't want to come out of this discussion is what I see continuously happening elsewhere—that is, the tendency to move into the highly intellectual without keeping in mind the realities of particular communities, especially those "away from the bridge," outside of Manhattan. The strategies that we are discussing here have to be formulated in a way that we can take them back to our outer borough communities and begin to change in some small way what is happening there. Let's remember that the public schools we are talking about have a high percentage of children of color in them. At Erasmus High School, Haitian children are crying every day, because English-speaking Caribbean children are ridiculing them every day. That's the reality. Okay? And I'm now doing what I call "laying down my bucket" right there in East Flatbush, and beginning to do the kind of work that I feel I'm going to be doing for the rest of my life. A white, gay person can't come into the community to do that work, so people of color have to take that responsibility. We need to be brave enough now to do some work right where we are, with whatever allies we have identified.

————It seems to me we need a way . . . an issue, a thing to talk about in our communities. In Boston, they used the basic question of child abuse. They said that what was happening in the schools was an issue of child abuse, lesbian and gay children being abused. And they were successful in getting programs in all the high schools, and having an ombudsperson or a counselor or somebody in each high school who lesbian and gay youth can go to. And they also provide programs for teenagers in the schools to increase their knowledge of lesbian and gay people.

————One of the things that I'm hearing is very depressing. On the one hand we're saying how important it is to be in a community, be in your neighborhood, and on the other, what a difficult process it is for lesbian and gay people to engage in doing that work, to be allowed to participate in a neighborhood or a community. I'm reminded of last year when we would sit and try to think about coalitions, and we would have conversations with different community organizers. Then we'd come back to the citywide meetings to plan the strategy and do the work; but the trouble was, the people were almost all white. The people who had the time and the energy to commit to the lesbian and gay issue were not people of color. Not because there's something especially homophobic about people of color, but we know how hard it is to do that work, and I almost feel like we need to suspend time in order to do it—because of the urgency of our other issues and the lack of resources. It takes effort away from your other priorities, okay? And sometimes people of color will say, "Well, you know, I need to take that issue of, say, homophobia, and put it over here right now, because I got to eat. I got a houseful of kids here. You know? And this is not an issue I got to deal with right now, okay? That's not a major issue for me, okay? What *is* a major issue is whether or not I got some Fruit Loops tomorrow morning and some milk to go with it, okay?

————All struggles are separate at the moment. The economic struggle, the struggle for quality education, the multicultural struggle, the struggle against homophobia, the struggle against child abuse. We need to put it all together, because we are potential allies. The thing is to get into the community, find out who your ally is, link up the struggle against homophobia to other struggles— like working to protect children in general, providing a safe environment for all children, a place where they can feel empowered.

————In terms of bringing people in, we also have to think about how you package whatever it is you're trying to sell. The perception exists that gay equals white men; so when you start talking about "gay" in a community of color, that's the "enemy." People are not going to automatically see the connection between homophobia and racism. For instance, if you're talking about an antiviolence committee for youth and you start by talking about antigay violence, Latinos and Blacks in particular probably are not going to go for that— because the perception is that kids are getting shot in school not because they're gay but because they happen to be in the wrong place at the wrong time, having nothing to do with their sexual orientation. So we need to be careful about how we present things.

————We can learn from the eras that have come before. We can learn that we need to be rooted in our own groups, and that we need somehow to link those groups. And we need to have patience with people, to let people feel able to say the things they're afraid to say. That way, we can move from what we're afraid of to where we want to be.

————One of the reasons why the Religious Right is able to make alliances with people and call it community, against what they perceive as the white gay and lesbian monolith, is because a lot of us white progressives did not do our homework. We supported the Children of the Rainbow Curriculum but a lot of us hadn't listened well to what was going on within our neighborhoods and what their concerns were. We really didn't make those alliances. More is involved than just finding allies around our issues, in this case the Children of the Rainbow issue. We need to be there on a regular basis, not disappear when issues around homophobia aren't directly on the table—be seen as regular activists listening to these communities, having more of an understanding of what's going on in these communities. Then it will be harder for demagogic organizations like the Christian Coalition to be able to paint our movement with such a broad brush.

————I think one of the successes of the Religious Right is that they have a set of universal values, religious tradition, and they appeal to those values regardless of race or culture or ethnicity or gender. And there are a lot of folks in this country who respond to that.

It sounds, on the one hand, like we are deeply committed to identity politics. And so we ask questions like, "What would a white lesbian or gay activist have to say to kids of color?" Yet on the other hand, we also all see the limits of identity politics. I think we're deeply conflicted, and I think this has profound practical implications. If we can't get this straight, we'll go nowhere. In 1990 I spent time in South Africa, and I talked to lesbian and gay activists and they said, "Look, the racial struggle is the primary struggle, and so we put our agenda on hold."

Now, I'm not saying that's great, and it certainly is very complicated, but I was so impressed by that degree of self-sacrifice and humility—to be able to say, "Here's the major problem, African American youth are being killed in this city, so as a white, gay man, I'll put my agenda on hold." How refreshing that would be if we could do that only once.

————I think what the right has is a false universalism. It's a universalism about anyone already in the tent, with everyone else scapegoated. The politics of identity are not about affirming a set of universal principles, but rather affirming human differences.

Using the example of school violence in discussing how we can create coalitions, I would try to get potential heterosexual allies to understand that my gay students all live in terror. And part of the reason gay students are scapegoated is that they're perceived as being weak. Most of the students in the school where I teach are kids who are filled with rage, anger and confusion, and they displace all that rage onto the gay students. We need to find a way of taking their rage, their anger, their frustration and addressing it to the real enemy, who, in my opinion, is the class enemy. Then, you know, things might be different.

B. Aging

46

Adult Development and Mental Health in Lesbians and Gay Men: Is Middle Age Necessary?

Robert M. Kertzner

A large number of self-identified lesbians and gay men who "came of age" during the inception of the modern gay rights movement are entering mid-adulthood. Little, however, is known about normative development and psychological well-being in these men and women who, like their heterosexual counterparts, may be experiencing important changes in their intimate relationships, work and family lives, sexuality, and physical health. Several markers that have been described as sine qua non of middle age—marriage, the maturation and emancipation of children, and the increasing awareness of personal mortality[1,2]—require modification in the lives of lesbians and gay men. Moreover, the classic notion of a midlife crisis that presents, for the first time, a serious challenge to personal identity does not pertain to the lives of many lesbians and gay men who have already undergone the transformation of coming out. As a result of these differences and others to be discussed, lesbians and gay men may sense less conventional change in their lives from youth to old age and may therefore want to consider the question: Is middle age necessary in gay lives?

Based on a cross-indexed literature review of "gay," "lesbian," "adult development," "midlife," and "mental health," the answer might appear to be no. Relatively little has been written about gay midlife compared to the more substantial literature on psychological change in younger and older lesbians and gay men. This is particularly true of psychological development in gay men (with a few notable exceptions);[3,4] in contrast, midlife development in lesbians has been explored more often.[5,6,7] Pioneering studies of psychological adjustment in older lesbians and gay men, while including middle-aged respondents, do not typically address midlife transitions as separate phenomena from the more general aging process.[8, 9] Moreover, because many of these studies predate the impact of HIV or do not specifically assess AIDS, their findings could not consider the effects of high rates of premature mortality on adult development.

Despite these limitations, an understanding of normative midlife development in lesbians and gay men is important because it provides a context in which to understand the impact of the HIV epidemic and, more generally, the psychosocial significance of maintaining a homosexual identity throughout the life span. For practitioners concerned with lesbian and gay mental health, an appreciation of age-related psychological adaptation provides a backdrop against which to evaluate and treat clinical problems.

Although much has been written about adult development in the general population, it is likely that adult development in lesbians and gay men differs significantly from that of heterosexuals, given the different social configuration of lesbian and gay lives, the lifelong psychological effects of stigmatization related to sexual orientation, and the profound effects of AIDS on life expectancy, and, more generally, life expectations. The extent to which gay adult development differs from heterosexual patterns, however, is not clear because of the lack of studies comparing gay and heterosexual middle age and the paucity of information about normative homosexual development beyond coming out. As Harry has written, "Coming out has little to say to adults and life seems to end at about age twenty-five with the rest of the lifespan left unanalyzed and unexplained."[10]

There are several reasons why little is known about gay adulthood and middle age. First, midlife is a relatively ambiguous stage of the life span without the clear biological markers that characterize childhood, adolescence, and late life.[11] Second, in the already heterogeneous setting of gay lives where gender, race, class, education, and residence impart distinctive features to psychological health, descriptions of gay midlife may pertain only to subpopulations of lesbians and gay men upon whom observations are based, typically cohorts of well-educated and primarily white urban residents. Third, historical and age cohorts effects limit generalizations that can be made about adult development; the current generation of middle-aged lesbians and gay men, for instance, has been uniquely influenced by Stonewall and the ascendance of AIDS. Finally, other developmental tasks such as coming out or living with HIV seem more urgent than midlife transitions and, understandably, have received more attention.

Paradoxically, both coming out and adapting to HIV are affected by prevalent if unrealized assumptions about gay midlife and aging. Implicit in the challenge to come out is the task of maintaining a homosexual identity throughout adulthood. Most young lesbians and gay men, however, lack information about gay aging, hold negative stereotypes about older gays, and have little sense of homosexual lives that are not rooted in youthful self-discovery; as Charles Kaiser writes, "Modern gay culture is only 23 years old. We still have grave problems in self-esteem, and many of us remain terrified of growing older." [12] The inability to envision a personal future may be associated with increased sexual risk behaviors for HIV transmission. [13] The relative lack of intergenerational families and social institutions in the gay community that provide contact between the young and old increases misperceptions about aging and may increase the isolation felt by older lesbians and gay men. [14]

Several studies of psychological health in older lesbians and gay men, however, contradict negative perceptions of aging; these studies describe a composite picture of psychological well-being, high levels of overall life satisfaction, and satisfaction with sexuality. [15,16,17] While it is true that these studies are subject to the possible biasing effect of better-adjusted lesbians and gay men being more likely to volunteer for research, these reports do nonetheless challenge prevailing stereotypes of poor psychological adaptation to aging in older gays. Unfortunately, few studies are based on large numbers of respondents or compare mental health findings in lesbians and gay men to the general population, thus further limiting their interpretation. In addition, no large-scale, systematic study of the general adult population has specifically inquired about sexual orientation, hence, the epidemiology of mental health in midlife and older lesbians and gay men is unknown.

Within populations of lesbians and gay men, certain mental health problems may be age-related. General mental health concerns and specific worries about illness and excessive responsibility are greater for middle-aged lesbians compared to younger lesbians, but long-term depression and anxiety are reported less frequently in older women. [18] Weinberg and Williams found no differences in depression, anxiety, or loneliness in a comparison of gay men over or under forty-five years of age; older men, in fact, reported less worry about disclosure of their sexual identity and were characterized as having more stable self-concepts. [19] Williams and her colleagues found high lifetime but not current rates of psychiatric disorder (primarily mood and substance abuse disorders) in a cohort of gay men, suggesting that early adulthood may be a time of increased emotional turmoil. [20] This interpretation would be consistent with the frequent occurrence of psychological distress associated with coming out, which usually occurs in adolescence or early adulthood.

Beyond the process of coming out, less is known about adult milestones in the lives of lesbians and gay men in which sexual orientation plays a prominent or specific role in shaping psychological adjustment. In first considering the sociodemographic markers of middle-aged Americans, we find that normative events may assume particular significance in the lives of lesbians and gay men. Most Americans between the age of thirty and sixty-five, for example, will lose one or both parents or will find themselves adjusting to their parents' aging and decline; [21] in the context of gay lives, these events may have particular significance. Deterioration in a parent's health, for example, may preclude the possibility of a long-deferred disclosure of a son's or daughter's sexual identity and the hope of a more open relationship with a parent before death.

Midlife adults also come to terms with a loss of their own youthfulness, a potent realization that can either provoke psychological distress or personal growth. Gay men may face particular difficulties with this loss, given the emphasis placed on youthful desirability in social and sexual interactions. Gagnon described a crisis experienced by gay men in their late thirties prompted by the awareness of growing older and the expectation of receiving fewer sexual and social rewards from other gays;[22] in harshest terms, some older men who participate in gay male sexual culture may be treated like "scraps of refuse."[23]

Of course, midlife heterosexuals also undergo changes in self-perception and reappraisals of social identity and the likelihood of social rewards. Traditional models of adult development, in fact, are based on these shifts of perception, albeit as experienced by heterosexual populations. Levenson, for example, found that his male respondents experienced middle age as a time during which personal limitations were realized and possibilities reassessed.[24] Middle-aged men and women studied by Neugarten became more inwardly focused, gradually distancing themselves, psychologically but not socially, from their environments.[25] Writing in a more theoretical vein, Jung described the task of midlife as accepting diminished capacity and increasing loss,[26] while Erikson emphasized how loss could be transformed through the cultivation of relationships that transmit personal experience, knowledge, and, hopefully, wisdom to younger generations; he called this process "generativity."[27]

Erikson believed that "generativity" was the hallmark of middle age in the lives of the presumably heterosexual men and women he studied. Despite the centrality of this concept, the relevance and expression of "generativity" in the lives of lesbians and gay men are unclear and warrant study. But a larger uncertainty is at hand: what is the broader applicability of traditional theories of adult development to lesbian and gay lives, given the generic limitations of these models and the specific dynamics of homosexual identity that create important variations in adult development? Lesbians and gay men establish an identity based on a minority and stigmatized sexual orientation; reconfigure traditional families and marriages; approach work with different considerations; and, particularly in HIV epicenters, question the assumption of good health that will last throughout middle age. Furthermore, even in the general population, not all individuals progress in the same developmental sequence, and unexpected factors skew individual development, for example, transitions occurring out of normal developmental sequence such as early "widowhood" and changes in role that are poorly mediated by culture.[28]

The formation of homosexual identity is the most striking and obvious departure from adult development in the general population and has several implications for midlife psychological health. The archetypal coming out process that occurs in late adolescence or early adulthood may constitute the most significant crisis in personal and social identity experienced by lesbians and gay men, more so than age-related changes in identity.[29,30] Coming out often results in lifelong patterns of psychological adaptation; lesbians and gay men, for example, may develop a "crises competence" and cultivate alternate sources of social support in response to real or imagined family rejection.

Acceptance of homosexual identity may never be fully resolved throughout the life span, depending on individual factors and the specific social context in which lesbians and gay men live. To the extent that stigmatization or discrimination are prevalent, optimal adult development is deflected if not precluded.[31] Indeed, the experience of stigmatization and discrimination may overlay the spectrum of adult development for most gay men and lesbians.[32] Whether one is able to participate openly in gay community life, teach younger generations, or adopt children is subject to the vagaries of law and social tolerance. Social oppression thus raises a critical question in gay midlife development: how can an aging person's acceptance of "loss" be considered normative if opportunities for self-acceptance and self-expression have never been fully permitted?

Perhaps resilience and adaptability, and changes in their expression across the life span, are more useful concepts in considering adult development in lesbians and gay men.[33] Indeed, mental health in lesbians and gay men may be strongly linked to a psychological resourcefulness necessary to overcome stigmatization and, more generally, to foster self-reliance, independence of thought, and the cultivation of supportive friends, families, and communities.[34, 35, 36] From this perspective, the overriding developmental task of gay adulthood may be to maintain a positive sense of self in "an assumptive world that negates their [lesbians' and gay men's] existence, and which directly or indirectly rewards their invisibility and punishes healthy disclosure."[37]

Lesbians and gay men, of course, are not just characterized by sexual orientation, and the integration and cultivation of other aspects of identity ideally proceed throughout adulthood. There may be important links between the tasks of general adult development, on the one hand, and homosexual identity formation and maintenance on the other, but how these developmental lines intertwine is not well established either in theory or in practice. The literature on homosexual identity formation and maintenance is not strongly linked to the main body of psychological theory concerned with adult development.[38] Conceivably, both developmental lines may reciprocally influence each other.

The consolidation of sexual identity for lesbians and gay men, for example, may occur ten to fourteen years after the first awareness of same-sex attraction.[39] The implications of this delay for subsequent adult development are unclear; arguably, the earlier lesbians and gay men are able to integrate their sexual orientation in young adulthood, the sooner and more completely other developmental tasks can proceed. Fear of intimacy in gay men, for example, is associated with greater difficulty in self-acceptance of homosexual identity.[40] As an example of more generic changes during adulthood reciprocally affecting gay identity, lesbians and gay men who came out as young adults may find themselves less concerned about social opinion and the disclosure of their sexual identity as they enter middle age; this change may reflect an increased sense of personal autonomy and environmental mastery associated with the passage from young adulthood to middle age, as has been found in the general population.[41]

Among the differences characterizing lesbian and gay lives that limit the applicability of traditional models of adult development, we must consider the social context of homosexuality. The lack of legal recognition of gay relationships, the absence of "built-in" intergenerational family ties, and the need for alternative sources of social support prompted by social stigmatization or rejection may lead to novel constructions of intimate relationships and families.[42,43] Lesbian and gay relationships, for example, may resemble traditional heterosexual marriages or be characterized by a greater tolerance of outside intimacy or involvement with ex-partners. Single status in middle age may have a different meaning in the context of heterosexual and homosexual lives, particularly in men. For instance, whereas single adult heterosexual men have higher rates of depression and mortality than their married counterparts,[44] single status, per se, in gay men does not necessarily imply psychological disadvantage.[45] This is not to say that midlife and older lesbians and gay men prefer to be single, but some may feel a greater need to be coupled in young adulthood during which time the establishment of relationships may be part of a larger exploration of homosexual identity.[46]

Although some middle-aged lesbians and gay men are parents either by biology, adoption, or other circumstance, most lesbians and gay men do not have children and thus expressions of "generativity," when present, may take other forms such as teaching, community activism, or establishing real or fictive kinships with children.[47] In addition, midlife lesbians and gay men may come to regard friendships as a particularly important source of pleasure and meaning in their lives; these friendships provide opportunities for mutual support and are sometimes referred to as families.

The career transitions of some midlife lesbians and gay men are also characterized by important differences from heterosexual patterns. Vaillant described a stage of "career consolidation" occurring in men's and women's late twenties or early thirties, after young adults achieve some proficiency in the developmental tasks of intimacy.[48] This sequence, however, may not apply to lesbians and gay men who either develop strong work identities before establishing intimate relationships, particularly if coming out is delayed, or experience a sense of "career consolidation" later in life when more basic questions of homosexual identity have been more fully addressed. In addition, the anticipation of ongoing rewards from work may have heightened significance for lesbians and gay men without other traditional sources of personal definition such as family or marriage; Harry found that attachment to work, for example, significantly mitigates concerns about growing older in gay men.[49]

AIDS has had a profound impact on the adult development of many midlife lesbians and gay men, particularly those residing in large urban areas. Cumulative mortality from AIDS has resulted in an inestimable loss of past, present, and potential lovers, friends, co-parents, protégés, and mentors. Important intergenerational links have been lost and opportunities for the realization of intimacy and "generativity" thereby diminished. HIV may delay normal development in young adulthood by confounding exploration with self-endangerment.[50] Perhaps the effects of HIV on adult development are most striking in HIV-infected gay men who simultaneously undertake developmental tasks usually resolved over the span of many years: consolidating personal identity, developing intimacies, cultivating the resources to provide for others, and preparing for the eventuality of death. Because of the ubiquity of premature mortality in AIDS epicenters, some HIV-infected as well as uninfected gay men have come to resemble geriatrics populations in sharing an orientation toward life typically associated with old age.[51]

With the above considerations in mind, we may focus on certain psychological difficulties that lesbians and gay men may have adapting to middle age and, more generally, the aging process. As described above, midlife is likely to pose several challenges to lesbians and gay men: accepting limitations inherent in having less time left in life, adjusting to the retreat of youthfulness and the emergence of physical changes associated with aging, and reconsidering the balance between work and personal life. For many gay men, the real or potential impact of AIDS heightens the immediacy of these concerns and foreshortens time remaining in life for engagement of these tasks.

With the increasing awareness of the finiteness of time, middle-aged adults frequently reevaluate life choices, and this process may result in significant psychological distress, particularly if certain choices have become impractical or impossible. In the lives of lesbians and gay men, the developmental lag attributable to overcoming a stigmatized sexual identity may result in a delayed readiness to develop careers or to establish relationships or families, yet opportunities to do so may be markedly diminished as individuals get older.

Sarah is a forty-three-year-old woman who describes a mixture of positive and negative appraisals of her life since turning forty. She is an underemployed artist working in another field and is apprehensive about her continuing ability to earn enough money to support her modest lifestyle; with a sense of resignation, she sees younger artists seizing the momentum of youth and establishing their reputations. Sarah regards her greatest accomplishment in life as "reworking" herself, by which she means overcoming long-standing critical feelings and difficulties accepting her lesbianism. She recently moved into a larger city, which has helped her struggle for self-acceptance, including her homosexuality; she says being gay has "quietly assumed a more comfortable position" in her life and she is less concerned about the opinions of others. As a single lesbian with estranged family relationships, she worries about being alone and whom she can depend on if she develops serious health or financial problems. Sarah currently considers herself to be depressed, a recurrent problem she has had since early adulthood. She regards her future with trepidation, feeling poised between hopefulness and "the old depressive me"; she wants to build her own family even if that entails a "parakeet and dog." Although she would like to be in a relationship, she expresses doubt about whether or not this is possible, given her perceptions of the insularity of lesbian relationships, which she finds intolerable.

All midlife adults experience narcissistic injuries associated with aging, such as the loss of youthful appearance and decreased physical stamina. When earlier problems in self-esteem have not been resolved, midlife reappraisal of self-image may add psychological insult to injury. In the context of gay men's lives, for example, early life experience of stigmatization and rejection may be rekindled by norms of gay culture that exalt youthfulness. To the extent that the ideal of youthfulness preserves reparative fantasies, individuals may experience aging as a revisitation of earlier feelings of exclusion. Gay men who are concerned about decreased success in attracting significantly younger sexual partners may, for example, perceive a diminution in meaningful attachments for the remainder of their lives, and this may create significant psychological distress as well as a sense of premature aging.[52, 53] Gay men entering middle age may also recognize a decreased ability or desire to compete with younger adults, and this may, in addition, precipitate feelings of inadequacy dating back to childhood and adolescence.

Frank is a forty-nine-year-old gay man who viewed his imminent fiftieth birthday with dread. Over recent months, he became increasingly agitated, thinking about all that he had not accomplished in his life; he was increasingly concerned about self-destructive behaviors, such as using recreational drugs despite occasional chest pain. His father had recently suffered a stroke; he felt unappreciated at work; and he felt increasingly envious of younger men's greater physical stamina and desirability. Frank felt turning fifty symbolized his personal obsolescence, and this enraged him. Despite these concerns, he was in a loving relationship and maintained close friendships. He felt guilty about being unhappy, citing his HIV-negative status, the love of his partner, and an ever-present awareness of life's calamities, such as AIDS, the cause of his ex-lover's death.

Work-related concerns may figure prominently in the mental health of midlife lesbians and gay men. Although lesbians are more likely to be employed in professional, technical, managerial, or administrative roles compared to all working women, gay women do not receive commensurate income; not surprisingly, they are five times as likely as other women their age to have money problems.[54] Many lesbians at all stages of the life cycle, including midlife, express worries about personal finances.

Some lesbians as well as gay men working in institutional or business settings resist greater identities as "company women" or "company men" as they ascend work hierarchies. For women and men who are "out" this may be based on an appraisal that career advancement beyond a certain stage may be unlikely because of their being different, not "one of the boys." Other lesbians and gay men with advanced degrees from colleges and universities may not promote themselves at work or may hold themselves back from advancement, fearing an exposure of their homosexuality. As such, a "lavender ceiling" may be just as much self-imposed as it is a reality of discrimination in the workplace.[55] Midlife lesbians and gay men may most resemble each other in work and career issues, including appraisals of discrimination, competition, self-employment, and the meaning of retirement.[56]

As the likelihood of engaging the health care system increases with age, lesbians and gay men may have concerns about discriminatory treatment by health care providers and institutions, including retirement facilities, and worries about who will take care of them if they become sick.[57,58] The most significant health issues for midlife lesbians and bisexual women, similar to younger and older lesbians, continue to result from invisibility, ignorance of medical professionals about lesbian health concerns, and lack of access to health care. Middle-aged lesbians have particular concerns about gynecological health, but many experience difficulties getting adequate health care because of their anticipation of, or experience with, insensitive or discriminatory treatment.[59]

In AIDS epicenters, the HIV epidemic has thrown into question the presumption of good health and, more pointedly, has challenged the assumption that one will be alive at forty.[60] HIV-infected gay men have been thrust into the roles of professional patient and political activist as they navigate the miasma of antiviral treatments. For many gay men, AIDS has decimated friendship networks and severed incipient and long-term relationships; this loss is compounded by the greater difficulty midlife and older gay men may experience in establishing friendships and relationships in middle age compared to young adulthood.[61] Moreover, some HIV-negative gay men, fearful of infection or emotional demands, are reluctant to enter into relationships with HIV-infected gay men despite the resultant decrease in the number of eligible partners.[62]

For some midlife gay men, staying alive or remaining uninfected are more immediate concerns than adjusting to middle or old age. As Michael Callen wrote, "I find myself studying the wizened or bloated naked bodies of Yiddish-chattering old men at my gym. I'm embarrassed to admit that I actually experience envy that they've lived so long. I've now developed a very clear image of what I would have looked like as an old man. It makes me smile to think of what a great old man I'd have made—cantankerous, opinionated, frisky."[63]

HIV has also increased the prevalence of couples who find themselves at disparate stages of adult development, as is typified by individuals in HIV serodiscordant relationships. Not infrequently an HIV-uninfected partner in his thirties or forties is engaged in building a life, while his HIV-infected partner is adapting to an uncertain future.

Peter is an HIV-positive designer who has been experiencing recent problems with his HIV-negative partner of four years, Ralph. Both men are presently in their early forties. With increasing health problems, Peter decided to leave his job with a firm, despite the momentum of a successful career. Ralph, a hardworking professional who has entered a time in his life of maximal career advancement, believes that all problems can and should be fixed. Ralph has difficulties with Peter's nonaggressive approach to seeking medical care; Peter feels the main problem in their relationship is Ralph's inability to tolerate the inevitable times when he is not feeling well. Peter dreads the prospect of becoming dependent on Ralph and the burdens his illness will impose on the relationship.

As a final example of problems encountered in middle age, lesbians and gay men who come out later in life often bring to midlife particular concerns related to the integration of their sexual identity with established identities such as parent, spouse, worker, or neighbor. Coming out as a middle-aged person may result in considerable anger and regret about missed opportunities in early adulthood, and this may impede other developmental tasks of midlife that are based on a gradual acceptance of limitations inherent in having less time left in life. Since the sexual identity of gay men compared to lesbians is less likely to emerge in the context of an emotionally intimate relationship and the implied emotional support of such bonds,[64] gay men who are first coming out in midlife may be at increased risk for psychological distress. In contrast, many midlife women experience their emergent lesbianism in the context of increasing personal independence or a strong commitment to feminism,[65] two factors that might enhance psychological adjustment to coming out in middle age.

Although I have focused on age-related influences on lesbian and gay psychological health, other factors strongly determine individual adult development in midlife. From a traditional mental health perspective, temperament, personality, constitutional factors, and previous psychiatric disorder all shape adult mental health as illustrated in the above cases. Furthermore, gender accounts for significant differences in adult development;[66] these differences persist between lesbians and gay men, although their expression is altered. Concerns about premature aging and decreased physical desirability, for instance, are more pronounced in gay men than lesbians, lesbians may be more likely than gay men to express "generativity" across the life span, reflecting the greater importance of relationships to personal identity in women.[67] Although a discussion of the broader effects of race, class, and education is beyond the scope of this essay, these factors significantly interact with other determinants of lesbians' and gay men's mental health and create separate pathways of adult development.[68] Prior education and work opportunities may provide particularly important advantages as lesbians and gay men gradually experience limitations associated with increasing age and less time remaining in life.

With these caveats in mind, midlife is arguably a time of maximal opportunities for some lesbians and gay men and, in this sense, homosexual adult development may depart from more classic descriptions of midlife in heterosexuals. Without the developmental "head start" of a conventional sexual orientation or the social facilitation of a gay identity, the developmental task of young adulthood may be to consolidate homosexual identity and to explore individual sexuality. Some lesbians and gay men thus enter midlife with a sense of having resolved basic questions of self-identity and feel ready to undertake, or catch up with, more expansive pursuits such as creating homes, kinships, and communities; maximizing fulfillment or focus in work, or, in the words of Michael Callen, "thriving *and* surviving HIV" (italics added).[69] In these ways, adult development may take an accelerated course during middle age, with the thirties or forties described as the best years of one's life.[70]

Conversely, continuing difficulty resolving homosexual identity or the lack of opportunity to do so may thwart psychological change throughout adulthood. Self-acceptance permits the engagement of other development tasks that, in turn, provide a base from which lesbians and gay men negotiate the relinquishments of middle age; without self-acceptance, there may be little "give" and thus little resilience. Moreover, certain realities of gay life, such as the lack of extended families, the emphasis on youth in the sexual culture of gay men, the financial constraints experienced by many lesbians, and the cumulative losses due to AIDS and other illness, may become more pronounced in middle age. For some lesbians and gay men, middle age may be a matter of survival, not of development, and may sorely test the notion of resilience described above.

Yet resilience may become increasingly important as lesbians and gay men face the opportunities and hazards of midlife. Further exploration of midlife will reveal how being homosexual and middle-aged optimally proceed together, to maximize psychological adaptation and health. Ideally, psychological adjustment will be enhanced by medical advances against HIV and the continuing evolution of social tolerance and legal rights, such as the recognition of domestic partnerships, parenting rights, and homosexual marriage, and the adoption of antidiscrimination measures. In a world of greater possibility, homosexual middle age represents a widening of developmental pathways undertaken by lesbians and gay men who, hopefully, bring to adulthood less encumbered homosexual identities. Perhaps more than a concept of necessity, homosexual middle age signifies the possibility of better beginnings and better endings for lesbian and gay lives.

References

1. Fowlkes MR: Single worlds and homosexual lifestyles: Patterns of sexuality and intimacy, in *Sexuality across the Life Course.* Edited by Rossi A. Chicago: University of Chicago Press, 1994, 151–84.

2. Nemiroff RA, Colarusso CA: Frontiers of adult development in theory and practice, in *New Dimensions in Adult Development.* Edited by Nemiroff RA, Colarusso CA. New York: Basic Books, 1990, 97–124.

3. Cornett CW, Hudson RA: Middle adulthood and the theories of Erikson, Gould, and Valliant: Where does the gay man fit in? *J Gerontological Social Work* 10 (3–4): 61–73, 1987.

4. Kimmel DC, Sang BE: Lesbians and gay men in midlife, *Lesbian, Gay, and Bisexual Identities over the Lifespan: Psychological Perspectives.* Edited by D'Augelli AR, Patterson CJ. New York: Oxford University Press, 1995.

5. Sang B: Moving toward balance and integration, in *Lesbians at Mid-life: The Creative Transition.* Edited by Sang B, Warshow J, Smith AJ. San Francisco: Spinster Books, 1991: 206–14.

6. Tully CT. Caregiving: What do midlife lesbians view as important? *J Gay and Lesbian Psychotherapy* 1 (1): 87–103, 1989.

7. Kirkpatrick M: Lesbians: A different middle age? in *New Psychoanalytic Perspectives. The Middle Years.* Edited by Oldham J, Liebert R. New Haven: Yale University Press, 1989, 135–48.

8. Berger RM: *Gay and Gray: The Older Homosexual Man.* Urbana-Champaign: University of Illinois Press, 1982.

9. Adelman M: Stigma, gay lifestyles, and adjustments to aging: A study of later-life gay men and lesbians, in *Gay Midlife and Maturity,* Edited by Lee JA. Binghamton, NY: Harrington Park, 1991.

10. Harry J: *Gay Children Grown Up.* New York: Praeger, 1982, 38.

11. Colarusso CA, Nemiroff RA: *Adult Development: A New Dimension in Psychoanalytic Theory and Practice.* New York: Plenum, 1981, 83–104.

12. Kaiser, Charles: Tempting the virus. *QW* magazine 52 (1): 23–26, 1992.

13. Frutchey C, Blankenstein W, Stall R: Ability to envision a future predicts safe sex among gay men, Poster presented at the Ninth International Conference on AIDS, Berlin PO-D06-3835, 1993.

14. Kimmel DC: Adult development and aging: A gay perspective. *J Social Issues* 34 (3): 113–30, 1978.

15. Berger, *op. cit.*

16. Pope M, Schulz R: Sexual attitudes and behavior in midlife and aging homosexual males, in *Gay Midlife and Maturity.* Edited by Lee, op. cit.

17. Quam JK, Whitford GS: Adaptation and age-related expectations of older gay and lesbian adults. *Gerontologist* 32 (3): 367–74, 1992.

18. Bradford J, Ryan C: Who we are: Health concerns of middle-aged lesbians, in *Lesbians at Mid-life.* Edited by Sang, B Warshow, J Smith, op. cit., 147–63.

19. Weinberg MS, Williams CJ: *Male Homosexuals: Their Problems and Adaptations.* New York: Penguin, 1975.

20. Williams JBW, Rabkin JG, Remien RH, Gorman JM, and Ehrhardt AA: Multidisciplinary baseline assessment of homosexual men with and without human immunodeficiency virus infection: II. Standardized clinical assessment current and lifetime psychopathology. *Archives of General Psychiatry* 48:124–30, 1991.

21. Bumpass LL, Aquilino WS: A social map of midlife: Family and work over the middle life course. Document published by the MacArthur Foundation Research Network on Successful Midlife Development, Vero Beach, Florida. March 1995.

22. Gagnon J, Simon W: *Sexual Conduct.* Chicago: Aldine, 1973, 149.

23. G. Rotello: Let's talk about sex. *Advocate,* 687–688: 120, 1995. Rotello describes a focus group discussion among gay men about sex and sexual culture.

24. Levenson DJ: *The Seasons of a Man's Life.* New York: Knopf, 1978.

25. Neugarten BL: The awareness of middle age, in *Middle Age and Aging.* Edited by Neugarten BL. Chicago: University of Chicago Press, 1968, 93–98.

26. Jung CG: *Modern Man in Search of a Soul.* New York: Harcourt, Brace and World, 1933.

27. Erikson EH: *Dimensions of a New Identity;* Jefferson Lectures. New York: Norton, 1973. Erikson wrote, "in youth you find out what you care to do and who you care to be—even in changing roles. In young adulthood you learn whom you care to be with—at work and in private life, not only exchanging intimacies but sharing intimacy. In adulthood, however, you learn to know what and whom you can take care of" (124).

28. Vaillant GE: The ego and adult development, in *The Wisdom of the Ego:* Cambridge: Harvard University Press, 1993, 141–74.

29. Kimmel, *op. cit.*

30. Hopcke RH: Midlife, gay men, and the AIDS epidemic. *Quadrant* 35 (1): 101–9, 1992.

31. Erikson EH: *Identity and the life cycle. Psychological Issues* 1 (1): 50–100, 1959; in discussing the effects of social intolerance on minorities, Erikson wrote of the "sad truth that in any system based on suppression, exclusion, and exploitation, the suppressed, excluded, and exploited unconsciously believe in the evil image which they are made to represent by those who are dominant."

32. Cohen CJ, Stein TS: Reconceptualizing individual psychotherapy with gay men and lesbians, in *Contemporary Perspectives on Psychotherapy with Lesbians and Gay Men.* (New York: Plenum Medical, 1986, 37.

33. Vaillant GE: Disadvantage, resilience, and mature defenses, in *The Wisdom of the Ego,* 284–325. In a discussion of the effects of social disadvantage on inner-city men who participated in a longitudinal study of adult development, George Vaillant argues that resilience is a critical factor distinguishing those men who successfully adapt to hardship. This concept might usefully be applied to lesbians and gay men, a stigmatized sexual minority. Erikson E: *Childhood and Society,* New York: Norton, 1950. Erikson describes ego integrity as "the acceptance of one's one and only life cycle as something that had to be and that, by necessity, permitted of no substitutions," 269.

34. Friedman R: *Male Homosexuality. A Contemporary Psychoanalytic Perspective.* New Haven: Yale University Press, 1988.

35. Bradford J, Ryan C, Rothblum ED: National lesbian health care survey: Implications for mental health care. *J Consulting and Clinical Psychology* 6 (2): 228–42, 1994.

36. Kertzner RM: Psychological adaptation in midlife lesbians and gay men. Poster presented at the American Psychological Association annual meeting, New York, 1995. Seventeen lesbians and gay men between forty and fifty five participated in a study of psychological adaptation to midlife, subjects who scored highest on an Eriksonian measure of adult development also conveyed greater independence of thought about their lives and a positive appraisal of the difficulties they experienced, often related to coming out.

37. Brooks WK: Research and the gay minority: Problems and possibilities, in *Lesbians and Gay Lifestyles.* Edited by Woodman NJ. New York: Irvinton, 1992, 211.

38. Gonsiorek JC, Rudolph JR: Homosexual identity: Coming out and other developmental events, in *Homosexuality: Research Implications for Public Policy,* Edited by Gonsoriek JC, Weinrich JD. Newbury Park, CA: Sage, 1991.

39. Coleman E: Developmental stages of the coming out process, in *Homosexuality and Psychotherapy: A Practitioner's Handbook of Affirmative Models.* Edited by Gonsiorek JC. New York: Haworth, 1985.

40. Frederick RJ, Gibbs MS: Fear of intimacy in gay men. Poster presented at the annual meeting of the American Psychological Association, New York, 1995.

41. Ryff CD: Happiness is everything, or is it? Explorations on the meaning of psychological well-being. *J Personality and Social Psychology* 57 (6): 1069–81, 1989.

42. McWhirter DP, Mattison AM: *The Male Couple: How Relationships Develop.* Englewood Cliffs, NJ: Prentice Hall, 1984.

43. Weston K: *Families We Choose.* New York: Columbia University Press, 1993.

44. Fowlkes, *op. cit.*

45. Bell AP, Weinberg MS: *Homosexualities: A Study of Diversity among Men and Women.* New York: Simon and Schuster, 1978.

46. Coleman, *op. cit.*

47. Kevin Farrell, The psychosocial adaptations of middle-aged gay men to being childless. Master's thesis, California State University, Long Beach, December 1992.

48. Vaillant, Ego and adult development, *op. cit.*

49. Harry, *op. cit.*

50. Isay RA: *Being Homosexual: Gay Men and Their Development.* New York: Farrar, Straus, and Giroux, 1989.

51. In his doctoral dissertation at Teachers' College, Mark Thomas assessed the Eriksonian psychosocial stages of generativity and integrity in a cohort of HIV-positive and HIV-negative gay men. He found that mean levels of generativity and integrity were high in both HIV-positive and HIV-negative men and did not significantly differ, these means were also comparable to generativity and integrity scores found in a geriatrics population.

52. Harry, *op. cit.*

53. Friend RA: The individual and social psychology of aging: Clinical implications for lesbians and gay men. *J Homosexuality* 14 (1–2): 307–31, 1987.

54. Bradford, Ryan, Rothblum, *op. cit.*

55. Horn M: Making your life your life's work. *Metrosource,* autumn–winter 1994, 52.

56. Kimmel and Sang, *op. cit.*

57. Bradford and Ryan, *op. cit.*

58. Quam and Whitford, *op. cit.*

59. Bradford and Ryan, *op. cit.*

60. Odets W: AIDS education and harm reduction for gay men: Psychological approaches for the 21st century. *AIDS Public Policy Journal* 9 (1): 1–18, 1994.

61. Kertzner, *op. cit.*

62. Kertzner RM, Todak G, Goetz R, Rabkin JG, Ehrhardt AA: Living in a sero-possible world: Adaptations of HIV-negative gay men. Poster presented at the Second Annual Biopsychosocial Conference on AIDS, Brighton, England, 1994.

63. Callen M: Dinosaur's diary: In my time of dying. *QW,* August 30, 1992, 45.

64. de Monteflores C: Coming out: Similarities and differences for lesbians and gay men. *J Social Issues* 34 (3): 59–72, 1978.

65. Charbonneau C, Lander PS: Redefining sexuality: Women becoming lesbian in midlife, in *Lesbians at Mid-life.* Edited by Sang, Warshow, Smith, op. cit. 35–43

66. Gilligan C. *In a Different Voice: Psychological Theory and Women's Development.* Cambridge: Harvard University Press, 1982.

67. Neugarten, *op. cit.*

68. Gutierrez FJ, Dworkin SH: Gay, lesbian, and African American: Managing the integration of identities, in *Counseling Gay Men and Lesbians: Journey to the End of the Rainbow.* Edited by Dworkin SH, Gutierrez FJ. Alexandria, VA: Association for Counseling and Development, 1992, 141–56. The authors describe bicultural personality development, which incorporates both an Eriksonian model of adult development and model of minority identity development.

69. Callen M: *Surviving AIDS.* New York: HarperCollins, 1990.

70. Kertzner, *op. cit.* Several gay men in a study of midlife psychological adaptation describe their late thirties and early forties as the years of greatest personal fulfillment.

47

The Virtual and Actual Identities of Older Lesbians and Gay Men

Arnold H. Grossman

Today more than 13 percent of the U. S. population is over the age of sixty-five, as contrasted to approximately 4 percent in 1900. This older adult population continues to grow, and it has become a significant political force in American society. These aging Americans are remarkably diverse; they vary according to age (i.e., young old, old old, oldest old), gender, race, ethnicity, culture, socioeconomic status, level of education, and sexual orientation. Society tends to promote images of some aging individuals, while others remain invisible.

Being Invisible

To many members of the gay and lesbian world, as well as the heterosexual society, there are no gay and lesbian older adults. As Vacha states, "The stereotype is that older gay men [and women] don't exist, they burn out like a candle at both ends, they die, they vanish, kaput!" Those who are now older lesbians and gay men have spent most of their lives being invisible. Some chose to live such a lifestyle primarily because of self-hate and a low self-image, while others did so from fear of losing their families, friends, and jobs. This invisibility effectively keeps older lesbians and gay men isolated from each other and segregated in all aspects of life.[1]

Kehoe has described older lesbians as a "triply invisible minority," based on their age, gender, and sexual orientation. A similar invisibility can be attributed to older gay men based on their age and sexual orientation or, as Altman states, the common belief that all gay men are dying from AIDS. Healey describes the invisibility as follows:

> Now that we are sixty years old and beyond, the experience of ageism is the primary circumstance which colors the lives of most old lesbians *now*. To illustrate, my lover and I can walk down the street holding hands and affectionately kissing—without an eyebrow being lifted because *no one notices us—we have become invisible!* Actions which previously would cause reprisals are now ignored. If by chance we are noticed, it would not matter anyhow because all old women are presumed to be asexual! We certainly do not regret the lack of reprisals. What is devastating is that with age we have become non-persons.

Living "Virtual" Identities

As indicated above, many older lesbians and gay men spend much energy managing their identities in such a way as to remain invisible. They have come to believe that their identities are discreditable in a society that condones homophobic antilocutions, discrimination, and oppression by many of its citizens and institutions. Even though these older people have survived with their "virtual" social identities intact until now, they know that they might be discredited in the future. Goffman distinguished between "virtual" and "actual" social identities: the former are assumed and unchallenged and the latter are demonstrated and proven. These older lesbians and gay men tend to fall into the categories that Friend identifies as "stereotypical" or "passing" gay and lesbian people.

The older lesbians and gay men who are located on the end of the continuum that Friend describes as "stereotypical" tend to believe the negative images of gay and lesbian people that have been promulgated by a heterosexist society. They view their homosexuality as secretive and their aging as punishment for an immoral life, and they remain distanced from their families by fear, ignorance, and sometimes self-loathing. Therefore, they conceal their "actual" identity and present a "virtual" identity, which embodies heterosexuality, to the world.

Friend's second category of adaptational styles is the "passing" older lesbians and gay men, located in the middle of the continuum. These individuals tend to believe that some of the homophobic antilocutions of society are true and that heterosexuality is the superior sexual orientation. They tend to feel valued for what others expect them to be, rather than for who they really are; therefore, they tend to hide the stigma attached to their sexual orientation by using a "cover." They marry and have children, considering such actions their only chance for happiness. When they get older, they fear causing pain to those they love, and consequently tend to remain in the closet. They may have extramarital affairs with members of the same sex or seek anonymous sex in tearooms and parks, at truck stops or other known cruising areas.

The third adaptational style identified by Friend is the "affirmative" one, which is located on the opposite end of the continuum from the "stereotypical." The older lesbians and gay men who embrace this style affirm their homosexual identity by fighting heterosexism, challenging its assumptions, forming same-sex long-term relationships, and establishing close same-sex friendships. In these relationships, they often confront rigid gender role stereotypes, and some become politically involved, advocating civil rights for gay and lesbian people. These older lesbians and gay men reconstruct what being homosexual means to them, and they often use the experiences learned through the process to develop lifelong skills that have been found helpful in adapting to aging. These skills may also prove helpful in times of crises and may have proved helpful in fostering the courage and stamina necessary to fight the HIV/AIDS epidemic.

Myths and Stereotypical Attitudes

Despite the research of Friend and other scholars,[2] many gays and lesbians of all ages continue to believe in the myths of aging, as well as the stereotypical attitudes related to aging in the lesbian and gay world. Some stereotypes that are attributed to aging have been found to be due not to aging but rather to disease, personality, or socioeconomic status.

Myths of Aging

Many myths related to growing old are believed by most people in the United States, and they form the basis of verbal and behavioral actions that are frequently labeled "ageism." They include the beliefs that being old is unattractive and ugly, out of date, over the hill, past history, and valueless, and that old people are asexual, mentally incompetent, and physically diminished. The myths also portray all old people as the same: complaining, rigid, and unwilling to change. In addition, as Healey states, "Old age is still viewed in white North American culture as a 'condition' requiring professional treatment rather than a natural and valuable part of the life cycle."

Stereotypical Attitudes about Older Gays and Lesbians

The most prominent stereotypes depict older lesbians and gay men as socially isolated and lonely; emotionally isolated, unhappy, or depressed; having low self-esteem and self-acceptance; and having lost their physical attractiveness. The stereotypes further portray older gay and lesbian people as being oversexed, but their sex lives are unsatisfactory; and as they are unable to form lasting relationships, most of their encounters with others are transient. If lesbians do establish relationships, they embrace roles of "butch" and "femme." Older lesbians and gay males are expected to grow old before their time because of the youthful emphasis in the gay male and lesbian cultures, and when they do grow old they become social embarrassments. Additional myths are that older lesbians and gay men exchange status, security, and financial favors for younger partners; that they are disengaged from the gay world and acquaintances in it; and if they were ever "out," they are retreating further and further into the closet—fearful of being discredited. The myths are summed up in the observations "He's an old queen. She's an old bitch."[3]

The Politics of Research

The invisibility, myths, and stereotypical attitudes about older lesbians and gay men are a form of social control that serves to keep this group powerless. If they remain in this position, they are not able to participate in community decision-making processes that affect their lives, and they are removed from the social function of being role models for younger gay and lesbian people. But most important, they are deprived of quality of life. They are not able to live in the moment, enjoying their "actual" identities in everyday life; concurrently, they are deprived of opportunities for life review, for recognizing the beauty and continuity of life, and for preparing for the end of life.

Research in the area of gay aging has examined the situations and experiences of older lesbians and gay men in the light of myths and stereotypes. It has included such issues as having sex lives and relationships in a sex-negative society with rigid gender role expectations; living with internalized homophobia and a conspiracy of silence around homosexuality; facing invisibility and aging in a society in which gay and lesbian lives are acknowledged only to a limited extent; growing up before gay liberation and constantly being confronted with the decision whether, to whom, and when to disclose one's sexual orientation; confronting loneliness and finding life satisfaction in a homophobic and heterosexist society; and facing great losses with limited traditional supportive networks.[4]

The limitations of the research are related to the fact that it has been based on convenience samples; and for the most part the participants have been white, middle-class, "affirming" older gay men (more recently, researchers have conducted studies exploring the life situations of older lesbians). These and other concerns are addressed by Berger in his study of older gays and lesbians. A first concern relates to the inability to obtain a representative sample of homosexuals because of the absence of a clear-cut definition of homosexuality; therefore, the studies traditionally use self-attribution of homosexuality as the most valid definition. A second concern enumerated by Berger is a bias in favor of homosexuals who had participated in at least one gay or lesbian organization or establishment, for example, a gay or lesbian bar; consequently, they tend to be people who are either "passing" or "affirming." A third concern relates to the refutation of stereotypes. As Berger puts it, "because stereotypes are by definition universal hypotheses about populations, any members of the population who do not correspond to the stereotype challenge it. A biased but diverse sample of the population is sufficient to refute stereotypes, as long as the findings are not interpreted as demographic representations of . . . homosexuals in general." A final concern, Berger states, is the fact that the research does not represent the diversity among older lesbians and gay men, specifically those related to ethnicity and socioeconomic status.

Some Research Findings Related to Older Gay Men

Limited though the research may be, a fair amount of it contradicts the standard stereotypes enumerated above. The findings of Kelly, for example, have shown that older gay men occasionally go out to bars, particularly those that serve their peer group (not in search of younger men), and that older gay men have many gay friends (and fewer heterosexual ones).

According to the research of Kimmel, older gay men report high life satisfaction, contradicting the stereotype of the lonely and segregated gay man. This finding is replicated by Berger, who reports that older gay men scored as high or higher on a life satisfaction index than other older persons in two surveys of the general population. Berger also found that most older gay men remain sexually active and are generally satisfied with their sex lives, that they prefer to socialize with peers (rather than younger men), and that they worry less about disclosure or the discovery of their homosexuality than younger men do. The latter relates to the fact that most of them are retired and therefore not involved in professional activities where disclosure might ruin their careers or their lives. Vacha, in a study conducted in England, found that relationships among older gay men are not transient. Some also have a high degree of intergenerational relationships, but they are not related to favors or financial rewards that older men could give to young men so as to hold on to them. In fact, Vacha points out that most of these older gay men were not rich and did not have the money or material favors to offer younger men. Vacha also found that older gay men reported having a greater sense of self-confidence and contentment in their later years than in their youth—again counteracting the stereotype.

Berger has found that most older gay men are integrated in supportive networks and have had a significant other or others for extended periods of their lifetimes. According to Vacha, most older gay men have a wide range of relationships, including lovers, ex-lovers, friends, and sometimes children who compose self-selected families. Berger also suggests that two of the strong predictors of good adjustment in old age are a commitment to homosexuality (unwillingness to change sexual orientation) and integration into the homosexual community; however, he also notes that gay men over forty tend to have a consistently lower attendance at political and social service organizations, bars, bathhouses, and social clubs than younger men in a comparable study. Despite current myths, internalized homophobia is one of the HIV/AIDS risk factors among elderly gay men. Kooperman has found that these individuals do not reach out to HIV/AIDS education and service organizations, and the efforts of these organizations do not reach such men. Two other risk factors identified by Kooperman are their denial of risk (i.e., they see AIDS as a young gay man's disease) and anonymous sexual encounters in bookstores, gay theaters, private club rooms, or with prostitutes. I have identified other risk factors, including substance abuse. (i.e., alcohol, illegal drugs, and prescription drugs) and blood transfusions due to ailments or medical complications associated with age-related illnesses.

In summary, many older gay men—again, drawn not in a random sample but a narrow one—are not without significant others or gay friends, report high life satisfaction and contentment, are involved in the gay community, and tend not to worry about disclosure of their homosexuality as much as younger gays.

Some Research Findings Related to Older Lesbians

The experiences of older lesbians have barely been researched. What research has been conducted is similar in its selectivity to the male cohorts, that is, with primarily white and middle-class participants.

Kehoe found that older lesbians establish families of choice to provide them with social support. Other scholars[5] have reported that older lesbians tend to form friendship networks. All of this contradicts the stereotype of isolated and lonely women. Kehoe has also discovered that the majority of older lesbians are highly satisfied with their lives, that they are not likely to be homebound, and that they are not afraid to go out alone. However, according to Jacobson, older lesbians are less likely than younger ones to frequent bars, and they are more likely than younger lesbians to congregate in homes of comparably successful lesbians. And although in the past, butch/femme roles were a common pattern for many lesbian relationships, Kehoe reports that such role playing is not supported or publicly acknowledged by most of the older lesbians in her study—contradicting another stereotype. On the other hand, most older lesbians report experiencing multiple repressions. As Healey states, "Being old and lesbian presents the very special lethal synergy of ageism and heterosexism."

In summary, older lesbians have established supportive networks and are satisfied or highly satisfied with their lives. They tend to go out, but less frequently to bars and more likely to homes of similarly successful peers than younger lesbians. Most report experiencing ageism, and most do not currently support butch/femme role playing.

Implications of Gay Liberation for Older Gays and Lesbians

According to Berger and Kelly, the research findings reported above focus on two central ideas: "crisis competence" and "mastery of stigma." In the former case, gay or lesbian youths realize that they are different from their peers;

when they leave their homes of origin, they are not likely to replace them with traditional families (i.e., get married like heterosexuals). They are faced with becoming independent at the commencement of their adult years, which creates a crisis of competence. When they are later faced with the losses of old age, for example, loss of job status and friends, they can call on the attitudes and skills they developed in response to the crisis of management to help them succeed. Similarly, the gay-positive researchers indicate that the crisis of stigma enables older gay and lesbian people to call on the "mastery" developed in coping with the negative reactions of a homophobic culture and the accompanying feelings of self-hate and self-doubt.

Gay liberation may have made these crises more severe for older gay and lesbian people, as well as for gay and lesbian youth—causing both groups increased emotional distress. As Rotello puts it,

> The rise in visibility is precisely what we've been fighting for, and it's great— provided you've come to terms with yourself, come out of the closet, and build some kind of support network. But when you're the only queer 15-year-old in a classroom of hostile straight kids [or the only 70-year-old lesbian in a senior center surrounded by homophobic aging men and women], losing cover can be devastating. In a sense the gay movement has "outed" a whole generation without compensating by making life any easier.

The research findings of Adelman in her 1991 study of heterosexual and homosexual men and women sixty years of age and older may indicate increased self-protective behaviors against the rise in gay and lesbian visibility. She found that low disclosure at work was related to high life satisfaction and that low disclosure to relatives was associated with lower self-criticism. Lee, after conducting a 1989 interview study, concluded that older gay men who remained in the closet were more likely to lead a happy old age. He did not find, however, any correlation between self-rated life satisfaction and how widely a person was known as gay.

As indicated earlier, it is difficult to describe the characteristics of older gays and older lesbians because it is impossible to get representative samples of these groups. Existing research does not include older gay and lesbian people who are not part of or attached to the traditional sources of research samples, for example, social service agencies, clubs, community-based organizations, national organizations. Therefore, although the data from extant research may be important to challenge negative views of gay and lesbian aging, they may also be skewed.

There are anecdotal reports of older gays and lesbians who are isolated and lonely, and who experience despair and depression. There are also accounts of many older gays and lesbians who use and abuse substances, including alcohol, prescription drugs, and street drugs. Furthermore, descriptions exist of homebound, homeless, and penniless older gay and lesbian individuals who live without hope and dignity. How many of these conditions are compounded by gay-related stressors—for example, discovery, disclosure, verbal and physical harassment—and are associated with increased gay and lesbian visibility is not known.

The majority of the research studies have focused on the resilient young old; small numbers of old old have been included at times. However, there is virtually no information available about the oldest old—those seventy years and above. Does the learning that results from the crisis of management and mastery of stigma continue to provide advantages as a person (1) joins an older cohort? (2) gets a number of chronic illnesses? and (3) "lives too long"— surviving all friends and loved ones.[6] As Berger and Kelly conclude, "It is one of the prerogatives of youth to believe that old age will bring with it the answers for which we long. But old age brings with it instead many new questions, and hopefully, the dignity to ponder them unanswered."

Working with Older Lesbians and Gay Men

It is important that professionals working with older gay and lesbian people attain a certain degree of understanding about being homosexual, being an aging person, and the intersection of the two. Members of all professions working with people who are aging should know that some of these individuals will have a gay or lesbian orientation, whether or not they decide to come out of the closet or continue their lifetime behaviors associated with passing. Growing up gay or lesbian in a homophobic society leads to hiding as part of the socialization process and to experiencing cognitive, emotional, and social isolation. Aging individuals who also grew up hearing that they are immoral, sick, sinful, or unnatural are not likely to come out when they are old and possibly vulnerable and dependent.[7]

Human service providers must also incorporate some of the basic assumptions and understandings about homosexuality into the framework of their professional practices. Ignorance of this knowledge often leads to biased, heterosexist, and prejudicial language and behaviors, which create hostile and threatening spaces. Some of the basic understandings are that

1. homosexuality is a normal variation of both sexual orientation and sexual behavior;

2. homosexuality is an orientation that includes emotional and social preferences, sexual attraction and fantasies, and self-identification;

3. understanding homosexuality does not require understanding its cause;

4. femininity and masculinity have nothing to do with sexual orientation;

5. homophobic attitudes, like other forms of prejudice, create pain, stress, fear, inner conflicts, and feelings of oppression among gay and lesbian people; and

6. homophobic attitudes lead to unequal regard and unequal treatment on the part of workers.

It is important to recognize that all older gay and lesbian people, like younger ones, pay a price for being different. The price may be higher if one also happens to be a person of color, disabled, female, poor, or Jewish. Many of these individuals react to the oppressions of ageism and homophobia by becoming dependent; others have reacted by developing personas characterized by self-reliance. This latter group of older gay and lesbian people expect professionals to accept and acknowledge them and to engage them in full partnership. Healey, writing as an "old lesbian," highlights this point. "When professionals . . . attempt to structure their interactions as experts rather than equals, they diminish rather than empower. That model of helping is disrespectful of my personhood and ageist in its stereotypic presumption that my years have made me incompetent and incapable."

In providing services to older gay and lesbian people social service personnel must create environments that are sensitive to cultural and sexual diversity, accessible, and affordable. In addition, the services must communicate that the privacy and confidentiality of all individuals will be preserved, as many older adults tend not to disclose their personal "business" for fear that their confidentiality might not be respected. As I have pointed out in my own work, this is especially true among older gay men who may have experienced verbal and physical abuse, entrapment and arrest, or discrimination when they previously disclosed their sexual orientation. And it is most important to remember that some issues and problems relate to living in society, and these may not be attributed to being an aging lesbian or gay individual.

According to Goffman, a "social identity" is based on relationships to other people, while a "personal identity" is related to an individual's personal biography. Both of these identities may be jeopardized by stigmas related to aging and to sexual orientation. These stigmas tend to expose discrepancies between virtual and actual selves; that is, the projected selves are exposed as untenable, and embarrassment ensues. The individuals are then called upon to manage the stigmas.

Many older gay and lesbian people try to manage two stigmas: their homosexual orientation in a heterosexist society and their aging in the gay and lesbian world. The various ways of managing the stigmas depend on a person's ability to control information. According to Goffman, the first and most often used strategy is concealment, while a second approach is establishing a cover, that is, passing by acting in an expected way. The third, disclosure, is a different type of strategy. Most of today's older gay and lesbian people have long ago selected the strategies of concealment and passing. This has led to their invisibility and isolation, and to the proliferation of myths and stereotypes about them. These forces have led researchers interested in aging gay and lesbian individuals to design studies aimed at combating the stereotypes, and for the most part they have succeeded in doing so.

The identity management strategy of disclosure is increasingly used by those older gay and lesbian people who have decided to affirm their identities. As Goffman indicates, the process of disclosing or flaunting a stigma changes individuals from being people with potentially stigmatizing information to manage to ones with difficult situations to get through, that is, from being people who are discreditable to those who are discredited.

Becoming an old "dyke" or "queen" in the lesbian and gay world may bring some hurtful remarks and rejection from younger members, and it may bring verbal and physical harassment from heterosexuals in one's life sphere. However, the feelings of satisfaction and empowerment resulting from being true to one's self have led many older lesbians and gay men to lead lives with which they are partly or highly satisfied. The challenge for social service professionals is to become allies and to share the goal of empowerment with these older lesbian and gay people.

Notes

The author expresses appreciation to Philip Bockman for his critical comments and helpful suggestions on an earlier draft of this manuscript.

1. See Berger (1982a), Dunker (1987), Healey (1994), and Vacha (1985).
2. For example, Berger (1982a, 1982b), Kehoe (1986a, 1986b, 1988), Kimmel (1979), and Vacha (1985).
3. See Berger (1982a, 1982b). Dawson (1982), Healey (1994); Kehoe (1986a, 1988); Kelly (1980); and Martin and Lyon (1984).
4. See Berger (1982a, 1982b, 1985); Berger and Kelly (1996); Kimmel (1978, 1979, 1992); Kehoe (1988), Martin and Lyon (1984); Minnigerode (1976), and Vacha (1985).
5. See Berger (1985), Kimmel (1992), and Lipman (1986).
6. See Norman (1996).
7. See Grossman (1994), Hetrick and Martin (1987), Hunter and Schaecher (1987), and Martin (1982).

References

Adelman, M. 1991. Stigma, gay lifestyles, and adjustment to aging: A study of later-life gay men and lesbians. In *Gay Midlife and Maturity,* ed. J. A. Lee, 7–32. New York: Harrington Park.

Altman, D. 1988. Legitimation through disaster: AIDS and the gay movement. In *AIDS: The Burdens of History,* ed. E. Fee and D. M. Fox, 301–15. Berkeley: University of California Press.

Berger, R. M. 1982a. *Gay and Gray: The Older Homosexual Man.* Urbana: University of Illinois Press.

———. 1982b. The unseen minority: Older gays and lesbians. *Social Work* 27 (3):236–42.

———. 1984. Realities of gay and lesbian aging. *Social Work* 29:57–62.

———. 1985. Rewriting a bad script: Older lesbians and gays. In *Lesbian and Gay*

Issues: A Resource Manual for Social Workers, ed. H. Hidalgo, T. L. Peterson, and N. J. Woodman. Silver Spring, MD: National Association of Social Workers.

Berger, R. M., and J. Kelly. 1996. Prologue: Gay and gray revisited. In *Gay and Gray: The Older Homosexual Man,* ed. R. M. Berger, 1–22. 2d ed. New York: Harrington Park.

Dawson, K. 1982. Serving the gay community. *SIECUS Report.* November, 5–6.

Dunker, B. 1987. Aging lesbians: Observations and speculations. In *Lesbian Psychologies: Explorations and Challenges,* ed. Boston Lesbian Psychologies Collective, 72–82. Chicago: University of Illinois Press.

Fowles, D. G., Researcher and compiler. 1991. *A Profile of Older Americans: 1991.* Washington, DC: Program Resources Department, American Association of Retired Persons, and U.S. Department of Health and Human Services, Administration on Aging.

Friend, R. A. 1989. Older lesbian and gay people: Responding to homophobia. *Marriage and Family Review* 14 (3–4): 241–63.

Goffman, E. 1963. *Stigma: Notes on the Management of Spoiled Identity.* Englewood Cliffs, NJ: Prentice-Hall.

Grossman, A. H. 1994. Hiding and coming out: Gay and lesbian youth at risk. In *Youth at Risk: Targeting In on Prevention,* ed. B. Cato, H. Gray, D. Nelson, and P. Varnes, 49–56. Reston, VA: American Association for Leisure and Recreation.

———. 1995. At risk, infected, and invisible: Older gay men and HIV/AIDS. *JANAC: Journal of the Association of Nurses in AIDS Care* 6 (6):13–19.

Healey, S. 1994. Diversity with a difference: On being old and lesbian. *Journal of Gay and Lesbian Social Services* 1 (1):109–17.

Hetrick, E. S., and A. D. Martin. 1987. Developmental issues and their resolution for gay and lesbian adolescents. *Journal of Homosexuality* 14 (1–2): 25–43.

Hunter, J., and R. Schaecher. 1987. Stresses on lesbian and gay adolescents in schools. *Social Work in Education* 9 (3): 180–86.

Jacobson, S. 1994. What do we know about the leisure of old lesbians? In *Invisible No More! Gay and Lesbian Aging 101.* Symposium at the meeting of the National Recreation and Park Association, Minneapolis, October.

Kehoe, M. 1986a. Lesbians over sixty-five: A triply invisible minority. *Journal of Homosexuality* 12 (3–4): 139–52.

———. 1986b. A portrait of the older lesbian. *Journal of Homosexuality* 12 (3–4): 157–61.

———. 1988. Lesbians over sixty speak for themselves. *Journal of Homosexuality* 16 (3–4): 1–111.

Kelly, J. 1980. Homosexuality and aging. *In Homosexual Behavior: A Modern Reappraisal,* ed. J. Marmor, 176–93. New York: Basic Books.

Kimmel, D. C. 1978. Adult development and aging: A gay perspective. *Journal of Social Issues* 34 (3): 113–30.

———. 1979. Life history interviews of aging gay men. *International Journal of Aging and Human Development* 10 (3): 239–48.

———. 1992. The families of older gays and lesbians. *Generations* 17:37–38.

Kooperman, L. (Speaker). 1993. *AIDS and the Elderly* (Cassette Recording). San Francisco: American Society on Aging.

Lee, J. A. 1989. Invisible men: Canada's aging homosexuals: Can they be assimilated into Canada's "liberated" gay communities? *Canadian Journal on Aging* 8 (1): 79–97.

Lipman, A. 1986. Homosexual relationships. *Generations* 10: 51–54.

Martin, A. D. 1982. Learning to hide: The socialization of the gay adolescent. In *Adolescent Psychiatry: Developmental and Clinical Studies,* vol. 10, ed. S. C.

Feinstein, J. G. Looney, A. Schwartzberg, and J. Sorosky, 52–65. Chicago: University of Chicago Press.

Martin, D., and P. Lyon. 1984. The older Lesbian. In *Positively Gay*, ed. B., Berzon, 134–45. Los Angeles: Mediamix Associates.

Minnigerode, F. A. 1976. Age-status labeling in homosexual men. *Journal of Homosexuality* 1 (3): 273–75.

Norman, M. 1996. Living too long. *New York Times Magazine*, January 14, 36–38.

Rotello, G. 1996. Last word: Trickle-down liberation. *Advocate*, February 20, 72.

Vacha, K. 1985. *Quiet Fire: Memoirs of Older Gay Men*. Trumansburg, NY: Crossing.

48

Living with Aging: Review and Prospects

Miriam Ehrenberg

In this youth-oriented culture, aging, which used to connote wisdom and command reverence, has taken on negative connotations, and the boundary defining "older" has dropped significantly. There is now not only a loss of respect for older people but a bias against the elderly as well (see Kite and Johnson's meta-analysis, 1988). The elderly are considered "over the hill," and the stereotypic image is of a "rigid," "less interesting," "confused," "cranky" person. Special labels such as "senior citizen" support this image, and the "golden years" have turned to dross for many. The negative image pertaining to the elderly in general becomes more markedly so in the popular imagination when applied to gays and lesbians. Older gay men are frequently viewed as depressed, lonely, rejected by family, spurned by younger men, oversexed and, thereby, also disgusting. Older lesbian women are also frequently viewed as lonely and family-less, but also as emotionally cold and physically unattractive. In the 1970s, motivated in good part by the desire to dispel the negative image of older homosexuals, researchers directed their attention specifically toward gay populations. It was felt that disdainful views of gay aging were bound to create greater difficulties for young homosexuals in developing a positive gay identity, and would stand in the way of acceptance of one's sexuality and one's self.

Research on Mental Health Issues for Aging Gays and Lesbians

An evaluation of the results of the research on homosexual aging is difficult primarily because of the samples used. The subjects for most of the studies were recruited through gay organizations and friendship networks and seldom included subjects who were socially isolated, as many elderly are. As Bell and Weinberg (1978) point out, the questionable representativeness of most homosexual samples greatly limits the generality of findings. Some of the studies consisted solely of white, middle- and upper-middle-class urban respondents who were, moreover, very involved in organized gay activities, itself a factor found to be related to mental health status. The age of the subjects also varied from study to study. Subjects in some studies were classified as "older" if over forty, and such studies did not necessarily break down responses in terms of age group. The earlier studies focused on male homosexuals, and only more recent studies have examined aging issues as related to female homosexuals. Because of these limitations, the research findings in this area offer some insights into aging issues for gays and lesbians, but do not provide any clear answers.

Kelly (1977), in a pioneering study of 241 gay men between the ages of sixteen and seventy-nine, concluded that the typical aging gay man does not fit into the popular stereotype of a socially isolated, fearful person who has lost his physical attractiveness and appeal to the young men he craves. Rather, Kelly maintained that older gays found their lives quite satisfactory, including their sex lives, and that they desired contact with men of their own age. The results presented, however, do not totally support this conclusion. Kelly's subjects were not involved at the time of the study in any lasting gay liaisons. Further, although the number of persons in emotionally gratifying liaisons initially increased with age, after age fifty-five these partnerships decreased to almost none. Kimmel (1978), in a study based on a sample of only fourteen men over the age of fifty-five, also drew positive conclusions, while recognizing that they were speculative and not based on solid data. Kimmel felt that the aging gay male has advantages over his heterosexual counterpart, including greater awareness of self-responsibility, no reliance on family, more "continuity of life" because of lack of interference by children, no limiting gender roles, experience in living alone and the ability therefore to cope with this state, and the possession of a friendship network for social support and sexual companionship. Berger (1982) interviewed 112 Midwestern gay men between the ages of forty-one and seventy-seven by questionnaire and selected 10 of these for an extensive interview. His data, however, are not always broken down by age. He found that the men in his study had excellent psychological adjustment and that the problems they experienced were generated by social factors, not by their own attitudes. Most were highly involved in the gay rights movement and manifested self-acceptance despite the homophobia they had experienced. His subjects saw no difference in aging for heterosexuals and homosexuals. The men in Berger's study were not lonely or isolated and felt that age brought them new freedom. They maintained their earlier level of sexual activity, although with fewer partners. Almost half, however, felt that younger gay men felt an aversion to them, but those who did not socialize with younger gays had the best adjustment. Other investigators, such as Friend (1980), Francher and Henkin (1973), and Weinberg (1970), have also reported on samples of older gay men whom they describe as psychologically well adjusted, adapting to the aging process, and self-accepting.

A less formal study of seventeen men over sixty was conducted by Vacha (1985). His subjects had experienced considerable harassment by families, police, and the military, had found the need to deny their homosexuality early on, were frequent users of drugs and alcohol, had difficulty achieving long-term partnerships, and had a high incidence of physical illness. Many also were wary of the gay rights movement and favored conciliation rather than militancy. Vacha's subjects accepted themselves and their aging and seemed quite sure of themselves despite very difficult lives.

Based on a longitudinal study of fifty-four gay men over fifty, Lee (1987, 1988) disputed the previously drawn conclusion that the difficulties endured by older gays helped them cope as they age, and related adjustment in later years to their good fortune or skill in avoiding stressful events. He also reported a generation gap between younger and older gays, leading to "invisibility" of older men who cannot accept the "hardness" of young gay lifestyles and gay liberation politics and who fear flaunting sexual preference. Lee's older subjects avoided labeling themselves gay, and he found no relation between disclosure of sexual orientation and life satisfaction.

Following in this vein, Grube (1990) interviewed thirty-five gay men, ranging in age from forty to ninety-two, from which he identified two different gay communities. According to Grube, older gay men identify with a traditional gay culture that tried to accommodate to the prevailing heterosexual world. Their relationships are based on mentor-protégé pairs, and they come into conflict with the new gay liberationists, whose relationships are modeled on organized institutional lines.

Research on mental health issues among lesbians followed in the late 1970s and 1980s. The first account was provided by Meyer (1979), who studied twenty lesbians aged fifty to seventy-three. She found five different responses to aging among her subjects, ranging from feeling fine about it to negativity. On the whole she found her participants to be flexible, sexually alive, and not lonely or isolated. Almvig (1982) studied seventy-four lesbians over fifty. Her study was weighted toward white, well-educated women who lived in urban settings. The study covered respondents' self-perceptions of their mental health, thoughts about aging, family relations and support systems, preparations for the future, and connections to the gay community. Most subjects felt they were mentally healthy, and were positive about their aging. They reported "great joy and satisfaction" in their lesbianism. Their fears related to loss of physical or mental capacities and of income. Many were involved in lesbian networks. This positive view was duplicated in a study by Kehoe (1986) focusing on lesbians over sixty-five. Her sample of fifty lesbians was similar to Almvig's, consisting of white, well-educated women of relatively high social/economic status with ties to the lesbian community. According to Kehoe, the typical lesbian over sixty-five "is a survivor, a balanced personality, coping with aging in a satisfactory manner" (139). A more comprehensive survey by Bradford et al. (1994) was conducted in 1984–85, and derived information from 1,925 lesbians from all fifty states. Only 3 percent of the sample consisted of women fifty-five or older, but responses were broken down by age group, and a primary mental health risk, factor explored was physical and sexual abuse. Slightly over a third of those fifty five and older had ever experienced abuse. Present concerns revolved around money, job and responsibility worries, and problems with lovers and/or family. Of the mental health symptoms explored, the older age group seemed relatively impervious compared to their younger compatriots. Only 4 percent indicated current problems with depression; 1 percent reported problems with anxiety, and 60 percent reported they never thought about suicide. On the negative side, however, both tobacco and alcohol use was found to increase with age. Older lesbians used other drugs less frequently, except for tranquilizers. Although a very small total number used them at all, those who used them daily were primarily forty-five or older. In an attempt to relate mental health status to lesbian identity, the study assessed "outness," which was determined by the number of family, homosexual friends, heterosexual friends, and coworkers who knew that the respondents were lesbians. The lowest outness scores were achieved by lesbians fifty-five years or older. The authors conclude that the "less frequent involvement among older lesbians with the lesbian and gay community and decreased openness about their sexual orientation may lead to increased reliance on alcohol to mitigate the long-term effects of isolation, lack of adequate support, and compartmentalization of their identity" (240). The authors, in this connection, do not comment on the relatively low rate of depression and anxiety in this older group. Still another study, by Deevey (1990), conducted from 1986 to 1988, surveyed seventy-eight lesbians over fifty. Again, the sample consisted primarily of well-educated women, all but one of whom were white. According to Deevey, most of the older women reported "excellent mental health." However, like Bradford et al., Deevey also found high alcohol consumption as well as extra weight in the older group. In a study of both older lesbians and gays, aged fifty to seventy-three and active in the gay and lesbian community, Quam and Whitford (1992) found acceptance of the aging process and high levels of life satisfaction.

Rather than trying to demonstrate that gays and lesbians are better adjusted than others, some researchers have tried to study the relationship between adjustment and styles of being gay. This was first done for younger gays, and Berger (1982) and Lee (1987) attempted to examine the relationship among older gays—and with different conclusions. Berger concluded that low disclosure of gay status leads to emotional problems, while Lee reported that greater self-concealment is correlated with greater life satisfaction. Adelman (1990) attempted to relate styles of being gay with adjustment patterns among both older gays and older lesbians. The data were based on a sample of twenty-seven homosexual men and twenty-five lesbian women living in the San Francisco Bay area, all of whom were white, and the majority of whom had a comfortable standard of living. The mean age of the gays was 65.63 years, and of the lesbians 64.48 years. Adelman found that adjustment to aging is related to satisfaction with being gay and the developmental sequence of early gay developmental events. The latter included low disclosure at work, low involvement with other gay people, plus early age of awareness of homosexual status, but a decrease in the importance of homosexuality in later years. Adelman suggests that these results reflect a generational rather than developmental pattern. The homosexuals who were in their sixties at the time the data were collected represent a pre-Stonewall group, and their life experiences with disclosure and its ramifications must be very different from those of future generations of people over sixty.

The general tenor of the various research studies suggests a population of sturdy people who have weathered the stresses of homophobia and discrimination and emerged better able to cope than their heterosexual age-mates. These conclusions probably reflect the mental health status of many white, affluent, physically fit gays and lesbians who constituted the majority of the samples used, but these participants, as Cruikshank noted in her review of gay and lesbian aging studies (1990), are quite likely to be "the most robust specimens" of their group. There are undoubtedly unhappy and lonely gay and lesbian seniors who have not come forward to talk about their lives. As Lee (1990) points out in his foreword to the special issue on Gay Midlife and Maturity of the *Journal of Homosexuality*, trying to persuade these older gays and lesbians "that they have superior capacities for adapting to old age (such as 'crisis competence') does a disservice. . . . Pollyanna mythology leaves the lonely homosexual senior asking 'What's wrong with me, if the research says all those other homosexuals are so cheerful in old age?' " (xiv). As Erwin (1993) notes, studies continue to show significantly higher rates of suicide, depression, substance abuse, as well as other indicators of psychological distress among lesbians and gays of all ages than among heterosexuals.

Some Theoretical Considerations

How can the developmental problems of the over sixty population in general — the decline in strength, health, memory; confusion and depression brought on by medications; changes in appearance (wrinkling, stooping, hair loss); drop in income through retirement; disengagement from the world and loss of stimulation through disability or lack of money — be expected to impact on gays and lesbians? Research only provides answers about more privileged gays and lesbians, but what about those who are not white, affluent, well educated, highly involved in the gay/lesbian community with a network of friends, and moreover, not particularly sturdy physically but, perhaps, in need of a caretaker?

Gays and lesbians who must depend on others for financial help or caretaking usually have no option but to turn to general community resources. The homosexual community cannot presently provide ongoing financial grants or homophilic institutional settings for the elderly. When gays and lesbians must rely on public resources they are very likely to come across discrimination and hostility. Most problematic is dependency on institutional care. Homophobia is rampant in many institutional settings; not only is there general disregard and among gaycontempt for older persons at large, but this is apt to be intensified in the case of gays and lesbians, who may therefore suffer from lack of attention and friendly input, if not outright neglect. Institutions tend to have little patience for partners and friends of homosexuals, particularly gays, may disregard requests of such persons for information or changes in procedures, and may actively interfere with or prevent physical interactions between homosexual residents and their guests. Displays of physical affection between gays may be considered "disgusting." Heterosexual patients as well as staff may shun and isolate the homosexual patient. If it should happen that two patients are drawn to each other and seek physical affection from each other, this is difficult for staff and other patients to tolerate. It has been demonstrated (Commons 1992) that professionals have little acceptance of sexual behavior between any institutionalized patients but are most condemning of homosexual acts. Ailing and financially needy homosexuals, thus, are clearly at risk for feeling rejected, isolated, and therefore easy prey to feelings of self-doubt. There are no data available for gays in terms of income. It is apparent, however, that despite the many high-profile wealthy gays, particularly in arts and entertainment, there are many more financially marginal gays in these fields—unemployed actors, designers, hairdressers—who can barely eke out a living while in their youth and may become destitute as they age. Data on lesbians (Bradford and Ryan, 1987) suggest that they are five times as likely as other women to have money problems and that their income level is not commensurate with their education and experience.

Social isolation, according to most gay and lesbian research studies of older people, is not a problem, but the participants whose responses led to this conclusion were primarily people active in homosexual activities and organizations. What about those gays and lesbians without such connections or in communities where such connections are not possible, such as those living in rural areas or in fundamentalist heartland territory? First, it is not that clear that older people who have access to organized homosexual activities avail themselves of these opportunities or that they are welcome if they do so. Younger gays and lesbians, like their heterosexual counterparts, are not immune to ageism and are not necessarily welcoming to their older brothers and sisters. Ray Schaffer (1973) described the hypocrisy of many gay liberationists in regard to the aged in his article "Will You Still Love Me When I'm 64?" While being active in the gay community may be an antidote to problems in accepting aging, the gay/lesbian community itself is not accepting of the aged. As both

Lee (1988) and Grube (1990) point out, liberated homosexual communities are not willing to make room for the elderly. There is a dearth of older gays in leadership positions in gay institutions, and their contributions to the gay liberation movement are not generally recognized or respected.

The generation gap in the homosexual community appears to have an effect both on general social acceptance and on intimate personal relationships. The gap also impacts differentially on gays and lesbians. Social isolation seems to afflict older gays more than older lesbians, probably reflecting the different social roles of men and women. Women live longer than men and are more likely to have surviving age-mates within their social circle. Women are also socialized to be caretakers and therefore lesbians are more likely than gays to find women who will be available as part of a support network. Homosexual men have been less rigid in adhering to stereotyped sex roles than heterosexual men, and AIDS has propelled many into the caretaker role. The continuing erosion of sex roles will probably equalize issues of isolation for future generations of gays and lesbians as they age.

Finding partners is another issue for older homosexuals that seems to be experienced differently by lesbians and gays. Older lesbians tend to feel that younger lesbians do not want them as partners, but bias against older partners is particularly marked among gay men. From an exhaustive review of the literature Symons (1979) concluded that there is a strong tendency among men, whether homosexual or not, to prefer younger partners, a tendency not noted among lesbians. Steinman (1990) gathered data between 1983 and 1985 on forty-six gay male couples with a gap in age of at least eight years. Even though these couples did not fit the stereotype of the "sugar daddy" who "keeps" a younger man (most of his younger subjects were not financially dependent on their partners), still the older partners were drawn by the sexual excitement offered by their younger partners and the latter were attracted to the generally greater economic resources of the older partners. The older partners generally wanted more sex than their younger partners would provide, and Steinman believes that the "refusal" of sex is one way the younger partner can counterbalance the control over financial resources exercised by the older partner. The attraction of younger men because of their intrinsic qualities and the valuation of older partners for the extrinsic rewards they can provide is a far cry from the mentor-protégé relationship that Grube (1990) found to exist traditionally.

Devaluation of older gays in terms of their intrinsic qualities is abetted by the "accelerated aging" that appears to exist among male homosexuals. Kelly (1977, 1980) found a tendency for gays to perceive "old age" starting earlier than heterosexual males perceived it, namely, at around fifty. In contrast, a study by Minnigerode (1976) found no difference between homosexual and heterosexual males in their perception of when old age begins, which his subjects put at around sixty-four years of age even though they classified themselves as "middle-aged" when they were in this age bracket. Bennett and Thompson's study (1990) offered a resolution of these seemingly contradictory results; their sample of gay men thought that other gays believe "old age" starts at fifty-four, and that these other gays also see them as older than they see themselves.

The search for younger partners among older gays is accompanied by a concern about appearance. Interestingly, the double standard of aging that applies to the population at large seems to be reversed for homosexuals. Gays seem more concerned about their appearance than lesbians are. The latter are generally free from appearance concerns and free from heterosexist male standards and fantasies that affect their heterosexual sisters. Many lesbians wear no makeup, shun high heels, and do not worry about being overweight, while many gays are much more invested in keeping up their looks and youthful appearance. This phenomenon, however, may be undergoing a generational shift and may not be applicable to younger gays and lesbians as they age.

It is possible that the search for younger partners by older gay men is, in part, a search for a surrogate son. The more traditional mentor-protégé relationship and the more contemporary version of older-younger partnering may be an expression of the need for generativity. Older men may look for a son in a sexualized relationship when they do not experience having a son any other way. Similarly "sons" may be looking for the father acceptance they were denied. Generativity and the search for connection to the younger generation are potentially more an issue among gay men than lesbians. One study (Bradford and Ryan 1987) indicates that a third of the older lesbian population have children, whereas most older gay men do not. Although the younger generations of homosexuals are tending to build families through adoption, artificial insemination, and other means, many—like the heterosexual youth of today—do not want children. This may become problematic for them when they age as the attempt to connect to younger people through gay and lesbian community activity does not seem a viable alternative for older gays and lesbians, who frequently are not welcomed. The need for connection and continuity, which runs strong in all people, may remain unsatisfied among gays and lesbians, leading to feelings of emptiness and reinforcing the sense of isolation that comes with age.

While Erikson (1950, 1968) and others have focused on relationships to future generations, the importance of connection to the past has been overlooked. Many gays and lesbians not only miss a sense of continuity with the future but are also discontinuous with the past. Families have tended to suppress the homosexual chapters of family history. Because gays and lesbians often feel they have not been created in the image of their parents, the closeting of other family homosexuals denies them an important link and a place in the family history, as well as role models.

A particular area of concern that seems to pose special mental health problems for lesbians and gays is coming to terms with one's life as one approaches the inevitability of death. The extra burden placed on gays and lesbians in this area is their relationship to their own homosexuality. Obviously gays and lesbians may stay closeted as they grow older for the same reasons they remained so while younger—fear of alienating others, losing a job, and so forth—but to the extent that gays and lesbians stay closeted they may experience a sense of self-betrayal. This, in turn, makes it difficult to reconcile oneself to the end of life if one feels it has not been openly lived. The data that exist suggest that older gays and lesbians have come out less than their younger peers and then mostly to their homosexual friends, not to family. It has been hypothesized that disclosure would be related to better adjustment. Friend (1990), for example, has developed a theory of successful aging based on different styles of identity formation and disclosure. His "stereotypic" older homosexual has internalized negative homophobic messages and remains closeted; he or she has a poor relationship to self and others and experiences loneliness and despair. Friend's "passing" older homosexuals marginally accept their homosexuality but distance themselves from anything lesbian or gay; these people have conditional self-acceptance and spend their energies in hiding. The "affirmative" older homosexuals reconstruct homosexuality into something positive and open and gain thereby self-empowerment. Research, however, has not borne out a relationship between openness to others and life satisfaction. As already noted, Berger (1982) found that low disclosure leads to emotional problems, whereas Lee (1987) found low disclosure related to greater life satisfaction. Adelman (1990), in a more detailed analysis, found that low disclosure at work as well as low involvement with other gays and lesbians are related to life satisfaction. Adelman also found that high disclosure to relatives is related to high self-criticism. Adjustment to aging was highly correlated to satisfaction with being gay, but also with a decreasing importance of homosexuality in later years. These somewhat contradictory results imply that fear of stigma and rejection, at least in the current generation of older homosexuals, seems to function more as an impediment to adjustment than does inability to live openly as a gay or lesbian person. Perhaps, as Adelman's findings suggest, older gays and lesbians deal with fear of disclosure by minimizing the importance of homosexuality as they age. Adelman also attributes the decreasing importance of homosexuality in later years to the decreasing importance of sexuality. Another alternative explanation is that homosexuality decreases in importance as the aging person increasingly defines herself or himself in terms beyond sexual orientation.

Prospects and Proposals

Most research on the mental health of older gays and lesbians has been based on relatively affluent, well-educated, and physically healthy respondents, and they have been found to be psychologically sturdy with good coping skills, and content with their lives, which include networks of supportive friends. We know very little about older gays and lesbians with limited financial resources, poor health, and few homosexual friends to whom to turn. It can only be assumed that their mental health status leaves much to be desired; this could be reflected in the relatively high rates of drug and alcohol use and suicide among gays and lesbians. The psychological resiliency of some older gays has been attributed to their affirmation of their homosexuality and their openness about their sexual orientation. Research findings, however, do not necessarily lead to that conclusion. The data could be interpreted to indicate that education and affluence lead to a more satisfying life and make it possible for one to live according to one's own dictates rather than comply with social standards. Status and financial security also help one find and keep partners of one's choice. Research indicates that older gay men gravitate toward younger, more physically attractive partners and are aided in their search if they command power and influence. Older gays and older lesbians have not usually found themselves welcomed by their younger compatriots, and tend to feel alienated. They may remain in the closet in part because they cannot identify with the more flamboyant and radical style of younger gays and lesbians, but they may also remain in the closet because they are not invited into the living room where their younger, supposed— comrades are interacting. What implications and applications can be drawn, then? Several concepts emerge:

1. It would be useful for gays and lesbians to give more attention to life issues within the gay and lesbian community as well as the struggle between it and the broader society. This is important not only for older homosexuals, but for younger lesbians and gays as well. If the gay and lesbian community is to be a genuine substitute for family, it needs the role modeling and lessons of experience that older gays and lesbians can provide. A family stays alive and vibrant to the extent that it offers its older members the possibility of interacting with youth to give them a sense of generativity and continuity.

2. Older gays and lesbians might consider keeping a journal of their experiences to pass on to others. For those who feel isolated, it provides a way of feeling connected, and the journal can be a valuable resource for younger homosexuals who need to hear from others about the different pathways life can follow. Such journals could be passed on from individual to individual and perhaps someday become the nucleus of a library of homosexual life to which everyone could have recourse.

3. Mental health professionals have to reexamine their assumptions about aging, about disclosure, and about what makes for life satisfaction and stability. Individuals vary greatly in their circumstances and not everyone has the tempermental predisposition, the support system, or the financial security to place themselves in potential jeopardy by disclosure. Openness with oneself is essentially more important than openness with what may be a hostile world.

4. Older gays and lesbians should consider conducting a life review that deals with what has been done well, as well as with what may not have been accomplished. If not dealt with previously, feelings about one's sexual orientation can still be explored at this time and the individual should try to accept her or his homosexuality before it is too late.

References

Adelman, M. 1990. Stigma, gay lifestyles, and adjustment to aging: A study of later-life gay men and lesbians. *Journal of Homosexuality* 20:7–32.

Almvig, C. 1982. *The Invisible Minority: Aging and Lesbianism.* New York: Utica College of Syracuse University.

Bell, A. P., and M. S. Weinberg. 1978. *Homosexualities.* New York: Simon and Schuster.

Bennett, K. C., and N. L. Thompson. 1990. Accelerated aging and male homosexuality: Australian evidence in a continuing debate. *Journal of Homosexuality* 20:65–75.

Berger, R. M. 1982. *Gay and Gray: The Older Homosexual Man.* Boston: Alyson.

Bradford, J. B., and C. Ryan. 1987. *National lesbian health care survey: Mental health implications for lesbians.* (Report no. PB88-201496/AS). Bethesda, MD: National Institute of Mental Health.

Bradford, J. B., C. Ryan, and E. A. Rothblum, 1994. National lesbian health care survey: Implications for mental health care. *Journal of Consulting and Clinical Psychology* 62:228–42.

Commons, M. L. 1992. Professionals' attitudes towards sex between institutionalized patients. *American Journal of Psychotherapy* 46:571–80.

Cruikshank, M. 1990. Lavender and gray: A brief survey of lesbian and gay aging studies. *Journal of Homosexuality* 20:77–87.

Deevey, S. 1990. Older lesbian women: An invisible minority. *Journal of Gerontological Nursing* 16:35–39.

Erikson, E. 1950. *Childhood and Society.* New York: Norton.

———. 1968. *Identity: Youth and Crisis.* New York: Norton.

Erwin, K. 1993. Interpreting the evidence: Competing paradigms and the emergence of lesbian and gay suicide as a social fact. *International Journal of Health Services* 23:437–53.

Francher, S. J. and J. Henkin. 1973. The menopausal queen. *American Journal of Orthopsychiatry* 43:670–74.

Friend, R. A. 1980. GAYging: Adjustment and the older gay male. *Alternative Lifestyles* 3:231–48.

———. 1990. Older lesbian and gay people: A theory of successful aging. *Journal of Homosexuality* 20:99–118.

Grube, J. 1990. Natives and settlers: An ethnographic note on early interaction of older homosexual men with younger gay liberationists. *Journal of Homosexuality* 20:119–35.

Kehoe, M. 1986. Lesbians over sixty-five: A triply invisible minority. *Journal of Homosexuality* 12:139–52.

Kelly, J. 1977. The aging male homosexual: Myth and reality. *Gerontologist* 17:16–79.

———. 1980. Homosexuality and aging. In *Homosexual Behavior: A Modern Reappraisal,* ed. J. Marmor. New York: Basic Books.

Kimmel, D. C. 1978. Adult development and aging: A gay perspective. *Journal of Social Issues* 34:113–30.

Kite, M. E. and B. T. Johnson. 1988. Attitudes toward older and younger adults: A meta-analysis. *Psychology and Aging,* 233–44.

Kurdek, L. A., and J. P. Schmidt. 1987. Perceived emotional support from family and friends in members of homosexual, married, and heterosexual cohabiting couples. *Journal of Homosexuality* 14:57–68.

Lee, J. A. 1987. What can gay aging studies contribute to theories of aging? *Journal of Homosexuality* 13:43–71.

———. 1988. Invisible lives of Canada's gray gays. In *Aging in Canada,* ed. V. Marshall, 138–55. Toronto: Fithenry and Whiteside.

Lee, J. A. 1990. Foreword. *Journal of Homosexuality* 20:xii–xix.

Meyer, M. 1979. *The Older Lesbian*. Master's thesis. Dominguez Hills: California State University.

Minnigerode, F. A. 1976. Age-status labelling in homosexual men. *Journal of Homosexuality* 1:273–76.

Quam, J. K., and G. S. Whitford. 1992. *Gerontologist* 32:367–74.

Schaffer, R. 1973. Will you still love me when I'm sixty-four? In *The Gay Liberation Book*. San Francisco: Ramparts Press.

Steinman, R. 1990. Social exchanges between older and younger gay male partners. *Journal of Homosexuality* 20:179–206.

Symons, D. 1979. *The Evolution of Human Sexuality*. New York: Oxford University Press.

Tully, C. T. 1989. Caregiving: What do midlife lesbians view as important? *Journal of Gay and Lesbian Psychotherapy* 1:87–103.

Vacha, L. 1985. *Quiet Fire: Memories of Older Gay Men*. Trumansburg, NY: Crossing.

Weinberg, M. S. 1970. The male homosexual: Age-related variations in social and psychological characteristics. *Social Problems* 17:527–37.

C. AIDS

49

Randy Shilts's Miserable Failure

Douglas Crimp

During the first week of April 1989, a young Dutchman on his way to the National Lesbian and Gay Health Conference and AIDS Forum in San Francisco was detained at the airport in Minneapolis-St. Paul when customs officials discovered he had AIDS. He was then incarcerated on the basis of a law barring entry to foreigners with contagious diseases, a category in which AIDS is now included. The Immigration and Naturalization Service ruled against a waiver for the Dutchman, stating, "The risk of harm by an AIDS-infected alien in the absence of humanitarian reasons for the temporary admission of aliens far outweighs the privilege of an alien to enter the United States to participate in a conference."[1] I think we all know how ludicrous this is, and how dangerous are its consequences. With the highest number of cases of AIDS of any country in the world, the United States is nevertheless one of only a very few countries that, against the recommendations of the World Health Organization, have enacted such a law. The law is based on a whole series of myths—that AIDS is contagious, that people with AIDS are ruthless, deliberate spreaders of disease, and that, in any case, people need not *routinely* take precautions against becoming infected or infecting others with HIV. These extremely pervasive myths directly result in not only bad laws, but bad policy, discrimination, and violence, and indirectly result in the deaths of thousands of people who are not being properly treated or educated.

The March 1989 issue of *Esquire* carried an article by Randy Shilts, which, while very largely a piece of self-puffery, purports to be about something more significant: the supposedly incomprehensible fact that although his book *And the Band Played On* made *him* a media celebrity, it nevertheless failed to affect the way AIDS is perceived by the populace, reported in the media, and dealt with at the levels of policy and funding. As Shilts put it, "Never before have I succeeded so well; never before have I failed so miserably." [2] He goes on to regale us with stories of his success interwoven with examples of his failure. The principal failure is the scandal of the National Institutes of Health's stone-walling about the hopelessly stalled development of drug treatments and the media's inability to see a story in this scandal. At the international AIDS conference in Stockholm, Shilts provided the hot tip of this story to his fellow journalists, since he himself was too busy with his book promotion tour to cover it. "One reporter responded to my tip," Shilts writes, "with the question: 'But who's going to play *you* in the miniseries?' " [3] "Clinical trials were not sexy," Shilts complains. "Clinical trials were boring." [4]

A second anecdote concerns Shilts's appearance on the *Morton Downey Show,* where, in spite of assurances that this was an issue Downey was not going to play games with because his brother had AIDS, Downey neverthe-less—hardly surprisingly—turned the show into a referendum on quarantine and fueled the flames of his audience's homophobia. Shilts gives his astute analysis of this situation: "For Morton Downey Jr., talking about AIDS was not an act of conscience; it was a ratings ploy." [5]

Story three is about a Palm Springs fund-raiser with various movie stars and socialites, where Shilts would receive an award for his valiant fight against AIDS. When receiving the award, Shilts launched into the series of AIDS jokes he'd been telling on the lecture circuit. These are all about Shilts's clever repartee with the yahoos who call in to talk shows with their absurd questions about how you "catch" AIDS. But this time, when he told the one about the woman who called in and asked, "What if a gay waiter took my salad back into the kitchen and ejaculated into my salad dressing?" a silence fell over the audience. Shilts explains, "Fears that I dismissed as laughable were the genuine concerns of my audience, I realized." [6]

The stories that Shilts tells reduce basically to two: the story of irrational fears of AIDS and loathing of those who have it, and the media's sense of the fascination of its audience with "sexy" stories about AIDS. What Shilts is thus describing are reactions to AIDS that I think we must recognize as unconscious and therefore extremely intractable, incapable of being rectified by what Shilts calls "the truth" or objective reporting of the facts.

I want to suggest here that it is only by taking account of reactions to AIDS that operate at the level of the unconscious and by unpacking Shilts's unproblematized notion of "the truth" or "objectivity" that we can understand why *And the Band Played On* is so deeply flawed.

Many people have written about why Shilts's book is, by his own admission, a miserable failure, or have addressed criticisms directly to Shilts when they encountered him on his celebrity tour. Needless to say, this is an aspect of being a celebrity that Shilts fails to report in his *Esquire* article. In spite of Shilts's own sense of failure, he arrogantly dismisses the questions raised by his critics. He still appears to feel that he has written the perfect book, the book that really tells the *true* story of the epidemic's first five years.

Let me give you just one example, taken from the transcripts of Shilts's book promotion appearance at the Institute of Contemporary Arts in London. Shilts was asked in some detail about his book's most widely criticized passages, those dealing with the story of Patient Zero, in an exchange with the writer Adam Mars-Jones.

"At what stage did you decide to give [the Patient Zero story] so much prominence?" Mars-Jones asked.

"Well, I don't think it is that prominent in the book . . ., but I thought it was a fascinating story . . . I think it represents very good investigative journalism."

"There are passages describing how [Patient Zero] would have sex with people in bathhouses, then turn the lights on and say, 'I'm going to die and so are you.'"

"Which he did! At the time he was doing that, I was hearing about it."

"But those were rumors."

"No, it wasn't rumors, I talked to people he did this to . . . I mean, he was doing it quite a bit. The fact is it all happened. The facts are not disputed."

"William Darrow of the CDC [Centers for Disease Control] does repudiate them."

"No, he does not. The fact is that William Darrow saw every word that was written about him and about the study [the 1982 CDC cluster study involving the so-called Patient Zero], and he approved every word of it. Now we're getting into very fine points of argument, and they're not very substantial."[7]

This exchange refers, in part, to a review of *And the Band Played On* that had just been published by Duncan Campbell in the *New Statesman*.[8] Campbell reports a telephone conversation with Darrow in which Darrow explained that the CDC cluster study, which sought to determine whether AIDS was caused by sexual transmission of an infectious agent, was based on speculation that the duration between infection and onset of symptoms was nine to eleven months. Having later learned, as all of us, including Shilts, did, that the period probably averages about eight *years*, Darrow claimed that he made it very clear to Shilts that the Patient Zero story was nonsense. He furthermore said that he pleaded with Shilts not to publish the name of Patient Zero, Gaeton Dugas, fearing that Dugas's family would suffer (and indeed the family later faced death threats).

Shilts cancelled an interview with Campbell when he learned what the *New Statesman* review would entail, and later attacked Campbell in an interview with the gay newspaper *Coming Up*, complaining that this was the

> typical crap I get from certain segments of the gay press . . . I go way back on working on this [epidemic]—and to get it from Campbell, who just came out of his comfortable closet a year ago. . . . I think he has ideological reasons. He's out front, he says it makes gay people look bad. The fact is Patient Zero did exist. . . . It's a brilliant book, superb. . . . [The review is] more snide than *The Bay Area Reporter*. It's a nasty, vindictive attack. It's the only place I've gotten a bad review; the mainstream press loved my book.[9]

Indeed, the mainstream press did love Shilts's book. What Shilts does not say, but what he nevertheless makes clear, is that he returns their love. Ultimately he dismisses the Campbell review by saying that the *New Statesman* (a British equivalent to the *Nation* in the United States) is insignificant, a marginal publication. Shilts's book is in every way a product of his identification with the dominant media and their claim to objectivity. It is this claim that allows Shilts, along with the *New York Times*, for example, to disregard the demands of people with AIDS that they not be called AIDS victims. To accede to their demands would be to give in to a special interest group, a group with an ideological bias. Other groups with ideological biases meriting Shilts's disdain, for which there is ample evidence in *And the Band Played On*, are gay community leaders and AIDS activists.

"Personally, I'm not an ideological person," Shilts said at the ICA. "I don't think you can be a journalist and really have a political ideology, because you tend to see the fallacies in all ideologies." Speaking from this dangerously naive or cynically disingenuous ideological position that calls itself "objective," Shilts explains that

> the whole problem of AIDS from the start was that liberals were trying to be sweet and not tell the whole story, and conservatives did not want to tell the whole story, and I felt what I wanted to do was get the whole story out. At some point I just have to say, I think my work has integrity. I think my work is honest.

Shilts's defense of the Patient Zero story hinges entirely on this naive notion of truth, on the fact, simply, that the story actually happened. But truth is never unproblematic, never a simple matter of empirical facts; it is always selective, always a particular construction, and always exists within a specific context. By the time the narrative of *And the Band Played On* ends, officially 6,079 people had died of AIDS in the United States. Shilts might have selected any one of those people's stories to tell. Among the very few he did select was that of Gaeton Dugas, which makes his story about one six-thousandth of the "truth."

Shilts selected Dugas's story, as he said at the ICA, because it was "fascinating." But what does it mean in the context of AIDS to be *fascinated?* What are the *unconscious* mechanisms that would account for this very selective will to truth? Is this not precisely what Shilts means when he says of the media that they are interested in sexy stories? Is this not, in fact, the recounting of a story we already know, the story of Typhoid Mary, the story of the murderously irresponsible, sexually voracious gay man? Is this not the story of Fabian Bridges, as told on the 1986 PBS *Frontline* special "AIDS: A National Inquiry," in which a black homeless gay man with AIDS, who was forced to support himself by hustling, was bribed by the PBS crew in order to get their story and then reported to the authorities? Is it not the story of the bisexual deliberately infecting "innocent women" in the *Midnight Caller* episode of December 13, 1988, whose producers defended themselves against the protests of the San Francisco gay community by citing the Patient Zero story as proof that such things really do happen?[10] Is it not the story of Rock Hudson, as it was recounted before a jury who would award his ex-lover millions of dollars in damages? Is it not the story of prostitutes and junkies as the media portrays them every day? Is it not ultimately the story of all people with AIDS as they haunt the imaginations of those whose fear and loathing Shilts is so unable to comprehend? Is it not, finally, in the eyes of the INS, the story of Hans Paul Verhoef, the Dutchman they feared would spread AIDS at the Lesbian and Gay Health Conference?

The problem with the Patient Zero story is not whether or not it is true. We now know, in any case, that it is not, at least insofar as we know that Gaeton Dugas had sex with the other men in the CDC cluster study after they had already been infected. Nor is it merely the problem that this story was selected by Shilts's publishers as the story that would sell the book, and that they therefore gave it pride of place in their publicity and had it serialized in *California Magazine.*[11] The real problem with Patient Zero is that he already existed as a phobic fantasy in the minds of Shilts's readers before Shilts ever wrote the story. And, thanks in part to *And the Band Played On*, that fantasy still haunts us—as it still haunts Shilts—today. "I had written a book to change the world," Shilts says in *Esquire.*[12] What he forgot was that this is a world in which people's fantasies of homosexuality include gay waiters running into the kitchen to ejaculate in the salad dressing, or of gay foreigners attending health conferences with no other purpose than to infect their fellow conferees with a deadly virus. Patient Zero is just such a fantasy, and it matters not one whit whether his story is true or not.

1996 Postscript: History as Musical Comedy?

The question posed to this CLAGS panel, "*And the Band Played On:* History as Mini-Series?" arose, no doubt, for two reasons, first, because *And the Band Played On* had been widely acclaimed as the definitive history of the epidemic up to 1985, and second, because the rights to *And the Band Played On* had been purchased by Esther Shapiro, producer of the popular nighttime television soap opera *Dynasty.* Shilts's book faithfully adopted the episodic form of the television series, itself a derivative of the Victorian serialized novel. Each of the stories Shilts's book recounts is interwoven with many others, and each passage of its telling leaves off at just the point where something especially dramatic is portended. Television's series format, in which each segment ends with the demand that we "tune in next time," is scrupulously followed by Shilts, keeping us in a constant state of suspenseful excitement.

When *And the Band Played On* finally made it to the television screen, however, it was not a miniseries but an HBO special movie in yet another television format, the docudrama. Perhaps this pseudo-documentary formula seemed to the team of scriptwriters a more appropriate form of historical reporting. In any case, the fact that the film was still made after such a long delay, and that it met with great success, is testimony to the durability of Shilts's version of events of the early years of the AIDS epidemic. My under-graduate students often cite the HBO film as their most important source of information about AIDS.

The HBO movie greatly reduces the dramatis personae of Shilts's book, and it revolves around a single hero, Don Francis, an honorable and dedicated CDC epidemiologist. Patient Zero is still there, but less prominent and less sensationally portrayed than he is in the book. His function now is that of the reluctant but finally cooperative, if arrogant, participant in the CDC's cluster study (the accuracy and relevance of whose findings are left uncontested in the film), just one of many moments in the story of a heroic scientist as he relentlessly pursues the truth about AIDS against the obstacles thrown in his way by tightfisted government bureaucrats, other scientists with more ego than integrity, profiteering blood-bank executives, and gay activists who care only about preserving their overheated sex lives. Shilts acted as a consultant for the film.

At about the same time that *And the Band Played On* aired on national television, another version of the Patient Zero story appeared on movie screens to provide an off-beat but eloquent critique of Shilts's account. *Zero Patience*, independent Canadian filmmaker John Greyson's wacky musical comedy, stars a ghost named Zero and a Toronto Natural History Museum taxidermist named Dick. The only living being who can see and hear Zero, Dick is the Victorian orientalist and explorer Sir Richard Francis Burton, famous for his translation of *The Thousand and One Nights*. As the narrator explains, Burton's unfortu-nate encounter with the Fountain of Youth in 1892 extended his life span indefinitely. Now engaged in constructing a "Hall of Contagion" at the mu-seum, Burton seizes on the story of "the man who brought AIDS to North America" as the crowning set piece of his exhibit. Zero's story is to be presented as a spectacular music video funded by a pharmaceutical company called Gilbert and Sullivan.

In preparing his video, Burton edits his filmed interviews in such a way as to distort his interlocutors' words, thus making them conform to his preconceived idea of Zero as a sexually insatiable gay "serial killer." Faced with Zero's mother's adamant refusal to be interviewed, Burton cajoles, "Think about how it could help someone else, another young man, another mother." Burton's camera surreptitiously records Madame Zero's reply: "That's just what the journalist said. Ever so smoothly, and I believed him. Well, he made it sound like Zero was the devil, bringing his boyfriends home, flaunting his life style under our noses. Zero never did that, not once." The beleaguered woman's words reappear in the edited tape: "Zero was the devil, bringing his boyfriends home, flaunting his life style under our noses."

"Sometimes the facts have to be rearranged to get at the real truth," argues Burton when Zero confronts him. But, contrary perhaps to our expectations, Greyson's critique of Shilts does not consist of this charge of rearranging and misrepresenting the facts. Unquestionably, Greyson does intend to clear Zero's name. He makes his protagonist sexy, charming, and adorable, and never more so than at the moment when, having learned the truth about the CDC cluster study from none other than "Miss HIV," he proclaims with a broad grin, "I'm innocent. I'm *not* the first, but I'm still the best." Not only do we, the film's viewers, fall in love with Zero, but so does Burton, who decides in the end to refashion his exhibit to clear Zero's name. Recording a new narration for his video, he says, "Patient Zero should be proclaimed a hero of the epidemic. Through his cooperation in the 1982 cluster study, he helped prove that AIDS was sexually transmitted. Thus Zero should be lauded as the slut who inspired safer sex."

"Thanks for nothing," Zero responds. "This has nothing to do with me, with what I was, with what I want. . . . This is just another of your lies." What Zero really desires, Burton cannot give him: Zero wants his life back.

The point is that whatever spin Burton puts on the events, it's never Zero's story, it's Burton's. This is the real thrust of Greyson's critique of Shilts, for unlike Shilts, Greyson makes us aware at every moment that his film is, after all, only a story. Not for nothing is the fate of Scheherazade the film's framing conceit: "Tell a story, save a life, just like Scheherazade," sings Zero in the opening Esther Williams–style water ballet. What might seem wildly eccentric in *Zero Patience* is in fact strategic. That the story's protagonists are a ghost and a nineteenth-century figure still alive in the present, that their story is told through musical numbers that include a pair of singing assholes, a song and dance performance whose characters are animals from the natural history museum's dioramas suddenly sprung to life, and an HIV virus portrayed by Michael Callen in drag and singing falsetto in a Busby Berkeley–style routine seen through a microscope—what could more fully alert us to the *artifice*, the *invention* of this version of the Patient Zero story?

While every storytelling is a construction relying on the codes of its chosen genre, certain genres seek to obscure their conventions, to naturalize them, in order to pose as direct, transparent accounts of the facts, to provide what might be called a truth-effect. This is the case of most mainstream journalism and documentary filmmaking, but surely it is less germane to so-called creative nonfiction and television docudrama. The latter fuses documentary and dramatic techniques to tell a story indistinguishable from fiction film, except that it is supposedly "a true story." The former derives its conventions from bourgeois fiction. Nevertheless, regarding the "creative" qualities of *And the Band Played On*, Shilts writes, "There has been no fictionalization. For purposes of narrative flow, I reconstruct scenes, recount conversations and occasionally attribute observations to people with such phrases as 'he thought' or 'she felt.' " [13] Thus, for Shilts, conventions meant to produce a truth-effect, even those clearly adopted from fiction, are mistaken for truth itself. His own labor to construct that "truth" is disavowed, and his only defense reinforces the disavowal: "The fact is, it all happened." "It was a fascinating story."

Zero Patience, too, tells a sexy story, but one that "happened" only through

John Greyson's vivid imagination, political consciousness, and deft manipulation of filmic conventions. But our fascination with *this* story does not return us to one we already know. This story asks us to question what we think we know, how we come to know, what and how else we might know. For Shilts, history is the story of what actually happened. For Greyson, history is what we make by telling a story.

Notes

Beyond a new postscript, this piece appears as I originally delivered it in April 1989, as part of a CLAGS-sponsored panel, *"And the Band Played On:* History as Mini-Series?" Rather than rework or "update" the talk, I prefer that it be read as very much the occasional piece it was, tied to a specific event, and a product of that historical moment.

1. "Alien with AIDS Is Ordered Freed," *New York Times,* April 8, 1989, A9.
2. Randy Shilts, "Talking AIDS to Death," *Esquire,* March 1989, 124.
3. Ibid., 128.
4. Ibid., 126.
5. Ibid., 128.
6. Ibid., 130.
7. See Tim Kingston, "Controversy Follows Shilts and 'Zero' to London," *Coming Up,* April 1988, 11.
8. Duncan Campbell, "An End to the Silence," *New Statesman,* March 4, 1988, 22–23.
9. Quoted in Kingston, 11.
10. "Mr. DiLello noted that Randy Shilts, in his acclaimed book about AIDS, 'And the Band Played On,' wrote about Gaetan Dugas, the man who may have brought AIDS to San Francisco and who continued to have a multitude of sexual partners even after learning that he was ill." Stephen Farber, "AIDS Groups Protest Series Episode," *New York Times,* December 8, 1988, C24.
11. October 1987 issue.
12. Shilts, 124.
13. Randy Shilts, *And the Band Played On* (New York: St. Martin's, 1987), 607. Shilts adopted the novelistic form for his biography of Harvey Milk, *The Mayor of Castro Street* (1982), and used it consistently right through *Conduct Unbecoming* (1993).

50

AIDS and Adolescence

Cindy Patton

The most heated exchange came when Abraham [the district attorney] and city Health Commissioner Robert K. Ross refused to say how many teenage boys had reported having sex with Savitz.

Officials vowed they would never say whether any of those teenagers were found to have contracted AIDS . . . Ross said it is difficult to ascertain how many teenagers engaged in highest-risk activity—unprotected anal sex with Savitz.

As reporters tried to get Ross to pinpoint how many youths might have been put at risk of AIDS by their contact with Savitz, the questioning was cut off and Ross was escorted from the podium. . . .

Before he left the podium, however, Ross continued to insist that the potential health threat was not as great as officials, including Abraham, had suggested. (*Philadelphia Inquirer*, April 3, 1992, B1, 3)

It is easy to start an AIDS panic.

Existing societal fears and stereotypes quickly amalgamate with misrepresentations of medical and sociological facts. Once started, AIDS panics take on a life of their own. Although we might believe that information can offset the public's fears, cultural narratives of perversion and contagion seem endlessly capable of turning apparently interpretation-proof facts into ammunition for panics and discrimination.

Panics are most volatile when a class of "innocent" victims can be constructed. But in the context of a largely sexually transmitted disease, the very notion of innocence is itself constituted by fears and convictions that have little to do with any actual possibility of transmitting an etiologic agent. I want to use the media coverage from a recent AIDS panic to unearth at least some of the cultural logic about sexuality that fuels rather than quells fears of large-scale contagion.

On March 25, 1992, "Uncle Eddie" Savitz, a Philadelphia man the media described as having been diagnosed with AIDS, was arrested for allegedly having sex with some large number of teenage boys. The boys' underage status and the allegation that Savitz had reportedly "lied" to one or more boys when asked whether he had AIDS produced Savitz as a sex monster and the teenagers as innocent victims. Bail was set at $20 million, a figure associated with organized crime figures or mass murderers. The story instantly made CNN and the *New York Times* and was, of course, almost daily front-page news in the *Philadelphia Inquirer* over the next weeks.

As frequently occurs when there is a high-profile AIDS-related story, hotlines reported a dramatic rise in calls from Philadelphians who thought they might have had sex with Savitz, and from countless others for whom the sensational media coverage and reported conflicts between the Public Health Commission and the district attorney raised the specter of their own infection. Equally unsurprising, violence against gays and others perceived to "have AIDS" reportedly increased, causing panic among the city's gay people and persons living with AIDS (PLWA).

Legally speaking, the term "sex charges" covers a wide range of activities, from unwanted touching to violent rape. The actual charges against Savitz were not specified for more than a week, and when they were finally enumerated they seemed rather less spectacular than the news coverage had suggested. As reported in the April 3 *Philadelphia Inquirer*, they appeared to include allegations of contact with only four boys, none of whom would testify to having joined Savitz in anal intercourse, the major HIV transmission-enabling sexual behavior. In addition, prosecutors would bring as evidence photographs of Savitz in "sexually suggestive poses with two 15 year old boys" taken on the day of his arrest, and testimony by one of those boys that Savitz "asked to have oral sex with him that day." A second boy stated that Savitz had "performed oral sex on him about nine times since September when the boy was 14." Another statement was made by a seventeen-year-old boy who says Savitz also photographed him and "paid him to let Savitz perform oral sex on him between 1989 and 1991." And finally there was "a roommate's statement that Savitz told him 'he had oral and anal sex' with an unspecified number of some 500 boys that the roommate says visited Savitz since 1989."

Police also claimed to have a deposition from a single boy, aged fifteen, who said he had had anal intercourse with Savitz "an unspecified number of times," but there was no indication whether the boy was the recipient or the insertor. In the same *Inquirer* account, defense attorneys are reported as stating that the police reports they had been given contained no mention of anal intercourse and "dispute that this man engaged in any intrusive sexual activity that wasn't protected."

From the first day of coverage, when Savitz was said to have had sex with hundreds, perhaps thousands, of Philadelphia "boys," to the ultimate enumeration of the charges, it appeared that most of the "contact" between Savitz and the boys consisted in his fellating the boys (from the standpoint of HIV transmission, constituting no risk to the boys). What seemed to upset some people was that Savitz had purchased boys' soiled underwear and feces samples, which he reportedly collected in separate, labeled pizza boxes.

Irrespective of the biology of transmission, the fact that a person living with AIDS was indicted on underage sex charges of any kind prompted panic that hundreds, perhaps thousands, of Philadelphia's male youth had been "exposed to AIDS."

Panic over the form of Savitz's sexual interests colluded with panic over AIDS generally. The *Inquirer*'s editorial slip—"highest-risk activity . . . anal intercourse with Savitz"—quite baldly displayed the underlying belief that any association with Savitz, much less any "contact," meant contagion. If HIV was not transmitted, perversion itself might be. Ironically, however, since intercourse, irrespective of gender, age, or other object choice attributes, is the most dangerous form of sex from the standpoint of HIV transmission, then it was the very dispersion of Savitz's sexual aim into scopophilia, fetishism, and oral servicing that provided the boys' safety from HIV infection. The news stories provide no good reason to believe that Savitz was not practicing "safer sex."

The Savitz case raises some interesting theoretical issues. The panic was grounded in a series of confusions. The difference between sexual object and sexual aim was lost; adolescents were constituted as "innocent"; and HIV was conflated with AIDS.

Together, these slippages engendered one category—"sexual contact"—from at least two. The first, scopophilia, fetishism, and fellatio, are dangerous only from the standpoint of cultural fears of sexual difference, while the second, intercourse, is dangerous from the standpoint of HIV infection. Lumping together "perverse" and "normal" sex as "dangerous" ignores the requirements for HIV transmission and slides directly into fear of any sexualized contact with a person living with AIDS. These blurrings generated a full-scale panic, however, only because Savitz's sexual objects were teenage boys.

Adolescent "innocence" is an unstable category. It is constructed in part by adults via a nostalgia for a mythological time before the onset of sexual knowledge. But adolescent innocence also includes the child's yearning to become an adult (i.e., sexual). The adolescent's sexual stirrings foretell but do not produce the sexual subject (adult). This is accomplished through sexual practice, understood as such.

Innocence is invented from memory, or lack of memory, in at least two ways. First, as Sigmund Freud (1918) describes cultural beliefs about virginity,

> The demand that the girl shall bring with her into marriage with one man no memory of sexual relations with another is after all nothing but a logical consequence of the exclusive right of possession over a woman which is the essence of monogamy—it is but an extension of this monopoly on to the past. (193)

Second, invention is constructed through the adult's nostalgia for the ever receding time before the mother was recognized as sexual, a moment the adult is sure existed but can never recall, and must perpetually reinvent.

Thus innocence, as well as those who break cultural taboos by overtly staking their erotic life on it, is a gnomon, a space left over after the production of sexual memory. Erotic practices in relation to innocence, and the complex social institutions designed to protect it, each chip away at the space of innocence by demanding whether innocence knows what it is, ever disqualifying the innocent by pressing him or her into the production of a narrative about innocence that is, of course, always retrospective, about innocence lost.

Innocence is linked principally with sexual knowledge. Traditionally, innocence concerns the acquisition of knowledge about sex in the transition from childhood to adulthood.

In AIDS discourse, notions of innocence are also involved in questions pertaining to the right to withhold information ("lie," "protect confidentiality") about HIV serostatus, and from whom. For the most part, adult sex is now caveat emptor, the exceptions being wives, but not unmarried female partners, of bisexual men. Single women are supposed to realize that any partner might have had sex with men, but the vows of matrimony are somehow supposed to supersede the possibility of spousal lying. For example, there have been difficult debates about whether states should institute contact tracing programs for people who test positive for the HIV antibody. While most states offer voluntary contact tracing programs, some states have passed laws enabling physicians to make contact if they believe the seropositive person will not do so. The major argument lodged in these cases seems to be that, because of the furtive nature of male bisexuals (as opposed to their better adjusted, "open" gay peers), they will not tell their wives.

Representing Sex/Representation as Sex: CNN's "Boy"

The sole "boy," a big and tough-sounding youth interviewed on CNN, casually states that it was widely known that you could make a few bucks by selling your briefs to Uncle Eddie. In the young man's account, Uncle Eddie is benign; if anything, viewers get the impression that his fetish for soiled youthful underwear made Savitz something of a victim to the young hustlers' mercantile schemes. By 1992, viewers were accustomed to associating sexual danger with the one-way exchange of pernicious bodily fluids from "carriers" to "innocent victims": the media's categories of innocence and volition were well established. Gay male to gay male sexual transmission and junky to junky needle-sharing transmission are considered victimless acts, side effects of deviant subcultures that people enter with their eyes open to the dangers. However, both gay or bisexual men and drug injectors are considered "carriers" who intentionally infect women/others through "ordinary" heterosexual intercourse or through luring (white, middle-class) adolescents into their lifestyle. Women sex workers are presumed to have been infected through drug injection and are thought to willfully infect their johns, doubly denying the reality that women, including sex workers, are at substantially greater risk from men during heterosexual intercourse if condoms are not used.

In this system of tropes, readers of the Savitz story had to exert a certain amount of decoding labor to interpret the exchange of money for dry, if soiled, underwear as dangerous sex. Nevertheless, CNN offers us the boy's account as evidence of Savitz's potential for rampant HIV transmission. The CNN boy reminds us that adolescents are supposedly sexually liminal, possessing (or possessed by) sexual desires but not yet engaging in fully sexual acts (i.e., intercourse). By way of his innocence, he stands as a symbol of the possibility of obtaining legal proof of Savitz's guilt as a potential sex murderer.

Where Savitz's perversions (homosexuality, pedophilia, scopophilia, a fixation on oral servicing) signify a derailed sexual trajectory, the boy's participation is largely thought of as a phase. Especially in regard to the selling of underwear, the boy seems not to register Savitz's oddities as sexual: part of the danger of teens' liminal sexuality is that they may inadvertently engage in behaviors they do not "know" are "sex" as they will later recognize it as an adult. Part of the difficulty faced by CNN's interviewer is that he cannot really ask the boy too much lest he provoke the boy into a recognition of his sexuality. This is what divides adults from adolescents: adults are subjects because they have sexuality, while adolescents cannot speak of their sexuality. The victims of sex crimes, in order to convict their violators and preserve the sanctity of innocence in general (the victim's is now lost), must tell us what happened, must narrate from the standpoint of a sexual object. But to confess the crime committed against them means they have knowledge, a memory, which de facto means they are no longer innocent.

CNN finds a novel solution to the problem of producing evidence against Savitz without participating in sexualizing the boy. Unlike the accused but not yet prosecuted Savitz, whose gentle if slightly troubled face was practically a household image, the boy's image was digitally obscured. The legal presumption that Savitz would be innocent until proven guilty is undercut by the evidentiary boy whose natural innocence serves as a prohibition to representing him. To make the innocent speak produces their sexual experiences as narrative, as text, too close to the voyeurism and snapshot pornography CNN has already considered tantamount to sex. Thus, the boy "speaks" without a face.

Teens and AIDS

This problem of the gnomon space of adolescent innocence caused AIDS education and policy to misdirect energies during the crucial mid-1980s, when young people, especially young people of color and young gay men, were rapidly acquiring HIV with no real recognition of their risk. Like CNN, educators had a hard time figuring out how to hail young people without producing them as sexual subjects (or, more commonly, "causing" them to have sex prematurely).

Sadly, for many young people who might eagerly have taken nonjudgmental and straightforward information under advisement, it is now too late. By 1990, 6,233 cases of AIDS were reported in persons aged twenty to twenty-five, and an additional 19,568 in people aged twenty-five to twenty-nine, most of whom would have been infected as teens during the early 1980s (Athey 1991, 523). Seroprevalence studies on army and Job Corps recruits conducted through the late 1980s showed rates of .15 percent nationally, with rates of 1.6 percent among minority youth in some major cities, while studies among runaway youth in metropolitan areas show rates as high as 10 percent (Boyer and Kegeles 1991, 12).

The Savitz case came on the heels of an almost hysterical interest in teens and AIDS. Nearly every network had some kind of special program on teens and AIDS after Magic Johnson's revelations. It appeared that the reality that persons between the ages of twelve and twenty one were contracting HIV in alarming numbers had just been discovered. However, there had been a steady trickle of articles about young people's risk for contracting HIV from 1985, and the Global Program on AIDS had designated the 1989 World AIDS Day for raising awareness about youth and AIDS.

One reason for the declared concern was scientific; it was not until the mid-1980s, following the discovery of HIV (then called LAV or HTLV-111) and a review of epidemiological data, especially the stored serum from a cohort of thousands of gay men who had been enrolled in a hepatitis B study begun in 1978, that researchers were able to realize that time from infection to AIDS diagnoses might be a decade or more, and that people diagnosed in their early to mid-twenties must have been infected as teenagers. However, the framing of the early concerns about young people suggests that additionai cultural factors prevented the constitution of teens *as a class* of people at special risk of contracting HIV through sex.

The initial articles addressing young people and HIV infection took two forms. The first were reports about whether infected "school children" should be allowed in the classroom ("AIDS Issue" 1985; "New Untouchables" 1985; "Lessening Fears" 1986.). These young people were represented as having been infected through transfusions or from blood products used in conjunction with clotting disorders. Here, teenagers were lumped together with elementary school children because their route of transmission was the same.

The most tenured figure in the schools debates was Ryan White, whose life with HIV was widely documented in the popular press. White initially came to the nation's attention because at age thirteen he was banned from school and was hooked up to his classrooms via telephone. We watched White grow into early manhood, including getting a girlfriend and becoming friends with rock stars like Michael Jackson and Elton John. There were a few comments in interviews that he was being actually cautious with his girlfriend. White, like men with clotting disorders generally, was never represented as a sexual being. His passage through adolescence seemed to keep him in a state of perpetual innocence instead. The terror of sexually active HIV-infected teenagers never emerged.

The second area of coverage of teens and HIV concerned the question of whether college students were "practicing safe sex" ("Campus Sex" 1985; Van Gelder and Brandt 1986). The age of students seemed less a concern than the general upswing of concern about "heterosexual AIDS" in the wake of Rock Hudson's death.

In all these cases, concerns centered on white middle-class young people, most of whom were "straight." But articles began to include token accounts of a now-infected gay-boy-next-door who had not realized that he, too, might be at risk (presumably from older, more culpable gay men). The *New York Times* (Gross 1987) produced a rare article about the plight of "gay teenagers," but these teens, since "many of them are not yet sexually active," were considered a subcategory of students. If stories that allowed nice gay boys to be counted as innocent teens suggested that homophobia had diminished, racism and sexism quickly filled the vacated space. A review of epidemiologic data clearly shows that among men of color reported as having AIDS, a large percentage must have contracted HIV while still in their teens. Likewise, women in general and especially women of color diagnosed with AIDS must have contracted HIV as teens.

In many popular media accounts young people of color were represented as culpable—not innocent victims—either because they were said to engage in adult behavior at much younger ages or because they live in the harsh inner city, an uncivilized world in which "primitive" behaviors were expected. A *Good Housekeeping* advice column ("Teenagers" 1990) answers the question, "Is your child at risk?" by providing "markers" as "guides" "to identify young-sters who are at risk." Along with the long-standing middle-class problem children—"[G]irls with early physical development" and "[A]dolescents with serious school problems"—the article states, "Youngsters living in poverty in inner cities are at very high risk. They are often under great social pressures to have sex early, and IV drugs may be rampant in their environment" (257). Thus, in AIDS discourse, "adolescence" virtually always referred to the white middle or working class. Teenage sex traders and drug injectors, who were often represented as part of the Black or Latino urban underclass, were a source of danger (and therefore adult) rather than a site of innocence. While the risk of transmission was partly an issue of age in the case of school attenders and experimenting college students, the actual grouping together of similarly aged people into the cross-transmission route at risk category "adolescent" did not occur until the early 1990s, in the context of Magic Johnson's announcement and the subsequent publicity given to a range of studies on adolescent drug use, underutilization of medical care, and mortality rates.

Adolescence between Innocence and Safety

There are several terms that cover the age group running roughly from twelve to twenty-one—teenager, adolescent, youth, adult. While each term and the concept it indexes carry connotations of the subject's relation to knowledge about adult matters, they all share a theory of human development, conceived in the mid-twentieth century, that imagines a stage between a natural and innocent childhood and an accomplished (worked for) adulthood. Anna Freud (1958) described this in-between period as a time of upheaval and liminality in which the normal and abnormal are reversed: "To be normal during the adolescent period is by itself abnormal" (275).

Western notions of adolescence are shot through with colonialist fantasies about liminal stages drawn from research on aboriginal cultures (Turner 1967). Adolescence—the space between childhood and adulthood—is represented as always in danger of collapse, impinged upon by the forces of modernity. Campaigns for child labor laws and mandatory school attendance, which served the evolving economic needs of industrial and postindustrial societies, are usually couched in terms of preserving childhood and adolescence as a time free from adult pressures like work and sex.

The general belief in adolescence—even given variations by gender, ethnicity, and geography—as a time of turmoil between a period of innocence (childhood) and one of accomplished identity and safety (adulthood) underlies AIDS discourse. Although commentators (Powers, Hauser, and Kilner 1989) note that the "storm and stress" (200) model of adolescence does not stand up under empirical investigation and is undergoing a paradigm shift, policy advocates and AIDS researchers seem to still believe that adolescence is a stage, however difficult to pin down, during which young people are exposed to features of a previously foreclosed adult lifestyle, but lack all the necessary skills to actually operate responsibly as adults. Even when actively engaged in supposedly adult-defining behaviors (sexual intercourse and drug injection), adolescents somehow perform them with childish attitudes, with a lack of full understanding of what they are doing. Adolescents' risk taking is explained away: teens are incapable of judging future consequences of current acts and believe they are immortal. While much of the data offered bear out these conclusions, it is unclear that most adults are any better at looking to their future or evaluating the consequences of proximate risks. Apparently, adults are allowed to choose self-destructive behaviors (alcohol consumption seems key here, followed by cigarette smoking, eating a bad diet, and overwork) that would count as impaired adolescent reasoning if engaged in by a slightly younger person.

This construction of adolescents as unbalanced and on the cusp of acting without full understanding underlies the confusion in the Savitz accounts concerning sexual object and aim. Freud defines the terms: "the person from whom sexual attraction proceeds [is] the sexual object and the act toward which the instinct tends [is] the sexual aim." The Savitz coverage and accounts of adolescence generally assume adolescence to be a time of *deflected* object and aim and consider accomplished or fixed object and aim to define adulthood.

The apparent decrease in homophobia in opinion polls and popular discourse about AIDS generally accepts homosexual object choice as valid or at least workable (i.e., susceptible to change toward safer sex). This can occur only because a gay male sexuality historically is analogized to the same trajectory from "innocence" to intercourse I have been describing. Here, the sexual revolution of the 1970s is equated with the meaningless play of burgeoning desires and inability to foresee future dire consequences thought to characterize the individual adolescent. As two early AIDS commentators (Fettner and Check 1984) describe it,

> the realities of AIDS may turn [gay men's] inchoate desires into a political consensus. . . . Gay men are being forced by AIDS to recognize their personal priorities, to put aside self-preoccupation and to turn their abilities outward to the good of a wider community. (243)

This description suggests that acceptance has occurred due to the emergence of an adult gay community characterized by altruism, political participation, and, tacitly, safe sex. A 1990 *Newsweek* feature on "The Future of Gay America" describes a party in which "5,000 condoms rained down on guests" (22) in a nightclub. This "encouraging sign that safe sex works" (23) uses the now-worn device of signifying safe sex through the mention of condoms. The persistent focus on condoms and their association with the new gay male sexuality of the AIDS era—"infection among gay men has been dropping since 1987" (23)—seems to insist that intercourse is now the mature and stable form of sex.

This belief in intercourse as a mark of adult homosexuality is quite recent. Freud (1905), reviewing early sexological findings, states that homosexual men and women have a deviation of object and of aim (11–12). Freud notes that men prefer manual sex (what is described in AIDS education as "mutual masturbation," an already value-laden term that reinforces the view of male homosexuality as a kind of projective narcissism) while women prefer kissing.

Whether this actually reflected any kind of numerical reality is impossible to determine. There are certainly celebrated cases of "sodomy" involving both lesbians and gay men that would have come to Freud's attention. Indeed, Henry Abelove (1992) argues that the dominance of intercourse as both the preferred method of sexual encounter and the act definitive of "real" sex around which "foreplay" and even "homosexual" acts were organized occurs quite late, and in tandem with the differentiation of work and leisure time. The need to organize sex in order to make room for work may have unconsciously motivated an insistence on intercourse as the proper aim and sexologists' use of male-female intercourse as the standard alongside which their favored "deviations" coexisted as "normal" abnormalities. Under the pressure of safe sex education in the context of AIDS, a homosexuality that was once doubly deviant has now "straightened out" its aim. Now homosexuality and heterosexuality differ only in gender of object choice: Savitz is a "deviant" homosexual.

Work and Sex

There is an inescapable logic to the tale of adolescent development. The adolescent does not legitimately own his or her body. That body is not a legitimate vessel for sexual pleasure. In neither sex nor work can an adolescent legitimately use it, improve it, wear it out, or destroy it as he or she elects. Adolescence ends only with the capacity to work and have sex. This sequence complicates the Savitz case.

If Savitz is supposed to have stolen the boys' innocence through premature sex, the CNN boy's casual suggestion that a lot of boys knew they could make money from Savitz reveals a rather calculating underground economy of teenage fetish-peddlers.

Media accounts of young people trading sex for money often cast them and their innocence as doubly lost. They have sex "prematurely" because of being driven to a need for remunerative work—the first loss of innocence. But having had sex, they develop an adult desire for both more sex and more money—the second loss of innocence.

Some elaboration of the consequences of these losses of innocence is warranted. Selling sex is understood differently in young women and men. For young men, hustling is a preliminary form of entrepreneurship. The fact of having sold his body to men does not imply that the entrepreneur is homosexual. The innocence lost pertains to work. He is no longer a work virgin, but not yet a sexually identifiable item. For a young woman, however, prostitution acts as a nonlegitimate replacement for the culturally sanctioned barter of matrimony. She loses her sexual innocence but maintains her work innocence. She ends up very much defined as a sexual object, but not as an entrepreneurial subject.

Having sex and achieving economic independence vie for premier place among the criteria for establishing the boy's adulthood. To see the boys as adults because of their commercial ventures implies consent, making them responsible (as adults) for insuring the safety of their own sexual activity. Here, the issue of Savitz's alleged "lying" takes on special significance. If "safe sex" is predicated on the "honesty" of one's partner, Savitz's "lie" enhances his status as contagious. For example, a *Good Housekeeping* editorial ("Teenagers" 1990) suggests that parents "make it clear how important it is to select a partner carefully" (257), and the surgeon general's report (1988), sent to households in most states, contains a section called "What about Dating?" that advises,

> You are going to have to be careful about the person you become sexually involved with, making your own decision based on your own best judgment. That can be difficult.

Has this person had any sexually transmitted diseases? How many people have they been to bed with? Have they experimented with drugs? All these are sensitive, but important, questions. But you have a personal responsibility to ask. (4)

This injunction to "know your partner" is itself complicated, and it generates further complications regarding questions of complicity and innocence. For instance, most advice pamphlets produced outside the gay community advise avoiding sex with persons with HIV. As I have argued elsewhere (1990, 1992), most advice to heterosexuals suggests that any sex act is safe with a person known to be HIV negative, while no act is safe (only safer) with a person of unknown or positive HIV serostatus. This advice pointedly ignores a huge number of always-safe activities—voyeurism, intercourse with dildos, manual stimulation, and so forth. But it also implies that one cannot know of them without having lost one's innocence. Knowledge of those safe activities must be gained through illegitimate channels.

The advice also leaves open a vast terrain of people who don't know, don't know they should know, or won't tell you—dumb innocents or false innocents.

It is extremely difficult to establish a legal obligation to know one's HIV antibody status, especially when the modes of transmission are voluntary and the means of prevention so easy. Given the difficulty individuals outside the hardest-hit groups (urban gay men and urban drug injectors) have recognizing their own risk, and given that test taking does not reliably stimulate risk reduction, it seems particularly hazardous to hang the safety of heterosexual sex on the very innocent idea that one's partner will be willing to accurately share test results. Here, the sexual innocence attributed to adolescence has percolated upward and has destructively misshapen "adult messages" regarding safe sex practices.

As innocence is differentially distributed, so the apparent need for changes in sexual practices will also be differentially distributed. Curbing HIV transmission might require everyone to change their sexual practices. I have elsewhere shown (Patton 1990, 1992a, 1992b) that the changes in concepts of homosexual practice both inside and outside the gay community, as well as the emergence of a strongly felt sense of "heterosexual" identity among young Americans, serve as end runs around the need to confront this possibility.

Notions of innocence dovetail with notions of risk and are differentially constructed by gay versus straight cultures. At least on the ideological level, most urban gay men seem to accept that they will have to use condoms in order to engage in intercourse. A significant portion of gay men simply always have safe sex without revealing or inquiring about serostatus. Their heterosexual cohorts, by contrast, often continue to trust in their own capacity to distinguish the innocent from the complicit, that is, they continue to believe in innocence.

They develop ever more complex schemes for quizzing their partners or looking for signs of danger.

It is remarkable that there is no suggestion in the Savitz stories that the boys might be gay. They must be considered straight in order to be counted as victims.

Young people are generally considered heterosexuals, even as they "explore" homosexuality. One *works* at homosexuality, while heterosexuality, it seems, comes without practice. Thus, while Eddie is represented as a homosexual (the "roommate" who is to testify against him shores up this idea), the boys are not. Their mutual sexual activity might be described as homosexual, but the boys are "innocent." Therefore, their decision-making capacities are presumed to operate in the heterosexual, information-sparse, know-your-partner epi-steme. Eddie, on the other hand, operates in the homosexual, information-dense, always-practice-safe-sex episteme. In this complex of different quantities of available information and different strategies for arriving at decisions about safe sex, the source of a fall from innocence and the presumption of both having knowledge and having to share it falls on Savitz. Not only does he know, or, as a member of a "risk group," is *thought responsible to find out* his HIV serosta-tus, but also he is, ironically, someone constructed as occupying the position of pedagogue. He is thought responsible for conveying knowledge about safe sex that the innocent young men are presumably unable to have gotten in their homes, schools, or leisure activities.

HIV versus AIDS

Perhaps the most critical pedagogic error in the news coverage of the Savitz case was the blurring of the crucial distinction between Human Immunodefi-ciency Virus (HIV) and Acquired Immune Deficiency Syndrome. You do not "get AIDS" through *any* form of contact; rather, you contract HIV through specific, known, and relatively difficult routes—sexual intercourse in which there is ejaculation into the anus or vagina, or conversely, in which there is dramatic abrasion to the penis, permitting entry of the virus into the urethra; innoculation, either through transfusion or use of blood products, or through sharing hypodermic needles during medical or nonmedical procedures; and from mother to fetus. Health educators consider this distinction crucial in helping the public understand why they need not fear widespread contagion, decreasing fatalism about preventing HIV transmission to oneself, and improv-ing the situation of already infected people by encouraging them to take advan-tage of life-prolonging and quality of life enhancing measures (Aggleton et al. 1989, 57–59; Lawrence 1991).

Most scientists now believe that HIV, along with a potentially wide variety of cofactors, is the principal but not sufficient etiologic agent that may, some ten years after infection, result in immune system failure that renders the infected person susceptible to the some two dozen opportunistic infections that bring with them an AIDS diagnosis. Opportunistic infections or the generalized direct effects of HIV (wasting and encephalopathy) occur only after the crucial T-4 cells drop from the normal 800–1200 parts per milliliter to less than 200, losing about 100 parts per year. With prophylaxis for pneumocystis canini pneumonia, once the major cause of death in people diagnosed with AIDS, a significant number of long-infected people (ten to fifteen years) have T cell counts around 50 and still do not qualify for an AIDS diagnosis. HIV-infected individuals are presumably infectious for a decade or more before recognizable symptoms occur. This makes asking whether someone "has AIDS" less than helpful if one uses obtaining a medical history as a means of screening partners. While asking whether someone is HIV positive might be more useful, it is likely that many people simply do not know, or prefer not to tell and instead engage exclusively in risk-eliminating behavior.

The confusion between HIV and AIDS in the Savitz case is all the more remarkable because only five months earlier, the same news sources had gone out of their way to explain the crucial distinction during Magic Johnson's November 1991 revelation. Indeed, in the methadone clinics where I was working at that time, it became common for clients to describe HIV as "what Magic's got." Individuals whose HIV status becomes a public issue are recruited as narrative devices in explaining AIDS to consumers of news media. If Magic Johnson was to operate as a role model for living positively with HIV and a wholesome example to young people, he had to be produced as (still) a figure of health and strength who had not become monogamous soon enough. Similarly, for Savitz to play the role of monster in relation to innocent teens, he must be produced as always and already sick, even before he acquired HIV, if indeed he did not simply have it *sui generis* as a pervert. If the careful coverage of Magic Johnson's status momentarily taught a nation the difference between HIV and AIDS, the very same media's coverage of Savitz set HIV education back years.

AIDS Panics/AIDS Education

AIDS panics spur the consolidation of hazardous cultural logics. In the Savitz panic, this decreased the possibility of providing useful advice to young people. Much AIDS discourse and media coverage like that surrounding the Savitz case constitute intercourse as the identity-conveying adult sexual act. They also increase the anxiety about protecting the "innocent." That discourse seems to promote the most risk-enabling act while simultaneously issuing a gag order on explaining how to do it safely.

As long as the responsibility for "causing" HIV infection is laid at the door of the people with whom teenagers may have sex, the "know your partner" strategy will prevail. It will be promoted over strategies like condoms or the far from innocent choice of other pleasurable nonintercourse activities.

Freud was sure that inverts were doubly perverse, in both object and aim. A century later we may find that deviations of aim are a survival tactic, and gay men, no longer innocent, having normalized safe sex, may provide the best model for self-conscious, ingenuous sexual development.

References

Abelove, Henry. 1992. "Some Speculations on the History of 'Sexual Intercourse' during the 'Long Eighteenth Century' in England." In *Nationalisms and Sexualities,* ed. Andrew Parker, Mary Russo, Doris Sommer, and Patricia Yaeger. New York: Routledge.

Aggleton, Peter, Hilary Homans, Jan Mojsa, Stuart Watson, and Simon Watney. 1989. *AIDS. Scientific and Social Issues, A Resource for Health Educators.* London: Churchill Livingston.

"The AIDS Issue Hits the Schools." 1985. *Time,* September 9.

Athey, Jean L. 1991. "HIV Infection and Homeless Adolescents." *Child Welfare* 70 5.

Boyer, Cherrie B., and Susan M. Kegeles. 1991. "AIDS Risk and Prevention among Adolescents." *Social Science Medicine* 33.1.

"Campus Sex: New Fears." 1985. *Newsweek,* October 28.

Fettner, Anne Guidici, and William A. Check. 1984. *The Truth about AIDS: Evolution of an Epidemic.* New York: Holt, Rinehart, and Winston.

Freud, Anna. 1958. "Adolescence." In *Psychoanalytic Study of the Child.* New York: International Universities Press.

Freud, Sigmund. 1905. "The Sexual Aberrations." In *Three Essays on the Theory of Sexuality.* SE 7.

————1918. "The Taboo of Virginity." SE 11.

"The Future of Gay America." 1990. *Newsweek,* March 12.

Gross, Jane. 1987. "AIDS Threat Brings New Turmoil for Gay Teenagers." *New York Times,* October 21.

Lawrence, Raise. 1991. *Sex Talk: Reformulating AIDS Education for Adolescents.* Unpublished thesis. Amherst, Mass: Amherst College.

"Lessening Fears." 1986. *Time,* February 17.

"The New Untouchables." 1985. *Time,* September 23.

Patton, Cindy. 1990. *Inventing AIDS.* New York: Routledge.

————. 1992a. "From Nation to Family: Containing African AIDS." In *Nationalism and Sexualities,* ed. Andrew Parker, Mary Russo, Doris Sommer, and Patricia Yaeger. New York: Routledge.

————. 1992b. " 'With Champagne and Roses': Women at Risk from/in AIDS Discourse." In *Women and AIDS,* ed. Corrine Squire. Sage Women and Psychology Series. London: Sage.

Powers, Sally L., Stuart T. Hauser, and Linda A. Kilner. 1989. "Adolescent Mental Health." *American Psychologist* 44.2.

Surgeon General. 1988. "Understanding AIDS."

"Teenagers and AIDS." 1990. *Good Housekeeping,* May.

Turner, Victor. 1967. *The Forest of Symbols: Aspects of Ndembu Ritual.* Ithaca: NY: Cornell University Press.

Van Gelder, Lindsay, and Pam Brandt. 1986. "AIDS on Campus." *Rolling Stone,* September 25, 483.

51

Women and AIDS in Sub-Saharan Africa

Nellie Mathu

My entry point is the background within which women are exposed to the AIDS epidemic in Africa. Infection does not just happen. Since the first cases were identified in the early 1980s, there have been numerous theories about the disease's origin, and fingers have been pointed from one continent to the other. The frenzy about AIDS starting in Africa hinges on the fact that Africa has for a long time been known as the "Dark Continent."

Then, of course, fingers were pointed to special needs groups. "Oh, it only affects the gay community, so, in a way, it's all right." Or "It only affects the blacks, so in another way, maybe it's all right." People kept moving aside, until it started affecting the mainstream—what they call the "mainstream." Then people stopped pointing fingers, because the fingers were getting closer and closer to themselves. But all that time, while fingers were being pointed, and we were very busy apportioning blame, we were continuing to lose very valuable lives, and fear and denial were continuing to spread unchecked.

Stigmatization took the place of reason and compassion, and almost everybody ran amok. To a large extent people are still running amok—though at this point, many of us have realized that there is nowhere to hide. The spread of AIDS has shown us that it is impossible to live in isolation from the world community, as we are part of one planet, one system; AIDS, as somebody put it, does not need a visa to enter a homestead or even a country. It is predicted that each one of us living today will know a person infected with AIDS. For many of us, of course, this is no longer a prediction; it is a grim, painful reality.

Now, during the past decade, HIV has infected more than ten million people worldwide. As of 1992, approximately 81 percent of these infections are in the developing countries, which carry 76 percent of the world's population. The remaining 19 percent of cases are in the world's developed countries, with 24 percent of the world's population. While Africa carries only 11 percent of the world's population, it contains approximately 63 percent of the HIV-positive cases. In comparison, Asia, with 56 percent of the world's population, contains only 6 percent, although these figures are going higher every day. North and Latin America, with 5 percent and 8 percent of the world's population, respectively, contain only about 12 percent of HIV infections. Although statistics are necessary in order to give a general overview of the distribution of cases around the world, AIDS cannot fully be understood only through statistics.

The abstract nature of statistics obscures the human experiences of the epidemic. This approach strips the human experience of AIDS from its social, cultural, political, economic, historic, and personal contexts. The exclusion of these human experiences, especially in the study of women and AIDS in Africa, limits our understanding of how AIDS differentially impacts on their lives. Media representation of AIDS solely as a sexually transmitted disease in Africa is also inaccurate, in that it fosters victim-blaming attitudes and justifies inadequate national and international responses—most of which have been limited to condom distribution and abstract AIDS education and information programs.

In addition, epidemiological studies have included women in Africa in their research only out of concern for their roles as reproducers of children. This has resulted in women not being viewed as active agents of change, but as passive bearers of children and of the HIV virus. Women are blamed for perinatal and heterosexual transmission of AIDS, which, combined, accounts for 80 percent of all AIDS infections in Africa. Little effort is made to understand under which conditions the women themselves were infected. Feminist scholars take issue with these studies, because they maintain that women must be worthy of research because of their humanness, and not just because of their reproductive function in society.

Gender and class relations shaping women's multiple experiences of the pandemic must be seen as a valid starting point in AIDS research. It is social relations that mold and even determine the setting of each individual's exposure and susceptibility to infection. The African family differs from the nuclear family, comprising a father, a mother, and their children, in that it is a part of a larger kin group. The male members of the kin group have the familiar obligation to perpetuate the lineage. The prosperity and security of the lineage are closely linked to the members in the kin group, which makes children an essential requirement in any marriage. Marriage is therefore closely monitored by elders in the kin group. In many African cultures, too, marriages are exogamous, which means that the girl marries into a clan, or into a tribe, and she has to come from outside that clan. She is perceived as an outsider, a very lonely outsider, into that clan, until such time as she gives birth to children. It is through those children that she can claim her place in that kin group; and of course, we should note that in many rural setups, where girls do not go to school, they are socialized to look at marriage as the ultimate form of self-actualization.

Through marriage, the girl gains status as a wife and mother. She is no longer referred to by her name, but rather as the mother of so-and-so, or the wife of so-and-so. The birth of a baby boy, of course, is particularly prestigious, because he in turn will be an accountable member of the kin group, and he will in turn also have the responsibility to extend the kin group. From the man's perspective, marriage and children give him status in the lineage as he fulfills his obligation to continue it. Female fidelity is very important in these arrangements; it allows the kin group to maintain the purity of the lineage and insure the legitimacy of the members. Man's infidelity, on the other hand, is perceived as a sign of manhood, as it is an indication of additional wives and children.

The family size and fertility are controlled by the menfolk, and it is very unusual for a woman to initiate protection or contraception, especially if the method being used is the condom. The woman is reduced to the role of reproducer; she is appreciated only through her fertility. Here, motherhood legitimizes a woman's sexuality and, very often, her life. The multiple meanings of children to the woman, as well as the dilemmas women are faced with when asked to choose between motherhood and avoiding HIV infection, must therefore be clearly understood and appreciated.

Now let us look at the social realities that set the stage against which the epidemic is unfolding. With the coming of colonial domination in many of the African countries, traditional forms of livelihood were disrupted, discouraged, or outright forbidden. Men were forced to migrate to urban centers or neighboring countries in search of paid labor. Women were left to assume the responsibilities of heads of families without the control that goes with it. In the absence of her husband, it is likely that elders in the kin group will make decisions about her household instead of asking the woman to make those decisions.

Because of these extended separations, which could stretch from a few months to years, men took on additional wives within the towns where they worked. The women, on the other hand, constantly found themselves exchanging sexual favors for badly needed cash or other gifts. Closely linked with the above point is the takeover of African agricultural systems by capitalism. With capitalism came the amassing of wealth in the hands of a few, while the majority were left with nothing. Landlessness translated to malnutrition, hunger, and ultimate poverty. Constant wars resulted in young men being confined in military camps, while political upheavals made women and children flee for their lives. The refugee system reached epidemic proportions, and people were forced to live in subhuman conditions. Disease erupts in times of crisis and under living conditions such as these.

There is a direct relationship between economic turmoil, widespread unemployment, intense competition, women's low status, and the spread of sexually transmitted diseases, including AIDS. Like so many other diseases produced by socioeconomic and political conditions, AIDS is a disease of development and underdevelopment. The virus is only a biological agent, the effects of which are magnified by conditions of rapid urbanization, distorted development, and the current world crisis.

The organization African Women Against AIDS, which I currently chair, is a nongovernmental organization that provides advocacy on the plight of African women as they confront AIDS devastation, in addition to the poverty that they deal with on a day-to-day basis. Our founding members were concerned with the Western media representation of AIDS primarily as a sexually transmitted disease, without regard to the other factors that are at play. We recognized that AIDS prevention is both personal and political. Effective control will require a change in the economic and social status of women. Women's economic independence, personal autonomy, and control over interpersonal relations, including the power to negotiate sex, must be increased if we are to stop AIDS.

The gap that exists between AIDS education and behavior modification can be narrowed only if women's needs are addressed in their entirety. The lessons that were *supposedly* learned in many of the African countries from family planning programs is that you cannot just go to people and imagine that they are empty vessels, waiting to be filled with beautiful information—beautiful, as you see it; or that after you give them the information, they will automatically change behavior that puts them at risk. But this lesson does not seem to have been learned: AIDS information is being conveyed in the same manner.

Women in Africa are being told about the presence of this new disease; they know that there is this threat. But they are not changing behavior, and the question is why? Women are not being reached. You cannot just go and tell a woman who is hungry, who has a child—who is probably very sick and probably not going to school—"leave the income-generating activities that you are working with, leave the development activities that you are working with, and come tomorrow—we want to teach you about AIDS information and education." AIDS, as they see it, "is something that may come to me, or it may not come, but the hunger that I feel is an issue now."

It is not a matter of whether it will come or it will not come. When women have such low status, when women are the poorest of the poor in any given society, you cannot go and tell them to protect themselves tomorrow, without dealing with where they are today. You cannot lead people into tomorrow without knowing where they are coming from. And that has been a major omission in AIDS work.

Our organization, therefore, tries to involve ourselves with where women are *now*. We take where they are, and AIDS information and education, and blend the two together, so that they stop seeing AIDS as something out there, something they will deal with tomorrow. "I'll deal with you when I finish with the hunger. I'll deal with you when I finish with school fees."

We deal with them all together, because all are part of life, and all impact on their lives. UNICEF reported a case from Uganda (which is very badly devastated with AIDS) where women were seen to weep openly when they were told that they tested HIV negative. Why? They wept because if they had tested positive, their children would have been eligible for school subsidy; as long as they test negative, their children cannot be assisted. That is the context within which women are being told, abstractly, to protect themselves. If those women who are weeping were told that within that door there is AIDS, or the virus is in that door, what do you think they would do, very likely? Run there, get infected, get subsidy.

They would give their life so that their children may live. And if we do not want them to continue doing that, if we do not want them to continue engaging in activities that put them at risk—selling sexual favors, sleeping with their husbands even when they are coming from towns where they know that they have been exposed to HIV infection—then we must reach them in compassion, as human beings, and not just tell them, "Protect yourselves." Our main objective must be to promote the welfare of rural women through the improvement of their health status and quality of life.

52

On the Need for a Gay Reconstruction of Public Health

Walt Odets

A decade and a half into the epidemic, those who care about the human futures of gay men must begin to think about new alliances among disciplines that will reconstruct public health for gay men and help us take back and begin—within the realities of our lifelong epidemic—to remake our lives. The pervasive presence of traditional public health in gay culture has given the discipline inordinate influence on gay men's personal and interpersonal lives, their feelings about themselves, and their visions of—or lack of vision about—their futures. The "gay agenda" today is largely subsumed by the public health agenda. The pulses of our communities are now taken by epidemiologists, and our well-being and accomplishments are measured in seroprevalence and seroincidence statistics. But even as public health's necessary presence in gay communities has contributed to some reduction in HIV transmission and the sometimes useful treatment of those already infected, it has also become a huge humanly impoverishing force. The narrow understandings and purposes of traditional public health have been unable to help a despised, sexually identified minority envision viable ways to live humanly rich and intimate lives in an enduring, sexually vectored epidemic. *Those* visions are the foundations of lives worth living, and thus of lives worth protecting from infection. We have abdicated too much to the dictates of public health in hopes that it would save us, and it has not in any sense of the idea.

Much of human life has always been determined by others' anxious, narrow, or self-interested prescriptions. Gay men, who so often feel shame and guilt about their sexuality and need to make amends for the transgression, have, as a group, inordinate cravings for familial and social acceptance. This has historically made us particularly responsive to others' prescriptions, at least in public. But in the late 1960s, gay people began a movement in the United States that was aimed loosely at gaining political and social power on our own terms. Ultimately, the most important products of such power would have been the opportunity to begin an integration of our internal lives—and thus of our external lives with our internal lives—and out of this wholeness, a capacity to not feel about ourselves as others feel about us. We would, we hoped, no longer live lives profoundly distorted by the psychological internalization of others' hatred and self-hatred.

With this effort barely launched, an alarming matter came to light. It quickly seemed a matter directly connected to our sexuality, but one we hoped would be short-lived and allow us to return to issues of human liberation. In 1990, however, we entered a new decade of life in the epidemic, and the matter was still with us. It was now vigorous, now substantially threatening our future, and it had insidiously come to define our agenda. The "simple behavioral changes" that were to have ended the epidemic—described ad nauseum in public health education—had not ended it. Furthermore, careful observers were discovering that many younger men, having come to adulthood in the epidemic—with the behavioral information, but never having known a gay life without AIDS—were not, in their unconscious feelings, even entertaining the possibility of being gay and *not* being infected. Many older men who also had the behavioral information, but had actually seen the death and experienced the losses, were becoming infected through unconscious identification, depression, guilt, and a sense of the inevitability of infection. We discovered, to the surprise of many, that gay sex was not merely perverse recreation, but humanly compelling and essential, and that it was not being conducted in the ordinary, rational states of consciousness that traditional public health both assumed and insisted on.

Oddly, given the long-standing history of our political and social issues, AIDS has created an unexpected niche for gay men and their sexual behaviors in the popular consciousness. While this niche of acknowledgment *resembles* something gay liberation of the 1970s sought, it is in good part nothing more than the plausible elaboration of an erotophobic and homophobic mentality: a heightened popular consciousness of gay lives to be sure, but one preoccupied with gay lives contorted by transgression, illness, disfigurement, death, retribution, and contrition. These are lives the public has always fantasized about gay men and gay men have always feared for themselves, and the transition into the age of AIDS was a natural and easy one for both gay men and the general public. Today the parent warns his son, not that he is *going to hell*, but that he is *going to get AIDS*. What is too often, if not invariably, left out of this new consciousness of gay lives—because it is too unexpected by both them and us—is a perception of integrated, intimate, respected, and self-respected lives. Today we might be sympathetically perceived as caretakers, but we remain only rarely supported as lovers.

It is certainly true that the epidemic has allowed gay men to demonstrate considerable talent, intelligence, perseverance, and humanity in personal and community service, public policy, and public health. But from the beginning we have also been preoccupied with public appraisals of our "response" to the epidemic quite aside from the overwhelming necessity of that response. If we were going to be disfigured and tortured with AIDS for sexual transgression, we were determined to show that we were dealing with it particularly well. Our own long-standing conflicts about being gay left us ready to espouse, and sometimes even adopt, a newly approved, sanitary sex that eschewed the very fluids that made sex intimate. We were eager to have, or pretend to have, sex the way we were told to have it. We were ready to declare celibacy. We were ready to declare our contrition and accept penance. We were, after all, nothing more or less than virtually normal, and we were going to make that clear by doing good and being good under the worst of circumstances.

Such feelings—as intelligible as they are pervasive and destructive—have caused us to succumb to some of the most confusing and dangerous potentials of the epidemic. This is nowhere more clearly expressed than in our unqualified embracing of the values and purposes of traditional public health. We have basked in the praise of our "unprecedented public health success" and have thus failed to acknowledge and clarify some of the destructive sources and the human costs of that success. Behind the approbation—in our private lives and private consciousness, where both we and society have always insisted on confining our pain—our public health victories are grotesquely marred by new wounds and new scars. These include new fears and loathing of our own desires and intimacies, new disconnections between gay men, new kinds of loneliness and hopelessness, and new kinds of shame and guilt about new kinds of transgressions. In our wishes to be masters of public health, we have been unable to acknowledge that our public health victory has also been a human disaster.[1]

With beginnings as a "health police" in the tuberculosis epidemic of the late nineteenth century, public health has traditionally considered the individual, human issues of "carriers" secondary to the issues of the uninfected "public." Public health's unequivocal purpose was to protect the larger public from infection, with little regard to the consequences for those already infected. Although public health has expanded its vision and methods considerably during the past forty years, it has come to the AIDS epidemic still primarily centered on these narrow purposes. Regardless of the reality of the issue, much of public health's *perceived* role in the AIDS epidemic has been to protect the heterosexual mainstream from infection by minorities. In the context of such purposes, it is understandable that public health—which, like the mainstream values that inform it, is inclined anyway to treat gay sex dismissively, if not contemptuously—has patently ignored the human costs of gay men's public health victory. But it is a testimony to the power and tenacity of our own internal conflicts that a radical minority, significantly defined by the very behaviors public health sought to change and limit, has so readily embraced public health's narrow purposes for *its own* epidemic. It is now apparent that our internal conflicts have caused a majority of us to paradoxically identify with both "carrier" and "public," regardless of known HIV status. This confused identification has spawned an approach to HIV prevention in gay communities that is not only humanly destructive, but of too little utility in stemming infection itself.

If it were not clear before, the AIDS epidemic should make it obvious that the concepts of carrier and public are partly social constructions that express our feelings about each other. But within those social issues, there are also knowable, if not always known, medical realities: some gay men are now infected with HIV and others are not. The gay community's identification with the *public* in public health's paradigm is relatively understandable. *Our* public-to-be-protected is, after all, gay men who are still uninfected. But our complex identifications with each other as gay men, our identifications with gay community, and our identifications with culpability and shame for simply being and living as homosexuals have created an indiscriminate identification with the paradigm's *carrier* among a majority of gay men, whether infected or not. Such identifications are seen in the numbers of uninfected gay men who have inexplicable difficulty believing they are really uninfected; who have difficulty *saying*, without equivocation, that they are uninfected; who secretly doubt that they can stay uninfected; who have never seriously thought about staying uninfected; who repeatedly test for HIV without reason; who have never tested for HIV because they "already know"; and who are unable, after all, to remain uninfected. We were caught red-handed by an epidemic primarily vectored in our communities through the abhorred act of receptive anal sex, an act "committed" by many who remained uninfected, and an act identified with—in commission or abhorrence of—by all gay men. AIDS has simply confirmed that anal sex could, or would in the future, be as destructive and dangerous as we had always been told it was. Whether infected or not, we are part of the community that does the things that get people contaminated in every sense of the feeling.

One of the most destructive consequences of confused identifications with both carrier and public among gay men is the development—largely by gay men working in public health—of a peculiarly "undifferentiated" approach to AIDS prevention for their own communities. This approach pursues the traditional purposes of public health (protecting the uninfected from infection) by instructing all gay men to behave as both carrier and public.[2] While we have encouraged universal testing for HIV and used testing as the backbone of prevention,[3] men who test HIV-negative are paradoxically instructed to ignore the information in conducting their lives, their relationships, and their efforts to remain uninfected. The confused identifications of gay men with both carrier and public, and the paradoxes that result from this, are illustrated in a very typical piece of public health education for gay men, *Asians and AIDS:*

> We must face the fact that Asians are at risk, and we must do something about it. . . . We can find out the facts—how AIDS is transmitted and how it is not. We

then have a choice—do nothing about it or use this information by translating it into safer sex behavior. The AIDS virus is often transmitted through having unsafe sex or sharing needles with an infected person. . . . Playing safer means knowing how to protect ourselves and our partners. . . . AIDS is not only a threat to you and your partners, but also to your friends.[4]

Confused identifications are at first merely suggested by the idea that Asian's are "at risk." While here the term is intended to mean *at risk for HIV infection*, it is commonly used to speak of an HIV-infected man who is *at risk* for opportunistic infections. The confusion deepens, however, through the exclusive discussion of how *"AIDS is transmitted."* Although gay men may be universally *identified* with AIDS, it is not AIDS, but *HIV,* that is transmitted or contracted. Only men who already have HIV are at risk for AIDS. Furthermore, HIV is *contracted,* not "transmitted through having unsafe sex or sharing needles with an infected person." Finally, while the (presumably uninfected) reader is first told that he is at risk and that he can transmit—meaning contract—HIV by having sex with an infected person, he next learns that *he* should "protect [his] partner" and that AIDS is a threat to *"your* partners . . . [and] *your* friends." These confusions are all the more powerful because nowhere is the term "uninfected" or "HIV-negative" used, and nowhere is it simply stated that the purpose of the piece is to help uninfected men remain uninfected.

As confusing and paradoxical as it seems, this typical piece of education accurately expresses the public health model that has become standard for gay men in the United States. As almost universally applied by and for gay men, the model *would* have every gay man behave and experience himself as both carrier and public, regardless of circumstance, and regardless of what he knows—or does not know—about his or his partner's antibody status. The model thus dictates that every gay man live a lifetime—and thus often feel for a lifetime—as if he and all his partners were infected and at the same time needed to be protected from infection.

The model is usually rationalized against scrutiny by the assertion of the obvious truths that many gay men—probably one-third—do not know their real HIV status, and that others will unknowingly or intentionally misrepresent theirs. But this rationalization for the paradoxical model is nothing more than an assertion of the demand that all gay men live as if they *cannot* know their own or their partner's status simply because many *do not* know or misrepresent what they do know. And, indeed, if no behavioral benefits—such as the freedom to have ordinary, intimate, human sex disentangled from the specter of death and the latex paraphernalia of fear—*could* result from the knowledge of HIV status, why would one go to the trouble and risk of finding out? Such rationalizations of paradoxical, undifferentiated education discourage the knowledge that allows the consolidation of gay identities as uninfected, and thus discourage the very foundation of primary prevention. In fact, the paradoxical model seems to suggest that keeping men guessing about their HIV status contributes to their staying uninfected. In fact, the model needlessly exacerbates the feelings of plausibility or inevitability about having HIV that so many gay men experience—identifications that clearly contribute to new infections by making infection seem plausible or inevitable.

Public health has found a prevention model that exploits gay men's confused identifications. Unexamined, the model often feels like the most cautious approach for a world in which many do not know their antibody status, for it appears to provide the reassurance of erring on the safe side. Unfortunately, it is an approach built on public sentiment that would limit, dictate, or eliminate gay sexuality, and it expresses an altogether facile dismissal of the real-world, human importance of the issues. After a decade of life in the epidemic, gay men have watched the shame of homosexuality become almost seamlessly transformed and integrated into the "shame of AIDS." As one result, we have permitted public health to conduct education that makes paradoxical, often ridiculous demands, many of which are so impossible that many men are now abandoning any serious efforts to avoid even the very high-risk behaviors, effects that *could* be reasonably sustained over lifetimes. *These* results—the real-world consequences of our instruction—do not err on the safe side, and at this point in the epidemic they are, or ought to be, readily observable for all in public health. Do we really believe that the twenty-two-year-old gay man could be—or *ought* to be—educated into using condoms every time he has sex for the rest of his life with complete disregard for knowledge, context, or partner? And do we believe that he should experience himself as a "relapser" or "recidivist" when he does not?[5]

Such instruction is rooted in a homophobic dismissal of the human issues in gay lives and gay sex. Unfortunately, gay men have themselves participated in the development and promotion of such prescriptions, tried compliantly to heed them, and have insisted on finding them publicly reasonable, if privately impossible. Contrary to our general acceptance of the necessity of vaginal sex for heterosexuals—and billions of dollars spent on contraceptive methods to allow it without condoms *or* pregnancy—gay men have told gay men that "if you don't like condoms, don't fuck." Despite an almost complete lack of evidence to support concerns about oral HIV transmission and a huge body of data suggesting it is a minimal risk on a par with many other daily activities, gay men at San Francisco's STOP AIDS Project have persisted in instructing gay men to routinely "suck latex."[6] Gay educators at San Francisco's Center for AIDS Prevention Studies (CAPS), who posit a mutually monogamous relationship as a "most effective" prevention solution for heterosexuals,[7] tell us that for gay men it may be "negotiated danger."[8] And these same CAPS educators believe we will feel assured of their sensitivity to the human issues in HIV prevention by their statement that "although we have taken a strong stand on risk elimination, this does not mean that we advocate abandoning those individuals who are unable or unwilling to immediately cease all risky sexual behaviors."[9]

Contrary to the assertions of these educators, the undisputed desirability of reducing new infections among gay men does not justify the humanly destructive and relatively ineffective solutions that homophobic values so easily espouse. As a community in distress, we have wanted to feel that the interests of public health are—or might be made to be—simply synonymous with the interests and purposes of gay lives on the whole. The intense identifications of our political, social, psychological—and often, professional—lives with AIDS have influenced the gay man concerned with the future of his community to choose public health instead of the community organizing, teaching, sociology, writing, psychology, philosophy, or politics that might help clarify and nurture our lives in human senses. But to date, public health by and for gay men—what should truly be *our* public health—has largely reflected the narrow values of the larger society and our destructive internalization of those values. Even as it has saved lives, it has also marshaled our retreat into new rounds of shame, self-hatred, and amend-making.

We have given over our lives to the epidemic—including the epidemic as constructed by public health—in so many senses of the idea. The "responsible" gay man now tests and thus learns how to define himself in his community. Those who find that they live with HIV in their bodies are told to feel optimistic about that, to get treatment, and to thrive with HIV. They are told to not think about illness or death, but to experience it courageously should it come. Those who find that they live without HIV in their bodies are told to feel grateful—perhaps only undeserving, but lucky—and little else. We are *all* told to live the paradoxical sexual lives and relationships prescribed by public health. We are all expected to live with the preposterous—if humanely rooted—pretense that infected and uninfected men have no fear, ambivalence, or anger about each other in politics, relationships, or sexual intimacy. And even as those still uninfected are warned to avoid infection at any cost, we are all expected to tell each other that there is nothing "wrong" with being infected for fear that if we acknowledge that, it will call into question the "rightness" of homosexuality itself.

All these expectations and instructions about how to feel and live—and the long-standing shame and self-hatred that makes us compliant—have lured us from the pre-epidemic paths that had been leading toward an authentic gay liberation. Instead of authentic liberation, we are now apparently expected to believe the suggestion of public health educators that following their instruction and remaining free of HIV will, alone, provide us with viable human lives. Is it possible that even the narrowest purposes of prevention—much less the essential, broader human purposes—could really be built on the ugly foundation of shame, guilt, and self-hatred? Can we expect the very public health effort that has simultaneously obfuscated, exploited, and exacerbated such feelings to help gay men *take care* of themselves in any sense of the idea? Can we expect to save lives that are not experienced as worth saving?

We—gay men—are among the handful of groups in the United States who now have the most to lose in lives and quality of life at the hands of the epidemic and its current handling by public health. At the moment, we are perhaps also the group best positioned politically, economically, and education-ally to take the opportunity to radically reconstruct public health in a form that accounts for the realities of human lives. We already have the knowledge to create a public health that tells the truth, a public health that eschews erotopho-bia and homophobia and their exploitation for behavioral compliance, a public health that accounts for the social and interpersonal realities of our lives as gay men, a public health that comprehends the psychological experience in our lives, and a public health that helps clarify and nurture the complexity and richness of human life and human sexuality.

In order to actually do this we must reclarify the self-hatred that stymies our motivations, comprehension, and resolve, and coerces us to abdicate our lives to others' expectations and demands. In clarifying that, we will allow ourselves the opportunity to create the obvious: an alliance of disciplines that will bring sensitivity, insight, and respect to this important work. Public health, now merely about biological lives, can and must be about human life if it is to do the broader work it should do, as well as the narrower work it has to date only modestly accomplished. To do both, it must assist in the respectful clarification of lives so that those lives are experienced as worth protecting by those who live them. Gay men can and should thus reconstruct public health—for themselves, and for all others whose lives have been rendered miserable by the wonderful, if peculiar, predicament of conscious life in a human body that pulses, sleeps, eats, excretes, is warm, and makes love.

Notes

1. I have written more extensively on the psychological issues of gay men, AIDS, and prevention in Walt Odets, *In the Shadow of the Epidemic: Being HIV-Negative in the Age of AIDS* (Durham: Duke University Press, 1995); and idem, "AIDS Education and Harm Reduction for Gay Men: Psychological Approaches for the Twenty-first Century," *AIDS and Public Policy Journal* 9, no. 1 (1994): 3–15.

2. I have written in some detail on this subject in Walt Odets, "Why We Stopped Doing Primary Prevention for Gay Men in 1985," *AIDS and Public Policy Journal* 10, no. 1 (1995): 1–21.

3. Early medical intervention has been proposed as one reason for men to test, and for men who test positive there may be some benefit. Other reasons for testing, including the idea that "it is important to know," that it helps one "take control of one's life," or that it motivates one to "change behavior" are crude, broadly brushed, and partially specious.

4. *Asians and AIDS: What's the Connection* (San Francisco: Asian AIDS Project 1988).

5. Maria Ekstrand, Ron Stall, Susan Kegeles, Robert Hays, Michael DeMayo, and Thomas Coates, "Safer Sex among Gay Men: What Is the Ultimate Goal," *AIDS* 7(1993):281–82.

6. A 1995 campaign of the STOP AIDS Project of San Francisco.

7. Pamela DeCarlo, "Do Condoms Work?" in *HIV Prevention: Looking Back, Looking Ahead.* (Center for AIDS Prevention Studies, University of California, San Francisco and the Harvard AIDS Institute, 1995).

8. Ekstrand et al., 282. Although educators usually argue against "negotiated safety" (unprotected sex between partners of mutually known antibody status) because gay men are thought to be less monogamous than heterosexuals, the critical issue would be whether or not *protected* sex was practiced outside the relationship to prevent HIV from being introduced into the relationship. If protected sex would not serve this purpose, it would not prevent HIV from being transmitted within the relationship.

9. Ekstrand et al., 282.

Acknowledgments

My primary acknowledgement is to the more than a hundred contributors to *A Queer World* (and the second, forthcoming anthology *Queer Representations*). The individual authors worked with me generously and at length to recover, hone, and update the assorted panel remarks, colloquia presentations, and conference papers that marked their varied appearances at sponsored by the Center for Lesbian and Gay Studies (CLAGS).

These events, in turn, were the work of many hands. Over time, a large number of individuals associated with CLAGS, as well as the support staffs and volunteers connected to various sister organizations with whom we sometimes cosponsored, took on primary responsibility for putting together a particular occasion—ranging from single lectures to elaborate three-day conferences. It is they who created the venues in which the work represented in this volume was initially presented to the public. For their time-consuming and often behind-the-scenes efforts, I want especially to thank the following: David Bergman, Marcellus Blount, Peter Bowen, Brett Callis, Cheryl Clarke, Richard Elovich, Jeffrey Escoffier, Dan Evans, Stephanie Grant, Larry Gross, Ann Pollinger Haas, David M. Kahn, Robert Lang, Don Mengay, Framji Minwalla, Sylvia Molloy, Vivien Ng, Jay Prosser, Kelly Ready, Matthew Rottnek, James M. Saslow, Alisa Solomon, Ed Stein, Chris Straayer, Jan Strout, Sharon Thompson, Randolph Trumbach, and Robert Viscusi. In the mid to late eighties, Seymour. Kleinberg coordinated our monthly colloquia at which work-in-progress was presented for comment and critique; Gilda Zwerman followed him in that difficult job and built the colloquia series into a major venue for the presentation of cutting-edge scholarly work (some of which, in revised form, appears in this volume).

About a third of our one- to three-day conferences were cosponsored by sister organizations. In this regard I want to thank the Astraea National Lesbian Action Foundation; The American Society on Gerontology; ALGFAS (The Association of Lesbian and Gay Faculty, Administrators and Staff at New York University); Funders Concerned about AIDS; Funding Exchange/OUT Fund;

GMHC; the Humanities Institute of Brooklyn College; the Instituto Cervantes; the Lesbian and Gay Community Services Center; the PEN American Center, the Publishing Triangle; SAGE; and the Working Group on Funding Lesbian and Gay Issues.

For their help in varying ways, large and small, to gather, sort, and transcribe the vast original bulk of material that ultimately became this volume, and its companion volume, *Queer Representations*, I owe special thanks to Danny di Gia, John Morrone, Felice Picano, Matthew Rottnek, Richard Schneider, Eric Schwarz, and Ana Sequoia. For help in getting the final manuscript ready for production, I would also like to thank Despina Papazoglou Gimbel, Managing Editor of the NYU Press, and the volume's superb copy editor, Rosalie Morales Kearns.

Just as CLAGS, the organization, owes an incalculable debt to the various foundations and individuals who have funded our activities through the years, so the production of these two anthologies—which summarize so many of those activities—is indebted to state legislator Deborah Glick for a discretionary grant that allowed me to reduce a veritable ton of taped proceedings first to transcripts and then to a text of manageable proportions.

Finally, I owe special thanks to Jeffrey Escoffier and Esther Katz, the initial coeditors of the New York University Press/CLAGS Series in Lesbian and Gay Studies (of which this is the inaugural volume), and to Niko Pfund, Director of the New York University Press. All three, in an extended series of editorial meetings, provided the reinforcing energy that helped me shape (and reshape) the final contents of these readers.

Permissions

Introduction: © 1997 by Martin Duberman

Chapter 1: © 1997 by Judith Roof

Chapter 2: © 1997 by Jewelle L. Gomez

Chapter 3: © 1997 by Michael Moon

Chapter 4: © 1997 by Mariana Romo-Carmona

Chapter 5: © 1997 by Yukiko Hanawa. A different version of this essay is due to appear in *positions: east asian cultures critique* 4, no. 3 (winter 1996), published by Duke University Press, Durham, NC.

Chapter 6: From *Third Sex, Third Gender: Beyond Sexual Dimorphism in Culture and History*, ed. Gilbert Herdt (New York: Zone Books, 1994). © 1994 by Will Roscoe. Reprinted by permission.

Chapter 7: © 1997 by Serena Nanda

Chapter 8: © 1997 by Randolph Trumbach

Chapter 9: © 1997 by Gilbert Herdt

Chapter 10: From *Psychological Dialogues* 1, no. 4 (1992). © 1997 by Susan Coates. Reprinted by permission of Analytic Press.

Chapter 11: © 1997 by Nan Alamilla Boyd

Chapter 12: © 1997 by Suzanne Kessler

Chapter 13: © 1997 by Jonathan Ned Katz

Chapter 14: From *Radical History Review*, Queer Issue. © 1997 by Elizabeth Lapovsky Kennedy. Reprinted by permission.

Contributors

M. V. Lee Badgett is an assistant professor of economics at the University of Maryland at College Park. Among her many publications are "The Wage Effects of Sexual Orientation Discrimination," and the pamphlet *Beyond Biased Samples: Challenging the Myths on the Economic Status of Lesbians and Gay Men.*

Nan Alamilla Boyd is an assistant professor of history at the University of Colorado. She has recently completed a history of lesbian and gay San Francisco, and is currently at work on "transgendered bodies in motion." During 1995–96 she was a Rockefeller Humanities Fellow at the Center for Lesbian and Gay Studies (CLAGS).

Alan Bray is an independent scholar living in London. He is the author of *Homosexuality in Renaissance England* and is a member of the editorial collective of *History Workshop Journal.*

William Byne is the director of the Laboratory of Neuroanatomy in the Department of Psychiatry at the Mount Sinai School of Medicine, New York City, and a psychiatrist in private practice.

David Chang is a professor of law at the New York Law School. His many articles include "Ground between Conservative Republicans and Gay Rights Advocates" and "Á Critique of Judicial Supremacy."

Cheryl Clarke's books of poetry include *Narratives, Living as a Lesbian,* and *Humid Pitch.* Her poems, essays, and reviews have appeared in numerous publications, including *This Bridge Called My Back* and *Home Girls.* She is currently the director of the Office of Diverse Community Affairs and Lesbian and Gay Concerns at Rutgers University.

Susan Coates is the director of the Childhood Gender Identity Center in the Department of Psychiatry at St. Luke's/Roosevelt Hospital Center, and is an associate clinical professor of medical psychology at the College of Physicians and Surgeons, Columbia University.

Richard R. Cornwall teaches economics at Middlebury College. Starting with publications in mathematical economics (e.g., *Introduction to the Use of General Equilibrium Theory*), he has endeavored to model "transactions" between humans that promote or diminish socioeconomic inequality related to sexual orientation, gender, and race.

Douglas Crimp is a professor of visual and cultural studies at the University of Rochester. His work on AIDS includes the collection of essays *AIDS: Cultural Analysis/Cultural Activism, AIDS Demo Graphics*, and articles contributed to various journals and anthologies.

Martin Duberman is Distinguished Professor of History at Lehman College and the Graduate Center of the City University of New York. Founder of the Center for Lesbian and Gay Studies (CLAGS), he is the author of sixteen books, most recently *Midlife Queer, Stonewall, Cures*, and *Paul Robeson*.

Miriam Ehrenberg is an adjunct associate clinical professor of psychology at John Jay College, CUNY, and is also in private practice as a psychotherapist in New York City. She is the acting executive director of the Institute for Human Identity. She has coauthored several books, including *The Psychotherapy Maze*, and has written numerous articles on lesbian/gay concerns and women's issues.

Jeffrey Escoffier is an editor and writer living in New York City. He is the author of numerous articles and of *John Maynard Keynes;* his forthcoming book is entitled *American Homo: Essays on Cultural Politics, Sexuality and Capitalism*. He is on the board of the CUNY Center for Lesbian and Gay Studies.

Joshua Gamson is an assistant professor of sociology at Yale University. Along with a number of articles and reviews, he has written *Claims to Fame: Celebrity in Contemporary America* and is currently at work on *Freaks Talk Back: Television Talk Shows and Sexual Nonconformity*.

Amy Gluckman teaches social studies at an alternative high school in Lowell, Massachusetts, and is a member of the editorial collective that publishes *Dollars and Sense*, a progressive popular economics magazine.

Anne B. Goldstein is a professor of law at Western New England College of Law and has been a visiting professor at the University of Connecticut School of Law and the University of Texas School of Law.

Jewelle L. Gomez is the author of two collections of poetry, *The Lipstick Papers* and *Flamingoes and Bears,* and a novel, *The Gilda Stories.* She is currently working on a collection of her essays and completing a short biography of Audre Lorde.

Pat Griffin teaches in the Social Justice Education Program at the School of Education in the University of Massachusetts at Amherst.

Arnold H. Grossman is a professor of education at New York University. He is on the board of the Hetrick-Martin Institute and project director of the NYU AIDS/SIDA Mental Hygiene Project. In 1993 he received the Diego Lopez Award for Outstanding Service to People with AIDS. He is the author of numerous book chapters and articles related to gay, lesbian, and HIV/AIDS issues.

Yukiko Hanawa is a professor of women's studies at the University of Washington, Seattle. Among her publications are "Inventing Japanese Rural Women," in *Invention of Tradition, Japan,* ed. Stephen Vlatos.

Gilbert Herdt is a professor of human development at the University of Chicago. He is the author of a dozen books, including *Ritualized Homosexuality in Melanesia, Intimate Communications* (with Robert J. Stoller), and *Gay and Lesbian Youth,* and he also edited *Third Sex, Third Gender.*

Gregory M. Herek is an associate research psychologist at the University of California at Davis. He has published numerous scholarly articles on homophobia, antigay violence, and AIDS-related stigma, and has coedited (with Kevin T. Berrill) *Hate Crimes: Confronting Violence against Lesbians and Gay Men.*

Janice M. Irvine is an assistant professor of sociology at the University of Massachusetts at Amherst. She is the author of *Disorders of Desire* and *Sexuality Education across Cultures,* and editor of *Sexual Cultures and the Construction of Adolescent Identities.*

Jonathan Ned Katz is the author of the pioneering documentaries *Gay American History* and *Gay/Lesbian Almanac.* His articles and reviews have appeared in the *Village Voice,* the *Nation,* and the *Advocate.* His most recent work is *The Invention of Heterosexuality.*

Elizabeth Lapovsky Kennedy is an associate professor of American studies at the State University of New York at Buffalo, and a cofounder of the Buffalo Women's Oral History Project. She is the coauthor of *Feminist Scholarship: Kindling the Groves of Academe* and (with Madeline Davis) *Boots of Leather, Slippers of Gold.*

Jim Kepner is a pioneering gay activist and writer who began his movement work in 1952. He is a cofounder (and for many years the curator) of the International Gay and Lesbian Archives, now under the sponsorship of the University of California.

Robert M. Kertzner is an assistant clinical professor of psychiatry in the College of Physicians and Surgeons, Columbia University, and the training director of the Behavioral Sciences Research in HIV Infection Training Program at the New York State Psychiatric Institute. He is a member of the American Psychiatric Association Commission on AIDS.

Suzanne Kessler is a professor of psychology at the State University of New York at Purchase. With Wendy McKenna she is the coauthor of *Gender: An Ethnomethodological Approach.* The chapter in this volume extends her earlier analysis of the new medical management of intersexuality.

Karl Bruce Knapper is president of the board of directors of Frameline, which puts on the San Francisco International Lesbian and Gay Film Festival. He is also on the editorial collective of the *Socialist Review,* and works at the Martin Luther King Jr. Papers Project at Stanford.

Arthur S. Leonard is a professor at New York Law School, specializing in issues of labor and employment law, legal ethics, and sexuality and the law. He edits a monthly newsletter, *Lesbian/Gay Law Notes,* published by the Lesbian and Gay Law Association of Greater New York, and writes on lesbian/gay legal issues for *LGNY,* a community newspaper in New York City.

M. Susan Lindee teaches at the University of Pennsylvania. She has written *Suffering Made Real: American Science and the Survivors at Hiroshima* and has coauthored with Dorothy Nelkin *The DNA Mystique: The Gene as a Cultural Icon.*

Diana E. Long is a professor of history and the former director of women's studies at the University of Southern Maine. Her current research is on medical indexing and cultural change, 1880–1950.

Nellie Mathu is the chairperson of the African Women against AIDS Network.

Heino F. L. Meyer-Bahlburg teaches at the New York State Psychiatric Institute and the Department of Psychiatry, College of Physicians and Surgeons, Columbia University. He has written widely on psychoendocrine research and sexual orientation.

Michael Moon teaches in the English department of Duke University. He is the author of *Disseminating Whitman* and coeditor (with Cathy N. Davidson) of *Subjects and Citizens: Nation, Race and Gender from "Oroonoko" to Anita Hill.*

Bianca Cody Murphy is an associate professor of psychology at Wheaton College and a practicing psychologist with Newton Psychotherapy Associates. She has written several articles and book chapters on clinical issues concerning lesbian and gay couples.

Serena Nanda is a professor of anthropology at John Jay College, CUNY. She is the author of *Neither Man Nor Woman: The Hijras of India,* as well as *Cultural Anthropology* and *American Cultural Pluralism and Law,* a study of ethnicity, gender, and law in the United States.

Dorothy Nelkin holds a University Professorship at New York University, teaching in the Department of Sociology and the School of Law. A former president of the Society for the Social Studies of Science, she is the winner of their Bernal Prize. Her many books include *Science as Intellectual Property,* and *The DNA Mystique: The Gene as a Cultural Icon* (with M. Susan Lindee).

Joan Nestle is the cofounder of the Lesbian Herstory, Archives. She is the author of *A Restricted Country,* has edited *The Persistent Desire: A Femme-Butch Reader,* and has coedited *Women on Women* (which won a Lambda Award) and *Sister and Brother.*

Vivien Ng is an associate professor and the chair of women's studies at the State University of New York at Albany. She is currently finishing a book on the first generation of Chinese feminists, and her next project is on the politics of "pathologizing sex" in China in the 1920s.

Walt Odets is a clinical psychotherapist in private practice in Berkeley, California, and a member of the AIDS Task Force of the Gay and Lesbian Medical Association. He has written widely on AIDS education and prevention, and is the author of *In the Shadow of the Epidemic: Being HIV Negative in the Age of AIDS.*

Cindy Patton, an activist and writer, is an associate professor in the English

Department at Temple University. Her books include *Sex and Germs: The Politics of AIDS* and *Inventing AIDS*.

Michael Piore is a professor of economics and political science at the Massachusetts Institute of Technology. His most recent book is *Beyond Individualism*, and he has edited (with Richard Locke and Thomas Kochan) *Employment Relations in a Changing World Economy*.

Betsy Reed, a former editor of *Dollars and Sense* magazine, is managing editor of the *Boston Review*.

David A. J. Richards is Edwin D. Webb Professor of Law and the director of the Program for the Study of Law, Philosophy, and Social Theory at New York University. His books include *The Moral Criticism of Law* and *Conscience and the Constitution*. He is currently preparing a study of gender, sexual preference, and constitutional justice.

Ruthann Robson is a professor of law at the City University of New York School of Law. She is the author of *Lesbian (Out)Law: Survival under the Rule of Law*, two collections of lesbian fiction, *Eye of a Hurricane* and *Cecile*, and most recently a novel, *Another Mother*, about a lesbian attorney defending lesbian mothers.

Mariana Romo-Carmona is a Chilean lesbian writer of fiction in English and Spanish. She coedited *Cuentos: Stories by Latinas* and *Queer City*. She is on the M.F.A. faculty in the Writing Program at Goddard College, Vermont, and is managing editor of *Color Life* magazine in New York City.

Judith Roof is a professor of English at Indiana University, Bloomington. She is the author of *A Lure of Knowledge, Come As You Are*, and coeditor of *Who Can Speak? Authority and Critical Identity*.

Will Roscoe is the author of many articles and books, including *The Zuni Man-Woman* (winner of a Lambda Award) and *Queer Spirits: A Gay Men's Myth Guide*. He also edited *Living the Spirit: A Gay American Indian Anthology*, and *Radically Gay*. He was recently an affiliated scholar at the Institute for Research on Women and Gender at Stanford University.

Francesca Canadé Sautman is a professor of French, women's studies, and medieval studies at Hunter College and the Graduate School of the City University of New York. She has published *La Religion du Quotidien: Rites et croyances populaires de la fin du Moyen Age* and a wide range of articles on folk culture and women's cultural history in France, Italy, the Maghrib, and the United States.

Charles Silverstein is in private practice and is a member of the faculty of New York University Medical Center. He was the founding director of Identity House, the Institute for Human Identity, and the *Journal of Homosexuality*. He has published five books, including (with Felice Picano) the second edition of *The Joy of Gay Sex*.

Sean Strub is the founder of the marketing firm Strubco Inc. and also of *POZ* magazine.

Kendall Thomas is a professor of law at Columbia University, where he teaches constitutional law, legal philosophy, critical race theory, and law and sexuality. He is an editor of *Critical Race Theory: The Key Writings That Formed the Movement*.

Sharon Thompson is the author of *Going All the Way: Teenage Girls' Tales of Sex, Romance, and Pregnancy* and coeditor (with Ann Snitow and Christine Stansell) of the feminist classic *Powers of Desire: The Politics of Sexuality*. Her widely anthologized essays have appeared in *the Village Voice, Feminist Studies, Heresies*, and other magazines.

Randolph Trumbach, a professor of history at Baruch College and the Graduate Center of the City University of New York, is the author of a number of widely anthologized articles. His books include *The Rise of the Egalitarian Family*. He has completed the first of a two-volume work on *Sex and the Gender Revolution: Reputation and Variance in Eighteenth-Century London*.

Carmen Vazquez is the founding director of the San Francisco Women's Building, and was executive director of the National Network for Immigrant and Refugee Rights. She is currently the director of public policy for the Lesbian and Gay Community Services Center in New York City.

James Woods was an assistant professor of economics at the College of Staten Island, CUNY, until his death in 1995 from AIDS. He was the author of *The Corporate Closet* and coedited (with Larry Gross) a forthcoming anthology, *The Columbia Reader on Lesbians and Gay Men in American Media, Society and Politics*.

Gilbert Zicklin is on the faculty at Montclair State University, where he teaches the sociology of sexuality. He has recently (1995) written on lesbian and gay family relationships in the *Marriage and Family Review*.

Index